Exam 70-528: *Microsoft® .NET Framework 2.0—Web-Based Client Development*

Note: Exam objectives are subject to change at any time without prior notice and at Microsoft's sole discretion. Please visit the Microsoft Learning Certification Web site (*www.microsoft.com/learning/mcp/*) for the most current listing of exam objectives.

Microsoft®

Microsoft®

MCTS Self-Paced Training Kit (Exam 70-528):

Microsoft® .NET Framework 2.0 Web-Based Client Development

Glenn Johnson and Tony Northrup

PUBLISHED BY
Microsoft Press
A Division of Microsoft Corporation
One Microsoft Way
Redmond, Washington 98052-6399

Library of Congress Control Number 2006932076

ISBN-13: 978-0-7356-2334-7
ISBN-10: 0-7356-2334-1

Printed and bound in the United States of America.

1 2 3 4 5 6 7 8 9   QWT   1 0 9 8 7 6

Distributed in Canada by H.B. Fenn and Company Ltd.

A CIP catalogue record for this book is available from the British Library.

Microsoft Press books are available through booksellers and distributors worldwide. For further information about international editions, contact your local Microsoft Corporation office or contact Microsoft Press International directly at fax (425) 936-7329. Visit our Web site at www.microsoft.com/mspress. Send comments to tkinput@microsoft.com.

Microsoft, Active Directory, Internet Explorer, MSDN, MSN, PGR, Segoe, Visual Basic, Visual Studio, Visual Web Developer, Windows, and Windows Server are either registered trademarks or trademarks of Microsoft Corporation in the United States and/or other countries. Other product and company names mentioned herein may be the trademarks of their respective owners.

The example companies, organizations, products, domain names, e-mail addresses, logos, people, places, and events depicted herein are fictitious. No association with any real company, organization, product, domain name, e-mail address, logo, person, place, or event is intended or should be inferred.

This book expresses the author's views and opinions. The information contained in this book is provided without any express, statutory, or implied warranties. Neither the authors, Microsoft Corporation, nor its resellers, or distributors will be held liable for any damages caused or alleged to be caused either directly or indirectly by this book.

Acquisitions Editor: Ken Jones
Project Editor: Jenny Moss Benson
Editorial Production: nSight, Inc.
Copy Editor: Evan Gelder
Technical Reviewer: Thomas Keegan
Indexer: Nancy Guenther

Body Part No. X12-48741

Dedication

For Chris Geggis

−Tony Northrup

About the Authors

Glenn Johnson

Glenn Johnson is a professional trainer, consultant, and developer whose experience spans the past 20 years. As a consultant and developer, he has worked on several large projects, the latest being a successful conversion of a SmallTalk/GemStone system to C#/Microsoft SQL Server for a very large customer. This is Glenn's third .NET-related book, and he has also developed courseware for and taught classes in many countries on Microsoft ASP.NET, Visual Basic .NET, C#, and the .NET Framework.

Glenn holds the following Microsoft Certifications: MCT, MCPD, MCTS, MCAD, MCSD, MCDBA, MCP + Site Building, MCSE + Internet, MCP + Internet, and MCSE. You can find Glenn's Web site at *http://GJTT.com.*

Tony Northrup

Tony Northrup, MCTS, MCSE, CISSP, and Microsoft MVP, is a consultant and author. He has written more than a dozen books covering Windows networking, security, and development. Among other titles, Tony is coauthor of the MCSA/MCSE Self-Paced Training Kits for Exams 70-536 and 70-330/340.

When he's not consulting or writing, Tony enjoys cycling, hiking, and nature photography. Tony lives in Phillipston, Massachusetts, with his wife, Erica, his cat, Sam, and his dog, Sandi. You can learn more about Tony by visiting his Web site at *http://www.northrup.org.*

Contents at a Glance

Table of Contents

Acknowledgments

Glenn Johnson

To Jenny Moss Benson, thanks for your constructive feedback throughout the entire process of writing this book. Thanks for also having patience while the summer months were passing and my desire to play outweighed my desire to write.

Thanks to Ken Jones for persuading me to have a co-author on this book.

Tony Northrup, thanks for being a wonderful co-author, and thanks for your professionalism during all stages of writing this book.

To everyone at Microsoft Press who has played a role in getting this book to the public, thank you for your hard work and thanks for making this book venture a positive experience for me.

Tony Northrup

Many people helped me with this book by distracting me at the right times. My friends and family, especially Tara, John, and Emilie Banks; Kristin Casciato; Bob and Heather Dean; Mike, Michelle, Ray, and Sandi Edson; Chris and Diane Geggis; Bob Hogan; Sam Jackson; Tom and Heather Keegan; Kim Lively; Jenny Lozier; Eric and Alison Parucki; Skip and Chris Rice; Scott and Debbie Robichaud; Carol Whitney; and Jimmy and Gloria Young helped me enjoy my time away from the keyboard. More than anyone, I have to thank my wife, Erica, for being so patient during many long days of writing.

Introduction

This training kit is designed for developers who plan to take Microsoft Certified Technical Specialist (MCTS) exam 70-528, as well as for developers who need to know how to develop applications using the Microsoft .NET Framework 2.0. We assume that before you begin using this kit, you have a working knowledge of Microsoft Windows and Microsoft Visual Basic or C#.

By using this training kit, you'll see how to do the following:

- Create a Web application using Web server controls, event handlers, application state, and session state.
- Create custom Web server controls.
- Develop accessible Web applications that can be used by a global audience.
- Integrate a Web application with a back-end database.
- Create a Web application that stores user-specific information and preferences.
- Add authentication and authorization features to your application to improve security and add multiple access levels.
- Create Web applications that can be used from mobile phones and PDAs.

Hardware Requirements

The following hardware is required to complete the practice exercises:

- Computer with a 600 MHz or faster processor
- 192 MB of RAM or more
- 2 GB of available hard disk space
- DVD-ROM drive
- 1,024 x 768 or higher resolution display with 256 colors
- Keyboard and Microsoft mouse, or compatible pointing device

Software Requirements

The following software is required to complete the practice exercises:

- One of the following operating systems:
    - Microsoft Windows 2000 with Service Pack 4
    - Microsoft Windows XP with Service Pack 2
    - Microsoft Windows XP Professional x64 Edition (WOW)
    - Microsoft Windows Server 2003 with Service Pack 1
    - Microsoft Windows Server 2003, x64 Editions (WOW)
    - Microsoft Windows Server 2003 R2
    - Microsoft Windows Server 2003 R2, x64 Editions (WOW)
    - Microsoft Windows Vista
- Microsoft Visual Studio 2005 (A 90-day evaluation edition of Visual Studio 2005 Professional Edition is included on DVD with this book.)

Using the CD and DVD

A companion CD and an evaluation software DVD are included with this training kit. The companion CD contains the following:

- **Practice tests** You can reinforce your understanding of how to create .NET Framework 2.0 applications by using electronic practice tests that you customize to meet your needs from the pool of Lesson Review questions in this book. Or, you can practice for the 70-528 certification exam by using tests created from a pool of 300 realistic exam questions, which is enough to give you many different practice exams to ensure that you're prepared.
- **Code** Most chapters in this book include sample files associated with the lab exercises at the end of every lesson. For some exercises, you will be instructed to open a project prior to starting the exercise. For other exercises, you will create a project on your own and be able to reference a completed project in the event you experience a problem following the exercise.
- **An eBook** An electronic version (eBook) of this book is included for times when you don't want to carry the printed book with you. The eBook is in Portable Document Format (PDF); you can view it by using Adobe Acrobat or Adobe Reader.

The evaluation software DVD contains a 90-day evaluation edition of Visual Studio 2005 Professional Edition, in case you want to use it with this book.

How to Install the Practice Tests

To install the practice test software from the companion CD to your hard disk, do the following:

1. Insert the companion CD into your CD drive, and accept the license agreement. A CD menu appears.

    NOTE   If the CD menu doesn't appear

    If the CD menu or the license agreement doesn't appear, AutoRun might be disabled on your computer. Refer to the Readme.txt file on the CD-ROM for alternate installation instructions.

    ---

2. Click the Practice Tests item, and follow the instructions on the screen.

How to Use the Practice Tests

To start the practice test software, follow these steps:

1. Click Start | All Programs | Microsoft Press Training Kit Exam Prep. A window appears that shows all the Microsoft Press training kit exam prep suites installed on your computer.

2. Double-click the lesson review or practice test that you want to use.

    NOTE   Lesson reviews vs. practice tests

    Select the (70-528) Microsoft .NET Framework 2.0—Web-Based Client Development *lesson review* to use the questions from the "Lesson Review" sections of this book. Select the (70-528) Microsoft .NET Framework 2.0 — Web-Based Client Development *practice test* to use a pool of 300 questions similar to those in the 70-528 certification exam.

Lesson Review Options

When you start a lesson review, the Custom Mode dialog box appears so that you can configure your test. You can click OK to accept the defaults, or you can customize the number of questions you want, how the practice test software works, which exam objectives you want the questions to relate to, and whether you want your lesson review to be timed. If you're retaking a test, you can select whether you want to see all the questions again or only those questions you missed or didn't answer.

After you click OK, your lesson review starts.

- To take the test, answer the questions and use the Next, Previous, and Go To buttons to move from question to question.

- After you answer an individual question, if you want to see which answers are correct—along with an explanation of each correct answer—click Explanation.

- If you'd rather wait until the end of the test to see how you did, answer all the questions, and then click Score Test. You'll see a summary of the exam objectives you chose and the percentage of questions you got right overall and per objective. You can print a copy of your test, review your answers, or retake the test.

Practice Test Options

When you start a practice test, you choose whether to take the test in Certification Mode, Study Mode, or Custom Mode:

- **Certification Mode**   Closely resembles the experience of taking a certification exam. The test has a set number of questions, it's timed, and you can't pause and restart the timer.

- **Study Mode**   Creates an untimed test in which you can review the correct answers and the explanations after you answer each question.

- **Custom Mode**   Gives you full control over the test options so that you can customize them as you like.

In all modes, the user interface you see when taking the test is the basically the same, but with different options enabled or disabled depending on the mode. The main options are discussed in the previous section, "Lesson Review Options."

When you review your answer to an individual practice test question, a "References" section is provided that lists where in the training kit you can find the information that relates to that question; it also provides links to other sources of information. After you click Test Results to score your entire practice test, you can click the Learning Plan tab to see a list of references for every objective.

How to Uninstall the Practice Tests

To uninstall the practice test software for a training kit, use the Add Or Remove Programs option in Windows Control Panel.

How to Install the Code

To install the sample files referenced in the book's exercises from the companion CD to your hard disk, do the following:

1. Insert the companion CD into your CD drive, and accept the license agreement. A CD menu appears.

NOTE If the CD menu doesn't appear

If the CD menu or the license agreement doesn't appear, AutoRun might be disabled on your computer. Refer to the Readme.txt file on the CD-ROM for alternate installation instructions.

---

2. Click the Code item, and follow the instructions on the screen.

The code will be installed to \Documents and Settings*<user>*\My Documents \MicrosoftPress\70-528.

Microsoft Certified Professional Program

The Microsoft certifications provide the best method to prove your command of current Microsoft products and technologies. The exams and corresponding certifications are developed to validate your mastery of critical competencies as you design and develop, or implement and support, solutions with Microsoft products and technologies. Computer professionals who become Microsoft-certified are recognized as experts and are sought after industry-wide. Certification brings a variety of benefits to the individual and to employers and organizations.

MORE INFO All the Microsoft certifications

For a full list of Microsoft certifications, go to *http://www.microsoft.com/learning/mcp/default.asp*.

Technical Support

Every effort has been made to ensure the accuracy of this book and the contents of the companion CD. If you have comments, questions, or ideas regarding this book or the companion CD, please send them to Microsoft Press by using either of the following methods:

E-mail: tkinput@microsoft.com

Postal Mail:

Microsoft Press
Attn: *MCTS Self-Paced Training Kit (Exam 70-528): Microsoft .NET Framework 2.0 - Web-Based Client Development* Editor
One Microsoft Way
Redmond, WA 98052–6399

For additional support information regarding this book and the CD-ROM (including answers to commonly asked questions about installation and use), visit the Microsoft Press Technical Support website at *http://www.microsoft.com/learning/support/books/*. To connect directly to the Microsoft Knowledge Base and enter a query, visit *http://support.microsoft.com/search/*. For support information regarding Microsoft software, please connect to *http://support.microsoft.com*.

Evaluation Edition Software Support

The 90-day evaluation edition provided with this training kit is not the full retail product and is provided only for the purposes of training and evaluation. Microsoft and Microsoft Technical Support do not support this evaluation edition.

Information about any issues relating to the use of this evaluation edition with this training kit is posted to the Support section of the Microsoft Press Web site (*http://www.microsoft.com/learning/support/books/*). For information about ordering the full version of any Microsoft software, please call Microsoft Sales at (800) 426-9400 or visit *http://www.microsoft.com*.

Chapter 1
Introducing the ASP.NET 2.0 Web Site

Microsoft Visual Studio 2005 and ASP.NET 2.0 represent a major release for Microsoft. If you have previous experience with Visual Studio products, you will see the differences immediately when you attempt to create your first Web site. Even if you are new to Visual Studio 2005 and ASP.NET 2.0, you will be able to immediately take advantage of the productivity enhancements.

This chapter starts by introducing the Web site players (Web server, Web browser, and Hypertext Transfer Protocol [HTTP]). It explores the architecture of an ASP.NET Web site and then shows the various ways that you can create a Web site. After that, you will learn about some of the Web site configuration options in Visual Studio 2005.

Exam objectives in this chapter:
- Program a Web application.
    - Avoid performing unnecessary processing on a round trip by using a page's *IsPostBack* property.
- Create and configure a Web application.
    - Create a new Web application.
    - Add Web Forms pages to a Web application.
- Configure settings for a Web application.
    - Configure system-wide settings in the Machine.config file.
    - Configure settings for a Web application in the application's Web.config file.
    - Manage a Web application's configuration by using the Web Site Administration Tool.
- Optimize and troubleshoot a Web application.
    - Troubleshoot a Web application by using ASP.NET Trace.

Lessons in this chapter:

Before You Begin

To complete this chapter, you must:

- Be familiar with Microsoft Visual Basic or C#.

- Have Microsoft Windows XP, Internet Information Services (IIS) 5.1, and Visual Studio 2005 installed with Microsoft SQL Server 2005 Express Edition.

- Be familiar with the Visual Studio 2005 Integrated Development Environment (IDE).

- Understand how to make assemblies available to other applications.

- Have a basic understanding of Hypertext Markup Language (HTML) and client-side scripting.

Real World

Glenn Johnson

It's easier to learn how to develop Web clients once you understand who the players are. I have seen many people attempt to learn Web development without learning the roles of the Web browser, HTTP, and the Web server. It's not a pretty sight.

Lesson 1: Understanding the Players

It's important to get an understanding of the roles of the Web server, Web browser, and HTTP before starting your Web development. The typical communication process can be generalized into the following steps:

1. The Web browser initiates a request for a Web server resource.
2. HTTP is used to send the GET request to the Web server.
3. The Web server processes the request.
4. The Web server sends a response to the Web browser. HTTP protocol is used to send the HTTP response to the Web browser.
5. The Web browser processes the response, displaying the Web page.
6. The user enters data and performs an action, such as clicking a Submit button that causes the data to be sent back to the Web server.
7. HTTP is used to POST the data back to the server.
8. The Web server processes the data.
9. The Web server sends the response back to the Web browser.
10. HTTP is used to send the HTTP response to the Web browser.
11. The Web browser processes the response, displaying the Web page.

This section gives a brief description of how the Web browser exchanges communications with the Web server via HTTP. It also describes the responsibilities of both the Web browser and Web server.

After this lesson, you will be able to:

■ Describe the Web server's role in responding to requests for resources.

■ Describe the Web browser's role in collecting and presenting data to the user.

■ Describe HTTP's role in communicating to the Web server.

■ Describe how HTTP verbs are used to request resources from the Web server.

■ Describe the status-code groups that are implemented in HTTP.

■ Describe Distribute Authoring and Versioning.

■ Describe *PostBack*, the common method of sending data to the Web server.

■ Describe some methods for troubleshooting HTTP.

Estimated lesson time: 30 minutes

The Web Server's Role

Let's start with the *Web server*. The original Web servers were responsible for receiving and handling *requests* from the browsers via HTTP. Each Web server handled the request and sent a *response* back to the Web browser. After that, the Web server closed the connection and released all resources that were involved in the request. All resources were released because the Web server needed to be able to handle thousands of requests per minute, and the original Web pages were simple, static HTML pages. The Web environment was considered to be "stateless" because no data was held at the Web server between Web browser requests, and because the connection was closed after the response was sent (see Figure 1-1).

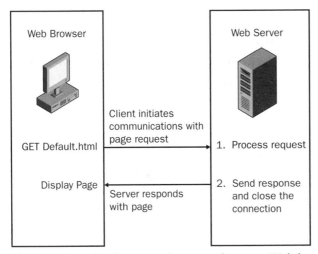

Figure 1-1   A simple request/response between Web browser and Web server in a stateless environment.

Today's Web servers deliver services that go far beyond the original Web servers. In addition to serving static HTML files, the Web servers can also handle requests for pages that contain code that will execute at the server; the Web servers will respond with the results of code execution, as shown in Figure 1-2. Web servers also have the ability to store data across Web page requests, which means that Web pages can be connected to form Web applications. Because many Web sites are set up as Web applications containing many Web pages, the idea of a Web server delivering a single page to the Web browser and closing the connection is rather outdated. Web servers now implement "keep alive" features for connections that make the Web servers keep the connections to the Web browsers open for a period of time with anticipation of additional page requests from a Web browser.

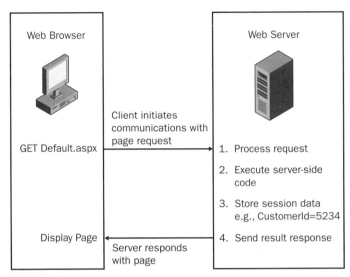

Figure 1-2   Web servers now store state between page requests to enable the creation of Web applications.

The Web Browser's Role

The *Web browser* provides a platform-independent means of displaying Web pages that were written with HTML. Platform-independent means that HTML was designed to be able to render within any operating system while placing no constraint on the window size. HTML was designed to "flow," wrapping text as necessary to fit into the browser window. The Web browser also needs to display images and respond to hyperlinks. Each Web page request to the Web server results in the Web browser clearing the browser screen and displaying the new Web page.

Although the Web browser's role is simply to present data and collect data, many new client-side technologies enable today's Web browsers to execute code such as Java-Script and to support plug-ins which improve the user's experience. Technologies such as Asynchronous JavaScript and XML (AJAX) allow the Web browsers to talk to the Web servers without clearing the existing Web pages from the browser window. These technologies make the user experience much better and more robust than the user experience provided by the original Web browsers.

Understanding Hypertext Transfer Protocol's Role

HTTP is a text-based communication protocol that is used to request Web pages from the Web server and send responses back to the Web browser. HTTP messages are typically sent between the Web server and Web browser using port 80, or, when using secure HTTP (HTTPS), port 443.

MORE INFO   HTTP/1.1 Specification

For more information on HTTP/1.1, see the HTTP/1.1 specification at *http://www.w3.org/Protocols/rfc2616/rfc2616.html*.

When a Web page is requested, a textual command like the following is sent to the Web server:

```
GET /default.aspx HTTP/1.1
Host: www.northwindtraders.com
```

Notice that the first line contains the *method*, also known as a verb or a command, called *GET*, and is followed by the Uniform Resource Locator (URL) of the Web page to be retrieved, which is followed by an indicator of the HTTP version to be used. The method indicates what action is to be performed by the Web server using the URL that follows the method. Table 1-1 contains a list of some of the common HTTP methods with a description of their uses. Note that, if *Distributed Authoring and Versioning (DAV)* is enabled on the Web site, many more verbs will be available, such as *LOCK* and *UNLOCK*.

The second line identifies the name of the host that may be used by the Web server if the Web server is hosting more than one Web site. This process is known as using host headers to identify the Web site that will handle the request(s).

Table 1-1   Common HTTP/1.1 Methods

HTTP Method	Description
OPTIONS	Used by client applications to request a lists of all supported verbs. Checks to see if a server allows a particular verb before wasting network bandwidth trying to send an unsupported request.
GET	Gets a URL from the server. A *GET* request for a specific URL, say, /test.htm, retrieves the test.htm file. Data retrieved using this verb is typically cached by the browser. *GET* also works with collections, such as those in directories that contain collections of files. If you request a directory, the server can be configured to return a default file, such as index.html, that may be representative of the directory.

Table 1-1   Common HTTP/1.1 Methods

HTTP Method	Description
HEAD	Retrieves the meta information for a resource. This information is typically identical to the meta information sent in response to a GET request, but the HEAD verb never returns the actual resource. The meta information is cacheable.
POST	Used to create a new, dynamically named resource. Data retrieved using this verb is typically not cached.
PUT	Allows a client to directly create a resource at the indicated URL on the server. The server takes the body of the request, creates the file specified in the URL, and copies the received data to the newly created file. If the file exists and is not locked, the content of the file will be overwritten.
DELETE	Used to delete a resource at the Web server. Requires write permissions on the directory.
TRACE	Used for testing or diagnostics; allows the client to see what is being received at the other end of the request chain. Responses to this method are never cached.
CONNECT	Reserved for use with a proxy that can dynamically switch to being a tunnel, such as Secure Socket Layer (SSL) protocol.
DEBUG	Is not defined in the HTTP/1.1 specification, but is used to start ASP.NET debugging. Informs Visual Studio 2005 of the process that the debugger will attach to.

Notice that Web-browser-to-Web-server communication is referred to as a *request*. In ASP.NET, the *Request* object represents the Web browser's communications to the Web server asking for a resource.

What Is Distributed Authoring and Versioning?

Distributed Authoring and Versioning (DAV) is a set of extensions to HTTP/1.1 that simplifies Web site development when working in a team scenario. DAV is an open standard and is available on numerous platforms. DAV provides the ability to lock and unlock files plus the ability to designate versions.

> DAV is built directly on HTTP/1.1, so no other protocols, such as File Transfer Protocol (FTP) or Server Message Block (SMB), are required. DAV also provides the ability to query the Web server for various resource properties such as file names, time stamps, and sizes. DAV also gives the developers the ability to perform server-side file copying and moving. For example, you can use the HTTP *GET* and *PUT* verbs to retrieve files from the Web servers and save them to different locations, or you can use the DAV's *COPY* verb to simply tell a server to copy the file.

The communication from the Web server back to the Web browser is commonly referred to as the *response*. In ASP.NET this is represented as the *Response* object. When the Web server responds to a request, the communication is typically in the following text-based format:

```
HTTP/1.1 200 OK
Server: Microsoft-IIS/6.0
Content-Type: text/html
Content-Length: 38
<html><body>Hello, world.</body><html>
```

The first line contains the protocol and version information, plus a status-code and reason. The three-digit status codes are grouped as shown in Table 1-2.

Exam Tip   Even if you don't memorize every status code, it's helpful to know the five status-code groupings in Table 1-2.

Table 1-2   Status-Code Groups

Status-Code Group	Description
1xx	Informational: Request received, continuing to process.
2xx	Success: The action was successfully received, understood, and accepted.
3xx	Redirect Command: Further action must be taken in order to complete the request.
4xx	Client Error: The request has a syntax error or the server does not know how to fulfill the request.
5xx	Server Error: The server failed to fulfill a request that appears to be valid.

In addition to the status-code groups, HTTP/1.1 defines unique status-codes and reasons. (A reason is nothing more than a very brief description of the status-code.) Table 1-3 shows a list of the common status-codes and reasons. Reason text can be modified without breaking the protocol.

Table 1-3   Common Status-Codes and Reasons

Status-Code	Reason
100	Continue
200	OK
201	Created
300	Multiple Choices
301	Moved Permanently
302	Found
400	Bad Request
401	Unauthorized
403	Forbidden
404	Not Found
407	Proxy Authentication Required
408	Request Time-out
413	Request Entity Too Large
500	Internal Server Error
501	Not Implemented

The second line of the response indicates the type of Web server. The third line (Content-Type) indicates the type of resource that is being sent to the Web browser. This indicator is in the form of a *Multipurpose Internet Mail Extensions* (MIME) type. In this case, the file is a static HTML text file. The MIME type is a two-part designator "type/subtype," in which the first part is the resource type and the second part is the resource subtype. Some common types are shown in Table 1-4.

Table 1-4   Common MIME Types

MIME Type	Description
text	Textual information. No special software is required to get the full meaning of the text, aside from support for the indicated character set. One subtype is *plain*, which means that the text can be read without requiring additional software. Other subtypes are *html* and *xml*, which indicate the appropriate file type(s).
image	Image data. Requires a display device (such as a graphical display or a graphics printer) to view the information. Subtypes are defined for two widely used image formats, *jpeg* and *gif*.
audio	Audio data. Requires an audio output device (such as a speaker or headphones) to "hear" the contents. An initial subtype called *basic* is defined for this type.
video	Video data. Requires the capability to display moving images, typically including specialized hardware and software. An initial subtype called *mpeg* is defined for this type.
application	Other kinds of data, typically either uninterpreted binary data or information to be processed by an application. The subtype, called *octet-stream*, is to be used in the case of uninterpreted binary data, in which the simplest recommended action is to offer to write the information into a file for the user. The *PostScript* subtype is also defined for the transport of PostScript material.

MORE INFO   MIME Types

The registry contains a list of MIME types/subtypes at the following location:
HKEY_CLASSES_ROOT\MIME\Database\Content Type.

After the content-length line, the response message is returned. This message is based on the MIME type. The browser attempts to handle the message based on its MIME type.

Submitting Form Data to the Web Server

The HTML <form> tag can be used to create a Web form that collects data and sends the data to the Web server. A typical use of <form> tag is as follows.

```
<form method="POST" action = "getCustomer.aspx" >
   Enter Customer ID:
   <input type="text" name="Id">
   <input type="submit" value="Get Customer">
</form>
```

This form prompts for a Customer ID, displays a text box that collects the desired customer ID, and also displays a submit button that initiates the sending of data to the Web server. The method of the form indicates the HTTP verb to use when sending the data to the server. The action is the relative URL of the resource that the data will be sent to.

There are two HTTP methods that can be used to submit the form data back to the Web server: *GET* and *POST*. When the *GET* verb is used, the *QueryString* containing the data is appended to the URL. The QueryString is a collection of key=value statements, separated by ampersand (&) characters that can be passed to the Web server by concatenating a question mark (?) to the end of the URL, and then concatenating the QueryString as follows:

```
GET /getCustomer.aspx?Id=123&color=blue HTTP/1.1
Host: www.northwindtraders.com
```

In this example, a *GET* request is made to the Web server for a Web page called getCustomer.aspx on the root of the Web site, and the QueryString contains the data that follows the question mark (?). An advantage to using the *GET* verb is that the complete URL and QueryString can be seen and modified in the address bar of the Web browser as needed. Keep in mind that, depending on the scenario, this could also be a disadvantage. The complete URL and QueryString are easy to save as a unit. For example, you can bookmark a Web page that has data that is included in the QueryString. One disadvantage is that the QueryString is limited in size by the Web browser and Web server being used. For example, when using Microsoft Internet Explorer and IIS, the limit is 1024 characters. Another consideration is that you may not want to allow a user to type the URL and QueryString directly into the address bar without navigating through other Web pages first.

When the *POST* verb is used to submit data back to the Web server, the data is placed into the message body as follows:

```
POST /getCustomer.aspx HTTP/1.1
Host: www.northwindtraders.com

Id=123&color=blue
```

Using the *POST* verb removes the size constraint on the data. We posted more than 10 megabytes of data to see if the Web server would accept the data. It worked, but sending that much data across the Internet can cause other problems, primarily bandwidth-related, such as timeout errors and performance problems. The *POST* verb does not allow the user to simply type the data, because this data is hidden in the message body. In most scenarios, using the *POST* verb is the more desirable way to send data to the Web server.

Sending data back to the server is often referred to as a *PostBack* to the server. Although its name comes from the *POST* verb, it is possible to perform a PostBack using the *GET* method described above. An ASP.NET Web page contains a property called *IsPostBack* that is used to determine if data is being sent back to the Web server or if the Web page is simply being requested.

HTTP Troubleshooting

You can easily view the exchange of HTTP messages by using a network sniffer. The sniffer captures all packets between the Web browser and the Web server, and you can simply view the packet data to read messages such as the requests and responses described in this section.

Real World

Glenn Johnson

I always keep Microsoft Network Monitor, which is a network packet sniffer that is included with Microsoft Server Opererating Systems and Microsoft Systems Management Server (SMS), installed on my computer so I can readily run this application to see the packet-by-packet conversation between my computer and other computers on the network. This is probably the best way to understand what's happening because you see the raw data packets that were exchanged.

Another tool that you can use for HTTP diagnostics is Telnet. Telnet is nothing more than a terminal emulator that sends and receives textual data on port 23, but you can specify port 80 to communicate to the Web server. With Telnet, you can type the HTTP commands and view the results.

There are also many applications you can download from the Internet to troubleshoot and analyze HTTP. Simply type **HTTP** as the keyword in a search on the site *http://www.download.com* to get a list of such applications.

Quick Check

1. What protocol is used to communicate between the Web browser and the Web server?

2. In ASP.NET, what does the *Request* object represent?

3. In ASP.NET, what does the *Response* object represent?

Quick Check Answers

1. HTTP

2. The *Request* object represents the communication from the Web browser to the Web server.

3. The *Response* object represents the communication from the Web server to the Web browser.

Lab: Exploring HTTP

In this lab, you explore the HTTP by using Telnet, which is the terminal emulation application that is built into Windows XP.

▶ **Exercise 1: Starting and Configuring Telnet**

In this exercise, you start Telnet and configure it to work with HTTP.

1. Open a command prompt. Do so by selecting Start | All Programs | Accessories | Command Prompt.

2. Clear the screen. Type the following command to clear the screen:

   ```
   CLS
   ```

3. Start Telnet. In the command prompt window, type the following command to start the Telnet client:

   ```
   Telnet.exe
   ```

4. Configure Telnet to echo type characters. Type the following command into the Telnet window, which will cause locally typed characters to be displayed while you type them:

```
set localecho
```

Telnet will respond with the following:

```
Local echo on
```

5. Set carriage return and line feed to On. Type the following command to instruct Telnet that it should treat the Enter key as a combination of carriage return and line feed.

```
set crlf
```

Telnet will respond with the following:

```
New line mode - Causes return key to send CR & LF
```

▶ **Exercise 2: Communicating with a Web Site**

In this exercise, you connect to a Web site, request the default page, and observe the result.

NOTE   **Take your time**

In this section, if you mistype a command, you will need to start over, so take your time entering each command.

---

1. In this exercise, you will open a connection to a Web site. Type the following command into the Telnet command window to open a connection to GJTT.com on port 80:

```
o GJTT.com 80
```

The Web server responds with the following:

```
Connecting To GJTT.com...
```

Note that this Telnet will not indicate that you are indeed connected.

2. Press the Enter key until the cursor is positioned on the next line.

3. Attempt to *GET* the default page. Type the following lines. After typing the second line, press the Enter key two times; this indicates the end of message to the Web server.

```
GET  /  HTTP/1.1
Host: GJTT.com
```

After pressing the Enter key two times, you will see the result shown in Figure 1-3. Notice that the status-code is 302 with a reason of Object Moved. The message body contains HTML with a hyperlink to the new location.

Figure 1-3   The response is a result code that indicates a redirect.

4. Try other sites. After pressing the Enter key, you will be back at the Telnet command prompt. Repeat the steps in this exercise to connect to other Web sites.

Lesson Summary

- The Web server is responsible for accepting a request for a resource and sending a response.

- The Web browser is responsible for displaying data to the user, collecting data from the user, and sending data to the Web server.

- HTTP is a text-based communication protocol that is used to communicate between Web browsers and Web servers, using port 80.

- Secure HTTP (HTTPS) uses port 443.

- Each HTTP command contains a method that indicates the desired action. Common methods are *GET* and *POST*.

- Sending data to the Web server is commonly referred to as a PostBack.

- You can troubleshoot HTTP by using the Telnet application or a packet sniffer.

Lesson Review

You can use the following question to test your knowledge of the information in Lesson 1, "Understanding the Players." The question is also available on the companion CD if you prefer to review it in electronic form.

NOTE Answers

An answer to this question and explanations of why each answer choice is right or wrong are located in the "Answers" section at the end of the book.

---

1. What is the name of the Web page property that you can query to determine that a Web page is being requested without data being submitted? (Choose one.)

    A. *FirstGet*

    B. *Initialized*

    C. *IncludesData*

    D. *IsPostBack*

Lesson 2: Creating a Web Site and Adding New Web Pages

This lesson presents methods that will help you create a new Web site using Visual Studio 2005. When you create a new Web site, you will be presented with options that are important for you to understand. You will learn how Visual Studio 2005 makes it easy to create the new Web site and add new Web pages.

After this lesson, you will be able to:

- Create a new Web site within Visual Studio 2005.
- Add new Web pages, which are also known as Web Forms, to a Web site.

Estimated lesson time: 60 minutes

Understanding the Visual Studio 2005 Web Site Types

Before creating your first Web site in Visual Studio 2005, let's look at the general architecture of a Web site. In Visual Studio 2005, the project structure has been changed to more accurately reflect the way Web Applications are typically constructed. Web projects are now called "Web Sites." You now have several options for running and testing your Web site, based on the type of Web site that you have. A new Web site can be file-based, FTP-based, local HTTP-based, or remote HTTP-based. These options simplify the system requirements on the developer's machine. Listed below is a description of each of the options.

NOTE   .NET 2.0

The Web site types are new in .NET 2.0.

- **File**   The file-based Web site consists of a folder, or folder structure, that contains all of the files for the Web site. This Web site uses the lightweight ASP.NET development server that is included in Visual Studio 2005, and does not use or require IIS on the local machine.
- **FTP**   The FTP-based Web site is used when you want to use FTP to manage the files on a local or remote Web site. This option is more frequently used when your Web site is hosted on a remote computer and your access to the files and folders on your Web site is via FTP instead of through Front Page Server Extensions.

- **Local HTTP**   The local HTTP-based Web site is used when you are working with IIS on your local machine. This Web site may be configured at the root of the IIS Web Server, or in a virtual directory that is configured as an application.

- **Remote HTTP**   The remote HTTP-based Web site is used when you have a remote site that is hosted on a remote server and gives you access to your Web files via Front Page Server Extensions.

The Visual Studio 2005 Solution Files

When a Web site is created, a solution file (.sln) and a hidden solution user options file (.suo) are created. By default, these files are created in the My Documents\Visual Studio 2005\Projects folder. The solution file is a text file that contains information such as the following:

- A list of the projects that are to be loaded into Visual Studio 2005

- A list of project dependencies

- Microsoft Visual SourceSafe information

- A list of add-ins that are available

The solution user options file is a binary file that contains various user settings related to the Integrated Development Environment (IDE), such as the following:

- The task list

- Debugger break points and watch window settings

- Visual Studio window locations

Note that the solution files are not located in your Web site's folder because they are Visual Studio 2005–specific and are not required in the deployed Web site. Also, a solution may contain many Web sites and Visual Studio projects, so it's best to keep the solution files in an independent folder. Solution files also can be developer-specific, meaning that developers may want to configure solution files based on their preferences.

Looking at the ASP.NET Page Structure

When an ASP.NET Web page is created, it must have an *.aspx* extension. The typical Web page is composed of three sections: page directives, code, and page layout. These sections are defined as follows:

- **Page Directives** This section is used to set up the environment, specifying how the page should be processed. For example, this is where you can import namespaces and load assemblies.

- **Code** This section contains code to handle events from the page or its controls. Code can be placed in a <script> tag. By default, script blocks contain client-side code but they may be designated as being server-side code by including the *runat="server"* attribute in the <script> tag. As a side note, code can also be contained in attached files, called code-behind files. All page code is compiled prior to execution. In addition, all pages can be precompiled to an assembly if the assembly is the only file that needs to be deployed.

- **Page Layout** The page layout is the HTML of the page, which includes the HTML body and its markup. The body can contain client and server controls as well as simple text.

A simple Web page may look like the following.

```
<!-page directives-->
<%@ Page Language="VB" %>
 <!--script-->
<script runat="server">
    Private Sub SayHi(ByVal sender As Object, ByVal args As EventArgs)
        Response.Write("Hello " + txtName.Value)
    End Sub
</script>

<!--layout-->
<html>
<head>
    <title>Say Hi Page</title>
</head>
<body>
    <form id="form1" runat="server">
     <input runat="server" id="txtName" type="text" />
     <input runat="server" id="btnSayHi" type="button"
        value="Say Hi" onserverclick="SayHi" />
    </form>
</body>
</html>
```

Notice the *runat="server"* attribute that is used. For the script block, this indicates that the code will run at the server. For the form and its controls, this indicates that ASP.NET will create server-side objects to match these HTML tags. A server-side object is capable of running server-side code and raising server-side events.

In-Line versus Code-Behind Programming Model

The previous Web page contains all the code and markup in a single file. This is called in-line programming. Although this model is simple, and might be a logical model to choose when you are converting an ASP application (that also has all of its code in a single file) to ASP.NET, new applications should always be implemented with the code-behind programming model. The code-behind programming model is always the preferred model because it provides clean separation between the client-side code and the server-side code.

The code-behind programming model adds another file to the Web page that is called the code-behind page. The code-behind page contains the server-side code, thus separating server-side code from the client-side code and markup.

NOTE .NET 2.0

Partial classes are new to ASP.NET version 2.0. The implementation of partial classes allowed the dynamic compilation to change in ASP.NET 2.0.

The code-behind files in ASP.NET 2.0 use a new language feature called partial classes, which allow code-behind files to be dynamically compiled with their associated ASPX pages into a single class type. This means you no longer need to declare member variables in the code-behind page for each control. This greatly simplifies maintenance of sites that use this code-separation technique.

Dynamic Web Site Compilation

ASP.NET 2.0 implements a new dynamic Web site compilation model. In ASP.NET 2.0, the code is not compiled until it is required by a user accessing your site. With dynamic compilation, the Web site doesn't produce a deployable executable assembly as its output when it is built in Visual Studio 2005. Instead, each page is compiled when it is requested. The compiled page has a dependency on the source file's timestamp. If the source code is changed, the page is recompiled the next time it is requested. Dynamic compilation offers the following advantages:

- The entire application does not need to be recompiled every time a change is made to a single page or component, which is especially great news to developers of large Web sites. Remember that each page is recompiled as needed based on the timestamp of the source code files.

- Pages that contain compile errors do not prevent other pages in the Web site from running. This means that you can test Web sites that contain pages still in development.

In Visual Studio 2005, when you compile a Web site, the Web site still gets built, but there is now verification that all the pages and their dependencies can be compiled. No assembly is created for running the Web site. Compiling in Visual Studio 2005 is more rigorous than in earlier versions of Visual Studio .NET because Visual Studio now verifies that the code can be compiled and finds errors in the markup syntax and Web.config file.

Creating a Web Site

We mentioned that there are four ways to create a Web site. This section demonstrates the creation of each of the Web site types: file, FTP, local HTTP, and remote HTTP. The basic steps for creating a new Web site in Visual Studio 2005 are as follows:

1. In Visual Studio 2005, use the menus to request the creation of a new Web site.
2. Select the Web site type, the default programming language, and the location.
3. Click OK. Enter additional information if prompted.

You can create a Web Site application by opening Visual Studio 2005 and selecting File | New | Web Site. The New Web Site dialog box appears, as shown in Figure 1-4.

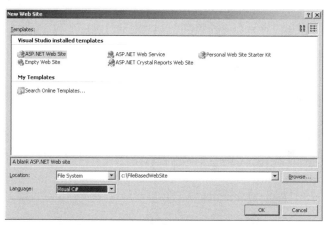

Figure 1-4   The New Web Site dialog box contains properties for setting the Web site type, location, and default language.

Creating a File-Based Web Site

In the New Web Site dialog box, change the Location drop-down list to File System, and type a valid location on a local drive. After that, select the default language for the Web site and click OK.

Visual Studio 2005 creates the folder for your site and a new page named Default.aspx. When the new page is created, Visual Studio 2005 displays the page in HTML Source view, where you can see the page's HTML elements.

Creating an FTP-Based Web Site

In the New Web Site dialog box, select FTP from the Location drop-down list, and type a valid local or remote location that uses FTP to manage the files. After that, select the default language for the Web site and click OK. You will be prompted for FTP parameters, as shown in Figure 1-5.

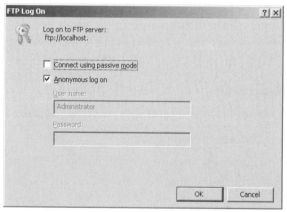

Figure 1-5   Configure the FTP parameters for Web site access.

Active Mode versus Passive Mode

FTP is TCP-based (has a connection) and has no UDP (connectionless) component. FTP requires two ports for communication: a command port and a data port. Port 21 is typically the command port at the server; port 20 is the typical data port when using active mode FTP.

Active mode FTP communications is the default and starts with the client selection of two ports: n and n+1. The client will use port n to initiate communications to port 21 of the server. When the server responds, the client sends a *port* command, which instructs the server of the port to use for data communications, as shown in Figure 1-6. It's the server that initiates data communications, from port 20 to the client's data port (n+1). If the client has a firewall installed, the server may be blocked from initiating communications to the client on the data port.

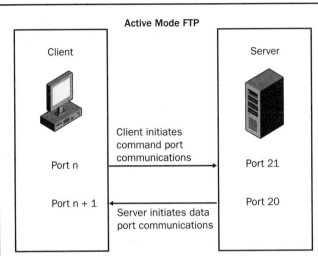

Figure 1-6 Active mode requires that the server initiate the connection on the data port.

Passive-mode FTP communications can be used to correct the problem with active-mode communications. Passive mode starts with the client selection of two ports: n and n+1. The client will use port n to initiate communications to port 21 of the server. When the server responds, the client sends a *pasv* command to the server. The server selects a random port p to use for data communications and sends the port number to the client. The client then initiates communications on the data port (n+1) to the server's data port (p), as shown in Figure 1-7.

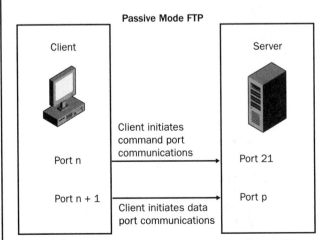

Figure 1-7 When using passive mode, the client initiates communications on the command and data ports.

> Notice that when using passive mode, the client initiates communications of the command port and the data ports. This fixes the problem of the client having a firewall installed that blocks the server's request to initiate communications on the data port.

Creating a Local or Remote HTTP-Based Web Site

In the New Web Site dialog box, change the Location drop-down list selection to HTTP and type a valid HTTP location, either localhost or a fully qualified remote location. If you enter a remote location, the remote server must have Front Page Server Extensions installed. After that, select the default language for the Web site and click OK.

Quick Check

1. Where are solution files created by default?
2. For new applications created with ASP.NET 2.0, what is the recommended programming model?

Quick Check Answers

1. In the My Documents\Visual Studio 2005\Projects folder.
2. The code-behind programming model.

What's in the Newly Created Web Site?

When you create a new Web site, Visual Studio 2005 creates a new page named Default.aspx. When the new page is created, Visual Studio 2005 displays the page in HTML Source view, where you can see the page's HTML elements.

The Default.aspx page that is created also has a code-behind page called Default.aspx.vb or Default.aspx.cs, depending on the programming language that you choose. Code-behind pages are optional files that contain server-side code. The programming language you choose is the default language for your Web site, but you can use multiple programming languages in the same Web application.

The new Web site also contains a special folder called App_Data. This folder is reserved for databases such as SQL Server 2005 Express Edition .mdf files. Table 1-5 contains a list of special folders that you can add to your Web site. A primary benefit of adhering to the suggested folder structure is that a user who attempts to browse to any of these folders (except App_Themes) will receive an HTTP 403 Forbidden error.

Table 1-5 ASP.NET 2.0 Special Folders

Folder Name	Description
App_Browsers	Contains browser definitions files (.browser) that ASP.NET uses to identify browsers and determine their capabilities.
App_Code	Contains source code for classes and business objects (.cs, .vb, and .jsl files) that you want to compile as part of your application.
App_Data	Contains application data files (.mdf and .xml files).
App_GlobalResources	Contains resources (.resx and .resources files) that are compiled into assemblies and have a global scope.
App_LocalResources	Contains resources (.resx and .resources files) that are scoped to a specific page, user control, or master page in an application.
App_Themes	Contains files (.skin and .css files, as well as image files and generic resources) that define the appearance of Web pages and controls.
App_WebReferences	Contains Web reference files (.wsdl, .xsd, .disco, and .discomap files) that define Web references.
Bin	Contains compiled assemblies (.dll files) for code that you want to reference in your application. Assemblies in the Bin folder are automatically referenced in your application.

Adding New Web Pages to the Web Site

After the Web site has been created, you can add as many Web pages as you need to create your Web site application. A Web page is also known as a *Web Form* and may be composed of a single file when using the in-line programming model or a pair of files when using the code-behind programming model. The steps for adding a new Web page to a Web site are as follows:

1. Using Visual Studio 2005 menus, request a new Web Form.

2. Assign a name to the Web Form.

3. Select the programming language for this Web Form.

4. Change other settings as necessary and click OK.

You can easily add new Web pages to the Web site by simply selecting Website | Add New Item. Select the Web Form, assign a name, and select the programming language, as shown in Figure 1-8. Notice that the option Place Code In Separate File allows you to indicate whether you want a code-behind file. Note that you can also assign a master page, which allows you to create a consistent look and feel for your Web site. We will cover master pages in more detail in Chapter 9, "Customizing and Personalizing a Web Application."

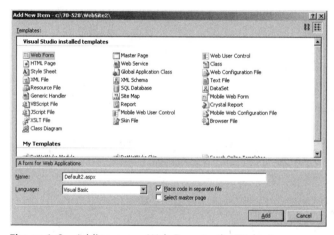

Figure 1-8   Adding a new Web Form to the Web site.

Lab: Create a New Web Site

In this lab, you will create a new Web site and explore its contents using Visual Studio 2005. After that, you will add a new Web page to the Web site.

▶ **Exercise 1: Creating a New Web Site**

1. Start Visual Studio 2005. Select Start | All Programs | Microsoft Visual Studio 2005 | Microsoft Visual Studio 2005.

2. Create a file-based Web site. Select File | New | Web Site. The New Web Site dialog box appears.

3. In the New Web Site dialog box, change the Location drop-down list to File System and type **C:\70-528\MyFirstSite** as the location on a local drive. Then select your preferred programming language for the Web site and click OK. This creates a new directory and subdirectory for the new Web site.

4. Explore the new Web site. In the Solution Explorer window, notice the special folder called App_Data and the Web page called Default.aspx. Click the plus (+) sign beside the Default.aspx file to reveal the code-behind page.

5. Explore the temporary files. Open the following folder with Windows Explorer:

    %WinDir%\Microsoft.NET\Framework\v2.0.50727\Temporary ASP.NET Files

    Notice that this folder contains a subdirectory called myfirstsite. This folder was dynamically created and contains files related to your new Web site. The first file is the Code Compile Unit (.ccu) file, which contains a serialized collection of source code objects that can be compiled. Next is the compiler (.compiled) file, which is an .xml file containing compiler information. This file indicates that the Code Compile Unit file is created from the Web page and its corresponding code-behind page. The last one is the Hash.web file, which contains a hash of the Web site.

6. While the temporary files folder is open and in view, build the Web site. In Visual Studio 2005, select Build | Build Web Site. Notice that the code files are being created, and then the newly created files are deleted and replaced with assemblies. After the build is completed, note the files that exist in the temporary files folder. A dynamic-link library (DLL) was created that contains the compiled Web page and its code-behind page. Also, a new compiled file has been created, containing the compiler settings that were used to create the DLL.

7. Browse the default.aspx page. In Visual Studio 2005, select Debug | Start Without Debugging. After a moment you should see your blank Web page. Notice that there are no new files in the temporary files folder because this page was already compiled and has not been changed. Leave these windows open if you are going to proceed to the next exercise.

▶ **Exercise 2: Adding a New Web Page**

In this exercise, you add a new Web page to the Web site that you just created.

1. Add a new Web page. In Visual Studio 2005, select Website | Add New Item. In the Add New Item dialog box, select Web Form, assign Page2.aspx as the name, select your preferred programming language, and click Add.

2. Observe the result in Visual Studio 2005. In the Solution Explorer window, a new file has been added called Page2.aspx. Click the plus (+) sign next to Page2.aspx to reveal the code-behind page.

3. Observe the result in the temporary files folder. Open the temporary files folder and notice that a new code compile unit file has been created. Also, a compiler file was created that contains the compiler settings that are required to create the code compiler unit file.

4. Browse the Default.aspx page. In Visual Studio 2005, select Debug | Start Without Debugging. After a moment, you should see your blank Web page. Notice that there are two new files in the temporary files folder. The .dll file is an assembly that contains the compiled Page2.aspx file and its code-behind file.

Lesson Summary

- ASP.NET 2.0 supports the file Web site type. This is a good option when IIS is not installed on the developer's computer and the developer wants to create a Web site without the use of a remote Web server.

- ASP.NET 2.0 supports the FTP Web site type. This option can be used when building a Web site that is being hosted on a remote computer that does not have Front Page Server Extensions installed.

- ASP.NET 2.0 supports the local HTTP Web site type. This option is a good choice when IIS is installed on the developer's computer and the developer has explicit IIS configuration settings that need to be tested.

- ASP.NET 2.0 supports the remote HTTP-based Web site type. This option is typically used when the Web site is being hosted on a remote computer that has Front Page Server Extensions installed.

- When using FTP in ASP.NET 2.0, active mode is the default. Passive mode can solve communication problems when the client has a firewall.

- ASP.NET 2.0 supports two programming models for Web pages: in-line and code-behind. With the in-line programming model, all of the Web page markup and code is in a single file. With the code-behind programming model, the server-side code for a Web page is separated into its own page, which is called the code-behind page.

- In ASP.NET 2.0, dynamic compilation refers to the delayed compilation of Web pages that takes place until the user requests the Web page.

- In ASP.NET 2.0, because each Web page produces its own DLL, Visual Studio 2005 allows you to select a programming language for each Web page.

- ASP.NET 2.0 defines several special folders. When a new Web site is created, the App_Data folder is created by default; it can contain a SQL Server 2005 Express Edition database, another database, or an .xml data file that will be used in the Web site.

- In ASP.NET 2.0 you can add new Web pages to a Web site using Visual Studio 2005. By default, each new Web page will contain a code-behind page.

Lesson Review

You can use the following questions to test your knowledge of the information in Lesson 2, "Creating a Web Site and Adding New Web Pages." The questions are also available on the companion CD if you prefer to review them in electronic form.

NOTE Answers

Answers to these questions and explanations of why each answer choice is right or wrong are located in the "Answers" section at the end of of the book.

1. If you want to create a Web site on a remote computer that does not have Front Page Server Extensions installed, which Web site type will you create? (Choose one.)

    A. Remote HTTP

    B. File

    C. FTP

    D. Local HTTP

2. If you want to create a new Web site on a Web server that is hosted by your ISP and the Web server has Front Page Server Extensions installed, what type of Web site would you create? (Choose one.)

    A. Local HTTP

    B. File

    C. FTP

    D. Remote HTTP

3. If you want to separate your server-side code from your client-side code on a Web page, what programming model should you implement? (Choose one.)

   A. Separation model

   B. Code-Behind model

   C. In-Line model

   D. ClientServer model

4. Joe created a new Web site using Visual Studio 2005, setting the Web site type to File, and the programming language to C#. Later, Joe received an elaborate Web page from his vendor, which consisted of the Vendor.aspx file and the Vendor.aspx.vb code-behind page. What must Joe do to use these files? (Choose one.)

   A. Joe can simply add the files into the Web site, because ASP.NET 2.0 supports Web sites that have Web pages that were programmed with different languages.

   B. The Vendor.aspx file will work, but Joe must rewrite the code-behind page using C#.

   C. Both files must be rewritten in C#.

   D. Joe must create a new Web site that contains these files and set a Web reference to the new site.

Lesson 3: Working with Web Configuration Files

Web sites are configured based on a hierarchy of XML configuration files, as shown in Figure 1-9. The first configuration file is the Machine.config file. This file is located in the configuration folder for the version of the .NET Framework installed on the computer, and is usually found at the following location:

%WINDIR%\Microsoft.NET\Framework*version*\Config\machine.config

The Machine.config file contains settings for all .NET application types, such as Windows, Console, ClassLibrary, and Web applications. These settings are global to the machine. Some of the settings in the Machine.config file can be overridden by settings in Web.config files that are in the hierarchy, while other settings are more global in nature. The global ones complete the .NET Framework, so they are protected and cannot be overridden by the Web.config files.

After this lesson, you will be able to:

- Understand the configuration file hierarchy.
- Use the GUI configuration tool to make changes to the configuration files.

Estimated lesson time: 20 minutes

The next file in the hierarchy is the Root Web.config file, which is located in the same directory as the Machine.config file. This file contains default Web server settings, some of which can override settings in the Machine.config file.

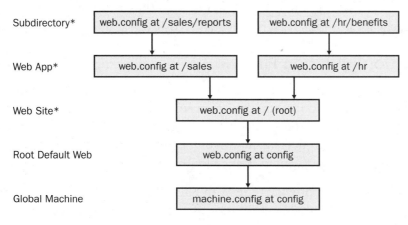

Figure 1-9 The configuration file hierarchy.

At the root directory of each Web site, you have the ability to add a Web.config file. This file is optional and can contain additional settings for the Web site as well as setting overrides. In each Web application, you can optionally have a Web.config file to provide more settings and override settings. Finally, each subdirectory in a Web application can optionally have a Web.config file where only a subset of the settings is valid.

Processing the Configuration Files

When you initially run your Web application, the runtime builds a cache of the effective settings for your Web application by flattening the layers of configuration files as follows:

1. The Machine.config file settings are retrieved.

2. The settings from the root Web.config file are added to the caches, overwriting any conflicting settings that were created earlier while reading the Machine.config file.

3. If there is a Web.config file at the root of the Web site, this file is read into the cache, overwriting existing entries.

4. If there is a Web.config file at the Web application, it is read into the caches, also overwriting any existing settings. The resulting cache contains the settings for this Web site.

5. If you have subdirectories in your Web application, the subdirectories can have a Web.conifg file that includes settings that are specific to the files and folders that are contained within this folder. To calculate the effective settings for the folder, the Web site settings are read (steps 1-4), and then this Web.config is read into the cache for this folder, overwriting (thereby overriding) any existing settings.

Modifying the Configuration Files

Because they are XML files, the configuration files can be opened and modified with any text editor or XML editor. You can also use the .NET Framework 2.0 Configuration snap-in with the Microsoft Management Console (MMC), which provides a graphical user interface (GUI) for modifying some of the configuration file settings that an administrator may want to change.

Visual Studio 2005 also provides the Web Site Administration Tool, which can be used to modify many of the configuration file settings. You can access this tool by selecting Website | ASP.NET Configuration.

The Web Site Administration Tool allows you to edit the following categories of the configuration files:

- **Security** This setting allows you to set up security for your Web site. In this category, you can add users, roles, and permissions for your Web site.

- **Application Configuration** This category is used to modify the application settings. Figure 1-10 shows the Web Site Administration Tool, which displays the Application tab.

- **Provider Configuration** This configuration file contains settings that allow you to specify the database provider to use for maintaining membership and roles.

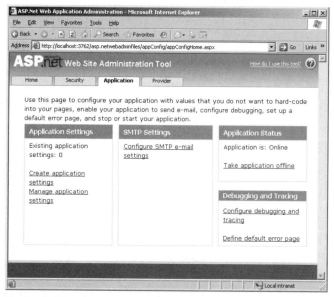

Figure 1-10 The Web Site Administration Tool showing the Application tab.

The Web Site Administration Tool lets you create and modify Web site settings that are not inherited. If a setting is inherited and cannot be overridden, it will appear, but it will be dimmed when the setting is disabled.

Quick Check

1. Is the format of a configuration file CSV, INI, XML, or DOC?

2. If a setting exists in the root Web.config file and also in the Web.config file at the Web application but with a different value, which Web.config file takes precedence?

Quick Check Answers

1. The configuration file is formatted with XML.

2. The Web.config file at the Web application takes precedence.

Lab: Modifying Your Web Site Configuration

In this lab, you use the Web Site Administration Tool to modify the Web site configuration by enabling debugging on the Web site. After that, you view the changes in the Web.config file.

▶ Exercise 1: Creating the New Web.Config File

In this exercise, you start Visual Studio 2005 and open the Web site from the previous lab.

1. Open the MyFirstSite from the previous lab. Alternatively, you can open the completed Lesson 2 lab project from the CD.

2. Note that this project does not contain a Web.config file yet. If the project does contain a Web.config file, delete it.

3. Open the Web Site Administration Tool by selecting Website | ASP.NET Configuration.

4. Click the Application tab to display the application settings.

5. Click the link to display the Configure debugging and tracing page, as shown in Figure 1-11.

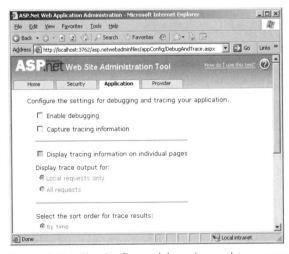

Figure 1-11   The Configure debugging and trace page.

6. Select the Enable Debugging check box. This will enable debugging for the current Web site. Notice that selecting this check box performs a PostBack to the Web server.

7. Close the Web Site Administration Tool.

8. A new Web.config file was created. Click the Refresh button at the top of the Solution Explorer window and the Web.config file will appear.

9. Open the Web.config file. The new Web.config file will contain the following:

```xml
<?xml version="1.0" encoding="utf-8"?>
<configuration
   xmlns="http://schemas.microsoft.com/.NetConfiguration/v2.0">
   <system.web>
       <compilation debug="true" />
   </system.web>
</configuration>
```

Notice that the file contains the setting to set debug to true.

Lesson Summary

- Web sites are configured based on a hierarchy of XML configuration files, starting with the Machine.config file, followed by the Web.config file that's in the same folder. After that, you may have a Web.config file in the root of the Web site, in each Web application, and in any subdirectory in a Web application.

- The configuration files may be edited with a text editor, an XML editor, the .NET Framework 2.0 Configuration snap-in with the MMC, or the Web Site Administration Tool.

- The Web Site Administration Tool is used to add and modify the Web site settings.

Lesson Review

You can use the following questions to test your knowledge of the information in Lesson 3, "Working with Web Configuration Files." The questions are also available on the companion CD if you prefer to review them in electronic form.

NOTE Answers

Answers to these questions and explanations of why each answer choice is right or wrong are located in the "Answers" section at the end of of the book.

---

1. You want to make a configuration setting change that will be global to all Web and Windows applications on the current computer. Which file do you change? (Choose one.)

   A. Global.asax

   B. Web.config

   C. Machine.config

   D. Global.asa

2. You want to make a configuration setting change that will affect only the current Web application. Which file will you change? (Choose one.)

   A. Web.config that is in the same folder as the Machine.config file

   B. Web.config in the root of the Web application

   C. Machine.config

   D. Global.asa

3. You want to make a configuration setting change that will affect only the current Web application, and you want to use a tool that has a user-friendly Graphical User Interface (GUI). Which tool should you use? (Choose one.)

   A. The Microsoft Management Utility

   B. Microsoft Word

   C. Visual Studio, using the | Tools | Options path

   D. Web Site Administration Tool

Lesson 4: Using ASP.NET Trace to Explore Web Pages

The trace facility that is included in ASP.NET can be used to troubleshoot and diagnose problems with your Web site. You can also use the trace facility to explore resource usage on each Web page. This lesson covers the enabling and configuring of the trace facility and then explores the data that is made available by the trace facility.

After this lesson, you will be able to:

■ Enable and configure the ASP.NET trace facility.

■ Understand the data that is available in the ASP.NET trace facility.

Estimated lesson time: 20 minutes

Enabling and Configuring the ASP.NET Trace Facility

The trace facility can be enabled in the Web.config file, but you can use the Web Site Administration Tool to provide a user-friendly GUI to enable and configure this option. This section demonstrates the enabling and setting of the ASP.NET trace facility options.

Enabling the Trace Facility Using the Web Site Administration Tool

The following steps identify how to enable and configure the trace facility using the Web Site Administration Tool:

1. Open the Web Site Administration Tool by selecting Website | ASP.NET Configuration.

2. Click the Application tab and click the Configure debugging and tracing link to view and modify the trace settings.

3. Click Capture Tracing Information. This enables the trace facility.

4. Change the settings as necessary. Table 1-6 describes each of the settings.

Table 1-6   ASP.NET Trace Settings

Web Site Administration Tool Setting	Web.Config Setting	Description
Capture tracing information	Enabled	Enables the trace facility. When this option is enabled, the other trace options are also enabled.
Display tracing information on individual pages	pageOutput	Displays the trace information directly on the Web page that is being traced. Depending on the page content, the trace information displays either at the bottom of the Web page or behind the regular Web page content.
Display trace output for	localOnly	Designates either Local requests only or All requests. When set to Local Requests Only, the trace facility only operates with requests and PostBacks from the computer that the Web server is running on. The All requests setting enables the trace facility to respond for all requests and PostBacks from any computer to the Web site.
Select the sort order for trace results	traceMode	Enables sorting of the trace output either by time or by category.
Number of trace requests to cache	requestLimit	Sets the quantity of items to hold in the cache.
Select which trace results to cache	mostRecent	Designates the Most Recent Trace Results or the Oldest Trace Results. When set to Most Recent Trace Results, the cache continues to update, holding the latest results. When set to Oldest Trace Results, as soon as the number of requests has been met, the cache no longer updates until after the Web application is restarted.

5. Run the Web application.

6. Navigate to the trace.axd page on the Web application (*http://server/application/trace.axd*). This is not a physical Web page. Instead, trace.axd is a virtual page that is constructed dynamically based on the Web pages you visited, and displays the trace data that is available.

Enabling the Trace Facility in the Web.Config File

The ASP.NET trace facility can also be enabled in the Web application's Web.config file. You do so using the following steps:

1. Open the Web.Config file for your site. This is an XML file that contains settings for the Web site.

2. Locate the trace element, which looks something like this.

```
<trace
    enabled="false"
    requestLimit="10"
    pageOutput="false"
    traceMode="SortByTime"
    localOnly="true"
    mostRecent="true"
/>
```

3. Change the settings as necessary. Table 1-6 describes each of the settings.

4. Run the Web application.

5. Navigate to the trace.axd page on the Web application (*http://server/application/trace.axd*) to display the trace data that is available.

Viewing the Trace Data

After turning on the ASP.NET trace facility, you can either view the trace output on each Web page (pageOutput="true"), or view the trace output by navigating to the trace.axd (*http://server/application/trace.axd*) page on the current Web application. When navigating to the trace.axd page, a summary page displays, which contains the list of results that are in the cache. Click on one of the cached results to view the result of a single page request, which is similar to the resultant information that is shown on each Web page when the page output is set to True.

Security Alert   If you opt for displaying the trace information on individual pages, the trace information can be displayed on any browser that makes a request. This is a potential security threat because sensitive information such as server variables will display. Be sure to disable page tracing on production Web servers.

The trace result page is broken into sections, as described in Table 1-7. This information can be very useful when you are trying to identify performance issues and resource usage.

Table 1-7   **Trace Result Sections**

Trace Result Section	Description
Request Details	Provides general details about the page request.
Trace Information	Displays performance information related to the Web page's life-cycle events. The From First(s) column displays the running time from when the page request started. The From Last(s) column shows the elapsed time since the previous event.
Control Tree	Displays information about each control on the Web page, such as the size of the rendered controls.
Session State	Displays all Session variables and their values.
Application State	Displays all Application variables and their states.
Request Cookies Collection	Displays the list of cookies that are passed to the server as part of the request.
Response Cookies Collection	Displays the list of cookies that are passed to the browser as part of the response.
Headers Collection	Displays the list of HTTP headers that are sent to the Web server as part of the request.
Form Collection	Displays the list of values that are posted back to the Web server.
QueryString Collection	Displays the list of values that are included in the query string.
Server Variables	Displays all server variables.

Quick Check
1. How can you make the trace data display on your Web page?
2. What is the name of the virtual page that you can request to view trace data when the trace data is not displayed on its corresponding Web page?

Quick Check Answers
1. Set pageOutput="true".
2. The virtual page is called Trace.axd.

Lab: Using the ASP.NET Trace Facility

In the following lab, you use the Web Site Administration Tool to modify the Web site configuration by enabling the ASP.NET trace facility on the Web site. After that, you browse your Web site and view the trace results.

▶ **Exercise 1: Enable the ASP.NET Trace Facility**

In this exercise, you start Visual Studio 2005 and open the Web site from the previous lab.

1. Open the MyFirstSite from the previous lab. Alternatively, you can open the completed Lesson 3 lab project from the CD.

2. Open the Web Site Administration Tool by selecting Website | ASP.NET Configuration.

3. Click the Application tab to display the application settings.

4. Click the link to display the Configure debugging and tracing page.

5. Click Capture tracing information. This enables the trace facility.

6. Make the following changes to cache the latest 50 local request results without displaying on the Web page:

   ❑ Select the Capture Tracing Information check box.

   ❑ Ensure the Display Tracing Information On Individual Pages check box is unchecked.

   ❑ Set the Display Trace Output For option to Local Requests Only.

   ❑ Set the Select The Sort Order For Trace Results option to By Time.

   ❑ Set the Number Of Trace Requests To Cache drop-down list to 50.

   ❑ Set the Select Which Trace Results To Cache option to Most Recent Trace Results.

7. Close the Web Site Administration Tool.

8. Open the Web.config file. The new Web.config file will contain the following:

```
<?xml version="1.0" encoding="utf-8"?>
<configuration
      xmlns="http://schemas.microsoft.com/.NetConfiguration/v2.0">
```

```
<system.web>
  <trace
    enabled="true"
    mostRecent="true"
    requestLimit="50" />
  <compilation debug="true" />
</system.web>
</configuration>
```

Notice that the file contains the trace element and attributes to enable tracing as described.

9. Press F5 to run the Web application. Although the default.aspx page is blank because it has no controls on it, the trace facility is still logging results. Press F5 a couple times to refresh the Web page.

10. In the Address bar, change the URL to point to the Page2.aspx file. Press F5 a couple times to refresh the Web page.

11. In the Address bar, change the URL to request the trace.axd page. You should see the trace summary page shown in Figure 1-12.

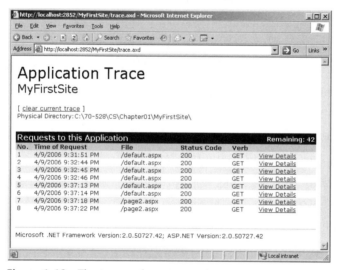

Figure 1-12   The trace.axd summary screen.

12. Click one of the links to open one of the trace result pages. Notice that Trace Information contains the timings for the events in the Web page life cycle as shown in Figure 1-13.

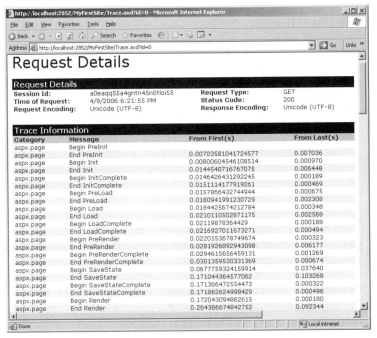

Figure 1-13   The detailed trace information.

Lesson Summary

- The trace facility that is included in ASP.NET can be used to troubleshoot and diagnose problems with your Web site.

- You can also use the trace facility to explore resource usage on each Web page.

- The Web Site Administration Tool can be used to enable and modify the ASP.NET trace facility settings.

- The ASP.NET trace facility can also be enabled and its settings can be changed by modifying the Web.config file in the Web application folder.

Lesson Review

You can use the following questions to test your knowledge of the information in Lesson 4, "Using ASP.NET Trace to Explore Web Pages." The questions are also available on the companion CD if you prefer to review them in electronic form.

NOTE Answers

Answers to these questions and explanations of why each answer choice is right or wrong are located in the "Answers" section at the end of of the book.

---

1. You want to identify which event in the Web page life cycle takes the longest time to execute. How can you accomplish this? (Choose one.)

   A. Turn on ASP.NET trace and run the Web application. After that, review the trace results.

   B. Add a line of code to each of the life-cycle events that will print the current time.

   C. In the Web.config file, add the *monitorTimings* attribute and set it to True.

   D. In the Web site properties, turn on the performance monitor and run the Web application. After that, open performance monitor to see the timings.

2. You want to run the trace continuously to enable you to quickly look at the 10 most recent traces from anyone using your Web site, but you are concerned about filling your hard drive with an excessive amount of data. Which of the following settings will accomplish your objective? (Choose one.)

   A.
   ```
   <trace
       enabled="false"
       requestLimit="10"
       pageOutput="false"
       traceMode="SortByTime"
       localOnly="true"
       mostRecent="true"
   />
   ```

   B.
   ```
   <trace
       enabled="true"
       requestLimit="10"
       pageOutput="true"
       traceMode="SortByTime"
       localOnly="true"
       mostRecent="true"
   />
   ```

   C.
   ```
   <trace
       enabled="true"
       requestLimit="10"
       pageOutput="false"
       traceMode="SortByTime"
       localOnly="true"
       mostRecent="false"
   />
   ```

    D.
```
<trace
    enabled="true"
    requestLimit="10"
    pageOutput="false"
    traceMode="SortByTime"
    localOnly="false"
    mostRecent="true"
/>
```

3. You are interested in examining the data that is posted to the Web server. What trace result section can you use to see this information? (Choose one.)

    A. Control Tree

    B. Headers Collection

    C. Form Collection

    D. Server Variables

Chapter Review

To further practice and reinforce the skills you learned in this chapter, you can perform the following tasks:

- Review the chapter summary.
- Review the list of key terms introduced in this chapter.
- Complete the case scenarios. These scenarios set up real-world situations involving the topics of this chapter and ask you to create solutions.
- Complete the suggested practices.
- Take a practice test.

Chapter Summary

- The Web server is responsible for accepting a request resource and sending a response.
- The Web browser is responsible for displaying data to the user, collecting data from the user, and sending data to the Web server.
- HTTP is a text-based communication protocol that is used to communicate between the Web browser and the Web server.
- A common way of communicating data to the Web server is referred to as a Post-Back.
- ASP.NET 2.0 supports four Web site types: File, FTP, local HTTP, and remote HTTP.
- ASP.NET 2.0 supports two programming models for Web pages: in-line and code-behind.
- Dynamic compilation refers to delayed compilation of Web pages that does not take place until the user requests the Web page.
- Visual Studio 2005 allows you to select a programming language for each Web page.
- New Web pages can be added to a Web site using Visual Studio 2005.
- ASP.NET 2.0 contains a hierarchy of configuration files that can be modified to adjust the settings.
- The ASP.NET trace facilities can be used to monitor performance and resource usage.

Key Terms

Do you know what these key terms mean? You can check your answers by looking up the terms in the glossary at the end of the book.

- Distributed Authoring and Versioning (DAV)
- Hypertext Transfer Protocol (HTTP)
- IsPostBack
- method
- Multipurpose Internet Mail Extensions (MIME) type
- PostBack
- QueryString
- request
- response
- Web browser
- Web Form
- Web server

Case Scenarios

In the following case scenarios, you will apply what you've learned in this chapter. You can find answers to these questions in the "Answers" section at the end of this book.

Case Scenario 1: Creating a New Web Site

You are assembling a group of developers to create a new Web site for a company named Wide World Importers. On each of the developer machines, you will install Visual Studio 2005. You want each developer to be able to debug the Web application independently, but you don't want to install IIS on each of the developer machines.

1. What type of Web site will you create, and why does the Web site type fulfill the requirements?

Case Scenario 2: Placing Files in the Proper Folders

You have created the new Web site for a company named Wide World Importers. The new site will use a third-party component, called ShoppingCart.dll, to process customer purchases. This component requires SQL Server 2005 Express Edition database files, which are called Purchases.mdf (data file) and Purshases.ldf (transaction log file). In addition, you will add a new class file called ShoppingCartWrapper.vb or ShoppingCart-Wrapper.cs, which will be used to simplify the use of the ShoppingCart.dll component.

   1. In what folder(s) will you place these files? What is benefit of using these locations?

Suggested Practices

To successfully master the Program a Web Application exam objective, Create and Configure a Web Application exam objective, Configure Settings for a Web Application exam objective, and Optimize and Troubleshoot a Web Application exam objective, complete the following tasks.

Create a New Web Site Using Visual Studio 2005

For this task, you should complete at least Practice 1. If you want a more well-rounded understanding of all of the Web site types, you should also complete Practice 2.

- **Practice 1**   Become familiar with Web sites by creating a file-based Web site. Also create a local HTTP-based Web site and explore the differences.
- **Practice 2**   You will need a remote computer with IIS, FTP, and Front Page Server Extensions installed. Create an FTP-based Web site and explore the options. Create a remote HTTP Web site and explore the options.

Add a Web Page to the Web Site

For this task, you should complete at least Practice 1. If you want a more well-rounded understanding of adding a Web page, you should also complete Practice 2.

- **Practice 1**   Create any type of Web site. Add a Web page that has a code-behind page. Add a Web page that does not have a code-behind page.
- **Practice 2**   Add another Web page, selecting a different programming language.

Program a Web Application

For this task, you should complete the previous practices first.

- **Practice 1**   In a Web page that you have created, add code to test the *IsPostBack* property of the Web page and display a message if the Web page is posted back.

Configure Settings for a Web Application

For this task, you should complete Practice 1 from the previous section.

- **Practice 1**
    - ❑ Locate the Machine.config file and open it with Notepad.
    - ❑ Explore the various settings that exist in the Machine.config file.
    - ❑ Locate and open the Web.config file that exists in the same folder as the Machine.config file.
    - ❑ Examine the settings that exist in this file.

Optimize and Troubleshoot a Web Application

For this task, you should complete all four practices.

- **Practice 1** Create any type of Web site. Add a Web page.
- **Practice 2** Turn on tracing in the Web page and run the Web application to see the trace.
- **Practice 3** Turn on tracing in the Web.config file and run the Web application to see the trace.
- **Practice 4** In the Web.config file, set the page output to False and use trace.axd to see the trace output.

Take a Practice Test

The practice tests on this book's companion CD offer many options. For example, you can test yourself on just the content covered in this chapter, or you can test yourself on all the 70-528 certification exam content. You can set up the test so it closely simulates the experience of taking a certification exam, or you can set it up in study mode so you can look at the correct answers and explanations after you answer each question.

MORE INFO **Practice tests**

For details about all the practice test options available, see the "How to Use the Practice Tests" section in this book's Introduction.

Chapter 2

Adding and Configuring Server Controls

Web site development provides many challenges that other application development projects don't have. One such challenge is for the developer to create a Web site application that provides seamless communication between the Web browser and the Web server. By seamless, we mean being able to move data back and forth in a way that gives the user the impression that the Web browser and server are one. ASP.NET helps the developer with this challenge by supplying server controls that provide automatic communication to the Web server when an event takes place.

This chapter starts with a description of the two primary types of server controls that are available in ASP.NET: Hypertext Markup Language (HTML) and Web. After that, this chapter dives deeply into the Web page and server control life cycle to help you understand the operation of a server control. Lastly, this chapter covers some of the controls that are available in ASP.NET 2.0.

Exam objectives in this chapter:
- Add and configure Web server controls.
    - Create HTML server controls in the designer.
    - Set HTML server control properties programmatically.
    - Use HTML server controls to programmatically access HTML tags.
    - Create HTML controls as elements in an HTML document.
    - Add Web server controls to a Web Form.
    - Configure the properties of Web server controls programmatically.
    - Configure Web server control properties by using the Microsoft Visual Studio Property Editor.
    - Specify whether events of a control cause a Web Form to post to the server.
    - Configure a control to receive postback events.
    - Access controls in Web Forms pages when working with naming containers and child controls.

❑ Use the Label Web server control to display customized text on a Web page.

❑ Enable users to type information into a Web Form by using the TextBox Web server control.

❑ Use the Button Web server control to send a command to the server when a button is clicked.

❑ Implement the CheckBox Web server control.

❑ Create a mutually exclusive set of choices by using the RadioButton Web server control.

❑ Dynamically add Web server controls to a Web Forms page programmatically.

■ Create event handlers for pages and controls.

❑ Create event handlers for a page or control at design time.

❑ Program a Web application.

❑ Convert HTML server controls to HTML elements.

Lessons in this chapter:

Before You Begin

To complete the lessons in this chapter, you should be familiar with Microsoft Visual Basic or C# and:

■ Have a basic understanding of HTML and client-side scripting.

■ Know how to create a new Web site.

Real World

Glenn Johnson

On many occasions, I've seen developers select the wrong server control for the functionality that needed to be implemented. The problem was that these developers tended to use only a select few controls for most tasks. The end result is that they spent excessive amounts of time developing something that already existed in a different control.

Lesson 1: Using a Server Control

A *server control* is a control that is programmable by writing server-side code to respond to events from the control. Server controls automatically maintain their state between calls to the server and are easily identified by their *runat="server"* attribute. A server control must have an ID attribute for you to reference it in code. ASP.NET provides two primary types of server controls: HTML and Web. All server controls, including the Web page class itself, inherit from the *System.Web.UI.Control* class. Figure 2-1 shows the class hierarchy of the *Control* class with its primary child classes.

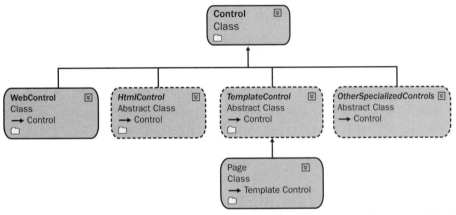

Figure 2-1   The *Control* class with its primary child classes. Note that *OtherSpecializedControls* is not a class; it's simply an indicator that there are other specialized controls that inherit from the *Control* class.

This section covers the life cycle of the Web page and its controls. After that, HTML and Web server controls are covered.

After this lesson, you will be able to:

- Describe the life cycle of the Web page and its controls.
- Describe *ViewState*.
- Explain the order and purpose of the primary events that take place when a page is requested.

Estimated lesson time: 30 minutes

Understanding the Life Cycle of the Web Page and Its Controls

To thoroughly understand how server controls operate, it's important to have a good understanding of the life cycle of a Web page and its controls. The life cycle starts when the browser requests a Web page from a Web site. The Web server constructs the Web page object and all of its child control objects and uses these objects to render the Web page to the browser. After that, the objects are destroyed. The Web page object and its child control objects are destroyed to free up resources. This allows the Web server to scale nicely but poses problems when you're trying to hold onto object data, or *state*, between calls to the server. This is where *ViewState* comes to the rescue.

What Is *ViewState*?

ViewState is the mechanism by which Web page object and child control object data can be maintained between page requests. Any object data that cannot be represented as HTML in the Web page is eligible to be placed into *ViewState*. For example, when a user clicks the Submit button on a Web page, a Postback occurs, sending all form data back to the Web server. *ViewState* is implemented by using a hidden form field called "__ViewState" to store the data. At the server, *ViewState* is used to reconstruct the Web page and its server controls.

Using *EnableViewState* to Minimize *ViewState* Size

Adding lots of data to *ViewState* can cause performance problems because the data is sent to the browser when a page is requested and back to the server when the data is posted back. To minimize the data that is in *ViewState*, you can set the *EnableViewState* property, which your server controls to *false*. Be careful, however, because setting this property to *false* means that you need to write code to repopulate the control yourself between page calls.

Control and Data State Separation

In ASP.NET 2.0, controls have the ability to separate data state and control state. Previous versions of ASP.NET stored data and control state together, and when a control's *EnableViewState* property was set to *false*, the control lost its appearance along with the data. What this means is that, in ASP.NET 2.0 you can set a control's *EnableViewState* to *false* and you lose the data but not the control's appearance. This also means that a control may still be contributing to the size of the __ViewState input even when the *EnableViewState* property is set to *false*.

NOTE .NET 2.0

Control state and data state separation is new in ASP.NET version 2.0.

Identifying *ViewState* Contributors

One problem that plagues many Web pages is that *ViewState* becomes bloated, which causes performance problems when receiving and posting pages. You can use the ASP.NET trace facility to examine the controls that contribute to *ViewState*. The trace facility also displays the *ViewState* size for each control, which means that you can easily identify the source of the bloat.

To use the ASP.NET trace facility to identify *ViewState* contributors, follow these steps:

1. Enable the trace facility as described in Chapter 1, "Introducing the ASP.NET 2.0 Web Site."

2. Browse the Web site, visiting the Web pages that you are interested in obtaining *ViewState* information for.

3. View the trace information; the Control Tree section indicates the *ViewState* size and the *ControlState* size for each control on the Web page.

Web Page and Server Control Events

All server controls have methods and events that execute during their life cycles, as their pages are being created and destroyed. Because the Web page derives from the *Control* class, it also has methods and events that execute as it is being created and destroyed. Table 2-1 contains an ordered list of the methods that execute and the events that take place when a page is requested. This table also contains the method names that correspond to the event. This list is specifically focused on *ViewState* and its availability during the control's life cycle.

Table 2-1 Web Page/Server Control Life Cycle Methods and Events

Method (Event)	Description
1. *OnInit (Init)*	Initializes each child control of the current control.

Table 2-1 Web Page/Server Control Life Cycle Methods and Events

Method (Event)	Description
2. *LoadControlState*	Loads the *ControlState* of the control. To use this method, the control must call the *Page.RegisterRequiresControlState* method in the *OnInit* method of the control.
3. *LoadViewState*	Loads the *ViewState* of the control.
4. *LoadPostData*	Is defined on interface *IPostBackDataHandler*. Controls that implement this interface use this method to retrieve the incoming form data and update the control's properties accordingly.
5. *Load (OnLoad)*	Allows actions that are common to every request to be placed here. Note that the control is stable at this time; it has been initialized and its state has been reconstructed.
6. *RaisePostDataChangedEvent*	Is defined on the interface *IPostBackData-Handler*. Controls that implement this interface use this event to raise change events in response to the Postback data changing between the current Postback and the previous Postback. For example, if a TextBox has a *TextChanged* event and AutoPostback is turned off, clicking a button causes the *TextChanged* event to execute in this stage before handling the click event of the button, which is raised in the next stage.
7. *RaisePostbackEvent*	Handles the client-side event that caused the Postback to occur.

Table 2-1 Web Page/Server Control Life Cycle Methods and Events

Method (Event)	Description
8. *PreRender (OnPreRender)*	Allows last-minute changes to the control. This event takes place after all regular Post-back events have taken place. This event takes place before saving *ViewState*, so any changes made here are saved.
9. *SaveControlState*	Saves the current control state to *ViewState*. After this stage, any changes to the control state are lost. To use this method, the control must call the *Page.RegisterRequiresControlState* method in the *OnInit* method of the control.
10. *SaveViewState*	Saves the current data state of the control to *ViewState*. After this stage, any changes to the control data are lost.
11. *Render*	Generates the client-side HTML, Dynamic Hypertext Markup Language (DHTML), and script that are necessary to properly display this control at the browser. In this stage, any changes to the control are not persisted into *ViewState*.
12. *Dispose*	Accepts cleanup code. Releases any unmanaged resources in this stage. Unmanaged resources are resources that are not handled by the .NET common language runtime, such as file handles and database connections.
13. *UnLoad*	Accepts cleanup code. Releases any managed resources in this stage. Managed resources are resources that are handled by the runtime, such as instances of classes created by the .NET common language runtime.

Creating Event Handlers

The Web page and its server controls have a default event. For example, the Web page's default event is *Load* event, and the button's default event is the *Click* event. In the Microsoft Visual Studio 2005 design time environment, you can add an event handler method for the default event by simply double-clicking the design surface of the object. An event handler is created in the code-behind file. For example, if you double-click on the Web page (don't double-click a server control), a *Page_Load* event handler method is created in the code-behind page, and you can simply add your custom code into this method.

The VB.NET and C# Web page designers differ when it comes to creating event handlers for other events, including *PostBack* events.

Adding the VB.NET Event Handler   For VB.NET, use the following steps to create an event handler for the Init event, assuming that you are currently looking at the Web page:

1. Right-click the Web page and click View Code. This opens the code-behind page without inserting any code.

2. In the code-behind file, click the object drop-down list and click Page Events, as shown in Figure 2-2.

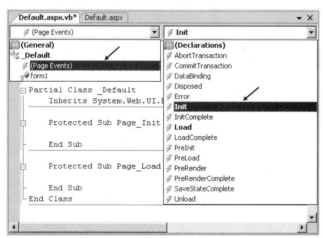

Figure 2-2   Add the *Init* event handler to a VB.NET Web page.

3. Click the event drop-down list and click the *Init* event that adds the following event handler code:

```
Protected Sub Page_Init(ByVal sender As Object, ByVal e As System.EventArgs) _
    Handles Me.Init

End Sub
```

Adding the C# Event Handler   In C#, the event handler drop-down list only contains existing events, not all events. This means that you need to explicitly type the event handler methods for Page events, but there is a way to use the Graphical User Interface (GUI) to add event handlers for the server controls that are on the Web page. To add the *Init* event handler to a C# Web page, follow these steps:

1. Type the following code into the code-behind page. The Web page has its *Auto-EventWireup* property set to *true* in the @*Page* directive at the top of the Source view, which means that the runtime automatically connects to the event handler that you create as long as the method name is in the form *Page_Event*.

```
private void Page_Init(object sender, EventArgs e)
{

}
```

2. To add an event handler for a server control that's on the Web page, in Design view, click the server control to select it.

3. In the Properties windows, click the Events icon, which is the button that has the yellow lightning bolt. This changes the Properties window to the events view.

4. Locate the Init event. Double-click anywhere on the line that contains the Init event, which opens the code-behind page and inserts the following event handler code as shown in Figure 2-3.

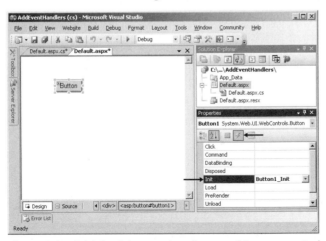

Figure 2-3   Add the *Init* event handler to a C# server control.

Making the Decision: HTML or Web Server Controls?

The following sections cover HTML and Web server controls. Frequently, the question arises: which one should I use? Here is some guidance that can help you choose the proper control type.

Consider using the HTML server controls when any of the following conditions exist:

- You are migrating existing ASP pages to ASP.NET.

- The control needs to have custom client-side JavaScript attached to the control's events.

- The Web page has lots of client-side JavaScript and that is referencing the control.

In all other cases, you should consider using the more powerful Web server controls.

MORE INFO   HTML and Web server controls

For more information about the differences between HTML server controls and Web server controls, visit *http://msdn2.microsoft.com/en-us/zsyt68f1.aspx*.

HTML Server Controls

An *HTML server control* looks like its matching HTML tag, but it also contains the *runat="server"* attribute. HTML server controls provide server-side objects that you can programmatically access. In the Web browser, they typically render as single HTML tags. The primary reason to use HTML server controls is to provide an easy conversion of older Web sites to ASP.NET. Figure 2-4 shows the class hierarchy of the common HTML server controls.

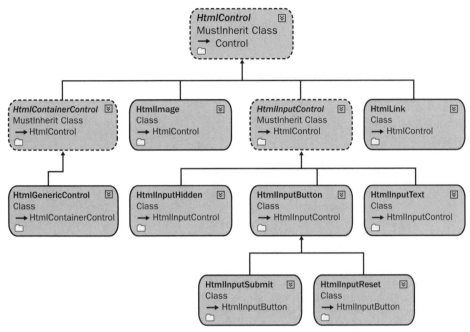

Figure 2-4   The class hierarchy of the common HTML server controls.

Creating HTML Control Elements in an HTML Document

You can easily create HTML controls as elements in an HTML document. Consider the following Web page on an existing ASP Web site.

Old ASP Web Page

```
<html>
    <head><title>Customer Page</title></head>
    <body>
        <form name="Form1" method="post" action="update.asp" id="Form1" >
            <input type="text" name="CustomerName"
                id="CustomerName" >
            <input type="submit" name="SubmitButton"
                value="Submit" id="SubmitButton" >
        </form>
    </body>
</html>
```

This is a form that has a text box and a submit button. The user can type a customer name and click the submit button to POST the data back to the update.asp page at the Web server.

Using HTML controls, you can easily convert the Web page to ASP.NET 2.0, resulting in the following.

Converted ASP.NET 2.0 Web Page

```
<html>
   <head><title>Customer Page</title></head>
   <body>
     <form name="Form1" method="post" id="Form1" runat="server">
        <input type="text" name="CustomerName"
           id="CustomerName" runat="server" >
        <input type="submit" name="SubmitButton"
           value="Submit" id="SubmitButton" runat="server">
     </form>
   </body>
</html>
```

Notice that there is a one-to-one conversion from the HTML tag to the HTML server control, but the *runat="server"* attribute was added. In essence, HTML controls were created by simply modifying the elements of the HTML document. Also, notice that the action attribute was removed from the form tag, because it's customary to send the data back to the same page.

Creating HTML Server Controls in the Designer

To create an HTML server control using the Visual Studio 2005 designer, perform the following steps:

1. Click the HTML tab in the Toolbox.

2. Drag an HTML element to either the Design or Source view of the Web page.

3. Convert the element to an HTML server control. In Source view, add the *runat="server"* attribute. In Design view, right-click the HTML element and click Run As Server Control. A glyph appears on the upper-left corner of the control in Design view to indicate that it is a server control.

NOTE   Location of HTML Server Controls

An HTML server control must be located inside a form element that has the *runat="server"* attribute to operate properly.

If you decide that you no longer need to program an HTML server control in server code, you should convert it back to a plain HTML element. Each HTML server control in a page uses resources, so it is a good practice to minimize the number of controls that the ASP.NET page has to work with. In Design view, right-click the control and clear the check mark next to Run As Server Control. In Source view, remove the *runat="server"* attribute from the control's tag. If the HTML element is referenced by client script, you should not remove the *ID* attribute.

Setting the HTML Server Control Properties

By default, HTML elements within an ASP.NET file are treated as literal text. You cannot reference them in server-side code until you convert the HTML element into an HTML server control. You should also set the element's *ID* attribute to give you a way to programmatically reference the control. Table 2-2 contains a list of the properties that all HTML server controls have in common. You can set the properties of the HTML server control by setting the attributes in the Source view, by setting the properties in the Design view, or by setting the properties programmatically in code. This section examines all three methods.

Table 2-2   Common HTML Server Control Properties

Property	Description
Attributes	A list of all attribute name/value pairs expressed on a server control tag within a selected ASP.NET page. This is accessible via code.
Disabled	A value that indicates whether the disabled attribute is included when an HTML control is rendered on the browser, which makes the control read-only when true.
Id	The programmatic identification of the control.
Style	A list of all cascading style sheet (CSS) properties that are applied to the specified HTML server control.
TagName	The element name of a tag that contains a *runat="server"* attribute.
Visible	A value that indicates whether the HTML server control is displayed on the page. If this value is set to *false*, the control does not render any HTML to the browser.

Setting Properties in Source View   In Source view, you set the properties of an HTML control by adding the appropriate HTML attribute to the HTML server control's element. Consider the following HTML server control button.

```
<input type="button"
    id="myButton"
    runat="server"
    style="position: absolute; top: 50px; left: 100px;"
    value="Click Me"
    visible="true" />
```

Notice that this server control has many of the same attributes that an HTML input button element has, except it has the *runat="server"* attribute and the *visible* attribute. The ID sets the programmatic identification to myButton, the *style* attribute sets the location of the control, the value of Click Me displays on the button face, and the button is visible. The rendered HTML looks like the following:

```
<input
    id="myButton"
    name="myButton"
    type="button"
    style="position: absolute; top: 50px; left: 100px;"
    value="Click Me" />
```

Notice that the *visible* attribute is missing. The fact that the input element was in the rendered HTML is an indicator that the *visible* attribute was set to *true*. If the *visible* attribute was set to *false*, the input element would be missing from the rendered HTML at the browser. Also, if the *name* attribute is not explicitly set, the *name* attribute is set to the *ID* attribute's value.

Setting Properties in Design View   In Design view, the properties of an HTML control are set by clicking the server control and modifying the desired properties in the Properties window. Figure 2-5 shows the same button configured using the Properties window. Changes that are made in the Properties window are reflected in the Source view, and changes in the Source view are reflected in the Properties window in Design view.

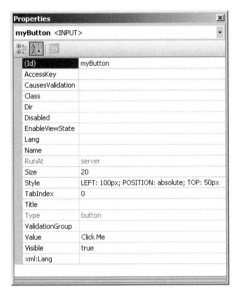

Figure 2-5 Setting the HTML input button properties using the Properties window.

Setting Properties Programmatically in Code   To set the properties of an HTML server control programmatically, use the dot notation to refer to the HTML server control by its *ID* property, and specify the property that you wish to change. All properties are essentially strings, integers, or boolean except the *style* property, which is a collection of keys as strings and values as strings. The following code was added to the *Page_Load* event handler; it sets the *visible* and *style* properties of the button that has the ID myButton:

```VB
'VB
myButton.Visible = True
myButton.Style.Add("position", "absolute")
myButton.Style.Add("left", "75px")
myButton.Style.Add("top", "150px")
```

```C#
//C#
myButton.Visible = true;
myButton.Style.Add("position", "absolute");
myButton.Style.Add("left", "75px");
myButton.Style.Add("top", "150px");
```

Using HTML Server Controls to Programmatically Access HTML Tags   If you need to access the properties of an HTML tag from a server control, the HTML tag must be converted to an HTML server control by adding the *runat="server"* attribute. The following steps demonstrate how clicking the HTML Button Input reads the value from an HTML Text Input and sets the *innerText* of an HTML Div:

1. Add an HTML Text Input and an HTML Div from the Toolbox.

2. Position these HTML elements as shown in Figure 2-6.

NOTE   Setting the Layout to Absolute Positioning

If you want to enable absolute positioning of controls on your Web pages, you can change the default positioning by selecting Layout | Positioning | Auto-position Options to display the Options window. Locate the HTML Designer | CSS Positioning options and set the positioning options to Absolutely positioned for controls added using the Toolbox, paste, or drag-and-drop options.

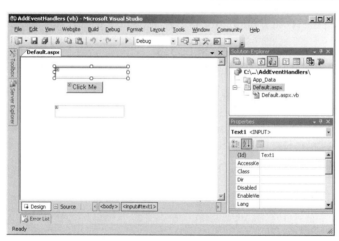

Figure 2-6   Add HTML elements to the page and convert to HTML server controls.

3. Right-click the HTML Text Input and HTML Div and click Run As Server Control.

4. Double-click myButton to add the Click event handler and add code to read from the HTML Text Input and place its value into the HTML Div's *innerText* property.

```
'VB
Protected Sub myButton_ServerClick(ByVal sender As Object, _
     ByVal e As System.EventArgs) _
     Handles myButton.ServerClick
   DIV1.InnerText = Text1.Value
End Sub
```

```
//C#
protected void myButton_ServerClick(object sender,
     System.EventArgs e)
{
   DIV1.InnerText = Text1.Value;
}
```

Best Practices for Using HTML Server Controls

HTML server controls are also useful when your control needs to have client-side Java-Script events attached.

There are a couple of disadvantages to using HTML server controls. One disadvantage is that HTML controls don't have a programming model that is consistent with Win-Form programming. For example, in WinForm programming, the data that is typed in the text box is available via the *Text* property, whereas the HTML server control's text box data is available via the *Value* property.

Another disadvantage to HTML server controls is that an HTML server control directly maps to a single HTML tag. Wouldn't it be great if you could add a single server control to a Web page and it would be rendered as many HTML tags? Web server controls are the answer.

Web Server Controls

Web server controls offer more functionality and a more consistent programming model than HTML server controls. Web server controls may also render as many HTML tags and may also include client-side JavaScript code. This means that it is possible to create very elaborate Web server controls, such as a calendar control or a data grid control.

Most, but not all, Web server controls inherit from the *WebControl* class. Figure 2-7 shows the class hierarchy of some of the more common Web server controls.

Web server controls have the ability to detect the Web browser's capabilities and render appropriately based on those capabilities. This means that the Web server controls can use the Web browser to its fullest potential.

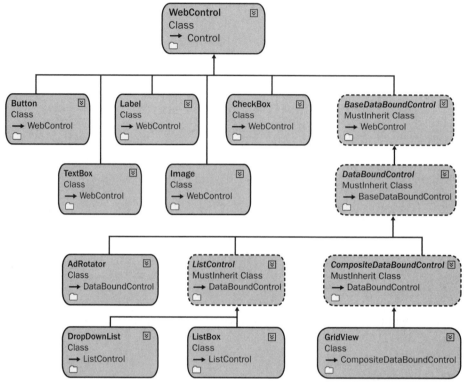

Figure 2-7   The class hierarchy of some of the common Web server controls.

In the design environment, a typical Web server control's source markup might look like the following.

```
<asp:textbox attributes runat="server" />
```

The attributes of the Web server control are used to control the look and behavior of the Web server control. These attributes may not render as attributes in the HTML that is rendered to the Web browser.

Adding Web Server Controls to the Web Page

A Web server control can be added to a Web page using Visual Studio 2005 Design view or Source view, or the Web server controls can be added dynamically via code. This section covers each of these methods.

Adding Web Server Controls Using Design View

Use these steps to add a Web server control to a Web page using the Design view:

1. Open the Web page in Visual Studio 2005.
2. Click the Design tab on the bottom of the Web page.
3. Open the Toolbox and click the tab called Standard.
4. Drag and drop a Web server control on the Web page.

Adding Web Server Controls Using Source View

Use these steps to add a Web server control to a Web page using the Source view:

1. Open the Web page in Visual Studio 2005.
2. Click the Source view tab on the bottom of the Web page.
3. Perform either step 4 or steps 5 and 6.
4. In the Source View of the Web page, type the Web server control element and its attributes.
5. Open the Toolbox and click the Standard tab.
6. In the Source View of the Web page, drag and drop a Web server control.

Like the HTML server control, the Web server control must be located within a form element that has the *runat="server"* attribute.

Adding Web Server Controls Dynamically Via Code

In addition to adding Web server controls using Visual Studio 2005, you can also programmatically add Web server controls to the Web page dynamically. It is important to understand the Web page and server control life cycle described in Table 2-1 to assure that the control operates properly. Notice that the *OnInit(Init)* method and event are typically used to initiate child controls. The following steps demonstrate the implementation of dynamically generated Web controls:

1. Open the Web page's code-behind page in Visual Studio 2005.
2. Click the Source view tab on the bottom of the Web page.
3. In the *Page_Init* method, add code to create a new instance of the Web server control.
4. After creating the instance, add code to make the control visible.

5. Add the control to the *Controls* collection of form1. Your code should look like the following.

```vb
'VB
Protected Sub Page_Init(ByVal sender As Object, _
        ByVal e As System.EventArgs) Handles Me.Init
    Dim c As New TextBox()
    c.ID = "txtUserName"
    c.Visible = True
    form1.Controls.Add(c)
End Sub
```

```csharp
//C#
protected void Page_Init(object sender,
        System.EventArgs e)
{
    TextBox c = new TextBox();
    c.ID = "txtUserName";
    c.Visible = true;
    form1.Controls.Add(c));
}
```

Setting the Web Server Control Properties

Most, but not all Web Server controls inherit from the *WebControl* class. All Web server controls must contain a valid ID to give you a way to programmatically reference the control. Table 2-3 contains a list of the properties that all Web server controls have in common. You can set the properties of the Web server control by setting the attributes in the Source view, by setting the properties in the Design view, or by setting the properties programmatically in code. This section examines all three methods.

Table 2-3   Common Web Server Control Properties

Property	Description
AccessKey	The keyboard shortcut key. It can specify a single letter or number that the user can press while holding down Alt. For example, specify "Q" if you want the user to press Alt+Q to access the control. The property is supported only in Microsoft Internet Explorer 4.0 and later.

Table 2-3 Common Web Server Control Properties

Property	Description
Attributes	A collection of additional attributes on the control that is not defined by a public property, but that should be rendered in the primary HTML element of this control. This allows you to use an HTML attribute that is not directly supported by the control. This property is accessible programmatically; it cannot be set in the designer.
BackColor	The background color of the control, which can be set using standard HTML color identifiers, such as "red" or "blue," or RGB values expressed in hex format ("#ffffff").
BorderColor	The border color of the control, which can be set using standard HTML color identifiers, such as "black" or "red," or RGB values expressed in hex format ("#ffffff").
BorderWidth	The width of the control's border in pixels. Not fully supported for all controls in browsers earlier than Internet Explorer 4.0.
BorderStyle	The border style, if there is any. Possible values are: NotSet, None, Dotted, Dashed, Solid, Double, Groove, Ridge, Inset, and Outset.
CssClass	The cascading style sheet (CSS) class to assign to the control.
Style	A list of all cascading style sheet (CSS) properties that are applied to the specified HTML server control.
Enabled	An attribute that disables the control when set to false. This dims the control and makes it inactive. It doesn't hide the control.
EnableTheming	The default of true, which enables themes for this control.
EnableViewState	The default of true, which enables view state persistence for the control.

Table 2-3   Common Web Server Control Properties

Property	Description
Font	An attribute that contains subproperties that you can declare using the property-subproperty syntax in the opening tag of a Web server control element. For example, you can make a Web server control's text italic by including the *Font-Italic* attribute in its opening tag.
ForeColor	The foreground color of the control. It is not fully supported for all controls in browsers earlier than Internet Explorer 4.0.
Height	The control's height. It is not fully supported for all controls in browsers earlier than Internet Explorer 4.0.
SkinID	The skin to apply to the control.
TabIndex	The control's position in the tab order. If this property is not set, the control's position index is 0. Controls with the same tab index can be tabbed according to the order in which they are declared in the Web page. This works only in Internet Explorer 4.0 and later.
ToolTip	The text that appears when the user hovers the mouse pointer over a control. The *ToolTip* property does not work in all browsers.
Width	The width of the control. The possible units are: Pixel, Point, Pica, Inch, Mm, Cm, Percentage, Em, and Ex. The default unit is pixels.

Setting Properties in Source View   In Source view, the properties of a Web server control are set by adding the appropriate attributes to the Web server control's element. Consider the following Web server control button:

```
<asp:Button ID="btnWebButton"
   runat="server"
   Style=" position: absolute; top: 50px; left: 300px;"
   Text="WebButton" />
```

Notice that this server control has different attributes from its HTML counterpart. For example, the *Text* property on the Web server control coincides with the value property on the HTML server control. The difference is an attempt to provide a consistent programming model among Web server controls and Windows Forms controls. As with HTML server controls, the *ID* property sets the programmatic identification. The *style* attribute sets the location of the control, and the *Text* of WebButton displays on the button face. The rendered HTML looks like the following:

```
<input id="btnWebButton"
   type="submit"
   name="btnWebButton"
   value="WebButton"
   style=" position: absolute; top: 50px; left: 300px;" />
```

Notice that the rendered HTML creates an HTML input element that is configured as a submit button, and the *value* attribute becomes the *Text* property on the Web server control. Also, if the *name* attribute is not explicitly set, the *name* attribute is automatically set to the ID.

Setting Properties in Design View   In Design view, the properties of a Web control are set by clicking the server control and modifying the desired properties in the Properties window. Figure 2-8 shows the same button configured using the Properties window. It's rather interesting to note that the *Style* property is not available in the Properties window. Changes that are made in the Properties window are reflected in the Source view; changes in the Source view are reflected in the Properties window in Design view.

Figure 2-8   Setting the Web server *Button* control properties using the Properties window.

Setting Properties Programmatically in Code   To set the properties of a Web server control programmatically, use the dot notation to refer to the Web server control by its *ID* property and specify the property that you wish to change. The following code was added to the *Page_Load* event handler; it sets the *visible* and *style* properties of the button that has the ID of *btnWebButton*.

```
'VB
btnWebButton.Visible = True
btnWebButton.Style.Add("position", "absolute")
btnWebButton.Style.Add("top", "200px")
btnWebButton.Style.Add("left", "350px")
```

```
//C#
btnWebButton.Visible = true
btnWebButton.Style.Add("position", "absolute");
btnWebButton.Style.Add("top", "200px");
btnWebButton.Style.Add("left", "350px");
```

Notice that the Style property is available for programmatic access and that changing the top and left values causes the control to be relocated.

Controlling Automatic PostBack

Some server controls always cause a PostBack when a specific event occurs. For example, the *Button* control's *Click* event always causes a PostBack. Other controls, such as the *TextBox*, have events that do not cause an automatic PostBack, but they are configurable to do so as required. For example, the *TextBox* contains a default event called *TextChanged*. By default, the *TextChanged* event does not cause an automatic PostBack, but the event is not lost. Instead, the event is raised when a different control, such as a *Button*, causes a PostBack.

When working with events that do not cause automatic PostBacks, it's important to understand when these events are raised with regard to the Web page life cycle that was defined in Table 2-1. Any postponed events, that is, events that do not cause automatic PostBacks, execute before the events that caused the PostBacks. For example, if the text is changed in a *TextBox* and a Button is clicked, the Button causes a PostBack, but the *TextChanged* event of the *TextBox* executes and then the *Click* event of the Button executes.

If you want to change a postponed event to an immediate event, set the *AutoPostBack* property of the control to *true*. You can do so in the Properties window, via code, or by adding the *AutoPostBack="True"* attribute to the Web server control element in Source view.

Working with Naming Containers and Child Controls

A Web page is made up of a hierarchy of controls. The *System.Web.UI.Control* class, which is the class that the Web page and its controls inherit from, has a *Controls* collection property. This means that the Web page has a *Controls* collection, each of the controls in that collection has its own *Controls* collection, and so on.

The Web page is a *naming container* for the controls that are added to it. A naming container defines a unique namespace for control names. Within a naming container, every control must be uniquely identifiable. Typically, this is accomplished by assigning a unique value to the server control's *ID* property. The *ID* is the programmatic name of the control instance. For example, if you set the *ID* property of a *Label* control to *lblMessage*, you can reference the control in code as *lblMessage* and there cannot be another control in this naming container that has the *ID* of *lblMessage*.

Many data-bound controls, such as the *GridView* control, are containers for child controls. For example, when the *GridView* control is instantiated, it generates multiple instances of child controls to represent the row and column data. How can multiple *GridView* controls be added to a Web page, and then, when their child controls are created, each has its own unique *ID* property? This is because the *GridView* control is a naming container.

The naming container for a given child control is a control above it (parent or higher) in the hierarchy that implements the *INamingContainer* interface. A server control implements this interface to create a unique namespace for populating the *UniqueID* property values of its child server controls. The *UniqueID* property contains the fully qualified name of the control. The difference between this property and the *ID* property is that the *UniqueID* property is generated automatically by the *NamingContainer* and contains the *NamingContainer* information.

Searching for Controls   If you want to locate a child control within a given *NamingContainer*, use the *FindControl* method of the *NamingContainer*. The *FindControl* method recursively searches the underlying child controls, but the searches do not enter the *Controls* collection of any child control that is a *NamingContainer*. The following code snippet shows how to find a control named *lblMessage* on the Web page.

```
'VB
Dim c As Control = FindControl("lblMessage")
```

```
//C#
Control c = FindControl("lblMessage");
```

This code snippet may not have much value because you can simply access lblMessage directly by its *ID*. The *FindControl* method is most valuable when you need to locate a control that has been dynamically created. If a control is created dynamically, you are not able to directly reference it by its *ID* property. Instead, you need to find the control, based on its *ID* property, and assign the returned value to a control variable that you can use to access the control. For example, the *GridView* dynamically creates its child controls using the format "ctl" plus *n*, where *n* is a numeric index for each control. To access a child control called *ctl08*, use the following code.

```
'VB
Dim c As Control = GridView1.FindControl("ctl08")
```

```
//C#
Control c = GridView1.FindControl("ctl08");
```

Quick Check

1. What property do you modify on a server control to minimize the size of the *ViewState* data?
2. What happens in the *OnInit* method of a control?
3. If you are migrating ASP pages to ASP.NET, what type of server controls would you use?

Quick Check Answers

1. Set *EnableViewState* to *false*.
2. Each child control of the current control is initialized.
3. Use HTML server control.

Lab: Exploring Web Page and Server Control Life Cycle Events

In this lab, you explore the Web page and server control life cycle events to gain an understanding of these events.

▶ **Exercise 1: Configuring Web page event handlers**

In this exercise, you configure some of the Web page and server control events by adding event handlers for some of the primary events and running the Web page to display the order of the events.

1. Open Visual Studio 2005 and create a new Web site called LifeCycleEvents using your preferred programming language. The new Web site is created and a Web page called Default.aspx is displayed.

2. Double-click the Default.aspx Web page to create a *Page_Load* event handler.

3. In the *Page_Load* event handler, add the following code.

```
'VB
Protected Sub Page_Load(ByVal sender As Object, _
        ByVal e As System.EventArgs) Handles Me.Load
    System.Diagnostics.Debug.Write("Page_Load<br>")
End Sub

//C#
protected void Page_Load(object sender, EventArgs e)
{
    System.Diagnostics.Debug.Write("Page_Load<br>");
}
```

4. Use the following procedure to add event handlers for the *PreInit*, *Init*, *PreRender*, and *Unload* events, placing Debug.Write code in each event handler that writes the name of the event handler to the Debug window.

   VB.NET

   a. In the code-behind file, click the object drop-down list and click Page Events, as shown in Figure 2-2.

   b. Click the event drop-down list and click the desired event, which adds the event handler code.

   c. Add the following event handler code, taking care to replace the event handler name string with the actual name of the event handler.

```
System.Diagnostics.Debug.Write("HandlerName")
```

   d. Your code should look like the following:

```
Partial Class _Default
    Inherits System.Web.UI.Page

    Protected Sub Page_Init(ByVal sender As Object, _
            ByVal e As System.EventArgs) Handles Me.Init
        System.Diagnostics.Debug.WriteLine("Page_Init")
    End Sub

    Protected Sub Page_Load(ByVal sender As Object, _
            ByVal e As System.EventArgs) Handles Me.Load
```

```
            System.Diagnostics.Debug.WriteLine("Page_Load")
        End Sub

        Protected Sub Page_PreInit(ByVal sender As Object, _
                ByVal e As System.EventArgs) Handles Me.PreInit
            System.Diagnostics.Debug.WriteLine("Page_PreInit")
        End Sub

        Protected Sub Page_PreRender(ByVal sender As Object, _
                ByVal e As System.EventArgs) Handles Me.PreRender
            System.Diagnostics.Debug.WriteLine("Page_PreRender")
        End Sub

        Protected Sub Page_Unload(ByVal sender As Object, _
                ByVal e As System.EventArgs) Handles Me.Unload
            System.Diagnostics.Debug.WriteLine("Page_Unload")
        End Sub
    End Class
```

C#

  a. Type the code for each of the events. The code is in the following format, but be sure to replace Event with the name of the event name:

```
protected void Page_Event(object sender, EventArgs e)
{
}
```

  b. Add the following event handler code, taking care to place the event handler name in string:

```
System.Diagnostics.Debug.Write("HandlerName");
```

  c. Your code should look like the following:

```
using System;
using System.Data;
using System.Configuration;
using System.Web;
using System.Web.Security;
using System.Web.UI;
using System.Web.UI.WebControls;
using System.Web.UI.WebControls.WebParts;
using System.Web.UI.HtmlControls;

public partial class _Default : System.Web.UI.Page
{
    protected void Page_Load(object sender, EventArgs e)
    {
        System.Diagnostics.Debug.WriteLine("Page_Load");
```

```
    }

    protected void Page_Init(object sender, EventArgs e)
    {
        System.Diagnostics.Debug.WriteLine("Page_Init");
    }

    protected void Page_PreRender(object sender, EventArgs e)
    {
        System.Diagnostics.Debug.WriteLine("Page_PreRender");
    }

    protected void Page_PreInit(object sender, EventArgs e)
    {
        System.Diagnostics.Debug.WriteLine("Page_PreInit");
    }

    protected void Page_Unload(object sender, EventArgs e)
    {
        System.Diagnostics.Debug.WriteLine("Page_Unload");
    }
}
```

5. Press F5 to run the Web application. You then receive a prompt stating that the Web site cannot be debugged without adding a Web.config file with debugging enabled. Click OK. The Web page is displayed, although it is blank because no controls were added.

6. Locate the Output window in Visual Studio 2005. In the Output window, you should see the following list of events. Notice the order of the events.

```
Page_PreInit
Page_Init
Page_Load
Page_PreRender
Page_Unload
```

Lesson Summary

- A server control is a control that is programmable by writing server-side code to respond to events from the control.

- Server controls contain the *runat="server"* attribute.

- HTML server controls are useful when ASP Web pages need to be migrated to ASP.NET 2.0 pages.

- HTML server controls are also useful when the server control has a lot of client-side JavaScript.

- Web server controls are much more powerful than HTML controls because a single Web server control can render as many HTML elements and JavaScript code blocks.

- *ViewState* is the mechanism by which Web page object and child control object data can be maintained between page requests.

Lesson Review

You can use the following questions to test your knowledge of the information in Lesson 1, "Using a Server Control." The questions are also available on the companion CD if you prefer to review them in electronic form.

NOTE   Answers

Answers to these questions and explanations of why each answer choice is right or wrong are located in the "Answers" section at the end of the book.

---

1. To add an HTML Web server control to the Web page, you must drag an HTML element from the ToolBox to the Web page and then perform which of the following tasks? (Choose one.)

   A. Right-click the HTML element and click Run=Server.

   B. Double-click the HTML element to convert it to an HTML server control.

   C. Right-click the HTML element and click Run As Server Control.

   D. Click the HTML element and set *ServerControl* to *true* in the Properties window.

2. You noticed that clicking a CheckBox does not cause a PostBack; you need the CheckBox to PostBack so you can update the Web page based on server-side code. How do you make the CheckBox cause a PostBack? (Choose one.)

   A. Set the *AutoPostBack* property to *true*.

   B. Add JavaScript code to call the *ForcePostBack* method.

   C. Set the *PostBackAll* property of the Web page to *true*.

   D. Add server-side code to listen for the click event from the client.

3. After writing code to create a new instance of a *TextBox* server control, what do you need to do to get the *TextBox* to display on the Web page? (Choose one.)

  A. Call the *ShowControl* method on the *TextBox*.

  B. Set the *VisibleControl* to true on the *TextBox*.

  C. Add the *TextBox* instance to the *form1.Controls* collection.

  D. Execute the *AddControl* method on the Web page.

Lesson 2: Exploring Common Web Server Controls

ASP.NET 2.0 provides many Web server controls that can be used to increase productivity. This lesson briefly covers some of the more common Web server controls.

After this lesson, you will be able to:

■ Use the Following Web server controls:

❑ *Label*

❑ *TextBox*

❑ *Button*

❑ *CheckBox*

❑ *RadioButton*

Estimated lesson time: 60 minutes

Real World

Glenn Johnson

A friend of mine asked me to review his Web site, so I navigated to his site and did some exploring to get acquainted with it. It didn't take long for me to see that I was able to enter <script> tags into some of the *TextBoxes* on the site; and that the script was stored in the database. When someone else visited the site, the script was loaded from the database and executed. This Web site contained numerous Cross Site Scripting (XSS) vulnerabilities that could be exploited to allow hackers to steal users' identity information.

Fortunately, the site wasn't in production, so he was able to correct the problems and avoid the embarrassment that this could have caused him and his company.

The *Label* Control

The *Label* control displays text at a specific location on the Web page using the properties that the control has been assigned. Use the *Label* control when server code changes the text or the properties. If you only need to display static text, use HTML or the *Literal* control instead of using a *Label* control. The *Literal* control also displays text and the text can be changed by server code, but the *Literal* control does not support styles, themes, and skins.

Labels can be used as the caption of the *TextBox* or other controls in a situation where using the access key for the *Label* moves the focus to the control to the right of the *Label*.

Security Alert Populating the *Label* control with data from an untrusted source can create Cross Site Scripting (XSS) vulnerabilities. Use the *HttpUtility.HtmlEncode* or the *Server.HtmlEncode* method to encode the untrusted data that is placed in the *Text* property.

To add a *Label* Web server control to a Web page, perform the following steps:

1. If you are in the Source view of the Web page, type an *<asp:Label>* element. If you are in the Design view of the Web page, drag the *Label* control from the Standard tab of the ToolBox to the Web page.

2. Set the control's *Text* property. You can include HTML formatting in the property. For example, you can underline portions of the text by placing the *<u>* element around the text.

The *TextBox* Control

The *TextBox* control collects text from the user. The *Text* property gets or sets the contents of the *TextBox* control.

The *TextBox* contains a *TextMode* property that you can set to SingleLine (default), MultiLine, or Password. SingleLine allows the user to enter a single line of text, MultiLine allows the user to enter many lines of text, and Password creates a single-line text box that masks the value entered by the user.

The *Columns* property sets the maximum width of the *TextBox*; the *Rows* property sets the maximum height of a multiline TextBox.

The *MaxLength* property limits the number of characters that can be entered; the *Wrap* property automatically continues the text on the next line when the end of the text box is reached.

The *Button* Control

The *Button* control displays a push button on the Web page that the user can click to trigger a PostBack to the Web server. A *Button* can be either a submit (default) button or a command button.

A submit button does not have its *CommandName* property set and simply performs a PostBack to the server. You provide an event handler for the *Click* event to control the actions performed when the user clicks the submit button.

You can use a *Button* as a command button by assigning a command name, such as *ChangeChannel* or *FastFoward*, to the *CommandName* property. Using the *Command-Name* property allows you to create multiple *Button* controls on a Web page; you can programmatically determine which *button* is clicked in the event handler for the *Command* event. You can also use the *CommandArgument* property to provide additional information about the command to perform, such as *ChannelUp*, *ChannelDown*, *x2* (FastForward x 2), or *x3* (FastForward x 3). Simply provide an event handler for the *Command* event to control the actions performed when a command button is clicked.

The *Button* control also contains a *CausesValidation* property that is set to true by default, which causes page validation to be performed when a *Button* control is clicked. Set the *CausesValidation* property to *false* when you want a *button* to bypass validation. Reset and help buttons are examples of buttons that typically bypass validation.

The *CheckBox* Control

The *CheckBox* control gives the user the ability to select between true and false. The *CheckBox* control's *Text* property specifies its caption. Use the *TextAlign* property to specify on which side that the caption appears. The *Checked* property is used to set and get the status of the *CheckBox* control.

Security Alert   Populating the *CheckBox* control's *Text* property with data from an untrusted source can create Cross Site Scripting (XSS) vulnerabilities. Use the *HttpUtility.HtmlEncode* or *Server.HtmlEncode* method to encode the untrusted data that is placed in the *Text* property.

The *CheckedChanged* event is raised when the state of the *CheckBox* control changes, but by default, the *AutoPostBack* property of the *CheckBox* control is set to *false*. This means that changing the checked state does not cause a PostBack, but the *Check-Changed* event is raised when another control performs a PostBack.

Exam Tip   If you need to create groups of *CheckBox* controls, consider using the *CheckBoxList* control. The *CheckBox* provides better layout control, but the *CheckBoxList* control is easier to use when binding with data.

The *RadioButton* Control

The *RadioButton* control gives the user the ability to select between mutually exclusive *RadioButton* controls in a group. To group multiple *RadioButton* controls together, specify the same *GroupName* for each *RadioButton* control. Grouping radio buttons together only allows a mutually exclusive selection from the group.

Security Alert   Populating the *RadioButton* control's *Text* property with data from an untrusted source can create Cross Site Scripting (XSS) vulnerabilities. Use the *HttpUtility.HtmlEncode* or *Server.HtmlEncode* method to encode the untrusted data that is placed in the *Text* property.

The *RadioButton* control's *Text* property specifies its caption. Use the *TextAlign* property to specify the side that the caption appears on. The *Checked* property is used to set and get the status of the *RadioButton* control.

Exam Tip   Be sure to also consider using the *RadioButtonList*. The *RadioButton* provides better layout control, but the *RadioButtonList* control is easier to use when binding with data.

Quick Check

1. What are the two types of Web server buttons that can be created?
2. How do you create a *TextBox* that retrieves a password from the user?
3. How do you make a *CheckBox* cause immediate PostBack?

Quick Check Answers

1. The two types of buttons are Submit and Command.
2. Set *TextMode* to *Password*.
3. Set its *AutoPostBack* property to *true*.

Lab: Working With Web Server Controls

In this lab, you work with the Web server controls that are defined in this chapter.

▶ **Exercise 1: Adding Controls to the Web Page**

In this exercise, you add Web page controls to the Web page that was created in the previous lab.

1. Open Visual Studio 2005 and open the Web site called LifeCycleEvents that you created in the previous lab. Alternatively, you can open the completed Lesson 1, Exercise 1 project from the CD.

2. Open the Default.aspx Web page in Design view.

3. Drag a *Label*, *TextBox*, *Button*, *CheckBox*, and three *RadioButtons* onto the Web page. Change the *Text* properties of these controls to match Figure 2-9, which shows how the Web page should look.

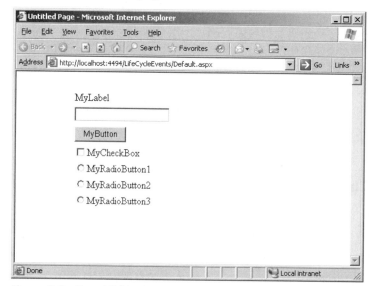

Figure 2-9   Drag Web server controls onto the Web page as shown.

4. Right-click the Web page and click View Code to open the code-behind page. Notice that no additional code was added to the code-behind page.

5. Press F5 to run the Web application.

6. Try clicking the *Button*, *CheckBox*, and *RadioButton* controls. Observe the behavior of these controls. Notice that the *Button* is the only control that performs a PostBack to the Web server. Also notice that the *RadioButton* controls are not mutually exclusive.

7. Double-click the *Button* control to add the Button's *Click* event handler. Add the following code to populate the *Label* with any text that has been typed into the *TextBox*. Be sure to take the security warnings seriously and use the *HtmlEncode* method. The code should look like the following.

```
'VB
Protected Sub Button1_Click(ByVal sender As Object, _
    ByVal e As System.EventArgs) Handles Button1.Click
  Label1.Text = Server.HtmlEncode(TextBox1.Text)
End Sub

//C#
protected void Button1_Click(object sender, EventArgs e)
{
    Label1.Text = Server.HtmlEncode(TextBox1.Text);
}
```

8. Double-click the *CheckBox* control to add the *CheckedChanged* event handler. Add code to replace its *Text* property with the current date and time if the *CheckBox* is selected. Your code should look like the following.

```
'VB
Protected Sub CheckBox1_CheckedChanged(ByVal sender As Object, _
    ByVal e As System.EventArgs) Handles CheckBox1.CheckedChanged
  If (CheckBox1.Checked) Then
      CheckBox1.Text = DateTime.Now.ToString()
  End If
End Sub

//C#
protected void CheckBox1_CheckedChanged(object sender, EventArgs e)
{
    if (CheckBox1.Checked)
    {
        CheckBox1.Text = DateTime.Now.ToString();
    }
}
```

9. To make the *RadioButton* controls mutually exclusive, these controls must have the same *GroupName* property setting, as long as the setting is not empty. Assign "MyGroup" to the *GroupName* property of all three *RadioButton* controls.

10. Add a single event handler for the *CheckedChanged* event of the three *RadioButtons*. You can do so by selecting all three *RadioButton* controls, and then clicking the lightning bolt icon in the Properties window to see the events that are available. In the *CheckedChanged* event, type **RadioChanged** and press Enter. This adds an

event hander to the code-behind page. In the event handler, add code to copy the text of the selected *RadioButton* into the *TextBox* control. The event handler should look like the following.

```
'VB
Protected Sub RadioChanged(ByVal sender As Object, _
    ByVal e As System.EventArgs) _
    Handles RadioButton1.CheckedChanged, _
        RadioButton2.CheckedChanged, _
        RadioButton3.CheckedChanged
  Dim r As RadioButton = CType(sender, RadioButton)
  TextBox1.Text = r.Text
End Sub

//C#
protected void RadioChanged(object sender, EventArgs e)
{
    RadioButton r = (RadioButton)sender;
    TextBox1.Text = r.Text;
}
```

11. Press F5 to run the Web application. The Web page is displayed.

12. Type something into the *TextBox* control and click the *Button* control. You should see the contents of the *TextBox* control in the *Label* control.

13. Click the CheckBox several times. Notice that nothing seems to happen. Make sure that the CheckBox is selected and then click the Button. Notice that the *CheckBox* control's *Text* property now contains the current date and time. The *CheckBox* does not have *AutoPostBack* set to true.

14. Type different text into the *TextBox*. Click RadioButton2. Notice that nothing happens because *AutoPostBack* is not enabled for the *RadioButton* controls. Click the *Button*. Notice that the *TextBox* is updated to RadioButton2 and the *Label* also contains RadioButton2. This behavior is predictable because the event that caused the PostBack always follows the events that did not cause the *AutoPostBack*.

15. Select the CheckBox and the RadioButtons and set the *AutoPostBack* to *true*.

16. Press F5 to run the Web application. The Web page is displayed.

17. Click the CheckBox. Notice that this control performs a PostBack, and the date and time are updated when the CheckBox is selected.

18. Click each of the *RadioButton* controls. Notice that these controls perform a Post-Back and the *TextBox* is updated to show the *RadioButton* that was clicked.

Lesson Summary

- The *Label* control displays text at a specific location on the Web page using the properties that have been assigned to the *Label* control.

- The *TextBox* control collects text from the user.

- The *Button* control displays a push button on the Web page that can be clicked to trigger a PostBack to the Web server.

- The *CheckBox* control gives the user the ability to select between true and false.

- The *RadioButton* control gives the user the ability to select between mutually exclusive *RadioButton* controls in a group.

Lesson Review

You can use the following questions to test your knowledge of the information in Lesson 2, "Exploring Common Web Server Controls." The questions are also available on the companion CD if you prefer to review them in electronic form.

Answers   Answers to these questions and explanations of why each answer choice is right or wrong are located in the "Answers" section at the end of the book.

---

1. If you want multiple *RadioButton* controls to be mutually exclusive, what property must you set? (Choose one.)

    A. *Exclusive*

    B. *MutuallyExclusive*

    C. *Grouped*

    D. *GroupName*

2. You are creating a Web page that has several related buttons, such as fast forward, reverse, play, stop, and pause. You want to create a single event handler that processes the PostBack from these *Button* controls. Other than the normal Submit button, what type of button can you create as a solution? (Choose one.)

    A. OneToMany

    B. Command

    C. Reset

    D. ManyToOne

3. When in Design view, what is the simplest way to create an event handler for the default event of a server control? (Choose one.)

    A. Open the code-behind page and write the code.

    B. Right-click the control and select Create Handler.

    C. Drag an event handler from the ToolBox to the desired control.

    D. Double-click the control.

Chapter Review

To further practice and reinforce the skills you learned in this chapter, you can perform the following tasks:

- Review the chapter summary.
- Review the list of key terms introduced in this chapter.
- Complete the case scenarios. These scenarios set up real-world situations involv-
  ing the topics of this chapter and ask you to create solutions.
- Complete the suggested practices.
- Take a practice test.

Chapter Summary

- A server control is a control that is programmable by writing server-side code to
  respond to events from the control.
- There are two types of server controls: HTML and Web.
- *ViewState* is the mechanism by which Web page object and child control object
  data can be maintained between page requests.
- The *Label*, *TextBox*, *Button*, *CheckBox*, and *RadioButton* are common Web server
  controls that can increase developer productivity.

Key Terms

Do you know what these key terms mean? You can check your answers by looking up
the terms in the glossary at the end of the book.

- HTML server control
- naming container
- server control
- ViewState
- Web server control

Case Scenarios

In the following case scenarios, you will apply what you've learned in this chapter. You can find answers to these questions in the "Answers" section at the end of this book.

Case Scenario 1: Determining the Type of Controls to Use

You are creating a new Web page that collects customer data. This Web page needs to capture customer names and addresses, plus indicators of which customers are active. You also need to display several vertical market categories and give the data entry person the ability to place the customer into all matching categories. You also prompt the data entry person for the quantity of computers that the customer has, based on sever ranges, such as 0–5, 6–50, 51–250, 251–1000, and 1001 or more.

1. Define the type of controls that you will use and why.

Case Scenario 2: Selecting the Proper Events to Use

You want to create controls dynamically, based on information from the database. The database also contains data that is assigned to the properties of these controls, but the data for one control may come from a different control, so you want to make sure that all of the server controls are instantiated before the properties are set.

1. In what event handler should you place code to dynamically create the controls? Why?

2. Where should you place code to set the properties? Why?

Suggested Practices

To successfully master the Add and Configure Web Server Controls exam objective, complete the following tasks.

Create a New Web Page Using Server Controls

For this task, you should complete at least Practice 1. If you want a more well-rounded understanding of all of the Web site types, you should also complete Practice 2.

- **Practice 1** Create a new Web page and add the Web server controls that have been defined in this chapter.

- **Practice 2** Obtain an existing ASP page and convert this page to ASP.NET by changing all existing HTML elements to HTML controls.

Create Event Handlers for Pages and Controls

For this task, you should complete at least Practice 1.

- **Practice 1**   Create a new Web page and add the Web server controls that have been defined in this chapter. Add event handlers for the default events and explore the other events that are available in each control.
- **Practice 2**   Add event handlers for the *Init* and *Load* event on the Web page.

Program a Web Application

For this task, you should complete Practice 1.

- **Practice 1**   Create a new Web page and add some of the HTML server controls that have been defined in this chapter. Practice converting the HTML server controls back to HTML elements.

Take a Practice Test

The practice tests on this book's companion CD offer many options. For example, you can test yourself on just the content covered in this chapter, or you can test yourself on all of the 70-528 certification exam content. You can set up the test so that it closely simulates the experience of taking a certification exam, or you can set it up in study mode so that you can look at the correct answers and explanations after you answer each question.

MORE INFO   **Practice tests**

For details about all the practice test options available, see the "How to Use the Practice Tests" section in this book's Introduction.

Chapter 3
Exploring Specialized Server Controls

It wasn't that long ago when creating a calendar on a Web page was a time-consuming task involving the creation of Hypertext Markup Language (HTML) tables with hyperlinks on each date and JavaScript to process the selection of a date. Today, with ASP.NET, common tasks such as creating a calendar are simple drag-and-drop operations.

The previous chapter provided an introduction to server controls and discussed some of the common Web server controls. This chapter explores the more specialized controls that are available in ADO.NET 2.0.

Exam objectives in this chapter:
- Add and configure Web server controls.
    - Use the *AdRotator* Web server control to manage banners and pop-up windows.
    - Display a calendar on a Web page by using the *Calendar* Web server control.
    - Implement the *FileUpload* Web server control.
    - Display an image on a Web form by using the *Image* Web server control.
    - Implement a button on a Web form by using the *ImageButton* Web server control.
    - Define hotspot regions within an image by using the *ImageMap* Web server control.
    - Display a hyperlink style button on a Web Form by using the *LinkButton* Web server control.
    - Display lists of information by using controls that derive from the *ListControl* class.

❑ Create a Web Form with static text by using the *Literal* Web server control.

❑ Use the *Panel* Web server control to group controls on a page.

❑ Create a container for a group of *View* controls by using the *MultiView* Web server control.

❑ Use the *View* Web server control.

❑ Construct a table by using the *Table*, *TableRow*, and *TableCell* Web server controls.

❑ Create a wizard by using the *Wizard* Web server control to collect data through multiple steps of a process.

❑ Use the *XML* Web server control to create Extensible Markup Language (XML) data at the location of the control.

❑ Customize the appearance of ASP.NET server controls by using Web control templates.

■ Implement data-bound controls.

❑ Use tabular data source controls to return tabular data.

❑ Use hierarchical data source controls to display hierarchical data.

❑ Display data by using simple data-bound controls.

❑ Display data by using composite data-bound controls.

❑ Display data by using hierarchical data-bound controls.

❑ Use the *FormView* control to display the values of a single table record from a data source.

Lessons in this chapter:

Before You Begin

To complete the lessons in this chapter, you should be familiar with Microsoft Visual Basic (VB) or C# and be comfortable with the following tasks:

- Have Microsoft Windows XP and Microsoft Visual Studio 2005 installed with SQL Server 2005 Express Edition and Internet Information Services (IIS).

- Be familiar with the Visual Studio 2005 Integrated Development Environment (IDE).

- Have a basic understanding of HTML and client-side scripting.

- Know how to create a new Web site.

- Be able to add Web server controls to a Web page.

Real World

Glenn Johnson

I have seen many Web sites that attempt to collect lots of data by simply presenting the user with a Web page that contains a vertical list of *Label:TextBox* prompts. Many users become frustrated with the amount of data that needs to be entered. As a result, these sites have a high rate of abandonment.

Lesson 1: Exploring Specialized Web Server Controls

This lesson covers many of the specialized Web server controls, meaning controls that don't directly convert to single HTML tags and are in ASP.NET 2.0.

After this lesson, you will be able to:

■   Use the following Web server controls:

❑   *Literal*

❑   *Table, TableRow,* and *TableCell*

❑   *Image*

❑   *ImageButton*

❑   *ImageMap*

❑   *Calendar*

❑   *FileUpload*

❑   *Panel*

❑   *MultiView*

❑   *View*

❑   *Wizard*

Estimated lesson time: 60 minutes

The *Literal* Control

The *Literal* control is similar to the *Label* control, as both controls are used to display static text on the Web page. The *Literal* control does not inherit from *WebControl*, as shown in the *Literal* control's object model in Figure 3-1. The *Literal* control does not provide substantial functionality and does not add any HTML elements to the Web page where the *Label* is rendered as a <span> tag. This means that the *Literal* does not have a *Style* property, and you cannot apply any styles, including positioning, to its content.

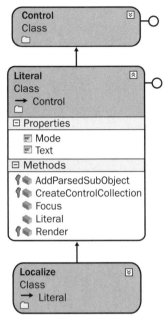

Figure 3-1   The *Literal* control object model.

Security Alert   By default, populating the *Literal* control with data from untrusted sources can create Cross Site Scripting (XSS) vulnerabilities. Set the *Mode* property to *Encode* to provide HTML encoding of untrusted data that will be placed into the *Text* property.

The *Literal* control contains the *Mode* property, which is used to specify particular handling of the content of the *Text* property, as shown in Table 3-1.

Table 3-1   The *Literal* Control's *Mode* Property

Mode	Description
PassThrough	The *Text* content is rendered as is.
Encode	The *Text* content is HTML-encoded.
Transform	The *Text* content is converted to match the markup language of the requesting browser, such as HTML, Extensible Hypertext Markup Language (XHTML), Wireless Markup Language (WML), or Compact Hypertext Markup Language (cHTML). If the markup language is HTML or XHTML, the content is passed through to the browser. For other markup languages, invalid tags are removed.

Take, for example, a Web page that was created and the words Transform, PassThrough, and Encode were added. A *Literal* control was placed beside each of the words. The following code was added to the code-behind page to demonstrate the use of the *Literal* control and the effect of the *Mode* property:

```VB
'VB
Partial Class LiteralControl
    Inherits System.Web.UI.Page

    Protected Sub Page_Load(ByVal sender As Object, _
            ByVal e As System.EventArgs) Handles Me.Load
        Literal1.Text = _
            "This is <font size=7>cool</font><script>alert(""Hi"");</script>"
        Literal2.Text = _
            "This is <font size=7>cool</font><script>alert(""Hi"");</script>"
        Literal3.Text = _
            "This is <font size=7>cool</font><script>alert(""Hi"");</script>"
        Literal1.Mode = LiteralMode.Transform
        Literal2.Mode = LiteralMode.PassThrough
        Literal3.Mode = LiteralMode.Encode
    End Sub
End Class
```

```C#
//C#
using System;
using System.Data;
using System.Configuration;
using System.Collections;
using System.Web;
using System.Web.Security;
using System.Web.UI;
using System.Web.UI.WebControls;
using System.Web.UI.WebControls.WebParts;
using System.Web.UI.HtmlControls;

public partial class LiteralControl : System.Web.UI.Page
{
    protected void Page_Load(object sender, EventArgs e)
    {
        Literal1.Text =
            @"This is <font size=7>cool</font><script>alert(""Hi"");</script>";
        Literal2.Text =
            @"This is <font size=7>cool</font><script>alert(""Hi"");</script>";
        Literal3.Text =
            @"This is <font size=7>cool</font><script>alert(""Hi"");</script>";
        Literal1.Mode = LiteralMode.Transform;
        Literal2.Mode = LiteralMode.PassThrough;
        Literal3.Mode = LiteralMode.Encode;
    }
}
```

Figure 3-2 shows the rendered output of the *Literal* control when the Web page is displayed. The alert message was displayed twice: once for *Transform* and once for *PassThrough*.

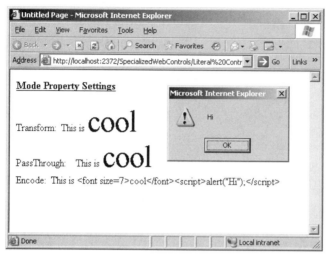

Figure 3-2 *Literal* controls rendered using different *Mode* settings.

The best use for the *Literal* control is in scenarios where you want to render text and controls directly into a page without any additional markup.

The *Table*, *TableRow*, and *TableCell* Controls

Tables provide a way to format information that is displayed on the Web page. The information can be tabular data, but it can also consist of graphics and controls that are to be displayed on the Web page.

NOTE .NET 2.0

The *Table*, *TableRow*, and *TableCell* controls are new in ASP.NET version 2.0.

Although you can configure the *Table* control to display static information while in Design view, the *Table* control's real power comes from the ability to programmatically add *TableRow* and *TableCell* controls at run time. If you only need to display static information, consider using the HTML table tag instead.

Exam Tip   An *HtmlTable* control can be created from the table tag by adding the *runat="server"* attribute to the tag and assigning an ID to the control, but the *Table* control is easier to use because it provides a programming model that is consistent with the *TableRow* and *TableCell* controls.

If you need to programmatically add rows and cells to a table at run time, the *Table* control may be the right choice, but *TableRow* and *TableCell* objects that are added to the *Table* control need to be programmatically re-created when *PostBack* occurs. If you need the rows and cells to survive *PostBacks*, you may want to consider using the *DataList* or *GridView* control. As a result, the *Table* control is usually considered to be best suited for control developers who use the table as part of a custom control that they build.

Security Alert   By default, populating the *TableCell* control with data from untrusted sources can create XSS vulnerabilities. Be sure to HTML encode all data using either the *Server.HtmlEncode* or the *HttpUtility.HtmlEncode* method.

The *Table* control provides an object model that is consistent with other Web controls. Figure 3-3 shows the *Table* control's object model.

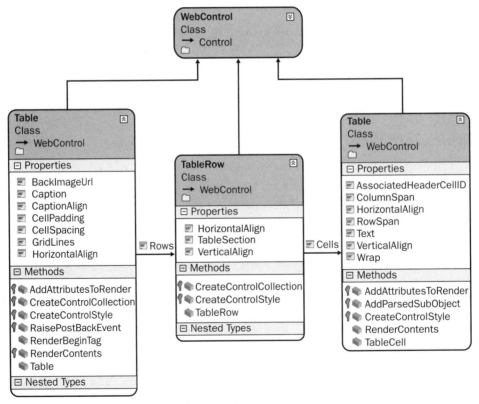

Figure 3-3   The *Table* control's object model.

Notice that the *Table* control contains a *Rows* collection property, which is a collection of *TableRow* controls. The *TableRow* control contains a *Cells* collection property, which is a collection of *TableCell* controls. You can programmatically add and delete *TableRows* and *TableCells* to these collections to build your *Table* control.

The *Table*, *TableRow*, and *TableCell* inherit from the *WebControl* class, which contains format properties such as *Font*, *BackColor*, and *ForeColor*. If you set these properties at the *Table*, you can override them in the *TableRow*, and the *TableRow* settings can be overridden in the *TableCell*.

As mentioned earlier, if you are writing a custom control, the *Table*, *TableRow*, and *TableCell* might be the classes for you, but if you are simply planning on dragging and dropping the *Table* onto the Web page, you should consider using one of the other list controls, such as the *Repeater*, *DataList*, or *GridView*, because these controls typically render as HTML tables and provide more functionality.

Adding Rows and Cells Dynamically to a *Table* Control

The following steps show how to dynamically add *TableCell* and *TableRow* objects to an existing *Table* control:

1. Create a *TableRow* object that corresponds to a row in the table.
2. Create a *TableCell* object and populate it with data by either setting the *Text* property or by adding controls to the *TableCell* object's *Controls* collection.
3. Add the *TableCell* object that you created in step 2 to the *TableRow* object's *Cells* collection.
4. Repeat steps 2 and 3 for each cell that needs to be created in the row.
5. Add the *TableRow* objects that you created in step 1 to the *Table* object's *Rows* collection.
6. Repeat steps 1 through 5, as necessary, for all rows and cells in the table.

In this example, a Web page was created and a *Table* control was added to the page. The following code was added to the code-behind page to demonstrate the dynamic addition of *TableRow* and *TableCell* controls to the *Table* control.

```
'VB
Partial Class Table__TableRow__and_TableCell_Controls
    Inherits System.Web.UI.Page

    Protected Sub Page_Load(ByVal sender As Object, _
        ByVal e As System.EventArgs) Handles Me.Load
        Table1.BorderWidth = 1
```

```
        For row As Integer = 0 To 4
            Dim tr As New TableRow()
            For column As Integer = 0 To 2
                Dim tc As New TableCell()
                tc.Text = String.Format("Row:{0} Cell:{1}", row, column)
                tc.BorderWidth = 1
                tr.Cells.Add(tc)
            Next column
            Table1.Rows.Add(tr)
        Next row
    End Sub
End Class

//C#
using System;
using System.Data;
using System.Configuration;
using System.Collections;
using System.Web;
using System.Web.Security;
using System.Web.UI;
using System.Web.UI.WebControls;
using System.Web.UI.WebControls.WebParts;
using System.Web.UI.HtmlControls;

public partial class Table__TableRow__and_TableCell_Controls : System.Web.UI.Page
{
    protected void Page_Load(object sender, EventArgs e)
    {
        Table1.BorderWidth = 1;
        for (int row = 0; row < 5; row++)
        {
            TableRow tr = new TableRow();
            for (int column = 0; column < 3; column++)
            {
                TableCell tc = new TableCell();
                tc.Text = string.Format("Row:{0} Cell:{1}", row, column);
                tc.BorderWidth = 1;
                tr.Cells.Add(tc);
            }
            Table1.Rows.Add(tr);
        }
    }
}
```

In the code example, notice that the code starts by setting the *BorderWidth* property of the *Table* control to one that causes the *Table* to have a line around its outside edges. The *TableCell* objects also have their *BorderWidth* set to one that causes each *TableCell* to be outlined as well. When the Web page is displayed, it will look like the page shown in Figure 3-4.

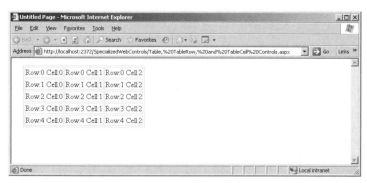

Figure 3-4   This Web page shows the result of dynamically creating *TableRow* and *TableCell* controls.

The *Image* Control

The *Image* control is used to display an image on a Web page. This control generates an <*img*> element when rendering to HTML. The *Image* control inherits directly from the Web control class, and the *ImageMap* and *ImageButton* inherit from the *Image* control, as shown in Figure 3-5.

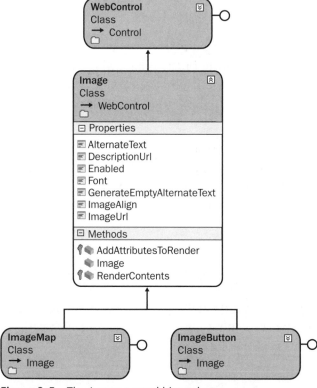

Figure 3-5   The *Image* control hierarchy.

The *Image* control's primary property, *ImageUrl*, indicates the path to the image that is downloaded from the browser and displayed. This property maps directly to the *href* attribute of the <img> element in HTML. It's important to understand that the *Image* is not embedded to the Web page; instead, when the browser encounters the <img> element with the *href* attribute, the browser initiates a separate request for the image from the server.

The *Image* control also contains a property called *AlternateText* that you can set to display a text message when the image is not available.

The *Image* control does not have a *Click* event, but in situations where the *Click* event is necessary, you can use the *ImageButton* or *ImageMap* instead. These controls allow you to retrieve the x- and y-coordinates of the user's click as well.

The *Image* control is represented as the <asp:Image> element in the HTML source and has no content, so you can write this element as a singleton (closing the tag with /> instead of using a separate closing tag).

The *ImageAlign* property can be set to *NotSet*, *Left*, *Right*, *Baseline*, *Top*, *Middle*, *Bottom*, *AbsBottom*, *AbsMiddle*, or *TextTop*. These settings specify the alignment of the image in relation to the other objects on the Web page.

The *DescriptionUrl* property is an accessibility feature that is used to provide further explanation of the content and meaning of the image when using nonvisual page readers. This property sets the *longdesc* attribute of the <img> element that is generated. This property should be set to the URL of a page that contains details of the image in text or audio format.

Setting the *GenerateEmptyAlternateText* property to true will add the attribute *alt*="" to the <img> element that the *Image* control generates. From the accessibility perspective, any image that does not contribute to the meaning of the page, such as a blank image or a page-divider image, should always carry this attribute, which causes nonvisual page readers to simply ignore the image.

Take the following example: A Web page was created and an *Image* control was added to the page. Also, an image file called Girl.gif was added to a new folder called images and an HTML page was created ImageDescription.htm, which contains a description that can be used by nonvisual page readers. The following code was added to the code-behind page to show how the *Image* control's properties can be set programmatically:

```vb
'VB
Partial Class Image_Control
    Inherits System.Web.UI.Page

  Protected Sub Page_Load(ByVal sender As Object, ByVal e As System.EventArgs) Handles Me.Load
      Image1.ImageUrl = "~/Images/Girl.gif"
      Image1.DescriptionUrl = "~/ImageDescription.htm"
      Image1.AlternateText = "This is a picture of a girl"
   End Sub
End Class
```

```csharp
//C#
using System;
using System.Data;
using System.Configuration;
using System.Collections;
using System.Web;
using System.Web.Security;
using System.Web.UI;
using System.Web.UI.WebControls;
using System.Web.UI.WebControls.WebParts;
using System.Web.UI.HtmlControls;

public partial class Image_Control : System.Web.UI.Page
{
    protected void Page_Load(object sender, EventArgs e)
    {
        Image1.ImageUrl = "~/Images/Girl.gif";
        Image1.DescriptionUrl = "~/ImageDescription.htm";
        Image1.AlternateText = "This is a picture of a girl";
    }
}
```

This code is simply setting properties. The tilde (~) indicates the current Web application folder. Figure 3-6 shows the rendered Web page, including the alternate text, which is displayed as a ToolTip.

Figure 3-6   The rendered *Image* control displaying the *AlternateText* property as a ToolTip.

The *ImageButton* Control

The *ImageButton* control is used to display a clickable image on a Web page that can be used to post back to the Web server when the image is clicked. This control generates an *<input type="image">* element when rendering to HTML. The *ImageButton* control inherits directly from the *Image* control class, as shown in Figure 3-7.

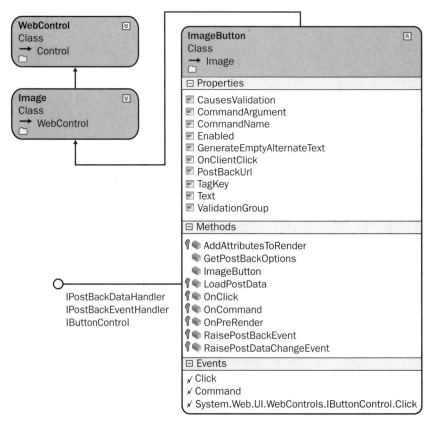

Figure 3-7   The *ImageButton* control hierarchy.

Like the *Image* control, the *ImageButton* control's primary property, *ImageUrl*, indicates the path to an image that can be downloaded from the browser and displayed. This property maps directly to the *src* attribute of the *<input>* element in HTML.

Because the *ImageButton* inherits from the *Image* control, it also contains the *AlternateText*, *DescriptionUrl*, *ImageAlign*, and *GenerateEmptyAlternateText* properties.

The *ImageButton* control has a *Click* and *Command* event that functions like the *Button* control. The second argument of the *Click* event has a data type of *ImageClickEventArgs*, which lets you retrieve the x- and y-coordinates of the user's click.

The *ImageButton* control is represented as the *<asp:ImageButton>* element in source view and has no content, so you can write this element as a singleton element.

Here's another example: A Web page was created and an *ImageButton* control was added to the page. This control also uses the same image file called Girl.gif and HTML page called ImageDescription.htm that were used in the previous *Image* control example. The following code was added to the code-behind page to show how the *Image-Button* control's properties can be set programmatically and the *Click* event can be implemented.

```
'VB
Partial Class ImageButton_Control
    Inherits System.Web.UI.Page

    Protected Sub ImageButton1_Click(ByVal sender As Object, ByVal e As
System.Web.UI.ImageClickEventArgs) Handles ImageButton1.Click
        ImageButton1.AlternateText = _
            String.Format("Button Clicked at {0},{1}", e.X, e.Y)
    End Sub

    Protected Sub Page_Load(ByVal sender As Object, ByVal e As System.EventArgs) Handles Me.Load
        ImageButton1.ImageUrl = "~/Images/Girl.gif"
        ImageButton1.DescriptionUrl = "~/ImageDescription.htm"
        ImageButton1.AlternateText = "This is a picture of a girl"
    End Sub
End Class
```

```
//C#
using System;
using System.Data;
using System.Configuration;
using System.Collections;
using System.Web;
using System.Web.Security;
using System.Web.UI;
using System.Web.UI.WebControls;
using System.Web.UI.WebControls.WebParts;
using System.Web.UI.HtmlControls;

public partial class ImageButton_Control : System.Web.UI.Page
{
    protected void Page_Load(object sender, EventArgs e)
    {
        ImageButton1.ImageUrl = "~/Images/Girl.gif";
        ImageButton1.DescriptionUrl = "~/ImageDescription.htm";
```

```
        ImageButton1.AlternateText = "This is a picture of a girl";
    }
    protected void ImageButton1_Click(object sender, ImageClickEventArgs e)
    {
        ImageButton1.AlternateText =
            string.Format("Button Clicked at {0},{1}", e.X, e.Y);
    }
}
```

This code sets the *ImageButton* control properties in the *Page_Load* event handler. In the *ImageButton1_Click* event handler, the x- and y-coordinates are retrieved and placed into the *AlternateText* property, as shown in Figure 3-8.

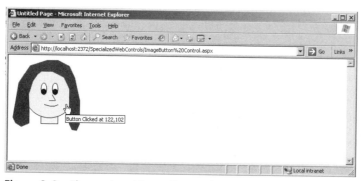

Figure 3-8   The rendered *ImageButton* displaying the *AlternateText* message after the *ImageButton* was clicked.

The *ImageMap* Control

The *ImageMap* control is used to display a clickable image on a Web page that can be used to post back to the Web server when the image is clicked. This control differs from the *ImageButton* control in that the *ImageMap* control allows you to define regions or "hot spots" that cause *PostBack*, whereas clicking anywhere on the *Image-Button* causes *PostBack*. This control generates an *<img usemap="#myMap">* element. In addition, a *<map name="myMap">* element with nested *<area>* elements is also created when rendering to HTML. The *ImageMap* control inherits directly from the *Image* control class, as shown in Figure 3-9.

Like the *Image* control, the *ImageMap* control's primary property, *ImageUrl*, indicates the path to the image that can be downloaded from the browser and displayed. This property maps directly to the *src* attribute of the *<img>* element in HTML.

Since the *ImageMap* inherits from the *Image* control, it also contains the *AlternateText*, *DescriptionUrl*, *ImageAlign*, and *GenerateEmptyAlternateText* properties.

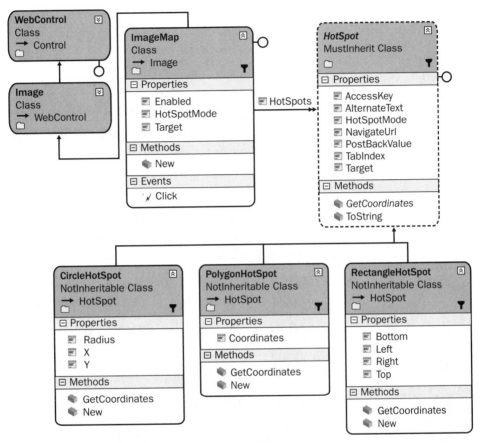

Figure 3-9 The *ImageMap* and *HotSpot* control hierarchy.

The *ImageMap* control has a *Click* event that functions like the *Button* control. The second argument of the *Click* event has a data type of *ImageMapEventArgs*, which lets you retrieve the *PostBackValue* of the associated hot spot that the user clicked.

In the source view, the *ImageMap* control is represented as the *<asp:ImageMap>* element and has nested hot spot elements that can be *CircleHotSpot*, *RectangleHotSpot*, and *PolygonHotSpot* elements.

Working with *HotSpot* Controls

A *hot spot* is a predefined area on an image that can be clicked to perform an action. Hot spots can be created to define areas on the image that are displayed by the *ImageMap* control. You can define many overlapping areas, with each layer based on the *HotSpot* definition order. The first *HotSpot* defined takes precedence over the last

HotSpot defined. The *HotSpot* object model is shown in Figure 3-9. The classes that inherit from the *HotSpot* are the *CircleHotSpot*, *RectangleHotSpot*, and *PolygonHotSpot*. Table 3-2 contains the list of *HotSpot* properties.

Table 3-2   *HotSpot* Properties

Property	Description
AccessKey	A tool that specifies the keyboard shortcut for a *HotSpot*. You can place only a single character into this property. If this property contains "C," for example, a Web user can press Alt+C to navigate to the *HotSpot*.
AlternateText	The text that is displayed for a *HotSpot* when the image is unavailable or renders to a browser that does not support images. This also becomes the *ToolTip*.
HotSpotMode	A tool that specifies the behavior of the *HotSpot* when it is clicked. Can be *NotSet*, *Inactive*, *Navigate*, or *PostBack*.
NavigateUrl	The URL to navigate to when a *HotSpot* object is clicked.
PostBackValue	The string that is passed back to the Web server and is available in the event argument data when the *HotSpot* is clicked.
TabIndex	The tab index number of the *HotSpot*.
Target	The target window or frame that displays the Web page and is linked to the *HotSpot*.

Understanding the *HotSpotMode* Property

The *HotSpotMode* property is used to specify how the *HotSpot* behaves when the *HotSpot* is clicked. You can specify the *HotSpotMode* on either the *HotSpot* or the *ImageMap* control. If you set the *HotSpotMode* on the *HotSpot* and the *ImageMap*, the *HotSpot* takes precedence. This means that you can specify the *HotSpotMode* on the *ImageMap* control to set a default *HotSpot* behavior, but the *HotSpotMode* of the *HotSpot* must be set to *NotSet* to inherit the behavior from the *HotSpot*.

Specifying *Navigate* for the *HotSpotMode* causes the *HotSpot* to navigate to a URL when the *HotSpot* is clicked. The *NavigateUrl* property specifies the URL to navigate to.

NOTE *HotSpotMode* Default

If the *ImageMap* and *HotSpot* have their *HotSpotModes* set to *NotSet*, the *HotSpots* default to *Navigate*.

Specifying *PostBack* for the *HotSpotMode* causes the *HotSpot* to generate a *PostBack* to the server when the *HotSpot* is clicked. The *PostBackValue* property specifies a string that is passed back to the Web server in the *ImageMapEventArgs* event data when the *HotSpot* is clicked and the *Click* event is raised.

Specifying *Inactive* for the *HotSpotMode* indicates that the *HotSpot* does not have any behavior when it is clicked. This is used to create an inactive *HotSpot* region within a larger active *HotSpot*, thus allowing you to create complex *HotSpot* zones within an *ImageMap* control. You must specify the inactive *HotSpot* before you designate the active *HotSpot* in the *ImageMap* control.

In this example, a Web page was created and a *Label* and *ImageMap* control were added to the page. The *ImageMap* control uses the same image file called Girl.gif and HTML page called ImageDescription.htm that were used in the previous *Image* and *ImageButton* control examples. The following code was added to the code-behind page to show how the *ImageMap* control's properties can be set programmatically and the *Click* event can be implemented to display the *HotSpot* that is clicked.

```vb
'VB
Partial Class ImageMap_Control
    Inherits System.Web.UI.Page

  Protected Sub Page_Load(ByVal sender As Object, ByVal e As System.EventArgs) Handles Me.Load
        ImageMap1.ImageUrl = "~/Images/Girl.gif"
        ImageMap1.DescriptionUrl = "~/ImageDescription.htm"
        ImageMap1.AlternateText = "This is a picture of a girl"
        ImageMap1.HotSpotMode = HotSpotMode.PostBack
        Dim chs As CircleHotSpot
        Dim rhs As RectangleHotSpot
        Dim phs As PolygonHotSpot
        chs = New CircleHotSpot()
        chs.X = 75
        chs.Y = 75
        chs.Radius = 6
        chs.PostBackValue = "Left Eye Center"
        ImageMap1.HotSpots.Add(chs)

        chs = New CircleHotSpot()
        chs.X = 100
        chs.Y = 75
        chs.Radius = 6
```

```
      chs.PostBackValue = "Right Eye Center"
      ImageMap1.HotSpots.Add(chs)

      phs = New PolygonHotSpot()
      phs.Coordinates = "76,57,82,64,81,76,76,82,71,76,70,63"
      phs.PostBackValue = "Left Eye"
      ImageMap1.HotSpots.Add(phs)

      phs = New PolygonHotSpot()
      phs.Coordinates = "99,57,105,64,104,76,99,82,94,76,93,63"
      phs.PostBackValue = "Right Eye"
      ImageMap1.HotSpots.Add(phs)

      rhs = New RectangleHotSpot()
      rhs.Top = 101
      rhs.Bottom = 110
      rhs.Left = 74
      rhs.Right = 110
      rhs.PostBackValue = "Mouth"
      ImageMap1.HotSpots.Add(rhs)

      phs = New PolygonHotSpot()
      phs.Coordinates = "92,82,101,95,85,95"
      phs.PostBackValue = "Nose"
      ImageMap1.HotSpots.Add(phs)

      phs = New PolygonHotSpot()
      phs.Coordinates = _
        "28,150,17,141,10,129,22,57,46,21,80,9," _
        + "103,9,129,22,141,47,152,93,152,142,144,156," _
        + "135,154,128,142,129,71,117,47,93,34,69,34," _
        + "51,56,42,81,44,140"
      phs.PostBackValue = "Hair"
      ImageMap1.HotSpots.Add(phs)

      chs = New CircleHotSpot()
      chs.X = 87
      chs.Y = 81
      chs.Radius = 50
      chs.PostBackValue = "Face"
      ImageMap1.HotSpots.Add(chs)

      rhs = New RectangleHotSpot()
      rhs.Top = 127
      rhs.Bottom = 142
      rhs.Left = 69
      rhs.Right = 107
      rhs.PostBackValue = "Neck"
      ImageMap1.HotSpots.Add(rhs)
    End Sub

    Protected Sub ImageMap1_Click(ByVal sender As Object, ByVal e As
System.Web.UI.WebControls.ImageMapEventArgs) Handles ImageMap1.Click
```

```
        Label1.Text = "You clicked the " + e.PostBackValue
    End Sub
End Class
```

```csharp
//C#
using System;
using System.Data;
using System.Configuration;
using System.Collections;
using System.Web;
using System.Web.Security;
using System.Web.UI;
using System.Web.UI.WebControls;
using System.Web.UI.WebControls.WebParts;
using System.Web.UI.HtmlControls;

public partial class ImageMap_Control : System.Web.UI.Page
{
    protected void Page_Load(object sender, EventArgs e)
    {
        ImageMap1.ImageUrl = "~/Images/Girl.gif";
        ImageMap1.DescriptionUrl = "~/ImageDescription.htm";
        ImageMap1.AlternateText = "This is a picture of a girl";
        ImageMap1.HotSpotMode = HotSpotMode.PostBack;
        CircleHotSpot chs;
        RectangleHotSpot rhs;
        PolygonHotSpot phs;

        chs = new CircleHotSpot();
        chs.X = 75;
        chs.Y = 75;
        chs.Radius = 6;
        chs.PostBackValue = "Left Eye Center";
        ImageMap1.HotSpots.Add(chs);

        chs = new CircleHotSpot();
        chs.X = 100;
        chs.Y = 75;
        chs.Radius = 6;
        chs.PostBackValue = "Right Eye Center";
        ImageMap1.HotSpots.Add(chs);

        phs = new PolygonHotSpot();
        phs.Coordinates = "76,57,82,64,81,76,76,82,71,76,70,63";
        phs.PostBackValue = "Left Eye";
        ImageMap1.HotSpots.Add(phs);

        phs = new PolygonHotSpot();
        phs.Coordinates = "99,57,105,64,104,76,99,82,94,76,93,63";
        phs.PostBackValue = "Right Eye";
        ImageMap1.HotSpots.Add(phs);
```

```
            rhs = new RectangleHotSpot();
            rhs.Top = 101;
            rhs.Bottom = 110;
            rhs.Left = 74;
            rhs.Right = 110;
            rhs.PostBackValue = "Mouth";
            ImageMap1.HotSpots.Add(rhs);

            phs = new PolygonHotSpot();
            phs.Coordinates = "92,82,101,95,85,95";
            phs.PostBackValue = "Nose";
            ImageMap1.HotSpots.Add(phs);

            phs = new PolygonHotSpot();
            phs.Coordinates =
              "28,150,17,141,10,129,22,57,46,21,80,9,"
            + "103,9,129,22,141,47,152,93,152,142,144,156,"
            + "135,154,128,142,129,71,117,47,93,34,69,34,"
            + "51,56,42,81,44,140";
            phs.PostBackValue = "Hair";
            ImageMap1.HotSpots.Add(phs);

            chs = new CircleHotSpot();
            chs.X = 87;
            chs.Y = 81;
            chs.Radius = 50;
            chs.PostBackValue = "Face";
            ImageMap1.HotSpots.Add(chs);

            rhs = new RectangleHotSpot();
            rhs.Top = 127;
            rhs.Bottom = 142;
            rhs.Left = 69;
            rhs.Right = 107;
            rhs.PostBackValue = "Neck";
            ImageMap1.HotSpots.Add(rhs);
        }

    protected void ImageMap1_Click(object sender, ImageMapEventArgs e)
    {
        Label1.Text = "You clicked the " + e.PostBackValue;
    }

}
```

In the sample code, clicking a *HotSpot* on the *ImageMap* causes a *PostBack* of the *PostBackValue* to the server. The *ImageMapEventArgs* contains the *PostBackValue*, which is placed into the *Text* property of the *Label*. Notice that many *HotSpot* objects overlap in this example. For example, the center of each eye overlaps the rest of that eye, and the eyes overlap the face. The hair also overlaps the face, and the face overlaps the neck.

Remember that the *HotSpot* objects that are added first override the later *HotSpots* in the *ImapeMap* control's *HotSpots* collection. Figure 3-10 shows the *ImageMap* after the hair has been clicked.

Figure 3-10   The rendered *ImageMap* displaying the *PostBackValue* message in the Label after the hair was clicked on the *ImageMap*.

The *Calendar* Control

The *Calendar* control displays a calendar for either the current month or a selected month. It allows the user to select dates and move to the next or previous month. The *SelectionChanged* event causes a *PostBack* when the user selects a new date, and the *VisibleMonthChanged* event causes a *PostBack* when the user selects a different month to be viewed. This is a complex Web server control that generates a *<table>* element when rendering to HTML. The *Calendar* control inherits directly from the *WebControl* class, as shown in Figure 3-11.

The *Calendar* control is represented as the *<asp:Calendar>* element in source view and can contain style elements to change the look of the control.

The *Calendar* control has a *DayRender* event that allows you to add text or controls to the day being rendered. This allows you to use the *Calendar* control to display appointments and other controls for any date by inserting these items into the day that is being rendered.

Calendar   ⊠
Class
→ Web Control
⌂

⊟ Properties

- ▤ Caption
- ▤ CaptionAlign
- ▤ CellPadding
- ▤ CellSpacing
- ▤ DayHeaderStyle
- ▤ DayNameFormat
- ▤ DayStyle
- ▤ FirstDayOfWeek
- ▤ NextMonthText
- ▤ NextPrevFormat
- ▤ NextPrevStyle
- ▤ OtherMonthDayStyle
- ▤ PrevMonthText
- ▤ SelectedDate
- ▤ SelectedDates
- ▤ SelectedDayStyle
- ▤ SelectionMode
- ▤ SelectMonthText
- ▤ SelectorStyle
- ▤ SelectWeekText
- ▤ ShowDayHeader
- ▤ ShowGridLines
- ▤ ShowNextPrevMonth
- ▤ ShowTitle
- ▤ TitleFormat
- ▤ TitleStyle
- ▤ TodayDayStyle
- ▤ TodaysDate
- ▤ UseAccessibleHeader
- ▤ VisibleDate
- ▤ WeekendStyle

⊟ Methods

- 🔷 Calendar
- ⚐🔷 CreateControlCollection
- ⚐🔷 HasWeekSelectors
- ⚐🔷 LoadViewState
- ⚐🔷 OnDayRender
- ⚐🔷 OnPreRender
- ⚐🔷 OnSelectionChanged
- ⚐🔷 OnVisibleMonthChanged
- ⚐🔷 RaisePostBackEvent
- ⚐🔷 Render
- ⚐🔷 SaveViewState
- ⚐🔷 TrackViewState

⊟ Events

- ⚡ DayRender
- ⚡ SelectionChanged
- ⚐⚡ VisibleMonthChanged

CalendarDay   ⊠
Class
⌂

⊟ Properties

- ▤ Date
- ▤ DayNumberText
- ▤ IsOtherMonth
- ▤ IsSelectable
- ▤ IsSelected
- ▤ IsToday
- ▤ IsWeekend

⊟ Methods

- 🔷 CalendarDay

Figure 3-11   The *Calendar* control hierarchy.

The *Calendar* control contains many properties that can be used to adjust the format and behavior of this control. Table 3-3 contains a list of the *Calendar* properties and their associated descriptions.

Table 3-3 *Calendar* **Properties**

Calendar Property	Description
Caption	The text that is rendered in the *Calendar*.
CaptionAlign	The alignment of the caption: *Top, Bottom, Left, Right*, or *NotSet*.
CellPadding	The space between each cell and the cell border.
CellSpacing	The spacing between each cell.
DayHeaderStyle	The style to be applied to days of the week.
DayNameFormat	The format for the names of the days of the week: *FirstLetter, FirstTwoLetters, Full, Short, Shortest*.
DayStyle	The default style for a calendar day.
FirstDayOfWeek	The day of the week to display in the first column of the *Calendar* control.
NextMonthText	The text to be displayed in the next month navigation control; ">" is the default. This only works if *ShowNextPrevMonth* property is *true*.
NextPrevFormat	The tool that sets the format of the next and previous navigation controls. Can be set to *CustomText* (default), *FullMonth* (for example, January), or *ShortMonth* (for example, Jan).
NextPrevStyle	The style to be applied to the next and previous navigation controls.
OtherMonthDayStyle	The tool that specifies the style for days on the calendar that are displayed and are not in the current month.
PrevMonthText	The text to be displayed in the previous month navigation control, which defaults as "<". This only works if the *ShowNextPrevMonth* property is *true*.

Table 3-3 *Calendar* **Properties**

Calendar Property	Description
SelectedDate	The date selected by the user. Can also be set by the user.
SelectedDates	A collection of *DataTime* values that represent all of the dates that were selected by the user. This property contains only a single date if the *SelectionMode* property is set to *CalendarSelectionMode.Day*, which allows only single date selection.
SelectedDayStyle	The style of the selected day.
SelectionMode	A value that indicates how many dates can be selected. Value can be *Day*, *DayWeek*, *DayWeekMonth*, or *None*.
SelectMonthText	The text displayed for the month selection column. The default value is ">>".
SelectorStyle	The style for the week and month selectors.
SelectWeekText	The text of the week selection in the week selector.
ShowDayHeader	An indicator that shows whether the day header should be displayed.
ShowGridLines	An indicator that tells whether grid lines should be displayed.
ShowNextPrevMonth	An indicator for whether the next and previous month selectors should be displayed.
ShowTitle	An indicator for whether the title should be displayed.
TitleFormat	A tool that sets the format for displaying the month (*Month*), or the month and year (*MonthYear*).
TitleStyle	The style for the title.
TodayDayStyle	The style of the today's date.
TodaysDate	Today's date.

Table 3-3 *Calendar* Properties

Calendar Property	Description
UseAccessibleHeader	A control which, when set to *true*, generates *<th>* for day headers (default), or, when set to *false*, generates *<td>* for day headers to be compatible with 1.0 of .NET Framework.
VisibleDate	A display that specifies which month to display in the *Calendar* control.
WeekendDayStyle	The style of weekend days.

The *Calendar* control can be used to select a single date, or multiple dates. The *SelectionMode* property can be set to one of the following settings:

- **Day** Allows selection of a single date.
- **DayWeek** Allows the selection of either a single date or a complete week.
- **DayWeekMonth** Allows selection of single date, a complete week, or the whole month.
- **None** Does not allow you to select any date.

After a selection is made, the *SelectionChanged* event handler lets you access the selected dates via the *SelectedDates* property. The *SelectedDate* property simply points to the date in *SelectedDates* collection.

Many people think that the *Calendar* control is only used as a date picker control, but the *Calendar* control can also be used to display a schedule. The trick to using the *Calendar* control to display scheduled items and special days is to make the control large enough to display text in each day, and then add *Label* controls (or other controls) to the *Cell* object's *Controls* collection in the *DayRender* event handler.

The following example shows how a *Calendar* control can be used as a schedule display showing special days. In this example, a Web page was created and a *Calendar* control was added to the page. The following code was added to the code-behind page to show how the *Calendar* control's properties can be set programmatically and the *Calendar* control events can be used.

```
'VB
Partial Class Calendar_Control
    Inherits System.Web.UI.Page
```

```
Dim schedule As New Hashtable()

Protected Sub Page_Load(ByVal sender As Object, _
        ByVal e As System.EventArgs) Handles Me.Load
    GetSchedule()
    Calendar1.Style.Add("position", "absolute")
    Calendar1.Style.Add("left", "5px")
    Calendar1.Style.Add("top", "50px")
    Calendar1.Caption = "Special Days"
    Calendar1.FirstDayOfWeek = WebControls.FirstDayOfWeek.Sunday
    Calendar1.NextPrevFormat = NextPrevFormat.ShortMonth
    Calendar1.TitleFormat = TitleFormat.MonthYear
    Calendar1.ShowGridLines = True
    Calendar1.DayStyle.HorizontalAlign = HorizontalAlign.Left
    Calendar1.DayStyle.VerticalAlign = VerticalAlign.Top
    Calendar1.DayStyle.Height = New Unit(75)
    Calendar1.DayStyle.Width = New Unit(100)
    Calendar1.OtherMonthDayStyle.BackColor = System.Drawing.Color.WhiteSmoke
    Calendar1.TodaysDate = New DateTime(2006, 12, 1)
    Calendar1.VisibleDate = Calendar1.TodaysDate
End Sub

Private Sub GetSchedule()
    schedule("11/23/2006") = "Thanksgiving"
    schedule("12/5/2006") = "Birthday"
    schedule("12/16/2006") = "First day of Chanukah"
    schedule("12/23/2006") = "Last day of Chanukah"
    schedule("12/24/2006") = "Christmas Eve"
    schedule("12/25/2006") = "Christmas"
    schedule("12/26/2006") = "Boxing Day"
    schedule("12/31/2006") = "New Year's Eve"
    schedule("1/1/2007") = "New Year's Day"
End Sub

Protected Sub Calendar1_SelectionChanged(ByVal sender As Object, _
        ByVal e As System.EventArgs) Handles Calendar1.SelectionChanged
    Response.Write("Selection changed to: " _
      + Calendar1.SelectedDate.ToShortDateString())
End Sub

Protected Sub Calendar1_VisibleMonthChanged(ByVal sender As Object, _
        ByVal e As System.Web.UI.WebControls.MonthChangedEventArgs) _
        Handles Calendar1.VisibleMonthChanged
    Response.Write("Month changed to: " + e.NewDate.ToShortDateString())
End Sub

Protected Sub Calendar1_DayRender(ByVal sender As Object, _
        ByVal e As System.Web.UI.WebControls.DayRenderEventArgs) _
        Handles Calendar1.DayRender

    If Not schedule(e.Day.Date.ToShortDateString()) Is Nothing Then
        Dim lit = New Literal()
        lit.Visible = True
```

```
            lit.Text = "<br />"
            e.Cell.Controls.Add(lit)
            Dim lbl = New Label()
            lbl.Visible = True
            lbl.Text = CType(schedule(e.Day.Date.ToShortDateString()), String)
            e.Cell.Controls.Add(lbl)
        End If

    End Sub
End Class


//C#
using System;
using System.Data;
using System.Configuration;
using System.Collections;
using System.Web;
using System.Web.Security;
using System.Web.UI;
using System.Web.UI.WebControls;
using System.Web.UI.WebControls.WebParts;
using System.Web.UI.HtmlControls;

public partial class Calendar_Control : System.Web.UI.Page
{
    Hashtable schedule = new Hashtable();

    protected void Page_Load(object sender, EventArgs e)
    {
        GetSchedule();
        Calendar1.Style.Add("position", "absolute");
        Calendar1.Style.Add("left", "5px");
        Calendar1.Style.Add("top", "50px");
        Calendar1.Caption = "Special Days";
        Calendar1.FirstDayOfWeek = FirstDayOfWeek.Sunday;
        Calendar1.NextPrevFormat = NextPrevFormat.ShortMonth;
        Calendar1.TitleFormat = TitleFormat.MonthYear;
        Calendar1.ShowGridLines = true;
        Calendar1.DayStyle.HorizontalAlign = HorizontalAlign.Left;
        Calendar1.DayStyle.VerticalAlign = VerticalAlign.Top;
        Calendar1.DayStyle.Height = new Unit(75);
        Calendar1.DayStyle.Width = new Unit(100);
        Calendar1.OtherMonthDayStyle.BackColor =
            System.Drawing.Color.WhiteSmoke;
        Calendar1.TodaysDate = new DateTime(2006, 12, 1);
        Calendar1.VisibleDate = Calendar1.TodaysDate;
    }

    private void GetSchedule()
    {
        schedule["11/23/2006"] = "Thanksgiving";
        schedule["12/5/2006"] = "Birthday";
        schedule["12/16/2006"] = "First day of Chanukah";
```

```
    schedule["12/23/2006"] = "Last day of Chanukah";
    schedule["12/24/2006"] = "Christmas Eve";
    schedule["12/25/2006"] = "Christmas";
    schedule["12/26/2006"] = "Boxing Day";
    schedule["12/31/2006"] = "New Year's Eve";
    schedule["1/1/2007"] = "New Year's Day";
}

protected void Calendar1_SelectionChanged(object sender, EventArgs e)
{
    Response.Write("Selection changed to: "
        + Calendar1.SelectedDate.ToShortDateString());
}

protected void Calendar1_VisibleMonthChanged(object sender,
    MonthChangedEventArgs e)
{
    Response.Write("Month changed to: " + e.NewDate.ToShortDateString());
}

protected void Calendar1_DayRender(object sender, DayRenderEventArgs e)
{
    Literal lit = new Literal();
    lit.Visible = true;
    lit.Text = "<br />";
    e.Cell.Controls.Add(lit);

    if (schedule[e.Day.Date.ToShortDateString()] != null)
    {
        Label lbl = new Label();
        lbl.Visible = true;
        lbl.Text = (string)schedule[e.Day.Date.ToShortDateString()];
        e.Cell.Controls.Add(lbl);
    }
}
}
```

This code sets the *Calendar* control properties, such as style and size, in the *Page_Load* event handler. A method called *GetSchedule* is added to populate a collection of special dates. In the *Calendar1_DayRender* event handler, the Date and Cell of the day that is being rendered is available. If a special date is found, a *Label* is created that contains the special date, and it is added to the *Cell* object's *Controls* collection. When the Web page is displayed, the special dates are rendered on the *Calendar* controls, as shown in Figure 3-12.

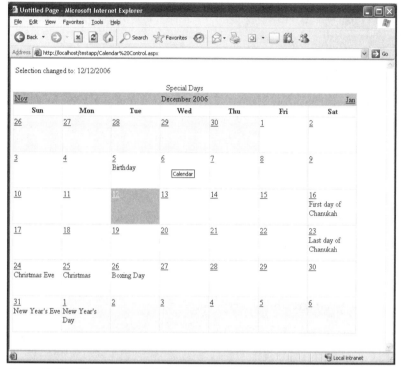

Figure 3-12 The rendered *Calendar* control displaying special days and having a selected date.

The *FileUpload* Control

The *FileUpload* control is used to display a TextBox and Browse button that allows a user to either type a file name and path, or click Browse and select a file and path. This control generates an *<input type="file">* element when rendering to HTML. The *FileUpload* control inherits directly from the *WebControl* class, as shown in Figure 3-13.

The *FileUpload* control is represented as the *<asp:FileUpload>* element in source view and has no content, so you can write this element as a singleton element.

The *FileUpload* control does not cause a *PostBack* to the Web server. After the user selects a file, the user needs to cause a *PostBack* via a different control, such as a *Button*. The *PostBack* causes the file to be uploaded to the server as posted data. At the server, the page code does not run until the file is uploaded to server memory.

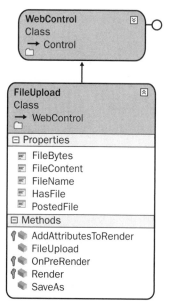

Figure 3-13   The *FileUpload* control hierarchy.

The following properties give you flexible ways to access the uploaded file:

- ■ *FileBytes*   The file is exposed as a byte array.
- ■ *FileContent*   The file is exposed as a stream.
- ■ *PostedFile*   The file is exposed as an object of type *HttpPostedFile*. This object has properties, such as *ContentType* and *ContentLength* properties.

You need to examine any file that is uploaded to determine if it should be saved; you can examine characteristics such as the file name, size, and MIME type. *MIME* stands for Multipurpose Internet Mail Extensions and specifies the type of file that is being uploaded. When you're ready to save the file, you can use the *SaveAs* method on the *FileUpload* control or the *HttpPostedFile* object.

You can save the file in any location for which you have permissions to create files. By default, the *requireRootedSaveAsPath* attribute of the *httpRuntime* configuration element in the Web.config file is set to *true*, which means that you need to provide an absolute path to save the file. You can get an absolute path by using the *MapPath* method of the *HttpServerUtility* class and passing to the method the tilde (˜) operator, which represents the application root folder.

The maximum size file that can be uploaded depends on the value of the *MaxRequest-Length* attribute of the *httpRuntime* configuration element in the Web.config file. If users attempt to upload a file that is larger than the *MaxRequestLength*, the upload fails.

Security Alert   The *FileUpload* control allows users to upload files but makes no attempt to validate the safety of the uploaded files. The *FileUpload* control doesn't provide a means to filter the file types that can be uploaded by a user, but you can examine the file characteristics, such as the file name and extension, as well as the *ContentType*, after the file has been uploaded.

Although you can provide client-side script to examine the file that is being submitted, remember that client-side validation is a convenience for the honest user. A hacker can easily strip the Web page of client-side code to bypass this validation.

In this example, a Web page was created and a *FileUpload* control was added to the page. In addition, a *Button* was added to the Web page that is used to submit the file to the Web server via *PostBack*. A folder was added to the Web site called Uploads. The following code was added to the code-behind page to show how the *FileUpload* control's properties can be set programmatically, and a file can be uploaded and saved.

```vb
'VB
Partial Class FileUpload_Control
    Inherits System.Web.UI.Page

    Protected Sub Button1_Click(ByVal sender As Object, _
            ByVal e As System.EventArgs) Handles Button1.Click
        If (FileUpload1.HasFile) Then
            Label1.Text = "File Length: " _
                + FileUpload1.FileBytes.Length.ToString() _
                + "<br />" _
                + "File Name: " _
                + FileUpload1.FileName _
                + "<br />" _
                + "MIME Type: " _
                + FileUpload1.PostedFile.ContentType
            FileUpload1.SaveAs( _
                MapPath("~/Uploads/" + FileUpload1.FileName))
        Else
            Label1.Text = "No file received."
        End If
    End Sub
End Class
```

```csharp
//C#
using System;
using System.Data;
using System.Configuration;
using System.Collections;
```

```
using System.Web;
using System.Web.Security;
using System.Web.UI;
using System.Web.UI.WebControls;
using System.Web.UI.WebControls.WebParts;
using System.Web.UI.HtmlControls;

public partial class FileUpload : System.Web.UI.Page
{
    protected void Button1_Click(object sender, EventArgs e)
    {
        if (FileUpload1.HasFile)
        {
            Label1.Text = "File Length: "
                + FileUpload1.FileBytes.Length
                + "<br />"
                + "File Name: "
                + FileUpload1.FileName
                + "<br />"
                + "MIME Type: "
                + FileUpload1.PostedFile.ContentType;
            FileUpload1.SaveAs(
                MapPath("~/Uploads/" + FileUpload1.FileName));
        }
        else
        {
            Label1.Text = "No file received.";
        }
    }
}
```

The Web page is shown in Figure 3-14. When a file is selected and the Submit button is clicked, the code checks to see if a file has been uploaded. If a file has been uploaded, information about the file is placed into the *Label* control for display. The file is then saved to the Uploads folder. The Web site requires an absolute path, and *MapPath* performs the conversion from the relative path supplied to an absolute path. Finally, the file is saved.

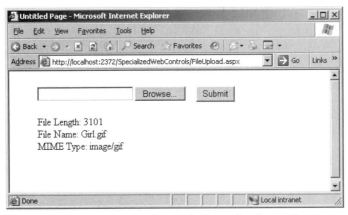

Figure 3-14   The *FileUpload* control after uploading a file.

The *Panel* Control

The *Panel* control is used as a control container and is useful when you have controls that you want to display and hide as a group. The *Panel* generates a *<div>* element when rendering as HTML. In source view, the Panel *control* is represented as the *<asp:Panel>* element and can contain many controls. The *Panel* control inherits directly from the *WebControl* class, as shown in Figure 3-15.

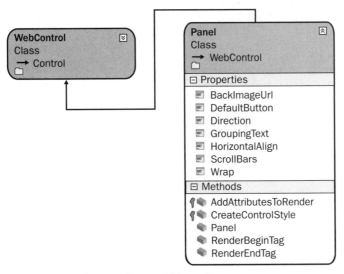

Figure 3-15   The *Panel* control hierarchy.

The *BackImageUrl* property can be used to display a background image in the *Panel* control. The *HorizontalAlignment* property lets you set the horizontal alignment of the controls that are in the *Panel*, and the *Wrap* property specifies whether items in the *Panel* automatically continue on the next line when a line is longer than the width of the *Panel* control. The *DefaultButton* property specifies the button that is clicked when the *Panel* control has focus and the user presses the Enter key. The *DefaultButton* property can be set to the ID of any control that implements the *IButtonControl* interface.

In this example, a Web page was created and a *Panel* control was added to the page. A *Label* control, a *TextBox* control, and a *Button* control were inserted into the *Panel*. In addition, a *Button* was added to the Web page that is used to toggle the *Visible* property's state of the *Panel* control, and *Button* controls were added to move the *Panel* left or right.

```vb
'VB
Partial Class Panel_Control
    Inherits System.Web.UI.Page

    Protected Sub Button2_Click(ByVal sender As Object, _
        ByVal e As System.EventArgs) Handles Button2.Click
        Panel1.Visible = Not Panel1.Visible
    End Sub

    Protected Sub Button3_Click(ByVal sender As Object, _
        ByVal e As System.EventArgs) Handles Button3.Click
        Dim left As New Unit(Panel1.Style("left"))
        left = New Unit(CType(left.Value, Double) - 10, left.Type)
        Panel1.Style("left") = left.ToString()
    End Sub

    Protected Sub Button4_Click(ByVal sender As Object, _
        ByVal e As System.EventArgs) Handles Button4.Click
        Dim left As New Unit(Panel1.Style("left"))
        left = New Unit(CType(left.Value, Double) + 10, left.Type)
        Panel1.Style("left") = left.ToString()
    End Sub
End Class
```

```csharp
//C#
using System;
using System.Data;
using System.Configuration;
using System.Collections;
using System.Web;
using System.Web.Security;
using System.Web.UI;
using System.Web.UI.WebControls;
using System.Web.UI.WebControls.WebParts;
using System.Web.UI.HtmlControls;

public partial class Panel_Control : System.Web.UI.Page
```

```
{
    protected void Button2_Click(object sender, EventArgs e)
    {
        Panel1.Visible = !Panel1.Visible;
    }

    protected void Button3_Click(object sender, EventArgs e)
    {
        Unit left = new Unit(Panel1.Style["left"]);
        left = new Unit((double)left.Value - 10,left.Type);
        Panel1.Style["left"] = left.ToString();
    }
    protected void Button4_Click(object sender, EventArgs e)
    {
        Unit left = new Unit(Panel1.Style["left"]);
        left = new Unit((double)left.Value + 10, left.Type);
        Panel1.Style["left"] = left.ToString();
    }
}
```

The example Web page is shown in Figure 3-16. Clicking the *Show/Hide* button hides the *Panel* and all of its controls, and clicking again displays the *Panel* and its controls. When the Move Left or Move Right buttons are clicked, the current location of the *Panel* control is retrieved from the *Style* property and updated to move the *Panel* and its controls.

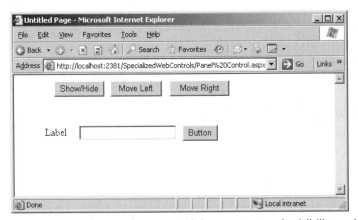

Figure 3-16   The *Panel* control with buttons to toggle visibility and move the *Panel* control.

The *MultiView* and *View* Controls

The *View* control is a control container; it's useful when you have controls that you want to display and hide as a group. It is also helpful when you hide one *View* control with its controls, because then you typically show a different *View* control. *View* controls are contained in a *MultiView* control. The *MultiView* and the *View* don't generate any elements when rendering as HTML because these controls are essentially server-side controls that manage the visibility of the child controls. In source view, the *MultiView* control is represented as the *<asp:MultiView>* element, and the *View* control is represented as the *<asp:View>* element. The *MultiView* and *View* controls inherit directly from the *Control* class, as shown in Figure 3-17.

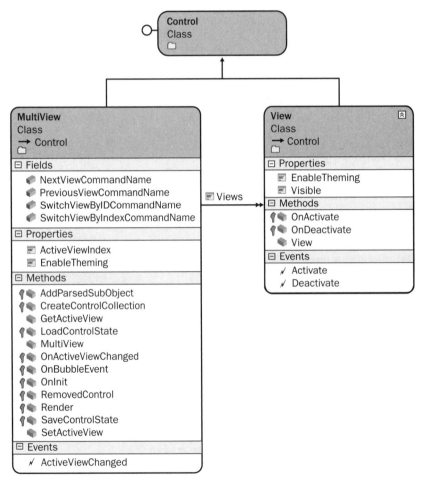

Figure 3-17   The *MultiView* and *View* control hierarchy.

NOTE   **.NET 2.0**

The *MultiView* and *View* controls are new in ASP.NET version 2.0.

You can use the *ActiveViewIndex* property or the *SetActiveView* method to change the *View* programmatically. If the *ActiveViewIndex* is set to -1, no *View* controls are displayed. If you pass an invalid *View* or a null (Nothing) value into the *SetActiveView* method, an *HttpException* is thrown. Note that only one *View* control can be active at any time.

The *MultiView* control is also used to create wizards, where each *View* control in the *MultiView* control represents a different step or page in the wizard.

The *MultiView* control is also suitable for use when developing multiple-screen applications for mobile devices, as the *MultiView* control provides the same functionality as the ASP.NET mobile *Form* control in .NET Framework version 1.1.

In this example, a Web page was created and a *MultiView* control and three *View* controls were added to the page. Next, a *Button* control was added to each of the *View* controls. The *Button* controls were staggered within each *View* control to visually help identify the current active *View* control. The *Text* property of the *Button* control was set to *Button1*, *Button2*, and *Button3*, respectively, as shown in Figure 3-18.

Figure 3-18   The *MultiView* and *View* control Web page contains a Button in each View.

After the controls were added to the Web page, the following code was added to the code-behind page:

```
'VB
Partial Class MultiView_and_View_Controls
    Inherits System.Web.UI.Page
```

```
    Protected Sub Button1_Click(ByVal sender As Object, _
        ByVal e As System.EventArgs) Handles Button1.Click
      MultiView1.ActiveViewIndex = 1
    End Sub

    Protected Sub Button2_Click(ByVal sender As Object, _
        ByVal e As System.EventArgs) Handles Button2.Click
      MultiView1.ActiveViewIndex = 2
    End Sub

    Protected Sub Button3_Click(ByVal sender As Object, _
        ByVal e As System.EventArgs) Handles Button3.Click
      MultiView1.SetActiveView(CType(Me.FindControl("View1"), View))
    End Sub

    Protected Sub Page_Load(ByVal sender As Object, _
        ByVal e As System.EventArgs) Handles Me.Load
      If (Not IsPostBack) Then
        MultiView1.ActiveViewIndex = 0
      End If
    End Sub
End Class

//C#
using System;
using System.Data;
using System.Configuration;
using System.Collections;
using System.Web;
using System.Web.Security;
using System.Web.UI;
using System.Web.UI.WebControls;
using System.Web.UI.WebControls.WebParts;
using System.Web.UI.HtmlControls;

public partial class MultiView_and_View_Controls : System.Web.UI.Page
{
    protected void Button1_Click(object sender, EventArgs e)
    {
       MultiView1.ActiveViewIndex = 1;
    }
    protected void Button2_Click(object sender, EventArgs e)
    {
       MultiView1.ActiveViewIndex = 2;
    }
    protected void Button3_Click(object sender, EventArgs e)
    {
       MultiView1.SetActiveView((View)MultiView1.FindControl("View1"));
    }
```

```
protected void Page_Load(object sender, EventArgs e)
{
    if (!IsPostBack)
    {
        MultiView1.ActiveViewIndex = 0;
    }
}
}
```

When the Web page is displayed, only *Button1* is visible, as shown in Figure 3-19.
Clicking *Button1* changes the active view to *View2*, which displays *Button2*. Clicking
Button2 changes the active view to *View3*, which displays *Button3*. Clicking *Button3*
changes the active view back to *View1*, which displays *Button1*.

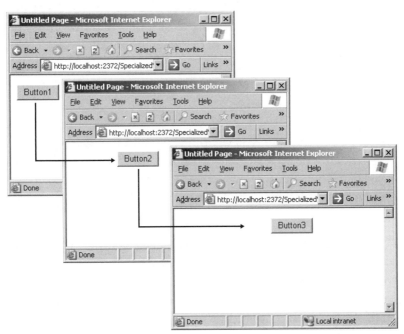

Figure 3-19   The *MultiView* is used to switch between the *View* controls.

The *Wizard* Control

The *Wizard* control is a complex control that is used to display a series of *WizardStep*
controls to a user, one after the other. Probably the most significant use of the *Wizard*
control is to prompt the user for a significant amount of data by breaking the data into

logical chunks, or steps, and presenting the user with the steps that can be validated, either at the end or between steps. You certainly can accomplish the same result by using separate Web pages for each logical chunk of data, but the *Wizard* consolidates the data collection process into a single Web page.

More Info   For more information about the *Wizard* control, visit *http://msdn2.microsoft.com /en-us/library/fs0za4w6.aspx.*

You can programmatically control which step is displayed, which means that you are not constrained to navigating through the steps in a linear fashion.

The *Wizard* control builds on the *MultiView* and *View* controls, providing logic to assure that only one *WizardStep* control is visible at a time and providing the ability to customize most aspects of the *Wizard* and *WizardStep* controls.

NOTE .NET 2.0

The *Wizard* control is new in ASP.NET version 2.0.

The *Wizard* control inherits from the *Control* class, and the *BaseWizardStep* inherits from *View*, as shown in Figure 3-20. The *Wizard* control has a *WizardSteps* collection of steps that contains the user interface for each step that is created by the developer. The built-in navigation capabilities determine which buttons to display based on the *StepType* value.

The *Wizard* control contains a header area that can be customized to display information specific to the step that the user is currently on. The *Wizard* control also contains a sidebar area that can be used to quickly navigate to steps in the control. As you can see from the many styles than can be assigned to parts of the *Wizard* control, the *Wizard* control can be significantly customized.

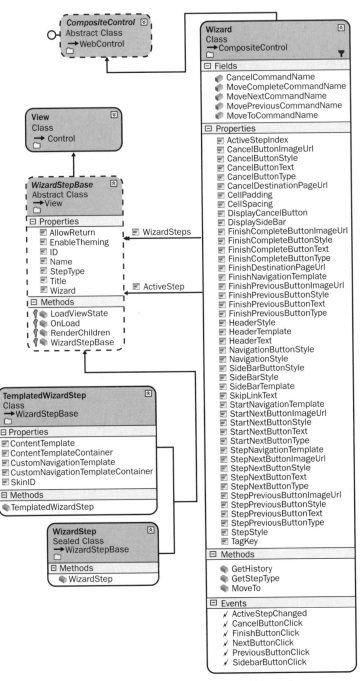

Figure 3-20   The *Wizard* and *WizardStep* control hierarchy.

The *BaseWizardStep* contains the *StepType* property that can be set to one of the following values:

- **WizardStepType.Auto**   This renders navigation buttons based on the location of the set within the *WizardSteps* collection property of the *Wizard*. This is the default.

- **WizardStepType.Complete**   This is the last step to appear. No navigation buttons are rendered.

- **WizardStepType.Finish**   This is the final data-collection step; the Finish and Previous buttons are rendered for navigation.

- **WizardStepType.Start**   This is the first one to appear, and only the Next button is rendered.

- **WizardStepType.Step**   This is a step between the Start and the Finish step. The Previous and Next buttons are rendered.

This is an example of a wizard that gives the user the ability to select options when selecting a vehicle. In a typical real vehicle-selection scenario, many more options are available, thus dictating the need to simplify the option selection for the user.

To create this example, a Web page was created and a *Wizard* control was added to the page. *WizardStep* controls were added for exterior, interior, options, and summary. The exterior selection step contains three *RadioButton* controls for selection of red, blue, or black exterior. The interior selection step contains two *RadioButton* controls for selection of leather or cloth seats. The options selection step contains *CheckBox* controls for selection of AM/FM radio, heated seats, and air freshener. The summary step contains a *Label* control that is populated with the selections that were made in the previous steps. The populated *WizardStep* controls are shown in Figure 3-21.

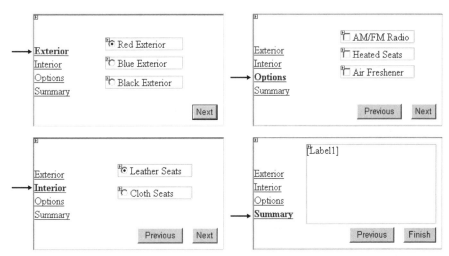

Figure 3-21   The *WizardStep* controls are populated with the controls to be displayed to the user.

After the *WizardStep* controls were created and each step was populated, code was added to the code-behind page to populate the *Label* control in the summary step. Also, code was added to the *Form_Load* event handler to assure that the *Wizard* starts at the first step, and finally, code was added to the *Wizard1_FinishButtonClick* event handler to display the results. The code-behind page is as follows:

```
'VB
Partial Class Wizard_Control
    Inherits System.Web.UI.Page

    Protected Sub Wizard1_FinishButtonClick(ByVal sender As Object, _
        ByVal e As System.Web.UI.WebControls.WizardNavigationEventArgs) Handles
Wizard1.FinishButtonClick

        Wizard1.Visible = False
        Response.Write("Finished<br />" + Label1.Text)
    End Sub

    Protected Sub Wizard1_NextButtonClick(ByVal sender As Object, _
        ByVal e As System.Web.UI.WebControls.WizardNavigationEventArgs) Handles
Wizard1.NextButtonClick

        If (Wizard1.WizardSteps(e.NextStepIndex).Title = "Summary") Then
            Label1.Text = String.Empty
            For Each ws As WizardStep In Wizard1.WizardSteps
                For Each c As Control In ws.Controls
                    If (TypeOf c Is System.Web.UI.WebControls.CheckBox) Then
                        Dim cb As CheckBox = CType(c, CheckBox)
                        If (cb.Checked) Then
```

```
                        Label1.Text += cb.Text + "<br />"
                    End If
                End If
            Next
        Next
    End If
End Sub

Protected Sub Page_Load(ByVal sender As Object, _
        ByVal e As System.EventArgs) _
        Handles Me.Load
    If Not IsPostBack Then
        Wizard1.ActiveStepIndex = 0
    End If
End Sub

End Class

//C#
using System;
using System.Data;
using System.Configuration;
using System.Collections;
using System.Web;
using System.Web.Security;
using System.Web.UI;
using System.Web.UI.WebControls;
using System.Web.UI.WebControls.WebParts;
using System.Web.UI.HtmlControls;

public partial class Wizard_Control : System.Web.UI.Page
{
    protected void Page_Load(object sender, EventArgs e)
    {
        if (!IsPostBack)
        {
            Wizard1.ActiveStepIndex = 0;
        }
    }
    protected void Wizard1_FinishButtonClick(object sender,
        WizardNavigationEventArgs e)
    {
        Wizard1.Visible = false;
        Response.Write("Finished<br />" + Label1.Text);
    }
    protected void Wizard1_NextButtonClick(object sender,
        WizardNavigationEventArgs e)
    {
        if (Wizard1.WizardSteps[e.NextStepIndex].Title == "Summary")
        {
            Label1.Text = String.Empty;
            foreach (WizardStep ws in Wizard1.WizardSteps)
```

```
{
    foreach (Control c in ws.Controls)
    {
        if (c is CheckBox)
        {
            CheckBox cb = (CheckBox)c;
            if (cb.Checked)
            {
                Label1.Text += cb.Text + "<br />";
            }
        }
    }
}
}
```

When the Web page is displayed, the user sees the first (Exterior) step, as shown in Figure 3-21. The user can go from step to step, and finally, press the Finish button. In the Summary step, the *Label* control displays the current selections. After the user presses the Finish button, the *Wizard* control is hidden and the summary information is displayed.

The *Xml* Control

The *Xml* control is used to display the contents of an XML document or the results of executing an Extensible Stylesheet Language (XSL) Transform. The *Xml* control hierarchy is shown in Figure 3-22.

The XML document to display is specified by setting either the *DocumentSource* property or the *DocumentContent* property. The *DocumentSource* property accepts a string that specifies the location of an XML file to be loaded into the control. The *DocumentContent* property accepts a string that contains actual XML content. If the *DocumentContent* and the *DocumentSource* are both set, the last property that is set is the property that is used.

The *TransformSource* property accepts an optional string that contains the location of an XSL transformation file to apply to the XML document. The *Transform* property accepts a *Transform* object that can be used to perform the transformation as well. If both of these properties are set, the last property set is used.

The *Xml* control also contains the *TransformArgumentList* property, which is used to pass arguments to the XSL transformation.

Figure 3-22 The *Xml* control hierarchy.

The following is an example of using the *Xml* control to display the contents of an XML file after applying an XSL transformation. This XML file and the XSL transformation file are as follows:

XML File – CarList.xml

```
<?xml version="1.0" encoding="utf-8" ?>
<CarList>
    <Car Vin="1A59B" Make="Chevrolet" Model="Impala" Year="1963" Price="1125.00" />
    <Car Vin="9B25T" Make="Ford" Model="F-250" Year="1970" Price="1595.00" />
    <Car Vin="3H13R" Make="BMW" Model="Z4" Year="2006" Price="55123.00" />
    <Car Vin="7D67A" Make="Mazda" Model="Miata" Year="2003" Price="28250.00" />
    <Car Vin="4T21N" Make="VW" Model= "Beetle" Year="1956" Price="500.00" />
</CarList>
```

XSL Transformation File – CarList.xsl

```
<?xml version="1.0" encoding="utf-8" ?>
<xsl:stylesheet version="1.0"
xmlns:xsl="http://www.w3.org/1999/XSL/Transform"
xmlns:msxsl="urn:schemas-microsoft-com:xslt"
xmlns:labs="http://labs.com/mynamespace">
```

```xml
<xsl:template match="/">
   <html>
      <head>
         <title>Car List</title>
      </head>
      <body>
         <center>
            <h1>Car List</h1>
            <xsl:call-template name="CreateHeading"/>
         </center>
      </body>
   </html>
</xsl:template>

<xsl:template name="CreateHeading">
   <table border="1" cellpadding="5">
      <tr >
         <th bgcolor="yellow">
            <font size="4" >
               <b>VIN</b>
            </font>
         </th>
         <th bgcolor="yellow">
            <font size="4" >
               <b>Make</b>
            </font>
         </th>
         <th  bgcolor="yellow">
            <font size="4" >
               <b>Model</b>
            </font>
         </th>
         <th  bgcolor="yellow">
            <font size="4">
               <b>Year</b>
            </font>
         </th>
         <th  bgcolor="yellow">
            <font size="4" >
               <b>Price</b>
            </font>
         </th>
      </tr>
      <xsl:call-template name="CreateTable"/>
   </table>
</xsl:template>

<xsl:template name="CreateTable">
   <xsl:for-each select="/CarList/Car">
      <tr>
         <td align="center">
            <xsl:value-of select="@Vin"/>
         </td>
```

```
            <td align="center">
               <xsl:value-of select="@Make"/>
            </td>
            <td>
               <xsl:value-of select="@Model"/>
            </td>
            <td>
               <xsl:value-of select="@Year"/>
            </td>
            <td align="right">
               <xsl:value-of select="format-number(@Price,'$#,##0.00')"/>
            </td>
         </tr>
      </xsl:for-each>
   </xsl:template>
</xsl:stylesheet>
```

In this example, an *Xml* control was added to a Web page and the following code was added to the code-behind page to display the XML file after applying the XSL transformation:

```vb
'VB
Partial Class Xml_Control
    Inherits System.Web.UI.Page

   Protected Sub Page_Load(ByVal sender As Object, ByVal e As System.EventArgs) Handles Me.Load
      Xml1.DocumentSource = "~/App_Data/CarList.xml"
      Xml1.TransformSource = "~/App_Data/CarList.xsl"
   End Sub
End Class
```

```csharp
//C#
using System;
using System.Data;
using System.Configuration;
using System.Collections;
using System.Web;
using System.Web.Security;
using System.Web.UI;
using System.Web.UI.WebControls;
using System.Web.UI.WebControls.WebParts;
using System.Web.UI.HtmlControls;

public partial class Xml_Control : System.Web.UI.Page
{
    protected void Page_Load(object sender, EventArgs e)
    {
        Xml1.DocumentSource = "~/App_Data/CarList.xml";
        Xml1.TransformSource = "~/App_Data/CarList.xsl";
    }
}
```

When the Web page is displayed, the XML and XSL files are loaded and the resulting transformation is shown in Figure 3-23.

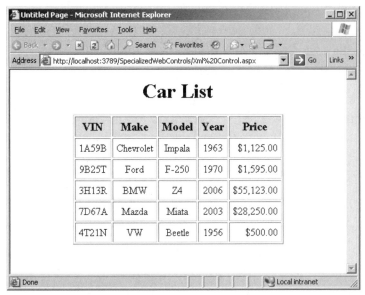

Figure 3-23 The result of applying the XSL transformation to the XML file.

Quick Check

1. What control provides the best implementation of a schedule of special dates?

2. You want to create a Web page that prompts the user to input lots of data, and you want the data input to be spread across multiple screens. What is the best control to use to implement this solution on a single Web page?

3. Your customer wants the home page to contain an image of the world and require users to click their specific countries. This redirects the users to the Web sites for their respective countries. What control will you use?

Quick Check Answers

1. The *Calendar* control

2. The *Wizard* control

3. The *ImageMap* control

Lab: Work with Specialized Web Controls

In this lab, you use the specialized Web controls that have been defined in this lesson to create a Web page for selecting a room in your house that needs to be serviced and a service date.

▶ **Exercise 1: Create the Web Site and Add the Controls**

In this exercise, you create the Web site and add the controls to the site.

1. Open Microsoft Visual Studio 2005 and create a new Web site, called UsingSpecializedControls, using your preferred programming language. Create the new Web site so that a Web page called Default.aspx is displayed.

2. Add a *Wizard* control to the Default.aspx Web page so that it displays the Wizard Tasks window.

3. In the Wizard Tasks window, click Add/Remove Wizard Steps to display the WizardStep Collection Editor.

4. Change the *Title* property of step 1 to **Select Room**.

5. Change the *Title* property of step 2 to **Service Date**.

6. Click the Add button to add another step and change its *Title* property to **Summary**. Click OK to close the WizardStep Collection Editor.

7. In the Solution Explorer window, right-click the project node and click New Folder. Rename the folder Images.

8. Add the following files to the Images folder. These files are available in sample code on this book's CD-ROM.

   ❑ House Dining Room.gif

   ❑ House Family Rooom.gif

   ❑ House Foyer.gif

   ❑ House Kitchen.gif

   ❑ House Office.gif

   ❑ House.gif

9. In Design view, click the *Wizard* control, set the *Height* property to 250px, and set the *Width* property to 425px.

10. In Design view, click the link for Select Room in the *Wizard* control to assure that this is the current step.

11. Add an *ImageMap* control to this step. After adding the *ImageMap* control, press Enter twice and type **Room Selected:**. After the text, add a *Label* control and remove its text from the *Text* property. Regardless of the language you choose, your ASPX source for this step should look like the following:

ASPX Source – Select Room
```
<asp:WizardStep runat="server" Title="Select Room">
    <br /> 
    <asp:ImageMap ID="ImageMap1" runat="server"
        ImageUrl="~/Images/House.gif">
    </asp:ImageMap>
    <br /><br />  
    Room Selected:
    <asp:Label ID="Label1" runat="server"></asp:Label>
</asp:WizardStep>
```

12. In Design view, click the Service Date link in the *Wizard* control to make this the active step.

13. In this step, press Enter, type **Select Service Date:**, and press Enter again. Add a *Calendar* control. Your ASPX source for this step should look like the following:

ASPX Source – Service Date
```
<asp:WizardStep runat="server" Title="Service Date">
    <br />Select Service Date:<br /> 
    <asp:Calendar ID="Calendar1" runat="server" >
    </asp:Calendar>
</asp:WizardStep>
```

14. In Design view, click the Summary link in the *Wizard* control to make this the active step.

    In this step, add a *Label* control and size it to the fill the *WizardStep* control. Your ASPX source for this step should look like the following:

ASPX Source – Service Date
```
<asp:WizardStep runat="server" Title="Summary">
    <asp:Label ID="Label2" runat="server" Height="225px" Width="325px">
    </asp:Label>
</asp:WizardStep>
```

15. In the Wizard Tasks window, click AutoFormat. Click Professional and click OK. The final result is shown in Figure 3-24.

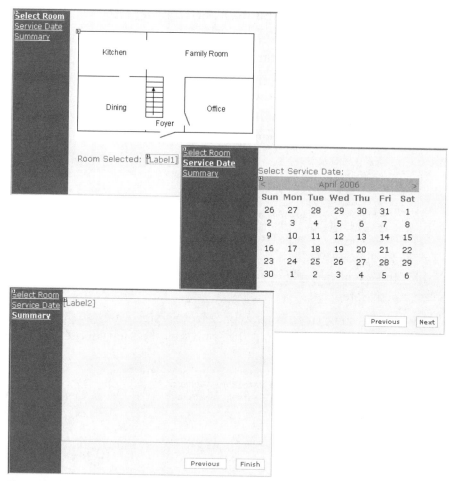

Figure 3-24   The completed Wizard user interface.

▶ **Exercise 2: Add to the Code-Behind Page**

In this exercise, you add code to the code-behind page to initialize the Wizard and the ImageMap hot spots and display a summary after the Wizard has completed its actions.

1. In Design view, double-click an empty area of the Web page to go to the code-behind page and insert the *Page_Load* event handler.

2. In the *Page_Load* event handler, add an *if* statement that tests whether the Web page is posted back. Inside the *if* statement, add code to set the *ActiveStepIndex* of the *Wizard* to the first *WizardStep*. Also add code to set the HotSpot mode of

the ImageMap to perform a *PostBack*. Finally, declare a local *RectangularHotSpot* variable and add code to create hot spots, as described in Table 3-4.

Table 3-4 *RectangularHotSpot* Controls

PostBackValue	Left	Top	Right	Bottom
Kitchen	4	3	113	73
Family Room	113	3	286	73
Dining Room	4	73	113	160
Office	176	73	286	160
Foyer	113	73	176	160

3. In Design view, double-click the ImageMap to create the *ImageMap1_Click* event handler in the code-behind page. Add code to this method that places the *PostBackValue* into *Label2*. Also add code that changes the *ImageUrl* of the ImageMap to display the current room that has been selected.

4. In Design view, double-click the *Wizard* to add the *Wizard1_FinishButtonClick* event handler in the code-behind page. In this method, add code to hide the *Wizard* and display a thank-you message.

5. In Design view, select the *Wizard* and click the Events button in the Properties window. Double-click the *ActiveStepChanged* event to add the *Wizard1_ActiveStepChanged* event handler. Add code to this method to find out if the active step is the summary, and if it is, populate *Label2* with a message that shows the current selection. Your final code-behind page should look like the following:

```
'VB
Partial Class _Default
    Inherits System.Web.UI.Page

    Protected Sub Page_Load(ByVal sender As Object, ByVal e As System.EventArgs) Handles
Me.Load
        If (Not IsPostBack) Then
            Wizard1.ActiveStepIndex = 0
            ImageMap1.HotSpotMode = HotSpotMode.PostBack
            Dim hs As RectangleHotSpot
            hs = New RectangleHotSpot()
            hs.PostBackValue = "Kitchen"
            hs.Left = 4
            hs.Top = 3
            hs.Right = 113
            hs.Bottom = 73
```

```
        ImageMap1.HotSpots.Add(hs)
        hs = New RectangleHotSpot()
        hs.PostBackValue = "Family Room"
        hs.Left = 113
        hs.Top = 3
        hs.Right = 286
        hs.Bottom = 73
        ImageMap1.HotSpots.Add(hs)
        hs = New RectangleHotSpot()
        hs.PostBackValue = "Dining Room"
        hs.Left = 4
        hs.Top = 73
        hs.Right = 113
        hs.Bottom = 160
        ImageMap1.HotSpots.Add(hs)
        hs = New RectangleHotSpot()
        hs.PostBackValue = "Office"
        hs.Left = 176
        hs.Top = 73
        hs.Right = 286
        hs.Bottom = 160
        ImageMap1.HotSpots.Add(hs)
        hs = New RectangleHotSpot()
        hs.PostBackValue = "Foyer"
        hs.Left = 113
        hs.Top = 73
        hs.Right = 176
        hs.Bottom = 160
        ImageMap1.HotSpots.Add(hs)
    End If
End Sub

Protected Sub ImageMap1_Click(ByVal sender As Object, _
        ByVal e As System.Web.UI.WebControls.ImageMapEventArgs) _
        Handles ImageMap1.Click
    Label1.Text = e.PostBackValue
    ImageMap1.ImageUrl = "~/Images/House " _
        + e.PostBackValue + ".gif"
End Sub

Protected Sub Wizard1_FinishButtonClick(ByVal sender As Object, _
        ByVal e As System.Web.UI.WebControls.WizardNavigationEventArgs) _
        Handles Wizard1.FinishButtonClick
    Wizard1.Visible = False
    Response.Write("Thank you for your order")
End Sub

Protected Sub Wizard1_ActiveStepChanged(ByVal sender As Object, _
        ByVal e As System.EventArgs) _
        Handles Wizard1.ActiveStepChanged
    If (Wizard1.ActiveStep.Title = "Summary") Then
        Label2.Text = "Summary Info:<br />" _
        + "Room: " + Label1.Text + "<br />" _
```

```
                + "Delivery Date: " _
                + Calendar1.SelectedDate.ToShortDateString()
          End If
      End Sub

End Class

//C#
using System;
using System.Data;
using System.Configuration;
using System.Collections;
using System.Web;
using System.Web.Security;
using System.Web.UI;
using System.Web.UI.WebControls;
using System.Web.UI.WebControls.WebParts;
using System.Web.UI.HtmlControls;

public partial class _Default : System.Web.UI.Page
{
    protected void Page_Load(object sender, EventArgs e)
    {
        if (!IsPostBack)
        {
            Wizard1.ActiveStepIndex = 0;
            ImageMap1.HotSpotMode = HotSpotMode.PostBack;
            RectangleHotSpot hs;
            hs = new RectangleHotSpot();
            hs.PostBackValue = "Kitchen";
            hs.Left = 4;
            hs.Top = 3;
            hs.Right = 113;
            hs.Bottom = 73;
            ImageMap1.HotSpots.Add(hs);
            hs = new RectangleHotSpot();
            hs.PostBackValue = "Family Room";
            hs.Left = 113;
            hs.Top = 3;
            hs.Right = 286;
            hs.Bottom = 73;
            ImageMap1.HotSpots.Add(hs);
            hs = new RectangleHotSpot();
            hs.PostBackValue = "Dining Room";
            hs.Left = 4;
            hs.Top = 73;
            hs.Right = 113;
            hs.Bottom = 160;
            ImageMap1.HotSpots.Add(hs);
            hs = new RectangleHotSpot();
            hs.PostBackValue = "Office";
            hs.Left = 176;
            hs.Top = 73;
```

```
            hs.Right = 286;
            hs.Bottom = 160;
            ImageMap1.HotSpots.Add(hs);
            hs = new RectangleHotSpot();
            hs.PostBackValue = "Foyer";
            hs.Left = 113;
            hs.Top = 73;
            hs.Right = 176;
            hs.Bottom = 160;
            ImageMap1.HotSpots.Add(hs);
        }
    }

    protected void Wizard1_FinishButtonClick(
        object sender, WizardNavigationEventArgs e)
    {
        Wizard1.Visible = false;
        Response.Write("Thank you for your order");
    }

    protected void Wizard1_ActiveStepChanged(
        object sender, EventArgs e)
    {
        if (Wizard1.ActiveStep.Title=="Summary")
        {
            Label2.Text = "Summary Info:<br />"
            + "Room: " + Label1.Text + "<br />"
            + "Delivery Date: "
            + Calendar1.SelectedDate.ToShortDateString();
        }
    }

    protected void ImageMap1_Click(
        object sender, ImageMapEventArgs e)
    {
        Label1.Text = e.PostBackValue;
        ImageMap1.ImageUrl = "~/Images/House "
            + e.PostBackValue + ".gif";
    }
}
```

6. Test the Web page by pressing F5 to display the page.

7. Try clicking each room and observe the results. You should see the image and the label should update to show the selected room.

8. Click the Service Date link or the Next button to display the *Calendar* control. Click a date.

9. Click the Summary link or the Next button to display a summary of your selections.

10. Click the Finish button to see the thank-you message.

Lesson Summary

- The *Literal* control is used to display static text on the Web page.

- The *Table*, *TableRow*, and *TableCell* controls provide ways to format tabular and graphical information that is displayed on the Web page.

- The *Image* control is used to display an image on a Web page.

- The *ImageButton* control is used to display a clickable image on a Web page that can be used to post back to the Web server when the image is clicked.

- The *ImageMap* control is used to display a clickable image on a Web page that can be used to post back to the Web server when the image is clicked.

- The *Calendar* control displays a calendar for a user's month of choice and allows the user to select dates and move to the next or previous month.

- The *FileUpload* control is used to display a TextBox and Browse button that allows a user to either type a file name and path, or click Browse and select a file and path.

- The *Panel* control is used as a control container and is useful when you have controls that you want to display and hide as a group.

- The *View* control is a control container and is useful when you have controls that you want to display and hide as a group.

- The *MultiView* control contains a collection of *View* controls; the *MultiView* control provides behavior that allows you to switch between *View* controls.

- The *Wizard* control is a complex control that is used to display a series of *Wizard-Step* controls to a user, one after the other.

Lesson Review

You can use the following questions to test your knowledge of the information in Lesson 1, "Exploring Specialized Web Server Controls." The questions are also available on the companion CD if you prefer to review them in electronic form.

NOTE Answers

Answers to these questions and explanations of why each answer choice is right or wrong are located in the "Answers" section at the end of the book.

---

1. Which of the following represents the best use of the *Table*, *TableRow*, and *TableCell* controls? (Choose one.)

   A. To create and populate a Table in Design view

   B. To create a customized control that needs to display data in a tabular fashion

   C. To create and populate a Table with images

   D. To display a tabular result set

2. Your graphics department just completed an elaborate image that shows the product lines that your company sells. Some of the product line graphics are circular, while others are rectangular, and others are complex shapes. You want to use this image as a menu on your Web site. What is the best way to incorporate the image into your Web site? (Choose one.)

   A. Use *ImageButton* and use the x- and y-coordinates that are returned when the user clicks to figure out what product line the user clicked.

   B. Use the *Table*, *TableRow*, and *TableCell* controls, break the image into pieces that are displayed in the cells, and use the *TableCell* control's *Click* event to identify the product line that was clicked.

   C. Use the *MultiView* control and break up the image into pieces that can be displayed in each *View* control for each product line. Use the *Click* event of the *View* to identify the product line that was clicked.

   D. Use an *ImageMap* control and define hot spot areas for each of the product lines. Use the *PostBackValue* to identify the product line that was clicked.

3. You are writing a Web site that collects lots of data from your users, and the data collection spreads over multiple Web pages. When the user reaches the last page, you need to gather all of data, validate the data, and save the data to the database. You notice that it can be rather difficult to gather the data that is spread over multiple pages and you want to simplify this application. What is the easiest control to implement that can be used to collect the data on a single Web page? (Choose one.)

   A. The *View* control

   B. The *TextBox* control

   C. The *Wizard* control

   D. The *DataCollection* control

Lesson 2: Working with Data-Bound Web Server Controls

The next chapter covers ADO.NET and XML, so we need to cover data-bound controls in this chapter so we can use them in the examples for ADO.NET and XML.

This lesson explores data binding and the Web server controls that are used in ASP.NET 2.0 to bind, or connect, to data.

After this lesson, you will be able to:

■ Use the following Web server controls:

❑ *ListControl*, and its child classes

❑ *AdRotator*

❑ *XML*

❑ *GridView*

❑ *FormView*

❑ *TreeView*

❑ *Menu*

Estimated lesson time: 60 minutes

Using a Collection to Perform Data-Binding

To keep things simple, the examples in this lesson use a collection of *Car* objects that can be bound to a control. The *Car* class is shown in the following code sample:

```vb
'VB
Imports Microsoft.VisualBasic
Imports System.Collections.Generic

Public Class Car
    Public Sub New(ByVal vin As String, ByVal make As String, _
        ByVal model As String, ByVal year As Integer, _
        ByVal price As Decimal)
      Me.Vin = vin : Me.Make = make : Me.Model = model
      Me.Year = year : Me.Price = price
    End Sub

    Public Property Vin() As String
      Get
          Return _vin
      End Get
      Set(ByVal value As String)
         _vin = value
      End Set
```

```vb
   End Property
   Private _vin As String

   Public Property Make() As String
      Get
         Return _make
      End Get
      Set(ByVal value As String)
         _make = value
      End Set
   End Property
   Private _make As String

   Public Property Model() As String
      Get
         Return _model
      End Get
      Set(ByVal value As String)
         _model = value
      End Set
   End Property
   Private _model As String

   Public Property Year() As Decimal
      Get
         Return _year
      End Get
      Set(ByVal value As Decimal)
         _year = value
      End Set
   End Property
   Private _year As Decimal

   Public Property Price() As Decimal
      Get
         Return _price
      End Get
      Set(ByVal value As Decimal)
         _price = value
      End Set
   End Property
   Private _price As Decimal

   Public Shared Function GetList() As List(Of Car)
      Dim carList As New List(Of Car)
      carList.Add(New Car("1A59B", "Chevrolet", "Impala", 1963, 1125.0))
      carList.Add(New Car("9B25T", "Ford", "F-250", 1970, 1595.0))
      carList.Add(New Car("3H13R", "BMW", "Z4", 2006, 55123.0))
      carList.Add(New Car("7D67A", "Mazda", "Miata", 2003, 28250.0))
      carList.Add(New Car("4T21N", "VW", "Beetle", 1956, 500.0))
      Return carList
   End Function
```

```
End Class

//C#
using System;
using System.Data;
using System.Configuration;
using System.Web;
using System.Web.Security;
using System.Web.UI;
using System.Web.UI.WebControls;
using System.Web.UI.WebControls.WebParts;
using System.Web.UI.HtmlControls;
using System.Collections.Generic;

/// <summary>
/// Summary description for Car
/// </summary>
public class Car
{
   public Car() { }

public Car(string vin, string make, string model, int year, decimal price)
{
      Vin = vin;  Make = make; Model = model; Year = year; Price = price;
}

   public string Vin
   {
      get { return vin; }
      set { vin = value; }
   }
   private string vin;

   public string Make
   {
      get { return make; }
      set { make = value; }
   }
   private string make;

   public string Model
   {
      get { return model; }
      set { model = value; }
   }
   private string model;

   public int Year
   {
      get { return year; }
      set { year = value; }
   }
```

```
    private int year;

    public decimal Price
    {
       get { return price; }
       set { price = value; }
    }
    private decimal price;

    public static List<Car> GetList()
    {
       List<Car> carList = new List<Car>();
       carList.Add(new Car("1A59B","Chevrolet", "Impala", 1963, 1125.00M));
       carList.Add(new Car("9B25T","Ford", "F-250", 1970, 1595.00M));
       carList.Add(new Car("3H13R","BMW", "Z4", 2006, 55123.00M));
       carList.Add(new Car("7D67A","Mazda", "Miata", 2003, 28250.00M));
       carList.Add(new Car("4T21N","VW", "Beetle", 1956, 500.00M));
       return carList;
    }

}
```

Notice that the *GetList* method returns a list of *Car* objects that can be used as needed.

Introducing Data-Bound Controls

Data-bound controls are controls that need to bind, or connect, to data. The data-bound controls are classified as simple, composite, or hierarchical controls. Simple data-bound controls are the controls that inherit from the *ListControl* and the *AdRotator* controls. Composite data-bound controls are classes that inherit from *Composite-DataBoundControl*, such as the *GridView*, *DetailsView*, and *FormsView* controls. Hierarchical data-bound controls are the *Menu* and *TreeView* controls.

The .NET framework provides several base classes that are used to provide common properties and behavior for the concrete data-bound controls. Figure 3-25 shows the hierarchy of the base classes.

The *HierarchicalDataBoundControl* inherits from the *BaseDataBoundControl* and is the parent class to controls that display hierarchical data, such as the *Menu* and *TreeView* controls.

The *DataBoundControl* inherits from the *BaseDataBoundControl* and is the parent class to the *CompositeDataBoundControl* and the *ListControl*, which are parent classes to other controls that display tabular data, such as the *GridView* and *DropDownList*. The *DataBoundControl* control's *DataMember* property is a string data type that is used when the *DataSource* contains more than one tabular result set. In this scenario, the *DataMember* property is set to the name of the tabular result set that is to be displayed.

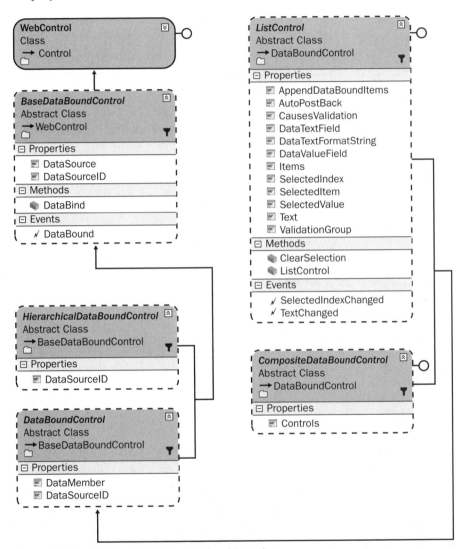

Figure 3-25 The base data-bound class hierarchy.

The *DataBoundControl* class has a method called *DataBind*. You call this method when the data is ready to be read from the data source. When this method is called on a control, this method is recursively called on all child controls. Calling the *DataBind* method on the Web page recursively calls the *DataBind* method on all controls on the Web page.

Using *DataSource* Objects

The *BaseDataBoundControl* is the first control in the hierarchy, inheriting from *WebControl*. The class contains the *DataSource* and *DataSourceID* properties. The *DataSource* property gets or sets the object that the data-bound control uses to retrieve a list of data items. The *DataSource* object is typically an instance of a class that implements *IEnumerable*, *IListSource*, *IDataSource*, or *IHierarchicalDatasource*. The *DataSourceID* property gets or sets the ID of a control that contains the source of the data, such as the *SqlDataSource* control. You typically set either the *DataSource* or the *DataSourceID*. If both properties are set, the *DataSourceID* takes precedence. The data-bound control automatically connects to the data source control at run time by calling the *DataBind* method on this control, which also raises the *DataBound* method.

NOTE .NET 2.0

Graphical User Interface (GUI)-based data sources are new in ASP.NET version 2.0.

The GUI-based data sources are controls that inherit from *DataSourceControl* or *HierarchicalDataSourceControl* and implement the *IDataSource* and *IListSource* interfaces. These controls provide a consistent means to bind any data source to a data-bound control. The class hierarchies for the *DataSourceControl* and *HierarchicalDataSourceControl* are shown in Figure 3-26.

The following is a description of each of the GUI-based data sources that you can use to bind, or connect, to a data-bound control:

- **AccessDataSource**   Provides binding to a Microsoft Access database file that has the .mdb extension.

- **SqlDataSource**   Provides binding to an Open Database Connectivity (ODBC), Object Linking and Embedding Database (OLEDB), SQL Server, Oracle, or other database that uses Structured Query Language (SQL). You can even attach to a SQL Server database file by simply including it in your project.

- **XmlDataSource**   Provides binding to an XML file in your project folder. You can specify a transform file that can be used to modify the XML file before it is bound to a control. You can also provide an XPath expression to retrieve a subset of the data in the XML file.

- **ObjectDataSource**   Provides binding to an object. The ObjectDataSource can connect to a middle-tier business object or *DataSet* object in the Bin or App_Code directory of your application. When using this option, you can select a class that you have access to, and an instance of the class is created for you each time that data is required. In addition to selecting a class, you must choose the methods you want to execute to select, insert, update, and delete. The select method should return a single object that implements *IEnumerable*, *IListSource*, *IDataSource*, or *IHierarchicalDatasource*. This means that a *DataTable* object, a *DataSet* object, or a collection object can be used. If the select method returns a *DataSet* object, the first *DataTable* object in the *DataSet* is used.

- **SitemapDataSource**   You can connect to the site navigation tree for your application. This option requires a valid sitemap file at the application root.

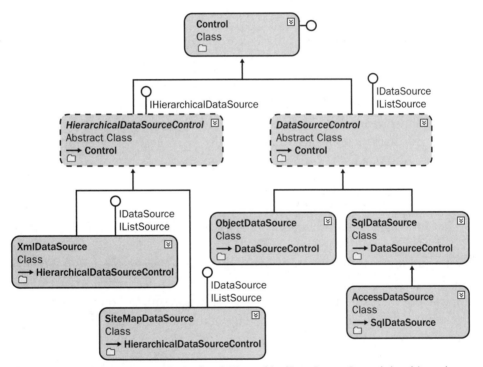

Figure 3-26   The *DataSourceControl* and *HierarchicalDataSourceControl* class hierarchy.

Mapping Fields to Templates

Templated binding can be used on controls that support templates. A template control is a control that has no default user interface. The control simply provides the mechanism for binding to data. The developer supplies the user interface in the form of inline templates. The template can contain declarative elements such as HTML and Dynamic Hypertext Markup Language (DHTML). The template can also contain

ASP.NET data-binding syntax to insert data from the data source. Controls that support templates include *GridView*, *DetailsView*, and *FormView*. A typical control may allow the following templates to be programmed:

- **HeaderTemplate**   This is an optional header, which is rendered at the top of the control.

- **FooterTemplate**   This is an optional footer, which is rendered at the bottom of the control.

- **ItemTemplate**   The item template is rendered for each row in the data source.

- **AlternatingItemTemplate**   This is an optional alternating item template; if implemented, every other row is rendered using this template.

- **SelectedItemTemplate**   This is an optional selected item template; if implemented, the template is used to render a row that has been selected.

- **SeparatorTemplate**   This is an optional separator template that defines the separation of each item and alternate item.

- **EditItemTemplate**   This is an optional edit item template that is used to render a row that is in edit mode. This usually involves displaying the data in a *TextBox* instead of a *Label* control.

Using the *DataBinder* Class

The *DataBinder* class provides a static method called *Eval*, which can simplify access to data, especially when you are using templated controls. The *Eval* method uses reflection to perform a lookup of the *DataItem* property's underlying type by looking at the type metadata that is stored in the type's assembly. After the metadata is retrieved, the *Eval* method determines how to connect to the given field. The end result is that *Eval* provides a consistent method of binding to the data. The following code shows the binding to the *Vin* property of the *Car* object:

```
<%# Eval("Vin") %>
```

The *Eval* method provides an overloaded method that allows a format string to be assigned. The *Price* can be modified to provide currency formatting, as shown in the following code:

```
<%# Eval("Vin", "{0:C}" ) %>
```

The problem with the *Eval* method is that it provides one-way, or read-only binding, but the new *Bind* method fixes that problem.

NOTE .NET 2.0

The *Bind* method is new in ASP.NET version 2.0.

The *Bind* method provides two-way data binding, which makes this method desirable for use when editing or inserting records. Just like the *Eval* method, the *Bind* method has two overloads, which means that you can use it with or without the *"format"* parameter. The following code shows the use of the *Bind* method to the *Vin* property of the *Car* object:

```
<%# Bind("Vin") %>
```

The *Bind* method provides an overloaded method that allows a format string to be assigned. The *Price* can be modified to provide currency formatting, as shown in the following code:

```
<%# Bind("Vin", "{0:C}" ) %>
```

Notice that the syntax for the *Bind* method is the same as for the *Eval* method. Also, the *GridView*, *DetailsView*, and *FormView* controls are the only controls that allow use of the *Bind* method.

NOTE Be Sure to Set the ID

A control that is data-bound using the *Bind* syntax must have the *ID* property set to a user-defined value.

Exploring the *ListControl*

The *ListControl* is an abstract base class that provides common functionality for its inherited classes, as shown in Figure 3-27. The *ListControl* contains an *Items* collection, which is a collection of *ListItem* objects. The *ListItem* contains a *Text* property that is displayed to the user and a *Value* property that is posted back to the Web server. The *ListItem* objects can be populated by adding new *ListItems* objects in code or by setting the *DataSource* and *DataMember* properties. If you set the *DataSource* and *DataMember* properties, you can choose the fields in your tabular result that you will bind to the *ListItem.Text* and *ListItem.Value* properties by setting the *DataTextField* and *DataValueField* properties, respectively. The text displayed for each item in the list control can be formatted by setting the *DataTextFormatString* property.

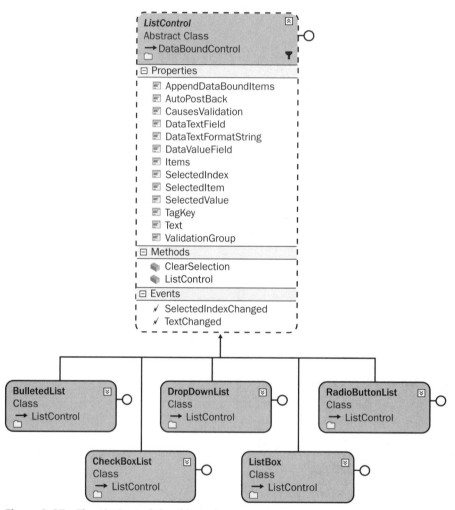

Figure 3-27   The *ListControl* class hierarchy.

The *SelectedIndex* property lets you get or set the index of the selected item in the *ListControl*. Using the *SelectedItem* property, you can access the selected *ListItem* object's properties. If you only need to access the value of the selected *ListItem*, use the *SelectedValue* property. The *ListControl* also provides the *SelectedIndexChanged* event, which is raised when the selection in the list control changes between posts to the server.

NOTE   **.NET 2.0**

AppendDataBoundItems is new in ASP.NET version 2.0.

The *ListControl* also contains a new property called *AppendDataBoundItems* that can be set to *true* to keep all items that are currently in the *ListControl* in addition to appending the items from the data binding. Setting this property to *false* clears the *Items* property prior to binding the data.

The *DropDownList* Control

The *DropDownList* control is used to display a list of items to the user who can make a single selection. The *DropDownList* control inherits from the *ListControl* control, as shown in Figure 3-28.

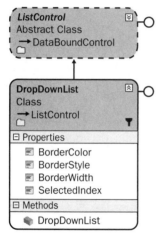

Figure 3-28 The *DropDownList* control hierarchy.

The *Items* collection contains the collection of *ListItem* objects contained in the *DropDownList* control. To determine the item that is selected, you can retrieve the *SelectedValue*, *SelectedItem*, or *SelectedIndex* property.

Security Alert   By default, populating the *DropDownList* control with data from an untrusted source can create XSS vulnerabilities. Be sure to HtmlEncode untrusted data that is placed into each *ListItem*.

The following example shows how to data-bind the *DropDownList* control to the *Car* collection. The Web page contains a *DropDownList* control, a *Button* control, and a *Label* control:

```
'VB
Imports System.Collections.Generic
```

```
Partial Class DropDownList_Control
    Inherits System.Web.UI.Page

  Private carList As List(Of Car) = Car.GetList()

  Protected Sub Page_Load(ByVal sender As Object, _
        ByVal e As System.EventArgs) Handles Me.Load
    If Not IsPostBack Then
        DropDownList1.DataSource = carList
        DropDownList1.DataTextField = "Price"
        DropDownList1.DataValueField = "Price"
        DropDownList1.DataTextFormatString = "Price: {0:C}"
        DropDownList1.DataBind()
    End If
  End Sub


  Protected Sub Button1_Click(ByVal sender As Object, _
        ByVal e As System.EventArgs) Handles Button1.Click
    Label1.Text = DropDownList1.SelectedValue
  End Sub
End Class

//C#
using System;
using System.Data;
using System.Configuration;
using System.Collections;
using System.Web;
using System.Web.Security;
using System.Web.UI;
using System.Web.UI.WebControls;
using System.Web.UI.WebControls.WebParts;
using System.Web.UI.HtmlControls;
//added
using System.Collections.Generic;

public partial class DropDownList_Control : System.Web.UI.Page
{
    private List<Car> carList = Car.GetList();

    protected void Page_Load(object sender, EventArgs e)
    {
        if (!IsPostBack)
        {
            DropDownList1.DataSource = carList;
            DropDownList1.DataTextField = "Price";
            DropDownList1.DataValueField = "Price";
            DropDownList1.DataTextFormatString = "Price: {0:C}";
            DropDownList1.DataBind();
        }
    }
```

```
protected void Button1_Click(object sender, EventArgs e)
{
    Label1.Text = DropDownList1.SelectedValue;
}
}
```

In the example shown in Figure 3-29, the user makes a selection in the *DropDownList* control, and the *Button* control is clicked to display the results in the *Label* control. Note that the *DropDownList* control is being populated only on the first request for the Web page. If the *DropDownList* control is repopulated, the selected item is discarded, resulting in no item being selected.

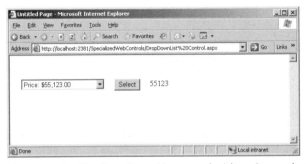

Figure 3-29 The *DropDownList* control with an item selected and copied to the *Label* control.

The *ListBox* Control

The *ListBox* control is used to display a list of items to the user, who can make a single selection or multiple selections. The *ListBox* control inherits from the *ListControl* control, as shown in Figure 3-30. The *SelectionMode* property is used to enable multiple-item selection by setting this property to *ListSelectionMode.Multiple*.

The *ListBox* control has the *Rows* property, which is used to specify the height of the *ListBox* control, based on specifying the quantity of data items to display.

The *Items* collection contains the collection of *ListItem* objects contained in the *ListBox* control. To determine the items that are selected, you can enumerate the *ListItem* objects in the *Items* collection by examining the *Selected* value for each *ListItem* element.

Security Alert By default, populating the *ListBox* control with data from an untrusted source can create XSS vulnerabilities. Be sure to HtmlEncode untrusted data that will be placed into each *ListItem*.

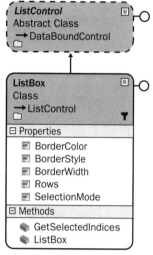

Figure 3-30   The *ListBox* control hierarchy.

The following example shows how to data-bind the *ListBox* control to the *Car* collection. The Web page contains two *ListBox* controls with a *Button* control between them. The *ListBox* controls have their *SelectionMode* properties set to *Multiple*.

```vb
'VB
Imports System.Collections.Generic

Partial Class ListBox_Control
    Inherits System.Web.UI.Page

    Private carList As List(Of Car) = Car.GetList()

    Protected Sub Page_Load(ByVal sender As Object, _
            ByVal e As System.EventArgs) Handles Me.Load
        ListBox1.SelectionMode = ListSelectionMode.Multiple
        ListBox2.SelectionMode = ListSelectionMode.Multiple
        If Not IsPostBack Then
            ListBox1.DataSource = carList
            ListBox1.DataTextField = "Price"
            ListBox1.DataValueField = "Price"
            ListBox1.DataTextFormatString = "Price: {0:C}"
            ListBox1.DataBind()
        End If
    End Sub

    Protected Sub Button1_Click(ByVal sender As Object, _
            ByVal e As System.EventArgs) Handles Button1.Click
        For Each item As ListItem In ListBox1.Items
            If item.Selected Then
                ListBox2.Items.Add(item)
```

```
        End If
      Next
      ListBox2.DataBind()
   End Sub
End Class

//C#
using System;
using System.Data;
using System.Configuration;
using System.Collections;
using System.Web;
using System.Web.Security;
using System.Web.UI;
using System.Web.UI.WebControls;
using System.Web.UI.WebControls.WebParts;
using System.Web.UI.HtmlControls;
//added
using System.Collections.Generic;

public partial class ListBox_Control : System.Web.UI.Page
{
   private List<Car> carList = Car.GetList();

   protected void Page_Load(object sender, EventArgs e)
   {
      ListBox1.SelectionMode = ListSelectionMode.Multiple;
      ListBox2.SelectionMode = ListSelectionMode.Multiple;
      if (!IsPostBack)
      {
         ListBox1.DataSource = carList;
         ListBox1.DataTextField = "Price";
         ListBox1.DataValueField = "Price";
         ListBox1.DataTextFormatString = "Price: {0:C}";
         ListBox1.DataBind();
      }
   }

   protected void Button1_Click(object sender, EventArgs e)
   {
      foreach (ListItem item in ListBox1.Items)
      {
         if (item.Selected)
         {
            ListBox2.Items.Add(item);
         }
      }
      ListBox2.DataBind();
   }
}
```

In the example shown in Figure 3-31, the user makes selections in the first *ListBox* control and clicks the *Button* control to display the results in the second *ListBox* control. Note that the first *ListBox* control is only being populated on the first request for the Web page. If the *ListBox* control is repopulated, the selected items are discarded, resulting in no items being selected.

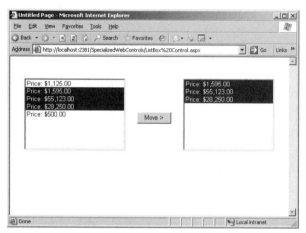

Figure 3-31   The *ListBox* control with items selected and copied to the second control.

The *CheckBoxList* and *RadioButtonList* Controls

The *CheckBoxList* and *RadioButtonList* controls are very similar and are used to display lists of items to the users, who can make single selections (*RadioButtonList*) or multiple selections (*CheckBoxList*). These controls inherit from the *ListControl* control, as shown in Figure 3-32.

These controls contain a *RepeatColumns* property that is used to size the control horizontally. In addition, the *RepeatDirection* can be set to *Vertical* or *Horizontal* to indicate which way the data is rendered.

The *Items* collection contains the collection of *ListItem* objects, which are inside the *CheckBoxList* and the *RadioButtonList* controls. Use the *SelectedValue* property to determine the item that has been selected for the *RadioButtonList*. To find the selected *CheckBoxList* items, you can enumerate the *ListItem* objects in the *Items* collection by examining the value of the *Selected* property for each *ListItem* element.

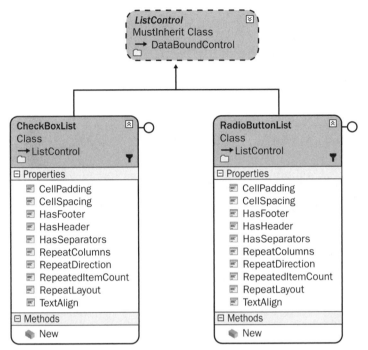

Figure 3-32   The *CheckBoxList* and *RadioButtonList* control hierarchy.

Security Alert   By default, populating the *CheckBoxList* and *RadioButtonList* controls with data from an untrusted source can create XSS vulnerabilities. Be sure to HtmlEncode untrusted data that will be placed into each *ListItem*.

The following example shows how to data-bind the *CheckBoxList* and *RadioButtonList* controls to the *Car* collection. The Web page contains one of each of the controls, plus a *ListBox* control. All of these controls have been bound to the *Car* collection. The *ListBox* shows the order of the *Car* collection. The *CheckBoxList* has the *RepeatColumns* set to 3 and the *RepeatDirection* set to *Horizontal*. The *RadioButtonList* also has the *RepeatColumns* set to 3, but the *RepeatDirection* property is set to *Vertical*.

```
'VB
Imports System.Collections.Generic

Partial Class CheckBoxList_and_RadioButtonList_Controls
    Inherits System.Web.UI.Page

    Private carList As List(Of Car) = Car.GetList()

    Protected Sub Page_Load(ByVal sender As Object, ByVal e As System.EventArgs) Handles Me.Load
```

```
        RadioButtonList1.RepeatColumns = 3
        RadioButtonList1.RepeatDirection = RepeatDirection.Vertical
        CheckBoxList1.RepeatColumns = 3
        CheckBoxList1.RepeatDirection = RepeatDirection.Horizontal

        If Not IsPostBack Then
            If Not IsPostBack Then
                ListBox1.DataSource = carList
                ListBox1.DataTextField = "Make"
                ListBox1.DataValueField = "Price"
                RadioButtonList1.DataSource = carList
                RadioButtonList1.DataTextField = "Make"
                RadioButtonList1.DataValueField = "Price"
                CheckBoxList1.DataSource = carList
                CheckBoxList1.DataTextField = "Make"
                CheckBoxList1.DataValueField = "Price"
                DataBind()
            End If
        End If
    End Sub

End Class


//C#
using System;
using System.Data;
using System.Configuration;
using System.Collections;
using System.Web;
using System.Web.Security;
using System.Web.UI;
using System.Web.UI.WebControls;
using System.Web.UI.WebControls.WebParts;
using System.Web.UI.HtmlControls;
//added
using System.Collections.Generic;

public partial class CheckBoxList_and_RadioButtonList_Controls : System.Web.UI.Page
{
    private List<Car> carList = Car.GetList();

    protected void Page_Load(object sender, EventArgs e)
    {
        RadioButtonList1.RepeatColumns = 3;
        RadioButtonList1.RepeatDirection = RepeatDirection.Vertical;
        CheckBoxList1.RepeatColumns = 3;
        CheckBoxList1.RepeatDirection = RepeatDirection.Horizontal;
        if (!IsPostBack)
        {
            ListBox1.DataSource = carList;
            ListBox1.DataTextField = "Make";
            ListBox1.DataValueField = "Price";
            RadioButtonList1.DataSource = carList;
```

```
    RadioButtonList1.DataTextField = "Make";
    RadioButtonList1.DataValueField = "Price";
    CheckBoxList1.DataSource = carList;
    CheckBoxList1.DataTextField = "Make";
    CheckBoxList1.DataValueField = "Price";
    DataBind();
    }
  }
}
```

In the example shown in Figure 3-33, the user makes selections in the first *ListBox* control and the *Button* control is clicked to display the results in the second *ListBox* control. Note that the first *ListBox* control is only populated on the first request for the Web page. If the *ListBox* control is repopulated, the selected items are discarded, resulting in no items being selected.

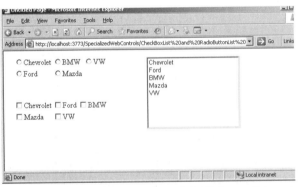

Figure 3-33   The *CheckBoxList* and *RadioButtonList* controls, showing the use of the Repeat-Columns and RepeatDirection.

The *BulletedList* Control

The *BulletedList* control displays an unordered or ordered list of items that renders as HTML *ul* or *ol* elements, respectively. The *BulletedList* control inherits from the *ListControl* control, as shown in Figure 3-34. This control renders as either bullets or numbers based on the *BulletStyle* property.

If the control is set to render as bullets, you can select the bullet style of *Disc*, *Circle*, or *Square*. Note that the *BulletStyle* settings are not compatible with all browsers. A custom image can be displayed instead of the bullet.

If the *BulletList* control is set to render numbers, you can set the *BulletStyle* to *Lower-Alpha*, *UpperAlpha*, *LowerRoman*, and *UpperAlpha* fields. You can also set the *FirstBullet-Number* property to specify the starting number for the sequence.

Figure 3-34   The *BulletedList* control hierarchy.

The *DisplayMode* property can be set to *Text*, *LinkButton*, or *HyperLink*. If set to *Link-Button* or *HyperLink*, the control performs a PostBack when a user clicks an item to raise the *Click* event.

Security Alert   By default, populating the *BulletedList* control with data from an untrusted source can create XSS vulnerabilities. Be sure to HtmlEncode untrusted data that is placed into each *List-Item*.

The following example shows how to data-bind the *BulletedList* control to the *Car* collection. The Web page contains a *BulletedList* control and two *ListBox* controls. The first *ListBox* control contains the list of *BulletStyle* options and the second *ListBox* contains the *DisplayMode* settings. These *ListBox* controls demonstrate the formatting options that are available.

```
'VB
Imports System.Collections.Generic

Partial Class BulletedList_Control
```

```
    Inherits System.Web.UI.Page

    Private carList As List(Of Car) = Car.GetList()

    Protected Sub ListBox1_SelectedIndexChanged(ByVal sender As Object, ByVal e As
System.EventArgs) Handles ListBox1.SelectedIndexChanged
        BulletedList1.BulletStyle = _
            CType([Enum].Parse( _
            GetType(BulletStyle), _
            ListBox1.SelectedValue), BulletStyle)
    End Sub

    Protected Sub ListBox2_SelectedIndexChanged(ByVal sender As Object, ByVal e As
System.EventArgs) Handles ListBox2.SelectedIndexChanged
        BulletedList1.DisplayMode = _
            CType([Enum].Parse( _
            GetType(BulletedListDisplayMode), _
            ListBox2.SelectedValue), BulletedListDisplayMode)
    End Sub

    Protected Sub Page_Load(ByVal sender As Object, _
            ByVal e As System.EventArgs) Handles Me.Load
        ListBox1.AutoPostBack = True
        ListBox2.AutoPostBack = True
        If (Not IsPostBack) Then
            BulletedList1.DataSource = carList
            BulletedList1.DataTextField = "Make"
            BulletedList1.DataValueField = "Price"
            ListBox1.DataSource = _
                [Enum].GetNames(GetType(BulletStyle))
            ListBox2.DataSource = _
                [Enum].GetNames(GetType(BulletedListDisplayMode))
            DataBind()
        End If

    End Sub
End Class

//C#
using System;
using System.Data;
using System.Configuration;
using System.Collections;
using System.Web;
using System.Web.Security;
using System.Web.UI;
using System.Web.UI.WebControls;
using System.Web.UI.WebControls.WebParts;
using System.Web.UI.HtmlControls;
//added
using System.Collections.Generic;
```

```
public partial class BulletedList_Control : System.Web.UI.Page
{
    private List<Car> carList = Car.GetList();

    protected void Page_Load(object sender, EventArgs e)
    {
        ListBox1.AutoPostBack = true;
        ListBox2.AutoPostBack = true;
        if (!IsPostBack)
        {
            BulletedList1.DataSource = carList;
            BulletedList1.DataTextField = "Make";
            BulletedList1.DataValueField = "Price";
            ListBox1.DataSource =
                Enum.GetNames(typeof(BulletStyle));
            ListBox2.DataSource =
                Enum.GetNames(typeof(BulletedListDisplayMode));
            DataBind();
        }
    }

    protected void ListBox1_SelectedIndexChanged(object sender,
        EventArgs e)
    {
        BulletedList1.BulletStyle =
            (BulletStyle)Enum.Parse(
            typeof(BulletStyle),
            ListBox1.SelectedValue);
    }
    protected void ListBox2_SelectedIndexChanged(object sender,
        EventArgs e)
    {
        BulletedList1.DisplayMode =
            (BulletedListDisplayMode)Enum.Parse(
            typeof(BulletedListDisplayMode),
            ListBox2.SelectedValue);
    }

}
```

In the example shown in Figure 3-35, you can select a *BulletStyle* and a *DisplayMode* to see the rendered output. Keep in mind that the *BulletStyle* settings are not compatible with all browsers.

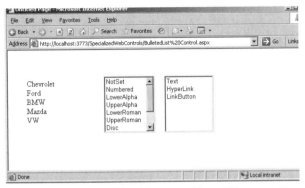

Figure 3-35 The *BulletedList* control has different setting options available.

The *AdRotator* Control

The *AdRotator* control is used to display randomly selected advertisement banners on a Web page. In Source view, the *AdRotator* control is created as an *<asp:AdRotator>* element. This control generates *<a>* and *<img>* elements when rendering to HTML. The *AdRotator* control inherits directly from the *DataBoundControl* class, as shown in Figure 3-36.

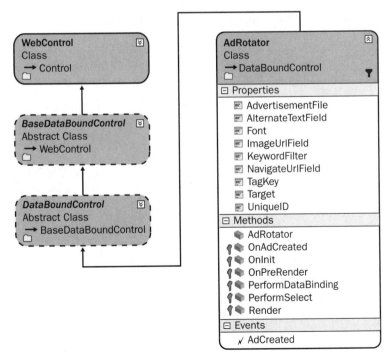

Figure 3-36 The *AdRotator* control hierarchy.

The advertisement information can be retrieved from an XML file or from a database. Table 3-5 describes the elements that can be placed in the XML file for each advertisement.

Table 3-5   Ad Elements

Element Name	Description
Keyword	The category key of the ad. This can be used to filter for specific ads.
ImageUrl	The URL of the advertisement image to display.
NavigateUrl	The URL to navigate to when the ad is clicked.
AlternateText	The text to display if the image is unavailable; is displayed as a ToolTip.
Impressions	A number that is used to weight the frequency of this ad being displayed. The sum of all of the impressions values must be less than 2,048,000,000.
Height	This is an optional value that specifies the pixel height of the ad. This value overrides the *AdRotator Height* property.
Width	This is an optional value that specifies the pixel width of the ad. This value overrides the *AdRotator Width* property.

You must be careful with the configuration, naming, and location of the advertisement file to assure that you don't cause security vulnerabilities. Listed below are some guidelines for this file:

1. Locate the advertisement file in the App_Data folder because ASP.NET does not allow browsers to request files in this folder.

2. Use a file extension, such as .config, that ASP.NET does not allow a browser to request.

3. Set permissions on the advertisement file to allow the ASP.NET account to have read-only access.

4. The ad file is not validated by the *AdRotator* control, so always check the data to assure that it does not contain malicious scripts before the data is released to production.

The *Impressions* element controls the frequency of advertisement display. A higher number increases the frequency relative to other advertisements in the file.

In this example, a Web page was created and an *AdRotator* control was added to the page. The advertisement file contains ad entries for Adventure Works, Contoso, and Northwind Traders. Listed below is the XML file, which was placed into the App_Data folder.

Sample Ads.config XML File

```
<?xml version="1.0" encoding="utf-8" ?>
<Advertisements
 xmlns="http://schemas.microsoft.com/AspNet/AdRotator-Advertisement-File-1.2">
    <Ad xmlns="">
       <Keyword>AdventureWorks</Keyword>
       <ImageUrl>~/images/AdventureWorks.gif</ImageUrl>
       <NavigateUrl>http://www.adventure-works.com</NavigateUrl>
       <AlternateText>Ad for Adventure Works Web site</AlternateText>
       <Impressions>100</Impressions>
    </Ad>
    <Ad xmlns="">
       <Keyword>Contoso</Keyword>
       <ImageUrl>~/images/Contoso.gif</ImageUrl>
       <NavigateUrl>http://www.contoso.com/</NavigateUrl>
       <AlternateText>Ad for Contoso Ltd. Web site</AlternateText>
       <Impressions>100</Impressions>
    </Ad>
    <Ad xmlns="">
       <Keyword>Northwind</Keyword>
       <ImageUrl>~/images/NorthwindTraders.gif</ImageUrl>
       <NavigateUrl>http://http://www.northwindtraders.com</NavigateUrl>
       <AlternateText>Ad for Northwind Traders Web site</AlternateText>
       <Impressions>50</Impressions>
    </Ad>
</Advertisements>
```

Next, full banner images (468 pixels wide by 60 pixels high) were added to the Images folder for Adventure Works, Contoso, and Northwind Traders, and the following code was added to the code-behind page to configure that *AdRotator* control:

```vb
'VB
Partial Class AdRotator_Control
    Inherits System.Web.UI.Page

    Protected Sub Page_Load(ByVal sender As Object, _
        ByVal e As System.EventArgs) Handles Me.Load
       AdRotator1.AdvertisementFile = "~/App_Data/Ads.config"
       AdRotator1.Height = 60
```

```
        AdRotator1.Width = 468
    End Sub
End Class

//C#
using System;
using System.Data;
using System.Configuration;
using System.Collections;
using System.Web;
using System.Web.Security;
using System.Web.UI;
using System.Web.UI.WebControls;
using System.Web.UI.WebControls.WebParts;
using System.Web.UI.HtmlControls;

public partial class AdRotator_Control : System.Web.UI.Page
{
    protected void Page_Load(object sender, EventArgs e)
    {
        AdRotator1.AdvertisementFile = "~/App_Data/Ads.config";
        AdRotator1.Height = 60;
        AdRotator1.Width = 468;
    }
}
```

When this Web page is displayed, one of the advertisements is displayed, as shown in Figure 3-37.

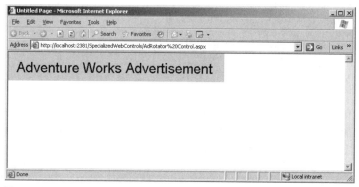

Figure 3-37   The rendered *AdRotator* displays an advertisement.

The *CompositeDataBoundControl* Control

The *CompositeDataBoundControl* control serves as a base class for controls that contain other data-bound controls. The most significant aspect of this class is that it implements the *INamingContainer* interface, which means that an inheritor of this class is a naming container for its child controls.

The classes that inherit from *CompositeDataBoundControl* are *FormsView*, *DetailsView*, and *GridView*, as shown in Figure 3-38. These controls are introduced in this lesson and will be further discussed as they are used with ADO.NET in Chapter 4, "Using ADO.NET and XML with ASP.NET."

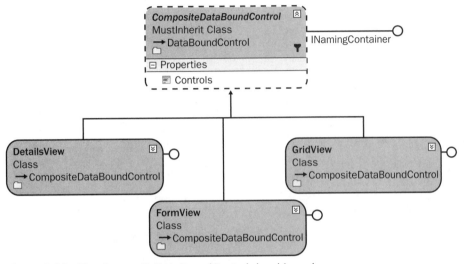

Figure 3-38   The *CompositeDataBoundControl* class hierarchy.

The *GridView* Control

The *GridView* control is used to display data in a tabular, rows-and-columns format. The *GridView* renders in the browser as an HTML table. The *GridView* control makes it easy to configure features such as paging, sorting, and editing without having to write much, if any, code. The *GridView* class hierarchy is shown in Figure 3-39.

NOTE   .NET 2.0

The *GridView* is new in ASP.NET version 2.0.

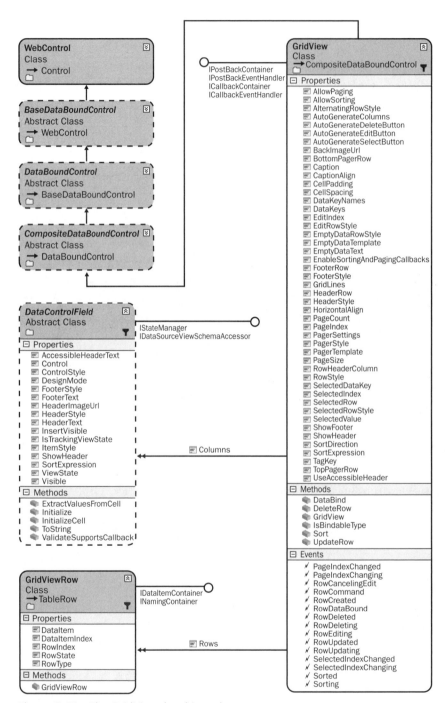

Figure 3-39   The *GridView* class hierarchy.

The basic structure of the *GridView* is shown in Figure 3-40. The *GridView* control consists of a collection of *GridViewRow* (row) objects and a collection of *DataControlField* (column) objects. The *GridViewRow* object inherits from the *TableRow* object, which contains the *Cells* property, which is a collection of *DataControlFieldCell* objects.

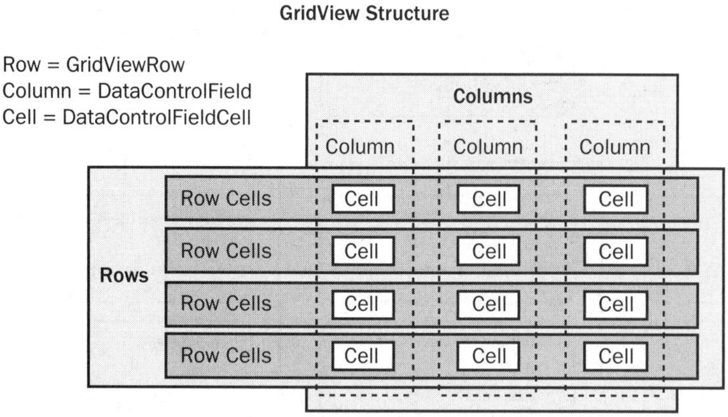

Figure 3-40   The basic *GridView* control structure.

Although the *GridViewRow* object holds the collection of cells, each *DataControlField* (column) object provides the behavior to initialize cells of a specific type in the *DataControlField* object's *InitializeCell* method. The column classes that inherit from *DataControlField* override the *InitializeCell* method. The *GridView* control has an *InitializeRow* method that is responsible for creating a new *GridViewRow* and the row's cells by making calls to the overridden *InitializeCell* method when the row is being created.

The *DataControlField* class hierarchy is shown in Figure 3-41. The derived classes are used to create a *DataControlFieldCell* with the proper contents. Remember that you don't define cell types for your *GridView* control; you define column types and your column object supplies a cell object to the row using the *InitializeCell* method.

The *DataControlField* class hierarchy shows the different column types that are available in a *GridView* control.

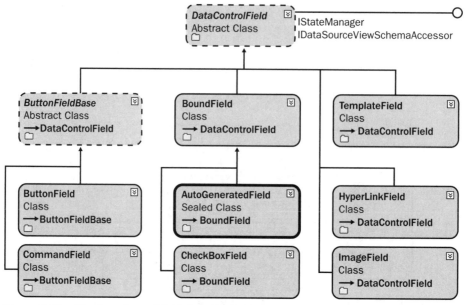

Figure 3-41   The *DataControlField* class hierarchy.

Using Styles to Format the *GridView* Control

You use styles to format the *GridView*. Figure 3-42 shows the style hierarchy. The *Row-Created* and *RowDataBound* events can be used to control the style programmatically. In either of these event handlers, the *Cells* collection on the newly created row can be used to apply a style to a single cell in the row. The difference between the two events is that the *RowCreated* event takes place first, but the data is not available at this time. You can use the *RowDataBound* event when you need to apply a different style to a cell based on the data in the cell. These events fire after the styles are applied, which means you can override any existing styles. Applying a different style to a cell based on the data in the cell allows you to apply business rules to determine whether a cell should stand out from other cells (such as making negative "quantity on hand" numbers red, but only when an item is shipped more than once per month).

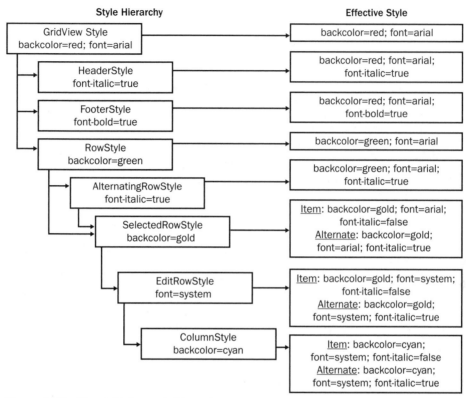

Figure 3-42 The *GridView* style hierarchy.

The following is an example of using the *GridView* with an *ObjectDataSource* to browse and edit data. This example uses a newly created class called *CarList* to connect to the *ObjectDataSource* control. The *CarList* class file is added and the code is as follows:

```vb
'VB
Imports Microsoft.VisualBasic
Imports System.Collections.Generic

Public Class CarList

    Private Shared carList As List(Of Car)

    Public Shared Sub Initialize()
        carList = Car.GetList()
    End Sub
```

```vb
    Public Function [Select]() As List(Of Car)
        Return carList
    End Function

    Public Sub Update(ByVal updateCar As Car)
        current = updateCar
        Dim carFound As Car = carList.Find(AddressOf MatchId)
        carFound.Make = updateCar.Make
        carFound.Model = updateCar.Model
        carFound.Year = updateCar.Year
        carFound.Price = updateCar.Price
    End Sub

    Private current As Car
    Private Function MatchId(ByVal _car As Car) As Boolean
        Return IIf(current.Vin = _car.Vin, True, False)
    End Function

    Public Sub Insert(ByVal _car As Car)
        carList.Add(_car)
    End Sub

    Public Sub Delete(ByVal deleteCar As Car)
        current = deleteCar
        Dim carFound As Car = carList.Find(AddressOf MatchId)
        carList.Remove(carFound)
    End Sub

    Public Function Count() As Integer
        Return carList.Count
    End Function
End Class
```

```csharp
//C#
using System;
using System.Data;
using System.Configuration;
using System.Web;
using System.Web.Security;
using System.Web.UI;
using System.Web.UI.WebControls;
using System.Web.UI.WebControls.WebParts;
using System.Web.UI.HtmlControls;
//added
using System.Collections.Generic;

/// <summary>
/// Summary description for EmployeeList
/// </summary>
public class CarList
{
    private static List<Car> carList;
```

```csharp
public static void Initialize()
{
    carList = Car.GetList();
}

    public List<Car> Select()
    {
        return carList;
    }

    public void Update(Car updateCar)
    {
        Car carFound = carList.Find(
            delegate(Car car) { return car.Vin == updateCar.Vin; });
        carFound.Make = updateCar.Make;
        carFound.Model = updateCar.Model;
        carFound.Year = updateCar.Year;
        carFound.Price = updateCar.Price;
    }

    public void Insert(Car car)
    {
        carList.Add(car);
    }

    public void Delete(Car deleteCar)
    {
        Car carFound = carList.Find(
            delegate(Car car) { return car.Vin == deleteCar.Vin; });
        carList.Remove(carFound);
    }

    public int Count()
    {
        return carList.Count;
    }
}
```

A *GridView* control, *ObjectDataSource*, and *Button* are added to a Web page. The *Object-DataSource* is configured to use the *CarList* as its data source. The *GridView* control is configured to use the *ObjectDataSource* as its data source. The *Button* is used to populate the *CarList* with sample data because the *GridView* control does not natively support the ability to add to the data source. The following is the declarative markup for the Web page form element that works with VB.NET and C#:

ASPX Declarative Markup

```
<form id="form1" runat="server">
  <div>
    <asp:ObjectDataSource ID="ObjectDataSource1" runat="server"
      DataObjectTypeName="Car" TypeName="CarList"
```

```
            SelectMethod="Select" UpdateMethod="Update"
            DeleteMethod="Delete" InsertMethod="Insert">
            <InsertParameters>
                <asp:Parameter Name="vin" Type="String" />
                <asp:Parameter Name="make" Type="String" />
                <asp:Parameter Name="model" Type="String" />
                <asp:Parameter Name="year" Type="Int32" />
                <asp:Parameter Name="price" Type="Decimal" />
            </InsertParameters>
        </asp:ObjectDataSource>
        <asp:GridView ID="GridView1" runat="server"
            Style="z-index: 100; left: 20px; position: absolute; top: 75px"
            AllowPaging="True" AutoGenerateColumns="False"
            DataSourceID="ObjectDataSource1" Width="135px" CellPadding="4"
            DataKeyNames="Vin" ForeColor="#333333" GridLines="None">
            <Columns>
                <asp:CommandField ShowDeleteButton="True"
                    ShowEditButton="True" ShowSelectButton="True" />
                <asp:BoundField DataField="Vin" HeaderText="Vin"
                    SortExpression="Vin" ReadOnly="True" />
                <asp:BoundField DataField="Make" HeaderText="Make"
                    SortExpression="Make" />
                <asp:BoundField DataField="Model" HeaderText="Model"
                    SortExpression="Model" />
                <asp:BoundField DataField="Year" HeaderText="Year"
                    SortExpression="Year" />
                <asp:BoundField DataField="Price" DataFormatString="{0:C}"
                    HeaderText="Price" HtmlEncode="False"
                    SortExpression="Price">
                    <ItemStyle HorizontalAlign="Right" />
                </asp:BoundField>
            </Columns>
            <FooterStyle BackColor="#5D7B9D" Font-Bold="True"
                ForeColor="White" />
            <RowStyle BackColor="#F7F6F3" ForeColor="#333333" />
            <EditRowStyle BackColor="#999999" />
            <SelectedRowStyle BackColor="#E2DED6" Font-Bold="True"
                ForeColor="#333333" />
            <PagerStyle BackColor="#284775" ForeColor="White"
                HorizontalAlign="Center" />
            <HeaderStyle BackColor="#5D7B9D" Font-Bold="True"
                ForeColor="White" />
            <AlternatingRowStyle BackColor="White" ForeColor="#284775" />
        </asp:GridView>
           
        <asp:Button ID="Button1" runat="server" OnClick="Button1_Click"
            Style="z-index: 102; left: 20px; position: absolute; top: 45px"
            Text="Load Cars" />
    </div>
</form>
```

In the declarative markup, the *ObjectDataSource* is configured to use the *CarList* class, which is a collection of *Car* objects. The *GridView* is configured to allow editing, deleting, and selecting *Car* rows. The *Vin* property is configured to display as read-only, and the *Price* property is configured to be right-aligned and display as currency.

The code-behind page only contains code to populate the car list when the *Button* control is clicked, as follows:

```
'VB
Partial Class GridView_Control
    Inherits System.Web.UI.Page

    Protected Sub Button1_Click(ByVal sender As Object, _
         ByVal e As System.EventArgs) Handles Button1.Click
      CarList.Initialize()
      GridView1.DataBind()
    End Sub

End Class
```

```
//C#
using System;
using System.Data;
using System.Configuration;
using System.Collections;
using System.Web;
using System.Web.Security;
using System.Web.UI;
using System.Web.UI.WebControls;
using System.Web.UI.WebControls.WebParts;
using System.Web.UI.HtmlControls;

public partial class GridView_Control : System.Web.UI.Page
{
    protected void Button1_Click(object sender, EventArgs e)
    {
      CarList.Initialize();
      GridView1.DataBind();
    }
}
```

When this Web page is executed and displayed, the Web page displays only the *Button* control. Click the *Button* to populate the *CarList* collection and display the contents in the *GridView*. Click the Edit link on one of the rows to place the row into edit mode, as shown in Figure 3-43.

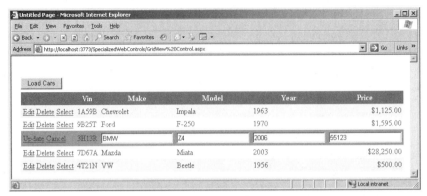

Figure 3-43   The *GridView* control in edit mode is populated from an *ObjectDataSource* and *CarList* object.

The *DetailsView* Control

The *DetailsView* control is used to display the values of a single record from a data source in an HTML table, where each table row represents a field of the record. The *DetailsView* control allows you to edit, delete, and insert records. If the *AllowPaging* property is set to *true*, the *DetailsView* can be used by itself to navigate the data source, but the *DetailsView* can also be used in combination with other controls, such as the *GridView*, *ListBox*, or *DropDownList*, for scenarios in which you want to display a master detail. The *DetailsView* class hierarchy is shown in Figure 3-44.

NOTE   .NET 2.0

The *DetailsView* is new in ASP.NET version 2.0.

The *DetailsView* does not support sorting, whereas the *GridView* does. The *GridView* does not support inserting new records, whereas the *DetailsView* does.

The *DetailsView* supports the same formatting options that are available with the *GridView* control. You can format the *DetailsView* control using the *HeaderStyle*, *RowStyle*, *AlternatingRowStyle*, *CommandRowStyle*, *FooterStyle*, *PagerStyle*, and *EmptyDataRowStyle* properties.

The following is an example of using the *DetailsView* to display the *CarList* collection that was defined in the previous *GridView* example. This example is very much like the *GridView* example, but the *DetailsView* control is used instead, so you can easily see the differences between the controls.

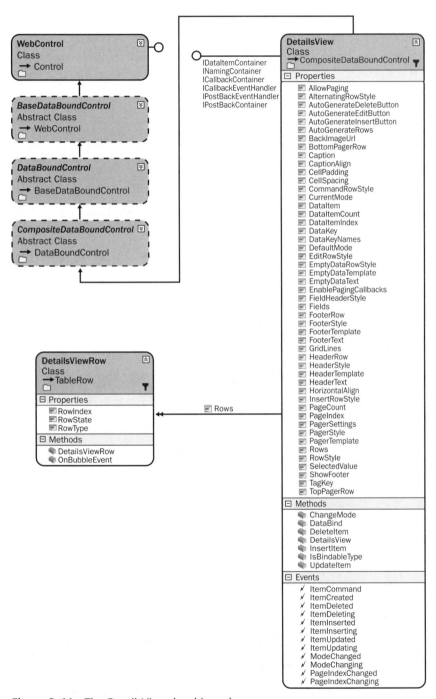

Figure 3-44   The *DetailsView* class hierarchy.

The code for the *CarList* class must be added as shown in the previous *GridView* example. A *DetailsView*, *ObjectDataSource*, and *Button* control are added to the Web page and configured. The following is the Web page markup, showing everything inside the form element:

ASPX Declarative Markup

```
<form id="form1" runat="server">
   <div>
      <asp:ObjectDataSource ID="ObjectDataSource1" runat="server"
         DataObjectTypeName="Car" TypeName="CarList"
         SelectMethod="Select" UpdateMethod="Update"
         DeleteMethod="Delete" InsertMethod="Insert">
      </asp:ObjectDataSource>
      <asp:Button ID="Button1" runat="server" OnClick="Button1_Click"
         Style="z-index: 101; left: 20px; position: absolute; top: 45px"
         Text="Load Cars" />
      <asp:DetailsView ID="DetailsView1" runat="server"
         AllowPaging="True" CellPadding="4"
         DataSourceID="ObjectDataSource1" ForeColor="#333333"
         GridLines="None" Height="50px"
         Style="z-index: 103; left: 20px;
            position: absolute; top: 85px" Width="305px"
         AutoGenerateRows="False" DataKeyNames="Vin">
         <FooterStyle BackColor="#5D7B9D" Font-Bold="True"
            ForeColor="White" />
         <CommandRowStyle BackColor="#E2DED6" Font-Bold="True" />
         <EditRowStyle BackColor="#999999" />
         <RowStyle BackColor="#F7F6F3" ForeColor="#333333" />
         <PagerStyle BackColor="#284775" ForeColor="White"
            HorizontalAlign="Center" />
         <Fields>
            <asp:BoundField DataField="Vin" HeaderText="Vin"
               SortExpression="Vin" ReadOnly="True" />
            <asp:BoundField DataField="Make" HeaderText="Make"
               SortExpression="Make" />
            <asp:BoundField DataField="Model" HeaderText="Model"
               SortExpression="Model" />
            <asp:BoundField DataField="Year" HeaderText="Year"
               SortExpression="Year" />
            <asp:BoundField DataField="Price" HeaderText="Price"
               SortExpression="Price" DataFormatString="{0:C}"
               HtmlEncode="False" >
               <ItemStyle HorizontalAlign="Right" />
            </asp:BoundField>
            <asp:CommandField ShowDeleteButton="True"
               ShowEditButton="True" ShowInsertButton="True" />
         </Fields>
         <FieldHeaderStyle BackColor="#E9ECF1" Font-Bold="True" />
         <HeaderStyle BackColor="#5D7B9D" Font-Bold="True"
            ForeColor="White" />
         <AlternatingRowStyle BackColor="White" ForeColor="#284775" />
```

```
    </asp:DetailsView>
  </div>
</form>
```

In the declarative markup, the *ObjectDataSource* is configured to use the *CarList* class, which is a collection of *Car* objects. The *DetailsView* is configured to allow editing, deleting, and inserting *Car* rows. The *Vin* property is configured to display as read-only, and the *Price* property is configured to be right-aligned and displayed as currency.

The code-behind page only contains code to populate the car list when the *Button* control is clicked, as follows:

```vb
'VB
Partial Class DetailsView_Control
    Inherits System.Web.UI.Page

    Protected Sub Button1_Click(ByVal sender As Object, _
        ByVal e As System.EventArgs) Handles Button1.Click
      CarList.Initialize()
      DetailsView1.DataBind()
    End Sub
End Class
```

```csharp
//C#
using System;
using System.Data;
using System.Configuration;
using System.Collections;
using System.Web;
using System.Web.Security;
using System.Web.UI;
using System.Web.UI.WebControls;
using System.Web.UI.WebControls.WebParts;
using System.Web.UI.HtmlControls;

public partial class DetailsView_Control : System.Web.UI.Page
{
    protected void Button1_Click(object sender, EventArgs e)
    {
        CarList.Initialize();
        DetailsView1.DataBind();
    }
}
```

When this Web page is executed and displayed, the Web page displays only the *Button* control unless you have already populated the *CarList*. Click the *Button* to populate the *CarList* collection and display the contents in the *DetailsView*. Click the New link on the bottom of the control to add a new row and place the row into edit mode, as shown in Figure 3-45.

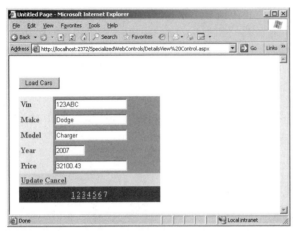

Figure 3-45 The *DetailsView* control in edit mode after clicking the New link is populated from an *ObjectDataSource* and *CarList* object.

The *FormView* Control

Like the *DetailsView*, the *FormView* control is used to display a single record from a data source, except that it displays user-defined templates instead of row fields. Different user-defined templates can be assigned for viewing, editing, and updating records. Creating your own templates gives you the greatest flexibility in controlling how the data is displayed. Figure 3-46 shows the *FormView* class hierarchy.

NOTE .NET 2.0

The *FormView* is new in ASP.NET version 2.0.

Although the *FormView* control gives you the greatest flexibility when choosing whether to use the *GridView*, *DetailsView*, or *FormView*, you have the most work to do when setting up the *FormView*, so you should take a close look at the *GridView* and *DetailsView* before choosing this control.

The following is an example of using the *FormView* control to display the *CarList* collection that was defined in the previous *GridView* example. This example is very much like the *DetailsView* example, but the *FormView* control is used instead, which allows you to compare the *GridView*, *DetailsView*, and *FormView* controls.

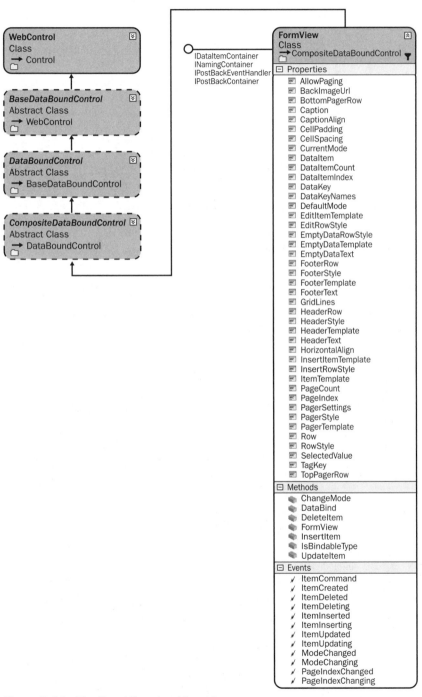

Figure 3-46 The *FormView* class hierarchy.

The code for the *CarList* class must be added as shown in the prior *GridView* example. A *FormView*, *ObjectDataSource*, and *Button* control are added to the Web page and configured. The following is the Web page markup, showing everything inside the form element:

ASPX Declarative Markup

```
<form id="form1" runat="server">
   <div>
      <asp:ObjectDataSource ID="ObjectDataSource1" runat="server"
         DataObjectTypeName="Car" TypeName="CarList"
         SelectMethod="Select" UpdateMethod="Update"
         DeleteMethod="Delete" InsertMethod="Insert">
      </asp:ObjectDataSource>
      <br /> <br /> <br />        
      <asp:Button ID="Button1" runat="server" OnClick="Button1_Click"
         Style="z-index: 101; left: 20px; position: absolute; top: 45px"
         Text="Load Cars" />
   </div>
   <asp:FormView ID="FormView1" runat="server" AllowPaging="True"
      DataKeyNames="Vin" DataSourceID="ObjectDataSource1"
      Width="100%">
      <ItemTemplate>
        <table>
        <tr ><td align="center"><hr />
        <span style="font-weight: bold; color: blue">VIN:</span> 
        <asp:Label ID="VinLabel"  Width="105px" runat="server"
           Text='<%# Eval("Vin") %>'>
        </asp:Label>  
        <span style="font-weight: bold; color: blue">Make:</span> 
        <asp:Label ID="MakeLabel" Width="105px" runat="server"
           Text='<%# Eval("Make") %>'>
        </asp:Label>  
        <span style="font-weight: bold; color: blue">Model:</span> 
        <asp:Label ID="ModelLabel" Width="105px" runat="server"
           Text='<%# Eval("Model") %>'>
        </asp:Label>  
       <span style="font-weight: bold; color: blue">Year:</span> 
        <asp:Label ID="YearLabel" Width="105px" runat="server"
           Text='<%# Eval("Year") %>'>
        </asp:Label><br /></td></tr>
        <tr ><td align="center">
        <span style="font-weight: bold; font-size: x-large; color: blue">
           Price: </span>
        <span style="font-weight: bold; font-size: x-large"> 
        <asp:Label   ID="PriceLabel"  Width="105px"  runat="server"
           Text='<%# Eval("Price","{0:C}") %>'>
        </asp:Label></span></td></tr>
        <tr><td align="center"><hr />
           <asp:LinkButton ID="LinkButton1" runat="server"
              CausesValidation="False" CommandName="Edit" Text="Edit">
           </asp:LinkButton>
```

```
            <asp:LinkButton ID="LinkButton2" runat="server"
               CausesValidation="False" CommandName="New" Text="New">
            </asp:LinkButton>
            <asp:LinkButton ID="LinkButton3" runat="server"
               CausesValidation="False" CommandName="Delete" Text="Delete">
            </asp:LinkButton> </td></tr> </table>
</ItemTemplate>
<EditItemTemplate>
  <table>
  <tr><td align="center"><hr />
   <span style="font-weight: bold; color: blue">VIN:</span> 
   <asp:Label ID="VinLabel"  Width="105px" runat="server"
      Text='<%# Eval("Vin") %>'>
   </asp:Label>  
   <span style="font-weight: bold; color: blue">Make:</span> 
   <asp:TextBox ID="EditMakeTextBox" Width="100px" runat="server"
      Text='<%# Bind("Make") %>'>
   </asp:TextBox>  
   <span style="font-weight: bold; color: blue">Model:</span> 
   <asp:TextBox ID="EditModelTextBox" Width="100px" runat="server"
      Text='<%# Bind("Model") %>'>
   </asp:TextBox>  
   <span style="font-weight: bold; color: blue">Year:</span> 
   <asp:TextBox ID="EditYearTextBox" Width="100px" runat="server"
      Text='<%# Bind("Year") %>'>
   </asp:TextBox><br />   </td></tr>
   <tr><td align="center">
   <span style="font-weight: bold; font-size: large; color: blue">
      Price: </span>
   <span style="font-weight: bold; font-size: large"> 
   <asp:TextBox ID="EditPriceTextBox" Width="100px" runat="server"
      Text='<%# Bind("Price") %>'>
   </asp:TextBox></span></td></tr>
   <tr><td align="center"><hr />
    <asp:LinkButton ID="LinkButton1" runat="server"
       CausesValidation="True" CommandName="Update" Text="Update">
    </asp:LinkButton>
    <asp:LinkButton ID="LinkButton2" runat="server"
       CausesValidation="False" CommandName="Cancel" Text="Cancel">
    </asp:LinkButton></td></tr></table>
</EditItemTemplate>
<EmptyDataTemplate>
  <table width="655px">
  <tr><td align="center" ><hr />
   <span style="font-weight: bold; font-size: x-large; color: blue">
      No Cars For Sale - Chack Back Soon! </span>
   <tr><td align="center"><hr />
      <asp:LinkButton ID="LinkButton2" runat="server"
         CausesValidation="False" CommandName="New" Text="New">
      </asp:LinkButton></td></tr></table>
</EmptyDataTemplate>
<InsertItemTemplate>
    <table>
```

```
      <tr><td align="center"><hr />
       <span style="font-weight: bold; color: blue">VIN:</span> 
       <asp:TextBox ID="InsertVinTextBox" Width="100px" runat="server"
         Text='<%# Bind("Vin") %>'>
       </asp:TextBox>  
       <span style="font-weight: bold; color: blue">Make:</span> 
       <asp:TextBox ID="InsertMakeTextBox" Width="100px" runat="server"
         Text='<%# Bind("Make") %>'>
       </asp:TextBox>  
       <span style="font-weight: bold; color: blue">Model:</span> 
       <asp:TextBox ID="InsertModelTextBox" Width="100px" runat="server"
         Text='<%# Bind("Model") %>'>
       </asp:TextBox>  
       <span style="font-weight: bold; color: blue">Year:</span> 
       <asp:TextBox ID="InsertYearTextBox" Width="100px" runat="server"
         Text='<%# Bind("Year") %>'>
       </asp:TextBox><br />   </td></tr>
      <tr><td align="center">
       <span style="font-weight: bold; font-size: large; color: blue">
         Price: </span>
       <span style="font-weight: bold; font-size: large"> 
         <asp:TextBox ID="InsertPriceTextBox" Width="100px" runat="server"
           Text='<%# Bind("Price") %>'></asp:TextBox></span></td></tr>
      <tr><td align="center"><hr />
        <asp:LinkButton ID="LinkButton1" runat="server"
          CausesValidation="True" CommandName="Insert" Text="Insert">
        </asp:LinkButton>
        <asp:LinkButton ID="LinkButton2" runat="server"
          CausesValidation="False" CommandName="Cancel" Text="Cancel">
        </asp:LinkButton></td></tr></table>
    </InsertItemTemplate>
    <HeaderTemplate>
      <table><tr><td align="center">
      <span style="font-weight: bold; font-size: x-large; color: blue">
        Car For Sale</span></td></tr>
      <tr><td>
    </HeaderTemplate>
    <FooterTemplate>
      </td></tr></table>
    </FooterTemplate>
  </asp:FormView>
       <br />
</form>
```

In the declarative markup, the *ObjectDataSource* is configured to use the *CarList* class, which is a collection of *Car* objects. The *FormView* control is configured to allow editing, deleting, and inserting *Car* rows. The *Vin* property is configured to display as read-only when editing, and the *Price* property is configured to display as currency. To show that you have lots of flexibility using templates with this control, the header, footer, item, edit item, insert item, and empty data templates are configured.

The code-behind page only contains code to populate the car list when the *Button* control is clicked, as follows:

```vb
'VB
Partial Class FormView_Control
    Inherits System.Web.UI.Page

    Protected Sub Button1_Click(ByVal sender As Object, _
        ByVal e As System.EventArgs) Handles Button1.Click
      CarList.Initialize()
      FormView1.DataBind()
    End Sub

End Class
```

```csharp
//C#
using System;
using System.Data;
using System.Configuration;
using System.Collections;
using System.Web;
using System.Web.Security;
using System.Web.UI;
using System.Web.UI.WebControls;
using System.Web.UI.WebControls.WebParts;
using System.Web.UI.HtmlControls;

public partial class FormView : System.Web.UI.Page
{
    protected void Button1_Click(object sender, EventArgs e)
    {
        CarList.Initialize();
        FormView1.DataBind();
    }
}
```

When this Web page is executed and displayed, the Web page displays the *Button* control and the empty data template unless you have already populated the *CarList*. Click the *Button* to populate the *CarList* collection and display the contents in the *FormView*, using the item template. Click the New link on the bottom of the control to add a new row and place the row into edit mode, as shown in Figure 3-47.

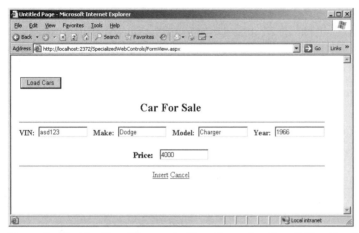

Figure 3-47   The *FormView* control in edit mode after clicking the New link is populated from an *ObjectDataSource* and *CarList* object.

The *HierarchicalDataBoundControl* Control

The *HierarchicalDataBoundControl* control serves as a base class for controls that render data in a hierarchical fashion. The classes that inherit from *HierarchicalDataBound-Control* are *TreeView* and *Menu*, as shown in Figure 3-48.

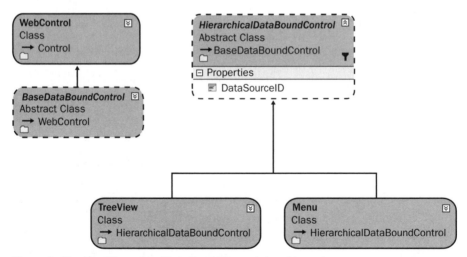

Figure 3-48   The *HierarchicalDataBoundControl* class hierarchy.

The *TreeView* Control

The *TreeView* is a data-bound control that is used to display hierarchical data, such as a listing of files and folders, or a table of contents in a tree structure. The nodes of this control can be bound to XML, tabular, or relational data. This control can also provide site navigation when used with the *SiteMapDataSource* control. The *TreeView* control class hierarchy is shown in Figure 3-49.

NOTE .NET 2.0

The *TreeView* is new in ASP.NET version 2.0.

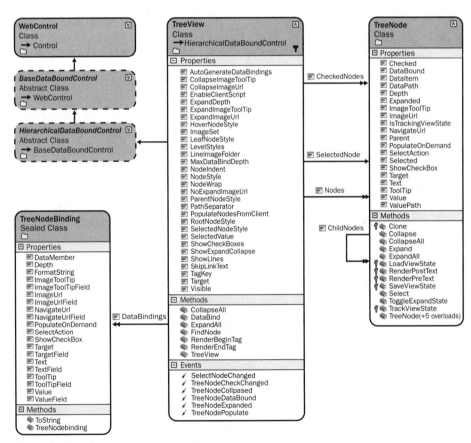

Figure 3-49 The *TreeView* control hierarchy.

You can programmatically access and control the properties of the *TreeView* control. The *TreeView* can also be populated via client-side script on Internet Explorer 5.0 and later, and on Netscape 6.0 and later. In addition, nodes can be displayed as either plain text or hyperlinks, and you can optionally display a check box next to each node.

Each entry in the tree is called a node and is represented by a *TreeNode* object. A node that contains other nodes is called a *parent node*. A node that is contained by another node is called a *child node*. A node can be a parent node and a child node. A node that has no children is called a *leaf node*. A node that is not contained by any other node but is the ancestor to all the other nodes is the *root node*.

The typical *TreeView* tree structure has only one root node, but you can add multiple root nodes to the tree structure. This means that you can display a tree hierarchy without being forced to have a single root node.

The *TreeNode* has a *Text* property that is populated with the data that is to be displayed. The *TreeNode* also has a *Value* property that is used to store the data that is posted back to the Web server.

A node can be configured to be a selection node or a navigation node by setting the *NavigateUrl* property. If the *NavigateUrl* property is set to an empty string (*string.Empty*), it is a selection node, where clicking the node simply selects it. If the *NavigateUrl* property is not set to an empty string, it is a navigation node, where clicking the node attempts to navigate to the location that is specified by the *NavigateUrl* property.

Populating the *TreeView* Control

The *TreeView* control can be populated using static data or by data binding to the control. To populate the *TreeView* control with static data, you can use declarative syntax by placing opening and closing *<Nodes>* tags in the *TreeView* element, and then creating a structure of nested *<asp:TreeNode>* elements within the *<Nodes>* element. Each *<asp:TreeNode>* has properties that you can set by adding attributes to the *<asp:TreeNode>* element.

To use data binding to populate the *TreeView* control, you can use any data source that implements the *IHierarchicalDataSource* interface, such as an *XmlDataSource* control or a *SiteMapDataSource* control. Simply set the *DataSourceID* property of the *TreeView* control to the ID value of the data source control, and the *TreeView* control automatically binds to the specified data source control.

You can also bind to an *XmlDocument* object or a *DataSet* object that contains *DataRelation* objects by setting the *DataSource* property of the *TreeView* control to the data source, and then calling the *DataBind* method.

The *TreeView* control contains a *DataBindings* property that is a collection of *TreeNodeBinding* objects that define the binding between a data item and the *TreeNode*. You can specify the criteria for binding and the data item property to display in the node. This is useful when binding to XML elements where you are interested in binding to an attribute of the element.

Security Alert   The *TreeView* control performs client-side JavaScript callbacks when expanding nodes. A malicious user can craft a callback to get *TreeView* data that you may have tried to hide using the *MaxDataBindDepth* property, so don't use the *MaxDataBindDepth* as a means to hide sensitive data.

The following is an example of using the *TreeView* control to display customer data from a new file called Customers.xml, which contains a list of customers, their orders and invoices, and the order items for each order. This data is stored in a hierarchical format in the XML file. The Customers.xml file looks like the following:

Customers.xml File

```
<?xml version="1.0" encoding="utf-8" ?>
<Customers>
    <Customer CustomerId="1" Name="Northwind Traders">
        <Orders>
            <Order OrderId="1" ShipDate="06-22-2006">
                <OrderItems>
                    <OrderItem OrderItemId="1" PartNumber="123"
                        PartDescription="Large Widget" Quantity="5"
                        Price="22.00" />
                    <OrderItem OrderItemId="2" PartNumber="234"
                        PartDescription="Medium Widget" Quantity="2"
                        Price="12.50" />
                </OrderItems>
            </Order>
            <Order OrderId="2" ShipDate="06-25-2006">
                <OrderItems>
                    <OrderItem OrderItemId="5" PartNumber="432"
                        PartDescription="Small Widget" Quantity="30"
                        Price="8.99" />
                    <OrderItem OrderItemId="4" PartNumber="234"
                        PartDescription="Medium Widget" Quantity="2"
                        Price="12.50" />
                </OrderItems>
            </Order>
        </Orders>
```

```
            <Invoices>
                <Invoice InvoiceId="6" Amount="99.37" />
                <Invoice InvoiceId="7" Amount="147.50" />
            </Invoices>
        </Customer>
        <Customer CustomerId="2" Name="Tailspin Toys">
            <Orders>
                <Order OrderId="8" ShipDate="07-11-2006">
                    <OrderItems>
                        <OrderItem OrderItemId="9" PartNumber="987"
                            PartDescription="Combo Widget" Quantity="2"
                            Price="87.25" />
                        <OrderItem OrderItemId="10" PartNumber="654"
                            PartDescription="Ugly Widget" Quantity="1"
                            Price="2.00" />
                    </OrderItems>
                </Order>
                <Order OrderId="11" ShipDate="08-21-2006">
                    <OrderItems>
                        <OrderItem OrderItemId="12" PartNumber="999"
                            PartDescription="Pretty Widget" Quantity="50"
                            Price="78.99" />
                        <OrderItem OrderItemId="14" PartNumber="575"
                            PartDescription="Tiny Widget" Quantity="100"
                            Price="1.20" />
                    </OrderItems>
                </Order>
            </Orders>
            <Invoices>
                <Invoice InvoiceId="26" Amount="46.58" />
                <Invoice InvoiceId="27" Amount="279.15" />
            </Invoices>
        </Customer>
</Customers>
```

An *XmlDataSource* and a *TreeView* control are added to the Web page and configured. The following is the Web page markup, showing everything inside the form element:

ASPX Declarative Markup

```
<form id="form1" runat="server">
    <div>
        <asp:XmlDataSource ID="XmlDataSource1" runat="server"
            DataFile="~/App_Data/Customers.xml">
        </asp:XmlDataSource>
        <asp:TreeView ID="TreeView1" runat="server"
            DataSourceID="XmlDataSource1"
            ShowLines="True" ExpandDepth="0">
            <DataBindings>
              <asp:TreeNodeBinding DataMember="Customer"
               TextField="Name" ValueField="CustomerId" />
              <asp:TreeNodeBinding DataMember="Order"
               TextField="ShipDate" ValueField="OrderId" />
```

```
            <asp:TreeNodeBinding DataMember="OrderItem"
             TextField="PartDescription" ValueField="OrderItemId" />
            <asp:TreeNodeBinding DataMember="Invoice"
             TextField="Amount" ValueField="InvoiceId"
             FormatString="{0:C}" />
          </DataBindings>
       </asp:TreeView>
     </div>
</form>
```

In this example, the configuration was kept to a minimum, but configuration was required in order to display information that is more important than the XML element name, such as the customer's name instead of the XML element name (Customer). The following code was added to the code-behind page to simply display the value of the selected node:

```vb
'VB
Partial Class TreeView_Control
    Inherits System.Web.UI.Page

    Protected Sub TreeView1_SelectedNodeChanged(ByVal sender As Object, _
        ByVal e As System.EventArgs) Handles TreeView1.SelectedNodeChanged
        Response.Write("Value:" + TreeView1.SelectedNode.Value)
    End Sub
End Class
```

```csharp
//C#
using System;
using System.Data;
using System.Configuration;
using System.Collections;
using System.Web;
using System.Web.Security;
using System.Web.UI;
using System.Web.UI.WebControls;
using System.Web.UI.WebControls.WebParts;
using System.Web.UI.HtmlControls;

public partial class TreeView_Control : System.Web.UI.Page
{
    protected void TreeView1_SelectedNodeChanged(object sender, EventArgs e)
    {
        Response.Write("Value:" + TreeView1.SelectedNode.Value);
    }
}
```

When the Web page is displayed, the *Customers* node is visible, but you can click the plus (+) sign to expand the node as shown in Figure 3-50.

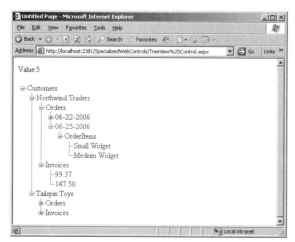

Figure 3-50   The *TreeView* displays the nodes as configured.

The *Menu* Control

The *Menu* control is a data-bound control that is used to display hierarchical data in the form of a menu system. The *Menu* control is often used in combination with a *SiteMapDataSource* control for navigating a Web site. The *Menu* control class hierarchy is shown in Figure 3-51.

NOTE .NET 2.0

The *Menu* is new in ASP.NET version 2.0.

The *Menu* control can be populated using static data or by data binding to the control. To populate the *Menu* control with static data, you can use declarative syntax by placing opening and closing *<Items>* tags in the *Menu* element, and then you can create a structure of nested *<asp:MenuItem>* elements within the *<Items>* element. Each *<asp:MenuItem>* has properties that you can set by adding attributes to the *<asp:MenuItem>* element.

To use data binding to populate the *Menu* control, you can use any data source that implements the *IHierarchicalDataSource* interface, such as an *XmlDataSource* control or a *SiteMapDataSource* control. Simply set the *DataSourceID* property of the *Menu* control to the ID value of the data source control, and the *Menu* control automatically binds to the specified data source control.

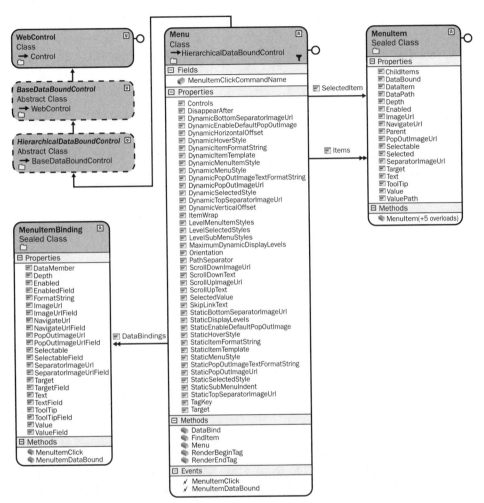

Figure 3-51 The *Menu* control hierarchy.

You can also bind to an *XmlDocument* object or a *DataSet* object that contains *DataRelation* objects by setting the *DataSource* property of the *Menu* control to the data source, and then call the *DataBind* method.

The *Menu* control contains a *DataBindings* property that is a collection of *MenuItem-Binding* objects that define the binding between data items and *TreeNodes*. You can specify the criteria for binding and the data item properties to display in the nodes. This is useful when binding to XML elements where you are interested in binding to an attribute of the element.

The following is an example of using the *Menu* control to display menu data from a new file called MenuItems.xml, which contains a list of the menu items to be displayed. The data is stored in a hierarchical format in the XML file. The MenuItems.xml file looks like the following:

MenuItems.xml File

```xml
<?xml version="1.0" encoding="utf-8" ?>
<MenuItems>
    <Home display="Home"  url="~/" />
    <Products display="Products" url="~/products/">
        <SmallWidgets display="Small Widgets"
            url="~/products/smallwidgets.aspx" />
        <MediumWidgets display="Medium Widgets"
            url="~/products/mediumwidgets.aspx" />
        <BigWidgets display="Big Widgets"
            url="~/products/bigwidgets.aspx" />
    </Products>
    <Support display="Support"  url="~/Support/">
        <Downloads display="Downloads"
            url="~/support/downloads.aspx" />
        <FAQs display="FAQs"
            url="~/support/faqs.aspx" />
    </Support>
    <AboutUs display="About Us" url="~/aboutus/">
        <Company display="Company"
            url="~/aboutus/company.aspx" />
        <Locations display="Location"
            url="~/aboutus/locations.aspx" />
    </AboutUs>
</MenuItems>
```

An *XmlDataSource*, a *Menu*, and a *Label* control are added to the Web page. The *XmlDataSource* is configured to use the XML file. The *Menu* control is configured to use the *XmlDataSource*. The following is the Web page markup, showing everything inside the form element:

ASPX Declarative Markup

```
<form id="form1" runat="server">
    <div>
        <asp:Menu ID="Menu1" runat="server" DataSourceID="XmlDataSource1"
            OnMenuItemClick="Menu1_MenuItemClick">
        </asp:Menu>
        <asp:XmlDataSource ID="XmlDataSource1" runat="server"
            DataFile="~/App_Data/MenuItems.xml"
```

```
        XPath="/MenuItems/*"></asp:XmlDataSource>
      <br />
    </div>
    <asp:Label ID="Label1" runat="server" Text="Label"></asp:Label>
</form>
```

In this example, showing the *MenuItems* root node in the XML file was not desirable, so an XPath expression was supplied to retrieve the nodes that exist under the *MenuItems* element. The following code was added to the code-behind page to simply display the *ValuePath* property of the selected *MenuItem*:

'VB
```
Partial Class Menu_Control
    Inherits System.Web.UI.Page

    Protected Sub Menu1_MenuItemClick(ByVal sender As Object, _
          ByVal e As System.Web.UI.WebControls.MenuEventArgs) _
          Handles Menu1.MenuItemClick
      Label1.Text = e.Item.ValuePath
    End Sub
End Class
```

//C#
```
using System;
using System.Data;
using System.Configuration;
using System.Collections;
using System.Web;
using System.Web.Security;
using System.Web.UI;
using System.Web.UI.WebControls;
using System.Web.UI.WebControls.WebParts;
using System.Web.UI.HtmlControls;

public partial class Menu_Control : System.Web.UI.Page
{
    protected void Menu1_MenuItemClick(object sender, MenuEventArgs e)
    {
        Label1.Text = e.Item.ValuePath;
    }
}
```

When the Web page is displayed, the *Menu* displays and you can hover above a menu item to see its child menu items, as shown in Figure 3-52.

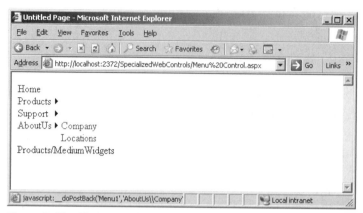

Figure 3-52   The *Menu* displays the nodes as configured.

> ## Quick Check
>
> 1. What method should you call on a data-bound control when the data is ready to be read from the data source?
> 2. What method is used in a *FormView* to perform a two-way data binding?
> 3. What GUI object can provide a data source that allows you to connect middle-tier objects to data-bound controls?
> 4. What must you do to minimize cross-site scripting vulnerabilities when displaying untrusted data in a *RadioButtonList* control?
>
> ### Quick Check Answers
> 1. The *DataBind* method.
> 2. The *Bind* method.
> 3. The *ObjectDataSource* control.
> 4. You must HtmlEncode the data.

Lab: Use the *GridView* and *DetailsView* Controls

In this lab, you use the *GridView* and *DetailsView* controls together to create a master/detail page. The *GridView* is used to display a list of customer names and IDs, with a select link for each customer. The *DetailsView* displays all of the customer information for editing while providing the ability to add new customers.

▶ **Exercise 1: Create the *Site* and the *Data* Classes**

In this exercise, you create a new Web site and add the data classes for the customers.

1. Open Visual Studio 2005 and create a new Web site called UsingDataBound-Controls, using your preferred programming language. When the new Web site is created, a Web page called Default.aspx is displayed.

2. In the Solution Explorer, right-click the Web Site and select Add New Item. Add a class, and name it **Customer**. You will be prompted to add this into an App_Code folder; click Yes.

3. Add public properties and private fields for the following customer attributes:

Property	DataType
Id	*Int32*
Name	*String*
City	*String*
State	*String*
Phone	*String*

4. Keep the existing parameterless constructor, and add a constructor for the class that accepts all of the data that was defined in the previous step. The *Customer* class should look like the following:

```
'VB
Imports Microsoft.VisualBasic

Public Class Customer

    Public Property Id() As Integer
        Get
            Return _id
        End Get
        Set(ByVal value As Integer)
            _id = value
        End Set
    End Property
    Private _id As Integer

    Public Property Name() As String
        Get
            Return _name
        End Get
```

```vb
        Set(ByVal value As String)
            _name = value
        End Set
    End Property
    Private _name As String

    Public Property City() As String
        Get
            Return _city
        End Get
        Set(ByVal value As String)
            _city = value
        End Set
    End Property
    Private _city As String

    Public Property State() As String
        Get
            Return _state
        End Get
        Set(ByVal value As String)
            _state = value
        End Set
    End Property
    Private _state As String

    Public Property Phone() As String
        Get
            Return _phone
        End Get
        Set(ByVal value As String)
            _phone = value
        End Set
    End Property
    Private _phone As String

    Public Sub New()
    End Sub

    Public Sub New(ByVal _id As Integer, ByVal _name As String, _
        ByVal _city As String, ByVal _state As String, ByVal _phone As String)
        Id = _id : Name = _name : City = _city
        State = _state : Phone = _phone
    End Sub

End Class

//C#
using System;
using System.Data;
using System.Configuration;
using System.Web;
using System.Web.Security;
using System.Web.UI;
```

```csharp
using System.Web.UI.WebControls;
using System.Web.UI.WebControls.WebParts;
using System.Web.UI.HtmlControls;

public class Customer
{
    public Int32 Id
    {
        get { return id; }
        set { id = value; }
    }
    private Int32 id;

    public string Name
    {
        get { return name; }
        set { name = value; }
    }
    private string name;

    public string City
    {
        get { return city; }
        set { city = value; }
    }
    private string city;

    public string State
    {
        get { return state; }
        set { state = value; }
    }
    private string state;

    public string Phone
    {
        get { return phone; }
        set { phone = value; }
    }
    private string phone;

public Customer()
{
}

    public Customer(int id, string name, string city,
        string state, string phone)
    {
        Id = id; Name = name; City = city;
        State = state; Phone = phone;
    }
}
```

5. Add another class to the App_Code folder called CustomerList. Add a private shared field (in C#, use static keyword) called *custList* and initialize it.

6. Add a method called *Select* that returns the *custList*.

7. Add a method called *Update* that accepts a *Customer* as a parameter. Search the *custList* for a match based on the the *Id* property. After finding the customer, update all of the properties except the *Id*. (Hint: In C#, the search can be performed using an anonymous method, but in VB.NET, you need to create a helper method to perform the find.)

8. Add a method called *Insert* that accepts a *Customer* parameter. In this method, add the *Customer* to the *custList*.

9. Add a method called *Delete* that accepts a *Customer* parameter. In this method, find the matching *Customer* object and delete it.

10. Add a method called *SelectSingle* that accepts an *id* as *Int32* parameter. In this method, return nothing (in C#, null) if the *id* parameter is -1; else, return the customer whose *Id* property matches the *id* parameter.

Your *CustomerList* should look like the following:

```
'VB
Imports Microsoft.VisualBasic
Imports System.Collections.Generic

Public Class CustomerList

    Private Shared custList As New List(Of Customer)()

    Public Function [Select]() As List(Of Customer)
        Return custList
    End Function

    Public Function SelectSingle(ByVal selectCustomerId As Integer) As Customer
        If selectCustomerId = -1 Then Return Nothing
        current = New Customer() : current.Id = selectCustomerId
        Return custList.Find(AddressOf MatchId)
    End Function

    Public Sub Update(ByVal updateCustomer As Customer)
        current = updateCustomer
        Dim customerFound As Customer = custList.Find(AddressOf MatchId)
        customerFound.Id = updateCustomer.Id
        customerFound.Name = updateCustomer.Name
        customerFound.City = updateCustomer.City
        customerFound.State = updateCustomer.State
        customerFound.Phone = updateCustomer.Phone
    End Sub
```

```
Private current As Customer
Private Function MatchId(ByVal _customer As Customer) As Boolean
    Return IIf(current.Id = _customer.Id, True, False)
End Function

Public Sub Insert(ByVal _customer As Customer)
    custList.Add(_customer)
End Sub

Public Sub Delete(ByVal deleteCustomer As Customer)
    current = deleteCustomer
    Dim customerFound As Customer = custList.Find(AddressOf MatchId)
    custList.Remove(customerFound)
End Sub

End Class
```

```
//C#
using System;
using System.Data;
using System.Configuration;
using System.Web;
using System.Web.Security;
using System.Web.UI;
using System.Web.UI.WebControls;
using System.Web.UI.WebControls.WebParts;
using System.Web.UI.HtmlControls;
using System.Collections.Generic;

public class CustomerList
{
    private static List<Customer> custList = new List<Customer>();

    public List<Customer> Select()
    {
        return custList;
    }

    public Customer SelectSingle(int selectCustomerId)
    {
        if (selectCustomerId == -1) return null;
        return custList.Find(
          delegate(Customer customer)
          { return customer.Id == selectCustomerId; });
    }

    public void Update(Customer updateCustomer )
    {
        Customer customerFound = custList.Find(
          delegate(Customer customer)
          { return customer.Id == updateCustomer.Id; });
        customerFound.Id = updateCustomer.Id;
        customerFound.Name = updateCustomer.Name;
```

```
        customerFound.City = updateCustomer.City;
        customerFound.State = updateCustomer.State;
        customerFound.Phone = updateCustomer.Phone;
    }

    public void Insert(Customer _customer)
    {
        custList.Add(_customer);
    }

    public void Delete(Customer deleteCustomer)
    {
        Customer customerFound = custList.Find(
            delegate(Customer customer)
            { return customer.Id == deleteCustomer.Id; } );
        custList.Remove(customerFound);
    }
}
```

11. Build the Web site to assure that there are no errors.

▶ **Exercise 2: Add and Configure the Controls**

In this exercise, you create a new Web site and add the data classes for the customers.

1. Open Visual Studio 2005 and open the Web site called UsingDataBoundControls that you created in the previous exercise. Alternatively, you can open the completed Lesson 2, Exercise 1 project from the CD.

2. Open the Default.aspx Web page in Design view.

3. Drag and drop two *ObjectDataSource* controls, a *GridView*, and a *DetailsView* onto the Web page.

4. Click the symbol in the upper-left corner of the *ObjectDataSource1* control to display the ObjectDataSource Tasks window. Click Configure Data Source link to start the Wizard.

5. In the Choose Business Object screen, select the CustomerList, and click Next.

6. In the Define Data Methods screen, choose the *Select* method for the Select tab. On the Update tab, select the *Update* method. On the Insert tab, select the *Insert* method, and on the Delete tab, select the *Delete* method. Click Finish.

7. Click the symbol in the upper-left corner of the *ObjectDataSource2* control to display the ObjectDataSource Tasks window. Click Configure Data Source link to start the Wizard.

8. In the Choose Business Object screen, select the CustomerList, and click Next.

9. In the Define Data Methods screen, choose the *SelectSingle* method for the Select tab. When prompted for the *select* parameter, set the Parameter Source to Control, the Control ID to GridView1, and set a Default Value of -1. On the Update tab, select the *Update* method. On the Insert tab, select the *Insert* method, and on the Delete tab, select the *Delete* method. Click Finish.

10. Click the symbol in the upper-left corner of the *GridView* control to display the GridView Tasks window. Choose ObjectDataSource1 as the Data Source.

11. Click Enable Paging and Enable Selection.

12. Click Edit Columns. Delete all the fields from the Selected Fields list except Select, Id, and Name.

13. In the GridView Properties window, set the DataKeyNames to Id.

14. Set the *EnableViewState* property to *false*.

15. Right-click the GridView and click AutoFormat. Select the Professional format and click OK.

16. Click the symbol in the upper-left corner of the *DetailsView* control to display the DetailsView Tasks window. Choose ObjectDataSource2 as the Data Source.

17. Click Enable Inserting, Enable Editing, and Enable Deleting.

18. Click Edit Fields and order the fields as Id, Name, City, State, and Phone.

19. Click the Id field and set the *ReadOnly* property to *true*.

20. Click Edit Templates and select the EmptyData Template. Type **No Customer Selected** and add a *LinkButton*. Set the *LinkButton* control's *CausesValidation* property to *false*. Set its *CommandName* property to New. Set its *Text* property to New. In the DetailView Tasks window, click End Template Editing.

21. In the DetailsView Properties window, set the DataKeyNames to Id.

22. Right-click the DetailsView and click AutoFormat. Select the Professional format and click OK.

    The completed Web page is shown in Figure 3-53.

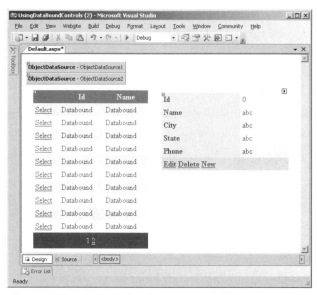

Figure 3-53   The completed master/detail form.

23.   Press F5 to run the Web application.

24.   No customers exist, so you should see the message that states that no customer has been selected. Click New LinkButton, and enter several customers.

25.   Notice that the *GridView* is updated to show the added customers.

26.   In the *GridView*, click one of the Select links. This causes the details to be displayed in the *DetailsView*, as shown in Figure 3-54.

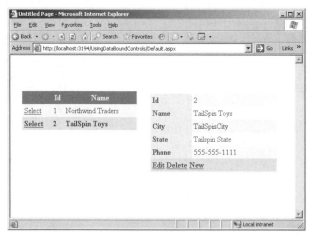

Figure 3-54   Clicking the Select link on the *GridView* displays the customer in the *DetailsView* control.

Lesson Review

You can use the following questions to test your knowledge of the information in Lesson 2, "Working with Data-Bound Web Server Controls." The questions are also available on the companion CD if you prefer to review them in electronic form.

NOTE Answers

Answers to these questions and explanations of why each answer is right or wrong are located in the "Answers" section at the end of the book.

---

1. You want to display an image that is selected somewhat randomly from a collection of images. What is the best approach to implementing this? (Choose one.)

   A. Use the *ImageMap* control and randomly select a *HotSpot* to show or hide.

   B. Use the *Image* control to hold the image and a *Calendar* control to randomly select a date for each image to be displayed.

   C. Use the *AdServer* control and create an XML file with configuration of the control.

   D. Use an *ImageButton* control to predict randomness of the image to be loaded based on the clicks of the control.

2. You want to display a list of suppliers on a Web page. The supplier list displays 10 suppliers at a time, and you require the ability to edit the suppliers. Which Web control is the best choice for this scenario? (Choose one.)

   A. The *DetailsView* control

   B. The *Table* control

   C. The *GridView* control

   D. The *FormView* control

3. You want to display a list of parts in a master/detail scenario where the user can select a part number using a list that takes a minimum amount of space on the Web page. When the part is selected, a *DetailsView* control displays all the information about the part and allows the user to edit the part. Which Web control is the best choice to display the part number list for this scenario? (Choose one.)

    A. The *DropDownList* control

    B. The *RadioButtonList* control

    C. The *FormView* control

    D. The *TextBox* control

Lesson Summary

- The *AdRotator* control is used to display randomly selected advertisement banners on a Web page.

- Simple data-bound controls consist of the *AdRotator* control and the controls that inherit from the *ListControl*.

- Composite data-bound controls consist of the *GridView*, *DetailsView*, and the *FormView* control.

- Hierarchical data-bound controls consist of the *Menu* and the *TreeView* controls.

- Many data-bound controls can be modified by providing templates to control the appearance of the control.

Chapter Review

To further practice and reinforce the skills you learned in this chapter, you can perform the following tasks:

- Review the chapter summary.
- Review the list of key terms introduced in this chapter.
- Complete the case scenarios. These scenarios set up real-world situations involving the topics of this chapter and ask you to create a solution.
- Complete the suggested practices.
- Take a practice test.

Chapter Summary

- ASP.NET 2.0 provides many specialized controls that can help you solve your development problems quickly and easily.
- The *Literal*, *Table*, *Image*, *ImageButton*, *ImageMap*, *AdRotator*, *Calendar*, *FileUpload*, *Panel*, *MultiView*, *View*, and *Wizard* represent some of the specialized Web server controls that can increase developer productivity.
- Data-bound controls are controls that permit you to display more than one field in a data record. Some data-bound controls permit you to see many data records as well.

Key Terms

Do you know what these key terms mean? You can check your answers by looking up the terms in the glossary at the end of the book.

- child node
- leaf node
- parent node
- root node

Case Scenarios

In the following case scenarios, you will apply what you've learned in this chapter. You can find answers to these questions in the "Answers" section at the end of this book.

Case Scenario 1: Determining How to Prompt for Data

You are creating a new Web page that will be used to price a car insurance policy. There are many factors that go into pricing the policy, but the customer information can be placed into the following categories:

- Location
- Vehicles
- Other Drivers
- Accident History
- Motor Vehicle Violations

You are concerned that a prospective customer may leave the site before all of the information is entered. List some of the ways that you can prompt the user for this information in an organized fashion, keeping the displayed prompts to a minimum so the customer does not feel inundated with too many prompts.

Case Scenario 2: Implementing a Calendar Solution

You are a training provider who is creating a Web site that will be used to schedule training contractors to work at different locations. The application will prompt you for the contractor information and the training class dates. You can view a schedule showing all of your training classes and which contractors are scheduled for which times. Also, a contractor can log in and see the training classes that have been assigned to him or her.

1. Where can you use the *Calendar* control in this solution?
2. Would you need to use a *Table* control?

Case Scenario 3: Implementing a Master/Detail Solution

You are a developer who is creating a Web page for displaying customers and their orders in a master/detail scenario. The top of the Web page will provide a list of customers that contains the customer numbers and names. The bottom of the Web page will provide a list of the orders containing the order numbers, the order dates, the order amounts, and the ship dates. The orders will be displayed for the customer that is selected.

1. What controls would you use to display the customer and orders? If you want to use this Web page to add customers and orders, what are some ways that you can provide this functionality?

Suggested Practices

To help you successfully master the Add and Configure Web Server Controls and Implement Data-Bound Controls exam objectives, complete the following tasks.

Create New Web Pages Using Each of the Server Controls

For this task, you should complete Practice 1.

- **Practice 1** Create a new Web page and add the Web server controls that are defined in this chapter. Add event handlers for the default events, plus explore the other events that are available in each control.

Create a Master/Detail Solution Using the Data-Bound Server Controls

For this task, you should complete Practice 1.

- **Practice 1** Create a new Web site that has a Web page that is configurable as a master/detail to provide data access to data that is related, such as customers/ orders, owners/vehicles, employees/sick days, and albums/songs. Use the composite data-bound controls to provide the desired behaviors.

Modify the Appearance of a Data-Bound Control Using Templates

For this task, you should complete Practice 1.

- **Practice 1** Open a Web page that uses a composite data-bound control. Try converting one of the fields to a template field and modify the field to change its appearance.

Take a Practice Test

The practice tests on this book's companion CD offer many options. For example, you can test yourself on just the content covered in this chapter, or you can test yourself on all the 70-528 certification exam content. You can set up the test so that it closely simulates the experience of taking a certification exam, or you can set it up in study mode so that you can look at the correct answers and explanations after you answer each question.

MORE INFO   **Practice tests**

For details about all the practice test options available, see the "How to Use the Practice Tests" section in this book's Introduction.

Chapter 4

Using ADO.NET and XML with ASP.NET

Probably the most important facet of any application is the retrieval and storage of data. At the end of the day, virtually all applications exist for the purpose of data retrieval or data storage.

The previous chapter covered data-bound controls and demonstrated their uses with object data, primarily using the objects and the ObjectDataSource to populate the control.

This chapter covers the classes that are available in ADO.NET, which are split into two categories: connected and disconnected. Like the data-bound controls that were covered in the previous chapter, you can use the disconnected classes without ever connecting to a database, while the connected classes are specific to the database that you're connecting to. Figure 4-1 shows the major disconnected and connected classes. This chapter covers these classes as well as other ADO.NET classes.

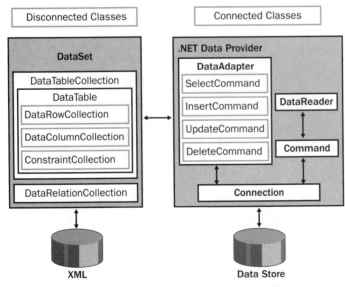

Figure 4-1   The major disconnected and connected classes.

The use of Extensible Markup Language (XML) is rapidly growing among companies that read and write data to XML files and also those that send and receive data in XML formatted messages. This chapter also covers the classes that are available in XML and their roles in providing data storage and retrieval.

Exam objectives in this chapter:

- Manage connections and transactions of databases.
    - ❏ Configure a connection to a database graphically by using the Connection Wizard.
    - ❏ Configure a connection by using the Server Explorer.
    - ❏ Configure a connection to a database by using the *connection* class.
    - ❏ Connect to a database by using specific database *connection* objects.
    - ❏ Enumerate through instances of Microsoft SQL Server by using the *DbProviderFactories.GetFactoryClasses* method.
    - ❏ Open a connection by using the *Open* method of a *connection* object.
    - ❏ Close a connection by using the *connection* object.
    - ❏ Secure a connection to protect access to your data source.
    - ❏ Create a connection designed for reuse in a connection pool.
    - ❏ Control connection pooling by configuring *ConnectionString* values based on database type.
    - ❏ Use *connection* events to detect database information.
    - ❏ Handle connection exceptions when connecting to a database.
    - ❏ Perform transactions using the ADO.NET *Transaction* object.
- Create, delete, and edit data in a connected environment.
    - ❏ Retrieve data by using a *DataReader* object.
    - ❏ Build SQL commands visually in Server Explorer.
    - ❏ Build SQL commands in code.
    - ❏ Create parameters for a *command* object.
    - ❏ Perform database operations by using a *command* object.

- ❏ Retrieve data from a database by using a *command* object.
- ❏ Perform asynchronous operations by using a *command* object.
- ❏ Perform bulk copy operations to copy data to a SQL Server computer.
- ❏ Store and retrieve binary large object (BLOB) data types in a database.
- Create, delete, and edit data in a disconnected environment.
  - ❏ Create an instance of the *DataSet* class programmatically.
  - ❏ Create a *DataSet* graphically.
  - ❏ Create a *DataSet* programmatically.
  - ❏ Add a *DataTable* to a *DataSet*.
  - ❏ Add a relationship between tables.
  - ❏ Navigate a relationship between tables.
  - ❏ Merge *DataSet* contents.
  - ❏ Copy *DataSet* contents.
  - ❏ Create a strongly typed *DataSet*.
  - ❏ Create *DataTables*.
  - ❏ Manage data within a *DataTable*.
  - ❏ Create and use *DataViews*.
  - ❏ Represent data in a *DataSet* by using XML.
  - ❏ Access an ADO Recordset or Record by using the *OleDbDataAdapter* object.
  - ❏ Generate *DataAdapter* commands automatically by using the *Command-Builder* object.
  - ❏ Generate *DataAdapter* commands programmatically.
  - ❏ Populate a *DataSet* by using a *DataAdapter*.
  - ❏ Update the database by using a *DataAdapter*.
  - ❏ Resolve conflicts between a *DataSet* and a database by using the *Data-Adapter*.

❑ Respond to changes made to data at the data source by using *DataAdapter* events.

❑ Perform batch operations by using *DataAdapters*.

■ Manage XML data with the XML Document Object Model (DOM).

❑ Read XML data into the DOM by using the *Load* method.

❑ Modify an XML document by adding and removing nodes.

❑ Modify nodes in an XML document.

❑ Write data in XML format from the DOM.

❑ Work with nodes in the XML DOM by using *XmlNamedNodeMap* and the *XmlNodeList*.

❑ Handle *DOM* events.

❑ Modify XML declaration.

■ Read and write XML data by using the *XmlReader* and *XmlWriter*.

❑ Read XML data by using the *XmlReader*.

❑ Read all XML element and attribute content.

❑ Read specific element and attribute content.

❑ Read XML data by using the *XMLTextReader* class.

❑ Read node trees by using the *XmlNodeReader*.

❑ Validate XML data by using the *XmlValidatingReader*.

❑ Write XML data by using the *XmlWriter*.

Lessons in this chapter:

Before You Begin

To complete the lessons in this chapter, you should be familiar with Microsoft Visual Basic or C# and be comfortable with the following tasks:

- Have Microsoft Windows XP and Microsoft Visual Studio 2005 installed with Microsoft SQL Server 2005 Express Edition.

- Be familiar with the Visual Studio 2005 Integrated Development Environment (IDE).

- Have a basic understanding of Hypertext Markup Language (HTML) and client-side scripting.

- Be able to add Web server controls to a Web page.

- Be familiar with SQL Server.

Real World

Glenn Johnson

Developers spend lots of time creating controls that are specific to the tasks that need to be accomplished, but in many cases, the specialized data-bound controls that are built-in can be used with simple formatting and configuration changes.

Lesson 1: Using the ADO.NET Disconnected Classes

This lesson covers the disconnected data access classes that are instantiated within the Web application and can be used without ever connecting to a data store. When working with disconnected data, you must at least use the *DataTable* object, so this lesson starts by covering the *DataTable* and the objects that the *DataTable* object works with. After covering the *DataTable*, the *DataSet* and the *DataTableReader,* this chapter covers objects.

After this lesson, you will be able to:

■   Identify and use the following disconnected data classes in your Web application:

❑   *DataTable*

❑   *DataColumn*

❑   *DataRow*

Estimated lesson time: 60 minutes

Getting Started with the *DataTable* Object

The *DataTable* object represents tabular data as rows, columns, and constraints. Use the *DataTable* object to hold data in memory while performing disconnected data operations. The *DataTable* object can be explicitly created by instantiating the *DataTable* class, adding *DataColumn* objects that define the data to be held, and then adding *DataRow* objects, which are objects that contain the data. The *DataTable* object must contain *DataColumn* objects before any data can be added to the *DataTable* object. The *DataColumn* objects also contain *constraints,* which maintain data integrity by limiting the data that can be placed into a column. The following code creates an employee *DataTable* and adds *DataColumn* objects:

```vb
'VB
Private Function GetDataTable() As DataTable
    'Create the DataTable named "Employee"
    Dim employee As New DataTable("Employee")

    'Add the DataColumn using all properties
    Dim eid As New DataColumn("Eid")
    eid.DataType = GetType(String)
    eid.MaxLength = 10
    eid.Unique = True
    eid.AllowDBNull = False
```

```
        eid.Caption = "EID"
        employee.Columns.Add(eid)

        'Add the DataColumn using defaults
        Dim firstName As New DataColumn("FirstName")
        firstName.MaxLength = 35
        firstName.AllowDBNull = False
        employee.Columns.Add(firstName)
        Dim lastName As New DataColumn("LastName")
        lastName.AllowDBNull = False
        employee.Columns.Add(lastName)

        'Add the decimal DataColumn using defaults
        Dim salary As New DataColumn("Salary", GetType(Decimal))
        salary.DefaultValue = 0.0
        employee.Columns.Add(salary)

        'Derived column using expression
        Dim lastNameFirstName As New DataColumn("LastName and FirstName")
        lastNameFirstName.DataType = GetType(String)
        lastNameFirstName.MaxLength = 70
        lastNameFirstName.Expression = "lastName + ', ' + firstName"
        employee.Columns.Add(lastNameFirstName)

    Return employee
End Function

//C#
private DataTable GetDataTable()
{
    //Create the DataTable named "employee"
    DataTable employee = new DataTable("Employee");

    //Add the DataColumn using all properties
    DataColumn eid = new DataColumn("Eid");
    eid.DataType = typeof(string);
    eid.MaxLength = 10;
    eid.Unique = true;
    eid.AllowDBNull = false;
    eid.Caption = "EID";
    employee.Columns.Add(eid);

    //Add the DataColumn using defaults
    DataColumn firstName = new DataColumn("FirstName");
    firstName.MaxLength = 35;
    firstName.AllowDBNull = false;
    employee.Columns.Add(firstName);
    DataColumn lastName = new DataColumn("LastName");
    lastName.AllowDBNull = false;
    employee.Columns.Add(lastName);
```

```
        //Add the decimal DataColumn using defaults
        DataColumn salary = new DataColumn("Salary", typeof(decimal));
        salary.DefaultValue = 0.00m;
        employee.Columns.Add(salary);

        //Derived column using expression
        DataColumn lastNameFirstName = new DataColumn("LastName and FirstName");
        lastNameFirstName.DataType = typeof(string);
        lastNameFirstName.MaxLength = 70;
        lastNameFirstName.Expression = "lastName + ', ' + firstName";
        employee.Columns.Add(lastNameFirstName);

        return employee;
}
```

In this example, the *DataType* is a string for all *DataColumn* objects except salary, which is a *decimal* object that contains currency. The *MaxLength* property constrains the length of string data. The string data is truncated if you exceed this length and no exception is thrown. If the *Unique* property is set to *true*, an index is created to prevent duplication of entries. The *AllowDBNull* property is set to *false* to mandate the population of the column with data. The *Caption* property is a string that holds the column heading that is to be displayed when this *DataTable* object is used with Web server controls. The *lastNameFirstName DataColumn* object shows how an expression column is created, in this case, by assigning an expression. *Expression columns* are also known as calculated or derived columns. Adding a derived column is especially beneficial when data is available but not in the correct format.

The following is a list of the default values for *DataColumn* properties if you create a *DataColumn* without specifying a value for a property:

- **DataType**   String
- **MaxLength**   −1, which means that no maximum length check is performed
- **Unique**   False, which allows duplicate values
- **AllowDBNull**   True, which means that the *DataColumn* does not need to have a value
- **Caption**   The *DataColumn* object, which is the *ColumnName* property value

Creating Primary Key Columns

The *primary key* of a *DataTable* object consists of one or more columns, which have data that provides a unique identity for each data row. In the Employee example, the employee identification (Eid) is considered to be a unique key that can be used to retrieve the data for a given employee. In some scenarios, a unique key might require combining two or more fields to achieve uniqueness. For example, a sales order typically contains line items. The primary key for each of the Line Item rows would typically be a combination of the order number and the line number. The *PrimaryKey* property must be set to an array of *DataColumn* objects to accommodate composite (multiple) keys. The following code shows how to set the *PrimaryKey* property for the Employee *DataTable* object:

```
'VB
'Set the Primary Key
employee.PrimaryKey = new DataColumn(){eid}
```

```
//C#
//Set the Primary Key
employee.PrimaryKey = new DataColumn[] {eid};
```

Adding Data with *DataRow* Objects

After the *DataTable* is created with its schema, the *DataTable* is populated by adding *DataRow* objects. A *DataRow* object is created by a *DataTable* because the *DataRow* must conform to constraints of the *DataTable* object's columns.

Adding Data to the *DataTable*   The *DataTable* object contains a *Rows* collection, which contains a collection of *DataRow* objects. You can insert data into the *Rows* collection by using the *Add* method on the *Rows* collection or by using the *Load* method on the *DataTable* object.

The *Add* method contains an overload that accepts an array of objects instead of a *DataRow* object. The array of objects must match the quantity and data type of *DataColumn* objects in the *DataTable*.

The *Load* method can be used to update existing *DataRow* objects or load new *DataRow* objects. The *PrimaryKey* property must be set so the *DataTable* object can locate the *DataRow* that is to be updated. The *Load* method expects an array of objects and a *LoadOption* enumeration value that has one of the following values:

- ■ *OverwriteRow*   Overwrites the original *DataRowVersion* and the current *DataRowVersion* and changes the *RowState* to *Unchanged*. New rows also have the *RowState* of *Unchanged*.

- ■ *PreserveCurrentValues* **(default)**   Overwrites the original *DataRowVersion*, but does not modify the current *DataRowVersion*. New rows have the *RowState* of *Unchanged* as well.

- **UpdateCurrentValues**   Overwrites the current *DataRowVersion*, but does not modify the original *DataRowVersion*. New rows have the *RowState* of *Added*. Rows that had a *RowState* of *Unchanged* have the *RowState* of *Unchanged* if the current *DataRowVersion* is the same as the original *DataRowVersion*, but if they are different, the *RowState* is *Modified*.

The following code snippet demonstrates the methods of creating and adding data to the employee *DataTable*:

```
'VB
'Add New DataRow by creating the DataRow first
Dim newemployee As DataRow = employee.NewRow()
newemployee("Eid") = "123456789A"
newemployee("FirstName") = "Nancy"
newemployee("LastName") = "Davolio"
newemployee("Salary") = 10.0
employee.Rows.Add(newemployee)

'Add New DataRow by simply adding the values
employee.Rows.Add("987654321X", "Andrew", "Fuller", 15.0)

'Load DataRow, replacing existing contents, if existing
employee.LoadDataRow( _
    New Object() {"987654321X", "Janet", "Leverling", 20.0}, _
    LoadOption.OverwriteChanges)
```

```
//C#
//Add New DataRow by creating the DataRow first
DataRow newemployee = employee.NewRow();
newemployee["Eid"] = "123456789A";
newemployee["FirstName"] = "Nancy";
newemployee["LastName"] = "Davolio";
newemployee["Salary"] = 10.00m;
employee.Rows.Add(newemployee);

//Add New DataRow by simply adding the values
employee.Rows.Add("987654321X", "Andrew", "Fuller", 15.00m);

//Load DataRow, replacing existing contents, if existing
employee.LoadDataRow(
    new object[] { "987654321X", "Janet", "Leverling", 20.00m },
    LoadOption.OverwriteChanges);
```

This code adds new *DataRow* objects to the Employee *DataTable*. The first example explicitly creates a new *DataRow* using the *NewRow* method on the Employee *DataTable*. The next example adds a new *DataRow* by simply passing the values into the *employee.Rows.Add* method. Remember that nothing has been permanently stored to a database. We will cover that later in this chapter.

Binding to the *DataTable*   A *DataTable* object is bound to any of the data-bound controls by assigning it to the *DataSource* property of the data-bound control and executing the *DataBind* method of the control to render the data as follows:

```vb
'VB
Protected Sub Button1_Click(ByVal sender As Object, _
      ByVal e As System.EventArgs) _
      Handles Button1.Click
   'add grid to form
   Dim gv As New GridView()
   gv.Style.Add("position", "absolute")
   gv.Style.Add("left", "275px")
   gv.Style.Add("top", "20px")
   gv.EnableViewState = false
   form1.Controls.Add(gv)
   'get the table and display
   gv.DataSource = GetDataTable()
   gv.DataBind()
End Sub
```

```csharp
//C#
protected void Button1_Click(object sender, EventArgs e)
{
   //add grid to form
   GridView gv  = new GridView();
   gv.Style.Add("position", "absolute");
   gv.Style.Add("left", "275px");
   gv.Style.Add("top", "20px");
   gv.EnableViewState = false;
   form1.Controls.Add(gv);
   //get the table and display
   gv.DataSource = GetDataTable();
   gv.DataBind();
}
```

This rendered DataTable is shown in Figure 4-2.

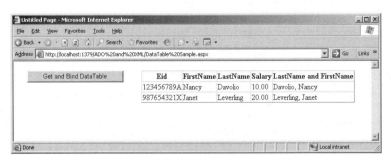

Figure 4-2   The employee *DataTable* object is bound to the *GridView* control.

If you are working with any controls that inherit from *ListControl*, such as the *ListBox*, you also need to set the *DataTextField* and *DataValueField* properties.

Using *DataRowState* with the *DataRow* Object   The *DataRow* has a *RowState* property that can be viewed and filtered at any time and can be any of the following *DataRowState* enumeration values:

- **Detached**   *DataRow* is created but not added to a *DataTable*.
- **Added**   *DataRow* is added to a *DataTable*.
- **Unchanged**   *DataRow* has not changed since the last call to the *AcceptChanges* method. The *DataRow* changes to this state when the *AcceptChanges* method is called.
- **Modified**   *DataRow* has been modified since the last time the *AcceptChanges* method was called.
- **Deleted**   *DataRow* is deleted using the *Delete* method of the *DataRow*.

Figure 4-3 shows the *RowState* transitions at different times in the *DataRow* object's life.

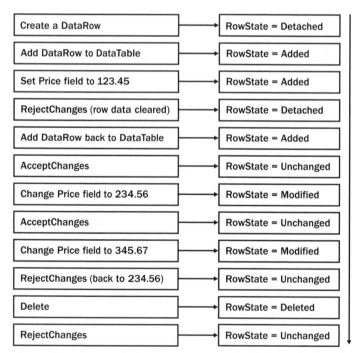

Figure 4-3   The *RowState* changes during the lifetime of a *DataRow* object.

Notice that, after the Price is assigned a value of 123.45, the *RowState* does not change to *Modified*. The *RowState* is still *Added* because *RowState* is an indicator of an action required to send an update of this data to the database. The fact that 123.45 was placed into the Price is not as important as the fact that a *DataRow* needs to be added to the database.

Holding Multiple Copies of Data with the *DataRowVersion*   The *DataRow* can hold up to three versions, or copies, of the data: Original, Current, and Proposed. When the *DataRow* is created, it contains a single copy of the data, which is the Current version. When the *DataRow* is placed into edit mode by executing its *BeginEdit* method, changes to the data are placed in a second version of the data, called the Proposed version. When the *EndEdit* method is executed, the Current version becomes the Original version, the Proposed version becomes the Current version, and the Proposed version no longer exists. After *EndEdit* has completed its execution, there are two versions of the *DataRow* data: Original and Current. If the *BeginEdit* method is called again, the Current version of the data is copied to a third version of the data, which is the Proposed version. Calling *EndEdit* again causes the Proposed version to become the Current version and the Proposed version to no longer exist.

When you retrieve data from the *DataRow*, the *DataRowVersion* you want to retrieve can also be specified as follows:

- **Current**   This is the current value of the *DataRow*, even after changes have been made. This version exists in all situations, except when the *RowState* property is *Deleted*. If you attempt to retrieve the Current version and the *RowState* is *Deleted*, an exception is thrown.

- **Default**   If the *RowState* is *Added* or *Modified*, the default version is Current. If the *RowState* is *Deleted*, an exception is thrown. If the *BeginEdit* method has been executed, the default version is Proposed.

- **Original**   This is the value at the time the last *AcceptChanges* method was executed. If the *AcceptChanges* method was never executed, the Original version is the value that was originally loaded into the *DataRow*. Note that this version is not populated until the *RowState* becomes *Modified*, *Unchanged*, or *Deleted*. If the *RowState* is *Deleted*, this information is still retrievable. If the *RowState* is *Added*, a *VersionNotFoundException* is thrown.

■ **Proposed**   This is the value at the time of editing the *DataRow*. If the *RowState* is *Deleted*, an exception is thrown. If the *BeginEdit* method has not been explicitly executed, or if *BeginEdit* was implicitly executed via editing a detached *DataRow* (an orphaned *DataRow* object that has not been added to a *DataTable* object), a *VersionNotFoundException* is thrown.

You can also query the *HasVersion* method on the *DataRow* object to test for the existence of a particular *DataRowVersion*. You can use this method to test for the existence of a *DataRowVersion* before attempting to retrieve a version that does not exist. The following code snippet demonstrates how to retrieve a string using the *RowState* and the *DataRowVersion*:

```vb
'VB
Private Function GetDataRowInfo( _
      ByVal row As DataRow, ByVal columnName As String) _
      As String

   Dim retVal As String = String.Format( _
      "RowState: {0} <br />", row.RowState)

   Dim versionString As String
   For Each versionString In [Enum].GetNames( _
         GetType(DataRowVersion))
      Dim version As DataRowVersion = _
         CType([Enum].Parse(GetType(DataRowVersion), _
         versionString), DataRowVersion)
      If (row.HasVersion(version)) Then
         retVal += String.Format( _
            "Version: {0} Value: {1} <br />", _
            version, row(columnName, version))
      Else
         retVal += String.Format( _
            "Version: {0} does not exist.<br />", _
            version)
      End If
   Next
   Return retVal
End Function
```

```csharp
//C#
private string GetDataRowInfo(DataRow row, string columnName)
{
   string retVal = string.Format(
      "RowState: {0}<br />",
      row.RowState);

   foreach (string versionString in
      Enum.GetNames(typeof(DataRowVersion)))
   {
```

```
        DataRowVersion version = (
          DataRowVersion)Enum.Parse(
            typeof(DataRowVersion), versionString);

        if (row.HasVersion(version))
        {
          retVal += string.Format(
            "Version: {0} Value: {1}<br />",
            version, row[columnName, version]);
        }
        else
        {
          retVal += string.Format(
            "Version: {0} does not exist.<br />",
            version);
        }
    }
    return retVal;
}
```

Resetting the *RowState* with *AcceptChanges* and *RejectChanges*   The *AcceptChanges* method is used to reset the *DataRow* state to *Unchanged*. This method exists on the *DataRow*, *DataTable*, and *DataSet* objects. (We cover *DataSet* later in this chapter.) After data has been loaded from the database, the *RowState* property of the loaded rows is set to *Added*. Calling *AcceptChanges* on the *DataTable* resets the *RowState* of all of the *DataRow* objects to *Unchanged*. If you modify the *DataRow* objects, their *RowState* changes to *Modified*. When you are ready to save the data, you can easily query the *DataTable* object for its changes by using the *GetChanges* method on the *DataTable* object, which returns a *DataTable* that is populated only with the *DataRow* objects that have changed since the last time that *AcceptChanges* was executed. Only the changes need to be sent to the data store.

After the changes have been successfully sent to the data store, change the state of the *DataRow* objects to *Unchanged* by calling the *AcceptChanges* method, which indicates that the *DataRow* objects are synchronized with the data store. Note that executing the *AcceptChanges* method also causes the *DataRow* object's Current *DataRowVersion* to be copied to the *DataRow* object's Original version. Consider the following code snippet:

```
'VB
Protected Sub Button2_Click(ByVal sender As Object, _
    ByVal e As System.EventArgs) Handles Button2.Click
  'add label to form
  Dim lbl As New Label()
  lbl.Style.Add("position", "absolute")
```

```
    lbl.Style.Add("left", "275px")
    lbl.Style.Add("top", "20px")
    lbl.EnableViewState = false
    form1.Controls.Add(lbl)
    'get the first row to play with
    Dim dr As DataRow = GetDataTable().Rows(0)
    'clear the rowstate
    dr.AcceptChanges()
    'make change in a single statement
    dr("FirstName") = "Marie"
    'start making changes that may span multiple statements
    dr.BeginEdit()
    dr("FirstName") = "Marge"
    lbl.Text = GetDataRowInfo(dr, "FirstName")
    dr.EndEdit()
End Sub
```

//C#
```
protected void Button2_Click(object sender, EventArgs e)
{
    //add label to form
    Label lbl = new Label();
    lbl.Style.Add("position", "absolute");
    lbl.Style.Add("left", "275px");
    lbl.Style.Add("top", "20px");
    lbl.EnableViewState = false;
    form1.Controls.Add(lbl);
    //get the first row to play with
    DataRow dr = GetDataTable().Rows[0];
    //clear the rowstate
    dr.AcceptChanges();
    //make change in a single statement
    dr["FirstName"] = "Marie";
    //start making changes that may span multiple statements
    dr.BeginEdit();
    dr["FirstName"] = "Marge";
    lbl.Text = GetDataRowInfo(dr, "FirstName");
    dr.EndEdit();
}
```

This code starts by adding a *Label* control to the Web page that holds the results of this test. Next, the first *DataRow* object in the employee *DataTable* is retrieved. The *DataRow* has an initial *RowState* of *Added*, and the *AcceptChanges* method clears the *RowState* to *Unchanged*. Next, the *FirstName* is modified in a single statement, which causes the *RowState* to become *Modified*. At this time, the Current version contains the modified data and the Original version contains the data values that exist after the *AcceptChanges* method is executed. Next, the *BeginEdit* method is executed to place the *DataRow* in an edit mode and the *FirstName* is changed again. At this time, the Proposed version contains the current data and executing the *GetDataRowInfo* method displays the results shown in Figure 4-4.

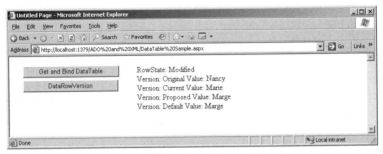

Figure 4-4　The *DataRow* information after making changes.

The *RejectChanges* method is used to roll back the *DataRow* to the point in time when you last called the *AcceptChanges* method. The *AcceptChanges* method overwrites the Original *DataRowVersion,* which means that you cannot roll back to a point in time that is earlier than the last time *AcceptChanges* was called.

Explicitly Changing *RowState* with the *SetAdded* and *SetModified* Methods　The *SetAdded* and *SetModified* methods on the *DataRow* allow you to explicitly set the *RowState*. This is useful when you want to force a *DataRow* to be stored in a data store that is different from the data store from which the *DataRow* was originally loaded.

**Deleting and Undeleting the *DataRow*　**The *Delete* method on the *DataRow* is used to set the *RowState* of the *DataRow* to *Deleted*. A *DataRow* object that has a *RowState* of *Deleted* indicates that the row needs to be deleted from the data store.

There are many scenarios where you need to undelete a *DataRow*. The *DataRow* object doesn't have an undelete method, but you can use the *RejectChanges* method to perform an undelete that may satisfy some scenarios. The problem is that executing the *RejectChanges* method copies the Original *DataRowVersion* to the Current *DataRowVersion,* which effectively restores the *DataRow* object to its state at the time the last *AcceptChanges* method was executed. This means that any changes that were made to the data prior to deleting are lost.

Copying and Cloning the *DataTable*

You often need to create a full copy of a *DataTable* in your application, possibly to pass it to another application, or to use as a scratch pad for operations that may be thrown out later. For example, you may want to assign a *DataTable* object to a *GridView* control to allow a user to edit the data, but you also may want to provide a cancel button that aborts all changes on the Web page. A simple way to implement this functionality is to create a copy of your *DataTable* object and use the copy for editing. If the user clicks the cancel button, the *DataTable* copy is thrown out. If the user decides to keep the changes, you can replace the original *DataTable* object with the edited copy.

To create a copy of a *DataTable* object, use the *Copy* method on the *DataTable,* which copies the *DataTable* object's schema and data. The following code snippet shows how to invoke the *Copy* method:

```
'VB
Dim copy as DataTable = employee.Copy( )
```

```
//C#
DataTable copy = employee.Copy( );
```

You often require a copy of the *DataTable* schema without the data. You can accomplish this by invoking the *Clone* method on the *DataTable*. Use this method when an empty copy of the *DataTable* is required and to which *DataRow* objects will be added at a later time. The following code shows the *Clone* method:

```
'VB
Dim clone as DataTable = employee.Clone( )
```

```
//C#
DataTable clone = employee.Clone( );
```

Importing *DataRow* Objects into a *DataTable*

The *ImportRow* method on the *DataTable* object copies a *DataRow* from a *DataTable* that has the same schema. The *ImportRow* method also imports Current and Original version data. If you attempt to import a *DataRow* that has a primary key value that already exists in the *DataTable* object, a *ConstraintException* is thrown. The following code snippet shows the process for cloning the *DataTable* and then copying a single *DataRow* to the cloned copy:

```
'VB
Dim clone as DataTable = employee.Clone( )
clone.ImportRow(employee.Rows(0))
```

```
//C#
DataTable clone = employee.Clone();
clone.ImportRow(employee.Rows[0]);
```

Using the *DataTable* with XML Data

You can use the *WriteXml* method of a *DataTable* to write the contents of the *Data-Table* to an XML file or stream. This method should be used with the *Server.MapPath* method to convert a simple filename to the Web site path, as shown in the following code snippet:

```vb
'VB
Protected Sub Button5_Click(ByVal sender As Object, _
      ByVal e As System.EventArgs) Handles Button5.Click
   Dim employee As DataTable = GetDataTable()
   employee.WriteXml(Server.MapPath("employee.xml"))
   Response.Redirect("employee.xml")
End Sub
```

```csharp
//C#
protected void Button5_Click(object sender, EventArgs e)
{
    DataTable employee = GetDataTable();
    employee.WriteXml(Server.MapPath("employee.xml"));
    Response.Redirect("employee.xml");
}
```

MORE INFO   Changes to the *DataTable*

The following Microsoft link provides more information about the changes to the *DataTable* in ADO.NET 2.0: *http://msdn.microsoft.com/msdnmag/issues/05/11/DataPoints.*

When this method is executed, the employee.xml file is produced, which looks like the following:

```xml
<?xml version="1.0" standalone="yes"?>
<DocumentElement>
  <Employee>
    <Eid>123456789A</Eid>
    <FirstName>Nancy</FirstName>
    <LastName>Davolio</LastName>
    <Salary>10</Salary>
    <LastName_x0020_and_x0020_FirstName>
        Davolio, Nancy
    </LastName_x0020_and_x0020_FirstName>
  </Employee>
  <Employee>
    <Eid>987654321X</Eid>
    <FirstName>Janet</FirstName>
    <LastName>Leverling</LastName>
```

```
    <Salary>20</Salary>
    <LastName_x0020_and_x0020_FirstName>
        Leverling, Janet
    </LastName_x0020_and_x0020_FirstName>
  </Employee>
</DocumentElement>
```

This example uses *DocumentElement* as the root element and uses repeating *Employee* elements for each *DataRow*. The data for each *DataRow* is nested as an element within each *Employee* element. Also notice that an XML element name cannot have spaces, so *LastName* and *FirstName* are automatically encoded (converted) to *LastName_x0020_and_x0020_FirstName*.

You can fine-tune the XML output by providing an XML schema or by setting properties on the *DataTable* and its objects. To change the name of the repeating element for the *DataRow* objects from *Employee* to *Person*, you can change the *DataTable* object's *TableName*. The *DataColumn* has a *ColumnMapping* property you can use to configure the output of each column by assigning one of the following *MappingType* enumeration values:

- **Attribute**   Places the column data into an XML attribute.
- **Element**   Is the default. Places the column data into an XML element.
- **Hidden**   Is the column data that is not sent to the XML file.
- **SimpleContent**   Is the column data that is stored as text within the row's element tags and does not include element tags for the column.

To change the *Eid*, *LastName*, *FirstName*, and *Salary* to XML attributes, you can set each *DataColumn* object's *ColumnMapping* property to *MappingType.Attribute*. The LastName and FirstName column is an expression column, so its data does not need to be stored. Therefore, its *ColumnMapping* property can be set to *MappingType.Hidden*. The following snippets show the necessary code and the resulting XML file contents:

```
'VB
Protected Sub Button6_Click(ByVal sender As Object, _
    ByVal e As System.EventArgs) Handles Button6.Click
  Dim employee As DataTable = GetDataTable()
  employee.TableName = "Person"
  employee.Columns("Eid").ColumnMapping = MappingType.Attribute
  employee.Columns("FirstName").ColumnMapping = MappingType.Attribute
  employee.Columns("LastName").ColumnMapping = MappingType.Attribute
  employee.Columns("Salary").ColumnMapping = MappingType.Attribute
  employee.Columns("LastName and FirstName").ColumnMapping = _
    MappingType.Hidden
```

```
        employee.WriteXml(Server.MapPath("Person.xml"))
        Response.Redirect("Person.xml")
End Sub
```

```
//C#
protected void Button6_Click(object sender, EventArgs e)
{
    DataTable employee = GetDataTable();
    employee.TableName = "Person";
    employee.Columns["Eid"].ColumnMapping = MappingType.Attribute;
    employee.Columns["FirstName"].ColumnMapping = MappingType.Attribute;
    employee.Columns["LastName"].ColumnMapping = MappingType.Attribute;
    employee.Columns["Salary"].ColumnMapping = MappingType.Attribute;
    employee.Columns["LastName and FirstName"].ColumnMapping =
        MappingType.Hidden;
    employee.WriteXml(Server.MapPath("Person.xml"));
    Response.Redirect("Person.xml");
}
```

```
XML
<?xml version="1.0" standalone="yes"?>
<DocumentElement>
<Person Eid="123456789A" FirstName="Nancy" LastName="Davolio" Salary="10" />
<Person Eid="987654321X" FirstName="Janet" LastName="Leverling" Salary="20" />
</DocumentElement>
```

Although the resulting XML file is compact, the data types aren't saved, so all data is considered to be string data. You can use the *XmlWriteMode.WriteSchema* enumeration value to store the XML schema with the data, as shown here:

```
'VB
Protected Sub Button7_Click(ByVal sender As Object, _
        ByVal e As System.EventArgs) Handles Button7.Click
    Dim employee As DataTable = GetDataTable()
    employee.TableName = "Person"
    employee.Columns("Eid").ColumnMapping = MappingType.Attribute
    employee.Columns("FirstName").ColumnMapping = MappingType.Attribute
    employee.Columns("LastName").ColumnMapping = MappingType.Attribute
    employee.Columns("Salary").ColumnMapping = MappingType.Attribute
    employee.Columns("LastName and FirstName").ColumnMapping = _
        MappingType.Hidden
    employee.WriteXml(Server.MapPath("PersonWithSchema.xml"), _
        XmlWriteMode.WriteSchema)
    Response.Redirect("PersonWithSchema.xml")
End Sub
```

```
//C#
protected void Button7_Click(object sender, EventArgs e)
{
    DataTable employee = GetDataTable();
    employee.TableName = "Person";
    employee.Columns["Eid"].ColumnMapping = MappingType.Attribute;
```

```
    employee.Columns["FirstName"].ColumnMapping = MappingType.Attribute;
    employee.Columns["LastName"].ColumnMapping = MappingType.Attribute;
    employee.Columns["Salary"].ColumnMapping = MappingType.Attribute;
    employee.Columns["LastName and FirstName"].ColumnMapping =
        MappingType.Hidden;
    employee.WriteXml(Server.MapPath("PersonWithSchema.xml"),
        XmlWriteMode.WriteSchema);      Response.Redirect("PersonWithSchema.xml");
}
```

XML

```
<?xml version="1.0" standalone="yes"?>
<NewDataSet>
  <xs:schema id="NewDataSet" xmlns="" xmlns:xs="http://www.w3.org/2001/XMLSchema"
xmlns:msdata="urn:schemas-microsoft-com:xml-msdata">
    <xs:element name="NewDataSet" msdata:IsDataSet="true"
            msdata:MainDataTable="Person" msdata:UseCurrentLocale="true">
      <xs:complexType>
        <xs:choice minOccurs="0" maxOccurs="unbounded">
          <xs:element name="Person">
            <xs:complexType>
              <xs:attribute name="Eid" msdata:Caption="EID" use="required">
                <xs:simpleType>
                  <xs:restriction base="xs:string">
                    <xs:maxLength value="10" />
                  </xs:restriction>
                </xs:simpleType>
              </xs:attribute>
              <xs:attribute name="FirstName" use="required">
                <xs:simpleType>
                  <xs:restriction base="xs:string">
                    <xs:maxLength value="35" />
                  </xs:restriction>
                </xs:simpleType>
              </xs:attribute>
              <xs:attribute name="LastName" type="xs:string" use="required" />
              <xs:attribute name="Salary" type="xs:decimal" default="0.00" />
              <xs:attribute name="LastName_x0020_and_x0020_FirstName"
                  msdata:ReadOnly="true"
                  msdata:Expression="lastName + ', ' + firstName"
                  use="prohibited">
                <xs:simpleType>
                  <xs:restriction base="xs:string">
                    <xs:maxLength value="70" />
                  </xs:restriction>
                </xs:simpleType>
              </xs:attribute>
            </xs:complexType>
          </xs:element>
        </xs:choice>
      </xs:complexType>
      <xs:unique name="Constraint1" msdata:PrimaryKey="true">
```

```
      <xs:selector xpath=".//Person" />
      <xs:field xpath="@Eid" />
    </xs:unique>
  </xs:element>
 </xs:schema>
 <Person Eid="123456789A" FirstName="Nancy" LastName="Davolio"
    Salary="10.00" />
 <Person Eid="987654321X" FirstName="Janet" LastName="Leverling"
    Salary="20.00" />
</NewDataSet>
```

With the XML Schema included in the file, the data types are defined. Notice that the XML schema also includes the maximum length settings for *Eid* and *FirstName*. A *DataTable* can be loaded with this XML file, and the resulting *DataTable* is the same as the *DataTable* that was saved to the file. The following code snippet reads the XML file into a new *DataTable* object:

```vb
'VB
Protected Sub Button8_Click(ByVal sender As Object, _
      ByVal e As System.EventArgs) Handles Button8.Click
   'add grid to form
   Dim gv As New GridView()
   gv.Style.Add("position", "absolute")
   gv.Style.Add("left", "275px")
   gv.Style.Add("top", "20px")
   gv.EnableViewState = False
   form1.Controls.Add(gv)
   'get the table and display
   Dim xmlTable as New DataTable()
   xmlTable.ReadXml(Server.MapPath("PersonWithSchema.xml"))
   gv.DataSource = xmlTable
   gv.DataBind()
End Sub
```

```csharp
//C#
protected void Button8_Click(object sender, EventArgs e)
{
    //add grid to form
    GridView gv = new GridView();
    gv.Style.Add("position", "absolute");
    gv.Style.Add("left", "275px");
    gv.Style.Add("top", "20px");
    gv.EnableViewState = false;
    form1.Controls.Add(gv);
    //get the table and display
    DataTable xmlTable = new DataTable();
    xmlTable.ReadXml(Server.MapPath("PersonWithSchema.xml"));
    gv.DataSource = xmlTable;
    gv.DataBind();
}
```

Although the data for the LastName and FirstName column was not saved, the column data is populated because this column is derived and the schema contains the expression to re-create this column data.

Opening a *DataView* Window in a *DataTable*

The *DataView* object provides a window into a *DataTable* that can be sorted and filtered using the *Sort*, *RowFilter*, and *RowStateFilter* properties. A *DataTable* can have many *DataView* objects assigned to it, allowing the data to be viewed in many different ways without requiring the data to be reread from the database. The *DataView* object also contains the *AllowDelete*, *AllowEdit*, and *AllowNew* properties to constrain user input as needed.

If you look at the *DataView* object's internal structure, you will find that it is essentially an index. You can provide a sort definition to sort the index in a certain order, and you can provide a filter to filter the index entries.

Ordering Data Using the *Sort* Property   The *Sort* property requires a sort expression. The default order for the sort is ascending, but you can specify ASC or DESC with a comma-separated list of columns to be sorted. In the following code snippet, the employee *DataTable* is retrieved, additional rows are added, and a *DataView* is created on the employee *DataTable* with a compound sort on the LastName column and the FirstName column in ascending order and on the Salary column in descending order.

```
'VB
Protected Sub Button9_Click(ByVal sender As Object, _
     ByVal e As System.EventArgs) Handles Button9.Click
   'add grid to form
   Dim gv As New GridView()
   gv.Style.Add("position", "absolute")
   gv.Style.Add("left", "275px")
   gv.Style.Add("top", "20px")
   gv.EnableViewState = False
   form1.Controls.Add(gv)
   'get datatable
   Dim employee As DataTable = GetDataTable()
   'Add New DataRow by adding the values
   employee.Rows.Add("ABC345DEF1", "Thomas", "Andersen", 25.00)
   employee.Rows.Add("123ABC345D", "Sean", "Chai" , 20.00)
   employee.Rows.Add("345DEF123A", "Erik", "Andersen", 22.00)
   employee.Rows.Add("DEF123ABC3", "Nancy", "Andersen", 8.00)
   'sort and display
   Dim view As New DataView(employee)
```

```
    view.Sort = "LastName ASC, FirstName ASC, Salary  DESC"
    gv.DataSource = view
    gv.DataBind()
End Sub
```

```csharp
//C#
protected void Button9_Click(object sender, EventArgs e)
{
    //add grid to form
    GridView gv = new GridView();
    gv.Style.Add("position", "absolute");
    gv.Style.Add("left", "275px");
    gv.Style.Add("top", "20px");
    gv.EnableViewState = false;
    form1.Controls.Add(gv);
    //get datatable
    DataTable employee = GetDataTable();
    //Add New DataRow by adding the values
    employee.Rows.Add("ABC345DEF1", "Thomas", "Andersen", 25.00m);
    employee.Rows.Add("123ABC345D", "Sean", "Chai" , 20.00m);
    employee.Rows.Add("345DEF123A", "Erik", "Andersen", 22.00m);
    employee.Rows.Add("DEF123ABC3", "Nancy", "Andersen", 8.00m);
    //sort and display
    DataView view = new DataView(employee);
    view.Sort = "LastName ASC, FirstName ASC, Salary  DESC";
    gv.DataSource = view;
    gv.DataBind();
}
```

Figure 4-5 shows the sorted *DataView* when the Web page is run.

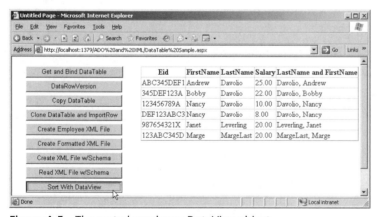

Figure 4-5   The sorted employee *DataView* object.

Narrowing the Search with the *RowFilter* and *RowStateFilter* Properties   The *DataView* filters comprise a *RowFilter* and a *RowStateFilter*. The *RowFilter* is set to a SQL "WHERE" clause without the word "WHERE." The following code shows a filter on the LastName column for employees whose names begin with the letter A and on the Salary column for employees whose salaries are greater than 15.

```
'VB
view.RowFilter = "LastName like 'A%' and Salary > 15"
```

```
//C#
view.RowFilter = "LastName like 'A%' and Salary > 15";
```

The *RowStateFilter* provides a filter based on the *DataRow* object's *RowState* property. This filter provides an extremely easy way to retrieve specific version information within the *DataTable* using one of the *DataViewRowState* enumeration values, which are as follows:

- **Added**   Retrieves the Current *DataRowVersion* of *DataRow* objects that have a *RowState* of *Added*.

- **CurrentRows**   Retrieves all *DataRow* objects that have a Current *DataRowVersion*.

- **Deleted**   Retrieves the Original *DataRowVersion* of *DataRow* objects that have a *RowState* of *Deleted*.

- **ModifiedCurrent**   Retrieves the Current *DataRowVersion* of *DataRow* objects that have a *RowState* of *Modified*.

- **ModifiedOriginal**   Retrieves the Original *DataRowVersion* of *DataRow* objects that have a *RowState* of *Modified*.

- **None**   Clears the *RowStateFilter* property.

- **OriginalRows**   Retrieves the *DataRow* objects that have an Original *DataRow-Version*.

- **Unchanged**   Retrieves *DataRow* objects that have a *RowState* of *Unchanged*.

Using a *DataSet* Object

The *DataSet* is a memory-based relational representation of data and is the primary disconnected data object. The *DataSet* contains a collection of *DataTable* and *DataRelation* objects, as shown in Figure 4-6. The *DataTable* objects can contain unique and foreign key constraints to enforce data integrity. The *DataSet* also provides methods for cloning the *DataSet* schema, copying the *DataSet*, merging with other *DataSet* objects, and retrieving changes from the *DataSet*.

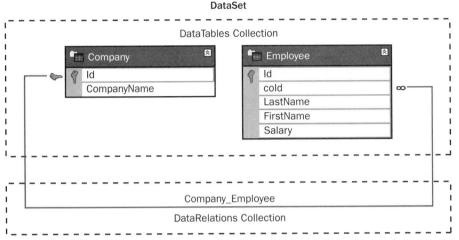

Figure 4-6 The *DataSet* object contains a collection of *DataTable* and *DataRelation* objects.

You can create the *DataSet* schema programmatically or by providing an XML schema definition. The following code demonstrates the creation of a simple *DataSet* containing a *DataTable* for companies and a *DataTable* for employees. The two *DataTable* objects are joined using a *DataRelation* named Company_Employee. (The *DataRelation* is discussed in more detail in the next section of this chapter.)

```
'VB
    Private Function GetDataSet() As DataSet

        Dim companyData As New DataSet("CompanyList")

        Dim company As DataTable = companyData.Tables.Add("company")
        company.Columns.Add("Id", GetType(Guid))
        company.Columns.Add("CompanyName", GetType(String))
        company.PrimaryKey = New DataColumn() {company.Columns("Id")}

        Dim employee As DataTable = companyData.Tables.Add("employee")
        employee.Columns.Add("Id", GetType(Guid))
        employee.Columns.Add("companyId", GetType(Guid))
        employee.Columns.Add("LastName", GetType(String))
        employee.Columns.Add("FirstName", GetType(String))
        employee.Columns.Add("Salary", GetType(Decimal))
        employee.PrimaryKey = New DataColumn() {employee.Columns("Id")}

        companyData.Relations.Add( _
            "Company_Employee", _
```

```
        company.Columns("Id"), _
        employee.Columns("CompanyId"))

    Return companyData
  End Function
```

```
//C#
private DataSet GetDataSet()
{
  DataSet companyData = new DataSet("CompanyList");

  DataTable company = companyData.Tables.Add("company");
  company.Columns.Add("Id", typeof(Guid));
  company.Columns.Add("CompanyName", typeof(string));
  company.PrimaryKey = new DataColumn[] { company.Columns["Id"] };

  DataTable employee = companyData.Tables.Add("employee");
  employee.Columns.Add("Id", typeof(Guid));
  employee.Columns.Add("companyId", typeof(Guid));
  employee.Columns.Add("LastName", typeof(string));
  employee.Columns.Add("FirstName", typeof(string));
  employee.Columns.Add("Salary", typeof(decimal));
  employee.PrimaryKey = new DataColumn[] { employee.Columns["Id"] };

  companyData.Relations.Add(
     "Company_Employee",
     company.Columns["Id"],
     employee.Columns["CompanyId"]);
  return companyData;
}
```

After the *DataSet* is created, the *DataTable* objects are populated with sample data, as shown in the following code sample. This code populates the Id columns by creating a new globally unique identifier. After a company is created and added to the company *DataTable*, the employee names for that company are created and added.

```
'VB
Public Sub PopulateDataSet(ByVal ds As DataSet)

  Dim company As DataTable = ds.Tables("Company")
  Dim employee As DataTable = ds.Tables("Employee")

  Dim coId, empId As Guid
  coId = Guid.NewGuid()
  company.Rows.Add(coId, "Northwind Traders")
  empId = Guid.NewGuid()
  employee.Rows.Add(empId, coId, "JoeLast", "JoeFirst", 40.00)
  empId = Guid.NewGuid()
  employee.Rows.Add(empId, coId, "MaryLast", "MaryFirst", 70.00)
  empId = Guid.NewGuid()
```

```
    employee.Rows.Add(empId, coId, "SamLast", "SamFirst", 12.00)

    coId = Guid.NewGuid()
    company.Rows.Add(coId, "Contoso")
    empId = Guid.NewGuid()
    employee.Rows.Add(empId, coId, "SueLast", "SueFirst", 20.00)
    empId = Guid.NewGuid()
    employee.Rows.Add(empId, coId, "TomLast", "TomFirst", 68.00)
    empId = Guid.NewGuid()
    employee.Rows.Add(empId, coId, "MikeLast", "MikeFirst", 18.99)

End Sub
```

```
//C#
private void PopulateDataSet(DataSet ds)
{
    DataTable company = ds.Tables["Company"];
    DataTable employee = ds.Tables["Employee"];

    Guid coId, empId;
    coId = Guid.NewGuid();
    company.Rows.Add(coId, "Northwind Traders");
    empId = Guid.NewGuid();
    employee.Rows.Add(empId, coId, "JoeLast", "JoeFirst", 40.00);
    empId = Guid.NewGuid();
    employee.Rows.Add(empId, coId, "MaryLast", "MaryFirst", 70.00);
    empId = Guid.NewGuid();
    employee.Rows.Add(empId, coId, "SamLast", "SamFirst", 12.00);

    coId = Guid.NewGuid();
    company.Rows.Add(coId, "Contoso");
    empId = Guid.NewGuid();
    employee.Rows.Add(empId, coId, "SueLast", "SueFirst", 20.00);
    empId = Guid.NewGuid();
    employee.Rows.Add(empId, coId, "TomLast", "TomFirst", 68.00);
    empId = Guid.NewGuid();
    employee.Rows.Add(empId, coId, "MikeLast", "MikeFirst", 18.99);
}
```

Using the Globally Unique Identifier (GUID) as a Primary Key

The previous code sample creates and populates a *DataSet*. Notice the use of the *Guid* data type for the Id columns. Although this option is not mandatory, you should consider implementing this option, especially when working with disconnected data. This can help you deal with the following issues:

■ If you use an auto-number Id column and if many people are creating new *DataRow* objects, it will be difficult for you to merge data later because there may be many duplicate keys.

■ The *Guid* data type is a "surrogate" key, meaning that its only purpose is to define uniqueness of the row and aid in connecting multiple tables together via relationships. This means that there is no reason for a user to see and change this value, which simplifies maintenance of the *DataSet*. If you allow the user to change the primary key on a row, you have to propogate the change down to all of the related tables. For example, changing the CompanyId value requires the update of the Company Id value in the Employee table.

■ The use of the *Guid* can simplify the joining of tables, which is better than the scenarios where you use compound keys that are based on the actual data. Compound keys typically result in smaller data footprints because the key is based on actual data, whereas joining tables is usually more difficult because compound joins are required. Remember that if you are using compound keys that are based on the actual data, you inevitably need to deal with recursive updates.

GetLabel and *GetGridView* Methods

The sample code in this chapter makes calls to the *GetLabel* and *GetGridView* methods. Instead of placing a *GridView* or *Label* control on the form to display the sample code output, these methods are used to dynamically create the proper output control as needed, which simplifies the sample code. The code for these methods is as follows.

```vb
'VB
Private Function GetLabel(ByVal left As Integer, _
      ByVal top As Integer) As Label
   Dim lbl As New Label()
   lbl.Style.Add("position", "absolute")
   lbl.Style.Add("left", left.ToString() + "px")
   lbl.Style.Add("top", top.ToString() + "px")
   lbl.EnableViewState = False
   form1.Controls.Add(lbl)
   Return lbl
End Function

Private Function GetGridView(ByVal left As Integer, _
      ByVal top As Integer) As GridView
   Dim gv As New GridView()
   gv.Style.Add("position", "absolute")
   gv.Style.Add("left", left.ToString() + "px")
   gv.Style.Add("top", top.ToString() + "px")
   gv.EnableViewState = False
   form1.Controls.Add(gv)
   Return gv
End Function
```

```csharp
//C#
private Label GetLabel(int left, int top)
{
    Label lbl = new Label();
    lbl.Style.Add("position", "absolute");
    lbl.Style.Add("left", left.ToString() + "px");
    lbl.Style.Add("top", top.ToString() + "px");
    lbl.EnableViewState = false;
    form1.Controls.Add(lbl);
    return lbl;
}

private GridView GetGridView(int left, int top)
{
    GridView gv = new GridView();
    gv.Style.Add("position", "absolute");
    gv.Style.Add("left", left.ToString() + "px");
    gv.Style.Add("top", top.ToString() + "px");
    gv.EnableViewState = false;
    form1.Controls.Add(gv);
    return gv;
}
```

Binding to the *DataSet* Object

Assign the *DataSet* to the *DataSource* property of a data-bound control to display the contents of a *DataSet*. The first *DataTable* in the *DataSet* is rendered when you issue the *DataBind* method on the control, but you can be more specific about the *DataTable* to use by assigning the name of the *DataTable* to the *DataMember* property of the data-bound control. The following code snippet uses the *GetGridView*, which dynamically creates a *GridView* and adds it to the form. This method is called to create a *GridView* for the Company table and another *GridView* for the Employee table. The code sample retrieves the populated *DataSet*, retrieves the populated *DataSet*, and binds the *DataSet* to the *GridView* controls:

```vb
' VB
Protected Sub Button1_Click(ByVal sender As Object, _
    ByVal e As System.EventArgs) Handles Button1.Click
  'add grids to form
  Dim gvCompany As GridView = GetGridView(275, 20)
  Dim gvEmployee As GridView = GetGridView(275, 125)

  'get the dataset and display
  Dim companyList As DataSet = GetDataSet()
  PopulateDataSet(companyList)

  'display
```

```
      gvCompany.DataSource = companyList
      gvCompany.DataMember = "Company"
      gvEmployee.DataSource = companyList
      gvEmployee.DataMember = "Employee"
      gvCompany.DataBind()
      gvEmployee.DataBind()
End Sub

//C#
protected void Button1_Click(object sender, EventArgs e)
{
    //add grids to form
    GridView gvCompany = GetGridView(275, 20);
    GridView gvEmployee = GetGridView(275, 125);

    //get the dataset and populate
    DataSet companyList = GetDataSet();
    PopulateDataSet(companyList);

    //display
    gvCompany.DataSource = companyList;
    gvCompany.DataMember = "Company";
    gvEmployee.DataSource = companyList;
    gvEmployee.DataMember = "Employee";
    gvCompany.DataBind();
    gvEmployee.DataBind();
}
```

Figure 4-7 shows the result after the Web page is displayed and the button is clicked.

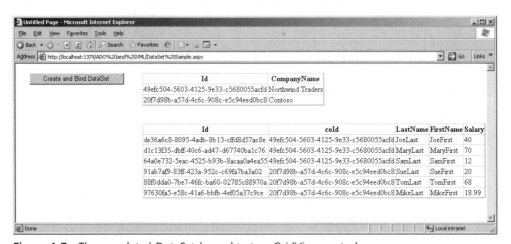

Figure 4-7   The populated *DataSet*, bound to two *GridView* controls.

Using Typed *DataSets*

After the *DataSet* object's schema is created, you can access any of the *DataTable* objects by using the table name (as shown in the following example) that retrieves the *Company DataTable* from the *saleData DataSet* object:

```
'VB
Dim companyTable as DataTable = salesData.Tables("Company")
```

```
//C#
DataTable companyTable = salesData.Tables["Company"];
```

If the name of the table is misspelled, an exception is thrown, but not until runtime. You can be notified of an error when you build your project by creating a new, specialized *DataSet* class that inherits from *DataSet,* and by adding a property for each of the tables. For example, a specialized *DataSet* class might contain a property called *Company* that can be accessed as follows:

```
'VB
Dim companyTable as DataTable = vendorData.Company
```

```
//C#
DataTable companyTable = vendorData.Company;
```

In this example, a compile error is generated if Company is not spelled correctly. (Keep in mind that you probably won't misspell the *Company* property because Visual Studio's IntelliSense displays the *Company* property for quick selection when the line of code is being typed.)

You can provide an XML Schema Definition (XSD) file to generate the typed *DataSet* class. You can use the DataSet Editor to graphically create and modify an XSD file, which, in turn, can be used to generate the typed *DataSet* class. Figure 4-8 shows the CompanyList *DataSet* that is loaded into the DataSet Editor.

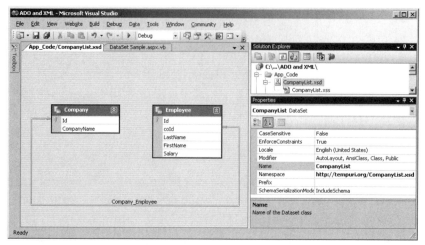

Figure 4-8   The DataSet template contains an XML schema definition and generates source code to create a typed *DataSet*.

Navigating *DataTable* Objects with *DataRelation* Objects

The *DataRelation* object is used to join two *DataTable* objects that are in the same *DataSet*, thus providing a navigable path between the two *DataTable* objects. The *DataRelation* can be traversed from parent *DataTable* to child *DataTable* or from child *DataTable* to parent *DataTable*. The following code example populates the Company and Employee *DataTable* objects and then performs *DataRelation* object navigation:

```vb
'VB
Protected Sub Button2_Click(ByVal sender As Object, _
    ByVal e As System.EventArgs) Handles Button2.Click
    'add a label to the form
    Dim lbl As Label = GetLabel(275, 20)

    'get the dataset and populate
    Dim companyList As DataSet = GetDataSet()
    PopulateDataSet(companyList)

    'get the relationship
    Dim dr As DataRelation = companyList.Relations("Company_Employee")

    'display second company
    Dim companyParent As DataRow = companyList.Tables("company").Rows(1)
    lbl.Text = companyParent("CompanyName") + "<br />"

    'display employees
    For Each employeeChild As DataRow In companyParent.GetChildRows(dr)
        lbl.Text += "   " + employeeChild("Id").ToString() + " " _
            + employeeChild("LastName") + " " _
```

```
            + employeeChild("FirstName") + " " _
            + String.Format("{0:C}", employeeChild("Salary")) + "<br />"
    Next

    lbl.Text += "<br /><br />"

    'display second employee
    Dim employeeParent As DataRow = companyList.Tables("employee").Rows(1)
    lbl.Text += employeeParent("Id").ToString() + " " _
        + employeeParent("LastName") + " " _
        + employeeParent("FirstName") + " " _
        + String.Format("{0:C}", employeeParent("Salary")) + "<br />"

    'display company
    Dim companyChild As DataRow = employeeParent.GetParentRow(dr)
    lbl.Text += "   " + companyChild("CompanyName") + "<br />"
End Sub
```

//C#
```
protected void Button2_Click(object sender, EventArgs e)
{
    //add a label to the form
    Label lbl = GetLabel(275, 20);

    //get the dataset and populate
    DataSet companyList = GetDataSet();
    PopulateDataSet(companyList);

    //get the relationship
    DataRelation dr = companyList.Relations["Company_Employee"];

    //display second company
    DataRow companyParent = companyList.Tables["company"].Rows[1];
    lbl.Text = companyParent["CompanyName"] + "<br />";

    //display employees
    foreach (DataRow employeeChild in companyParent.GetChildRows(dr))
    {
        lbl.Text += "   " + employeeChild["Id"] + " "
            + employeeChild["LastName"] + " "
            + employeeChild["FirstName"] + " "
            + string.Format("{0:C}", employeeChild["Salary"]) + "<br />";
    }

    lbl.Text += "<br /><br />";

    //display second employee
    DataRow employeeParent = companyList.Tables["employee"].Rows[1];
    lbl.Text += employeeParent["Id"] + " "
        + employeeParent["LastName"] + " "
        + employeeParent["FirstName"] + " "
        + string.Format("{0:C}", employeeParent["Salary"]) + "<br />";
```

```
    //display company
    DataRow companyChild = employeeParent.GetParentRow(dr);
    lbl.Text += "   " + companyChild["CompanyName"] + "<br />";
}
```

In this code example, the previously declared Company_Employee *DataRelation* navigates from parent to child and then from child to parent. The result is shown in Figure 4-9.

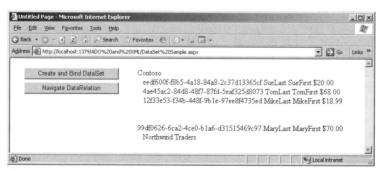

Figure 4-9 The *DataRelation* object is used to navigate the *DataTable* objects from parent to child or child to parent.

Primary and Foreign Key Constraint Creation   When you create a *DataRelation* object without unique and foreign key constraints, its sole purpose is to navigate between parent and child *DataTable* objects. The *DataRelation* constructor allows for the creation of a unique constraint on the parent *DataTable* object and a foreign key constraint on the child *DataTable* object.

Cascading Updates and Deletes   There are many scenarios where you want the deletion of a parent *DataRow* object to force the deletion of child *DataRow* objects. You can accomplish this by setting the *DeleteRule* on the *ForeignKeyConstraint* to *Cascade* (default). The following is a list of the *Rule* enumeration members:

- **Cascade**   Default. Deletes or updates the child *DataRow* objects when the *DataRow* object is deleted or its unique key is changed.

- **None**   Throws an *InvalidConstraintException* if the parent *DataRow* object is deleted or its unique key is changed.

- **SetDefault**   Sets the foreign key column(s) value to the default value of the *Data-Column* object(s) if the parent *DataRow* object is deleted or its unique key is changed.

- **SetNull** Sets the foreign key column(s) value to *DbNull* if the parent *DataRow* object is deleted or its unique key is changed.

As with deleting, on some occasions, you'll want to cascade changes to a unique key in the parent *DataRow* object to the child *DataRow* object's foreign key. You can set the *ChangeRule* to a member of the *Rule* enumeration to get the appropriate behavior.

Serializing and Deserializing *DataSet* Objects

A *DataSet* can be serialized as XML or as binary data to a stream or file. The *DataSet* can also be deserialized from XML or binary data from a stream or file. The serialized data can be transferred across a network via many protocols, including HTTP. This section looks at the various methods of transferring data.

Serializing the *DataSet* Object as XML You can serialize a *DataSet* to an XML file by executing the *DataSet* object's *WriteXml* method. The following code snippet uses the populated companyList *DataSet* that was created earlier in this chapter and writes the contents to an XML file. The resulting XML file contents are also shown.

```
'VB
Protected Sub Button4_Click(ByVal sender As Object, _
      ByVal e As System.EventArgs) Handles Button4.Click
   'get dataset and populate
   'get the dataset and populate
   Dim companyList As DataSet = GetDataSet()
   PopulateDataSet(companyList)

   'write to xml file
   companyList.WriteXml(MapPath("CompanyList.xml"))

   'display file
   Response.Redirect("CompanyList.xml")
End Sub

//C#
protected void Button4_Click(object sender, EventArgs e)
{
   //get dataset and populate
   //get the dataset and populate
   DataSet companyList = GetDataSet();
   PopulateDataSet(companyList);

   //write to xml file
   companyList.WriteXml(MapPath("CompanyList.xml"));

   //display file
```

```
    Response.Redirect("CompanyList.xml");
}
```

XML

```xml
<?xml version="1.0" standalone="yes"?>
<CompanyList>
  <company>
    <Id>c2a464fb-bdce-498a-a216-fb844dfb05a5</Id>
    <CompanyName>Northwind Traders</CompanyName>
  </company>
  <company>
    <Id>aa40966c-18b7-451b-acea-237eaa5e08af</Id>
    <CompanyName>Contoso</CompanyName>
  </company>
  <employee>
    <Id>7ad2a59c-dd3a-483b-877c-b4fe0d0c9bbe</Id>
    <coId>c2a464fb-bdce-498a-a216-fb844dfb05a5</coId>
    <LastName>JoeLast</LastName>
    <FirstName>JoeFirst</FirstName>
    <Salary>40</Salary>
  </employee>
  <employee>
    <Id>343d98b0-e6aa-432d-9755-2c9501cd1ace</Id>
    <coId>c2a464fb-bdce-498a-a216-fb844dfb05a5</coId>
    <LastName>MaryLast</LastName>
    <FirstName>MaryFirst</FirstName>
    <Salary>70</Salary>
  </employee>
  <employee>
    <Id>d69af78c-8f2e-4d4f-9fd0-e0ebca6fccaa</Id>
    <coId>c2a464fb-bdce-498a-a216-fb844dfb05a5</coId>
    <LastName>SamLast</LastName>
    <FirstName>SamFirst</FirstName>
    <Salary>12</Salary>
  </employee>
  <employee>
    <Id>3cc2b9da-3087-47de-99eb-9f924f1edb0d</Id>
    <coId>aa40966c-18b7-451b-acea-237eaa5e08af</coId>
    <LastName>SueLast</LastName>
    <FirstName>SueFirst</FirstName>
    <Salary>20</Salary>
  </employee>
  <employee>
    <Id>c5804b95-c498-45ab-91b4-07fc50154f2a</Id>
    <coId>aa40966c-18b7-451b-acea-237eaa5e08af</coId>
    <LastName>TomLast</LastName>
    <FirstName>TomFirst</FirstName>
    <Salary>68</Salary>
  </employee>
  <employee>
    <Id>ad3ca5ac-eac9-4bec-88d2-5d32522abd41</Id>
    <coId>aa40966c-18b7-451b-acea-237eaa5e08af</coId>
    <LastName>MikeLast</LastName>
```

```
    <FirstName>MikeFirst</FirstName>
    <Salary>18.99</Salary>
  </employee>
</CompanyList>
```

The XML document is well formed and its root node is called *CompanyList*, which you can change by changing the *DataSetName* property.

Notice that the single *Company DataRow* object is represented in the XML file by the single *Company* element, while the *Employee DataRow* objects are represented in the XML file by the repeating *Employee* elements. The column data is represented as elements within the element for the *DataRow*, but you can change this by changing the *ColumnMapping* property of the *DataColumn* objects.

You can nest the *Employee* elements inside the *Company* object that has the employees by setting the *Nested* property of the *DataRelation* object to *true*. In the following code snippet, the XML format is changed substantially by nesting the data and setting all of the *DataColumn* objects to *Attribute*. The resulting XML file is also shown.

```vb
'VB
Protected Sub Button5_Click(ByVal sender As Object, _
     ByVal e As System.EventArgs) Handles Button5.Click
  'get dataset and populate
  'get the dataset and populate
  Dim companyList As DataSet = GetDataSet()
  PopulateDataSet(companyList)

  'format xml
  companyList.Relations("Company_Employee").Nested = True
  For Each dt As DataTable In companyList.Tables
     For Each dc As DataColumn In dt.Columns
        dc.ColumnMapping = MappingType.Attribute
     Next
  Next

  'write to xml file
  companyList.WriteXml(MapPath("CompanyList.xml"))

  'display file
  Response.Redirect("CompanyList.xml")
End Sub
```

```csharp
//C#
protected void Button5_Click(object sender, EventArgs e)
{
  //get dataset and populate
  //get the dataset and populate
  DataSet companyList = GetDataSet();
  PopulateDataSet(companyList);
```

```
    //format xml
    companyList.Relations["Company_Employee"].Nested = true;
    foreach (DataTable dt in companyList.Tables)
    {
        foreach (DataColumn dc in dt.Columns)
        {
            dc.ColumnMapping = MappingType.Attribute;
        }
    }

    //write to xml file
    companyList.WriteXml(MapPath("CompanyListNested.xml"));

    //display file
    Response.Redirect("CompanyListNested.xml");
}
```

XML
```
<?xml version="1.0" standalone="yes"?>
<CompanyList>
  <company Id="63cd2a1e-c578-4f21-a826-c5dfb50258b0"
      CompanyName="Northwind Traders">
    <employee Id="a2e7bbba-20ba-4b73-86b3-2d0cca4f1bbb"
        coId="63cd2a1e-c578-4f21-a826-c5dfb50258b0"
        LastName="JoeLast" FirstName="JoeFirst" Salary="40" />
    <employee Id="5cf475e8-1d97-4784-b72f-84bfbf4a8e14"
        coId="63cd2a1e-c578-4f21-a826-c5dfb50258b0"
        LastName="MaryLast" FirstName="MaryFirst" Salary="70" />
    <employee Id="55ff1a2b-8956-4ded-99a4-68610134b774"
        coId="63cd2a1e-c578-4f21-a826-c5dfb50258b0"
        LastName="SamLast" FirstName="SamFirst" Salary="12" />
  </company>
  <company Id="0adcf278-ccd3-4c3d-a78a-27aa35dc2756"
      CompanyName="Contoso">
    <employee Id="bc431c32-5397-47b6-9a16-0667be455f02"
        coId="0adcf278-ccd3-4c3d-a78a-27aa35dc2756"
        LastName="SueLast" FirstName="SueFirst" Salary="20" />
    <employee Id="5822bf9f-49c1-42dd-95e0-5bb728c5ac60"
        coId="0adcf278-ccd3-4c3d-a78a-27aa35dc2756"
        LastName="TomLast" FirstName="TomFirst" Salary="68" />
    <employee Id="1b2334a4-e339-4255-b826-c0453fda7e61"
        coId="0adcf278-ccd3-4c3d-a78a-27aa35dc2756"
        LastName="MikeLast" FirstName="MikeFirst" Salary="18.99" />
  </company>
</CompanyList>
```

In the example, the XML file is written, but the XML file contains no information that describes the data types of the data. When not specified, the default data type for all data is *string*. If the XML file is read into a new *DataSet*, all data, including *DateTime* data and numeric data, is loaded as string data. Use the *XmlWriteMode.WriteSchema* enumeration value when saving because it stores the data type information with the XML file, as shown in the following code snippet:

```
'VB
'write to xml file with schema
companyList.WriteXml( _
    MapPath("CompanyListNestedWithSchema.xml"), _
    XmlWriteMode.WriteSchema)
```

```
//C#
//write to xml file with schema
companyList.WriteXml(
    MapPath("CompanyListNestedWithSchema.xml"),
    XmlWriteMode.WriteSchema);
```

The XML file is substantially larger than what's presented here. Instead of embedding the schema in the XML file, you can create a separate XSD file to load before loading the data. You can use the *DataSet* object's *WriteXmlSchema* method to extract the XML schema definition to a separate file, as shown here:

```
'VB
'write to xsd file
companyList.WriteXmlSchema( _
    MapPath("CompanyListSchema.xsd"))
```

```
//C#
//write to xsd file
companyList.WriteXmlSchema(
    MapPath("CompanyListSchema.xsd"));
```

Serializing a Changed *DataSet* Object as a DiffGram   A *DiffGram* is an XML document that contains all of the data from your *DataSet* object, including the original *DataRow* object information. To save as a DiffGram, use the *XmlWriteMode.DiffGram* enumeration value when serializing a *DataSet* object. This snippet shows the creation of company rows with changes that make it so that one is inserted, one is updated, one is deleted, and one is unchanged. Then the *DataSet* is written as a DiffGram.

```
'VB
Protected Sub Button8_Click(ByVal sender As Object, _
    ByVal e As System.EventArgs) Handles Button8.Click
        'get the dataset and populate
    Dim companyList As DataSet = GetDataSet()
    Dim company as DataTable = companyList.Tables("company")
    company.Rows.Add(Guid.NewGuid(), "UnchangedCompany")
    company.Rows.Add(Guid.NewGuid(), "ModifiedCompany")
    company.Rows.Add(Guid.NewGuid(), "DeletedCompany")
```

```
        companyList.AcceptChanges()
        company.Rows(1)("CompanyName") = "ModifiedCompany1"
        company.Rows(2).Delete()
        company.Rows.Add(Guid.NewGuid(), "AddedCompany")

        'format xml
        companyList.Relations("Company_Employee").Nested = True
        For Each dt As DataTable In companyList.Tables
            For Each dc As DataColumn In dt.Columns
                dc.ColumnMapping = MappingType.Attribute
            Next
        Next

        'write to xml diffgram file
        companyList.WriteXml( _
            MapPath("companyListDiffGram.xml"), XmlWriteMode.DiffGram)

        'display file
        Response.Redirect("companyListDiffGram.xml")
    End Sub

//C#
protected void Button8_Click(object sender, EventArgs e)
{
    //get the dataset and populate
    DataSet companyList = GetDataSet();
    DataTable company = companyList.Tables["company"];
    company.Rows.Add(Guid.NewGuid(), "UnchangedCompany");
    company.Rows.Add(Guid.NewGuid(), "ModifiedCompany");
    company.Rows.Add(Guid.NewGuid(), "DeletedCompany");
    companyList.AcceptChanges();
    company.Rows[1]["CompanyName"] = "ModifiedCompany1";
    company.Rows[2].Delete();
    company.Rows.Add(Guid.NewGuid(), "AddedCompany");

    //format xml
    companyList.Relations["Company_Employee"].Nested = true;
    foreach (DataTable dt in companyList.Tables)
    {
        foreach (DataColumn dc in dt.Columns)
        {
            dc.ColumnMapping = MappingType.Attribute;
        }
    }

    //write to xml diffgram file
    companyList.WriteXml(
        MapPath("CompanyListDiffGram.xml"), XmlWriteMode.DiffGram);
```

```
    //display file
    Response.Redirect("CompanyListDiffGram.xml");
}
```

The DiffGram is mostly used in an environment where a user occasionally connects to a database to synchronize a disconnected *DataSet* object with the current information that is contained in the database. When the user is not connected to the database, the *DataSet* object is stored locally as a DiffGram to ensure that you still have the original data, because the original data is needed when it's time to send your changes back to the database.

The DiffGram contains all of the *DataRowVersion* information, as shown in the following XML document. Company1 has not been modified. Notice that Company2 has been modified, and its status is indicated as such. Also notice that the bottom of the XML document contains the original information for *DataRow* objects that have been modified or deleted. This XML document also shows Company3 as deleted because Company3 has "before" information but not current information. Company4 is an inserted *DataRow* object as indicated, so this *DataRow* object has no "before" information.

```xml
<?xml version="1.0" standalone="yes"?>
<diffgr:diffgram xmlns:msdata="urn:schemas-microsoft-com:xml-msdata"
      xmlns:diffgr="urn:schemas-microsoft-com:xml-diffgram-v1">
  <CompanyList>
    <company diffgr:id="company1" msdata:rowOrder="0"
        Id="09b8482c-e801-4c63-82f6-0f5527b3768b"
        CompanyName="UnchangedCompany" />
    <company diffgr:id="company2" msdata:rowOrder="1"
        diffgr:hasChanges="modified"
        Id="8f9eceb3-b6de-4da7-84dd-d99a278a23ee"
        CompanyName="ModifiedCompany1" />
    <company diffgr:id="company4" msdata:rowOrder="3"
        diffgr:hasChanges="inserted"
        Id="65d28892-b8af-4392-8b64-718a612f6aa7"
        CompanyName="AddedCompany" />
  </CompanyList>
  <diffgr:before>
    <company diffgr:id="company2" msdata:rowOrder="1"
        Id="8f9eceb3-b6de-4da7-84dd-d99a278a23ee"
        CompanyName="ModifiedCompany" />
    <company diffgr:id="company3" msdata:rowOrder="2"
        Id="89b576d2-60ae-4c36-ba96-c4a7a8966a6f"
        CompanyName="DeletedCompany" />
  </diffgr:before>
</diffgr:diffgram>
```

Deserializing a *DataSet* from XML   You can deserialize an XML file or stream into a *DataSet* object by loading the schema and reading the stream. You can use the following code to read the schema file and the load the XML file:

```vb
'VB
Protected Sub Button9_Click(ByVal sender As Object, _
        ByVal e As System.EventArgs) Handles Button9.Click
    'add grids to form
    Dim gvCompany As GridView = GetGridView(275, 20)
    Dim gvEmployee As GridView = GetGridView(275, 125)

    'get the dataset and populate schema
    Dim companyList as new DataSet()
    companyList.ReadXmlSchema(MapPath("CompanyListSchema.xsd"))
    'populate from file
    companyList.ReadXml(MapPath("CompanyListNested.xml"))

    'display
    gvCompany.DataSource = companyList
    gvCompany.DataMember = "Company"
    gvEmployee.DataSource = companyList
    gvEmployee.DataMember = "Employee"
    gvCompany.DataBind()
    gvEmployee.DataBind()
End Sub
```

```csharp
//C#
protected void Button9_Click(object sender, EventArgs e)
{
    //add grids to form
    GridView gvCompany = GetGridView(275, 20);
    GridView gvEmployee = GetGridView(275, 125);

    //get the dataset and populate schema
    DataSet companyList = new DataSet();
    companyList.ReadXmlSchema(MapPath("CompanyListSchema.xsd"));
    //populate from file
    companyList.ReadXml(MapPath("CompanyListNested.xml"));

    //display
    gvCompany.DataSource = companyList;
    gvCompany.DataMember = "Company";
    gvEmployee.DataSource = companyList;
    gvEmployee.DataMember = "Employee";
    gvCompany.DataBind();
    gvEmployee.DataBind();
}
```

When reading an XML file, you can optionally pass an *XmlReadMode* enumeration value. If this value is not passed, the default is *XmlReadMode.IgnoreSchema*. This means that if the XML data file contains an XML schema definition, it is ignored. Listed below are the other options of the *XmlReadMode* enumeration:

- **Auto** The XML source is examined by the *ReadXml* method and the appropriate mode is selected.

- **DiffGram** If the *XmlFile* contains a *DiffGram*, the changes are applied to the *DataSet* using the same semantics that the *Merge* method uses. (*Merge* is covered in more detail in the next section.)

- **Fragment** This option causes the XML to be read as a fragment. Fragments can contain multiple root elements. *FOR XML* in SQL Server is an example of something that produces fragments.

- **IgnoreSchema** This causes any schema that is defined within the XML data file to be ignored.

- **InferSchema** Using this option, the XML file is read, and the *DataTable* objects and *DataColumn* objects are created based on the data. If the *DataSet* currently has *DataTable* objects and *DataColumn* objects, they are used and extended to accommodate new tables and columns that exist in the XML document, but don't exist in the *DataSet* object. All data types of all *DataColumn* objects are a string.

- **InferTypedSchema** Using this option, the XML file is read, and the schema is created based on the data. An attempt is made to identify the data type of each column, but if the data type cannot be identified, it is a string.

- **ReadSchema** Using this option, the XML file is read, and then embedded schema is searched for. If the *DataSet* already has *DataTable* objects with the same name, an exception is thrown. All other existing tables remain.

Inferring a schema simply means that the *DataSet* attempts to create a schema for the data based on looking for patterns of XML elements and attributes.

Serializing the *DataSet* Object as Binary Data The size of an XML file that is produced when serializing a *DataSet* object can cause problems with resources, such as memory and drive space or bandwidth, when you move this data across the network. If XML is not required and you want the best performance, the *DataSet* can be serialized as a binary file. The following code snippet writes the contents of the *vendorData DataSet* that we previously defined and populated to a binary file:

```vb
'VB
'Added the following Imports statements to the top of the file
Imports System.Runtime.Serialization.Formatters.Binary
Imports System.IO

Protected Sub Button10_Click(ByVal sender As Object, _
        ByVal e As System.EventArgs) Handles Button10.Click
    'get dataset and populate
    'get the dataset and populate
    Dim companyList As DataSet = GetDataSet()
    PopulateDataSet(companyList)

    'set output to binary else this will be xml
    companyList.RemotingFormat = SerializationFormat.Binary

    'write to binary file
    Using fs As New FileStream( _
        MapPath("CompanyList.bin"), FileMode.Create)
    Dim fmt As New BinaryFormatter()
    fmt.Serialize(fs, companyList)
End Using

    'feedback
    Dim lbl As Label = GetLabel(275, 20)
    lbl.Text = "File Saved."

End Sub
```

```csharp
//C#
//Added the following using statements to the top of the file
using System.Runtime.Serialization.Formatters.Binary;
using System.IO;

protected void Button10_Click(object sender, EventArgs e)
{
    //get dataset and populate
    //get the dataset and populate
    DataSet companyList = GetDataSet();
    PopulateDataSet(companyList);

    //set output to binary else this will be xml
    companyList.RemotingFormat = SerializationFormat.Binary;

    //write to binary file
    using (FileStream fs =
        new FileStream(MapPath("CompanyList.bin"), FileMode.Create))
    {
```

```
        BinaryFormatter fmt = new BinaryFormatter();
        fmt.Serialize(fs, companyList);
    }

    //feedback
    Label lbl = GetLabel(275, 20);
    lbl.Text = "File Saved.";
}
```

NOTE   New in ADO.NET 2.0

The *RemotingFormat* property, which provides true binary serialization, is new in ADO.NET 2.0.

The *DataSet* object's *RemotingFormat* property must be set to ensure binary serialization. This property is also available on the *DataTable* object for scenarios where only a single *DataTable* is to be binary serialized. Be careful when making the choice to serialize as XML or binary, because binary files contain more initial overhead (about 20 kilobytes) than XML files. For large *DataSet* objects, binary serialization always produces a smaller file, but for small *DataSet* objects, binary serialization may not produce the desired result.

Deserializing a *DataSet* from Binary Data   You can easily deserialize the binary data file that we created in the previous example into a *DataSet* from a file or stream. The *BinaryFormatter* stores the schema automatically, so there is no need to load a schema first. The *BinaryFormatter* automatically identifies the file as having been saved as *BinaryXml*. You can use the following code to load the binary file and display the *companyList*:

```
'VB
Protected Sub Button11_Click(ByVal sender As Object, _
        ByVal e As System.EventArgs) Handles Button11.Click
    'add grids to form
    Dim gvCompany As GridView = GetGridView(275, 20)
    Dim gvEmployee As GridView = GetGridView(275, 125)

    'get the dataset from the file
    Dim companyList As DataSet
    Using fs As New FileStream( _
            MapPath("CompanyList.bin"), FileMode.Open)
        Dim fmt As New BinaryFormatter()
        companyList = CType(fmt.Deserialize(fs), DataSet)
    End Using

    'display
    gvCompany.DataSource = companyList
```

```
    gvCompany.DataMember = "Company"
    gvEmployee.DataSource = companyList
    gvEmployee.DataMember = "Employee"
    gvCompany.DataBind()
    gvEmployee.DataBind()
End Sub
```

```
//C#
protected void Button11_Click(object sender, EventArgs e)
{
    //add grids to form
    GridView gvCompany = GetGridView(275, 20);
    GridView gvEmployee = GetGridView(275, 125);

    //get the dataset from the file
    DataSet companyList;
    using (FileStream fs = new FileStream(
        MapPath("CompanyList.bin"), FileMode.Open))
    {
        BinaryFormatter fmt = new BinaryFormatter();
        companyList = (DataSet)fmt.Deserialize(fs);
    }

    //display
    gvCompany.DataSource = companyList;
    gvCompany.DataMember = "Company";
    gvEmployee.DataSource = companyList;
    gvEmployee.DataMember = "Employee";
    gvCompany.DataBind();
    gvEmployee.DataBind();
}
```
Using Merge to Combine DataSet Data

On many occasions, data available in one *DataSet* must be combined with another *DataSet*. For example, an expense application might need to combine serialized *DataSet* objects (expense reports) received by e-mail from a number of people. It's also common within an application and (based on the user clicking Update) can merge the modified version back to the original *DataSet*.

The *Merge* method on the *DataSet* is used to combine data from multiple *DataSet* objects. The *Merge* method has several overloads that allow data to be merged from *DataSet, DataTable,* or *DataRow* objects. The following code example demonstrates how to use the *Merge* method to combine changes from one *DataSet* into another *DataSet*:

```
'VB
Protected Sub Button12_Click(ByVal sender As Object, _
    ByVal e As System.EventArgs) Handles Button12.Click
```

```vb
    'add grids to form
    Dim gvcompany As GridView = GetGridView(275, 20)
    Dim gvemployee As GridView = GetGridView(275, 125)

    'get the dataset
    Dim original As DataSet = GetDataSet()
    'add AdventureWorks
    original.Tables("Company").Rows.Add( _
        Guid.NewGuid(), "AdventureWorks")

    'copy the dataset
    Dim copy as DataSet = original.Copy()

    'modify the copy
    Dim aw as DataRow = copy.Tables("Company").Rows(0)
    aw("CompanyName") = "AdventureWorks Changed"
    Dim empId as Guid
    empId = Guid.NewGuid()
    copy.Tables("Employee").Rows.Add(empId, aw("Id"), _
        "MarkLast", "MarkFirst", 90.00)
    empId = Guid.NewGuid()
    copy.Tables("Employee").Rows.Add(empId, aw("Id"), _
        "SueLast", "SueFirst", 41.00)

    'merge changes back to the original
    original.Merge(copy, False, MissingSchemaAction.AddWithKey)

    'display
    gvcompany.DataSource = original
    gvcompany.DataMember = "company"
    gvemployee.DataSource = original
    gvemployee.DataMember = "employee"
    gvcompany.DataBind()
    gvemployee.DataBind()
End Sub
```

```csharp
//C#
protected void Button12_Click(object sender, EventArgs e)
{
    //add grids to form
    GridView gvcompany = GetGridView(275, 20);
    GridView gvemployee = GetGridView(275, 125);

    //get the dataset
    DataSet original = GetDataSet();
    //add AdventureWorks
    original.Tables["Company"].Rows.Add(
        Guid.NewGuid(), "AdventureWorks");

    //copy the dataset
    DataSet copy = original.Copy();
```

```
    //modify the copy
    DataRow aw = copy.Tables["Company"].Rows[0];
    aw["CompanyName"] = "AdventureWorks Changed";
    Guid empId;
    empId = Guid.NewGuid();
    copy.Tables["Employee"].Rows.Add(empId, aw["Id"],
        "MarkLast", "MarkFirst", 90.00m);
    empId = Guid.NewGuid();
    copy.Tables["employee"].Rows.Add(empId, aw["Id"],
        "SueLast", "SueFirst", 41.00m);

    //merge changes back to the original
    original.Merge(copy, false, MissingSchemaAction.AddWithKey);

    //display
    gvcompany.DataSource = original;
    gvcompany.DataMember = "Company";
    gvemployee.DataSource = original;
    gvemployee.DataMember = "Employee";
    gvcompany.DataBind();
    gvemployee.DataBind();
}
```

The *Merge* method is always called on the *DataSet* that you will merge into; it takes three parameters, and is then called. The first parameter is the *Copy* object. The second parameter is a Boolean called *preserveChanges*, which specifies whether updates from the copy *DataSet* should overwrite changes made in the original object. The last parameter is a *MissingSchemaAction* enumeration member. The *AddSchemaWithKey* is selected, which means that if a new *DataTable* is added to the copy *DataSet* object, the new *DataTable* and its data are added to the original *DataSet* object. The following is a list of the *MissingSchemaAction* enumeration members:

- **Add** Adds the necessary *DataTable* and *DataColumn* objects to complete the schema.

- **AddWithPrimaryKey** Adds the necessary *DataTable*, *DataColumn*, and *PrimaryKey* objects to complete the schema.

- **Error** Shows when an exception is thrown if a *DataColumn* does not exist in the *DataSet* that is being updated.

- **Ignore** Ignores data that resides in *DataColumns* that are not in the *DataSet* being updated.

When you use the *Merge* method, make sure each of the *DataTable* objects has a primary key. Failure to set the *PrimaryKey* property of the *DataTable* object results in a *DataRow* object being appended rather than an existing *DataRow* object being modified.

Quick Check

1. When working with disconnected data, what primary data object must you always have at least one of?

2. You have a *DataSet* with *Order* and *OrderDetail DataTable* objects. You want to be able to retrieve the *OrderDetail* rows for a specific *Order*. What data object can you use to navigate from the *Order* row to the *OrderDetail* rows?

3. You want to save a *DataSet* object to an XML file, but you are concerned that you may lose the original version of the *DataRow* object. How should you save the *DataSet* object?

Quick Check Answers

1. A *DataTable* object.

2. The *DataRelation* object.

3. Save it as a DiffGram.

Lab: Working with Disconnected Data

In this lab, you create and use a typed *DataSet* that you add graphically to your Web site. This *DataSet* populates a *GridView* control with *Customer* rows.

▶ **Exercise 1: Create the Web Site and the Typed *DataSet***

In this exercise, you create the Web site and add the controls to the site.

1. Open Visual Studio 2005 and create a new Web site called **WorkingWith DisconnectedData,** using your preferred programming language. The new Web site is created, and a Web page called Default.aspx is displayed.

2. In the Solution Explorer, add a typed *DataSet* graphically by right-clicking the Web site project and selecting Add New Item. Select *DataSet*, name the *DataSet* **Sales.xsd,** and click OK. When prompted to create the App_Code folder, click Yes. You will also be prompted to select a database connection; click Cancel.

3. Drag a *DataTable* from the ToolBox and drop it onto the DataSet Editor surface.

4. Select the *DataTable.* In the Properties window, set the name of the *DataTable* to **Customer**.

5. Add the following columns to the Customer Table by right-clicking the *Data-Table*, selecting Add, and selecting Column.

Column Name	Data Type
Id	*System.Guid*
CustomerName	*System.String*

6. Close and save the Sales type instance called *DataSet*.

▶ **Exercise 2: Add *GridView* and *DataSet***

In this exercise, you add a *GridView* control to the Default.aspx page. In the code-behind page, you instantiate the *Sales DataSet*, populate it, and bind it to the *GridView* control.

1. Open the Web site that you created in Exercise 1. Alternatively, you can open the completed Lesson 1, Exercise 1 project from the CD.

2. Add a *GridView* control to the Default.aspx Web page. Regardless of the language you choose, your .aspx source for the form element should look like the following:

```
<form id="form1" runat="server">
    <div>
        <asp:GridView ID="GridView1" runat="server"
            Style="z-index: 100; left: 55px; position: absolute;top: 15px">
        </asp:GridView>
    </div>
</form>
```

3. Double-click an empty location on the Web page to go to the code-behind page. In the code-behind page, add code to create and populate an instance of the *Sales DataSet*, and assign the *DataSet* object to the *GridView*. This code only needs to execute when the page is not being posted back and should look like the following:

```
'VB
Partial Class _Default
    Inherits System.Web.UI.Page

    Protected Sub Page_Load(ByVal sender As Object, _
            ByVal e As System.EventArgs) Handles Me.Load
        If Not IsPostBack Then
            Dim salesDataSet As New Sales()
            salesDataSet.Customer.Rows.Add(Guid.NewGuid(), "Acme")
            salesDataSet.Customer.Rows.Add(Guid.NewGuid(), "Northwind Traders")
            salesDataSet.Customer.Rows.Add(Guid.NewGuid(), "TailSpin Toys")
            salesDataSet.Customer.Rows.Add(Guid.NewGuid(), "Coho Winery")
            salesDataSet.Customer.Rows.Add(Guid.NewGuid(), "Litware, Inc.")
            GridView1.DataSource = salesDataSet
            GridView1.DataMember = "Customer"
```

```
        DataBind()
    End If
  End Sub
End Class

//C#
using System;
using System.Data;
using System.Configuration;
using System.Web;
using System.Web.Security;
using System.Web.UI;
using System.Web.UI.WebControls;
using System.Web.UI.WebControls.WebParts;
using System.Web.UI.HtmlControls;

public partial class _Default : System.Web.UI.Page
{
    protected void Page_Load(object sender, EventArgs e)
    {
        if (!IsPostBack)
        {
            Sales salesDataSet = new Sales();
            salesDataSet.Customer.Rows.Add(Guid.NewGuid(), "Acme");
            salesDataSet.Customer.Rows.Add(Guid.NewGuid(), "Northwind Traders");
            salesDataSet.Customer.Rows.Add(Guid.NewGuid(), "TailSpin Toys");
            salesDataSet.Customer.Rows.Add(Guid.NewGuid(), "Coho Winery");
            salesDataSet.Customer.Rows.Add(Guid.NewGuid(), "Litware, Inc.");
            GridView1.DataSource = salesDataSet;
            GridView1.DataMember = "Customer";
            DataBind();
        }
    }
}
```

4. Run the Web page. Figure 4-10 shows the results.

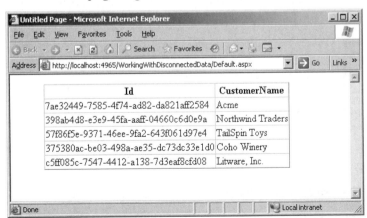

Figure 4-10 The typed *DataSet* is populated and bound to the *GridView* control.

Lesson Summary

- This lesson provides a detailed overview of ADO.NET's disconnected classes. When you work with disconnected data, a *DataTable* object is always a requirement.

- The *DataTable* object contains *DataColumn* objects, which define the schema, and *DataRow* objects, which contain the data. *DataRow* objects have *RowState* and *DataRowVersion* properties.

- You use the *RowState* property to indicate whether the *DataRow* should be inserted, updated, or deleted from the data store if the data is ever persisted to a database.

- The *DataRow* object can contain up to three copies of its data, based on the *DataRowVersion*. This feature allows the data to be rolled back to its original state, and you can use it when you write code to handle conflict resolution.

- The *DataSet* object is an in-memory, relational data representation. The *DataSet* object contains a collection of *DataTable* objects and a collection of *DataRelation* objects.

- *DataSet* and *DataTable* objects can be serialized and deserialized to and from a binary or XML file or stream. Data from other *DataSet*, *DataTable*, and *DataRow* objects can be merged into a *DataSet* object.

Lesson Review

You can use the following questions to test your knowledge of the information in Lesson 1, "Using the ADO.NET Disconnected Classes." The questions are also available on the companion CD if you prefer to review them in electronic form.

NOTE Answers

Answers to these questions and explanations of why each answer choice is right or wrong are located in the "Answers" section at the end of the book.

---

1. You have a *DataSet* containing a *Customer DataTable* and an *Order DataTable*. You want to easily navigate from an *Order DataRow* to the *Customer* who placed the order. What object will allow you to easily navigate from the *Order* to the *Customer*?

   A. The *DataColumn* object

   B. The *DataTable* object

    C. The *DataRow* object

    D. The *DataRelation* object

2. Which of the following is a requirement when merging modified data into a *DataSet*?

    A. A primary key must be defined on the *DataTable* objects.

    B. The *DataSet* schemas must match in order to merge.

    C. The destination *DataSet* must be empty prior to merging.

    D. A *DataSet* must be merged into the same *DataSet* that created it.

3. You are working with a *DataSet* and want to be able to display data, sorted different ways. How do you do so?

    A. Use the *Sort* method on the *DataTable* object.

    B. Use the *DataSet* object's *Sort* method.

    C. Use a *DataView* object for each sort.

    D. Create a *DataTable* for each sort, using the *DataTable* object's *Copy* method, and then *Sort* the result.

Lesson 2: Using the ADO.NET Connected Classes

The ADO.NET libraries contain *provider classes*, which are classes that you can use to transfer data between a data store and the client application. There are many different kinds of data stores, meaning that there is a need for specialized code to provide the necessary bridge between the disconnected data access classes and a particular data store. The provider classes fulfill this need.

This lesson focuses on these specialized classes, starting with the most essential, such as *DbConnection* and *DbCommand,* and concludes with the more elaborate classes that have been added in ADO.NET 2.0, such as *DbProviderFactory* and *DbProviderFactories.*

After this lesson, you will be able to:

■ Identify and use the following connected data classes in your Web application:

❑ *DbConnection*

❑ *DbCommand*

❑ *DbDataAdapter*

❑ *DbProviderFactory*

❑ *DbProviderFactories*

Estimated lesson time: 60 minutes

Using Provider Classes to Move Data

The classes that are responsible for the movement of data between the disconnected data classes in the client application and the data store are referred to as connected classes or provider classes. The Microsoft .NET Framework contains the following providers:

■ **OleDb**   Contains classes that provide general-purpose data access to many data sources. You can use this provider to access SQL Server 6.5 (and earlier versions), SyBase, DB2/400, and Microsoft Access.

■ **Odbc**   Contains classes for general-purpose data access to many data sources. This provider is typically used when no newer provider is available.

■ **SQL Server**   Contains classes that provide functionality similar to the generic *OleDb* provider. The difference is that these classes are tuned for SQL Server 7.0 and later data access. SQL Server 6.5 and earlier must use the *OleDb* provider.

■ *Oracle* Contains classes for accessing Oracle 8i and later servers. This provider is similar to the *OleDb* provider but provides better performance.

You can also use third-party providers, such as *DB2* and *MySql*, which you can download from the Web.

Table 4-1 lists the primary provider classes and interfaces. The classes are subclassed by the provider, which replaces the *Db* prefix with a provider prefix, such as *Sql, Oracle, Odbc,* or *OleDb*. You can use the base classes with factory classes to create client code that is not provider-specific. The following sections describe many of these classes.

Table 4-1 Primary Provider Classes and Interfaces in ADO.NET

Base Classes	*SqlClient* Classes	Generic Interface
DbConnection	*SqlConnection*	*IDbConnection*
DbCommand	*SqlCommand*	*IDbCommand*
DbDataReader	*SqlDataReader*	*IDataReader/IDataRecord*
DbTransaction	*SqlTransaction*	*IDbTransaction*
DbParameter	*SqlParameter*	*IDbDataParameter*
DbParameterCollection	*SqlParameterCollection*	*IDataParameterCollection*
DbDataAdapter	*SqlDataAdapter*	*IDbDataAdapter*
DbCommandBuilder	*SqlCommandBuilder*	
DbConnectionString-Builder	*SqlConnectionStringBuilder*	
DBDataPermission	*SqlPermission*	

Getting Started with the *DbConnection* Object

To access a data store, you need a valid, open connection object. The *DbConnection* class is an abstract class that the provider-specific connection classes inherit from. The connection class hierarchy is shown in Figure 4-11.

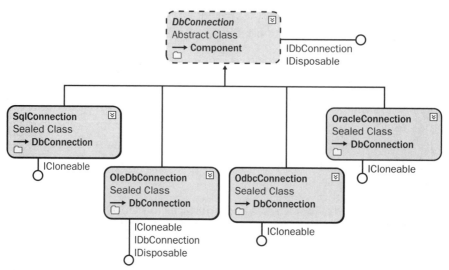

Figure 4-11   The *DbConnection* class hierarchy.

To create a connection, you must have a valid connection string. The following code snippet shows how to create the connection object and then assign the connection string. When you are finished working with the connection object, you must close the connection to free up the resources being held. The *pubs* sample database is used in this example. The *pubs* and *Northwind* sample databases are available from the Microsoft download site and are also included on the sample disc.

```vb
'VB
Dim connection as DbConnection = new SqlConnection()
connection.ConnectionString = _
   "Server=.;Database=pubs;Trusted_Connection=true"
connection.Open()
'Do lots of cool work here
connection.Close()
```

```csharp
//C#
DbConnection connection = new SqlConnection();
connection.ConnectionString =
   "Server=.;Database=pubs;Trusted_Connection=true";
connection.Open();
   //Do lots of cool work here
connection.Close();
```

Creating an instance of the *SqlConnection* class using the SQL Server .NET provider creates the *DbConnection*. The *ConnectionString* property is initialized to use the local machine (".") and the database is set to *pubs*. Lastly, the connection uses a trusted connection for authentication when connecting to SQL Server.

The connection must be opened before you can send commands to the data store, and you must always close the connection when you're done to prevent orphaned connections to the data store. You can close the connection by executing the *Close* method or by executing the *Dispose* method. It's common to create a "using" block to force the *Dispose* method to execute, as shown in the following code snippet.

NOTE   New in ASP.NET 2.0

The using block is new to Visual Basic in 2.0 of the .NET Framework, but it has always been in C#.

```
'VB
using (connection)
   connection.Open()
   'cool commands here...
End Using
```

```
//C#
using (connection)
{
   connection.Open();
   //cool commands here...
}
```

You can place the using block inside a try/catch block to force the connection to be disposed, which typically provides a cleaner implementation than the try/catch/finally block.

Regardless of the programming language used, the connection string is the same. The following sections explain how to configure a connection string using each of the .NET providers.

Configuring an ODBC Connection String   Open Database Connectivity (ODBC) is one of the older technologies that the .NET Framework supports, primarily because there are still many scenarios where the .NET Framework is required to connect to older database products that have ODBC drivers. Table 4-2 describes the most common ODBC connection string settings.

Table 4-2   **ODBC Connection String Keywords**

Keyword	Description
Driver	The ODBC driver to use for the connection.

Table 4-2   ODBC Connection String Keywords

Keyword	Description
DSN	A data source name, which can be configured via Control Panel | Administrative Tools | Data Sources (ODBC).
Server	The name of the server to connect to.
Trusted_Connection	A description that specifies what security is based on using the domain account of the currently logged-on user.
Database	The database to connect to.
DBQ	Typically, the physical path to a data source.

Working with Sample ODBC Connection Strings   The following connection string instructs the text driver to treat the files that are located in the C:\Sample\MySample-Folder subdirectory as tables in a database.

```
Driver={Microsoft Text Driver (*.txt; *.csv)};
   DBQ=C:\\Sample\\MySampleFolder;
```

The following connection string instructs the Access driver to open the *Northwind* database file that is located in the C:\Program Files\mySampleFolder folder.

```
Driver={Microsoft Access Driver (*.mdb)};
   DBQ=C:\\program files\\mySampleApp\\northwind.mdb
```

The following connection string uses the settings that have been configured as a data source name (DSN) on the current machine.

```
DSN=My Application DataSource
```

The following is a connection to an Oracle database on the ORACLE8i7 servers. The name and password are passed in as well.

```
Driver={Microsoft ODBC for Oracle};
   Server=ORACLE8i7;
   UID=john;
   PWD=s3$W%1Xz
```

The following connection string uses the Excel driver to open the MyBook.xls file.

```
Driver={Microsoft Excel Driver (*.xls)};
   DBQ=C:\\Samples\\MyBook.xls
```

The following connection string uses the SQL Server driver to open the *Northwind* database on MyServer using the passed-in user name and password.

```
DRIVER={SQL Server};
   SERVER=MyServer;
   UID=AppUserAccount;
   PWD=Zx%7$ha;
   DATABASE=northwind;
```

This connection string uses the SQL Server driver to open the *Northwind* database on MyServer using SQL Server's trusted security.

```
DRIVER={SQL Server};
   SERVER=MyServer;
   Trusted_Connection=yes
   DATABASE=northwind;
```

Configuring an OLEDB Connection String   Another common, but older, technology that is used to access databases is Object Linking and Embedding for Databases (OLEDB). Table 4-3 describes the most common OLEDB connection string settings.

Table 4-3   OLEDB Connection String Keywords

Keyword	Description
Data Source	The name of the database or physical location of the database file.
File Name	The physical location of a file that contains the real connection string.
Persist Security Info	A setting which, if set to *true*, retrieves the connection string and returns the complete connection string that was originally provided. If set to *false*, the connection string contains the information that was originally provided, minus the security information.
Provider	The vendor-specific driver to use for connecting to the data store.

Working with Sample OLEDB Connection Strings   This connection string uses the settings stored in the MyAppData.udl file. (The .udl extension stands for universal data link.)

```
FILE NAME=C:\Program Files\MyApp\MyAppData.udl
```

This connection string uses the Jet driver, which is the Access driver, and opens the demo database file. Retrieving the connection string from the connection returns the connection that was originally passed in, minus the security information.

```
Provider=Microsoft.Jet.OLEDB.4.0;
   Data Source=C:\Program Files\myApp\demo.mdb;
   Persist Security Info=False
```

Configuring a SQL Server Connection String   The SQL Server provider allows you to access SQL Server 7.0 and later. If you need to connect to SQL Server 6.5 and earlier, use the OLEDB provider. Table 4-4 describes the most common SQL Server connection string settings.

Table 4-4   SQL Server Connection String Keywords

Keyword	Description
Data Source, addr, address, network address, server	The name or IP address of the database server.
Failover Partner	A support provider for database mirroring in SQL Server 2005.
AttachDbFilename, extended properties, initial file name	The full or relative path and name of a file containing the database to be attached to. The path supports the keyword string |*DataDirectory*|, which points to the application's data directory. The database must reside on a local drive. The log file name must be in the format <database-File-Name>_log.ldf or it will not be found. If the log file is not found, a new log file is created.
Initial Catalog, database	The name of the database to use.

Table 4-4   SQL Server Connection String Keywords

Keyword	Description
Integrated Security, trusted_connection	A secure connection to SQL Server, in which authentication is via the user's domain account. Can be set to *true*, *false*, or *sspi*. The default is false.
Persist Security Info, persistsecurityinfo	A setting that, if set to *true*, causes a retrieval of the connection string to return the complete connection string that was originally provided. If set to *false*, the connection string contains the information that was originally provided, minus the security information. The default is false.
User ID, uid, user	The user name to use to connect to the SQL Server when not using a trusted connection.
Password, pwd	The password to use to log onto SQL Server when not using a trusted connection.
Enlist	When set to *true*, this pooler automatically enlists the connection into the caller thread's ongoing transaction context.
Pooling	A setting that, when set to *true*, causes the request for a new connection to be drawn from the pool. If the pool does not exist, one is created.
Max Pool Size	A setting that specifies the maximum allowed connections in the connection pool. The default is 100.
Min Pool Size	A setting that specifies the minimum number of connections to keep in the pool. The default is 0.
Asynchronous Processing, async	A setting that, when set to *true*, enables execution of asynchronous commands on the connection. (Synchronous commands should use a different connection to minimize resource usage.) The default is false.

Table 4-4   SQL Server Connection String Keywords

Keyword	Description
Connection Reset	A setting that, when set to *true*, indicates that the database connection is reset when the connection is removed from the pool. The default is true. A setting of false results in fewer round-trips to the server when creating a connection, but the connection state is not updated.
MultipleActiveResultSets	A setting that, when set to *true*, allows for the retrieval of multiple forward-only, read-only result sets on the same connection. The default is false.
Replication	A setting that is used by SQL Server for replication.
Connect Timeout, connection timeout, timeout	The time in seconds to wait while an attempt is made to connect to the data store. The default is 15 seconds.
Encrypt	A setting in which, if *Encrypt* is set to *true* and SQL Server has a certificate installed, all communication between the client and server is SSL-encrypted.
Load Balance Timeout, connection lifetime	The maximum time in seconds that a pooled connection should live. The maximum time is checked only when the connection is returned to the pool. This setting is useful in getting load-balanced cluster configurations to force a balance between a server that is online and a server that has just started. The default is 0.
Network Library, net, network	The network library DLL to use when connecting to SQL Server. Allowed libraries include dbmssocn (TCP/IP), dbnmpntw (Named Pipes), dbmsrpcn (Multiprotocol), dbmsadsn (Apple Talk), dbmsgnet (VIA), dbmsipcn (Shared Memory), and dbmsspxn (IPX/SPX). The default is dbmssocn (TCP/IP), but if a network is not specified and either "." or "(local)" is specified for the server, shared memory is used as the default.

Table 4-4 SQL Server Connection String Keywords

Keyword	Description
Packet Size	The size in bytes for each packet that is sent to SQL Server. The default is 8192.
Application Name, app	The name of the application. If not set, this defaults to .NET SQL Client Data Provider.
Current Language, language	The SQL Server language record name.
Workstation ID, wsid	The name of the client computer that is connecting to SQL Server.

Working with Sample SQL Server Connection Strings The following connection string connects to the *northwind* database on the current computer (localhost) using integrated security. This connection must be made within 30 seconds or an exception is thrown. The security information is not persisted.

```
Persist Security Info=False;
   Integrated Security=SSPI;
   database=northwind;
   server=localhost;
   Connect Timeout=30
```

This next connection string uses the TCP sockets library (DBMSSOCN) and connects to the *MyDbName* database on the computer located at IP address 192.168.1.5, using port 1433. Authentication is based on using MyUsername as the user name and u$2hJq@1 as the password.

```
Network Library=DBMSSOCN;
   Data Source=192.168.1.5,1433;
   Initial Catalog=MyDbName;
   User ID=myUsername;
   Password= u$2hJq@1
```

Attaching to a Local SQL Database File with SQL Express Microsoft SQL Server 2005 Express Edition is installed as part of the default Visual Studio 2005 installation, which makes it an excellent database to use when you're developing applications that are destined to be used on SQL Server 2005 Express Edition or SQL Server 2005. When you're building small Web sites and single-user applications, SQL Server 2005

Express Edition is a natural choice due to its XCOPY deployment capabilities, reliability, and high-performance engine. In addition, SQL Server 2005 Express Edition databases can easily be attached to SQL Server 2005. To attach a local database file, you can use the following connection string.

```
Data Source=.\SQLEXPRESS;
    AttachDbFilename=C:\MyApplication\PUBS.MDF;
    Integrated Security=True;
    User Instance=True
```

In this example, the Data Source is set to an instance of SQL Express called .\SQLEXPRESS. The database file name is set to the database file located at C:\MyApplication\PUBS.MDF. Note that the log file (PUBS_LOG.LDF) must also exist. Integrated security is used to authenticate with SQL Server 2005 Express Edition; setting User Instance to *true* starts an instance of SQL Server 2005 Express Edition using the current user's account.

Although you can use SQL Server to attach to a local file, SQL Server does not work with the User Instance=True setting. Also, SQL Server keeps the database attached when your application ends, so the next time you run SQL Server, an exception will be thrown because the data file is already attached.

AttachDBFilename can also understand the keyword |*DataDirectory*| to use the application's data directory. Here is the revised connection string.

```
Data Source=.\SQLEXPRESS;
    AttachDbFilename=|DataDirectory|\PUBS.MDF;
    Integrated Security=True;
    User Instance=True
```

For a Web application, the *DataDirectory* keyword resolves to the App_Data folder.

Storing the Connection String in the Web Configuration File   Connection strings should always be located outside your source code to simplify changes without requiring a recompile of your application. You can store connection strings in the machine or Web configuration file. You place the *<connectionStrings>* element under the *<configuration>* root element. This section supports the <add>, <remove>, and <clear> tags, as shown here:

```
<connectionStrings>
    <clear />
    <add name="PubsData"
        providerName="System.Data.SqlClient"
        connectionString=
        "Data Source=.\SQLEXPRESS;
```

```
                AttachDbFilename=|DataDirectory|PUBS.MDF;
                Integrated Security=True;
                User Instance=True"/>
</connectionStrings>
```

This example clears the list of *connectionStrings* that may have been defined in the machine configuration file, and then adds a new connection string setting called *Pubs-Data*. The *connectionStrings* can be accessed in code by using the static *Connection-Strings* collection on the *ConfigurationManager* class. In the following code sample, a *Label* control is dynamically created, the *PubsData* connection string is read from the Web.config file, and connection information is displayed in the *Label*:

```vb
'VB
Protected Sub Button1_Click(ByVal sender As Object, _
        ByVal e As System.EventArgs) Handles Button1.Click
    Dim lbl As Label = GetLabel(275, 20)
    'Get the settings from the configuration file
    Dim pubs As ConnectionStringSettings
    pubs = ConfigurationManager.ConnectionStrings("PubsData")
    'name = "PubsData"
    lbl.Text = "<p><b>Name:</b> " _
        + pubs.Name + "</p>"
    'provider = "System.Data.SqlClient"
    lbl.Text += "<p><b>Provider Name:</b> " _
        + pubs.ProviderName + "</p>"
    'cnString = "Data Source=.\SQLEXPRESS;
    '    AttachDbFilename=|DataDirectory|PUBS.MDF;
    '    Integrated Security=True;
    '    User Instance=True"
    lbl.Text += "<p><b>Connection String:</b> " _
        + pubs.ConnectionString + "</p>"
End Sub

Private Function GetLabel(ByVal left As Integer, _
        ByVal top As Integer) As Label
    Dim lbl As New Label()
    lbl.Style.Add("position", "absolute")
    lbl.Style.Add("left", left.ToString() + "px")
    lbl.Style.Add("top", top.ToString() + "px")
    lbl.EnableViewState = False
    form1.Controls.Add(lbl)
    Return lbl
End Function
```

```csharp
//C#
protected void Button1_Click(object sender, EventArgs e)
{
    Label lbl = GetLabel(275, 20);

    //Get the settings from the configuration file
```

```
        ConnectionStringSettings pubs =
            ConfigurationManager.ConnectionStrings["PubsData"];
        DbConnection connection = new SqlConnection(pubs.ConnectionString);
        //name = "PubsData"
        lbl.Text = "<p><b>Name:</b> "
            + pubs.Name + "</p>";
        //provider = "System.Data.SqlClient"
        lbl.Text += "<p><b>Provider Name:</b> "
            + pubs.ProviderName + "</p>";
        //cnString = "Data Source=.\SQLEXPRESS;
        //    AttachDbFilename=|DataDirectory|PUBS.MDF;
        //    Integrated Security=True;
        //    User Instance=True"
        lbl.Text += "<p><b>Connection String:</b> "
            + pubs.ConnectionString + "</p>";
    }

    private Label GetLabel(int left, int top)
    {
        Label lbl = new Label();
        lbl.Style.Add("position", "absolute");
        lbl.Style.Add("left", left.ToString() + "px");
        lbl.Style.Add("top", top.ToString() + "px");
        lbl.EnableViewState = false;
        form1.Controls.Add(lbl);
        return lbl;
    }
```

Working with Connection Pools   Creating and opening a connection to a data store can be a time-consuming and resource-intensive proposition, especially on Web-based systems, if you require separate connections to the data store on a user-by-user basis. It's easy to get into a situation where every user has one or more open connections to the database and the database server is consuming too many resources just managing connections. Ideally, the data store should be spending most of its time delivering data and as little time as possible maintaining connections. This is where connection pooling can help.

Connection pooling is the process of reusing existing active connections instead of creating new connections when a request is made to the database. It involves the use of a connection manager that is responsible for maintaining a list, or pool, of available connections. When the connection manager receives a request for a new connection, it checks its pool for available connections. If a connection is available, it is returned. If no connections are available, and the maximum pool size has not been reached, a new connection is created and returned. If the maximum pool size has been reached, the connection request is added to the queue and the next available connection is returned, as long as the connection timeout has not been reached.

Connection pooling is controlled by parameters placed into the connection string. The following is a list of parameters that affect pooling:

- **Connection Timeout** The time in seconds to wait while a connection to the data store is attempted. The default is 15 seconds.

- **Min Pool Size** The minimum amount of pooled connections to keep in the pool. The default is 0. It's usually good to set this to a low number, such as 5, when your application requires consistent, fast response—even if the application is inactive for long periods of time.

- **Max Pool Size** The maximum allowed number of connections in the connection pool. The default is 100, which is usually more than enough for most Web site applications.

- **Pooling** A setting in which a value of *true* causes the request for a new connection to be drawn from the pool. If the pool does not exist, it is created. The default is true.

- **Connection Reset** An indicator that the database connection is reset when the connection is removed from the pool. The default is true. A value of *false* results in fewer round-trips to the server when creating a connection, but the connection state is not updated.

- **Load Balancing Timeout, Connection Lifetime** The maximum time in seconds that a pooled connection should live. The maximum time is checked only when the connection is returned to the pool. This setting is useful in load-balanced cluster configurations to force a balance between a server that is online and a server that has just started. The default is 0.

- **Enlist** When this value is *true*, the connection is automatically enlisted into the creation thread's current transaction context. The default is true.

To implement connection pooling, you must follow a few rules:

- The connection string must be exactly the same, character-by-character, for every user or service that participates in the pool. Remember that each character must match in terms of lowercase and uppercase as well.

- The user ID must be the same for every user or service that participates in the pool. Even if you specify integrated security=true, the Windows user account of the process is used to determine pool membership.

- The process ID must be the same. It has never been possible to share connections across processes, and this limitation extends to pooling.

Where Is the Pool Located?   Connection pooling is a client-side technology, which means that the connection pool exists on the machine that initiates the *DbConnection* object's *Open* statement. The database server has no idea that there might be one or more connection pools involved in your application.

When Is the Pool Created?   A connection pool group is an object that manages the connection pools for a specific ADO.NET provider. When the first connection is instantiated, a connection pool group is created, but the first connection pool is not created until the first connection is opened.

Do Connections Stay in the Pool?   A connection is removed from the pool of available connections for use and then returned to the pool of available connections. When a connection is returned to the connection pool, it has a default idle lifetime of four to eight minutes, which is an intentionally random time span to ensure that idle connections are not held indefinitely. You can set the connection string's Min Pool Size to one or greater when you want to make sure that at least one connection is available when your application is idle for long periods.

Using the Load-Balancing Timeout   The connection string has a setting called the Load Balancing Timeout, which is also known as the Connection Lifetime. Connection Lifetime still exists for backward compatibility, but the new name better describes this setting's intended use. Use this setting only in an environment with clustered servers, because it's meant to aid in load-balancing database connections. This setting is only examined on closed connections. If the connection stays open longer than its Load Balancing Timeout setting, the connection is destroyed. Otherwise, the connection is added back into the pool.

The Load Balancing Timeout setting can be used to ensure that new connections are being created when you are using a database server cluster. If two database servers are clustered together and they appear heavily loaded, you may choose to add a third database server. After adding the third database server, you may notice that the original databases still seem overloaded and the new server has few or no connections.

The problem is that connection pooling is doing its job by maintaining connections to the existing database servers. Specify a Load Balancing Timeout setting that throws out some of the good connections so the new connection can go to the newly added database server. You lose a bit of performance because you destroy good connections, but the new connections potentially go to a new database server, which improves performance.

Using the Visual Studio 2005 GUI to Add a Connection   If you need to perform database-management tasks, you can add a connection to the database using the Server Explorer window and the Connection Wizard. A connection is automatically created for you for each database file that is added to your project, and you can also add connections manually. Figure 4-12 shows the Server Explorer window after the Pubs.mdf and Northwind.mdf files were added to the project, and after a connection was manually added to the *Northwind* database on the local copy of SQL Server 2005 by right-clicking the Connections node and selecting New Connection to start the Connection Wizard.

Figure 4-12   The Server Explorer window shows the connections that were added.

You can use the connection to perform maintenance, modify the database schema and data, and run queries. Also, controls such as the *SqlDataSource* allow you to select one of these connections when you add the control to the Web page.

Securing Connection Strings With Encryption   You store connections strings in your configuration files to make it easy to change the connection string without requiring a recompile of the application. The problem is that connection strings may contain login information such as user names and passwords.

The solution is to encrypt the connection string section of your configuration file by using the aspnet_regiis.exe utility. You can use the /? option to get help on the utility.

You encrypt and decrypt the contents of a Web.config file by using the System.Configuration.DPAPIProtectedConfigurationProvider, which uses the Windows Data Protection API (DPAPI) to encrypt and decrypt data, or the System.Configuration.RSAProtectedConfigurationProvider, which uses the RSA encryption algorithm to encrypt and decrypt data.

When you need to use the same encrypted configuration file on many computers in a Web farm, you must use the System.Configuration.RSAProtectedConfigurationProvider, which allows you to export the encryption keys used to encrypt the data. The encryption keys can be imported into another server. This is the default setting. A typical Web.config file might look like the following:

```
<?xml version="1.0"?>
<configuration xmlns="http://schemas.microsoft.com/.NetConfiguration/v2.0">
    <appSettings/>
    <connectionStrings>
        <add name="ConnectionString"
            connectionString="Data Source=.\SQLEXPRESS;
            AttachDbFilename=|DataDirectory|\northwnd.mdf;
            Integrated Security=True;User Instance=True"
            providerName="System.Data.SqlClient" />
    </connectionStrings>
    <system.web>
        ...
    </system.web>
</configuration>
```

The *connectionStrings* element can be encrypted by running the Visual Studio 2005 Command Prompt, executing the following command, and specifying the full path to your Web site folder:

```
aspnet_regiis -pef "connectionStrings" "C:\...\EncryptWebSite"
```

Note that the *–pef* switch requires you to pass the physical Web site path, which is the last parameter. Be sure to verify the path to your Web.config file. The encrypted Web.config file will look like the following:

```
<?xml version="1.0"?>
<configuration xmlns="http://schemas.microsoft.com/.NetConfiguration/v2.0">
    <protectedData>
        <protectedDataSections>
            <add name="connectionStrings"
                provider="RsaProtectedConfigurationProvider"
                inheritedByChildren="false" />
        </protectedDataSections>
    </protectedData>
    <appSettings/>
    <connectionStrings>
        <EncryptedData Type="http://www.w3.org/2001/04/xmlenc#Element"
        xmlns="http://www.w3.org/2001/04/xmlenc#">
            <EncryptionMethod
                Algorithm="http://www.w3.org/2001/04/xmlenc#tripledes-cbc" />
            <KeyInfo xmlns="http://www.w3.org/2000/09/xmldsig#">
                <EncryptedKey Recipient=""
                    xmlns="http://www.w3.org/2001/04/xmlenc#">
```

```
        <EncryptionMethod
            Algorithm="http://www.w3.org/2001/04/xmlenc#rsa-1_5" />
        <KeyInfo xmlns="http://www.w3.org/2000/09/xmldsig#">
            <KeyName>Rsa Key</KeyName>
        </KeyInfo>
        <CipherData>
<CipherValue>PPWA1TkWxs2i698Dj07iLUberpFYIj6wBhbmqfmNK/plarau4i1k+xq5bZzB4VJW8
OkhwzcIIdZIXff6INJ1w1Zz76ZV1DIbRzbH71t6d/L/qJtuOexXxTi2LrepreK/q3svMLpsJycnDPa
t9xaGoaLq4Cg3P19Z1J6HquFILeo=</CipherValue>
        </CipherData>
    </EncryptedKey>
  </KeyInfo>
  <CipherData>
<CipherValue>Q1re8ntDDv7/dHsvWbnIKdZF6COA1y3S91hmnhUN3nxYfrjSc7FrjEVyJfJh15EDX
4kXd8ukAjrqwuBNnQbsh1PAXNFDf1zB4FF+jyPKP/jm1Q9mDnmiq+NCuo3KpKj8F4vcHbcj+f3GYqq
B4pYbb1AvYnjPyPrrPmxLNT9KDtDr8pDbtGnKqAfcMnQPvA815w3BzPM4a73Vtt2kL/z9QJRu3Svd9
33taxOO/HufRJEnE2/hcBq3OWcBmEuXx3LFNjV+xVmuebrInhhxQgM2froBKYxgjwWiWNjIIjIeTI2
FQ8nZ8V8kzAVohmDYkZpCj4NQGdrjD996h97phI6NnHZYZHJ7oPRz</CipherValue>
        </CipherData>
    </EncryptedData>
  </connectionStrings>
  <system.web>
    ...
  </system.web>
</configuration>
```

If changes are made to the connectionStrings section using the GUI tools, the new connection is encrypted, which means that you won't have to run the aspnet_regiis utility again.

You can decrypt the *connectionStrings* section by using the following command:

```
aspnet_regiis -pdf "connectionStrings" "C:\...\EncryptWebSite"
```

After the *connectionStrings* section is decrypted, it looks just as it did before it was encrypted.

Using the *DbCommand* Object

The *DbCommand* object is used to send one or more Structured Query Language (SQL) statements to the data store. The *DbCommand* can be any of the following types:

- **Data Manipulation Language (DML)** Commands that retrieve, insert, update, or delete data.

- **Data Definition Language (DDL)** Commands that create tables or other database objects, or modify the database schema.

- **Data Control Language (DCL)** Commands that grant, deny, or revoke permissions.

The *DbCommand* object requires a valid open connection to issue the command to the data store. A *DbConnection* object can be passed into the *DbCommand* object's constructor or attached to the *DbCommand* object's *Connection* property after the *DbCommand* is created, but you should always consider using the *CreateCommand* method on the *DbConnection* object to limit the amount of provider-specific code in your application. The *DbConnection* automatically creates the appropriate provider-specific *DbCommand*.

The *DbCommand* also requires a valid value for its *CommandText* and *Command-Type* properties. The following code snippet shows how to create and initialize a *DbCommand*:

```vb
'VB
Protected Sub Button3_Click(ByVal sender As Object, _
    ByVal e As System.EventArgs) Handles Button3.Click
  Dim pubs As ConnectionStringSettings
  pubs = ConfigurationManager.ConnectionStrings("PubsData")
  Dim connection As DbConnection = New SqlConnection()
  connection.ConnectionString = pubs.ConnectionString
  Dim cmd As DbCommand = connection.CreateCommand()
  cmd.CommandType = CommandType.StoredProcedure
  cmd.CommandText = "uspGetCustomerById"
  Dim lbl as Label = GetLabel(275,20)
  lbl.Text = "Command Created"
End Sub
```

```csharp
//C#
protected void Button3_Click(object sender, EventArgs e)
{
    ConnectionStringSettings pubs =
       ConfigurationManager.ConnectionStrings["PubsData"];
    DbConnection connection =
      new SqlConnection(pubs.ConnectionString);
    DbCommand cmd = connection.CreateCommand();
    cmd.CommandType = CommandType.StoredProcedure;
    cmd.CommandText = "uspGetCustomerById";
    Label lbl = GetLabel(275, 20);
    lbl.Text = "Command Created";
}
```

This code creates a *SqlConnection* object and assigns it to the connection variable that has the data type of *DbConnection*. The *DbConnection* object is then used to create a *SqlCommand*, which is assigned to the *cmd* variable. The *DbConnection* must be opened before the command can be executed. To execute a stored procedure as shown, the *CommandText* property contains the name of the stored procedure, while the *CommandType* indicates that this is a call to a stored procedure.

Using *DbParameter* Objects to Pass Data   When you need to pass data to a stored procedure, you should use *DbParameter* objects. For example, a user-defined stored procedure called *uspGetCustomerById* might require a customer identification to retrieve the appropriate customer. You can create *DbParameter* objects by using the *Parameters.Add* method of the *Command* object, as shown here:

```vb
'VB
Protected Sub Button4_Click(ByVal sender As Object, _
      ByVal e As System.EventArgs) Handles Button4.Click
   Dim pubs As ConnectionStringSettings
   pubs = ConfigurationManager.ConnectionStrings("PubsData")
   Dim connection As DbConnection = New SqlConnection()
   connection.ConnectionString = pubs.ConnectionString
   Dim cmd As DbCommand = connection.CreateCommand()
   cmd.CommandType = CommandType.StoredProcedure
   cmd.CommandText = "uspGetCustomerById"
   Dim parm As DbParameter = cmd.CreateParameter()
   parm.ParameterName = "@Id"
   parm.Value = "AROUT"
   cmd.Parameters.Add(parm)
   Dim lbl As Label = GetLabel(275, 20)
   lbl.Text = "Command and Parmaters Created"
End Sub
```

```csharp
//C#
protected void Button4_Click(object sender, EventArgs e)
{
    ConnectionStringSettings pubs =
        ConfigurationManager.ConnectionStrings["PubsData"];
    DbConnection connection =
        new SqlConnection(pubs.ConnectionString);
    DbCommand cmd = connection.CreateCommand();
    cmd.CommandType = CommandType.StoredProcedure;
    cmd.CommandText = "uspGetCustomerById";
    DbParameter parm = cmd.CreateParameter();
    parm.ParameterName = "@Id";
    parm.Value = "AROUT";
    cmd.Parameters.Add(parm);
    Label lbl = GetLabel(275, 20);
    lbl.Text = "Command and Parmaters Created";
}
```

This code creates and configures a *DbConnection* object and a *DbCommand* object. A single parameter called *@Id* is created and assigned the value *AROUT*.

NOTE Be careful with parameter names and parameter order

The SQL provider requires that the parameter names match the parameter names defined in the stored procedure. The creation of the parameters is, therefore, not order-dependent.

The *OleDb* provider, on the other hand, requires the parameters to be defined in the same order that they are defined in the stored procedure. This means the name assigned to the parameter need not match the name defined in the stored procedure.

Use the name assigned to the *DbParameter* object to access the parameter through code. For example, to retrieve the value that is currently in the *SqlParameter* called *@Id*, use the following code:

```
'VB
Dim id as String = cmd.Parameters("@Id").Value
```

```
//C#
string id = (string)((DbParameter)cmd.Parameters["@Id"]).Value;
```

Building SQL Commands Using Server Explorer   The Server Explorer window can be used to create SQL Commands by right-clicking a connection and selecting New Query. This opens a four-pane window and prompts you to select tables, views, function, and synonyms to be added to the query. The four-paned window provides windows for the following:

- **Diagram Pane**   Visually shows the tables and views that have been selected, and also shows the relationships between them.
- **Criteria Pane**   Is a tabular pane that allows you to select the columns and specify attributes for each column, such as alias, sort, and filters.
- **SQL Pane**   Is a textual pane that shows the actual SQL statement that is being built.
- **Results Pane**   Is a tabular pane that shows the results after the query has been executed.

Using the *ExecuteNonQuery* Method   When you want to execute a *DbCommand* object and you don't expect a tabular result to be returned, you should use the *ExecuteNonQuery* method. Examples of SQL statements that don't return any rows are an insert, an update, or a delete query. This method returns an integer that represents the number of rows affected by the operation. The following example executes a SQL statement to increment the *qty* field in the sales table for sales with *qty* greater than 50; it returns the number of rows that were updated.

```vb
'VB
Protected Sub Button5_Click(ByVal sender As Object, _
        ByVal e As System.EventArgs) Handles Button5.Click
    Dim pubs As ConnectionStringSettings
    pubs = ConfigurationManager.ConnectionStrings("PubsData")
    Dim connection As DbConnection = New SqlConnection()
    connection.ConnectionString = pubs.ConnectionString
    Dim cmd As DbCommand = connection.CreateCommand()
    cmd.CommandType = CommandType.Text
    cmd.CommandText = _
        "UPDATE SALES SET qty = qty + 1 WHERE qty > 50"
    connection.Open()
    Dim count As Integer = cmd.ExecuteNonQuery()
    connection.Close()
    Dim lbl As Label = GetLabel(275, 20)
    lbl.Text = "Count = " + count.ToString()
End Sub
```

```csharp
//C#
protected void Button5_Click(object sender, EventArgs e)
{
    ConnectionStringSettings pubs =
        ConfigurationManager.ConnectionStrings["PubsData"];
    DbConnection connection = new SqlConnection(pubs.ConnectionString);
    DbCommand cmd = connection.CreateCommand();
    cmd.CommandType = CommandType.Text;
    cmd.CommandText = "UPDATE SALES SET qty = qty + 1 WHERE qty > 50";
    connection.Open();
    int count = cmd.ExecuteNonQuery();
    connection.Close();
    Label lbl = GetLabel(275, 20);
    lbl.Text = "Count = " + count.ToString();
}
```

Using the *ExecuteScalar* Method   You may execute a query that is expected to return a tabular result containing a single row and column, such as a query that retrieves the total sales for the day. In situations such as this, the results can be treated as a single return value. For example, the following SQL returns a result that consists of a single row with a single column:

```sql
SELECT COUNT(*) FROM Sales
```

If you use the *ExecuteScalar* method, the .NET runtime does not create an instance of a *DataTable* to hold the result, which means less resource usage and better performance.

The following code shows how to use the *ExecuteScalar* method to easily retrieve the number of rows in the Sales table into a variable called *count*:

```vb
'VB
Protected Sub Button6_Click(ByVal sender As Object, _
        ByVal e As System.EventArgs) Handles Button6.Click
    Dim pubs As ConnectionStringSettings
    pubs = ConfigurationManager.ConnectionStrings("PubsData")
    Dim connection As DbConnection = New SqlConnection()
    connection.ConnectionString = pubs.ConnectionString
    Dim cmd As DbCommand = connection.CreateCommand()
    cmd.CommandType = CommandType.Text
    cmd.CommandText = "SELECT COUNT(*) FROM Sales"
    connection.Open()
    Dim count As Integer = cmd.ExecuteScalar()
    connection.Close()
    Dim lbl As Label = GetLabel(275, 20)
    lbl.Text = "Count = " + count.ToString()
End Sub
```

```csharp
//C#
protected void Button6_Click(object sender, EventArgs e)
{
    ConnectionStringSettings pubs =
        ConfigurationManager.ConnectionStrings["PubsData"];
    DbConnection connection = new SqlConnection(pubs.ConnectionString);
    DbCommand cmd = connection.CreateCommand();
    cmd.CommandType = CommandType.Text;
    cmd.CommandText = "SELECT COUNT(*) FROM Sales";
    connection.Open();
    int count = (int)cmd.ExecuteScalar();
    connection.Close();
    Label lbl = GetLabel(275, 20);
    lbl.Text = "Count = " + count.ToString();
}
```

Using the *ExecuteReader* Method   The *ExecuteReader* method returns a *DbDataReader* instance that represents a forward-only, read-only, server-side cursor. *DbDataReader* objects can be created only by executing one of the *ExecuteReader* methods on the *DbCommand* object. (See the next section for more information on the *DbDataReader*.) The following example uses the *ExecuteReader* method to create a *DbDataReader* object with the query results and continuously loops through the results until the end of data has been reached (when the *Read* method returns *false*).

```vb
'VB
Protected Sub Button8_Click(ByVal sender As Object, _
        ByVal e As System.EventArgs) Handles Button8.Click
```

```
    Dim pubs As ConnectionStringSettings
    pubs = ConfigurationManager.ConnectionStrings("PubsData")
    Dim connection As DbConnection = New SqlConnection()
    connection.ConnectionString = pubs.ConnectionString
    Dim cmd As DbCommand = connection.CreateCommand()
    cmd.CommandType = CommandType.Text
    cmd.CommandText = "SELECT stor_id, ord_num FROM Sales"
    connection.Open()
    Dim rdr As DbDataReader = cmd.ExecuteReader()
    Dim lbl As Label = GetLabel(275, 20)
    While (rdr.Read())
        lbl.Text += rdr("stor_id") + ": " + rdr("ord_num") + "<br />"
    End While
    connection.Close()
End Sub
```

```
//C#
protected void Button8_Click(object sender, EventArgs e)
{
    ConnectionStringSettings pubs =
        ConfigurationManager.ConnectionStrings["PubsData"];
    DbConnection connection = new SqlConnection(pubs.ConnectionString);
    DbCommand cmd = connection.CreateCommand();
    cmd.CommandType = CommandType.Text;
    cmd.CommandText = "SELECT stor_id, ord_num FROM Sales";
    connection.Open();
    DbDataReader rdr = cmd.ExecuteReader();
    Label lbl = GetLabel(275, 20);
    while (rdr.Read())
    {
        lbl.Text += rdr["stor_id"] + ": " + rdr["ord_num"] + "<br />";
    }
    connection.Close();
}
```

Using the *DbDataReader* Object

A *DbDataReader* object provides a high-performance method of retrieving data from the data store. It delivers a forward-only, read-only, server-side cursor. This makes the *DbDataReader* object an ideal choice for populating *ListBox* controls, *DropDownList* controls, and even *GridView* controls that display read-only data. When you run reports, you can use the *DbDataReader* object to retrieve the data from the data store. The *DbDataReader* might not be a good choice when you are coding an operation that modifies data and needs to send the changes back to the database. For data modifications, the *DbDataAdapter* object, which is discussed in the next section, might be a better choice.

The *DbDataReader* contains a *Read* method that retrieves data into its buffer. Only one row of data is ever available at a time, which means that the data does not need to be completely read into the application before it is processed. The following code populates a new *DataTable* directly with the list of publishers from the *pubs* database:

```vb
'VB
Protected Sub Button9_Click(ByVal sender As Object, _
      ByVal e As System.EventArgs) Handles Button9.Click
   Dim pubs As ConnectionStringSettings
   pubs = ConfigurationManager.ConnectionStrings("PubsData")
   Dim connection As DbConnection = New SqlConnection()
   connection.ConnectionString = pubs.ConnectionString
   Dim cmd As DbCommand = connection.CreateCommand()
   cmd.CommandType = CommandType.Text
   cmd.CommandText = "SELECT pub_id, pub_name FROM publishers"
   connection.Open()
   Dim rdr As DbDataReader = cmd.ExecuteReader()
   Dim publishers As New DataTable()
   publishers.Load(rdr, LoadOption.Upsert)
   connection.Close()
   Dim gv as GridView = GetGridView(275,20)
   gv.DataSource = publishers
   gv.DataBind()
End Sub
```

```csharp
//C#
protected void Button9_Click(object sender, EventArgs e)
{
    ConnectionStringSettings pubs =
       ConfigurationManager.ConnectionStrings["PubsData"];
    DbConnection connection = new SqlConnection(pubs.ConnectionString);
    DbCommand cmd = connection.CreateCommand();
    cmd.CommandType = CommandType.Text;
    cmd.CommandText = "SELECT pub_id, pub_name FROM Publishers";
    connection.Open();
    DbDataReader rdr = cmd.ExecuteReader();
    DataTable publishers = new DataTable();
    publishers.Load(rdr, LoadOption.Upsert);
    connection.Close();
    GridView gv = GetGridView(275, 20);
    gv.DataSource = publishers;
    gv.DataBind();
}
```

Notice that the *DataTable* object's *Load* method contains a *LoadOption* parameter. The *LoadOption* gives you the option of deciding which *DataRowVersion* should get the incoming data. For example, if you load a *DataTable* object, modify the data, and then save the changes back to the database, you might encounter concurrency errors if someone else has modified the data between the time you got the data and the time you attempted to save the data. One option is to load the *DataTable* object again, using the default *PreserveCurrentValues* enumeration value, which loads the original *DataRowVersion* with the data from the database while leaving the current *DataRowVersion* untouched. Next, you can simply execute the *Update* method again and the update will succeed.

For this to work properly, the *DataTable* must have a *PrimaryKey* defined. Failure to define a *PrimaryKey* results in duplicate *DataRow* objects being added to the *DataTable* object. The *LoadOption* enumeration members are as follows:

- **OverwriteChanges** Overwrites the original *DataRowVersion* and the current *DataRowVersion* and changes the *RowState* to *Unchanged*. New rows have a *RowState* of *Unchanged* as well.

- **PreserveChanges** (default) Overwrites the original *DataRowVersion*, but does not modify the current *DataRowVersion*. New rows have a *RowState* of *Unchanged* as well.

- **Upsert** Overwrites the current *DataRowVersion*, but does not modify the original *DataRowVersion*. New rows have a *RowState* of *Added*. Rows that had a *RowState* of *Unchanged* have a *RowState* of *Unchanged* if the current *DataRowVersion* is the same as the original *DataRowVersion*, but if they are different, the *RowState* is *Modified*.

NOTE **New in ASP.NET 2.0**

Multiple Active Result Sets (MARS) is new in version 2.0 of the .NET Framework.

Using Multiple Active Result Sets (MARS) to Execute Multiple Commands on a Connection One of the problems with the *DbDataReader* is that it keeps an open server-side cursor while you are looping through the results of your query. If you try to execute another command while the first command is still executing, you receive an *InvalidOperationException* stating that "There is already an open DataReader associated with this Connection which must be closed first." You can avoid this exception by setting the *MultipleActiveResultSets* connection string option to *true* when connecting to MARS-enabled hosts, such as SQL Server 2005. For example, the following connection string shows how this setting is added into a new connection string called *PubsDataMars*:

```
<connectionStrings>
   <clear />
   <add name="PubsData"
      providerName="System.Data.SqlClient"
      connectionString=
      "Data Source=.\SQLEXPRESS;
         AttachDbFilename=|DataDirectory|PUBS.MDF;
         Integrated Security=True;
         User Instance=True"/>
   <add name="PubsDataMars"
      providerName="System.Data.SqlClient"
      connectionString=
      "Data Source=.\SQLEXPRESS;
         AttachDbFilename=|DataDirectory|PUBS.MDF;
         Integrated Security=True;
         User Instance=True;
         MultipleActiveResultSets=True"/>
</connectionStrings>
```

NOTE   MARS performance

MARS does not provide any performance gains, but it does simplify your coding efforts. As a matter of fact, setting *MultipleActiveResultSets=True* in the connection string has a negative performance impact, so you should not turn on MARS arbitrarily.

MARS is something that you can live without. MARS simply makes your programming easier. Think of a scenario in which you execute a query to get a list of authors and, while you are looping through a list of the authors that are returned, you want to execute a second query to get the total royalties for each author.

On a database server without MARS, you could first collect the list of authors into a collection and close the connection. After that, you could loop through the collection to get each author's ID and execute a query to get the total royalties for the author. This means that you would loop through the authors twice: once to populate the collection, and again to get each author's ID and execute a query to get the author's total of the royalties. A MARS solution is to simply create two connections: one for the author list and one for the total of royalties query.

Another benefit that MARS provides is for a situation in which you have purchased database client licenses that are based on the quantity of connections to the database. Without MARS, you would have to open a separate connection to the database for each command that needs to run at the same time, which means that you might need to purchase more client licenses.

The following code snippet shows how MARS can be used to perform the nested queries for the author list and the total of the royalties:

```vb
'VB
Protected Sub Button10_Click(ByVal sender As Object, _
    ByVal e As System.EventArgs) Handles Button10.Click
  Dim lbl As Label = GetLabel(275, 20)
  Dim pubs As ConnectionStringSettings
  pubs = ConfigurationManager.ConnectionStrings("PubsDataMars")
  Dim connection As DbConnection = New SqlConnection()
  connection.ConnectionString = pubs.ConnectionString
  Dim cmd As DbCommand = connection.CreateCommand()
  cmd.CommandType = CommandType.Text
  cmd.CommandText = "SELECT au_id, au_lname, au_fname FROM Authors"
  connection.Open()
  Dim rdr As DbDataReader = cmd.ExecuteReader()
  While rdr.Read()
     Dim salesCmd As DbCommand = connection.CreateCommand()
     salesCmd.CommandType = CommandType.Text
     salesCmd.CommandText = _
        "SELECT SUM(royaltyper) FROM TitleAuthor WHERE (au_id = @auId)"
     Dim parm As DbParameter = salesCmd.CreateParameter()
     parm.ParameterName = "@auId"
     parm.Value = rdr("au_id")
     salesCmd.Parameters.Add(parm)
     Dim qtySales As Object = salesCmd.ExecuteScalar()
     lbl.Text += rdr("au_lname").ToString() + ", " + rdr("au_fname").ToString() _
        + ": " + string.Format("{0:C}",qtySales) + "<br />"
  End While
  connection.Close()
End Sub
```

```csharp
//C#
protected void Button10_Click(object sender, EventArgs e)
{
  Label lbl = GetLabel(275, 20);
  ConnectionStringSettings pubs =
     ConfigurationManager.ConnectionStrings["PubsDataMars"];
  DbConnection connection = new SqlConnection(pubs.ConnectionString);
  DbCommand cmd = connection.CreateCommand();
  cmd.CommandType = CommandType.Text;
  cmd.CommandText = "SELECT au_id, au_lname, au_fname FROM Authors";
  connection.Open();
  DbDataReader rdr = cmd.ExecuteReader();
  while (rdr.Read())
  {
     DbCommand salesCmd = connection.CreateCommand();
     salesCmd.CommandType = CommandType.Text;
     salesCmd.CommandText =
        "SELECT SUM(royaltyper) FROM titleauthor WHERE (au_id = @auId)";
     DbParameter parm = salesCmd.CreateParameter();
     parm.ParameterName = "@auId";
```

```
        parm.Value = (string)rdr["au_id"];
        salesCmd.Parameters.Add(parm);
        object qtyRoyalties = salesCmd.ExecuteScalar();
        lbl.Text += (string)rdr["au_lname"] + ", " + (string)rdr["au_fname"]
            + ": " + string.Format("{0:C}",qtyRoyalties) + "<br />";
    }
    connection.Close();
}
```

Performing Bulk Copy Operations with the *SqlBulkCopy* Object

The *SqlBulkCopy* class provides a high-performance method for copying data to a table in a SQL Server database. The source of the copy is constrained to the overloads of the *WriteToServer* method, which can accept an array of *DataRow* objects, an object that implements the *IDbDataReader* interface, a *DataTable* object, or a *DataTable* and *DataRowState*, as shown in Figure 4-13. This variety of parameters means that you can retrieve data from most locations.

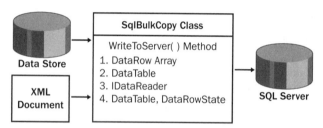

Figure 4-13   The *SqlBulkCopy* object can copy from a variety of sources to a SQL Server table.

NOTE   New in ASP.NET 2.0

The *SqlBulkCopy* object is new in version 2.0 of the .NET Framework.

The following code shows how you can use a *SqlBulkCopy* object to copy data from the Store table in the *pubs* database to the StoreList table:

```
'VB
Protected Sub Button11_Click(ByVal sender As Object, _
        ByVal e As System.EventArgs) Handles Button11.Click
    Dim pubs As ConnectionStringSettings
    pubs = ConfigurationManager.ConnectionStrings("PubsData")
    Dim connection As DbConnection = New SqlConnection()
    connection.ConnectionString = pubs.ConnectionString
    Dim bulkCopy As ConnectionStringSettings
    bulkCopy = ConfigurationManager.ConnectionStrings("PubsData")
    Dim bulkCopyConnection As DbConnection = New SqlConnection()
    bulkCopyConnection.ConnectionString = bulkCopy.ConnectionString
    Dim cmd As DbCommand = connection.CreateCommand()
    cmd.CommandType = CommandType.Text
```

```
    cmd.CommandText = "SELECT stor_name FROM Stores"
    connection.Open()
    bulkCopyConnection.Open()

    'make sure that table exists and is empty
    'in case button is clicked more that once
    Dim cleanup as SqlCommand = bulkCopyConnection.CreateCommand()
    cleanup.CommandText = _
        "IF EXISTS ( SELECT * FROM sys.objects " _
        + " WHERE object_id = OBJECT_ID('dbo.StoreList')   " _
        + " AND type in ('U')) " _
        + "DROP TABLE dbo.StoreList " _
        + "CREATE TABLE dbo.StoreList(stor_name varchar(40) NOT NULL )"
    cleanup.ExecuteNonQuery()

    'do the bulkcopy
    Dim rdr As DbDataReader = cmd.ExecuteReader()
    Dim bc As New SqlBulkCopy(bulkCopyConnection)
    bc.DestinationTableName = "StoreList"
    bc.WriteToServer(rdr)
    connection.Close()
    bulkCopyConnection.Close()
    Dim lbl as Label = GetLabel(275,20)
    lbl.Text = "Done with bulk copy"
End Sub

//C#
protected void Button11_Click(object sender, EventArgs e)
{
    ConnectionStringSettings pubs =
        ConfigurationManager.ConnectionStrings["PubsData"];
    DbConnection connection =
        new SqlConnection(pubs.ConnectionString);
    ConnectionStringSettings bulkCopy =
        ConfigurationManager.ConnectionStrings["PubsData"];
    SqlConnection bulkCopyConnection =
        new SqlConnection(bulkCopy.ConnectionString);
    DbConnection cmd = connection.CreateCommand();
    cmd.CommandType = CommandType.Text;
    cmd.CommandText = "SELECT stor_name FROM Stores";
    connection.Open();
    bulkCopyConnection.Open();

    //make sure that table exists and is empty
    //in case button is clicked more that once
    SqlCommand cleanup = bulkCopyConnection.CreateCommand();
    cleanup.CommandText =
        "IF EXISTS ( SELECT * FROM sys.objects "
        + " WHERE object_id = OBJECT_ID('dbo.StoreList')   "
        + " AND type in ('U')) "
        + "DROP TABLE dbo.StoreList "
        + "CREATE TABLE dbo.StoreList(stor_name varchar(40) NOT NULL )";
    cleanup.ExecuteNonQuery();
```

```
    //do the bulkcopy
    DbDataReader rdr = cmd.ExecuteReader();
    SqlBulkCopy bc = new SqlBulkCopy(bulkCopyConnection);
    bc.DestinationTableName = "StoreList";
    bc.WriteToServer(rdr);
    connection.Close();
    bulkCopyConnection.Close();
    Label lbl = GetLabel(275, 20);
    lbl.Text = "Done with bulk copy";
}
```

You should consider using the *IDbDataReader* parameter whenever possible to get the best performance with the least resources used. You can decide how much data should be copied based on the query that you use. For example, the preceding code sample retrieved only the store names and could have had a WHERE clause to further limit the data.

Using the *DbDataAdapter* Object

The *DbDataAdapter* object is used to retrieve and update data between a *DataTable* and a data store. The *DbDataAdapter* is derived from the *DataAdapter* class and is the base class of the provider-specific *DbDataAdapter* classes, as shown in Figure 4-14.

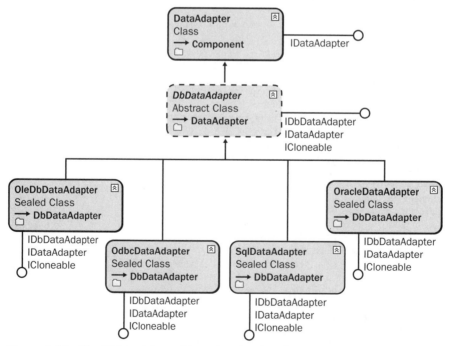

Figure 4-14   The *DbDataAdapter* hierarchy, showing the *DataAdapter* base class and the provider-specific derived classes

The *DbDataAdapter* has a *SelectCommand* property that you use when retrieving the data. The *SelectCommand* must contain a valid *DbCommand* object, which must have a valid connection.

The *DbDataAdapter* also has *InsertCommand*, *UpdateCommand*, and *DeleteCommand* properties, which can optionally contain *DbCommand* objects to send *DataTable* changes to the data store. You don't need to create these command objects if you only need to read data from the data store, but if you create one of these latter three commands, you must create all four of them.

Using the *Fill* Method   The *Fill* method moves data from the data store to the *Data-Table* object that you pass into this method. The *Fill* method has several overloads, some of which accept only a *DataSet* as a parameter. When a *DataSet* is passed to the *Fill* method, a new *DataTable* object is created in the *DataSet* if a source *DataTable* object is not specified.

The following code snippet shows how a *DataTable* can be loaded using the *Fill* method:

```vb
'VB
Protected Sub Button12_Click(ByVal sender As Object, _
      ByVal e As System.EventArgs) Handles Button12.Click
   Dim pubs As ConnectionStringSettings
   pubs = ConfigurationManager.ConnectionStrings("PubsData")
   Dim connection As DbConnection = New SqlConnection()
   connection.ConnectionString = pubs.ConnectionString
   Dim cmd As SqlCommand = CType(connection.CreateCommand(), SqlCommand)
   cmd.CommandType = CommandType.Text
   cmd.CommandText = "SELECT pub_id, pub_name FROM publishers"
   Dim pubsDataSet As New DataSet("Pubs")
   Dim da As New SqlDataAdapter(cmd)
   da.Fill(pubsDataSet, "publishers")
   Dim gv as GridView = GetGridView(275,20)
   gv.DataSource = pubsDataSet
   gv.DataMember = "publishers"
   gv.DataBind()
End Sub
```

```csharp
//C#
protected void Button12_Click(object sender, EventArgs e)
{
    ConnectionStringSettings pubs =
       ConfigurationManager.ConnectionStrings["PubsData"];
    DbConnection connection = new SqlConnection(pubs.ConnectionString);
    SqlCommand cmd = (SqlCommand)connection.CreateCommand();
    cmd.CommandType = CommandType.Text;
    cmd.CommandText = "SELECT pub_id, pub_name FROM Publishers";
```

```
    SqlDataAdapter da = new SqlDataAdapter(cmd);
    DataSet pubsDataSet = new DataSet("Pubs");
    da.Fill(pubsDataSet, "publishers");
    GridView gv = GetGridView(275, 20);
    gv.DataSource = pubsDataSet;
    gv.DataMember = "publishers";
    gv.DataBind();
}
```

Saving Changes to the Database Using the *Update* Method   The *Update* method
retrieves the changes from a *DataTable* object and executes the appropriate *InsertCommand*, *UpdateCommand*, or *DeleteCommand* to send each change to the data store on
a row-by-row basis. The *Update* method retrieves the *DataRow* objects that have been
changed by looking at the *RowState* property of each row. If the *RowState* is anything
but *Unchanged*, the *Update* method sends the change to the database.

For the *Update* method to work, all four commands must be assigned to the *DbData-
Adapter*. Normally, this means creating individual *DbCommand* objects for each command. You can easily create the commands by using the *DbDataAdapter* configuration
wizard, which starts when a *DbDataAdapter* is dropped onto the form. The wizard can
generate stored procedures for all four commands.

Another way to populate the *DbDataAdapter* object's commands is to use the *DbCommandBuilder* object. This object creates the *InsertCommand*, *UpdateCommand*, and
DeleteCommand as long as a valid *SelectCommand* exists. The *DbCommandBuilder* is
great for specific changes and demos, but it's generally better to use stored procedures
for all database access to eliminate security risk from SQL injection attacks. The following code demonstrates a simple update to the database using the *SqlDataAdapter*,
which is the SQL Server–specific version of the *DbDataAdapter*:

```
'VB
Protected Sub Button13_Click(ByVal sender As Object, _
        ByVal e As System.EventArgs) Handles Button13.Click
    Dim pubs As ConnectionStringSettings
    pubs = ConfigurationManager.ConnectionStrings("PubsData")
    Dim connection As DbConnection = New SqlConnection()
    connection.ConnectionString = pubs.ConnectionString
    Dim cmd As SqlCommand = _
        CType(connection.CreateCommand(), SqlCommand)
    cmd.CommandType = CommandType.Text
    cmd.CommandText = "SELECT * FROM publishers"
    Dim pubsDataSet As New DataSet("Pubs")
    Dim da As New SqlDataAdapter(cmd)
    Dim bldr As New SqlCommandBuilder(da)
```

```
   da.Fill(pubsDataSet, "publishers")
   'Modify data here - added time to assure change
   pubsDataSet.Tables("publishers").Rows(0)("pub_name") _
      = "Hello" + DateTime.Now.ToLongTimeString()
   'Add a row - use minutes and seconds for id
   pubsDataSet.Tables("publishers").Rows.Add( _
      "99" + DateTime.Now.Second.ToString(), _
      "Tailspin Toys", "Paris", Nothing, "France")
   da.Update(pubsDataSet, "publishers")
   Dim lbl As Label = GetLabel(275, 20)
   lbl.Text = "Update Complete"
End Sub

//C#
protected void Button13_Click(object sender, EventArgs e)
{
   ConnectionStringSettings pubs =
      ConfigurationManager.ConnectionStrings["PubsData"];
   DbConnection connection = new SqlConnection(pubs.ConnectionString);
   SqlCommand cmd = (SqlCommand)connection.CreateCommand();
   cmd.CommandType = CommandType.Text;
   cmd.CommandText = "SELECT * FROM Publishers";
   SqlDataAdapter da = new SqlDataAdapter(cmd);
   DataSet pubsDataSet = new DataSet("Pubs");
   SqlCommandBuilder bldr = new SqlCommandBuilder(da);
   da.Fill(pubsDataSet, "publishers");
   //Modify data here - added time to assure change
   pubsDataSet.Tables["publishers"].Rows[0]["pub_name"]
      = "Hello" + DateTime.Now.ToLongTimeString();
   //Add a row - use seconds in id
   pubsDataSet.Tables["publishers"].Rows.Add(
      "99" + DateTime.Now.Second.ToString(),
      "Tailspin Toys", "Paris", null, "France");
   da.Update(pubsDataSet, "publishers");
   Label lbl = GetLabel(275, 20);
   lbl.Text = "Update Complete";
}
```

Saving Changes to the Database in Batches   One way to increase update performance is to send the changes to the database server in batches instead of sending changes on a row-by-row basis. You can do this by assigning a value to the *DbDataAdapter* object's *UpdateBatchSize* property. This property defaults to 1, which causes each change to be sent to the server on a row-by-row basis. Setting the value to 0 instructs the *DbData-Adapter* object to create the largest possible batch size for changes, or you can set the value to the number of changes you want to send to the server in each batch. Setting the *UpdateBatchSize* to a number greater than the number of changes that need to be sent is equivalent to setting it to 0.

NOTE   New in ASP.NET 2.0

The *UpdateBatchSize* property is new in version 2.0 of the .NET Framework.

You can confirm that the changes are being sent to the database server in batches by adding a *RowUpdated* event to the *DbDataAdapter* object. The event handler method exposes the number of rows affected in the last batch. When the *UpdateBatchSize* is set to 1, the *RecordsAffected* property is always 1. In the following code snippet, the publishers' table contains eight rows. The *pubsDataSet* is filled, and then the *pub_name* field is modified on all eight rows. Before the *Update* method is executed, the *UpdateBatchSize* is changed to 3. When the *Update* method is executed, the changes are sent to the database as a batch of three changes, another batch of three changes, and finally, a batch of two changes. This code contains a *RowUpdated* event handler to collect batch information, which is displayed after the *Update* method is executed.

```vb
'VB
Public WithEvents da As New SqlDataAdapter()
Public sb As New System.Text.StringBuilder()

Private Sub rowUpdated(ByVal sender As Object, _
      ByVal e As SqlRowUpdatedEventArgs) Handles da.RowUpdated
   sb.Append("Rows: " & e.RecordsAffected.ToString() & vbCrLf)
End Sub

Protected Sub Button14_Click(ByVal sender As Object, _
      ByVal e As System.EventArgs) Handles Button14.Click
   Dim pubs As ConnectionStringSettings
   pubs = ConfigurationManager.ConnectionStrings("PubsData")
   Dim connection As DbConnection = New SqlConnection()
   connection.ConnectionString = pubs.ConnectionString
   Dim cmd As SqlCommand = _
      CType(connection.CreateCommand(), SqlCommand)
   cmd.CommandType = CommandType.Text
   cmd.CommandText = "SELECT * FROM publishers"
   Dim pubsDataSet As New DataSet("Pubs")
   da.SelectCommand = cmd
   Dim bldr As New SqlCommandBuilder(da)
   da.Fill(pubsDataSet, "publishers")
   'Modify data here
   For Each dr As DataRow In pubsDataSet.Tables("publishers").Rows
      dr("pub_name") = "Updated Toys " _
         + DateTime.Now.Minute.ToString() _
         + DateTime.Now.Second.ToString()
   Next
   da.UpdateBatchSize = 3
   da.Update(pubsDataSet, "publishers")
```

```
    Dim lbl As Label = GetLabel(275, 20)
    lbl.Text = sb.ToString()
End Sub
```

```csharp
//C#
public SqlDataAdapter da = new SqlDataAdapter();
public System.Text.StringBuilder sb = new System.Text.StringBuilder();

private void rowUpdated(object sender, SqlRowUpdatedEventArgs e)
{
    sb.Append("Rows: " + e.RecordsAffected.ToString() + "\r\n");
}

protected void Button14_Click(object sender, EventArgs e)
{
    //event subscription is normally placed in constructor but is here
    //to encapsulate the sample
    da.RowUpdated += new SqlRowUpdatedEventHandler(rowUpdated);
    ConnectionStringSettings pubs =
        ConfigurationManager.ConnectionStrings["PubsData"];
    DbConnection connection = new SqlConnection(pubs.ConnectionString);
    SqlCommand cmd = (SqlCommand)connection.CreateCommand();
    cmd.CommandType = CommandType.Text;
    cmd.CommandText = "SELECT * FROM Publishers";
    da.SelectCommand = cmd;
    DataSet pubsDataSet = new DataSet("Pubs");
    SqlCommandBuilder bldr = new SqlCommandBuilder(da);
    da.Fill(pubsDataSet, "publishers");
    //Modify data here
    foreach (DataRow dr in pubsDataSet.Tables["publishers"].Rows)
    {
        dr["pub_name"] = "Updated Toys "
            + DateTime.Now.Minute.ToString()
            + DateTime.Now.Second.ToString();
    }
    da.UpdateBatchSize = 3;
    da.Update(pubsDataSet, "publishers");
    //if event subscription is in the contructor, no need to
    //remove it here....
    da.RowUpdated -= new SqlRowUpdatedEventHandler(rowUpdated);
    Label lbl = GetLabel(275, 20);
    lbl.Text = sb.ToString();
}
```

Using the *OleDbDataAdapter* Object to Access ADO Recordset or Record   The *OleDb-DataAdapter* is similar to the *SqlDataAdapter*; however, the *OleDbDataAdapter* provides a unique feature: the ability to read a legacy ADO Recordset or Record into a *DataSet*. Consider the following code snippet:

```vb
'VB
Protected Sub Button7_Click(ByVal sender As Object, _
        ByVal e As System.EventArgs) Handles Button7.Click
    Dim da as  new OleDbDataAdapter()
    Dim ds as new DataSet()
    ' set reference to adodb.dll and
    ' add using ADODB
    Dim adoCn as new ADODB.Connection()
    Dim adoRs as new ADODB.Recordset()
    adoCn.Open( _
        "Provider=Microsoft.Jet.OLEDB.4.0;" _
        + "Data Source=" _
        + MapPath("App_Data/Northwind.mdb") + ";" _
        + "Persist Security Info=False", "", "", -1)
    adoRs.Open("SELECT * FROM Customers", _
        adoCn, ADODB.CursorTypeEnum.adOpenForwardOnly, _
        ADODB.LockTypeEnum.adLockReadOnly, 1)
    da.Fill(ds, adoRs, "Customers")
    adoCn.Close()
    Dim gv as GridView = GetGridView(275, 20)
    gv.DataSource = ds
    gv.DataMember = "Customers"
    gv.DataBind()
End Sub
```

```csharp
//C#
protected void Button7_Click(object sender, EventArgs e)
{
    OleDbDataAdapter da = new OleDbDataAdapter();
    DataSet ds = new DataSet();
    // set reference to adodb.dll and
    // add using ADODB
    ADODB.Connection adoCn = new ADODB.Connection();
    ADODB.Recordset adoRs = new ADODB.Recordset();
    adoCn.Open(
        "Provider=Microsoft.Jet.OLEDB.4.0;"
        + "Data Source="
        + MapPath("App_Data/Northwind.mdb") + ";"
        + "Persist Security Info=False", "", "", -1);
    adoRs.Open("SELECT * FROM Customers",
        adoCn, ADODB.CursorTypeEnum.adOpenForwardOnly,
        ADODB.LockTypeEnum.adLockReadOnly, 1);
    da.Fill(ds, adoRs, "Customers");
    adoCn.Close();
    GridView gv = GetGridView(275, 20);
    gv.DataSource = ds;
    gv.DataMember = "Customers";
    gv.DataBind();
}
```

This code sample is opening a connection to a Microsoft Access database called north-wind.mdb and retrieving the Customers table into an ADODB.Recordset. The recordset is passed to the *Fill* method on the *OleDbDataAdapter*, which uses the recordset as the source when filling the *DataSet* object.

The primary purpose of this feature is to support legacy data, which can be useful in situations where you have a legacy ADODB.Recordset and you want to display it using one of the .NET GUI controls, or if you want to save the data to a data store using one of the .NET providers.

Using the *DbProviderFactory* Classes

There are many reasons for writing an application that does not require database provider-specific code. A company might want the flexibility to upgrade from one database product to another, such as moving from Microsoft Access to SQL Server. A company might have a retail application that must allow connectivity to any data source.

ADO.NET provides base classes that the provider-specific classes inherit from, as shown earlier in Table 4-1. The .NET Framework supports only single inheritance, so this approach has limitations if you want to create your own base class, but for classes that will expand, providing base class inheritance is better than providing interface implementation. Note that interfaces are still provided for backward compatibility.

NOTE **New in ASP.NET 2.0**

The provider factory objects are new in version 2.0 of the .NET Framework.

The *DbProviderFactory* lets you create a factory object that is responsible for creating the appropriate provider objects. Each provider must supply a subclass of *DbProvider-Factory* that can be used to create instances of its provider classes. For example, you can use the *SqlClientFactory* to create instances of any of the SQL Server classes. Figure 4-15 shows the *DbProviderFactory* class hierarchy.

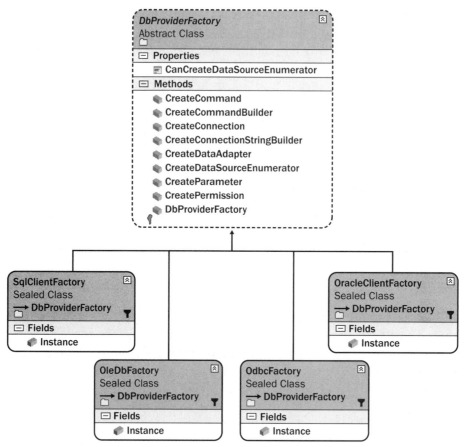

Figure 4-15   The *DbProviderFactory* and the *SqlClientFactory* classes.

The provider factory classes are implemented as singletons, where each class provides an *Instance* property that is used to access the methods and properties shown in Figure 4-15. For example, you can use the following code to create a new connection using the *SqlClientFactory*:

```vb
'VB
'Get the singleton instance
Dim factory As DbProviderFactory = SqlClientFactory.Instance

Public Function GetProviderConnection() As DbConnection
   Dim connection As DbConnection = factory.CreateConnection()
   connection.ConnectionString = "Data Source=.\SQLEXPRESS;" _
      & "AttachDbFilename=|DataDirectory|PUBS.MDF;" _
      & "Integrated Security=True;User Instance=True"
   Return connection
End Function
```

```
//C#
//Get the singleton instance
DbProviderFactory factory = SqlClientFactory.Instance;

public DbConnection GetProviderConnection()
{
    DbConnection connection = factory.CreateConnection();
    connection.ConnectionString = @"Data Source=.\SQLEXPRESS;"
        + "AttachDbFilename=|DataDirectory|PUBS.MDF;"
        + "Integrated Security=True;User Instance=True";
    return connection;
}
```

Using the *DbProviderFactories* Class

To query for the list of available factories, you can use the *DbProviderFactories* class. This class is a factory for obtaining factories. It contains a method called *GetFactory-Classes* that returns a *DataTable* that is populated with information describing all available providers. Retrieving the list of providers can be easily demonstrated by using the following code snippet:

```
'VB
Dim providersList As DataTable = Nothing

Protected Sub Button16_Click(ByVal sender As Object, _
        ByVal e As System.EventArgs) Handles Button16.Click
    providersList = DbProviderFactories.GetFactoryClasses()
    Dim gv As GridView = GetGridView(275, 20)
    gv.Width = 400
    gv.DataSource = providersList
    gv.DataBind()
End Sub
```

```
//C#
DataTable providersList = null;

protected void Button16_Click(object sender, EventArgs e)
{
    providersList = DbProviderFactories.GetFactoryClasses();
    GridView gv = GetGridView(275, 20);
    gv.Width = 400;
    gv.DataSource = providersList;
    gv.DataBind();
}
```

When the Web page is run and the button is clicked, the screen shown in Figure 4-16 is displayed.

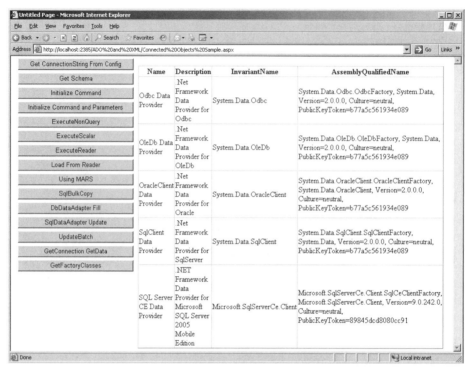

Figure 4-16   The available provider factory classes on an example computer.

The invariant column contains a string that you can use to retrieve a specific provider. The name and description provide information that you can use to display a friendly provider list to an application user. The listed assembly names are fully qualified. Any provider on the list must be located within the application's probing path. This means that the .NET runtime must be able to locate the provider. In most situations, the provider library is installed in the GAC or the application folder.

The provider list shown in Figure 4-16 is from the Machine.config file, which, by default, contains the following provider information within the *<configuration>* root element:

```
<system.data>
  <DbProviderFactories>
    <add name="Odbc Data Provider"
      invariant="System.Data.Odbc"
      description=".Net Framework Data Provider for Odbc"
      type="System.Data.Odbc.OdbcFactory, System.Data,
        Version=2.0.0.0, Culture=neutral, PublicKeyToken=b77a5c561934e089" />
    <add name="OleDb Data Provider"
      invariant="System.Data.OleDb"
```

```
          description=".Net Framework Data Provider for OleDb"
          type="System.Data.OleDb.OleDbFactory, System.Data,
             Version=2.0.0.0, Culture=neutral, PublicKeyToken=b77a5c561934e089" />
       <add name="OracleClient Data Provider"
          invariant="System.Data.OracleClient"
          description=".Net Framework Data Provider for Oracle"
            type="System.Data.OracleClient.OracleClientFactory,
               System.Data.OracleClient, Version=2.0.0.0, Culture=neutral,
               PublicKeyToken=b77a5c561934e089" />
       <add name="SqlClient Data Provider"
          invariant="System.Data.SqlClient"
          description=".Net Framework Data Provider for SqlServer"
          type="System.Data.SqlClient.SqlClientFactory, System.Data,
             Version=2.0.0.0, Culture=neutral, PublicKeyToken=b77a5c561934e089" />
       <add name="SQL Server CE Data Provider"
          invariant="Microsoft.SqlServerCe.Client"
          description=".NET Framework Data Provider for
             Microsoft SQL Server 2005 Mobile Edition"
          type="Microsoft.SqlServerCe.Client.SqlCeClientFactory,
             Microsoft.SqlServerCe.Client, Version=9.0.242.0,
             Culture=neutral, PublicKeyToken=89845dcd8080cc91" />
     </DbProviderFactories>
   </system.data>
```

Notice that *DbDatabaseProviderFactories* uses the *<add>* element. By using the *<add>* element, you can add more providers to the Machine.config file or the application's configuration file. You can also use the *<remove>* tag to remove providers from the default machine.config list. For example, the following is a sample App.config file that removes the ODBC provider from the defaults defined in Machine.config:

```
<configuration>
  <system.data>
    <DbProviderFactories>
        <remove invariant="System.Data.Odbc" />
    </DbProviderFactories>
  </system.data>
</configuration>
```

If very few specific providers (such as SQL Server and Oracle) are required, you can use the *<clear>* element to remove all of the providers in the Machine.config file and then use the *<add>* element to add the desired providers back into the list. The following example clears the provider list and adds the SQL Server provider back into the list:

```
<configuration>
  <system.data>
    <DbProviderFactories>
        <clear/>
        <add name="SqlClient Data Provider"
```

```
          invariant="System.Data.SqlClient"
          description=".Net Framework Data Provider for SqlServer"
          type="System.Data.SqlClient.SqlClientFactory, System.Data,
          Version=2.0.0.0, Culture=neutral,
          PublicKeyToken=b77a5c561934e089" />
    </DbProviderFactories>
  </system.data>
</configuration>
```

Enumerating Data Sources

Sometimes you want to display a list of the available data sources for a given provider. For example, if an application allows data to be read from one SQL Server and written to a different SQL Server, it might require a dialog box for selecting from a list of available SQL Servers for the source and destination servers. The following code snippet shows how to enumerate the data sources:

```
'VB
Protected Sub Button17_Click(ByVal sender As Object, _
      ByVal e As System.EventArgs) Handles Button17.Click
   Dim factory as DbProviderFactory  = _
      DbProviderFactories.GetFactory("System.Data.SqlClient")
   'get SQL Server instances
   Dim sources as DataTable = _
      factory.CreateDataSourceEnumerator().GetDataSources()
   Dim gv As GridView = GetGridView(275, 20)
   gv.DataSource = sources
   gv.DataBind()
End Sub
```

```
//C#
protected void Button17_Click(object sender, EventArgs e)
{
   DbProviderFactory factory =
      DbProviderFactories.GetFactory("System.Data.SqlClient");
   //get SQL Server instances
   DataTable sources =
      factory.CreateDataSourceEnumerator().GetDataSources();
   GridView gv = GetGridView(275, 20);
   gv.DataSource = sources;
   gv.DataBind();
}
```

Catching Provider Exceptions

All provider specific exceptions inherit from a common base class called *DbException*. When working with a provider-neutral coding model, your *try/catch* block can simply catch *DbException* generically instead of trying to catch each provider-specific exception.

The *DbException* object contains a *Data* collection property that contains information about the error; you can also use the *Message* property to retrieve information about the error. In the following example, a loop is created to show how you might want to retry a command on error. This code also demonstrates the use of the *try/catch* block and the *using* block.

```vb
'VB
Protected Sub Button19_Click(ByVal sender As Object, _
    ByVal e As System.EventArgs) Handles Button19.Click
  Dim lbl As Label = GetLabel(275, 20)
  Dim maxTries As Integer = 3
  For i As Integer = 1 To maxTries
    Dim pubs As ConnectionStringSettings = _
      ConfigurationManager.ConnectionStrings("PubsData")
    Dim connection As DbConnection = _
      New SqlConnection(pubs.ConnectionString)
    Dim cmd As DbCommand = connection.CreateCommand()

    Try
      Using (connection)
        Using (cmd)
          cmd.CommandType = CommandType.Text
          'choose the SQL statement; one causes error, other does not.
          cmd.CommandText = "RaisError('Custom Error',19,1) With Log"
          'cmd.CommandText = "Select @@Version"
          connection.Open()
          cmd.ExecuteNonQuery()
        End Using
      End Using
      lbl.Text += "Command Executed Successfully<br />"
      Return
    Catch xcp As DbException
      lbl.Text += xcp.Message + "<br />"
      for each item as DictionaryEntry in  xcp.Data
          lbl.Text += "  " + item.Key.ToString()
          lbl.Text += " = " + item.Value.ToString()
          lbl.Text += "<br />"
      Next
    End Try
  Next
  lbl.Text += "Max Tries Exceeded<br />"
End Sub

//C#
protected void Button19_Click(object sender, EventArgs e)
{
    Label lbl = GetLabel(275, 20);
    int maxTries = 3;
    for (int i = 0; i < maxTries; i++)
    {
        ConnectionStringSettings pubs =
```

```
        ConfigurationManager.ConnectionStrings["PubsData"];
    DbConnection connection =
        new SqlConnection(pubs.ConnectionString);
    DbCommand cmd = connection.CreateCommand();

    try
    {
        using (connection)
        {
            using (cmd)
            {
                cmd.CommandType = CommandType.Text;
                //choose the SQL statement; one causes error, other does not.
                cmd.CommandText = "RaiseError('Custom Error',19,1) With Log";
                //cmd.CommandText = "Select @@Version";
                connection.Open();
                cmd.ExecuteNonQuery();
            }
        }
        lbl.Text += "Command Executed Successfully<br />";
        return;
    }
    catch (DbException xcp)
    {
        lbl.Text += xcp.Message + "<br />";
        foreach (DictionaryEntry item in xcp.Data)
        {
            lbl.Text += "  " + item.Key.ToString();
            lbl.Text += " = " + item.Value.ToString();
            lbl.Text += "<br />";
        }
    }
    }
    lbl.Text += "Max Tries Exceeded<br />";
}
```

Detecting Information with the *Connection* Event   The connection classes contain an event called *InfoMessage* that can be used to retrieve general and error information from the database. You can use the *InfoMessage* event to view the results of SQL Print statements and any messages that are available as a result of the SQL RaiseError statement, regardless of the error level.

The following code snippet shows how this can be used to display information in a *Label* and a *GridView* by subscribing to the *InfoMessage* event when running a query that has informational messages:

```
'VB
Protected Sub Button18_Click(ByVal sender As Object, _
     ByVal e As System.EventArgs) Handles Button18.Click
```

```vbnet
    Dim errLabel As Label = GetLabel(275, 20)
    Dim errGrid As GridView = GetGridView(275, 100)
    Dim pubs As ConnectionStringSettings = _
        ConfigurationManager.ConnectionStrings("PubsData")
    Dim connection As New SqlConnection(pubs.ConnectionString)
    AddHandler connection.InfoMessage, AddressOf connection_InfoMessage
    Dim cmd As DbCommand = connection.CreateCommand()
    cmd.CommandType = CommandType.Text
    cmd.CommandText = "SELECT job_id, job_desc FROM Jobs;" _
        + "Print 'Hello Everyone';" _
        + "Raiserror('Info Error Occured', 10,1 )" _
        + "Print GetDate()"
    connection.Open()
    Dim rdr As DbDataReader = cmd.ExecuteReader()
    Dim publishers As New DataTable()
    publishers.Load(rdr, LoadOption.Upsert)
    connection.Close()
    Dim gv As GridView = GetGridView(275, 200)
    gv.DataSource = publishers
    gv.DataBind()
    errLabel.Text = errMessage
    errGrid.DataSource = errCollection
    errGrid.DataBind()
End Sub

Private errMessage As String = String.Empty
Private errCollection As New List(Of SqlError)

Private Sub connection_InfoMessage(ByVal sender As Object, _
        ByVal e As SqlInfoMessageEventArgs)
    errMessage += "Message: " + e.Message + "<br />"
    For Each err As SqlError In e.Errors
        errCollection.Add(err)
    Next
End Sub
```

```csharp
//C#
protected void Button18_Click(object sender, EventArgs e)
{
    Label errLabel = GetLabel(275, 20);
    GridView errGrid = GetGridView(275, 100);
    ConnectionStringSettings pubs =
        ConfigurationManager.ConnectionStrings["PubsData"];
    SqlConnection connection = new SqlConnection(pubs.ConnectionString);
    connection.InfoMessage +=
        new SqlInfoMessageEventHandler(connection_InfoMessage);
    DbCommand cmd = connection.CreateCommand();
    cmd.CommandType = CommandType.Text;
    cmd.CommandText = "SELECT job_id, job_desc FROM Jobs;"
      + "Print 'Hello Everyone';"
      + "Raiserror('Info Error Occured', 10,1 )"
      + "Print GetDate()";
    connection.Open();
```

```
DbDataReader rdr = cmd.ExecuteReader();
DataTable publishers = new DataTable();
publishers.Load(rdr, LoadOption.Upsert);
connection.Close();
GridView gv = GetGridView(275, 200);
gv.DataSource = publishers;
gv.DataBind();
errLabel.Text = errMessage;
errGrid.DataSource = errCollection;
errGrid.DataBind();
}

private string errMessage = string.Empty;
private List<SqlError> errCollection = new List<SqlError>();

void connection_InfoMessage(object sender, SqlInfoMessageEventArgs e)
{
    errMessage += "Message: " + e.Message + "<br />";
    foreach(SqlError err in e.Errors) errCollection.Add(err);
}
```

Using the ADO.NET *Transaction* Object

A *transaction* is an atomic unit of work that must be completed in its entirety. The transaction succeeds if it is committed and fails if it is aborted. Transactions have four essential properties: atomicity, consistency, isolation, and durability (known as the *ACID properties*).

- **Atomicity**   The work cannot be broken into smaller parts. Although a transaction might contain many SQL statements, it must be run as an all-or-nothing proposition, which means that, if a transaction is only partially complete when an error occurs, the work reverts to its state prior to the start of the transaction.

- **Consistency**   A transaction must operate on a consistent view of the data and must also leave the data in a consistent state. Any work in progress must not be visible to other transactions until the transaction has been committed.

- **Isolation**   A transaction should appear to be running by itself, the effects of other ongoing transactions must be invisible to this transaction, and the effects of this transaction must be invisible to other ongoing transactions.

- **Durability**   When a transaction is committed, it must be persisted so it is not lost in the event of a power failure or other system failure. Only committed transactions are recovered during power-up and crash recovery; uncommitted work is rolled back.

You can use the *DbConnection* object with the *BeginTransaction* method, which creates a *DbTransaction* object. The following code snippet shows how this is done:

```vb
'VB
Protected Sub Button20_Click(ByVal sender As Object, _
      ByVal e As System.EventArgs) Handles Button20.Click
   Dim lbl As Label = GetLabel(275, 20)
   Dim cnSetting As ConnectionStringSettings = _
      ConfigurationManager.ConnectionStrings("PubsData")
   Using cn As New SqlConnection()
      cn.ConnectionString = cnSetting.ConnectionString
      cn.Open()
      Using tran As SqlTransaction = cn.BeginTransaction()
         Try
            'work code here
            Using cmd As SqlCommand = cn.CreateCommand()
               cmd.Transaction = tran
               cmd.CommandText = "UPDATE jobs SET min_lvl=min_lvl * 1.1"
               Dim count As Integer = CInt(cmd.ExecuteNonQuery())
            lbl.Text = "Count = " + count.ToString()
            End Using
            'if we made it this far, commit
            tran.Commit()
         Catch xcp As Exception
            tran.Rollback()
            'cleanup code
            lbl.Text = xcp.Message
         End Try
      End Using
   End Using
End Sub
```

```csharp
//C#
protected void Button20_Click(object sender, EventArgs e)
{
   Label lbl = GetLabel(275, 20);
   ConnectionStringSettings cnSetting =
      ConfigurationManager.ConnectionStrings["PubsData"];
   using (SqlConnection cn = new SqlConnection())
   {
      cn.ConnectionString = cnSetting.ConnectionString;
      cn.Open();
      using (SqlTransaction tran = cn.BeginTransaction())
      {
         try
         {
            //work code here
            using (SqlCommand cmd = cn.CreateCommand())
            {
               cmd.Transaction = tran;
               cmd.CommandText = "UPDATE jobs SET min_lvl=min_lvl * 1.1";
               int count = (int)cmd.ExecuteNonQuery();
```

```
            lbl.Text = "Count = " + count.ToString();
          }
          //if we made it this far, commit
          tran.Commit();
        }
        catch (Exception xcp)
        {
          tran.Rollback();
          //cleanup code
          lbl.Text = xcp.Message;
        }
      }
    }
}
```

In this code, a *SqlConnection* object is created and opened, and the connection object is used to create a transaction object by executing the *BeginTransaction* method. The *try* block does the work and commits the transaction. If an exception is thrown, the *catch* block rolls back the transaction. Also, notice that the *SqlCommand* object must have its *Transaction* property assigned to the connection's transaction.

The scope of the transaction is limited to the code within the *try* block, but the transaction was created by a specific connection object, so the transaction cannot span to a different *Connection* object.

Asynchronous Data Access

Asynchronous access to data can greatly improve the performance or perceived performance (responsiveness) of your application. With asynchronous access, multiple commands can be executed simultaneously and notification of command completion can be accomplished by either polling, using *WaitHandles*, or delegating.

Synchronous vs. Asynchronous Access

Commands are normally executed synchronously, which causes the command to "block" program execution until the command has completed. Blocking execution keeps the program from continuing until the command has finished executing. This simplifies the writing of the code because the developer simply thinks about code execution in a rather procedural, step-by-step fashion, as shown in Figure 4-17. The problem arises with long-running commands, because blocking inhibits the program's ability to do other work such as performing additional commands or, more importantly, allowing the user to abort the command.

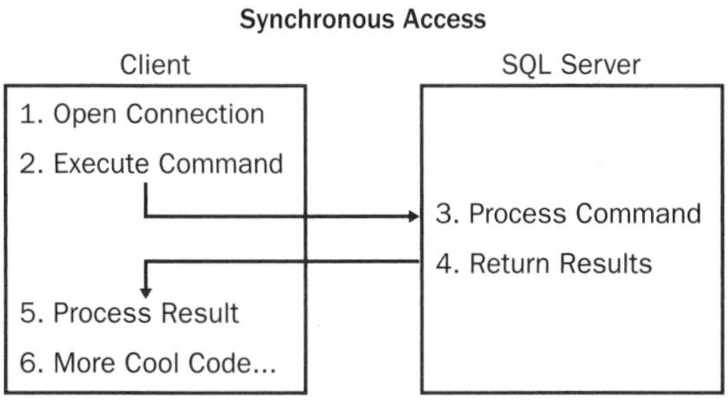

Figure 4-17 Synchronous data access.

Asynchronous command execution does not block program execution because it takes place on a new thread, which is another path of execution for your code. This means the original thread can continue executing while the new thread is waiting for its command to complete, as shown in Figure 4-18. The original thread is free to repaint the screen or listen for other events, such as button clicks.

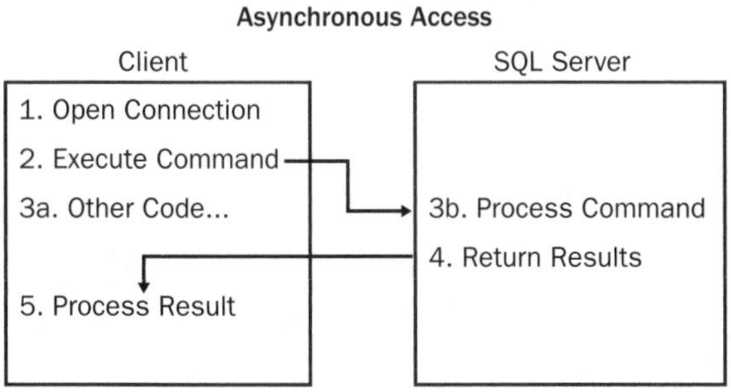

Figure 4-18 Asynchronous data access.

To demonstrate the difference between synchronous and asynchronous data access, the following code uses synchronous data access. This code simulates three long-running queries and then places a message in a label on the form.

```vb
'VB
Protected Sub Button21_Click(ByVal sender As Object, _
     ByVal e As System.EventArgs) Handles Button21.Click
  Dim lbl As Label = GetLabel(275, 20)
  Dim dtStart as DateTime = DateTime.Now
  Dim ver As String = string.Empty
  Dim cnSettings As SqlConnectionStringBuilder
  cnSettings = New SqlConnectionStringBuilder( _
     "Data Source=.;" _
        + "Database=PUBS;" _
        + "Integrated Security=True;" _
```

```
              + "Max Pool Size=5")
      Using cn1 As SqlConnection = _
            New SqlConnection(cnSettings.ConnectionString)
      Using cn2 As SqlConnection = _
            New SqlConnection(cnSettings.ConnectionString)
      Using cn3 As SqlConnection = _
            New SqlConnection(cnSettings.ConnectionString)
        Using cmd1 As SqlCommand = cn1.CreateCommand()
        Using cmd2 As SqlCommand = cn2.CreateCommand()
        Using cmd3 As SqlCommand = cn3.CreateCommand()
          cmd1.CommandText = _
              "WaitFor Delay '00:00:10' Select '1st Query<br />'"
          cmd2.CommandText = _
              "WaitFor Delay '00:00:10' Select '2nd Query<br />'"
          cmd3.CommandText = _
              "WaitFor Delay '00:00:10' Select '3rd Query<br />'"

          cn1.Open()
          Dim dr1 as SqlDataReader = cmd1.ExecuteReader()
          While dr1.Read()
              ver += dr1(0).ToString()
          End While
          dr1.Close()

          cn2.Open()
          Dim dr2 as SqlDataReader = cmd2.ExecuteReader()
          While dr2.Read()
              ver += dr2(0).ToString()
          End While
          dr2.Close()

          cn3.Open()
          Dim dr3 as SqlDataReader = cmd3.ExecuteReader()
          While dr3.Read()
              ver += dr3(0).ToString()
          End While
          dr3.Close()

        End Using
        End Using
        End Using
      End Using
      End Using
      End Using

      Dim dtEnd as DateTime = DateTime.Now
      ver += "Running Time: " _
          + (dtEnd - dtStart).ToString() + " Seconds<br />"
      lbl.Text = ver
End Sub

//C#
```

```csharp
protected void Button21_Click(object sender, EventArgs e)
{
    Label lbl = GetLabel(275, 20);
    DateTime dtStart = DateTime.Now;
    string ver = string.Empty;
    SqlConnectionStringBuilder cnSettings =
        new SqlConnectionStringBuilder(
    "Data Source=.;"
        + "Database=PUBS;"
        + "Integrated Security=True;"
        + "Max Pool Size=5");
    using( SqlConnection cn1 =
            new SqlConnection(cnSettings.ConnectionString))
    {
    using( SqlConnection cn2 =
            new SqlConnection(cnSettings.ConnectionString))
    {
    using( SqlConnection cn3 =
            new SqlConnection(cnSettings.ConnectionString))
    {
        using(SqlCommand cmd1 = cn1.CreateCommand())
        {
        using(SqlCommand cmd2 = cn2.CreateCommand())
        {
        using(SqlCommand cmd3 = cn3.CreateCommand())
        {
            cmd1.CommandText =
                "WaitFor Delay '00:00:10' Select '1st Query<br />'";
            cmd2.CommandText =
                "WaitFor Delay '00:00:10' Select '2nd Query<br />'";
            cmd3.CommandText =
                "WaitFor Delay '00:00:10' Select '3rd Query<br />'";

            cn1.Open();
            SqlDataReader dr1 = cmd1.ExecuteReader();
            while( dr1.Read())
            {
                ver += dr1[0].ToString();
            }
            dr1.Close();

            cn2.Open();
            SqlDataReader dr2 = cmd2.ExecuteReader();
            while( dr2.Read())
            {
                ver += dr2[0].ToString();
            }
            dr2.Close();

            cn3.Open();
            SqlDataReader dr3 = cmd3.ExecuteReader();
            while( dr3.Read())
```

```
        {
            ver += dr3[0].ToString();
        }
        dr3.Close();

    }
    }
    }
}
}
}

DateTime dtEnd = DateTime.Now;
ver += "Running Time: "
    + (dtEnd - dtStart).ToString() + " Seconds<br />";
lbl.Text = ver;
}
```

In this code, each of the three queries is run, one at a time. The running time displayed is approximately 30 seconds.

NOTE   New in ASP.NET 2.0

The *Asynchronous Processing* and *async* connection string keys are new in version 2.0 of the .NET Framework.

To use asynchronous code to run these queries, you must set the connection string to have *Asynchronous Processing=true* and *async=true,* or an exception is thrown. Next, one of the command object's *Begin* methods must be executed. The *SqlCommand* object provides the *BeginExecuteNoQuery, BeginExecuteReader,* and *BeginExecuteXmlReader* methods. The following code shows the asynchronous implementation:

```
'VB
Protected Sub Button22_Click(ByVal sender As Object, _
      ByVal e As System.EventArgs) Handles Button22.Click
    Dim lbl As Label = GetLabel(275, 20)
  Dim dtStart as DateTime = DateTime.Now
  Dim ver As String = string.Empty
  Dim cnSettings As SqlConnectionStringBuilder
  cnSettings = New SqlConnectionStringBuilder( _
     "Data Source=.;" _
        + "Database=PUBS;" _
        + "Asynchronous Processing=true;" _
        + "Integrated Security=True;" _
        + "Max Pool Size=5")
  Using cn1 As SqlConnection = _
        New SqlConnection(cnSettings.ConnectionString)
  Using cn2 As SqlConnection = _
        New SqlConnection(cnSettings.ConnectionString)
```

```
    Using cn3 As SqlConnection = _
        New SqlConnection(cnSettings.ConnectionString)
      Using cmd1 As SqlCommand = cn1.CreateCommand()
      Using cmd2 As SqlCommand = cn2.CreateCommand()
      Using cmd3 As SqlCommand = cn3.CreateCommand()
          cmd1.CommandText = _
              "WaitFor Delay '00:00:10' Select '1st Query<br />'"
          cmd2.CommandText = _
              "WaitFor Delay '00:00:10' Select '2nd Query<br />'"
          cmd3.CommandText = _
              "WaitFor Delay '00:00:10' Select '3rd Query<br />'"

          cn1.Open()
          cn2.Open()
          cn3.Open()
          Dim ar1 as IAsyncResult = cmd1.BeginExecuteReader()
          Dim ar2 as IAsyncResult = cmd2.BeginExecuteReader()
          Dim ar3 as IAsyncResult = cmd3.BeginExecuteReader()

          ar1.AsyncWaitHandle.WaitOne()
          Dim dr1 as SqlDataReader = cmd1.EndExecuteReader(ar1)
          While dr1.Read()
              ver += dr1(0).ToString()
          End While
          dr1.Close()

          ar2.AsyncWaitHandle.WaitOne()
          Dim dr2 as SqlDataReader = cmd2.EndExecuteReader(ar2)
          While dr2.Read()
              ver += dr2(0).ToString()
          End While
          dr2.Close()

          ar3.AsyncWaitHandle.WaitOne()
          Dim dr3 as SqlDataReader = cmd3.EndExecuteReader(ar3)
          While dr3.Read()
              ver += dr3(0).ToString()
          End While
          dr3.Close()

      End Using
      End Using
      End Using
    End Using
    End Using
    End Using

    Dim dtEnd as DateTime = DateTime.Now
    ver += "Running Time: " _
        + (dtEnd - dtStart).ToString() + " Seconds<br />"
    lbl.Text = ver
End Sub
```

```csharp
//C#
protected void Button22_Click(object sender, EventArgs e)
{
    Label lbl = GetLabel(275, 20);
    DateTime dtStart = DateTime.Now;
    string ver = string.Empty;
    SqlConnectionStringBuilder cnSettings =
        new SqlConnectionStringBuilder(
    "Data Source=.;"
        + "Database=PUBS;"
        + "Asynchronous Processing=true;"
        + "Integrated Security=True;"
        + "Max Pool Size=5");
    using (SqlConnection cn1 =
            new SqlConnection(cnSettings.ConnectionString))
    {
    using (SqlConnection cn2 =
            new SqlConnection(cnSettings.ConnectionString))
    {
    using (SqlConnection cn3 =
            new SqlConnection(cnSettings.ConnectionString))
    {
        using (SqlCommand cmd1 = cn1.CreateCommand())
        {
        using (SqlCommand cmd2 = cn2.CreateCommand())
        {
        using (SqlCommand cmd3 = cn3.CreateCommand())
        {
            cmd1.CommandText =
                "WaitFor Delay '00:00:10' Select '1st Query<br />'";
            cmd2.CommandText =
                "WaitFor Delay '00:00:10' Select '2nd Query<br />'";
            cmd3.CommandText =
                "WaitFor Delay '00:00:10' Select '3rd Query<br />'";

            cn1.Open();
            cn2.Open();
            cn3.Open();
            IAsyncResult ar1 = cmd1.BeginExecuteReader();
            IAsyncResult ar2 = cmd2.BeginExecuteReader();
            IAsyncResult ar3 = cmd3.BeginExecuteReader();

            ar1.AsyncWaitHandle.WaitOne();
            SqlDataReader dr1 = cmd1.EndExecuteReader(ar1);
            while (dr1.Read())
            {
                ver += dr1[0].ToString();
            }
            dr1.Close();

            ar2.AsyncWaitHandle.WaitOne();
            SqlDataReader dr2 = cmd2.EndExecuteReader(ar2);
            while (dr2.Read())
```

```
        {
            ver += dr2[0].ToString();
        }
        dr2.Close();

        ar3.AsyncWaitHandle.WaitOne();
        SqlDataReader dr3 = cmd3.EndExecuteReader(ar3);
        while (dr3.Read())
        {
            ver += dr3[0].ToString();
        }
        dr3.Close();

    }
    }
    }
}
}
}

DateTime dtEnd = DateTime.Now;
ver += "Running Time: "
    + (dtEnd - dtStart).ToString() + " Seconds<br />";
lbl.Text = ver;
}
```

MORE INFO **Asynchronous command execution**

The following Microsoft link provides more information about asynchronous command execution in ADO.NET 2.0:

http://msdn.microsoft.com/data/ref/adonet/default.aspx?pull=/library/en-us/dnvs05/html/async2.asp.

As you can see, the label is populated with the result of the queries, and the running time is only about 10 seconds. The *BeginExecuteReader* method was used to spawn each of the new threads. After the threads were spawned, the *IAsyncResult* object's *AsyncWaitHandle* property was used to wait until the command finished executing.

Storing and Retrieving Binary Large Object (BLOB) Data

When working with data, one challenge is to move large objects between the client application and the database server. In some scenarios, you might be able to treat large-object data just like any other data, but in many cases, you might be forced to look at alternative approaches.

In ADO.NET you can work with BLOBs by using a *SqlDataReader* object to return a result set, by using a *SqlDataAdapter* object to fill a *DataTable* object, or by using a *Sql-Parameter* configured as an output parameter. If an object is so large that you can't load it without running out of memory, you must deal with it by reading and processing it a chunk at a time.

Reading BLOB Data The normal operation of the *DataReader* object is to read one row at a time. When the row is available, all of the columns are buffered and available for you to access in any order.

To access the *DataReader* object in a stream fashion, you can change the *DbCommand* object's behavior to a sequential stream when you execute the *ExecuteReader* method. In this mode, you must get the bytes from the stream in the order of each column that is being returned, and you can't retrieve the data more than once. You essentially have access to the underlying *DataReader* object's stream.

To work with chunks of data, you should understand the operation of a stream object. When you read from a stream, you pass a byte array buffer that the stream populates. The stream does not have an obligation to populate the buffer, however. The stream's only obligation is to populate the buffer with at least one byte if the stream is not at its end. If the end has been reached, no bytes are read. When you use slow streams, such as a slow Internet network stream, data might not be available when you attempt to read the stream. In this case, the stream is not at its end, but no bytes are available, and the thread will block (wait) until one byte has been received. Based on the stream operation described, you should always perform stream reading in a loop that continues until no more bytes are read.

The following code sample reads all of the logos from the pub_info table in the *pubs* database and stores the logos to a GIF file:

```vb
'VB
Protected Sub Button23_Click(ByVal sender As Object, _
      ByVal e As System.EventArgs) Handles Button23.Click
   Const pubIdColumn As Integer = 0
   Const pubLogoColumn As Integer = 1
   'bufferSize must be bigger than oleOffset
   Const bufferSize As Integer = 100
   Dim buffer(bufferSize) As Byte
   Dim byteCountRead As Integer
   Dim currentIndex As Long = 0

   Dim pubSetting As ConnectionStringSettings = _
      ConfigurationManager.ConnectionStrings("PubsData")
   Using cn As New SqlConnection()
      cn.ConnectionString = pubSetting.ConnectionString
```

```
      cn.Open()

   Using cmd As SqlCommand = cn.CreateCommand()
      cmd.CommandText = _
         "SELECT pub_id, logo FROM pub_info"
      Dim rdr As SqlDataReader = cmd.ExecuteReader( _
         CommandBehavior.SequentialAccess)
      While (rdr.Read())

         Dim pubId As String = _
            rdr.GetString(pubIdColumn)
         Dim fileName As String = MapPath(pubId + ".gif")

         ' Create a file to hold the output.
         Using fs As New FileStream( _
            fileName, FileMode.OpenOrCreate, _
            FileAccess.Write)
            currentIndex = 0
            byteCountRead = _
               CInt(rdr.GetBytes(pubLogoColumn, _
               currentIndex, buffer, 0, bufferSize))
            While (byteCountRead <> 0)
               fs.Write(buffer, 0, byteCountRead)
               currentIndex += byteCountRead
               byteCountRead = _
                CInt(rdr.GetBytes(pubLogoColumn, _
                currentIndex, buffer, 0, bufferSize))
            End While
         End Using
      End While
   End Using
   End Using
   Dim lbl as Label = GetLabel(275,20)
   lbl.Text = "Done Writing Logos To Disk"
End Sub

//C#
protected void Button23_Click(object sender, EventArgs e)
{
   const int pubIdColumn = 0;
   const int pubLogoColumn = 1;
   //bufferSize must be bigger than oleOffset
   const int bufferSize = 100;
   byte[] buffer = new byte[bufferSize];
   int byteCountRead;
   long currentIndex = 0;

   ConnectionStringSettings pubSetting =
      ConfigurationManager.ConnectionStrings["PubsData"];
   using (SqlConnection cn = new SqlConnection())
   {
      cn.ConnectionString = pubSetting.ConnectionString;
```

```
            cn.Open();

            using (SqlCommand cmd = cn.CreateCommand())
            {
                cmd.CommandText =
                    "SELECT pub_id, logo FROM pub_info";
                SqlDataReader rdr = cmd.ExecuteReader(
                    CommandBehavior.SequentialAccess);
                while (rdr.Read())
                {
                    string pubId =
                        rdr.GetString(pubIdColumn);
                    string fileName = MapPath(pubId + ".gif");

                    //Create a file to hold the output.
                    using (FileStream fs = new FileStream(
                        fileName, FileMode.OpenOrCreate,
                        FileAccess.Write))
                    {
                        currentIndex = 0;
                        byteCountRead =
                            (int)rdr.GetBytes(pubLogoColumn,
                            currentIndex, buffer, 0, bufferSize);
                        while (byteCountRead != 0)
                        {
                            fs.Write(buffer, 0, byteCountRead);
                            currentIndex += byteCountRead;
                            byteCountRead =
                             (int)rdr.GetBytes(pubLogoColumn,
                             currentIndex, buffer, 0, bufferSize);
                        }
                    }
                }
            }
        }
        Label lbl = GetLabel(275, 20);
        lbl.Text = "Done Writing Logos To Disk";
    }
```

This code gives you the pattern for reading the BLOB and writing it to a file. The *ExecuteReader* method is executed with the *CommandBehavior.SequentialAccess* parameter. Next, a loop runs to read row data, and within the loop and for each row, the pub_id is read to create the file name. A new *FileStream* object is created, which opens the file for writing.

Next, a loop reads bytes into a byte array buffer, and then writes the bytes to the file. The buffer size is set to 100 bytes, which keeps the amount of data in memory to a minimum.

Writing BLOB Data   You can write BLOB data to a database by issuing the appropriate INSERT or UPDATE statement and passing the BLOB value as an input parameter. You can use the SQL Server *UPDATETEXT* function to write the BLOB data in chunks of a specified size. The *UPDATETEXT* function requires a pointer to the BLOB field being updated, so the SQL Server *TEXTPTR* function is first called to get a pointer to the field of the record to be updated.

The following code example updates the pub_info table, replacing the logo for pub_id 9999 with a new logo from a file:

```
'VB
Protected Sub Button24_Click(ByVal sender As Object, _
      ByVal e As System.EventArgs) Handles Button24.Click
  Const bufferSize As Integer = 100
  Dim buffer(bufferSize) As Byte
  Dim currentIndex As Long = 0
  Dim logoPtr() As Byte

  Dim pubString As ConnectionStringSettings = _
    ConfigurationManager.ConnectionStrings("PubsData")
  Using cn As New SqlConnection()
    cn.ConnectionString = pubString.ConnectionString
    cn.Open()

    Using cmd As SqlCommand = cn.CreateCommand()
      cmd.CommandText = _
  "SELECT TEXTPTR(Logo) FROM pub_info WHERE pub_id = '9999'"
      logoPtr = CType(cmd.ExecuteScalar(), Byte())
    End Using
    Using cmd As SqlCommand = cn.CreateCommand()
      cmd.CommandText = _
  "UPDATETEXT pub_info.Logo @Pointer @Offset null @Data"
      Dim ptrParm As SqlParameter = _
        cmd.Parameters.Add("@Pointer", SqlDbType.Binary, 16)
      ptrParm.Value = logoPtr
      Dim logoParm As SqlParameter = _
        cmd.Parameters.Add("@Data", SqlDbType.Image)
      Dim offsetParm As SqlParameter = _
        cmd.Parameters.Add("@Offset", SqlDbType.Int)
      offsetParm.Value = 0
      Using fs As New FileStream(MapPath("Logo.gif"), _
          FileMode.Open, FileAccess.Read)
        Dim count As Integer = fs.Read(buffer, 0, bufferSize)
        While (count <> 0)
          logoParm.Value = buffer
          logoParm.Size = count
          cmd.ExecuteNonQuery()
          currentIndex += count
```

```
                offsetParm.Value = currentIndex
                count = fs.Read(buffer, 0, bufferSize)
            End While
        End Using
    End Using
  End Using
  Dim lbl As Label = GetLabel(275, 20)
  lbl.Text = "Done Writing Logos To DB"
End Sub
```

```
//C#
protected void Button24_Click(object sender, EventArgs e)
{
  const int bufferSize = 100;
  byte[] buffer = new byte[bufferSize];
  long currentIndex = 0;
  byte[] logoPtr;

  ConnectionStringSettings pubString =
      ConfigurationManager.ConnectionStrings["PubsData"];
  using (SqlConnection cn = new SqlConnection())
  {
      cn.ConnectionString = pubString.ConnectionString;
      cn.Open();

      using (SqlCommand cmd = cn.CreateCommand())
      {
          cmd.CommandText =
  "SELECT TEXTPTR(Logo) FROM pub_info WHERE pub_id = '9999'";
          logoPtr = (byte[])cmd.ExecuteScalar();
      }
      using (SqlCommand cmd = cn.CreateCommand())
      {
          cmd.CommandText =
  "UPDATETEXT pub_info.Logo @Pointer @Offset null @Data";
          SqlParameter ptrParm =
              cmd.Parameters.Add("@Pointer", SqlDbType.Binary, 16);
          ptrParm.Value = logoPtr;
          SqlParameter logoParm =
              cmd.Parameters.Add("@Data", SqlDbType.Image);
          SqlParameter offsetParm =
              cmd.Parameters.Add("@Offset", SqlDbType.Int);
          offsetParm.Value = 0;
          using (FileStream fs = new FileStream(MapPath("Logo.gif"),
              FileMode.Open, FileAccess.Read))
          {
              int count = fs.Read(buffer, 0, bufferSize);
              while (count != 0)
              {
                  logoParm.Value = buffer;
                  logoParm.Size = count;
                  cmd.ExecuteNonQuery();
```

```
            currentIndex += count;
            offsetParm.Value = currentIndex;
            count = fs.Read(buffer, 0, bufferSize);
          }
        }
      }
    }
    Label lbl = GetLabel(275, 20);
    lbl.Text = "Done Writing Logos To DB";
}
```

This code opens a connection and retrieves a pointer to the logo that is to be updated by calling the *TEXTPTR* function using a *SqlCommand* object. Then, a new *SqlCommand* object is created, and its *CommandText* property is set to the following:

```
"UPDATETEXT pub_info.logo @Pointer @Offset null @Data "
```

Note that the *null* parameter defines the quantity of bytes to delete. Passing *null* indicates that all existing data should be deleted. Passing a *0* (zero) indicates that no data should be deleted; the new data simply overwrites the existing data. (You pass a number if you want to delete some of the data.) The other parameters represent the pointer to the start of the logo, the current offset to insert data, and the data being sent to the database.

After the file is opened, a loop starts that reads chunks of the file into the buffer and then sends the chunks to the database.

Quick Check

1. What two objects are required to send instructions to a SQL Server database?

2. What connected object is used to obtain the fastest access to SQL Server data?

3. When you need to copy large amonts of data to SQL Server, what object should you use?

Quick Check Answers

1. *SqlConnection* and *SqlCommand* objects

2. The *SqlDataReader* object

3. The *SqlBulkCopy* object

Lab: Working with Connected Data

In this lab, you will work with the Visual Studio 2005 GUI to create a Web page that displays the shippers in the *Northwind* database and supports inserts, updates, and deletes.

▶ **Exercise 1: Create the Web Site and the Typed *DataSet***

In this exercise, you will create the Web site and add the controls to the site.

1. Open Visual Studio 2005 and create a new Web site called **WorkingWithConnectedData** using your preferred programming language. The new Web site will be created and a Web page called Default.aspx is displayed.

2. In the Solution Explorer, right-click the App_Data folder and select Add Existing Item. Navigate to the Northwind.mdf file and select it.

3. Drag a *DetailsView* control onto the Web page and size it wide enough to display a company name.

4. Click the symbol in the upper-right corner of the *DetailsView* control to display the DetailsView Tasks window.

5. Click the Auto Format link and select Professional.

6. Click the Choose Data Source drop-down list and select New Data Source to start the Data Source Configuration Wizard. For the data source type, select Database and click OK.

7. On the Choose Your Data Connection screen, click New Connection. The Data-Source is set to Microsoft SQL Server (SqlClient). Click the Change button and select the Microsoft SQL Server Database File (SqlClient). In the Database File Name property, select the Northwind.mdf file that you just added to the App_Data folder and click Open. Click OK to accept the changes and go back to the Choose Your Data Connection screen. Click Next to go to the Save the Connection String to the Application Configuration File screen.

8. In the Save the Connection String to the Application Configuration File screen, change the connection string name to **nwConnection** and click Next.

9. In the Configure Select Statement screen, select the Shippers table from the Name drop-down list box and click the asterisk (*) to select all rows and columns.

10. While still in the Configure Select Statement screen, click Advanced and select the options for both Generate Insert, Update, And Delete statements and Use Optimistic Concurrency. Click OK.

11. In the Test Query screen, click the Test Query button to see the data. Click Finish to return to the DetailsView Tasks window.

12. Once you select the Enable Paging, Enable Inserting, Enable Editing, and Enable Deleting options, configuration of the *DetailsView* is complete.

13. Run the Web page. Notice that the data was retrieved and displayed.

14. Add a new shipper. Notice that the CompanyName and the Phone fields are displayed, but the ShipperID field is an autonumber field, so it's not displayed.

Lesson Summary

- Connected classes, also known as provider classes, are responsible for movement of data between the data store and the disconnected classes. A valid *DbConnection* object is required to use most of the primary provider classes.

- SQL Express is an excellent database server for development because the .mdf database file can be placed into the project and the file can be configured to be copied to the output folder every time the application is built and run.

- You use the *DbCommand* object to send a SQL command to a data store. You can also create parameters and pass them to the *DbCommand* object.

- The *DbDataReader* object provides a high-performance method of retrieving data from a data store by delivering a forward-only, read-only, server-side cursor.

- The *SqlBulkCopy* object can be used to copy data from a number of sources to a SQL Server table.

- You can use the *DbDataAdapter* object to retrieve and update data between a *DataTable* and a data store. The *DbDataAdapter* can contain a single *SelectCommand* for read-only data, or it can contain *SelectCommand*, *InsertCommand*, *UpdateCommand*, and *DeleteCommand* for fully updatable data.

- The *DbProviderFactory* object helps you create provider-independent code, which might be necessary when the data store needs to be quickly changeable.

- Connection pooling improves application responsiveness by allowing users to reuse existing active connections instead of creating new connections when a request is made to the database.

- A client-side connection manager maintains a list, or pool, of available connections that can be reused.

- Use the *using* statement to ensure that the *Dispose* method is called on the connection and command objects to avoid connection leaks.

- Asynchronous access to data can greatly improve the performance or perceived performance (responsiveness) of your application.

- To code asynchronous access in your application, use the Asynchronous Processing setting in the connection string and call one of the command object's *Begin* methods.

- You can use the *DbProviderFactories* object to obtain a list of the provider factories that are available on a computer.

- You can work with BLOBs using the same techniques you use for smaller data types, unless the objects are too large to fit into memory. When a BLOB is too large to fit into memory, you must use streaming techniques to move the data.

- Streaming involves "chunking" data, which means moving data in chunks to keep from using too much memory.

Lesson Review

You can use the following questions to test your knowledge of the information in Lesson 2, "Using the ADO.NET Connected Classes." The questions are also available on the companion CD if you prefer to review them in electronic form.

NOTE Answers

Answers to these questions and explanations of why each answer choice is right or wrong are located in the "Answers" section at the end of the book.

---

1. Which of the following ways can you proactively clean up a database connection's resources? (Choose two.)

   A. Execute the *DbConnection* object's *Cleanup* method.

   B. Execute the *DbConnection* object's *Close* method.

   C. Assign *Nothing* (C# *null*) to the variable that references the *DbConnection* object.

   D. Create a *using* block for the *DbConnection* object.

2. What event can you subscribe to if you want to display information from SQL Print statements? (Choose one.)

   A. *InfoMessage*

   B. *MessageReceived*

   C. *PostedMessage*

   D. *NewInfo*

3. To perform asynchronous data access, what must be added to the connection string?

   A. *BeginExecute=true*

   B. *MultiThreaded=true*

   C. *MultipleActiveResultSets=true*

   D. *Asynchronous=true*

Lesson 3: Working with XML Data

The .NET Framework provides vast support for XML. The implementation of XML is focused on performance, reliability, and scalability. The integration of XML with ADO.NET offers the ability to use XML documents as a data source. This lesson will cover many of the XML objects that are included in the .NET Framework.

After this lesson, you will be able to:

■ Use the Document Object Model to manage XML data.

■ Use the *XmlNamedNodeMap* object.

■ Use the *XmlNodeList* object.

■ Use the *XmlReader* and *XmlWriter* objects.

■ Use the *XmlNodeReader* to read node trees.

■ Validate Data with the *XmlValidatingReader*.

Estimated lesson time: 60 minutes

Real World

Glenn Johnson

The world has big plans for XML and its supporting technologies, with many companies already embracing XML, and many companies planning implementations of XML technologies in new applications. The World Wide Web Consortium (W3C) envisions the future Web as being completely based on XML technologies. XML is often the preferred format for data being stored to a file and for data being sent across the Internet because XML can represent hierarchical data, is text-based, and is not platform dependent.

The XML Document Object Model

The W3C has provided standards that define the structure and provide a standard programming interface that can be used in a wide variety of environments and applications for XML documents. This is called the *Document Object Model* (DOM). Classes that support the DOM are typically capable of random access navigation and modification of the XML document.

XML Namespace

The XML classes are accessible by setting a reference to the System.Xml.dll file and adding the Imports *System.Xml* (C# using *System.Xml;*) directive to the code.

The System.Data.dll file also extends the *System.Xml* namespace. This is the location of the *XmlDataDocument* class. If this class is required, a reference must be set to the System.Data.dll file.

XML Objects

This section covers the primary XML classes in the .NET Framework. Each of these classes offers varying degrees of functionality. It's important to look at each of the classes in detail in order to make the correct decision on which classes should be used. Figure 4-19 shows a high-level view of the objects that are covered.

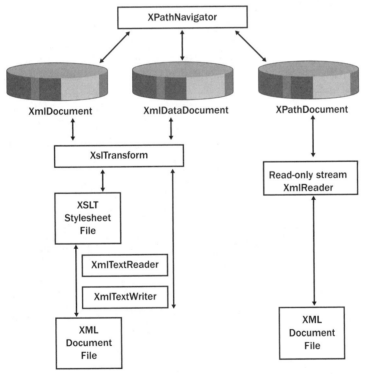

Figure 4-19   The primary XML objects that are covered in this lesson.

XmlDocument and XmlDataDocument   The *XmlDocument* and *XmlDataDocument* objects are in-memory representations of XML that use the Document Object Model (DOM) Level 1 and Level 2. These classes can be used to navigate and edit the XML nodes.

The *XmlDataDocument* inherits from the *XmlDocument* and also represents relational data. The *XmlDataDocument* can expose its data as a *DataSet* to provide relational and nonrelational views of the data. The *XmlDataDocument* is in the *System.Data.dll* assembly.

These classes provide many methods to implement the Level 2 specifications, and also contain methods to facilitate common operations. The methods are summarized in Table 4-5. The *XmlDocument* contains all of the methods for creating *XmlElements* and *XmlAttributes*.

Table 4-5   *XmlDocument* and *XmlDataDocument* Methods

Method	Description
CreateNodeType	Creates an XML node in the document. There are *Create* methods for each node type.
CloneNode	Creates a duplicate of an XML node. This method takes a Boolean argument called deep. If deep is *false*, only the node is copied. If deep is *true*, all child nodes are recursively copied as well.
GetElementByID	Locates and returns a single node based on its *ID* attribute. Note that this requires a Document Type Definition (DTD) that identifies an attribute as being an *ID* type. An attribute that has the name of *ID* is not an *ID* type by default.
GetElementsByTagName	Locates and returns an *XmlNodeList* containing all of the descendant elements based on the element name.

Table 4-5 *XmlDocument* and *XmlDataDocument* **Methods**

Method	Description
ImportNode	Imports a node from a different *XmlDocument* into this document. The source node remains unmodified in the original *XmlDocument*. This method takes a Boolean argument called deep. If deep is *false*, only the node is copied. If deep is *true*, all child nodes are recursively copied as well.
InsertBefore	Inserts an *XmlNode* immediately before the referenced node. If the referenced node is nothing, then the new node is inserted at the end of the child list. If the node already exists in the tree, the original node is removed when the new node is inserted.
InsertAfter	Inserts an XmlNode immediately after the referenced node. If the referenced node is nothing, then the new node is inserted at the beginning of the child list. If the node already exists in the tree, the original node is removed when the new node is inserted.
Load	Loads an XML document from a disk file, Uniform Resource Locator (URL), or stream.
LoadXml	Loads an XML document from a string.
Normalize	Assures that there are no adjacent text nodes in the document. This is like saving the document and reloading it. This method may be desirable when text nodes are being programmatically added to an *XmlDocument*, and the text nodes are side by side. Normalizing combines the adjacent text nodes to produce a single text node.

Table 4-5 *XmlDocument* and *XmlDataDocument* Methods

Method	Description
PrependChild	Inserts a node at the beginning of the child node list. If the new node is already in the tree, it is removed before it is inserted. If the node is an *XmlDocument-Fragment*, the complete fragment is added.
ReadNode	Loads a node from an XML document using an *XmlTextReader* or *XmlNodeReader* object. The reader must be on a valid node before executing this method. The reader reads the opening tag, all child nodes, and the closing tag of the current element. This repositions the reader to the next node.
RemoveAll	Removes all children and attributes from the current node.
RemoveChild	Removes the referenced child.
ReplaceChild	Replaces the referenced child with a new node. If the new node is already in the tree, it is removed first.
Save	Saves the XML document to a disk file, URL, or stream.
SelectNodes	Selects a list of nodes that match the XPath expression.
SelectSingleNode	Selects the first node that matches the XPath expression.
WriteTo	Writes a node to another XML document using an *XmlTextWriter*.
WriteContentsTo	Writes a node and all of its descendants to another XML document using an *XmlTextWriter*.

XPathDocument   The *XPathDocument* provides a cached read-only *XmlDocument* that can be used for performing quick XPath queries. This constructor for this class requires a stream object in order to create an instance of this object. The only useful method that this class exposes is the *CreateNavigator* method.

XmlConvert   The *XmlConvert* class has many static methods for converting between XSD data types and common language runtime (CLR) data types. This class is especially important when working with data sources that allow names that are not valid XML names. If a column in a database table is called List Price, trying to create an element or attribute with a space character throws an exception. Using *XmlConvert* to encode the name converts the space to _0x0020_, so the XML element name becomes *List_x0020_Price*. Later, this name can be decoded using the *XmlConvert.DecodeName* method.

The *XmlConvert* also provides many static methods for converting strings to numeric values.

XPathNavigator   The *DocumentNavigator* provides efficient navigation of an *XmlDocument* by providing XPath support for navigation. The *XPathNavigator* uses a cursor model and XPath queries to provide read-only random access to the data. The *XPathNavigator* supports XML Stylesheet Language Transforms (XSLT) and can be used as the input to a transform.

XmlNodeReader   The *XmlNodeReader* provides forward-only access to data in an *XmlDocument* or *XmlDataDocument*. It provides the ability to start at a given node in the *XmlDocument* and sequentially read each node.

XmlTextReader   The *XmlTextWrite* provides non-cached, forward-only access to XML data. It parses XML tokens but makes no attempt to represent the XML document as a Document Object Model (DOM). The *XmlTextReader* does not perform document validation, but it checks the XML data to ensure that it is well formed.

XmlTextWriter   The *XmlTextWriter* provides non-cached, forward-only writing of XML data to a stream of files, ensuring that the data conforms to the W3C XML 1.0 standard. The *XmlTextWriter* contains logic for working with namespaces and resolving namespace conflicts.

XmlValidatingReader   Obsolete; replaced by *XmlReader*.

XmlReader   The *XmlReader* provides an object for reading and validating against DTD, XML Schema Reduced (XDR), or Xml Schema Definition (XSD). The constructor expects a Reader or a string as the source of the XML to be validated.

XslTransform   The *XslTransform* can transform an XML document using an XSL stylesheet. The *XslTransform* supports XSLT 1.0 syntax and provides two methods: *Load* and *Transform*.

The *Load* method is used to load an XSLT stylesheet from a file or a stream. The *Transform* method is used to perform the transformation. The *Transform* method has several overloads but essentially expects a *XmlDocument* or *XmlNode* as the first argument, an *XsltArgumentList*, and an output stream.

Working with XML Documents

There are certainly many ways of working with XML data in the .NET Framework. This section covers some of the methods, such as creating a new XML file from scratch, reading and writing XML files, searching XML data, and transforming XML data.

Creating a New *XmlDocument* from Scratch   To create a new *XmlDocument*, start by creating an *XmlDocument* object. The *XmlDocument* object contains *CreateElement* and *CreateAttribute* methods that are used to add nodes to the *XmlDocument* object. The *XmlElement* contains the *Attributes* property, which is an *XmlAttributeCollection*. The *XmlAttributeCollection* inherits from the *XmlNamedNodeMap* class, which is a collection of names with corresponding values.

The following code shows how an *XmlDocument* can be created from scratch and saved to a file, and also uses the *GetLabel* method that was defined earlier in this chapter.

```
'VB
Protected Sub Button1_Click(ByVal sender As Object, _
    ByVal e As System.EventArgs) Handles Button1.Click
  'Declare and create new XmlDocument
  Dim xmlDoc As New XmlDocument()

  Dim el As XmlElement
  Dim childCounter As Integer
  Dim grandChildCounter As Integer

  'Create the xml declaration first
```

```
   xmlDoc.AppendChild( _
    xmlDoc.CreateXmlDeclaration("1.0", "utf-8", Nothing))

   'Create the root node and append into doc
   el = xmlDoc.CreateElement("myRoot")
   xmlDoc.AppendChild(el)

   'Child Loop
   For childCounter = 1 To 4
      Dim childelmt As XmlElement
      Dim childattr As XmlAttribute

      'Create child with ID attribute
      childelmt = xmlDoc.CreateElement("myChild")
      childattr = xmlDoc.CreateAttribute("ID")
      childattr.Value = childCounter.ToString()
      childelmt.Attributes.Append(childattr)

      'Append element into the root element
      el.AppendChild(childelmt)
      For grandChildCounter = 1 To 3
         'Create grandchildren
         childelmt.AppendChild(xmlDoc.CreateElement("GrandChild"))
      Next
   Next

   'Save to file
   xmlDoc.Save(MapPath("XmlDocumentTest.xml"))
   Dim lbl as Label = GetLabel(275, 20)
   lbl.Text = "XmlDocumentTest.xml Created"
End Sub
```

//C#
```
protected void Button1_Click(object sender, EventArgs e)
{
   //Declare and create new XmlDocument
   XmlDocument xmlDoc = new XmlDocument();

   XmlElement el;
   int childCounter;
   int grandChildCounter;

   //Create the xml declaration first
   xmlDoc.AppendChild(
    xmlDoc.CreateXmlDeclaration("1.0", "utf-8", null));

   //Create the root node and append into doc
   el = xmlDoc.CreateElement("myRoot");
   xmlDoc.AppendChild(el);

   //Child Loop
```

```
    for (childCounter = 1; childCounter <= 4; childCounter++)
    {
        XmlElement childelmt;
        XmlAttribute childattr;

        //Create child with ID attribute
        childelmt = xmlDoc.CreateElement("myChild");
        childattr = xmlDoc.CreateAttribute("ID");
        childattr.Value = childCounter.ToString();
        childelmt.Attributes.Append(childattr);

        //Append element into the root element
        el.AppendChild(childelmt);
        for (grandChildCounter = 1; grandChildCounter <= 3; grandChildCounter++)
        {
            //Create grandchildren
            childelmt.AppendChild(xmlDoc.CreateElement("GrandChild"));
        }
    }

    //Save to file
    xmlDoc.Save(MapPath("XmlDocumentTest.xml"));
    Label lbl = GetLabel(275, 20);
    lbl.Text = "XmlDocumentTest.xml Created";
}
```

This code started by creating an instance of an *XmlDocument*. Next, the XML declaration is created and placed inside the child collection. An exception is thrown if this is not the first child of the *XmlDocument*. The following is the XML file that was produced by running the code sample:

```
<?xml version="1.0" encoding="utf-8"?>
<myRoot>
  <myChild ID="1">
    <GrandChild />
    <GrandChild />
    <GrandChild />
  </myChild>
  <myChild ID="2">
    <GrandChild />
    <GrandChild />
    <GrandChild />
  </myChild>
  <myChild ID="3">
    <GrandChild />
    <GrandChild />
    <GrandChild />
  </myChild>
  <myChild ID="4">
    <GrandChild />
```

```
        <GrandChild />
        <GrandChild />
    </myChild>
</myRoot>
```

The previous code also works with the *XmlDataDocument*, but the *XmlDataDocument* has more features for working relational data. These features will be explored later in this lesson.

Parsing *XmlDocuments* Using the DOM   An *XmlDocument* can be parsed by using a recursive routine to loop through all elements. The following code is an example of parsing an *XmlDocument*:

```vb
'VB
Protected Sub Button2_Click(ByVal sender As Object, _
        ByVal e As System.EventArgs) Handles Button2.Click
    lbl = GetLabel(275, 20)
    Dim xmlDoc As New XmlDocument()
    xmlDoc.Load(MapPath("XmlDocumentTest.xml"))
    RecurseNodes(xmlDoc.DocumentElement)
End Sub

Public Sub RecurseNodes(ByVal node As XmlNode)
    'start recursive loop with level 0
    RecurseNodes(node, 0)
End Sub

Public Sub RecurseNodes(ByVal node As XmlNode, ByVal level As Integer)
    Dim s As String
    Dim n As XmlNode
    Dim attr As XmlAttribute

    s = String.Format("{0} <b>Type:</b>{1} <b>Name:</b>{2} <b>Attr:</b> ", _
        New String("-", level), node.NodeType, node.Name)
    For Each attr In node.Attributes
        s &= String.Format("{0}={1} ", attr.Name, attr.Value)
    Next
    lbl.Text += s & "<br>"
    For Each n In node.ChildNodes
        RecurseNodes(n, level + 1)
    Next
End Sub
```

```csharp
//C#
protected void Button2_Click(object sender, EventArgs e)
{
    lbl = GetLabel(275, 20);
    XmlDocument xmlDoc = new XmlDocument();
    xmlDoc.Load(MapPath("XmlDocumentTest.xml"));
    RecurseNodes(xmlDoc.DocumentElement);
}
```

```
public void RecurseNodes(XmlNode node)
{
    //start recursive loop with level 0
    RecurseNodes(node, 0);
}

public void RecurseNodes(XmlNode node, int level)
{
    string s;
    s = string.Format("{0} <b>Type:</b>{1} <b>Name:</b>{2} <b>Attr:</b> ",
        new string('-', level), node.NodeType, node.Name);
    foreach (XmlAttribute attr in node.Attributes)
    {
        s += string.Format("{0}={1} ", attr.Name, attr.Value);
    }
    lbl.Text += s + "<br>";
    foreach (XmlNode n in node.ChildNodes)
    {
        RecurseNodes(n, level + 1);
    }
}
```

The output of this code is shown in Figure 4-20. This code starts by loading an XML file and then calling a procedure called *RecurseNodes*. The *RecurseNodes* procedure is overloaded. The first call simply passes the xmlDoc's root node. The recursive calls pass the recursion level. Each time the *RecurseNodes* procedure executes, the node information is printed, and for each child that the node has, a recursive call is made.

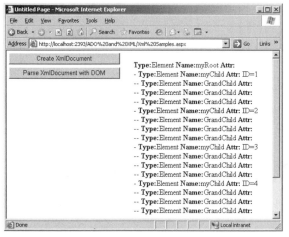

Figure 4-20   Parsing the XmlDocument.

Parsing XmlDocuments Using the *XPathNavigator*   The *XPathNavigator* provides an alternate method of walking the XML document recursively. This object does not use the methods that are defined in the DOM. Instead, it uses XPath queries to navigate the data and is in the *System.Xml.XPath* namespace. It offers many methods and properties that can be used, as shown in the following code example:

```vb
'VB
Protected Sub Button3_Click(ByVal sender As Object, _
    ByVal e As System.EventArgs) Handles Button3.Click

    lbl = GetLabel(275, 20)
    Dim xmlDoc As New XmlDocument()
    xmlDoc.Load(MapPath("XmlDocumentTest.xml"))

    Dim xpathNav As XPathNavigator = xmlDoc.CreateNavigator()
    xpathNav.MoveToRoot()
    RecurseNavNodes(xpathNav)

End Sub

Public Sub RecurseNavNodes(ByVal node As XPathNavigator)
    'start recursive loop with level 0
    RecurseNavNodes(node, 0)
End Sub

Public Sub RecurseNavNodes(ByVal node As XPathNavigator, _
 ByVal level As Integer)
    Dim s As String

    s = string.Format("{0} <b>Type:</b>{1} <b>Name:</b>{2} <b>Attr:</b> ", _
        New String("-", level), node.NodeType, node.Name)

    If node.HasAttributes Then
        node.MoveToFirstAttribute()
        Do
            s += string.Format("{0}={1} ", node.Name, node.Value)
        Loop While node.MoveToNextAttribute()
        node.MoveToParent()
    End If

    lbl.Text += s + "<br>"

    If node.HasChildren Then
        node.MoveToFirstChild()
        Do
            RecurseNavNodes(node, level + 1)
        Loop While node.MoveToNext()
        node.MoveToParent()
```

```
      End If
End Sub

//C#
protected void Button3_Click(object sender, EventArgs e)
{
   lbl = GetLabel(275, 20);
   XmlDocument xmlDoc = new XmlDocument();
   xmlDoc.Load(MapPath("XmlDocumentTest.xml"));

   XPathNavigator xpathNav = xmlDoc.CreateNavigator();
   xpathNav.MoveToRoot();
   RecurseNavNodes(xpathNav);
}

public void RecurseNavNodes(XPathNavigator node)
{
   //start recursive loop with level 0
   RecurseNavNodes(node, 0);
}

public void RecurseNavNodes(XPathNavigator node, int level)
{
   string s = null;

   s = string.Format("{0} <b>Type:</b>{1} <b>Name:</b>{2} <b>Attr:</b> ",
      new string('-', level), node.NodeType, node.Name);

   if (node.HasAttributes)
   {
      node.MoveToFirstAttribute();
      do
      {
         s += string.Format("{0}={1} ", node.Name, node.Value);
      } while (node.MoveToNextAttribute());
      node.MoveToParent();
   }

   lbl.Text += s + "<br>";

   if (node.HasChildren)
   {
      node.MoveToFirstChild();
      do
      {
         RecurseNavNodes(node, level + 1);
      } while (node.MoveToNext());
      node.MoveToParent();
   }
}
```

This is recursive code that works in a similar fashion to the DOM example that was previously covered. The difference is in the methods that are used to get access to each node.

To get access to the attributes, there is a *HasAttributes* property that is *true* if the current node has attributes. The *MoveToFirstAttribute* and *MoveToNextAttribute* methods are used to navigate the attributes. After the attribute list has been navigated, the *MoveToParent* method moves back to the element.

The *HasChildren* property returns *true* if the current node has child nodes. The *MoveToFirstChild* and *MoveToNext* are used to navigate the child nodes. After the children have been navigated, the *MoveToParent* method moves back to the parent element.

Depending on the task at hand, it may be more preferable to use the *XPathNavigator* instead of the DOM. In this example, other than syntax, there is little difference between the two methods.

Searching the *XmlDocument* Using the DOM   The DOM provides *GetElementByID* and the *GetElementsByTagName* methods for searching an *XmlDocument*. The *GetElementByID* method locates an element based on its ID. The ID refers to an ID type that has been defined in a DTD document. To demonstrate this, the following XML is used in many of the examples:

XML File – XmlSample.xml

```xml
<?xml version="1.0" encoding="utf-8"?>
<!DOCTYPE myRoot [
<!ELEMENT myRoot ANY>
<!ELEMENT myChild ANY>
<!ELEMENT myGrandChild EMPTY>
<!ATTLIST myChild
ChildID ID #REQUIRED
>
]>
<myRoot>
<myChild ChildID="ref-1">
<myGrandChild/>
<myGrandChild/>
<myGrandChild/>
</myChild>
<myChild ChildID="ref-2">
<myGrandChild/>
<myGrandChild/>
<myGrandChild/>
</myChild>
```

```
<myChild ChildID="ref-3">
<myGrandChild/>
<myGrandChild/>
<myGrandChild/>
</myChild>
<myChild ChildID="ref-4">
<myGrandChild/>
<myGrandChild/>
<myGrandChild/>
</myChild>
</myRoot>
```

The *ChildID* has been defined as an *ID* data type, and an ID is required to begin with a character, underscore, or colon. The following code performs a lookup of the element with an *ID* of *ref-3*:

```
'VB
Protected Sub Button4_Click(ByVal sender As Object, _
     ByVal e As System.EventArgs) Handles Button4.Click
  lbl = GetLabel(275, 20)
  Dim s As String
  'Declare and create new XmlDocument
  Dim xmlDoc As New XmlDocument()
  xmlDoc.Load(MapPath("XmlSample.xml"))

  Dim node As XmlNode
  node = xmlDoc.GetElementById("ref-3")

  s = string.Format("<b>Type:</b>{0} <b>Name:</b>{1} <b>Attr:</b>", _
   node.NodeType, node.Name)

  Dim a As XmlAttribute
  For Each a In node.Attributes
     s += string.Format("{0}={1} ", a.Name, a.Value)
  Next
  lbl.Text = s + "<br>"
End Sub
```

```
//C#
protected void Button4_Click(object sender, EventArgs e)
{
   lbl = GetLabel(275, 20);
   string s;
   //Declare and create new XmlDocument
   XmlDocument xmlDoc = new XmlDocument();
   xmlDoc.Load(MapPath("XmlSample.xml"));

   XmlNode node;
   node = xmlDoc.GetElementById("ref-3");

   s = string.Format("<b>Type:</b>{0} <b>Name:</b>{1} <b>Attr:</b>",
```

```
        node.NodeType, node.Name);

    foreach (XmlAttribute a in node.Attributes)
    {
        s += string.Format("{0}={1} ", a.Name, a.Value);
    }
    lbl.Text = s + "<br>";
}
```

The browser output is shown in Figure 4-21. When an *ID* data type is defined, the ID must be unique. This code locates *ref-3* and displays the node and attributes information.

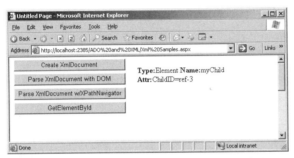

Figure 4-21   The browser output when the code is run to locate *ref-3* using the *GetElementById* method.

The *SelectSingleNode* method can also be used to locate an element. The *SelectSingle-Node* method requires an XPath query to be passed into the method. The previous code sample has been modified to call the *SelectSingleNode* method to achieve the same result using an XPath query. The sample code is as follows:

```
'VB
Protected Sub Button5_Click(ByVal sender As Object, _
        ByVal e As System.EventArgs) Handles Button5.Click
    lbl = GetLabel(275, 20)
    Dim s As String
    'Declare and create new XmlDocument
    Dim xmlDoc As New XmlDocument()
    xmlDoc.Load(MapPath("XmlSample.xml"))

    Dim node As XmlNode
    node = xmlDoc.SelectSingleNode("//myChild[@ChildID='ref-3']")

    s = String.Format("<b>Type:</b>{0} <b>Name:</b>{1} <b>Attr:</b>", _
      node.NodeType, node.Name)

    Dim a As XmlAttribute
    For Each a In node.Attributes
        s += String.Format("{0}={1} ", a.Name, a.Value)
```

```
      Next
      lbl.Text = s + "<br>"
End Sub
```

```
//C#
protected void Button5_Click(object sender, EventArgs e)
{
    lbl = GetLabel(275, 20);
    string s;
    //Declare and create new XmlDocument
    XmlDocument xmlDoc = new XmlDocument();
    xmlDoc.Load(MapPath("XmlSample.xml"));

    XmlNode node;
    node = xmlDoc.SelectSingleNode("//myChild[@ChildID='ref-3']");

    s = string.Format("<b>Type:</b>{0} <b>Name:</b>{1} <b>Attr:</b>",
     node.NodeType, node.Name);

    foreach (XmlAttribute a in node.Attributes)
    {
        s += string.Format("{0}={1} ", a.Name, a.Value);
    }
    lbl.Text = s + "<br>";
}
```

The *SelectSingleNode* method does not require a DTD to be provided and can perform an XPath lookup on any element or attribute where the *SelectSingleNode* requires an *ID* data type and a DTD.

The *GetElementsByTagName* method returns an *XmlNodeList* containing all matched elements. This following code returns a list of nodes which have the tag name of *myGrandChild*.

```
'VB
Protected Sub Button6_Click(ByVal sender As Object, _
      ByVal e As System.EventArgs) Handles Button6.Click

    lbl = GetLabel(275, 20)
    Dim s As String

    'Declare and create new XmlDocument
    Dim xmlDoc As New XmlDocument()
    xmlDoc.Load(MapPath("XmlSample.xml"))

    Dim elmts As XmlNodeList
    elmts = xmlDoc.GetElementsByTagName("myGrandChild")

    For Each node as XmlNode In elmts
        s = string.Format("<b>Type:</b>{0} <b>Name:</b>{1}", _
          node.NodeType, node.Name)
```

```
        lbl.Text += s + "<br>"
    Next
End Sub

//C#
protected void Button6_Click(object sender, EventArgs e)
{
    lbl = GetLabel(275, 20);
    string s;

    //Declare and create new XmlDocument
    XmlDocument xmlDoc = new XmlDocument();
    xmlDoc.Load(MapPath("XmlSample.xml"));

    XmlNodeList elmts;
    elmts = xmlDoc.GetElementsByTagName("myGrandChild");

    foreach (XmlNode node in elmts)
    {
        s = string.Format("<b>Type:</b>{0} <b>Name:</b>{1}",
         node.NodeType, node.Name);
        lbl.Text += s + "<br>";
    }
}
```

This code retrieves the list of elements that have the tag names of *myGrandChild*. The browser output is shown in Figure 4-22. This method does not require a DTD to be included, which makes this method a preference, even for a single node lookup when searching by tag name.

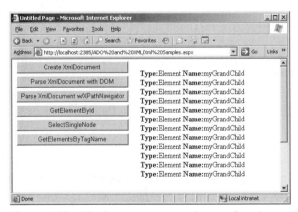

Figure 4-22   The browser output when performing a search for *myGrandChild* elements using the *GetElementsByTagName* method.

The *SelectNodes* method can also be used to locate an *XmlNodeList*. The *SelectNodes* method requires an XPath query to be passed into the method. The previous code sample has been modified to call the *SelectNodes* method to achieve the same result. The code is as follows:

```vb
'VB
Protected Sub Button7_Click(ByVal sender As Object, _
        ByVal e As System.EventArgs) Handles Button7.Click

            lbl = GetLabel(275, 20)
    Dim s As String

    'Declare and create new XmlDocument
    Dim xmlDoc As New XmlDocument()
    xmlDoc.Load(MapPath("XmlSample.xml"))

    Dim elmts As XmlNodeList
    elmts = xmlDoc.SelectNodes("//myGrandChild")
    For Each node As XmlNode In elmts
       s = String.Format("<b>Type:</b>{0} <b>Name:</b>{1}", _
       node.NodeType, node.Name)
       lbl.Text += s + "<br>"
    Next
End Sub
```

```csharp
//C#
protected void Button7_Click(object sender, EventArgs e)
{
    lbl = GetLabel(275, 20);
    string s;

    //Declare and create new XmlDocument
    XmlDocument xmlDoc = new XmlDocument();
    xmlDoc.Load(MapPath("XmlSample.xml"));

    XmlNodeList elmts;
    elmts = xmlDoc.SelectNodes("//myGrandChild");
    foreach (XmlNode node in elmts)
    {
       s = string.Format("<b>Type:</b>{0} <b>Name:</b>{1}",
       node.NodeType, node.Name);
       lbl.Text += s + "<br>";
    }
}
```

Note that this method can perform an XPath lookup on any element or attribute, with much more querying flexibility; whereas, the *SelectElementsByTagName* is limited to a tag name.

Using the *XPathNavigator* to Search XPathDocuments   The *XPathNavigator* offers much more flexibility for performing searches than what is available through the DOM. The *XPathNavigator* has many methods that are focused around XPath queries using a cursor model. The *XPathNavigator* works with the *XmlDocument*, but the *XPathDocument* object is tuned for the *XPathNavigator* and uses fewer resources than the *XmlDocument*. If the DOM is not required, use the *XPathDocument* instead of the *XmlDocument*. The following code example performs a search for the *myChild* element, where the *ChildID* attribute is equal to *ref-3*:

```vb
'VB
Protected Sub Button8_Click(ByVal sender As Object, _
        ByVal e As System.EventArgs) Handles Button8.Click
   lbl = GetLabel(275, 20)
   Dim s As String
   Dim xmlDoc As New XPathDocument(MapPath("XmlSample.xml"))
   Dim nav As XPathNavigator = xmlDoc.CreateNavigator()

   Dim expr As String = "//myChild[@ChildID='ref-3']"

   'Display the selection.
   Dim iterator As XPathNodeIterator = nav.Select(expr)
   Dim navResult As XPathNavigator = iterator.Current
   While (iterator.MoveNext())

       s = string.Format("<b>Type:</b>{0} <b>Name:</b>{1} ", _
       navResult.NodeType, navResult.Name)

       If navResult.HasAttributes Then
          navResult.MoveToFirstAttribute()
          s += "<b>Attr:</b> "
          Do
             s += string.Format("{0}={1} ", _
             navResult.Name, navResult.Value)
          Loop While navResult.MoveToNextAttribute()
       End If

       lbl.Text += s + "<br>"
   End While
End Sub

//C#
protected void Button8_Click(object sender, EventArgs e)
{
   lbl = GetLabel(275, 20);
   string s;
   XPathDocument xmlDoc = new XPathDocument(MapPath("XmlSample.xml"));
   XPathNavigator nav = xmlDoc.CreateNavigator();

   string expr = "//myChild[@ChildID='ref-3']";

   //Display the selection.
```

```
XPathNodeIterator iterator = nav.Select(expr);
XPathNavigator navResult = iterator.Current;
while (iterator.MoveNext())
{
    s = String.Format("<b>Type:</b>{0} <b>Name:</b>{1} ",
     navResult.NodeType, navResult.Name);

    if (navResult.HasAttributes)
    {
        navResult.MoveToFirstAttribute();
        s += "<b>Attr:</b> ";
        do
        {
            s += String.Format("{0}={1} ",
             navResult.Name, navResult.Value);
        } while (navResult.MoveToNextAttribute());
    }

    lbl.Text += s + "<br>";
  }
}
```

Figure 4-23 shows the browser output. This code uses an XPath query to locate the *myChild* element for which the *ChildID* attribute is equal to *ref-3*. The *Select* method is called with the query string. The *Select* method returns an *XPathNodeIterator* object, which allows navigation over the node or nodes that are returned. The *XPathNode-Iterator* has a property called *Current*, which represents the current node, and is in itself an *XPathNavigator* data type. Rather than use *iterator.Current* throughout the code, a variable called *navResult* is created and assigned a reference to *iterator.Current*. Note that the call to *MoveToParent* is not required when finishing the loop through the attributes. This is because the *iterator.MoveNext* doesn't care what the current location is, because it is simply going to the next node in its list.

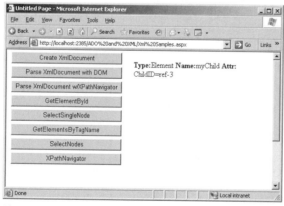

Figure 4-23 Using the XPathNavigator to search for a node.

Some of the real power of the *XPathNavigator* starts to show when the requirement is to retrieve a list of nodes and sort the output. Sorting involves compiling an XPath query string to an *XPathExpression* object, and then adding a sort to the compiled expressions. The following is an example of compiling and sorting:

```vb
'VB
Protected Sub Button9_Click(ByVal sender As Object, _
        ByVal e As System.EventArgs) Handles Button9.Click
    lbl = GetLabel(275, 20)
    Dim s As String
    Dim xmlDoc As New XPathDocument(MapPath("XmlSample.xml"))
    Dim nav As XPathNavigator = xmlDoc.CreateNavigator()

    'Select all myChild elements
    Dim expr As XPathExpression
    expr = nav.Compile("//myChild")

    'Sort the selected books by title.
    expr.AddSort("@ChildID", _
     XmlSortOrder.Descending, _
     XmlCaseOrder.None, "", _
     XmlDataType.Text)

    'Display the selection.
    Dim iterator As XPathNodeIterator = nav.Select(expr)
    Dim navResult As XPathNavigator = iterator.Current
    While (iterator.MoveNext())

        s = String.Format("<b>Type:</b>{0} <b>Name:</b>{1} ", _
         navResult.NodeType, navResult.Name)

        If navResult.HasAttributes Then
            navResult.MoveToFirstAttribute()
            s += "<b>Attr:</b> "
            Do
                s += String.Format("{0}={1} ", _
                 navResult.Name, navResult.Value)
            Loop While navResult.MoveToNextAttribute()
        End If

        lbl.Text += s + "<br>"
    End While
End Sub
```

```csharp
//C#
protected void Button9_Click(object sender, EventArgs e)
{
    lbl = GetLabel(275, 20);
    string s;
    XPathDocument xmlDoc = new XPathDocument(MapPath("XmlSample.xml"));
```

```
XPathNavigator nav = xmlDoc.CreateNavigator();

//Select all myChild elements
XPathExpression expr;
expr = nav.Compile("//myChild");

//Sort the selected books by title.
expr.AddSort("@ChildID",
 XmlSortOrder.Descending,
 XmlCaseOrder.None, "",
 XmlDataType.Text);

//Display the selection.
XPathNodeIterator iterator = nav.Select(expr);
XPathNavigator navResult = iterator.Current;
while (iterator.MoveNext())
{
    s = String.Format("<b>Type:</b>{0} <b>Name:</b>{1} ",
     navResult.NodeType, navResult.Name);

    if (navResult.HasAttributes)
    {
       navResult.MoveToFirstAttribute();
       s += "<b>Attr:</b> ";
       do
       {
          s += String.Format("{0}={1} ",
            navResult.Name, navResult.Value);
       } while (navResult.MoveToNextAttribute());
    }
    lbl.Text += s + "<br>";
}
}
```

Figure 4-24 shows the browser output. This code is similar to the previous example, with the exception of the creation of the *expr* variable. The *expr* variable is created by compiling the query string to an *XPathExpression*. After that, the *AddSort* method is used to sort the output in descending order, based on the *ChildID* attribute.

When working with XML, it may seem easier to use the *DOM* methods to access data, but there are limits to the search capabilities that could require walking the tree to get the desired output. On the surface, the *XPathNavigator* may appear to be more difficult to use, but having the ability to perform XPath queries and sorting make this the object of choice for more complex XML problem solving.

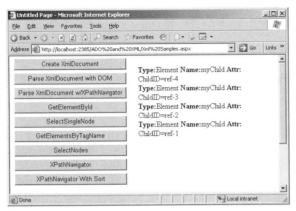

Figure 4-24 The browser output when the XPath query is compiled to an *XPathExpression* and sorted.

Writing a File Using the *XmlTextWriter* The *XmlTextWriter* can be used to create an XML file from scratch. This class has many properties that aid in the creation of XML nodes. The following sample creates an XML file called EmployeeList.xml and writes two employees to the file:

```vb
'VB
Protected Sub Button10_Click(ByVal sender As Object, _
     ByVal e As System.EventArgs) Handles Button10.Click
   Dim xmlWriter As New _
      XmlTextWriter(MapPath("EmployeeList.xml"), _
      System.Text.Encoding.UTF8)

   With xmlWriter
      .Formatting = Formatting.Indented
      .Indentation = 5

      .WriteStartDocument()
      .WriteComment("XmlTextWriter Test Date: " & _
      DateTime.Now.ToShortDateString())

      .WriteStartElement("EmployeeList")

      'New Employee
      .WriteStartElement("Employee")
      .WriteAttributeString("EmpID", "1")
      .WriteAttributeString("LastName", "JoeLast")
      .WriteAttributeString("FirstName", "Joe")
      .WriteAttributeString("Salary", XmlConvert.ToString(50000))

      .WriteElementString("HireDate", _
```

```
                        XmlConvert.ToString(#1/1/2003#, _
                        XmlDateTimeSerializationMode.Unspecified))

                .WriteStartElement("Address")
                .WriteElementString("Street1", "123 MyStreet")
                .WriteElementString("Street2", "")
                .WriteElementString("City", "MyCity")
                .WriteElementString("State", "OH")
                .WriteElementString("ZipCode", "12345")

                'Address
                .WriteEndElement()
                'Employee
                .WriteEndElement()

                'New Employee
                .WriteStartElement("Employee")
                .WriteAttributeString("EmpID", "2")
                .WriteAttributeString("LastName", "MaryLast")
                .WriteAttributeString("FirstName", "Mary")
                .WriteAttributeString("Salary", XmlConvert.ToString(40000))

                .WriteElementString("HireDate", _
                        XmlConvert.ToString(#1/2/2003#, _
                        XmlDateTimeSerializationMode.Unspecified))

                .WriteStartElement("Address")
                .WriteElementString("Street1", "234 MyStreet")
                .WriteElementString("Street2", "")
                .WriteElementString("City", "MyCity")
                .WriteElementString("State", "OH")
                .WriteElementString("ZipCode", "23456")

                'Address
                .WriteEndElement()
                'Employee
                .WriteEndElement()

                'EmployeeList
                .WriteEndElement()
                .Close()
        End With
        Response.Redirect("EmployeeList.xml")
    End Sub

//C#
protected void Button10_Click(object sender, EventArgs e)
{
    XmlTextWriter xmlWriter  = new
    XmlTextWriter(MapPath("EmployeeList.xml"),
    System.Text.Encoding.UTF8);

    xmlWriter.Formatting = Formatting.Indented;
```

```
xmlWriter.Indentation = 5;

xmlWriter.WriteStartDocument();
xmlWriter.WriteComment("XmlTextWriter Test Date: " +
    DateTime.Now.ToShortDateString());

xmlWriter.WriteStartElement("EmployeeList");

//New Employee
xmlWriter.WriteStartElement("Employee");
xmlWriter.WriteAttributeString("EmpID", "1");
xmlWriter.WriteAttributeString("LastName", "JoeLast");
xmlWriter.WriteAttributeString("FirstName", "Joe");
xmlWriter.WriteAttributeString("Salary", XmlConvert.ToString(50000));

xmlWriter.WriteElementString("HireDate",
    XmlConvert.ToString(DateTime.Parse("1/1/2003"),
    XmlDateTimeSerializationMode.Unspecified));

xmlWriter.WriteStartElement("Address");
xmlWriter.WriteElementString("Street1", "123 MyStreet");
xmlWriter.WriteElementString("Street2", "");
xmlWriter.WriteElementString("City", "MyCity");
xmlWriter.WriteElementString("State", "OH");
xmlWriter.WriteElementString("ZipCode", "12345");

//Address
xmlWriter.WriteEndElement();
//Employee
xmlWriter.WriteEndElement();

//New Employee
xmlWriter.WriteStartElement("Employee");
xmlWriter.WriteAttributeString("EmpID", "2");
xmlWriter.WriteAttributeString("LastName", "MaryLast");
xmlWriter.WriteAttributeString("FirstName", "Mary");
xmlWriter.WriteAttributeString("Salary", XmlConvert.ToString(40000));

xmlWriter.WriteElementString("HireDate",
    XmlConvert.ToString(DateTime.Parse("1/2/2003"),
    XmlDateTimeSerializationMode.Unspecified));

xmlWriter.WriteStartElement("Address");
xmlWriter.WriteElementString("Street1", "234 MyStreet");
xmlWriter.WriteElementString("Street2", "");
xmlWriter.WriteElementString("City", "MyCity");
xmlWriter.WriteElementString("State", "OH");
xmlWriter.WriteElementString("ZipCode", "23456");

//Address
xmlWriter.WriteEndElement();
//Employee
```

```
    xmlWriter.WriteEndElement();

    //EmployeeList
    xmlWriter.WriteEndElement();
    xmlWriter.Close();

    Response.Redirect("EmployeeList.xml");
}
```

This code starts by opening the file as part of the constructor for the *XmlTextWriter*. The constructor also expects an encoding type. Since an argument is required, passing *Nothing* causes the encoding type to be UTF-8, which is the same as the value that is explicitly being passed. The following is the EmployeeList.xml that is created.

The XmlTextWriter was used to produce this XML file

```
<?xml version="1.0" encoding="utf-8"?>
<!--XmlTextWriter Test Date: 8/16/2006-->
<EmployeeList>
    <Employee EmpID="1" LastName="JoeLast" FirstName="Joe" Salary="50000">
        <HireDate>2003-01-01T00:00:00</HireDate>
        <Address>
            <Street1>123 MyStreet</Street1>
            <Street2 />
            <City>MyCity</City>
            <State>OH</State>
            <ZipCode>12345</ZipCode>
        </Address>
    </Employee>
    <Employee EmpID="2" LastName="MaryLast" FirstName="Mary" Salary="40000">
        <HireDate>2003-01-02T00:00:00</HireDate>
        <Address>
            <Street1>234 MyStreet</Street1>
            <Street2 />
            <City>MyCity</City>
            <State>OH</State>
            <ZipCode>23456</ZipCode>
        </Address>
    </Employee>
</EmployeeList>
```

There are many statements that are doing nothing more than writing to the *xmlWriter*. Typing time is saved in the VB code by the use of *With xmlWriter* statement, which allows a simple dot to be typed to represent the *xmlWriter* object.

The *XmlTextWriter* handles the formatting of the document by setting the *Formatting* and *Indentation* properties.

The *WriteStartDocument* method writes the XML declaration to the file. The *WriteComment* writes a comment to the file.

When writing elements, you can use either the *WriteStartElement* method or the *WriteElementString* method. The *WriteStartElement* method only writes the starting element but keeps track of the nesting level and adds new elements inside this element. The element is completed when a call is made to the *WriteEndElement* method. The *WriteElementString* method simply writes a closed element to the file.

The *WriteAttribute* method takes a name and value pair and writes the attribute into the current open element.

When writing is complete, the *Close* method must be called to avoid losing data. The file is then saved.

Reading a File Using the *XmlTextReader* The *XmlTextReader* is used to read an XML file, node by node. The reader provides forward-only, non-caching access to an XML data stream. The reader is ideal for use when there is a possibility that the information that is desired is near the top of the XML file, and the file is large. If random access is required, use the *XPathNavigator* class or the *XmlDocument* class. The following code reads the XML file that was created in the previous example and displays information about each node:

```vb
'VB
Protected Sub Button11_Click(ByVal sender As Object, _
    ByVal e As System.EventArgs) Handles Button11.Click
  lbl = GetLabel(275, 20)
  Dim xmlReader As New _
    XmlTextReader(MapPath("EmployeeList.xml"))

  Do While xmlReader.Read()

    Select Case xmlReader.NodeType
      Case XmlNodeType.XmlDeclaration, _
       XmlNodeType.Element, _
       XmlNodeType.Comment
        Dim s As String
        s = String.Format("{0}: {1} = {2}<br>", _
          xmlReader.NodeType, _
          xmlReader.Name, _
          xmlReader.Value)
        lbl.Text += s
      Case XmlNodeType.Text
        Dim s As String
        s = String.Format(" - Value: {0}<br>", _
         xmlReader.Value)
        lbl.Text += s
    End Select
```

```vb
      If xmlReader.HasAttributes Then
          Do While xmlReader.MoveToNextAttribute()
              Dim s As String
              s = String.Format(" - Attribute: {0} = {1}<br>", _
               xmlReader.Name, xmlReader.Value)
              lbl.Text += s
          Loop
      End If
  Loop
  xmlReader.Close()
End Sub
```

```csharp
//C#
protected void Button11_Click(object sender, EventArgs e)
{
   lbl = GetLabel(275, 20);
   XmlTextReader xmlReader = new
       XmlTextReader(MapPath("EmployeeList.xml"));

   while( xmlReader.Read())
   {
      switch( xmlReader.NodeType)
      {
         case XmlNodeType.XmlDeclaration:
         case XmlNodeType.Element:
         case XmlNodeType.Comment:
         {
            string s;
            s = String.Format("{0}: {1} = {2}<br>",
               xmlReader.NodeType,
               xmlReader.Name,
               xmlReader.Value);
            lbl.Text += s;
            break;
         }
         case XmlNodeType.Text:
         {
            string s;
            s = String.Format(" - Value: {0}<br>",
             xmlReader.Value);
            lbl.Text += s;
            break;
         }
      }

      if( xmlReader.HasAttributes)
      {
         while (xmlReader.MoveToNextAttribute())
         {
            string s;
            s = String.Format(" - Attribute: {0} = {1}<br>",
             xmlReader.Name, xmlReader.Value);
            lbl.Text += s;
```

```
            }
        }
    }
    xmlReader.Close();
}
```

Figure 4-25 shows the browser output. This code opens the EmployeeList file, and then performs a simple loop, reading one element at a time until finished. For each node that is read, a check is made on the *NodeType*, and the node information is printed.

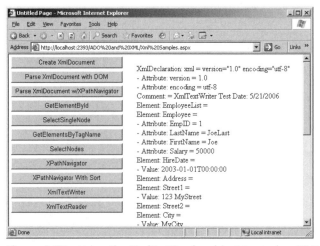

Figure 4-25 Using the *XmlTextReader* object to read an XML file and display each node's information.

When a node is read, its corresponding attributes are read as well. A check is made to see if the node has attributes, and they are displayed.

Modifying an XML Document

When the *XmlDocument* object is loaded, you can easily add and remove nodes. When removing a node, you simply need to locate the node and delete it from its parent. When adding a node, you need to create the node, search for the appropriate location to insert the node into, and insert the node. The following code snippet deletes an existing node and adds a new node:

```
'VB
Protected Sub Button12_Click(ByVal sender As Object, _
        ByVal e As System.EventArgs) Handles Button12.Click

    lbl = GetLabel(275, 20)
```

```
'Declare and load new XmlDocument
Dim xmlDoc As New XmlDocument()
xmlDoc.Load(MapPath("XmlSample.xml"))

'delete a mode
Dim node As XmlNode
node = xmlDoc.SelectSingleNode("//myChild[@ChildID='ref-3']")
node.ParentNode.RemoveChild(node)

'create a node and add it
Dim newElement as XmlElement = _
    xmlDoc.CreateElement("myNewElement")
node = xmlDoc.SelectSingleNode("//myChild[@ChildID='ref-1']")
node.ParentNode.InsertAfter(newElement, node)
xmlDoc.Save(MapPath("XmlSampleModified.xml"))
Response.Redirect("XmlSampleModified.xml")
End Sub
```

```
//C#
protected void Button12_Click(object sender, EventArgs e)
{
    lbl = GetLabel(275, 20);

    //Declare and load new XmlDocument
    XmlDocument xmlDoc = new XmlDocument();
    xmlDoc.Load(MapPath("XmlSample.xml"));

    //delete a mode
    XmlNode node;
    node = xmlDoc.SelectSingleNode("//myChild[@ChildID='ref-3']");
    node.ParentNode.RemoveChild(node);

    //create a node and add it
    XmlElement newElement =
        xmlDoc.CreateElement("myNewElement");
    node = xmlDoc.SelectSingleNode("//myChild[@ChildID='ref-1']");
    node.ParentNode.InsertAfter(newElement, node);
    xmlDoc.Save(MapPath("XmlSampleModified.xml"));
    Response.Redirect("XmlSampleModified.xml");
}
```

To delete a node, use the *SelectSingleNode* method to locate the node to delete. After the node is located, the node can be removed from its parent by using the *ParentNode* property's *RemoveChild* method.

To add a node, execute the *CreateElement* method on the *XmlDocument* object. Next, the insert location is searched and the *ParentNode* property's *InsertAfter* method is used to insert the new node. Figure 4-26 shows the resulting XML document.

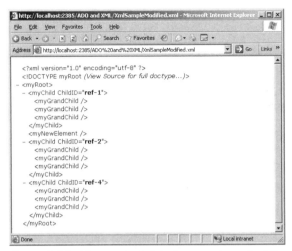

Figure 4-26   The result of deleting a node and adding a node.

Validating XML Documents

An important element to exchanging documents between disparate systems is the ability to define the structure of an XML document and then validate the XML document against its defined structure. The .NET Framework offers the ability to perform validation against a document type definition (DTD) or schema. Earlier versions of the .NET Framework used the *XmlValidatingReader* object to perform validation, but this object is now obsolete. Instead, this section explores XML document validation using the *XmlReader* class.

The *XmlReader* class performs forward-only reading and validation of a stream of XML. The *XmlReader* class contains a *Create* method that can be passed as a string or a stream, as well as an *XmlReaderSettings* object. To perform validation, the *XmlReader-Settings* object must be created and its properties set to perform validation. In the next example, the files XmlSample.xml and XmlBadSample.xml are validated using the following code:

```
'VB
Protected Sub Button13_Click(ByVal sender As Object, _
    ByVal e As System.EventArgs) Handles Button13.Click
  lbl = GetLabel(275, 20)
  If ValidateDocument(MapPath("XmlSample.xml")) Then
    lbl.Text += "Valid Document<br />"
  Else
    lbl.Text += "Invalid Document<br />"
```

```vb
      End If
   End Sub

   Protected Sub Button14_Click(ByVal sender As Object, _
         ByVal e As System.EventArgs) Handles Button14.Click
      lbl = GetLabel(275, 20)
      If ValidateDocument(MapPath("XmlBadSample.xml")) Then
         lbl.Text += "Valid Document<br />"
      Else
         lbl.Text += "Invalid Document<br />"
      End If
   End Sub

   Public Function ValidateDocument(ByVal fileName As String) _
         As Boolean
      Dim xmlSet As New XmlReaderSettings()
      xmlSet.ValidationType = ValidationType.DTD
      xmlSet.ProhibitDtd = False
      Dim vr As XmlReader = XmlReader.Create( _
            fileName, xmlSet)

      Dim xd As New XmlDocument()
      Try
         xd.Load(vr)
         Return True
      Catch ex As Exception
         lbl.Text += ex.Message + "<br />"
         Return False
      Finally
         vr.Close()
      End Try
   End Function

//C#
protected void Button13_Click(object sender, EventArgs e)
{
   lbl = GetLabel(275, 20);
   if (ValidateDocument(MapPath("XmlSample.xml")))
   {
      lbl.Text += "Valid Document<br />";
   }
   else
   {
      lbl.Text += "Invalid Document<br />";
   }
}

protected void Button14_Click(object sender, EventArgs e)
{
   lbl = GetLabel(275, 20);
   if (ValidateDocument(MapPath("XmlBadSample.xml")))
```

```csharp
      {
         lbl.Text += "Valid Document<br />";
      }
      else
      {
         lbl.Text += "Invalid Document<br />";
      }
   }

   private bool ValidateDocument(string fileName)
   {
      XmlReaderSettings xmlSet = new XmlReaderSettings();
      xmlSet.ValidationType = ValidationType.DTD;
      xmlSet.ProhibitDtd = false;
      XmlReader vr = XmlReader.Create(fileName, xmlSet);
      XmlDocument xd = new XmlDocument();
      try
      {
         xd.Load(vr);
         return true;
      }
      catch (Exception ex)
      {
         lbl.Text += ex.Message + "<br />";
         return false;
      }
      finally
      {
         vr.Close();
      }
   }
```

The XmlBadSample.xml file is as follows:

XML File – XmlBadSample.xml

```xml
<?xml version="1.0" encoding="utf-8"?>
<!DOCTYPE myRoot [
   <!ELEMENT myRoot ANY>
   <!ELEMENT myChild ANY>
   <!ELEMENT myGrandChild EMPTY>
   <!ATTLIST myChild
ChildID ID #REQUIRED
>
]>
<myRoot>
   <myChild ChildID="ref-1">
      <myGrandChild/>
      <myGrandChild/>
      <myGrandChild/>
   </myChild>
   <myChild ChildID="ref-2">
```

```
            <myGrandChild/>
            <myGrandChild/>
            <myGrandChild>this test</myGrandChild>
        </myChild>
        <myChild ChildID="ref-3">
            <myGrandChild/>
            <myGrandChild/>
            <myGrandChild/>
        </myChild>
        <myChild ChildID="ref-4">
            <myGrandChild/>
            <myGrandChild/>
            <myGrandChild/>
        </myChild>
    </myRoot>
```

This code simply opens the XML file with an *XmlReader,* and, while the *XmlDocument* is being read, the document is being validated. Since this code has an embedded DTD, the document is validated.

The DTD states that the *myGrandChild* element must be empty, but one of the *myGrandChild* elements of *myChild ref-1* has a *myGrandChild* element containing the word *Hi.* This causes an error, as shown in Figure 4-27. Attempts to read from the *Xml-Reader* when valid should always be within a *try/catch* block to catch possible validation exceptions.

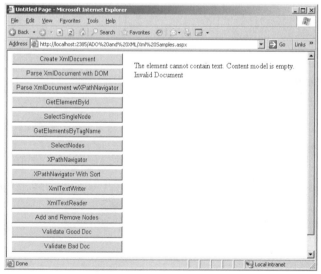

Figure 4-27 The *XmlReader* throws an exception when the document is not valid.

> ## Quick Check
>
> 1. What method can you execute to locate a single XML node by its tag name?
> 2. What method can you use to search for all elements that have a specific tag name and retrieve the results as an *XmlNodeList*?
> 3. What object should you use to perform XPath queries on large XML documents?
>
> ## Quick Check Answers
> 1. *SelectSingleNode*
> 2. *GetElementsByTagName* or *SelectNodes*
> 3. *XPathNavigator*

Lab: Working with XML Data

In this lab, you work with XML data to display a subset of an XML file in a *GridView* control, using the XmlDataSource and an XSL Transform file.

▶ **Exercise 1: Create the Web Site and the XML Files**

In this exercise, you create the Web site and XML file.

1. Open Visual Studio 2005; create a new Web site called **WorkingWithXmlData** using your preferred programming language. The new Web site will be created and a Web page called Default.aspx is displayed.

2. In the Solution Explorer, right-click the App_Data folder and select Add New Item. Select XML file, name the file **CarList.xml**, and click Add.

3. In the XML file, add the following:

```
XML File – CarList.xml
<?xml version="1.0" encoding="utf-8" ?>
<CarList>
    <Car Vin="1A59B" Make="Chevrolet" Model="Impala" Year="1963" Price="1125.00" />
    <Car Vin="9B25T" Make="Ford" Model="F-250" Year="1970" Price="1595.00" />
    <Car Vin="3H13R" Make="BMW" Model="Z-4" Year="2006" Price="55123.00" />
    <Car Vin="7D67A" Make="Mazda" Model="Miata" Year="2003" Price="28250.00" />
    <Car Vin="4T21N" Make="VW" Model="Bug" Year="1956" Price="500.00" />
</CarList>
```

4. Drag a *DetailsView* control onto the Web page and size it wide enough to display the car information.

5. Click the symbol in the upper-right corner of the *DetailsView* control to display the DetailsView Tasks window.

6. Click the Auto Format link and select Professional.

7. Click the Choose Data Source drop-down list and select New Data Source to start the Data Source Configuration Wizard. For the data source type, select XML file and click OK.

8. On the Configure Data Source page, click the browse button for the *Data* property and browse to the CarList.xml file in the App_Data folder.

9. Click OK.

10. Select the Enable Paging option. Configuration of the *DetailsView* is complete.

11. Run the Web page. Notice that the data is retrieved and displayed.

Lesson Summary

- XML documents can be accessed using the Document Object Model (DOM) Level 1 and Level 2.

- The *XPathNavigator* uses a cursor model and XPath queries to provide read-only, random access to the data.

- The *XmlReader* provides an object for validating against DTD, Xml Schema Reduced (XDR), or Xml Schema Definition (XSD) by setting the *XmlReaderSettings* object properties.

Lesson Review

You can use the following questions to test your knowledge of the information in Lesson 3, "Working with XML Data." The questions are also available on the companion CD if you prefer to review them in electronic form.

NOTE   Answers

Answers to these questions and explanations of why each answer choice is right or wrong are located in the "Answers" section at the end of the book.

---

1. Which class can be used to create an XML document from scratch?

    A. *XmlConvert*

    B. *XmlDocument*

    C. *XmlNew*

    D. *XmlSettings*

2. Which class can be used to perform data type conversion between .NET data types and XML types?

    A. *XmlType*

    B. *XmlCast*

    C. *XmlConvert*

    D. *XmlSettings*

Chapter Review

To further practice and reinforce the skills you learned in this chapter, you can perform the following tasks:

- Review the chapter summary.
- Review the list of key terms introduced in this chapter.
- Complete the case scenarios. These scenarios set up real-world situations involving the topics of this chapter and ask you to create solutions.
- Complete the suggested practices.
- Take a practice test.

Chapter Summary

- ADO.NET provides disconnected objects that can be used without ever creating a connection to a data store.
- ADO.NET provides connected objects that are provider-specific.
- ADO.NET provides access XML files using the classes in the *System.Xml* namespace.

Key Terms

Do you know what these key terms mean? You can check your answers by looking up the terms in the glossary at the end of the book.

- ACID properties
- connection pooling
- constraint
- *DataColumn*
- *DataRow*
- *DataTable*
- DiffGram
- Document Object Model (DOM)

- expression column
- primary key
- provider classes
- transaction

Case Scenarios

In the following case scenarios, you will apply what you've learned in this chapter. If you have difficulty completing this work, review the material in this chapter before beginning the next chapter. You can find answers to these questions in the "Answers" section at the end of this book.

Case Scenario 1: Determining Ways to Update the Database

You are creating a new Web page that allows users to upload XML files that contain expense report data. The expense report data contains general information about the expense report, such as the employee name and ID, the branch office number, and the week-ending date. The expense report file also contains information that describes each specific expense. For mileage, this data includes the date and the mile amount, and the and from locations. For entertainment, the data includes the location, the expense amount, and a description of the entertainment expense.

You need to import this data into a SQL Database and are looking for the easiest possible means. Define some methods of importing this data into the SQL Server database.

Case Scenario 2: Storing a DataSet to a Binary File

Your code populates a DataSet with more than 200,000 DataRows in several related DataTables. You want to store this DataSet object to a file, but you want the file to be as small as possible. What will you do to reduce the size of the file?

Suggested Practices

The following objectives have been addressed in this chapter:

- Manage connections and transactions of databases.
- Create, delete, and edit data in a connected environment.

- Create, delete, and edit data in a disconnected environment.
- Manage XML data with the XML Document Object Model (DOM).
- Read and write XML data by using the XmlReader and XmlWriter.

To successfully master these exam objectives, complete the following tasks.

Create a New Web Page For Updating Database Data

For this task, you should complete all three practices.

- **Practice 1** Create a new Web page and add Web server controls to prompt the user for a percentage increase (or decrease) for the price of the products in your database. Use the *Northwind* database, which has a Products table.
- **Practice 2** Add code to open a connection and execute a SQL query to increase or decrease the *UnitPrice* of all products based on the value submitted by the user.
- **Practice 3** Add code to perform the update of the Products table within a *SqlTransaction*.

Create a New Web Page For Editing Disconnected Data

For this task, you should complete this practice.

- **Practice 1** Create a new Web page and add a button to create a *DataTable* that contains a schema for employees, a button that adds a *DataRow* into the employees *DataTable*, a button that modifies an existing *DataRow,* and a button that deletes a *DataRow*.

Create a New Web Page For Editing Connected Data

For this task, you should complete both practices.

- **Practice 1** Create a new Web page and add a SqlDataSource configured to read data from a SQL Server or SQL Server 2005 Express Edition database and display the data in a *GridView* control.
- **Practice 2** Modify the Web page to enable inserts, updates and deletes.

Create a New Web Page Working with XML Data

For this task, you should complete both practices.

■ **Practice 1**   Create a Web page that uses an XmlDataSource to read data from an XML file and display the data in a *GridView* control.

■ **Practice 2**   Modify the Web page to enable inserts, updates, and deletes.

Create a New Web Page for Reading, Modifying, and Writing XML Data

For this task, you should complete all three practices.

■ **Practice 1**   Create an XML file that contains a list of products and their prices.

■ **Practice 2**   Create a new Web page and add Web server controls to prompt the user for a percentage increase (or decrease) for the price of the products in your XML file.

■ **Practice 3**   Add code to use the *XmlReader* to read the products file, modify the price, and then use the *XmlWriter* to write the data to a file.

Take a Practice Test

The practice tests on this book's companion CD offer many options. For example, you can test yourself on just the content covered in this chapter, or you can test yourself on all the 70-528 certification exam content. You can set up the test so that it closely simulates the experience of taking a certification exam, or you can set it up in study mode so that you can look at the correct answers and explanations after you answer each question.

MORE INFO   **Practice tests**

For details about all the practice test options available, see "How to Use the Practice Tests" in this book's Introduction.

Chapter 5
Creating Custom Web Controls

There are many controls in Microsoft Visual Studio 2005 that certainly save you lots of development time, but there are always opportunities for you to build your own controls to save even more development time. Many business problems require custom controls to simplify the development solution. Custom controls are typically required to obtain different functionality, new functionality, or the combined functionality of several controls. This chapter covers the types of custom controls that you can create in ASP.NET 2.0.

Exam objectives in this chapter:

- Create a composite Web application control.
    - Create a user control.
    - Convert a Web Forms page to a user control.
    - Include a user control in a Web Forms page.
    - Manipulate user control properties.
    - Handle user control events within the user control code-declaration block or code-behind file.
    - Create instances of user controls programmatically.
    - Develop user controls in a code-behind file.
    - Create a templated user control.
- Create a custom Web control that inherits from the *WebControl* class.
    - Create a custom Web control.
    - Add a custom Web control to the Toolbox.
    - Individualize a custom Web control.
    - Create a custom designer for a custom Web control.

- Create a composite server control.
    - ❏ Create a base class for composite controls.
    - ❏ Create a composite control.
- Develop a templated control.
    - ❏ Create a templated control.
    - ❏ Develop a templated data-bound control.

Lessons in this chapter:

Before You Begin

To complete the lessons in this chapter, you should be familiar with Microsoft Visual Basic or C# and be comfortable with the following tasks:

- Have Microsoft Windows XP and Microsoft Visual Studio 2005 installed on your computer with Microsoft SQL Server 2005 Express Edition.
- Be familiar with the Visual Studio 2005 Integrated Development Environment (IDE).
- Have a basic understanding of Hypertext Markup Language (HTML) and client-side scripting.

Real World

Glenn Johnson

Although we use the controls that are built-in to save time, we commonly don't see the opportunities to save more time by implementing custom controls to solve business problems. Custom controls not only save you time, but they also provide a consistent interface for your Web site.

Custom Web Control Types

There are three primary custom control types that will be covered in this chapter: user controls, custom Web controls, and composite controls. The following is a description of these controls:

- **user control**   A *user control* is a *template control* that provides extra behavior to allow constituent (individual) controls to be added to the user control in the Graphical User Interface (GUI) designer. These controls are added to the user control's template file, the .ascx file. The .ascx file is similar to the Web page's .aspx file and can have a code-behind page. To enable reuse, the .ascx and code-behind files must be included in each project that requires the user control.

- **custom Web control**   A *custom Web control* is a control that inherits from a Web control, where you either write all of the code to render the control, or inherit it from an existing Web control and provide extra behavior as necessary. The class file can be compiled to a .dll that can be shared among applications and can optionally be installed in the global assembly cache (GAC).

- **composite control**   A *composite control* is a custom Web control that can contain constituent controls; the constituent controls are added to the composite control via code to the class file that defines the control. The class file can be compiled to a .dll that can be shared among applications and can optionally be installed in the GAC.

Lesson 1: Working with User Controls

In this lesson, you learn how to create user controls and templated user controls. You also learn to make use of these controls in your Web page development efforts. This lesson starts by covering user controls, because they are the easiest to use. After that, the lesson covers templated user controls.

After this lesson, you will be able to:

- Create a user control.
- Add user controls to a Web page.
- Handle user control events within the user control code-declaration block or code-behind file.
- Create a templated user control.

Estimated lesson time: 60 minutes

Employing User Controls

A user control provides the easiest way to combine several controls onto a single control that can simply be dragged onto a Web page without writing much code.

Many times, pages contain similar controls. For example, when prompting a user for a billing address and a shipping address, the controls to retrieve the name, address, city, state, and zip code are duplicated. This is where user controls can be very handy. You can create a user control containing the name, address, city, state, and zip code and drop it onto a Web page where needed.

User controls are built using similar procedures to those that are required to build a standard Web page. Web pages can even be converted to user controls with little effort.

User controls inherit from the *UserControl* class, which inherits from the *Template-Control* class, which inherits from the *Control* class, as shown in Figure 5-1.

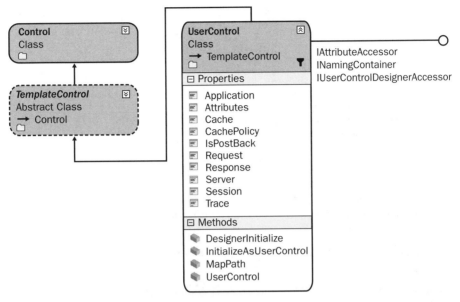

Figure 5-1 The *UserControl* class hierarchy.

MORE INFO User Controls

For more information on the User Controls, visit *http://msdn2.microsoft.com/en-us/library/ fb3w5b53.aspx.*

Creating a User Control

User controls have a standard naming convention, which uses an .ascx extension to ensure that the control is not executed in a stand-alone fashion. You can create a user control in Visual Studio 2005 by choosing Website, Add New Item, Web User Control. On the surface, it appears that a new Web page was added. However, a quick glance at the HTML reveals a *Control* directive instead of a *Page* directive, as follows:

```
'VB
<%@ Control Language="VB"
    AutoEventWireup="false"
    CodeFile="MyControl.ascx.vb"
    Inherits="MyControl" %>
```

```
//C#
<%@ Control Language="C#"
    AutoEventWireup="true"
    CodeFile="MyControl.ascx.cs"
    Inherits="MyControl" %>
```

All text and controls that are added to this user control are rendered on the page that the control is added to. For example, a *Label* called *lblName* and a *TextBox* called *txtName* are placed on the user control, as shown below, and the user control can be added to any Web page where required.

```
'VB
<%@ Control Language="VB" AutoEventWireup="false"
     CodeFile="MyControl.ascx.vb" Inherits="MyControl" %>
<asp:Label ID="lblName" runat="server" Text="Label">
</asp:Label>
<asp:TextBox ID="txtName" runat="server" ></asp:TextBox>
```

```
//C#
<%@ Control Language="C#" AutoEventWireup="true"
     CodeFile="MyControl.ascx.cs" Inherits="MyControl" %>
<asp:Label ID="lblName" runat="server" Text="Label">
</asp:Label>
<asp:TextBox ID="txtName" runat="server"></asp:TextBox>
```

Creating a User Control from a Web Page

In addition to explicitly creating a user control, you can also convert a Web page to a user control. The primary benefit is that you can do your prototyping and testing without having to deal with placing the control on a Web page.

The procedure for converting a Web page to a user control is as follows:

1. Remove the *<html>*, *<body>*, and *<form>* begin and end tags.
2. Change the *@Page* directive at the top of the file to an *@Control* directive.
3. Change the file extension of your Web page from .aspx to.ascx.
4. In the *@Control* directive, change Inherits="System.Web.UI.Page" to Inherits="System.Web.UI.UserControl".

Adding a User Control to a Page

You can add a user control to a Web page by simply dragging it from the Solution Explorer and dropping it on a Web page. When you add the user control to the page, a look at the HTML reveals the following additions to the page:

```
<%@ Page Language="language" AutoEventWireup="false"
     CodeFile="Default.aspx.language" Inherits="_Default" %>
<%@ Register Src="MyControl.ascx" TagName="MyControl" TagPrefix="ucl" %>
<!DOCTYPE html
   PUBLIC "-//W3C//DTD XHTML 1.0 Transitional//EN"
   "http://www.w3.org/TR/xhtml1/DTD/xhtml1-transitional.dtd">
```

```
<html xmlns="http://www.w3.org/1999/xhtml">
<head runat="server">
   <title>Untitled Page</title>
</head>
<body>
   <form id="form1" runat="server">
      <div>
          <ucl:MyControl ID="MyControl1" runat="server" />
      </div>
   </form>
</body>
</html>
```

Notice the *@Register* directive at the top of the page. This is a requirement to place the controls on the page. The *TagPrefix* attribute is a namespace identifier for the control. The default *TagPrefix* is *ucl* (as in User Control 1) and is changeable. The *TagName* attribute is the name of the control to use. The *Src* attribute is the location of the user control. The instance of *MyControl* is in the form tag. Notice that the ID is automatically created as *MyControl1*, the next instance will be called *MyControl2*, and so on.

Accessing Data from the User Control

If this user control is placed on a Web page, the *TextBox* and *Label* are visible to the user, but how can the name be retrieved? The *TextBox* and *Label* controls are declared as protected members on the Web page, which means that they are accessible only to the *MyControl* class and to classes that inherit from the control. To access the data for the *Label* and *TextBox*, you could expose the properties that are required, such as the *Text* property of the *txtName* TextBox and the *Text* property of the *lblName* Label. The user control is a class and can contain properties and methods. You can add properties to the user controls called *UserName* and *UserCaption*, as follows:

```
'VB
Partial Class MyControl
   Inherits System.Web.UI.UserControl

   Public Property UserCaption() As String
      Get
         Return lblName.Text
      End Get
      Set(ByVal value As String)
         lblName.Text = value
      End Set
   End Property

   Public Property UserName() As String
      Get
         Return txtName.Text
```

```
        End Get
        Set(ByVal value As String)
            txtName.Text = value
        End Set
    End Property

End Class
```

```
//C#
using System;
using System.Data;
using System.Configuration;
using System.Collections;
using System.Web;
using System.Web.Security;
using System.Web.UI;
using System.Web.UI.WebControls;
using System.Web.UI.WebControls.WebParts;
using System.Web.UI.HtmlControls;

public partial class MyControl : System.Web.UI.UserControl
{
    public string UserCaption
    {
        get { return lblName.Text; }
        set { lblName.Text = value;  }
    }

    public string UserName
    {
        get { return txtName.Text; }
        set { txtName.Text = value; }
    }
}
```

To demonstrate the new properties, the *MyControl* user control, a *Button* control, and a *Label* control are added to the Web page, and code is added to the code-behind page of the Web page to retrieve the *UserName*, as follows:

ASPX File

```
'VB
<%@ Page Language="VB" AutoEventWireup="true"
    CodeFile="MyControlPropertyTest.aspx.vb"
    Inherits="MyControlPropertyTest" %>

<%@ Register Src="MyControl.ascx" TagName="MyControl" TagPrefix="uc1" %>

<!DOCTYPE html PUBLIC "-//W3C//DTD XHTML 1.0 Transitional//EN"
"http://www.w3.org/TR/xhtml1/DTD/xhtml1-transitional.dtd">

<html xmlns="http://www.w3.org/1999/xhtml" >
<head runat="server">
```

```
    <title>Untitled Page</title>
</head>
<body>
    <form id="form1" runat="server">
    <div>
        <br />
        <asp:Button ID="Button1" runat="server" Text="Get Name"
            OnClick="Button1_Click" />
        <br />
        <br />
        <uc1:MyControl ID="MyControl1" runat="server" />
        <br />
        <br />
        <asp:Label ID="Label1" runat="server" ></asp:Label>
        </div>
    </form>
</body>
</html>
```

//C#
```
<%@ Page Language="C#" AutoEventWireup="true"
    CodeFile="MyControlPropertyTest.aspx.cs"
    Inherits="MyControlPropertyTest" %>
<%@ Register Src="MyControl.ascx" TagName="MyControl" TagPrefix="uc1" %>
<!DOCTYPE html PUBLIC "-//W3C//DTD XHTML 1.0 Transitional//EN"
    "http://www.w3.org/TR/xhtml1/DTD/xhtml1-transitional.dtd">

<html xmlns="http://www.w3.org/1999/xhtml" >
<head runat="server">
    <title>Untitled Page</title>
</head>
<body>
    <form id="form1" runat="server">
      <div>
        <br />
        <asp:Button ID="Button1" runat="server" Text="Get Name"
            OnClick="Button1_Click" /> <br />
        <br />
        <uc1:MyControl ID="MyControl1" runat="server" />
        <br />
        <br />
        <asp:Label ID="Label1" runat="server"></asp:Label>
        <br />
        <br />
      </div>
    </form>
</body>
</html>
```

Code-Behind
'VB
```
Partial Class MyControlPropertyTest
    Inherits System.Web.UI.Page
```

```
    Protected Sub Page_Load(ByVal sender As Object, _
        ByVal e As System.EventArgs) Handles Me.Load
      MyControl1.UserCaption = "Enter User Name:"
    End Sub

    Protected Sub Button1_Click(ByVal sender As Object, _
        ByVal e As System.EventArgs) Handles Button1.Click
      Label1.Text = MyControl1.UserName
    End Sub
End Class
```

```
//C#
using System;
using System.Data;
using System.Configuration;
using System.Collections;
using System.Web;
using System.Web.Security;
using System.Web.UI;
using System.Web.UI.WebControls;
using System.Web.UI.WebControls.WebParts;
using System.Web.UI.HtmlControls;

public partial class MyControlPropertyTest : System.Web.UI.Page
{
    protected void Page_Load(object sender, EventArgs e)
    {
        MyControl1.UserCaption = "Enter User Name:";
    }
    protected void Button1_Click(object sender, EventArgs e)
    {
        Label1.Text = MyControl1.UserName;
    }
}
```

Positioning User Controls

When a user control is dropped onto a Web page, you always position it using some of the same techniques as you would use to position other controls using Flow Layout, such as placing the user control in an HTML table.

You'll soon find that you cannot position the user control using Dynamic Hypertext Markup Language (DHTML) to set the absolute positioning using the *Style* property because the user control does not automatically add an outer tag for the contents of the control that could be assigned a *Style*. You can set the positioning using DHTML if you add a *Panel* control to the Web page and place the user control into the *Panel*. This allows the *Panel* and its contents to be positioned.

User Control Events

User controls can have their own events and cause a postback of the Web page's form data. It's interesting to note that user controls do not contain form server controls, since there can only be one form server control on a Web page. User controls are aware of the life cycle of the page, and the user control has many of the same events that the page has, such as the *Init* and *Load* events.

A user control can also handle its own events. In the following example, a user control called HiControl.ascx is created containing a *TextBox* control, a *Button* control, and a *Label* control. When the *Button* control is clicked, the user control handles the *Button* control's *Click* event to populate the *Label* control with a hello message.

ASCX File

'VB

```
<%@ Control Language="VB" AutoEventWireup="true"
      CodeFile="HiControl.ascx.vb" Inherits="HiControl" %>
<asp:TextBox ID="TextBox1" runat="server" ></asp:TextBox>
<asp:Button ID="Button1" runat="server" Text="Say Hi" />
<br />
<asp:Label ID="Label1" runat="server" Text="Label"></asp:Label>
```

//C#

```
<%@ Control Language="C#" AutoEventWireup="true"
      CodeFile="HiControl.ascx.cs" Inherits="HiControl" %>
<asp:TextBox ID="TextBox1" runat="server"></asp:TextBox>
<asp:Button ID="Button1" runat="server" Text="Say Hi"
      OnClick="Button1_Click" />
<br />
<asp:Label ID="Label1" runat="server" Text="Label"></asp:Label>
```

Code-Behind

'VB

```
Partial Class HiControl
    Inherits System.Web.UI.UserControl

    Protected Sub Button1_Click(ByVal sender As Object, _
          ByVal e As System.EventArgs) Handles Button1.Click
        Label1.Text = "Hi " + TextBox1.Text
    End Sub
End Class
```

//C#

```
using System;
using System.Data;
using System.Configuration;
using System.Collections;
using System.Web;
using System.Web.Security;
```

```
using System.Web.UI;
using System.Web.UI.WebControls;
using System.Web.UI.WebControls.WebParts;
using System.Web.UI.HtmlControls;

public partial class HiControl : System.Web.UI.UserControl
{
    protected void Button1_Click(object sender, EventArgs e)
    {
        Label1.Text = "Hi " + TextBox1.Text;
    }

}
```

It's interesting to note that the code for *Button* control's *Click* event has been encapsulated into the user control. Figure 5-2 shows the user control and the rendered output after the control was placed onto a simple Web page. Encapsulation of the user control's event code can help to simplify the page.

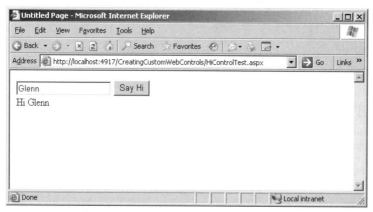

Figure 5-2   This user control contains encapsulated code to process the *Button* control's *Click* event.

Dynamically Loading Controls

Like other server controls, user controls can be loaded dynamically. Loading controls dynamically can be useful in situations where a variable quantity of user controls is displayed on the page. In the following example, the Web page loads two instances of *MyControl* onto the page. The *UserName* of the first instance is initialized.

```
'VB
Partial Class HiControlDynamicLoad
    Inherits System.Web.UI.Page
```

```
    Protected Sub Page_Load(ByVal sender As Object, _
        ByVal e As System.EventArgs) Handles Me.Load

      'Populate the form.
      Dim c1 As MyControl = _
        CType(LoadControl("MyControl.ascx"), MyControl)
      c1.UserName = "Glenn"
      form1.Controls.Add(c1)
      Dim c2 As MyControl = _
        CType(LoadControl("MyControl.ascx"), MyControl)
      form1.Controls.Add(c2)

    End Sub
End Class

//C#
using System;
using System.Data;
using System.Configuration;
using System.Collections;
using System.Web;
using System.Web.Security;
using System.Web.UI;
using System.Web.UI.WebControls;
using System.Web.UI.WebControls.WebParts;
using System.Web.UI.HtmlControls;

public partial class HiControlDynamicLoad : System.Web.UI.Page
{
    protected void Page_Load(object sender, EventArgs e)
    {
        //Populate the form.
        MyControl c1 =
            (MyControl)LoadControl("MyControl.ascx");
        c1.UserName = "Glenn";
        form1.Controls.Add(c1);
        MyControl c2 =
            (MyControl)LoadControl("MyControl.ascx");
        form1.Controls.Add(c2);
    }
}
```

The *LoadControl* method loads the control into memory, but this method returns a *System.Web.UI.Control*. To see the properties of *MyControl*, the returned *Control* object must be cast as a *MyControl* object. This is done using the *CType* function in Microsoft Visual Basic (VB) or the casting syntax in C#. The user control contains server controls, so it must be loaded into the controls collection of the form as shown.

Raising Events to the Page

A common requirement is to be able to place a control, such as a *Button* control, in the user control, but it's not known how the control will be implemented when the developer is creating the user control. This problem can be solved by raising the event to the Web page. For example, you may have a *Button* in the user control that raises an event when the *Button* is clicked and passes the contents of the *TextBox*. The following code shows a user control with a button called *btnMessage* that raises an event called *SendMessage*. The *SendMessage* event passes the name that was typed into the *TextBox*.

ASCX File
'VB
```
<%@ Control Language="VB" AutoEventWireup="false"
      CodeFile="MessageControl.ascx.vb" Inherits="MessageControl" %>
<asp:Label ID="lblName" runat="server" Text="Enter Name: "></asp:Label>
<asp:TextBox ID="txtName" runat="server" ></asp:TextBox>
<asp:Button ID="btnMessage" runat="server" Text="Send Message" />
```

//C#
```
<%@ Control Language="C#" AutoEventWireup="true"
      CodeFile="MessageControl.ascx.cs" Inherits="MessageControl" %>
<asp:Label ID="lblName" runat="server" Text="Enter Name: "></asp:Label>
<asp:TextBox ID="txtName" runat="server" ></asp:TextBox>
<asp:Button ID="btnMessage" runat="server" Text="Send Message"
      OnClick="btnMessage_Click" />
```

Code-Behind
'VB
```
Partial Class MessageControl
   Inherits System.Web.UI.UserControl

   Public Event SendMessage(ByVal UserName As String)

   Public Property UserName() As String
      Get
         Return txtName.Text
      End Get
      Set(ByVal Value As String)
         txtName.Text = Value
      End Set
   End Property

   Private Sub btnMessage_Click(ByVal sender As System.Object, _
         ByVal e As System.EventArgs) Handles btnMessage.Click
      RaiseEvent SendMessage(txtName.Text)
   End Sub

End Class
```

```
//C#
using System;
using System.Data;
using System.Configuration;
using System.Collections;
using System.Web;
using System.Web.Security;
using System.Web.UI;
using System.Web.UI.WebControls;
using System.Web.UI.WebControls.WebParts;
using System.Web.UI.HtmlControls;

public delegate void SendMessageHandler(string message);

public partial class MessageControl : System.Web.UI.UserControl
{
    public event SendMessageHandler SendMessage;
    protected void btnMessage_Click(object sender, EventArgs e)
    {
        if (SendMessage != null) SendMessage(txtName.Text);
    }
}
```

The event must always be declared as public at the top of the user control class. The *btnMessage* control's *Click* event handler has been programmed to raise the event, passing the contents of *txtName.Text*. The user control can be added to a Web page, and code can be added to subscribe to the *SendMessage* event, as shown in the following code sample:

ASPX File

```
'VB
<%@ Page Language="VB" AutoEventWireup="false"
    CodeFile="MessageControlTest.aspx.vb" Inherits="MessageControlTest" %>

<%@ Register Src="MessageControl.ascx"
    TagName="MessageControl" TagPrefix="uc1" %>

<!DOCTYPE html PUBLIC "-//W3C//DTD XHTML 1.0 Transitional//EN"
    "http://www.w3.org/TR/xhtml1/DTD/xhtml1-transitional.dtd">

<html xmlns="http://www.w3.org/1999/xhtml" >
<head runat="server">
    <title>Untitled Page</title>
</head>
<body>
    <form id="form1" runat="server">
    <div>
        <uc1:MessageControl ID="MessageControl1" runat="server" />
        <br />
        <br />
        <asp:Label ID="lblResult" runat="server" Text=""></asp:Label>
```

```
         </div>
       </form>
   </body>
   </html>
```

//C#
```
<%@ Page Language="C#" AutoEventWireup="true"
        CodeFile="MessageControlTest.aspx.cs" Inherits="MessageControlTest" %>

<%@ Register Src="MessageControl.ascx"
        TagName="MessageControl" TagPrefix="uc1" %>

<!DOCTYPE html PUBLIC "-//W3C//DTD XHTML 1.0 Transitional//EN"
        "http://www.w3.org/TR/xhtml1/DTD/xhtml1-transitional.dtd">

<html xmlns="http://www.w3.org/1999/xhtml" >
<head runat="server">
    <title>Untitled Page</title>
</head>
<body>
    <form id="form1" runat="server">
    <div>
        <uc1:MessageControl ID="MessageControl1" runat="server" />
        <br />
        <br />
        <asp:Label ID="lblResult" runat="server" Text=""></asp:Label>
    </div>
    </form>
</body>
</html>
```

Code-Behind
'VB
```
Partial Class MessageControlTest
    Inherits System.Web.UI.Page

    Protected Sub Page_Load(ByVal sender As Object, _
        ByVal e As System.EventArgs) Handles Me.Load
      AddHandler  MessageControl1.SendMessage, addressof MessageReceived
    End Sub

    private Sub MessageReceived(message as String)
       lblResult.Text = message
    End Sub
End Class
```

//C#
```
using System;
using System.Data;
using System.Configuration;
using System.Collections;
using System.Web;
```

```
using System.Web.Security;
using System.Web.UI;
using System.Web.UI.WebControls;
using System.Web.UI.WebControls.WebParts;
using System.Web.UI.HtmlControls;

public partial class MessageControlTest : System.Web.UI.Page
{
    protected void Page_Load(object sender, EventArgs e)
    {
        MessageControl1.SendMessage +=
            delegate(string message){ lblResult.Text = message;  };
    }

}
```

Figure 5-3 shows the completed Web page after a name was entered into the TextBox and the Button was clicked.

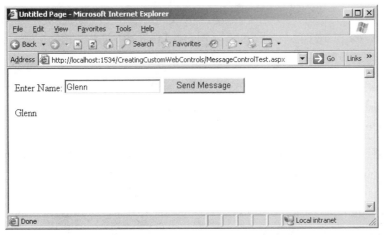

Figure 5-3   The user control raises the *SendMessage* event that can be handled by the Web page.

It's interesting to note the differences in implementation based on the programming language. In VB, the event was easy to create because the creation of an event causes the VB compiler to automatically create a delegate to handle the event, whereas C# requires you to create the delegate. When it's time to implement the user control and its *SendMessage* event, VB requires you to create an event handler method to populate the *Label* control with the message, whereas C# lets you implement an anonymous method to handle the event.

Creating a Templated User Control

A templated user control provides separation of control data from its presentation, meaning that a templated user control does not provide a default user interface. For example, if you know that you need to display your shipper's information, such as the shipper ID, the shipper name, and the shipper phone number, but you don't know how the page designer wants to format this information, you could create a templated user control called *ShipperControl* that allows the page designer to supply the format for the shipper data using a template.

Like user controls, the templated user control is only reusable in the same Web site. If you want reusability across multiple sites, consider implementing the templated control that's described near the end of this chapter.

The templated user control must provide a container class that is a naming container and has properties that are accessible to the host page. The template contains the user interface for the templated user control and is supplied by the page developer at design time. A template can contain controls and markup. You can create a templated user control by following these steps:

1. Add a user control file to your Web application.

2. In the .ascx file, place an ASP.NET *Placeholder* control where you want the template to appear.

3. In the code-behind file, implement a property of type *ITemplate*.

4. Add a new class to the App_Code folder in your Web site that contains the template's naming container class. This class inherits from *Control*, implements the *INamingContainer*, and contains a public property for each data element that is visible to the template. The container control contains an instance of the template when it is rendered.

5. Apply the *TemplateContainerAttribute* to the *ITemplate* property and pass the type of the template's naming container class as the argument to the constructor of the attribute.

6. Also, apply the *PersistenceModeAttribute* to the *ITemplate* property and pass the enumeration value of *PersistenceMode.InnerProperty* into its constructor.

7. In the user control's code-behind page, add public properties that let you pass your data to the template's naming container class so the data is available in the template.

8. In the *Page_Init* method of the user control, test for the *ITemplate* property being set. If the *ITemplate* property is set, create an instance of the naming container class and create an instance of the template in the naming container. Add the naming container instance to the *Controls* property of the *PlaceHolder* server control.

The following code sample defines a templated user control called *ShipperControl.ascx* that allows you to set a ShipperID, ShipperName, and ShipperPhone and allows the Web page developer to create a template to define the output.

ASCX File

```vb
'VB
<%@ Control Language="VB" CodeFile="ShipperControl.ascx.vb"
    Inherits="ShipperControl" %>
<asp:PlaceHolder ID="ShipperHolder" runat="server" />
```

```csharp
//C#
<%@ Control Language="C#" CodeFile="ShipperControl.ascx.cs"
    Inherits="ShipperControl"   %>
<asp:PlaceHolder ID="ShipperHolder" runat="server" />
```

Code-Behind

```vb
'VB
Partial Class ShipperControl
   Inherits System.Web.UI.UserControl

   <PersistenceMode(PersistenceMode.InnerProperty)> _
   <TemplateContainer(GetType(ShipperContainer))> _
   Public Property ShipperTemplate() As ITemplate
     Get
        Return _shipperTemplate
     End Get
     Set(ByVal value As ITemplate)
        _shipperTemplate = value
     End Set
   End Property
   Private _shipperTemplate As ITemplate

   Public Property ShipperId() As Integer
     Get
        Return _shipperId
     End Get
     Set(ByVal value As Integer)
        _shipperId = value
     End Set
   End Property
   Private _shipperId As Integer

   Public Property ShipperName() As String
     Get
```

```
            Return _shipperName
        End Get
        Set(ByVal value As String)
            _shipperName = value
        End Set
    End Property
    Private _shipperName As String

    Public Property ShipperPhone() As String
        Get
            Return _shipperPhone
        End Get
        Set(ByVal value As String)
            _shipperPhone = value
        End Set
    End Property
    Private _shipperPhone As String

    Public Sub Page_Init(ByVal sender As Object, _
            ByVal e As EventArgs) Handles Me.Init

        ShipperHolder.Controls.Clear()
        If ShipperTemplate Is Nothing Then
            ShipperHolder.Controls.Add( _
                New LiteralControl("No Template Defined"))
            Return
        End If
        Dim s As New ShipperContainer( _
            ShipperId, ShipperName, ShipperPhone)
        ShipperTemplate.InstantiateIn(s)
        ShipperHolder.Controls.Add(s)
    End Sub

End Class

//C#
using System;
using System.Web.UI;

public partial class ShipperControl : System.Web.UI.UserControl
{

    [PersistenceMode(PersistenceMode.InnerProperty)]
    [TemplateContainer(typeof(ShipperContainer))]
    public ITemplate ShipperTemplate
    {
        get { return _shipperTemplate; }
        set { _shipperTemplate = value; }
    }
    private ITemplate _shipperTemplate;

    public int ShipperId
    {
```

```csharp
      get { return _shipperId; }
      set { _shipperId = value; }
   }
   private int _shipperId;

   public string ShipperName
   {
      get { return _shipperName; }
      set { _shipperName = value; }
   }
   private string _shipperName;


   public string ShipperPhone
   {
      get { return _shipperPhone; }
      set { _shipperPhone = value; }
   }
   private string _shipperPhone;

   public void Page_Init()
   {
      ShipperHolder.Controls.Clear();
      if (ShipperTemplate == null)
      {
         ShipperHolder.Controls.Add(
           new LiteralControl("No Template Defined"));
         return;
      }
      ShipperContainer s = new ShipperContainer(
         ShipperId, ShipperName, ShipperPhone);
      ShipperTemplate.InstantiateIn(s);
      ShipperHolder.Controls.Add(s);
   }

}
```

Notice that this code requires a template-naming container called *ShipperContainer*. This code is placed in its own class file in the App_Code folder. The following is the contents of the *ShipperContainer* class:

```vb
'VB
Imports Microsoft.VisualBasic

Public Class ShipperContainer
   Inherits Control
   Implements INamingContainer

   Public Sub New(ByVal _shipperId As Integer, _
      ByVal _shipperName As String, ByVal _shipperPhone As String)
      Me._shipperId = _shipperId
      Me._shipperName = _shipperName
```

```
        Me._shipperPhone = _shipperPhone
     End Sub

     Public ReadOnly Property ShipperId() As Integer
        Get
           Return _shipperId
        End Get
     End Property
     Private _shipperId As Integer

     Public ReadOnly Property ShipperName() As String
        Get
           Return _shipperName
        End Get
     End Property
     Private _shipperName As String

     Public ReadOnly Property ShipperPhone() As String
        Get
           Return _shipperPhone
        End Get
     End Property
     Private _shipperPhone As String

End Class

//C#
using System;
using System.Web.UI;

public class ShipperContainer : Control, INamingContainer
{
   public ShipperContainer(int _shipperId,
      string _shipperName, string _shipperPhone)
   {
      ShipperId = _shipperId;
      ShipperName = _shipperName;
      ShipperPhone = _shipperPhone;
   }

   public int ShipperId
   {
      get { return _shipperId; }
      set { _shipperId = value; }
   }
   private int _shipperId;

   public string ShipperName
   {
      get { return _shipperName; }
      set { _shipperName = value; }
   }
   private string _shipperName;
```

```
   public string ShipperPhone
   {
      get { return _shipperPhone; }
      set { _shipperPhone = value; }
   }
   private string _shipperPhone;
}
```

Using the Templated User Control

Like the user control, the templated user must be used within the same project and can be used by dragging and dropping the templated user control from the Solution Explorer to a Web page. After the templated user control is added, you can set its properties and add a template. The following is a Web page that contains the *Shipper-Control* with a template to format the shipper data:

```
'VB
<%@ Page Language="VB" Debug="true"  AutoEventWireup="true"%>

<%@ Register TagPrefix="uc1" TagName="ShipperControl"
   Src="~/ShipperControl.ascx" %>
<!DOCTYPE html PUBLIC "-//W3C//DTD XHTML 1.0 Transitional//EN"
   "http://www.w3.org/TR/xhtml1/DTD/xhtml1-transitional.dtd">
<html xmlns="http://www.w3.org/1999/xhtml">

<script runat="server">
   Sub Page_Load()
      DataBind()
   End Sub 'Page_Load
</script>

<head runat="server">
   <title>ShipperControl Test</title>
</head>
<body>
   <form id="form1" runat="server">
      <uc1:ShipperControl ID="ShipperControl1" runat="server"
         ShipperId="1" ShipperName="Speedy Express"
         ShipperPhone="(503) 555-9831">
        <ShipperTemplate>
           <h1>Shipper Information</h1>
           <span style="background-color:Lime"> ID: </span>
           <%# Container.ShipperId %>
           <span style="background-color:Lime"> Name: </span>
           <%# Container.ShipperName %>
           <span style="background-color:Lime"> Phone: </span>
           <%# Container.ShipperPhone %>
```

```
        </ShipperTemplate>
    </ucl:ShipperControl>

  </form>
</body>
</html>
```

//C#
```
<%@ Page Language="C#" AutoEventWireup="true"  %>

<%@ Register Src="ShipperControl.ascx" TagName="ShipperControl"
   TagPrefix="ucl" %>
<!DOCTYPE html PUBLIC "-//W3C//DTD XHTML 1.0 Transitional//EN"
   "http://www.w3.org/TR/xhtml1/DTD/xhtml1-transitional.dtd">

<script runat="server">
   public void Page_Load()
   {
      DataBind();
   }
</script>

<html xmlns="http://www.w3.org/1999/xhtml" >

<head runat="server">
    <title>Untitled Page</title>
</head>
<body>
   <form id="form1" runat="server">
      <ucl:ShipperControl ID="ShipperControl1" runat="server"
           ShipperId="1" ShipperName="Speedy Express"
           ShipperPhone="(503) 555-9831">
         <ShipperTemplate>
           <h1>Shipper Information</h1>
           <span style="background-color:Lime"> ID: </span>
           <%# Container.ShipperId %>
           <span style="background-color:Lime"> Name: </span>
           <%# Container.ShipperName %>
           <span style="background-color:Lime"> Phone: </span>
           <%# Container.ShipperPhone %>
         </ShipperTemplate>
      </ucl:ShipperControl>
   </form>
</body>
</html>
```

Note that the templated user control does not display in Design view, but if you run the Web page, it displays properly, as shown in Figure 5-4.

Figure 5-4   The templated user control is rendered to display the supplier data.

Quick Check

1. What is the easiest way to combine several TextBoxes and Labels onto a single control that can be simply dragged onto a Web page without writing much code?

2. What type of control can be used to provide data that is to be rendered but allows the Web page designer to specify the format of the data?

Quick Check Answers

1. Create a *UserControl*.

2. A templated user control.

Lab: Working With User Controls

In this lab, you create a user control for collecting address information and implement the control to collect bill-to and ship-to information.

▶ **Exercise 1: Create the Web Site and the User Control**

In this exercise, you create the Web site and create the user control.

1. Open Visual Studio 2005; create a new Web site called **WorkingWithUserControls** using your preferred programming language. The new Web site is created, and a Web page called Default.aspx is displayed.

2. Add a Web User Control called AddressControl.ascx to the Web site by right-clicking the Web site in the Solution Explorer window, selecting Add New Item, and then selecting Web User Control; assign **AddressControl.ascx** as the name. An empty window is displayed for the new user control.

3. In the Source view of the user control, add the following markup to create an HTML table for the address information, and add controls to the table to collect the address information.

AddressControl.ascx File

```vb
'VB
<%@ Control Language="VB" AutoEventWireup="false"
    CodeFile="AddressControl.ascx.vb" Inherits="AddressControl" %>

<table>
    <tr>
        <td colspan="2">
            <asp:Label ID="lblTitle" runat="server" Text=""
            style="font-weight: bold; font-size: large;" >
            </asp:Label>
        </td>
    </tr>
    <tr>
        <td>
        Name:
        </td>
        <td>
            <asp:TextBox ID="txtName" width="300px"  runat="server">
            </asp:TextBox>
        </td>
    </tr>
    <tr>
        <td>
        Address:
        </td>
        <td >
            <asp:TextBox ID="txtAddress1" width="300px"  runat="server">
            </asp:TextBox>
        </td>
    </tr>
    <tr>
        <td>
         
        </td>
        <td >
            <asp:TextBox ID="txtAddress2" width="300px"  runat="server">
            </asp:TextBox>
        </td>
    </tr>
    <tr>
        <td colspan="2">
            City: <asp:TextBox ID="txtCity" width="150px" runat="server">
                </asp:TextBox> 
            State:
                <asp:DropDownList ID="ddlState" width="50px" runat="server">
                    <asp:ListItem Value="AK">AK</asp:ListItem>
```

```
                    <asp:ListItem Value="AZ">AZ</asp:ListItem>
                    <asp:ListItem Value="OH" Selected="True">OH</asp:ListItem>
                    <asp:ListItem Value="MA">MA</asp:ListItem>
                    <asp:ListItem Value="NH">NH</asp:ListItem>
                    <asp:ListItem Value="WA">WA</asp:ListItem>
                </asp:DropDownList> 
            Zip:    <asp:TextBox ID="txtZip" width="80px" runat="server">
                    </asp:TextBox> 
        </td>
    </tr>
</table>

//C#
<%@ Control Language="C#" AutoEventWireup="true"
CodeFile="AddressControl.ascx.cs" Inherits="AddressControl" %>

<table>
    <tr>
        <td colspan="2">
            <asp:Label ID="lblTitle" runat="server" Text=""
            style="font-weight: bold; font-size: large;" >
            </asp:Label>
        </td>
    </tr>
    <tr>
        <td>
        Name:
        </td>
        <td>
            <asp:TextBox ID="txtName" width="300px"  runat="server">
            </asp:TextBox>
        </td>
    </tr>
    <tr>
        <td>
        Address:
        </td>
        <td >
            <asp:TextBox ID="txtAddress1" width="300px"  runat="server">
            </asp:TextBox>
        </td>
    </tr>
    <tr>
        <td>
         
        </td>
        <td >
            <asp:TextBox ID="txtAddress2" width="300px"  runat="server">
            </asp:TextBox>
        </td>
    </tr>
    <tr>
```

```
        <td colspan="2">
          City: <asp:TextBox ID="txtCity" width="150px" runat="server">
                </asp:TextBox> 
          State:
                <asp:DropDownList ID="ddlState" width="50px" runat="server">
                  <asp:ListItem Value="AK">AK</asp:ListItem>
                  <asp:ListItem Value="AZ">AZ</asp:ListItem>
                  <asp:ListItem Value="OH" Selected="True">OH</asp:ListItem>
                  <asp:ListItem Value="MA">MA</asp:ListItem>
                  <asp:ListItem Value="NH">NH</asp:ListItem>
                  <asp:ListItem Value="WA">WA</asp:ListItem>
                </asp:DropDownList> 
          Zip:  <asp:TextBox ID="txtZip" width="80px" runat="server">
                </asp:TextBox> 
        </td>
      </tr>
    </table>
```

4. Figure 5-5 shows what the UI of your user control should look like in Design view.

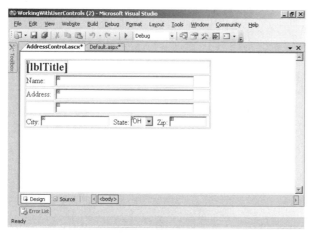

Figure 5-5   The UI of the AddressControl.ascx file in Design view.

5. In the code-behind for the user control, add public properties to allow the values of the Title, Name, Address1, Address2, City, State, and Zip to be read and set. Your code-behind page should look like the following:

```vb
'VB
Partial Class AddressControl
    Inherits System.Web.UI.UserControl

    Public Property Title() As String
        Get
```

```
            Return lblTitle.Text
        End Get
        Set(ByVal value As String)
            lblTitle.Text = value
        End Set
End Property

Public Property Name() As String
    Get
        Return txtName.Text
    End Get
    Set(ByVal value As String)
        txtName.Text = value
    End Set
End Property

Public Property Address1() As String
    Get
        Return txtAddress1.Text
    End Get
    Set(ByVal value As String)
        txtAddress1.Text = value
    End Set
End Property

Public Property Address2() As String
    Get
        Return txtAddress2.Text
    End Get
    Set(ByVal value As String)
        txtAddress2.Text = value
    End Set
End Property

Public Property City() As String
    Get
        Return txtCity.Text
    End Get
    Set(ByVal value As String)
        txtCity.Text = value
    End Set
End Property

Public Property State() As String
    Get
        Return ddlState.SelectedValue
    End Get
    Set(ByVal value As String)
        ddlState.SelectedValue = value
    End Set
End Property
```

```
      Public Property Zip() As String
         Get
            Return txtZip.Text
         End Get
         Set(ByVal value As String)
            txtZip.Text = value
         End Set
      End Property

End Class
```

```csharp
//C#
using System;
using System.Web.UI;

public partial class AddressControl : System.Web.UI.UserControl
{
    public string Title
    {
        get { return lblTitle.Text; }
        set { lblTitle.Text = value; }
    }

    public string Name
    {
        get { return txtName.Text; }
        set { txtName.Text = value; }
    }

    public string Address1
    {
        get { return txtAddress1.Text; }
        set { txtAddress1.Text = value; }
    }

    public string Address2
    {
        get { return txtAddress2.Text; }
        set { txtAddress2.Text = value; }
    }

    public string City
    {
        get { return txtCity.Text; }
        set { txtCity.Text = value; }
    }

    public string State
    {
        get { return ddlState.SelectedValue; }
        set { ddlState.SelectedValue = value; }
```

```
    }

    public string Zip
    {
        get { return txtZip.Text; }
        set { txtZip.Text = value; }
    }

}
```

▶ **Exercise 2: Employ the User Control**

In this exercise, you add multiple instances of AddressControl.ascx to the Default.aspx Web page and access their properties.

1. Open the Default.aspx Web page.

2. From the Solution Explorer window, drag the AddressControl.ascx file onto the Web page, change its *ID* property to **addBillTo**, and change the *Title* property to **Bill To Address**.

3. Add a *Button* control to the Web page and set its *Text* property to **Copy Bill To Address -> Ship To Address**.

4. From the Solution Explorer window, drag another AddressControl.ascx file onto the Web page, change its *ID* property to **addShipTo**, and change the *Title* property to **Ship To Address**. Figure 5-6 shows what your Web page should look like.

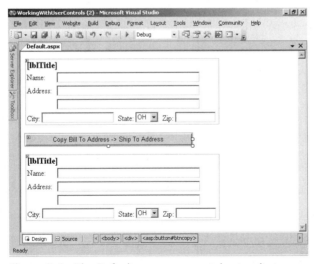

Figure 5-6 The Default.aspx page contains two instances of the AddressControl.ascx file.

5. Add code to the *Button* control's *Click* event handler that copies the address
    properties from the *addBillTo* control to *addShipTo* control. Your code-behind
    page should look like the following:

```vb
'VB
Partial Class _Default
    Inherits System.Web.UI.Page

    Protected Sub btnCopy_Click(ByVal sender As Object, _
        ByVal e As System.EventArgs) Handles btnCopy.Click
      addShipTo.Name = addBillTo.Name
      addShipTo.Address1 = addBillTo.Address1
      addShipTo.Address2 = addBillTo.Address2
      addShipTo.City = addBillTo.City
      addShipTo.State = addBillTo.State
      addShipTo.Zip = addBillTo.Zip
    End Sub
End Class
```

```csharp
//C#
using System;
using System.Web.UI;

public partial class _Default : System.Web.UI.Page
{
    protected void btnCopy_Click(object sender, EventArgs e)
    {
        addShipTo.Name = addBillTo.Name;
        addShipTo.Address1 = addBillTo.Address1;
        addShipTo.Address2 = addBillTo.Address2;
        addShipTo.City = addBillTo.City;
        addShipTo.State = addBillTo.State;
        addShipTo.Zip = addBillTo.Zip;
    }
}
```

6. View the Web page. Notice that the proper titles are displayed.

7. Try typing a bill-to address and clicking the *Button* control to copy the informa-
    tion to the ship-to address. This shows that the properties can be read and set.

Lesson Summary

■ The User Control enables a Web developer to easily combine controls onto a single control that can be dragged from the Solution Explorer window and dropped
onto a Web page.

■ Because the user control contains an .ascx markup file, a user control cannot be
compiled to a .dll and shared; it can only be shared within a Web site.

- You can expose properties, events, and methods in a user control.
- You can dynamically load a user control at run time by using the *LoadControl* method.
- You can create templated user controls, which allow the Web page designer to specify the formatting of data that the user control provides.

Lesson Review

You can use the following questions to test your knowledge of the information in Lesson 1, "Working with User Controls." The questions are also available on the companion CD if you prefer to review them in electronic form.

NOTE Answers

Answers to these questions and explanations of why each answer choice is right or wrong are located in the "Answers" section at the end of the book.

---

1. What file extension do you use to create a user control? (Choose one.)

   A. .ausr extension

   B. .aucx extension

   C. .asuc extension

   D. .ascx extension

2. You want to create a user control to display data, but you are concerned that you don't know how the Web page designers want to format the data. Also, some of the page designers mentioned that the format of the data might be different, depending on the Web page. How can you best create a user control to solve this problem? (Choose one.)

   A. Create a separate user control for each Web page and get each Web page designer to tell you the format to implement in each user control.

   B. Create a separate user control for each variation of the format once the Web page designers give you the desired formatting options.

   C. Create a templated user control that exposes the data to the Web page designers so they can specify their desired format.

   D. Create a user control that simply renders the data and let the Web page designers specify the style properties for the user control.

3. You want to employ a user control on one of your Web pages. What directive must be added to the top of the Web page to indicate that a user control is employed on the page? (Choose one.)

   A. *@Remember*

   B. *@Reference*

   C. *@Required*

   D. *@Register*

Lesson 2: Working with Custom Web Server Controls

In this lesson, you learn how to create custom controls that inherit from the *WebControl* class. These controls include composite controls and templated controls. You also learn to make use of these controls in your Web page development efforts.

> **After this lesson, you will be able to:**
> - Create a custom Web server control.
> - Add custom Web server controls to a Web page.
> - Individualize a custom Web server control.
> - Create a custom designer for a custom Web server control.
>
> **Estimated lesson time: 60 minutes**

Employing Custom Web Server Controls

A custom Web server control is a control that inherits from the *WebServer* control. This book has already covered many of the built-in Web server controls, so you should be familiar with the behaviors that they provide. Although you could specify that your custom control inherits from the *WebServer* class's parent class, the *Control* class, you should explore the class hierarchy and inherit from the class that provides the most useable benefits without going so far as to inherit from a class that provides many features that won't be used by your class. The primary benefit that the *WebControl* class provides is styles, which include UI-related properties such as *BackColor*, *ForeColor*, *Font*, *Height*, and *Width*.

An ASP.NET Web server control renders markup as well as client-side JavaScript. You can override the *Control* class' *Render* method to provide the markup via the HtmlTextWriter parameter that is passed to the method.

Creating a Custom Web Server Control

The two common approaches to creating a custom Web server control are to inherit from an existing control or to create a Web server control that inherits directly from *WebControl*. Regardless of the approach that you take, you should consider the reusability of the control. If you want to use your custom Web server control in multiple Web sites, you should place the new custom Web server control class in a Class Library project to create a .dll that you can share. If you only need to use the custom Web server control in the current Web site, you can simply add the class to the Web site.

Inheriting from Existing Web Server Controls

You can easily inherit from an existing control to add more properties, methods, and events. You can also override existing methods and properties to provide different behaviors. For example, maybe you want to create a labeled text box that exposes *LabelText* and *LabelWidth* properties and renders the *LabelText* in a span tag that has the width set before the performing the usual text box rendering. This can help minimize the use of tables for formatting because setting the width of the span tag assures that the *TextBox* controls line up vertically regardless of the text that is placed into the *LabelText* property. The following code shows how you can inherit from the *TextBox* control and add new properties called *LabelText* and *LabelWidth*. The *Render* method is overridden to add the span tag to the HTML output with the proper settings to call the *TextBox* control's *Render* method.

```vb
'VB
Imports Microsoft.VisualBasic

Public Class LabeledTextBox
    Inherits TextBox

    Public Property LabelText() As String
        Get
            Return _labelText
        End Get
        Set(ByVal value As String)
            _labelText = value
        End Set
    End Property
    Private _labelText As String

    Public Property LabelWidth() As Integer
        Get
            Return _labelWidth
        End Get
        Set(ByVal value As Integer)
            _labelWidth = value
        End Set
    End Property
    Private _labelWidth As Integer

    Protected Overrides Sub Render(ByVal writer As HtmlTextWriter)
        writer.Write( _
          "<span style=""display:inline-block;width:{0}px"">{1} </span>" _
          , LabelWidth, LabelText)
        MyBase.Render(writer)
    End Sub

End Class
```

```
//C#
using System;
using System.Web.UI;
using System.Web.UI.WebControls;

public class LabeledTextBox : TextBox
{
    public string LabelText
    {
        get { return _labelText; }
        set { _labelText = value; }
    }
    private string _labelText;

    public int LabelWidth
    {
        get { return _labelWidth; }
        set { _labelWidth = value; }
    }
    private int _labelWidth;

    protected override void Render(HtmlTextWriter writer)
    {
        writer.Write(
          @"<span style=""display:inline-block;width:{0}px"">{1} </span>"
          ,LabelWidth, LabelText);
        base.Render(writer);
    }

}
```

If this class is in the current Web site application, you can dynamically create instances of the control as shown in the following code sample for the LabeledText-BoxTest.aspx file:

```
'VB
Partial Class LabeledTextBoxTest
    Inherits System.Web.UI.Page

    Protected Sub Page_Init(ByVal sender As Object, _
            ByVal e As System.EventArgs) Handles Me.Init
        Dim width As Integer = 150
        Dim prompt1 As New LabeledTextBox()
        prompt1.LabelText = "Enter Name:"
        prompt1.LabelWidth = width
        form1.Controls.Add(prompt1)
        Dim brk As New LiteralControl("<br />")
        form1.Controls.Add(brk)
        Dim prompt2 As New LabeledTextBox()
        prompt2.LabelText = "Enter Address:"
```

```
        prompt2.LabelWidth = width
        form1.Controls.Add(prompt2)
    End Sub
End Class
```

```
//C#
using System;
using System.Web.UI;
using System.Web.UI.WebControls;

public partial class LabeledTextBoxTest : System.Web.UI.Page
{
    protected void Page_Init(object sender, EventArgs e)
    {
        int width = 150;
        LabeledTextBox prompt1 = new LabeledTextBox();
        prompt1.LabelText = "Enter Name:";
        prompt1.LabelWidth = width;
        form1.Controls.Add(prompt1);
        LiteralControl brk = new LiteralControl("<br />");
        form1.Controls.Add(brk);
        LabeledTextBox prompt2 = new LabeledTextBox();
        prompt2.LabelText = "Enter Address:";
        prompt2.LabelWidth = width;
        form1.Controls.Add(prompt2);
    }
}
```

Figure 5-7 shows the rendered Web page. When this Web page is run, the two *LabeledTextBox* controls have their *TextBox* controls lined up vertically because the *LabelWidth* property is set for these controls.

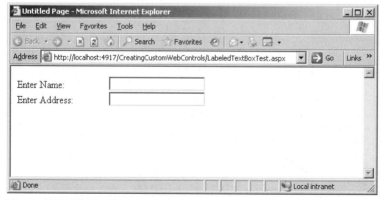

Figure 5-7   The rendered *LabeledTextBox* controls have *TextBox* controls that line up vertically.

Inheriting Directly from the *WebControl* Class

In addition to inheriting from an existing Web control, you can inherit directly from the *WebControl* class, which may be desirable when there is no control that currently provides behavior like the control that you want to implement.

When inheriting from the *WebControl* class, you must override the *Render* method to provide the desired output. The following is a code sample of *LogoControl* that contains a property for the *LogoUrl* and the *CompanyName*:

```vb
'VB
Imports Microsoft.VisualBasic

Public Class LogoControl
    Inherits WebControl

    Public Property LogoUrl() As String
        Get
            Return _logoUrl
        End Get
        Set(ByVal value As String)
            _logoUrl = value
        End Set
    End Property
    Private _logoUrl As String

    Public Property CompanyName() As String
        Get
            Return _companyName
        End Get
        Set(ByVal value As String)
            _companyName = value
        End Set
    End Property
    Private _companyName As String

    Protected Overrides Sub Render( _
        ByVal writer As System.Web.UI.HtmlTextWriter)
        writer.WriteFullBeginTag("div")
        writer.Write("<img src=""{0}"" /><br />", LogoUrl)
        writer.Write(CompanyName + "<br />")
        writer.WriteEndTag("div")
    End Sub

End Class
```

```csharp
//C#
using System;
using System.Web.UI;
using System.Web.UI.WebControls;
```

```
public class LogoControl : WebControl
{
    public LogoControl()
    {
    }

    public string LogoUrl
    {
        get { return _logoUrl; }
        set { _logoUrl = value; }
    }
    private string _logoUrl;

    public string CompanyName
    {
        get { return _companyName; }
        set { _companyName = value; }
    }
    private string _companyName;

    protected override void Render(HtmlTextWriter writer)
    {
        writer.WriteFullBeginTag("div");
        writer.Write(@"<img src=""{0}"" /><br />", LogoUrl);
        writer.Write(CompanyName + "<br />");
        writer.WriteEndTag("div");
    }
}
```

When this control is rendered, a *<div>* tag is output to the browser; the div tag contains a nested img tag with the src set to the *LogoUrl*. Also in the div tag is the CompanyName as text on the line that follows the image. Finally, the end tag is written for the div tag.

If this class is in the current Web site application, you can dynamically create instances of the control as shown in the following code sample for the LogoControl-Test.aspx file:

```
'VB
Partial Class LogoControlTest
    Inherits System.Web.UI.Page

    Protected Sub Page_Init(ByVal sender As Object, _
            ByVal e As System.EventArgs) Handles Me.Init
        Dim logo As New LogoControl()
        logo.CompanyName = "Northwind Traders"
        logo.LogoUrl = "NorthwindTraders.gif"
        form1.Controls.Add(logo)
    End Sub
End Class
```

```csharp
//C#
using System;
using System.Web.UI;
using System.Web.UI.WebControls;

public partial class LogoControlTest : System.Web.UI.Page
{
    protected void Page_Init(object sender, EventArgs e)
    {
        LogoControl logo = new LogoControl();
        logo.CompanyName = "Northwind Traders";
        logo.LogoUrl = "NorthwindTraders.gif";
        form1.Controls.Add(logo);
    }
}
```

This code creates an instance of the *LogoControl*, sets its properties, and adds the *Logo-Control* to the *form1* controls collection. The output is shown in Figure 5-8.

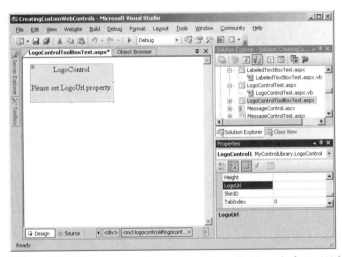

Figure 5-8   The rendered *LogoControl* inherits directly from *WebControl* and overrides the *Render* method.

Adding a Custom Web Server Control to the Toolbox

In the previous example, the control was added to the Web page dynamically by placing code in the code-behind page to instantiate and set the properties of the control. If you choose this method, you may also want to drag and drop your custom control from the Toolbox onto a Web page.

This basic requirement to having your Web control in the Toolbox is that the Web control be placed into a .dll file. In the case of the previous *LogoControl* example, the

LogoControl class has been added to a Class Library project called MyControlLibrary and placed into the default namespace of MyClassLibrary. You right-click the Toolbox, select Choose Items, and browse for the MyClassLibrary.dll file to add the controls that are contained in this .dll file to the Toolbox.

When the custom Web server control is added to the Toolbox, it uses the default icon. Add an attribute called *ToolboxBitmap* to specify the icon bitmap to use in the Toolbox. The bitmap must be 16 by 16 pixels in size. The path to the icon must be an absolute path with a drive letter specified. The bitmap path can also point to a .bmp file that is an embedded resource, as long as the name of the .bmp file has the same name as the fully qualified name of the class (classname.bmp). This means that you can add a .bmp file to the MyControlLibrary project called LogoControl.bmp, and, in the properties window, set the *Build Action* property to *Embedded Resource*.

The *ToolboxBitmapAttribute* class is located in the *System.Drawing* namespace in the *System.Drawing.dll* assembly. The following code snippet shows the *ToolboxBitmap* being set to a .bmp file that is configured to be an embedded resource. (When you use the *ToolBoxBitmapAttribute*, the *Attribute* suffix is optional.)

```vb
'VB
<ToolboxBitmap(GetType(LogoControl), "MyControlLibrary.LogoControl.bmp")> _
Public Class LogoControl
    Inherits WebControl
```

```csharp
//C#
[ToolboxBitmap(typeof(LogoControl), "MyControlLibrary.LogoControl.bmp")]
public class LogoControl : WebControl
```

The *DefaultProperty* attribute specifies the default property of the component (as the name implies). This is the property that is active in the Properties window when you drop a control onto the Web page.

Individualizing a Custom Web Server Control

You can further change the way your custom server control behaves when it is dropped onto the Web page by setting the *ToolboxDataAttribute* in your control class. This attribute is used to change the markup that is generated. The following code snippet shows the *ToolboxDataAttribute* implementation:

```vb
'VB
<ToolboxData( _
    "<{0}:LogoControl runat=""server"" CompanyName="" "" LogoUrl="" ""  />")> _
Public Class LogoControl
    Inherits WebControl
```

```
//C#
[ToolboxData(
    @"<{0}:LogoControl runat=""server"" CompanyName="" "" LogoUrl="" "" />")]
public class LogoControl : WebControl
```

The placeholder {0} contains the namespace prefix as defined by the Web page designer. Notice that the *CompanyName* and *LogoUrl* attributes are inserted automatically and assigned spaces.

You can also change the namespace prefix that is assigned by the Web page designer by assigning the *TagPrefixAttribute* to the assembly that contains your custom control. The following snippet shows the namespace prefix being changed to "mcl" for the controls in the MyControlLibrary project:

```
'VB
<Assembly: TagPrefix("MyControlLibrary", "mcl")>
```

```
//C#
[assembly: TagPrefix("MyControlLibrary", "mcl")]
```

With the previous changes to the *LogoControl*, dragging and dropping it on a Web page generates the following markup:

```
<mcl:LogoControl ID="LogoControl1" runat="server"
    CompanyName=" " LogoUrl=" " />
```

Creating a Custom Designer for a Custom Control

You can also specify a custom designer for your control that is used to render the control when in design mode by adding a reference to the *System.Design.dll* assembly and creating a class that inherits from the *ControlDesigner* class. This can be beneficial when the normal rendering of the control may not be visible due to code that needs to run to populate specific properties. For example, you may want to provide a custom designer for the *LogoControl* that provides a default rendering when the *LogoUrl* property has not been set, as shown in the following code sample:

```
'VB
imports System.ComponentModel

public class LogoControlDesigner
    Inherits System.Web.UI.Design.ControlDesigner

    private _logoControl as LogoControl

    public overrides function  GetDesignTimeHtml() as String
        _logoControl = Ctype(component, LogoControl)
        if (_logoControl.LogoUrl.Trim().Length = 0) then
```

```
                    return "<div id='mc11' " _
                        + "style='background-color:yellow;border-width:2px;' >" _
                        + "<center>LogoControl</center><br />" _
                        + "<center>Please set LogoUrl property.</center><br />" _
                        + "</div>"
                else
                    return mybase.GetDesignTimeHtml()
                End If
            end function

End Class
```

```csharp
//C#
using System;
using System.ComponentModel;
using System.Collections.Generic;
using System.Text;

namespace MyControlLibrary
{
    class LogoControlDesigner : System.Web.UI.Design.ControlDesigner
    {
        private LogoControl _logoControl;

        public override string GetDesignTimeHtml()
        {
            if (_logoControl.LogoUrl.Trim().Length == 0)
            {
                return "<div id=\'mc11\' "
                    + "style=\'background-color:yellow;border-width:2px;\' >"
                    + "<center>LogoControl</center><br />"
                    + "<center>Please set LogoUrl property.</center><br />"
                    + "</div>";
            }
            else
            {
                return base.GetDesignTimeHtml();
            }
        }

        public override void Initialize(IComponent component)
        {
            _logoControl = (LogoControl)component;
            base.Initialize(component);
            return;
        }
    }
}
```

After the class is created, you can assign the *DesignerAttribute* to the *LogoControl* class, as shown in the following code snippet:

```
'VB
<Designer("MyControlLibrary.LogoControlDesigner, MyControlLibrary")> _
Public Class LogoControl
    Inherits WebControl
```

```
//C#
[Designer("MyControlLibrary.LogoControlDesigner, MyControlLibrary")]
public class LogoControl : WebControl
```

When the *LogoControl* is dragged and dropped onto the Web page, the *LogoUrl* property is not set and the alternate rendering is provided. After the *LogoUrl* has been set, the default rendering is provided.

Creating a Composite Control

A composite control is a custom Web control that contains other controls. This sounds like a user control, but the composite control doesn't provide the designer screen and .ascx file that lets you drag and drop controls on it at design time. Instead, you inherit from the *CompositeControl* class and add constituent controls to the *Controls* collection of your class. The *CompositeControl* class hierarchy is shown in Figure 5-9. A composite control can fire, handle, and bubble up events raised by child controls.

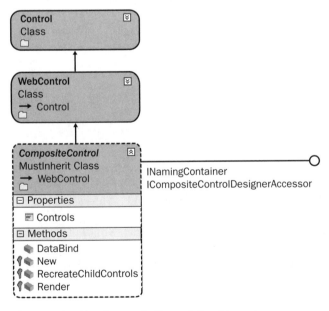

Figure 5-9   The *CompositeControl* class hierarchy.

A composite control is rendered out as a tree of constituent controls, each having its own life cycle and, together, forming a brand-new API. Because each of the child controls knows how to handle its own *ViewState* and *PostBack* data, you don't need to write extra code to deal with this.

To create a composite control, create a class that inherits from the *CompositeControl* class and overrides the *CreateChildControls* method. The *CreateChildControls* method needs to contain the code to instantiate the child controls and set their properties. If you want to be able to assign styles to the composite control, you should create an instance of the *Panel* class to provide a container that can have attributes assigned to it, add it to the *Controls* collection of your composite control, and then add your controls to the *Panel* control.

If you need to create many composite controls that have similar methods or properties, consider creating a base class for your composite controls that has the common code.

The following code sample shows a *UserPasswordControl* class that was added to the App_Code of the existing Web site. This control is used to prompt for a user name and password and also contains a submit button that can be subscribed to.

```vb
'VB
Imports System.Web.UI
Imports System.Web.UI.WebControls

Public Class UserPasswordControl
    Inherits CompositeControl
    Implements INamingContainer

    Public Event Submitted As System.EventHandler

    Public Property UserName() As String
        Get
            Dim txt As TextBox
            txt = CType(Me.FindControl("UserName"), TextBox)
            Return txt.Text
        End Get
        Set(ByVal Value As String)
            Dim txt As TextBox
            txt = CType(Me.FindControl("UserName"), TextBox)
            txt.Text = Value
        End Set
    End Property

    Public Property Password() As String
        Get
            Dim txt As TextBox
```

```vb
        txt = CType(Me.FindControl("Password"), TextBox)
        Return txt.Text
    End Get
    Set(ByVal Value As String)
        Dim txt As TextBox
        txt = CType(Me.FindControl("Password"), TextBox)
        txt.Text = Value
    End Set
End Property

Protected Overrides Sub CreateChildControls()
    Dim pnl As New Panel()
    Dim txtUserName As New TextBox()
    Dim txtPassword As New TextBox()
    Dim btnSubmit As New Button()
    AddHandler btnSubmit.Click, Addressof btnSubmit_Click

    'start control buildup
    Controls.Add(pnl)
    'add user name row
    pnl.Controls.Add(New LiteralControl("<table><tr><td>"))
    pnl.Controls.Add(New LiteralControl("User Name:"))
    pnl.Controls.Add(New LiteralControl("</td><td>"))
    pnl.Controls.Add(txtUserName)
    pnl.Controls.Add(New LiteralControl("</td></tr>"))
    'add password row
    pnl.Controls.Add(New LiteralControl("<tr><td>"))
    pnl.Controls.Add(New LiteralControl("Password:"))
    pnl.Controls.Add(New LiteralControl("</td><td>"))
    pnl.Controls.Add(txtPassword)
    pnl.Controls.Add(New LiteralControl("</td></tr>"))
    'add submit button row
    pnl.Controls.Add(New LiteralControl( _
 "<tr><td colspan=""2"" align=""center"" >"))
    pnl.Controls.Add(btnSubmit)
    pnl.Controls.Add(New LiteralControl("</td></tr></table>"))

    'setup control properties
    pnl.Style.Add("background-color", "silver")
    pnl.Style.Add("width", "275px")
    txtUserName.ID = "UserName"
    txtUserName.Style.Add("width", "170px")
    txtPassword.ID = "Password"
    txtPassword.TextMode = TextBoxMode.Password
    txtPassword.Style.Add("width", "170px")
    btnSubmit.Text = "Submit"

End Sub

Public Sub btnSubmit_Click(ByVal sender As Object, ByVal e As EventArgs)
    RaiseEvent Submitted(Me, e)
```

```
    End Sub
End Class

//C#
using System;
using System.ComponentModel;
using System.Web.UI;
using System.Web.UI.WebControls;
using System.Drawing;

public class UserPasswordControl : CompositeControl
{

    public event System.EventHandler Submitted;

    public string UserName
    {
        get
        {
            TextBox txt = (TextBox)FindControl("UserName");
            return txt.Text;
        }
        set
        {
            TextBox txt = (TextBox)FindControl("UserName");
            txt.Text = value;
        }
    }

    public string Password
    {
        get
        {
            TextBox pwd = (TextBox)FindControl("Password");
            return pwd.Text;
        }
        set
        {
            TextBox pwd = (TextBox)FindControl("Password");
            pwd.Text = value;
        }
    }

    protected override void CreateChildControls()
    {
        Panel pnl = new Panel();
        TextBox txtUserName = new TextBox();
        TextBox txtPassword = new TextBox();
        Button btnSubmit = new Button();
        btnSubmit.Click += new EventHandler(btnSubmit_Click);
```

```
//start control buildup
Controls.Add(pnl);
//add user name row
pnl.Controls.Add(new LiteralControl("<table><tr><td>"));
pnl.Controls.Add(new LiteralControl("User Name:"));
pnl.Controls.Add(new LiteralControl("</td><td>"));
pnl.Controls.Add(txtUserName);
pnl.Controls.Add(new LiteralControl("</td></tr>"));
//add password row
pnl.Controls.Add(new LiteralControl("<tr><td>"));
pnl.Controls.Add(new LiteralControl("Password:"));
pnl.Controls.Add(new LiteralControl("</td><td>"));
pnl.Controls.Add(txtPassword);
pnl.Controls.Add(new LiteralControl("</td></tr>"));
//add submit button row
pnl.Controls.Add(new LiteralControl(
    @"<tr><td colspan=""2"" align=""center"" >"));
pnl.Controls.Add(btnSubmit);
pnl.Controls.Add(new LiteralControl("</td></tr></table>"));

//setup control properties
pnl.Style.Add("background-color", "silver");
pnl.Style.Add("width", "275px");
txtUserName.ID = "UserName";
txtUserName.Style.Add("width", "170px");
txtPassword.ID = "Password";
txtPassword.TextMode = TextBoxMode.Password;
txtPassword.Style.Add("width", "170px");
btnSubmit.Text = "Submit";
}

void btnSubmit_Click(object sender, EventArgs e)
{
    if (Submitted != null) Submitted(this, e);
}
}
```

In this code, the *UserName* and *Password* properties are exposed to give you access to this data. An event called *Submitted* is also created so you can subscribe to the Submit button's *Click* event. The *CreateChildControls* method performs the work to instantiate the child controls for this composite control.

This control can be tested by adding it to a Web page using the same techniques described for custom Web controls. In the following code example, code is added in the code-behind page of the UserPassControlTest.aspx page to create a *UserPassword-Control* dynamically and set its properties. The *Submitted* event is used to simply display the user name and password.

```vb
'VB
Partial Class UserPasswordControlTest
   Inherits System.Web.UI.Page

   Protected Sub Page_Init(ByVal sender As Object, _
         ByVal e As System.EventArgs) Handles Me.Init
      Dim p As New UserPasswordControl()
      p.Style.Add("position", "absolute")
      p.Style.Add("left", "25px")
      p.Style.Add("top", "50px")
      form1.Controls.Add(p)
      AddHandler p.Submitted, AddressOf p_Submitted
   End Sub

   Public Sub p_Submitted(ByVal sender As Object, ByVal e As EventArgs)
      Dim p As UserPasswordControl = CType(sender, UserPasswordControl)
      Response.Write("User: " + p.UserName + "  Pass: " + p.Password)
   End Sub
End Class
```

```csharp
//C#
using System;
using System.Web.UI;
using System.Web.UI.WebControls;

public partial class UserPasswordControlTest : System.Web.UI.Page
{
   protected void Page_Init(object sender, EventArgs e)
   {
      UserPasswordControl p = new UserPasswordControl();
      p.Style.Add("position", "absolute");
      p.Style.Add("left", "25px");
      p.Style.Add("top", "50px");
      form1.Controls.Add(p);
      p.Submitted += new EventHandler(p_Submitted);
   }

   void p_Submitted(object sender, EventArgs e)
   {
      UserPasswordControl p = (UserPasswordControl)sender;
      Response.Write("User: " + p.UserName + "  Pass: " + p.Password);
   }
}
```

When this Web page is run, the *UserPasswordControl* displayed at the location is determined by the *Style* property. After typing a user name and password, click the Submit button to display that user name and password, as shown in Figure 5-10.

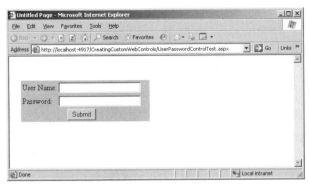

Figure 5-10   The *UserPasswordControl* collects the user name and password and exposes the *Submitted* event for processing of the data.

Creating a Templated Control

A templated control provides separation of control data from its presentation, which means that a templated control does not provide a default user interface. For example, if you know that you need to display product data, but you don't know how the page designer wants to format the product data, you could create a templated control called *ProductControl* that allows the page designer to supply the format for the product data as a template.

The templated control must provide a naming container and a class whose properties and methods are accessible to the host page. The template contains the user interface for the templated user control and is supplied by the page developer at design time. The templates can contain controls and markup. You can create a templated control using the following steps:

1. Create a ClassLibrary (.dll) project for your templated control.

2. Add a reference to the System.Web.dll library.

3. To your project, add a container class that has public properties for the data that you wish to be able to access via the *Container* object in your template.

4. In the container class file, import the System.Web.UI namespace (the C# syntax is "using").

5. Code your container class to inherit from the *System.Web.UI.Control* class and implement the *INamingContainer* interface.

6. Add a class to the project for your templated control.

7. In the class file, import the System.Web.UI namespace (the C# syntax is "using").

8. Code your templated control to inherit from the *System.Web.UI.Control* class and implement the *INamingContainer* interface.

9. Add the *ParseChildren(true)* attribute to the class. This attribute provides direction to the page parser to indicate that the nested content contained within the server control is parsed as a control and not used to set properties of the templated control.

10. Create one or more properties in the templated control class with the data type of *ITemplate* and that contain(s) a template as defined by the page designer. These properties need to have the *TemplateContainer* attribute set to the data type of the container, which might be the templated control, or, you could create a sub-container if you have repeating items to display in the template. Also, these properties have to have the *PersistenceMode* attribute set to *PersistenceMode.InnerProperty*, which allows page designers to add inner HTML elements to the HTML source of the templated control.

11. Add the desired properties to the template container that are to be accessible by the template.

12. The *DataBind* method must be overridden to call the *EnsureChildControls* method on the base *Control* class.

13. The *CreateChildControls* method must be overridden to provide the code to instantiate the template using the *InstantiateIn* method of the *ITemplate* interface. Code should also be provided for a default implementation if no template is provided.

The following code is placed in a *ClassLibrary* project called *MyControlLibrary*, which defines a templated control class called *ProductControl*. This control contains properties called *ProductId*, *ProductName*, *QtyPerUnit*, and *UnitPrice*. The values can be assigned at design time or at run time. The *ProductControl* class also contains a *ProductTemplate* property that allows the page designer to assign a template.

```vb
'VB
Imports System.Web.UI

<ParseChildren(True)> _
Public Class ProductControl
    Inherits Control
    Implements INamingContainer
```

```vb
Public Property ProductId() As Integer
    Get
        Return _productId
    End Get
    Set(ByVal value As Integer)
        _productId = value
    End Set
End Property
Private _productId As Integer

Public Property ProductName() As String
    Get
        Return _productName
    End Get
    Set(ByVal value As String)
        _productName = value
    End Set
End Property
Private _productName As String

Public Property QtyPerUnit() As String
    Get
        Return _qtyPerUnit
    End Get
    Set(ByVal value As String)
        _qtyPerUnit = value
    End Set
End Property
Private _qtyPerUnit As String

Public Property UnitPrice() As Decimal
    Get
        Return _unitPrice
    End Get
    Set(ByVal value As Decimal)
        _unitPrice = value
    End Set
End Property
Private _unitPrice As Decimal


<PersistenceMode(PersistenceMode.InnerProperty)> _
<TemplateContainer(GetType(ProductContainer))> _
Public Property ProductTemplate() As ITemplate
    Get
        Return _productTemplate
    End Get
    Set(ByVal value As ITemplate)
        _productTemplate = value
    End Set
End Property
Private _productTemplate As ITemplate
```

```vb
    Public Overrides Sub DataBind()
        EnsureChildControls()
        MyBase.DataBind()
    End Sub

    Protected Overrides Sub CreateChildControls()
        Controls.Clear()
        ' If there is a template, use it to create children.
        ' else just show the message.
        If Not (ProductTemplate Is Nothing) Then
            Dim p As New ProductContainer( _
               ProductId, ProductName, QtyPerUnit, UnitPrice)
            ProductTemplate.InstantiateIn(p)
            Controls.Add(p)
        Else
            Me.Controls.Add(New LiteralControl( _
                "No VB ProductTemplate Defined"))
        End If
    End Sub

End Class
```

```csharp
//C#
using System;
using System.Web;
using System.Web.UI;

namespace MyControlLibrary
{
    [ParseChildren(true)]
    public class ProductControl : Control, INamingContainer
    {

        public int ProductId
        {
            get { return _productId; }
            set { _productId = value; }
        }
        private int _productId;

        public String ProductName
        {
            get { return _productName; }
            set { _productName = value; }
        }
        private String _productName;

        public String QtyPerUnit
        {
            get { return _qtyPerUnit; }
            set { _qtyPerUnit = value; }
        }
```

```
    private String _qtyPerUnit;

    public decimal UnitPrice
    {
        get { return _unitPrice; }
        set { _unitPrice = value; }
    }
    private decimal _unitPrice;

    [PersistenceMode(PersistenceMode.InnerProperty)]
    [TemplateContainer(typeof(ProductContainer))]
    public ITemplate ProductTemplate
    {
        get { return _productTemplate; }
        set { _productTemplate = value; }
    }
    private ITemplate _productTemplate;

    public override void DataBind()
    {
        EnsureChildControls();
        base.DataBind();
    }

    protected override void CreateChildControls()
    {
        Controls.Clear();
        // If there is a template, use it to create children.
        // else just show the message.
        if (ProductTemplate != null)
        {
            ProductContainer p = new ProductContainer(
                ProductId, ProductName, QtyPerUnit, UnitPrice);
            ProductTemplate.InstantiateIn(p);
            Controls.Add(p);
        }
        else
        {
            this.Controls.Add(new LiteralControl(
                "No ProductTemplate Defined"));
        }
    }
  }//end class
}//end ns
```

Notice that the *ProductControl* creates a *ProductContainer* in the *CreateChildControls* method. This is the container class that exposes the data that is available to the template via the *Container* object. The code for the *ProductContainer* class is as follows:

'VB
```
Imports System.Web.UI
```

```vb
Public Class ProductContainer
    Inherits Control
    Implements INamingContainer

    Public Sub New()
    End Sub

    Public Sub New(ByVal _productId As Integer, ByVal _productName As String, _
    ByVal _qtyPerUnit As String, ByVal _unitPrice As Decimal)
        ProductId = _productId : ProductName = _productName
        QtyPerUnit = _qtyPerUnit : UnitPrice = _unitPrice
    End Sub


    Public Property ProductId() As Integer
        Get
            Return _productId
        End Get
        Set(ByVal value As Integer)
            _productId = value
        End Set
    End Property
    Private _productId As Integer

    Public Property ProductName() As String
        Get
            Return _productName
        End Get
        Set(ByVal value As String)
            _productName = value
        End Set
    End Property
    Private _productName As String

    Public Property QtyPerUnit() As String
        Get
            Return _qtyPerUnit
        End Get
        Set(ByVal value As String)
            _qtyPerUnit = value
        End Set
    End Property
    Private _qtyPerUnit As String

    Public Property UnitPrice() As Decimal
        Get
            Return _unitPrice
        End Get
        Set(ByVal value As Decimal)
            _unitPrice = value
        End Set
    End Property
    Private _unitPrice As Decimal
```

```
End Class

//C#
using System;
using System.Web;
using System.Web.UI;

namespace MyControlLibrary
{
    public class ProductContainer : Control, INamingContainer
    {
        public ProductContainer() { }

        public ProductContainer(int productId, string productName,
            string qtyPerUnit, decimal unitPrice)
        {
            ProductId = productId; ProductName = productName;
            QtyPerUnit = qtyPerUnit; UnitPrice = unitPrice;
        }

        public int ProductId
        {
            get { return _productId; }
            set { _productId = value; }
        }
        private int _productId;

        public String ProductName
        {
            get { return _productName; }
            set { _productName = value; }
        }
        private String _productName;

        public String QtyPerUnit
        {
            get { return _qtyPerUnit; }
            set { _qtyPerUnit = value; }
        }
        private String _qtyPerUnit;

        public decimal UnitPrice
        {
            get { return _unitPrice; }
            set { _unitPrice = value; }
        }
        private decimal _unitPrice;


    }//end class
}//end ns
```

Using the Templated Control

This class library project is compiled to a .dll, and the *ProductControl* can be added to the ToolBox by right-clicking the ToolBox and selecting the Choose Items option. Simply browse to and select the .dll file to add the *ProductControl* to your ToolBox.

In the following code example, a Web page is created called ProductControlTest.aspx and a *ProductControl* is added. After the *ProductControl* is added, the product's properties are set, and the *ProductTemplate* is defined in the HTML source of the page.

APSX File

```vb
'VB
<%@ Page Language="VB" AutoEventWireup="false" CodeFile="ProductControlTest.aspx.vb"
Inherits="ProductControlTest" %>

<%@ Register Assembly="MyControlLibrary" Namespace="MyControlLibrary" TagPrefix="cc1" %>

<!DOCTYPE html PUBLIC "-//W3C//DTD XHTML 1.0 Transitional//EN" "http://www.w3.org/TR/xhtml1/
DTD/xhtml1-transitional.dtd">

<script runat="Server">
    Public Sub Page_Load()
        DataBind()
    End Sub
</script>

<html xmlns="http://www.w3.org/1999/xhtml" >

<head runat="server">
    <title>Untitled Page</title>
</head>
<body>
    <form id="form1" runat="server">
    <div>
      <cc1:ProductControl ID="ProductControl1"
        runat="server" ProductId="925" ProductName="MyProduct"
        QtyPerUnit="12 per carton" UnitPrice="123.45">
        <ProductTemplate>
          <h1>Product ID: <%# Container.ProductId %></h1>
          <table border="1">
            <tr>
                <td>Name:</td>
                <td><%# Container.ProductName %></td>
            </tr>
            <tr>
                <td>Qty per Unit:</td>
                <td><%# Container.QtyPerUnit %></td>
            </tr>
            <tr>
                <td>Unit Price:</td>
```

```
                    <td align="right">
                        <%# Container.UnitPrice.ToString("C") %>
                    </td>
                </tr>
            </table>
        </ProductTemplate>
    </cc1:ProductControl>
  </div>
  </form>
</body>
</html>
```

```
//C#
<%@ Page Language="C#" AutoEventWireup="true" CodeFile="ProductControlTest.aspx.cs"
Inherits="ProductControlTest" %>

<%@ Register Assembly="MyControlLibrary" Namespace="MyControlLibrary" TagPrefix="cc1" %>

<!DOCTYPE html PUBLIC "-//W3C//DTD XHTML 1.0 Transitional//EN" "http://www.w3.org/TR/xhtml1/
DTD/xhtml1-transitional.dtd">

<script runat="server">
   public void Page_Load()
   {
      DataBind();
   }
</script>

<html xmlns="http://www.w3.org/1999/xhtml" >
<head runat="server">
    <title>Untitled Page</title>
</head>
<body>
    <form id="form1" runat="server">
    <div>
        <cc1:ProductControl ID="ProductControl1"
            runat="server" ProductId="925" ProductName="MyProduct"
            QtyPerUnit="12 per carton" UnitPrice="123.45">
            <ProductTemplate>
              <h1>Product ID: <%#Container.ProductId %></h1>
              <table border="1">
                <tr>
                    <td>Name:</td>
                    <td><%#Container.ProductName %></td>
                </tr>
                <tr>
                    <td>Qty per Unit:</td>
                    <td><%#Container.QtyPerUnit %></td>
                </tr>
                <tr>
                    <td>Unit Price:</td>
                    <td align="right">
                        <%#Container.UnitPrice.ToString("C") %>
```

```
                            </td>
                        </tr>
                    </table>
                </ProductTemplate>
            </cc1:ProductControl>
        </div>
        </form>
</body>
</html>
```

Notice that the top of the .aspx file contains a script with the *DataBind* call, which forces the rendering of the *ProductControl* with the product data. When the page is run, the product data is displayed using the *ProductTemplate* that was defined in the HTML source, as shown in Figure 5-11.

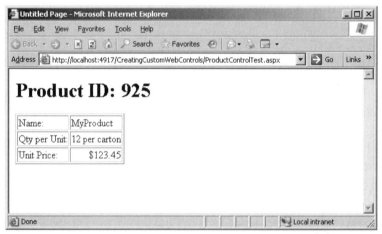

Figure 5-11   The rendered templated control shows the product data formatted using the *Product-Template*.

Quick Check

■ You want to create a control that can be distributed as a .dll. The control contains several *TextBox*, *Label*, and *Button* controls and you want to be able to add the control to the ToolBox. What is the best choice of control to create?

Quick Check Answer

■ Create a composite control.

Lab: Working With Custom Web Server Controls

In this lab, you create a custom Web server control called *StateControl* that displays a list of the states. This control is compiled into a .dll file and added to the ToolBox so it is available to all of your projects.

▶ **Exercise 1: Create the Class Library Project and the Control**

In this exercise, you create the *CustomControls* class library project. You also add the *StateControl* class to the project and add code to populate the *Items* collection with the list of states.

1. Open Visual Studio 2005; create a new class library project called **CustomControls** using your preferred programming language.

2. The new project creates a class called Class1. Delete this class.

3. Add a new class called **StateControl** to your project.

4. Add a reference to the *System.Web.dll* and the *System.Drawing.dll* assemblies.

5. Add the following statements to import namespaces into your project:

```
'VB
Imports System.Web.UI.WebControls
Imports System.Drawing

//C#
using System.Web.UI.WebControls;
using System.Drawing;
```

6. Add the StateControl.bmp file to the project and set its Build Action to Embedded Resource. This is a 16-by-6-pixel bitmap file showing the U.S. flag.

7. Add the *ToolboxBitmap* attribute above the *StateControl* to assign the StateControl.bmp file as the icon for the *StateControl* class.

8. In the constructor of the *StateControl*, add code to create an empty *ListItem* and a *ListItem* for each state, and add the *ListItems* to the *Items* collection of the *StateControl*. The *ListItem* for each state displays the full name of the state, but the posted value is the two-character state abbreviation. Your completed *StateControl* class should look like the following:

```
'VB
Imports System.Web.UI.WebControls
Imports System.Drawing

<ToolboxBitmap(GetType(StateControl), "StateControl.bmp")> _
```

```
Public Class StateControl
    Inherits DropDownList

    Public Sub New()
        Items.Add(New ListItem("", ""))
        Items.Add(New ListItem("Alabama", "AL"))
        Items.Add(New ListItem("Alaska", "AK"))
        Items.Add(New ListItem("Arizona", "AZ"))
        Items.Add(New ListItem("Arkansas", "AR"))
        Items.Add(New ListItem("California", "CA"))
        Items.Add(New ListItem("Colorado", "CO"))
        Items.Add(New ListItem("Connecticut", "CT"))
        Items.Add(New ListItem("Delaware", "DE"))
        Items.Add(New ListItem("District of Columbia", "DC"))
        Items.Add(New ListItem("Florida", "FL"))
        Items.Add(New ListItem("Georgia", "GA"))
        Items.Add(New ListItem("Hawaii", "HI"))
        Items.Add(New ListItem("Idaho", "ID"))
        Items.Add(New ListItem("Illinois", "IL"))
        Items.Add(New ListItem("Indiana", "IN"))
        Items.Add(New ListItem("Iowa", "IA"))
        Items.Add(New ListItem("Kansas", "KS"))
        Items.Add(New ListItem("Kentucky", "KY"))
        Items.Add(New ListItem("Louisiana", "LA"))
        Items.Add(New ListItem("Maine", "ME"))
        Items.Add(New ListItem("Maryland", "MD"))
        Items.Add(New ListItem("Massachusetts", "MA"))
        Items.Add(New ListItem("Michigan", "MI"))
        Items.Add(New ListItem("Minnesota", "MN"))
        Items.Add(New ListItem("Mississippi", "MS"))
        Items.Add(New ListItem("Missouri", "MO"))
        Items.Add(New ListItem("Montana", "MT"))
        Items.Add(New ListItem("Nebraska", "NE"))
        Items.Add(New ListItem("Nevada", "NV"))
        Items.Add(New ListItem("New Hampshire", "NH"))
        Items.Add(New ListItem("New Jersey", "NJ"))
        Items.Add(New ListItem("New Mexico", "NM"))
        Items.Add(New ListItem("New York", "NY"))
        Items.Add(New ListItem("North Carolina", "NC"))
        Items.Add(New ListItem("North Dakota", "ND"))
        Items.Add(New ListItem("Ohio", "OH"))
        Items.Add(New ListItem("Oklahoma", "OK"))
        Items.Add(New ListItem("Oregon", "OR"))
        Items.Add(New ListItem("Pennsylvania", "PA"))
        Items.Add(New ListItem("Rhode Island", "RI"))
        Items.Add(New ListItem("South Carolina", "SC"))
        Items.Add(New ListItem("South Dakota", "SD"))
        Items.Add(New ListItem("Tennessee", "TN"))
        Items.Add(New ListItem("Texas", "TX"))
        Items.Add(New ListItem("Utah", "UT"))
        Items.Add(New ListItem("Vermont", "VT"))
        Items.Add(New ListItem("Virginia", "VA"))
        Items.Add(New ListItem("Washington", "WA"))
```

```
            Items.Add(New ListItem("West Virginia", "WV"))
            Items.Add(New ListItem("Wisconsin", "WI"))
            Items.Add(New ListItem("Wyoming", "WY"))
            SelectedIndex = 0
    End Sub

End Class
```

```csharp
//C#
using System;
using System.Web.UI;
using System.Web.UI.WebControls;
using System.Drawing;

namespace CustomControls
{
    [ToolboxBitmap(typeof(StateControl),"StateControl.bmp")]
    class StateControl : DropDownList
    {
        public StateControl()
        {
            Items.Add(new ListItem("", ""));
            Items.Add(new ListItem("Alabama", "AL"));
            Items.Add(new ListItem("Alaska", "AK"));
            Items.Add(new ListItem("Arizona", "AZ"));
            Items.Add(new ListItem("Arkansas", "AR"));
            Items.Add(new ListItem("California", "CA"));
            Items.Add(new ListItem("Colorado", "CO"));
            Items.Add(new ListItem("Connecticut", "CT"));
            Items.Add(new ListItem("Delaware", "DE"));
            Items.Add(new ListItem("District of Columbia", "DC"));
            Items.Add(new ListItem("Florida", "FL"));
            Items.Add(new ListItem("Georgia", "GA"));
            Items.Add(new ListItem("Hawaii", "HI"));
            Items.Add(new ListItem("Idaho", "ID"));
            Items.Add(new ListItem("Illinois", "IL"));
            Items.Add(new ListItem("Indiana", "IN"));
            Items.Add(new ListItem("Iowa", "IA"));
            Items.Add(new ListItem("Kansas", "KS"));
            Items.Add(new ListItem("Kentucky", "KY"));
            Items.Add(new ListItem("Louisiana", "LA"));
            Items.Add(new ListItem("Maine", "ME"));
            Items.Add(new ListItem("Maryland", "MD"));
            Items.Add(new ListItem("Massachusetts", "MA"));
            Items.Add(new ListItem("Michigan", "MI"));
            Items.Add(new ListItem("Minnesota", "MN"));
            Items.Add(new ListItem("Mississippi", "MS"));
            Items.Add(new ListItem("Missouri", "MO"));
            Items.Add(new ListItem("Montana", "MT"));
            Items.Add(new ListItem("Nebraska", "NE"));
            Items.Add(new ListItem("Nevada", "NV"));
            Items.Add(new ListItem("New Hampshire", "NH"));
            Items.Add(new ListItem("New Jersey", "NJ"));
```

```
            Items.Add(new ListItem("New Mexico", "NM"));
            Items.Add(new ListItem("New York", "NY"));
            Items.Add(new ListItem("North Carolina", "NC"));
            Items.Add(new ListItem("North Dakota", "ND"));
            Items.Add(new ListItem("Ohio", "OH"));
            Items.Add(new ListItem("Oklahoma", "OK"));
            Items.Add(new ListItem("Oregon", "OR"));
            Items.Add(new ListItem("Pennsylvania", "PA"));
            Items.Add(new ListItem("Rhode Island", "RI"));
            Items.Add(new ListItem("South Carolina", "SC"));
            Items.Add(new ListItem("South Dakota", "SD"));
            Items.Add(new ListItem("Tennessee", "TN"));
            Items.Add(new ListItem("Texas", "TX"));
            Items.Add(new ListItem("Utah", "UT"));
            Items.Add(new ListItem("Vermont", "VT"));
            Items.Add(new ListItem("Virginia", "VA"));
            Items.Add(new ListItem("Washington", "WA"));
            Items.Add(new ListItem("West Virginia", "WV"));
            Items.Add(new ListItem("Wisconsin", "WI"));
            Items.Add(new ListItem("Wyoming", "WY"));
            SelectedIndex = 0;
        }
    }
}
```

9. Build the CustomControls project.

▶ **Exercise 2: Create the Class Library Project and the Control**

In this exercise, you create a Web site to test your *StateControl*.

1. Open Visual Studio 2005 and create a new ASP.NET Web site called **Working-WithCustomWebServerControls** using your preferred programming language. The new Web site is created and a Web page called Default.aspx is displayed.

2. Add the *StateControl* to the Toolbox by right-clicking the Toolbox and selecting Choose Items. Click the Browse button and locate the *CustomControls.dll* assembly. Select the *CustomControls.dll* assembly, and the *StateControl* is displayed in the Toolbox.

3. Drag the *StateControl*, and drop it onto the Default.aspx Web page.

4. Set the *Style* property of the *StateControl* to set the location of the *StateControl*, as shown in the following code sample:

```
'VB
<%@ Page Language="C#" AutoEventWireup="true"
    CodeFile="Default.aspx.cs" Inherits="_Default" %>

<%@ Register Assembly="CustomControls"
    Namespace="CustomControls" TagPrefix="cc1" %>
```

```
<!DOCTYPE html PUBLIC "-//W3C//DTD XHTML 1.0 Transitional//EN"
     "http://www.w3.org/TR/xhtml1/DTD/xhtml1-transitional.dtd">

<html xmlns="http://www.w3.org/1999/xhtml" >
<head runat="server">
    <title>Untitled Page</title>
</head>
<body>
    <form id="form1" runat="server">
    <div>
        <cc1:StateControl ID="StateControl1" runat="server"
          Style="z-index: 100; left: 80px; position: absolute; top: 30px">
        </cc1:StateControl>

    </div>
    </form>
</body>
</html>

//C#
<%@ Page Language="VB" AutoEventWireup="false"
     CodeFile="Default.aspx.vb" Inherits="_Default" %>

<%@ Register Assembly="CustomControls"
     Namespace="CustomControls" TagPrefix="cc1" %>

<!DOCTYPE html PUBLIC "-//W3C//DTD XHTML 1.0 Transitional//EN"
     "http://www.w3.org/TR/xhtml1/DTD/xhtml1-transitional.dtd">

<html xmlns="http://www.w3.org/1999/xhtml" >
<head runat="server">
    <title>Untitled Page</title>
</head>
<body>
    <form id="form1" runat="server">
    <div>
        <cc1:StateControl ID="StateControl1" runat="server"
          Style="z-index: 100; left: 80px; position: absolute; top: 30px">
        </cc1:StateControl>
    </div>
    </form>
</body>
</html>
```

5. Test the Web page by pressing F5 to display the page. You should see the *State-Control* in the location that was set with the *Style* property. The drop-down list box contains the list of states shown in Figure 5-12.

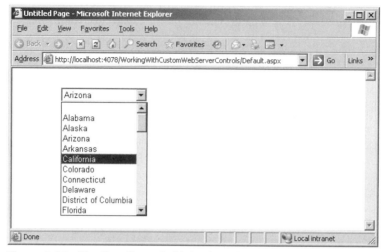

Figure 5-12   The *StateControl* with its drop down list of states.

Lesson Summary

- You can build a custom Web control by inheriting from the *WebControl* class.

- You can create a composite Web control by inheriting from the *CompositeControl* class.

- You can create a templated control by inheriting from the Web control class.

Lesson Review

You can use the following questions to test your knowledge of the information in Lesson 2, "Working with Custom Web Server Controls." The questions are also available on the companion CD if you prefer to review them in electronic form.

NOTE   Answers

Answers to these questions and explanations of why each answer choice is right or wrong are located in the "Answers" section at the end of the book.

---

1. Which of the following attributes can be used to set the image that is displayed in the Toolbox for your custom Web control? (Choose one.)

    A. *ToolboxIcon*

    B. *ToolboxData*

    C. *ToolboxBitmap*

    D. *ToolboxConfig*

2. You are going to create a custom Web server control that inherits directly from the *WebControl* class. Which method do you need to override to get your control to display in the browser window? (Choose one.)

    A. *Display*

    B. *Paint*

    C. *Build*

    D. *Render*

3. You are creating a composite control, so you create a class that inherits from the *CompositeControl* class. What method must be overridden so you can provide code to instantiate the child controls and set their properties? (Choose one.)

    A. *CreateChildControls*

    B. *InitChildren*

    C. *BuildChildControls*

    D. *RenderChildren*

Chapter Review

To further practice and reinforce the skills you learned in this chapter, you can perform the following tasks:

- Review the chapter summary.
- Review the list of key terms introduced in this chapter.
- Complete the case scenarios. These scenarios set up real-world situations involving the topics of this chapter and ask you to create a solution.
- Complete the suggested practices.
- Take a practice test.

Chapter Summary

- You can create user controls to make it easier to share code within a Web site.
- A templated user control can be created to separate the user control data from the presentation.
- You can create custom Web controls that inherit directly from *Control* or *WebControl*. Inheriting from Web controls gives you the ability to use properties like the *Style* property.
- The composite control is a custom Web control that has other controls and inherits from the *CompositeControl* class.
- The templated custom control inherits from *WebControl* and separates your data from the presentation.

Key Terms

Do you know what these key terms mean? You can check your answers by looking up the terms in the glossary at the end of the book.

- composite control
- custom Web control
- template control
- user control

Case Scenarios

In the following case scenarios, you apply what you've learned in this chapter. If you have difficulty completing this work, review the material in this chapter before beginning the next chapter. You can find answers to these questions in the "Answers" section at the end of this book.

Case Scenario 1: Sharing Controls Between Applications

You are creating a new Web site and find that you need to have a group of controls on many pages. These controls are used jointly to collect data from the user. Upon further investigation, you realize that your company uses these controls to collect user data on several other Web sites. Also, the company wants to standardize the layout and behavior of the user data-collection controls.

- What approach should you take to create a custom control that can be placed into the GAC and used by all Web sites on this production server?

Case Scenario 2: Providing Layout Flexibility

You are creating a single Web site for a customer and notice that there are several areas where you display customer information. Although the data that is displayed is the same, the layout for each area is different, and the Web page designers want the flexibility to change the layouts to keep the site design fresh.

- What is a quick way to create a control that offers the data to the Web page designers so they can create the layout?

Suggested Practices

To successfully master the Create a Composite Web Application Control exam objective, the Create a Composite Server Control exam objective, and the Develop a Templated Control exam objective, complete the following tasks.

Create a New Custom User Control

For this task, you should complete both Practices.

- **Practice 1** Create a new user control that has other controls and exposes properties. Practice adding the user control to several Web pages and write code to access the properties.

■ **Practice 2**   Add custom events to the user control and practice subscribing to the event.

Create a New Custom Web Server Control

For this task, you should complete both practices.

■ **Practice 1**   Create a class library project that contains a new custom Web server control that inherits from the *WebControl* class.

Add properties and methods to the custom Web server control class.

Compile and add the custom Web control to the ToolBox.

■ **Practice 2**   Practice adding the user control to several Web pages and write code to access the properties.

Create a New Composite Web Server Control

For this task, you should complete both practices.

■ **Practice 1**   Create a class library project that contains a new class that inherits from *System.Web.UI.CompositeContol* class.

Implement code to add constituent controls to your composite control and add properties to individualize the composite control.

Compile and add the custom Web control to the ToolBox.

■ **Practice 2**   Practice adding the composite control to several Web pages and write code to access the composite control properties.

Create a New Templated Control

For this task, you should complete both practices.

■ **Practice 1**   Create a class library project that contains a container class that inherits from *System.Web.UI.Contol* class and implements the *INamingContainer* interface.

Add a class for the templated control that contains at least one property that has a data type of *ITemplate*.

Compile and add the custom Web control to the ToolBox.

■ **Practice 2**   Practice adding the templated control to several Web pages and write code to access the templated control properties.

Take a Practice Test

The practice tests on this book's companion CD offer many options. For example, you can test yourself on just the content covered in this chapter, or you can test yourself on all the 70-528 certification exam content. You can set up the test so that it closely simulates the experience of taking a certification exam, or you can set it up in study mode so that you can look at the correct answers and explanations after you answer each question.

MORE INFO   **Practice tests**

For details about all the practice test options available, see the "How to Use the Practice Tests" section in this book's Introduction.

Chapter 6

Input Validation and Site Navigation

The previous chapters covered many Web server control and custom Web server controls. Those topics relate to building a Web page, and this chapter continues the Web page building process by covering input validation, which should be a mandatory requirement for all data that is collected from the user.

After the user input is validated and processed, you may want to navigate to a different Web page. This chapter covers the various means of navigating a Web site.

Exam objectives in this chapter:

- Program a Web application.
  - Redirect users to another page by using a server-side method.
  - Implement cross-page postbacks.
  - Assign focus to a control on a page when the page is displayed.
  - Avoid unnecessary client-side redirection by using the *HttpServerUtility* .*Transfer* method.
  - Avoid round trips by using client-side scripts.
- Implement site navigation and input validation.
  - Use the *SiteMap* Web server control to display a representation of a Web site's navigation structure.
  - Use validation controls to perform Web Forms validation.
  - Validate against values in a database for server controls by using a *CustomValidator* control.
  - Create a *CustomValidator* control and tie it to a custom function.
  - Test programmatically whether a user's input passes validation before running code.
  - Specify the location of a validation error message for server controls.
  - Format validation error messages for server controls.

❑ Specify the layout for in-place messages on server controls.

❑ Disable validation for server controls.

❑ Display custom error messages for server controls.

❑ Validate server controls programmatically.

■ Add and configure Web server controls.

❑ Create and manipulate links on a Web Form by using the *HyperLink* Web server control.

❑ Implement pagination for controls on a page by using the *Pager* Web server control.

Lessons in this chapter:

Before You Begin

To complete the lessons in this chapter, you should be familiar with Microsoft Visual Basic or C# and be comfortable with the following tasks:

■ Have Microsoft Windows XP and Microsoft Visual Studio 2005 installed with Microsoft SQL Server 2005 Express Edition.

■ Be familiar with the Visual Studio 2005 Integrated Development Environment (IDE).

■ Have a basic understanding of Hypertext Markup Language (HTML) and client-side scripting.

■ Know how to create a new Web site.

■ Be able to add Web server controls to a Web page.

Real World

Glenn Johnson

Recently, I was searching the Web for information on a couple of personal water-crafts. I performed my search and found three dealers that were nearby. I went to the first site; on their "Contact Us" page, I entered my e-mail address and the following message:

"Hi, I'm looking for two personal watercraft with a trailer. Please contact me."

I submitted my message and received a message stating that someone would get back to me.

I went to the second site and did the same thing. This time, when I submitted my message, I received a SQL syntax error. The problem is that my message has an apostrophe (single quote) in it. I changed my message to "...I am looking..." and re-submitted the message. The response was that someone would get back to me, so I decided that I would let them know about the problem when a salesperson contacted me. No one ever contacted me. This site probably still has this vulnerability.

You may be wondering what the big deal is. The problem is that this error is a blatant indicator that this Web site has a SQL injection vulnerability because the apostrophe is the string delimiter in a SQL statement. If an error is generated when the apostrophe is entered, it means that the developer did not take the necessary steps to escape the apostrophe. This means that the apostrophe that was entered by the user terminated the SQL string and SQL Server didn't know what to do with the characters that follow, so SQL Server threw a syntax error. A dishonest person could take advantage of this vulnerability to cause damage to the Web site or even to steal data from the Web site. Remember that it's important to perform input validation to ensure proper user input.

Lesson 1: Performing Input Validation

In this lesson, you will learn how the validation framework operates and how you can use the validation controls that are included in ASP.NET 2.0 to perform input validation.

After this lesson, you will be able to:

- Understand the validation framework.
- Add validation controls to a Web page.
- Configure validation controls.
- Implement the *CustomValidator* control.
- Test for valid user input.

Estimated lesson time: 60 minutes

Understanding the Validation Framework

We are often faced with the challenge of ensuring that the user has input the necessary data into all required fields and ensuring that the data is valid. The data-validation framework provides a simple way to accomplish this task with minimum coding. The validation controls that are built into ASP.NET 2.0 provide both client-side and server-side validation.

Client-side validation is a convenience to the user because it improves performance by checking the data at the browser before sending the data to the server. This avoids unnecessary round trips to the server, but client-side validation can be easily defeated by hackers.

Server-side validation provides a more secure means of validating the data that is posted back to the server. Using both client-side and server-side validation provides a better experience to the user and secure validation for the Web site.

To perform validation, the developer can simply attach one or more validator controls to each control that accepts user input. ASP.NET 2.0 provides several validation controls that automatically provide server-side and client-side validation. Figure 6-1 shows the validation control hierarchy.

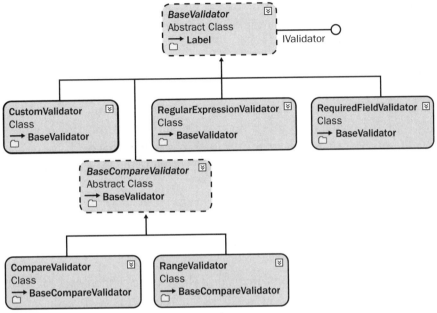

Figure 6-1 The validation control hierarchy.

You typically add a validation control to a Web page using the following steps:

1. Drag and drop the desired validator next to the control that is to be validated.

2. Name the validator control.

3. Set the *ControlToValidate* property to attach the validator to the control that will be validated.

4. Set the *ErrorMessage* property to a descriptive error message that the user will understand.

5. Copy the *ErrorMessage* property and paste it into the *ToolTip* property to display the error when the user hovers the pointer over the validator.

6. Set the *Text* property of the validator to a very short string, usually an asterisk (*), to minimize the space that is required by the validator when the control is not valid.

The validation framework contains the *ValidationSummary* control, which can be placed on the Web page to display all the validation error messages in one location. This is useful in scenarios where the Web page is crowded with other controls and displaying the validation error next to the invalid control is difficult. The *ValidationSummary* control can also be configured to display a pop-up message with the validation errors in lieu of, or in addition to, displaying the validation errors on the Web page.

The *Page* object has a *Validators* property that contains a collection of all validation controls. The Web page also has a *Validate* method that you can call to check all of the validator controls in the page. By default, the *Validate* method is called automatically, but this call takes place after the *Load* event handler method executes. The Web page has a property called *IsValid* that is set after the *Validate* method is executed. Although the *IsValid* property is set automatically for you, you need to check the *IsValid* property in every event handler to determine whether the code that you should run is based on the *IsValid* state.

NOTE   New in ASP.NET 2.0

The *Focus* and *SetFocusOnError* methods are new in ASP.NET 2.0.

The *Control* class has a method called *Focus* that can be called to set the focus to a specific control when the page is loaded. This method adds client-side JavaScript code that executes at the browser to set focus to the appropriate control. In addition to the new *Focus* method, a validation control has a similar method called *SetFocusOnError* that can be set to *true* to cause the invalid control to automatically receive focus.

Understanding the *BaseValidator* Class

The validation controls inherit from the *BaseValidator* abstract class. This class contains most of the validation functionality. Table 6-1 contains a list of the properties that the *BaseValidator* provides.

Table 6-1   *BaseValidator* Properties

BaseValidator Property	Description
ControlToValidate	Set this to the control that is to be validated.
Display	Set this to display the behavior of the validation message; it can be set to None (doesn't display the validation message), Static (displays the validation message and consumes the same space on the Web page even when the message does not display), or Dynamic (displays the validation message, but takes up no space if no message needs to be displayed).

Table 6-1 *BaseValidator* **Properties**

BaseValidator Property	Description
EnableClientSideScript	Set to *false* to disable client-side validation. Default is *true*.
ErrorMessage	Set to the text that displays when validation fails. If the *Text* property is set, the validation control displays the contents of the *Text* property, while the *ValidationSummary* control displays the *ErrorMessage* contents.
IsValid	The valid status of a control.

Set the *Enabled* property to *false* to completely disable the control. If a validation control is to supply information to the *ValidationSummary* control and not display its own information beside the invalid control, set the *Display* property of the control to *None*.

Understanding the *RequiredFieldValidator* Control

The *RequiredFieldValidator* is used to ensure that the user has placed non–white space data into a control. The other controls do not attempt to validate an empty field, so you frequently need to use the *RequiredFieldValidator* with one of the other controls to achieve the desired validation.

The *RequiredFieldValidator* provides an additional property called *InitialValue* that is used when the control that you are validating defaults to a value and you want to ensure that the user changes this value. For example, if you normally display a zero (0) value in a control for the age and you want to ensure that the user changes the age, set the *InitialValue* to zero so a validation error occurs if the user leaves the default value of the control set to zero.

Understanding the *BaseCompareValidator* Class

The *RangeValidator* and *CompareValidator* inherit from the *BaseCompareValidator* control, which contains common comparison behavior that is used by these controls.

The *BaseCompareValidator* contains the *Type* property, which you can set to the data type that the text is converted to before a comparison is made. The data types that are available are as follows:

- **Currency** The data is validated as *System.Decimal*, but currency symbols and grouping characters also can be entered.

- *Date*   The data is validated as a numeric date.
- *Double*   The data is validated as *System.Double*.
- *Integer*   The data is validated as *System.Int32*.
- *String*   The data is validated as *System.String*.

Using the *CompareValidator* Control

The *CompareValidator* control performs its validation by using comparison operators such as greater than and less than to compare the data with a constant or a value in a different control. In addition, the *CompareValidator* can verify that the data is of a certain type, such as a date.

The *ValueToCompare* property can be set to a constant that is used to perform the comparison.

The *Operator* property defines how to perform the comparison and can be set to *Equal*, *NotEqual*, *GreaterThan*, *GreaterThanEqual*, *LessThan*, *LessThanEqual*, or *DataTypeCheck*.

The *ControlToCompare* property can be set to a control that is used to perform the comparison. This property takes precedence if this property and the *ValueToCompare* properties are both set.

Using the *RangeValidator* Control

The *RangeValidator* control is used to verify that the data to be validated is within a specified range of values. To use this control effectively, you must set the *MinimumValue*, *MaximumValue*, and the *Type* properties.

The *Type* property causes the data to be converted to the proper data type prior to checking the range. The *Type* property defaults to *String*, so you must set the *Type* property to achieve proper range validation. For example, if you don't set the *Type* property, it defaults to *String*, and if a numeric range is being checked from 3 to 30, only strings that begin with the string letter 3 are considered valid.

Using the *RegularExpressionValidator* Control

The *RegularExpressionValidator* control performs its validation based on a regular expression. A regular expression is a powerful pattern-matching language that can be used to identify simple and complex character sequences that would otherwise require writing code to accomplish. This *ValidationExpression* property is set to a valid regular expression that is applied to the data that is to be validated. The data is validated if it matches the regular expression.

MORE INFO **Regular Expressions**

For more information about regular expressions such as tutorials and sample regular expressions, refer to the following URLs:

http://www.regexlib.com/

http://www.regular-expressions.info/

The *CustomValidator* Control

The *CustomValidator* control performs its validation based on custom validation code that you provide. You can write the client-side validation code using JavaScript or server-side validation code using your preferred .NET language.

The client-side validation code must contain a JavaScript function that has the following method signature:

```
function ClientFunctionName(source, arguments)
```

The *source* parameter contains a reference to the validation control that is performing the validation. The *arguments* parameter is an object that has a property called *Value* that contains the data to be validated and an *IsValid* property that you set to *false* if the data does not validate or *true* if the data does validate.

To attach your client-side code to the *CustomValidator*, set the *ClientFunctionName* property to the name of your validation function.

In the following code example, a Web page contains a *TextBox* called *txtPassword*, an associated *CustomValidator* called *cusCheckPassword*, and a *RequiredFieldValidator* called *reqPassword* because the custom script will not execute if a password is not entered. A valid password must be between 6 and 14 characters and must contain at least one uppercase letter, one lowercase letter, and one numeric character. A *ValidationSummary* has also been added to the bottom of the Web page to show the validation error.

JavaScript Client-Side Validation

```
<script language="javascript" type="text/javascript">
    function ValidatePassword(source, arguements)
    {
     var data = arguements.Value.split('');
```

```
        //start by setting false
        arguements.IsValid=false;

        //check length
        if(data.length < 6 || data.length > 14) return;

        //check for uppercase
        var uc = false;
        for(var c in data)
        {
           if(data[c] >= 'A' && data[c] <= 'Z')
           {
              uc=true; break;
           }
        }
        if(!uc) return;

        //check for lowercase
        var lc = false;
        for(var c in data)
        {
           if(data[c] >= 'a' && data[c] <= 'z')
           {
              lc=true; break;
           }
        }
        if(!lc) return;

        //check for numeric
        var num = false;
        for(var c in data)
        {
           if(data[c] >= '0' && data[c] <= '9')
           {
              num=true; break;
           }
        }
        if(!num) return;

        //must be valid
        arguements.IsValid=true;
     }
</script>
```

The Web page is run and lowercase letters are entered into the *txtPassword* control. When the *txtPassword* control loses focus, the client-side validation is executed, as shown in Figure 6-2.

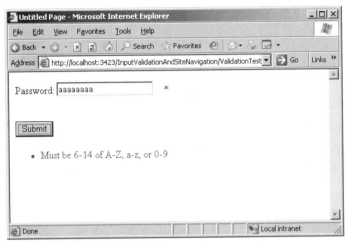

Figure 6-2   The client-side validation causes the *ValidationSummary* control to display the error.

The *CustomValidator* has an event called *ServerValidate* that is a server-side event. The following is an example of using the *ServerValidate* event to perform server-side validation:

ServerValidate Handler

```vb
'VB
Protected Sub cusCheckPassword_ServerValidate(ByVal source As Object, _
        ByVal args As System.Web.UI.WebControls.ServerValidateEventArgs) _
        Handles cusCheckPassword.ServerValidate
    Dim data As String = args.Value
    'start by setting false
    args.IsValid = False

    'check length
    If (data.Length < 6 Or data.Length > 14) Then Return

    'check for uppercase
    Dim uc As Boolean = False
    For Each c As Char In data
        If (c >= "A" And c <= "Z") Then

            uc = True : Exit For
        End If

    Next
    If Not uc Then Return

    'check for lowercase
    Dim lc As Boolean = False
    For Each c As Char In data
        If (c >= "a" And c <= "z") Then
```

```
                lc = True : Exit For
        End If
    Next
    If Not lc Then Return

    'check for numeric
    Dim num As Boolean = False
    For Each c As Char In data
        If (c >= "0" And c <= "9") Then
            num = True : Exit For
        End If
    Next
    If Not num Then Return

    'must be valid
    args.IsValid = True
End Sub
```

```
//C#
protected void cusCheckPassword_ServerValidate(object source,
    ServerValidateEventArgs args)
{
    string data = args.Value;
    //start by setting false
    args.IsValid = false;

    //check length
    if (data.Length < 6 || data.Length > 14) return;

    //check for uppercase
    bool uc = false;
    foreach (char c in data)
    {
        if (c >= 'A' && c <= 'Z')
        {
            uc = true; break;
        }
    }
    if (!uc) return;

    //check for lowercase
    bool lc = false;
    foreach (char c in data)
    {
        if (c >= 'a' && c <= 'z')
        {
            lc = true; break;
        }
    }
    if (!lc) return;

    //check for numeric
    bool num = false;
```

```
    foreach (char c in data)
    {
        if (c >= '0' && c <= '9')
        {
            num = true; break;
        }
    }
    if (!num) return;

    //must be valid
    args.IsValid = true;
}
```

Like client-side validation, server-side validation also provides access to the source validator and the *Value* to be validated, and the *IsValid* property can be set to false to indicate validation failure.

Note that, when using the *CustomValidator*, the server-side validation does need to provide the same validation at the client-side validation. For example, the custom client-side script for a *CustomValidator* that validates a five-character customer ID might simply test to ensure that five characters are provided within the acceptable range (uppercase, lowercase). The server-side validation may perform a database query to ensure that the customer ID is that of a valid customer in the database.

Ensuring Server-Side Validation

To test server-side validation, disable all client-side validation by setting the *EnableClientScript* property of the validation controls to false.

Server-side validation occurs after the *Load* event handler method is executed, at which time the runtime calls the *Validate* method on the Web page. You need to place code into your event handler methods to test the *IsValid* property, as shown in the following example:

```vb
'VB
Protected Sub Button1_Click(ByVal sender As Object, _
        ByVal e As System.EventArgs) _
        Handles Button1.Click
    If Not IsValid Then Return
    'use page data
End Sub
```

```csharp
//C#
protected void Button1_Click(object sender, EventArgs e)
{
    if (!IsValid) return;
    //use page data
}
```

Determining When to Validate

Although client-side validation is considered to be a convenience for the normal user and is certainly not secure, the primary benefit of client-side validation is that the page is not posted until all client-side validation has successfully occurred. This can be a problem when the user wants to press a cancel or help button and the page is not valid. The problem is that the default behavior of the button is to attempt *PostBack* to the server, but if the page is not valid, clicking the button won't cause *PostBack* to the server.

Controls that should be able to bypass validation can do so by setting their *CausesValidation* property to *false*. This property defaults to *true*.

Using Validation Groups

In earlier versions of ASP.NET, all of the validation controls were checked when a *PostBack* occurred. You could set the *CausesValidation* property to *false* on the control that caused the *PostBack* to occur, but you often wanted more control than that for scenarios where a Web page contained several sections and you only wanted a particular section to be validated.

NOTE New in ASP.NET 2.0

Validation groups are new in ASP.NET 2.0.

In ASP.NET 2.0, there is a new property called the *ValidationGroup* that can be assigned a string to specify a section. This property exists on the validation controls and on the controls that cause *PostBacks* to occur. When a control performs a *PostBack*, the validator controls that have a matching *ValidationGroup* property are validated.

On *PostBack*, the *IsValid* property on the *Page* object only reflects the validity of the validation controls that have been validated. By default, these are the validation controls that are in the same *ValidationGroup*, but you can call a validation control's *Validate* method to add that control to the set of controls that the *IsValid* reports on.

With the addition of the *ValidationGroup* property is a new overload to the *Page* object's *Validate* method that accepts a string to specify the *ValidationGroup* to authenticate. This overload is executed when a *PostBack* that causes validation occurs.

The *Page* object has a *GetValidators* method that accepts a string containing the name of the *ValidationGroup*. This method returns the list of validators in the *Validation-Group*.

Quick Check

1. Which validator control can be used to determine if data that is entered into a *TextBox* control is *Currency*?

2. What control can be used to display all validation errors in a pop-up window?

Quick Check Answers

1. The *CompareValidator* control.

2. The *ValidationSummary* control.

Lab: Working with Validation Controls

In this lab, you create a registration page that contains *TextBox* controls for the user name, password, confirm password, and Zip Code fields. All fields are required. The user name must be between 6 and 14 characters that can be uppercase, lowercase, numeric, or underscores. The password and confirm password will be 6 to 14 characters that must contain at least one uppercase letter, one lowercase letter, and one number, as described in the custom validator example. The Zip Code must be a valid U.S. Zip Code, which can be in the format 99999 or 99999-9999.

▶ **Exercise 1: Create the Web Site and add Controls**

In this exercise, you create the Web site and add the controls.

1. Open Visual Studio 2005 and create a new Web site called **WorkingWithVali-dationControls** using your preferred programming language. The new Web site is created, and a Web page called Default.aspx is displayed.

2. Add an HTML table to the Default.aspx Web page. This table will have four rows and two columns.

3. Add the descriptions in the first column of each of the four rows. The descriptions are **User Name**, **Password**, **Confirm Password**, and **Zip Code**.

4. Add a *TextBox* control into the second column of the four rows. Name the *Text-Box* controls **txtUser**, **txtPassword**, **txtConfirm**, and **txtZip**.

5. Set the *TextMode* property to **txtPassword** and *txtConfirm* to **Password**.

6. Add a *Button* control under the table. Set the *Text* of the *Button* control to **Submit**. Figure 6-3 shows the Web page.

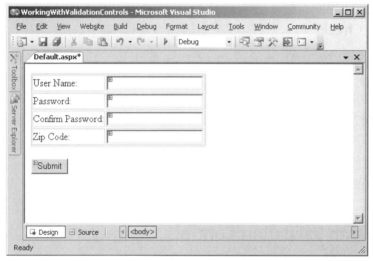

Figure 6-3 The registration page prior to adding validation.

▶ **Exercise 2: Add the Validation Controls**

In this exercise, you add and configure the validation controls.

1. Continue with the project from the previous exercise, or open the completed Lesson 1, Exercise 1 project from the CD.

2. All of the *TextBox* controls require user input, so add the *RequiredFieldValidator* next to each *TextBox* control.

3. For each of the *RequiredFieldValidator* controls, set the *ControlToValidate* property to the *TextBox* that is being validated.

4. For each of the *RequiredFieldValidator* controls, set the *ErrorMessage* property to **User name is required.**, **Password is required.**, **Confirm password is required.**, and **Zip code is required.**, respectively.

5. Add a *RegularExpression* control next to the *txtUser* control and set the *Control-ToValidate* property to **txtUser**. Set the *ErrorMessage* to **Must be 6-14 of A-Z, a-z, 0-9, or _**. Set the *ValidationExpression* to **\w{6,14}**.

6. Add a *CustomValidator* next to the *txtPassword* control. Set the *ControlToValidate* property to **txtPassword**. Set the *ErrorMessage* to **Must be 6-14 characters, at least 1 upper, 1 lower, and 1 number**.

7. Set the *ClientValidationFunction* to **ValidatePassword**. In the head section of the HTML source, add the client-side code from the listing "JavaScript Client-Side Validation," shown earlier in this lesson.

8. Add the *ServerValidate* event handler method to the code-behind page. In this method, add the code from the listing "ServerValidate Handler," shown earlier in this lesson.

9. The password and confirm password must be the same, so add a *CompareValidator* next to the *txtConfirm TextBox*. Set the *ControlToValidate* to the *txtConfirm* control. Set the *ControlToCompare* property to **txtPassword**. Set the *ErrorMessage* to **Password and Confirm Password must match**.

10. Add a *RegularExpressionValidator* beside the *txtZip* control. Set the *ControlToValidate* to the *txtZip* control. Set the *ErrorMessage* to **Must be formatted as 99999 or 99999-9999**. Set the *ValidationExpression* to U.S. Zip Code to provide a regular expression of \d{5}(-\d{4})?.

11. For each of the validator controls, set the *Display* property to **Dynamic**.

12. Copy the *ErrorMessage* contents to the *ToolTip* for each of the validator controls.

13. Notice that setting the *ErrorMessage* property changes the text that displays beside each *TextBox* control. The *ErrorMessage* should only be displayed in a *ValidationSummary* control at the bottom of the Web page, so set the *Text* property of each of the validator controls to an asterisk (*).

14. Add a *ValidationSummary* control to the bottom of the Web page. The completed Web page is shown in Figure 6-4.

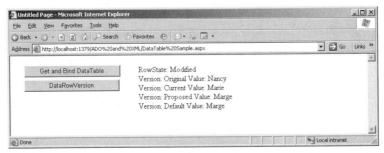

Figure 6-4   The completed Web page containing all validation controls.

▶ **Exercise 3: Test the Validation Controls**

In this exercise, you run the Web page and test the validation controls.

1. Continue with the project from the previous exercise, or open the completed Lesson 1, Exercise 2 project from the CD.

2. Run the Web page.

3. Before entering any information into the *TextBox* controls, press the Submit button. Verify that the *RequiredFieldValidators* are displayed by noting the errors that are displayed in the *ValidationSummary* control and by hovering your pointer over each of the asterisks to see each *ToolTip*.

4. Test the user name validation by typing fewer than six characters into *txtUser* and click the Submit button. Note the validation error. Also, try typing 15 or more characters. Attempt to type 10 characters, but use an invalid character, such as the apostrophe ('). Finally, attempt valid input to ensure the validator's ability to report valid input.

5. Test the password for the appropriate input by trying to input fewer than 6 characters or more than 14 characters. Also, attempt a password that is all lowercase, or all uppercase, or all numeric. Notice that special characters, such as plus sign (+), minus sign (-), and percent sign (%), are allowed in the password, but not required. Finally, attempt to enter a valid password.

6. Test the confirmation password by typing a confirmation password that does not match the password. Test again with a matching password.

7. Test the Zip Code by entering fewer than five characters, or characters that don't match the format specified in the regular expression. Finally, test with a valid Zip Code.

Lesson Summary

- The validation framework provides the ability to easily bind one or more validation controls to other Web controls.

- The validation controls provide client-side and server-side validation.

- Client-side validation can be disabled by setting the *EnableClientScript* property to *false*.

- The validator can be completely disabled by setting the *Enabled* property to *false*.

- The validation controls are *CustomValidator*, *CompareValidator*, *RangeValidator*, *RegularExpressionValidator*, and *RequiredFieldValidator*.

- The *ValidationSummary* control can be added to a Web page to provide a summary of the validation errors on the Web page and as a pop-up message.

- The *RegularExpressionValidator* is used to specify validation patterns.

- The *CustomValidator* allows you to provide your custom client-side and server-side code to perform validation. The client-side and server-side code need not match.

- The *CustomValidator* can be used to provide server-side lookups in a database or other location.

- The *Validate* method can be explicitly called to force validation.

- The Web page's *IsValid* property can be queried to verify that the page is valid before running code.

Lesson Review

You can use the following questions to test your knowledge of the information in Lesson 1, "Performing Input Validation." The questions are also available on the companion CD if you prefer to review them in electronic form.

NOTE Answers

Answers to these questions and explanations of why each answer choice is right or wrong are located in the "Answers" section at the end of the book.

---

1. You prompt the user to enter a code that exists in the database. How can you validate this input?

    A. Provide a *RegularExpressionValidator* and set the *ValidationExpression* property to */DbLookup{code}*.

    B. Provide a *RangeValidator* to and set the *MinValue* property to *DbLookup(code)* and set the *MaxVaue* property to *DbLookup(code)*.

    C. Provide a *CustomValidator* with server-side code to search the database for the code.

    D. Provide a *CompareValidator* and set the compare expression to the name of a server-side function that performs a database lookup of the code.

2. You created a Web page that contains many controls that are validated using validation controls. This page also contains *Button* controls that perform *PostBacks*. You disabled all of the client-side validation and noticed that when you clicked any of the *Button* controls, the code in the *Click* event handler was executing even when some of the controls did not have valid data. How can you best solve this problem to ensure code is not executed when invalid data exists?

A. In the *Click* event handler method for each of your *Button* controls, test the Web page's *IsValid* property and exit the method if this property is *false*.

B. In the *Load* event handler method of the Web page, test the Web page's *IsValid* property and exit the method if this property is *false*.

C. Re-enable the client-side script to disable *PostBack* until valid data exists.

D. Add the *runat="server"* attribute to all of the validation controls.

3. You have created an elaborate Web page that contains many validated controls. You want to provide a detailed message for each validation error, but you don't have space to provide the detailed message next to each control. What can you do to indicate an error at the control and list the detailed error messages at the top of the Web page?

A. Set the *Text* property of the validator control to the detailed message and set the *ErrorMessage* property to an asterisk. Place a *ValidationSummary* control at the top of the Web page.

B. Set the *ErrorMessage* property of the validator control to the detailed message and set the *Text* property to an asterisk. Place a *ValidationSummary* control at the top of the Web page.

C. Set the *ToolTip* property of the validator control to the detailed message and set the *ErrorMessage* property to an asterisk. Place a *ValidationSummary* control at the top of the Web page.

D. Set the *ToolTip* property of the validator control to the detailed message and set the *Text* property to an asterisk. Place a *ValidationSummary* control at the top of the Web page.

Lesson 2: Performing Site Navigation

Controls that perform *PostBacks* typically post to the same Web page as part of the typical Web page life cycle, but there are many scenarios where you want to collect data from the user while navigating from one Web page to another. Seamless navigation from one Web page to another is what makes a collection of Web pages feel like a Web application. In this lesson, you will learn the ways to navigate between Web pages on your site.

> **After this lesson, you will be able to:**
> - Assign focus to a control on a page when it is displayed.
> - Avoid round trips by using client-side scripts.
> - Redirect users to another page by using server-side methods.
> - Use the *SiteMap* Web server control to display a representation of a site's navigation structure.
> - Implement pagination for controls on a page by using the *Pager* Web server control.
>
> **Estimated lesson time: 60 minutes**

Is Site Navigation Necessary?

When collecting data from users, you can provide navigation to many Web pages to display prompts and collect the data, but you can also provide the illusion of navigating many pages to collect data. To provide the illusion of navigating many pages to display prompts to collect data, you may choose to use the *Wizard* control or *FormView*, which are covered in Chapter 3, "Exploring Specialized Server Controls." These controls provide a *Pager* control to navigate from one data collection screen to another, but both of the screens are on the same Web page, which means that it is somewhat easier to gather all of the data for processing.

The *Wizard* and *FormView* controls can simplify your data presentation and collection efforts but may not be suitable for every possible scenario.

Choosing a Method to Navigate Pages

There are many ways to navigate from page to page, so it's helpful to first identify these ways and then look at each in detail.

- **Provide client-side code or markup to request a new Web page.** Your client code or markup requests a new Web page in response to a client-side event, such as a button click.

- **Cross-page posting.** A control is configured to perform a *PostBack* to a different Web page.

- **Issue client-side browser redirect.** Your server-side code sends a message to the browser, informing the browser to request a different Web page.

- **Issue server-side transfer.** Your server-side code transfers control to a different Web page.

Providing Client-Side Code or Markup to Request a New Web Page

One of the easiest ways to navigate to a different Web page is to provide a *HyperLink* control on the form and set the *NavigateUrl* property to the desired destination. The *HyperLink* control generates an *<a>* element in the HTML and the *NavigateUrl* property is placed into the *href* attribute of the *<a>* element. The following example shows the source of a *HyperLink* control and its rendered HTML.

HyperLink Control: Source
```
<asp:HyperLink ID="HyperLink1"
runat="server" NavigateUrl="~/NavigateTest2.aspx">
Goto NavigateTest2
</asp:HyperLink>
```

HyperLink Control: Rendered HTML
```
<a id="HyperLink1" href="NavigateTest2.aspx">Goto NavigateTest2</a>
In this example, if this control is placed on a Web page called NavigateTest1.aspx, and the
HyperLink control is clicked, the browser simply requests the NavigateTest2.aspx page. This
means that no data is posted to NavigateTest2.aspx, and if data is required to pass to
NavigateTest2.aspx, you need to find a way to get the data to the page.
```

Your client-side code can also perform Web page navigation by changing the document object's location property to a new URL. The document object is the object that represents the Web page; setting its location property causes the browser to request the Web page at the new URL.

The following example contains an HTML *<input type="button">* element with a bit of client-side JavaScript to request the NavigateTest2.aspx page when the button is clicked.

```
<input id="Button1" type="button"
       value="Goto NavigateTest2"
       onclick="return Button1_onclick()" />
```

Notice that the *onclick* event is configured to call the client-side method (called *Button1_onclick*). The JavaScript source for the *Button1_onclick* method is added into the *<head>* element as follows:

```
<script language="javascript" type="text/javascript">
// <![CDATA[

function Button1_onclick() {
    document.location="NavigateTest2.aspx";
}

// ]]>

</script>
```

Once again, the NavigateTest2.aspx page is requested and no data is posted back to the Web server.

Cross-page Posting

Cross-page posting is frequently desired in a scenario where data is collected on one Web page and processed on another Web page that displays the results. In this scenario, a *Button* control has its *PostBackUrl* property set to the Web page to post back to. In the processing page, which is the Web page that you post back to, the data from the first Web page is available.

NOTE New in ASP.NET 2.0

The *Page* class's *PreviousPage* property is new in ASP.NET 2.0.

The processing page typically needs to access the data from the first page, which is possible by using the *PreviousPage* property of the *Page* object. The *PreviousPage* property is set if you are cross-page posting, and if the *PreviousPage* is set to *Nothing* (C# *null*), no cross-page posting occurs. You can access any of the controls in the previous page by using the *FindControl* method on the *NamingContainer* of the control that you are trying to locate.

In the following example, the Web page called NavigateTest2.aspx contains a *TextBox* control called *txtData* and a *Button* control with its *PostBackUrl* set to ~/ NavigateTest3.aspx. The NavigateTest3.aspx page contains a *Label* control called *lblData* that is populated with the data from *txtData* if NavigateTest3.aspx, which was called by using a cross-page *PostBack*, as shown in the following example:

```
'VB
Protected Sub Page_Load(ByVal sender As Object, _
    ByVal e As System.EventArgs) _
    Handles Me.Load
    If PreviousPage Is Nothing Then
        lblData.Text = "No PreviousPage"
    Else
        lblData.Text = _
            CType(PreviousPage.FindControl("txtData"), TextBox).Text
    End If
End Sub
```

```
//C#
protected void Page_Load(object sender, EventArgs e)
{
    if(PreviousPage == null)
    {
        lblData.Text = "No PreviousPage";
    }
    else
    {
        lblData.Text =
            ((TextBox)PreviousPage.FindControl("txtData")).Text;
    }
}
```

Accessing Strongly Typed Data

Another way to access the previous page data is to create public properties that expose the data that you need to access. After creating public properties, you need to set the *PreviousPageType* directive on the result page.

NOTE   New in ASP.NET 2.0

The *PreviousPageType* directive is new in ASP.NET 2.0.

In the following example, the NavigateTest3.aspx page performs a cross-page *PostBack* to NavigateTest4.aspx using a public property and the *PreviousPageType* directive. The NavigateTest3.aspx contains a *TextBox* control named *txtData* and a *Button* control on which the *PostBackUrl* property has been set to *~/NavigateTest4.aspx*. The following property was placed into the NavigateTest3.aspx code-behind page:

```
'VB
public readonly property PageData
    Get
        return txtData.Text
    End Get
End Property
```

```
//C#
public string PageData
{
    get { return txtData.Text; }}
```

In order to access this property, you need to set *PreviousPageType* directive in the NavigateTest4.aspx page. This directive is added after the *Page* directive and looks like this:

```
<%@ PreviousPageType VirtualPath="~/NavigateTest3.aspx" %>
```

The NavigateTest4.aspx page contains a *Label* control named *lblData* and is populated from the *PageData* property, as is shown in the following code snippet:

```
'VB
Protected Sub Page_Load(ByVal sender As Object, _
        ByVal e As System.EventArgs) Handles Me.Load
    If PreviousPage Is Nothing Then
        lblData.Text = "No PreviousPage"
    Else
        lblData.Text = _
            PreviousPage.PageData
    End If
End Sub
```

```
//C#
protected void Page_Load(object sender, EventArgs e)
{
    if (PreviousPage == null)
    {
        lblData.Text = "No PreviousPage";
    }
    else
    {
        lblData.Text =
            PreviousPage.PageData;
    }
}
```

When you attempt to enter this code snippet, you may find that IntelliSense doesn't show the *PageData* property. Simply build the page that causes the data type of the *PreviousPage* property to be set to *NavigateTest3_aspx*, and the *PageData* property is visible in the IntelliSense window.

Issuing Client-Side Browser Redirect

The *Response* object has a method called *Redirect* that you can use in your server-side code to instruct the browser to request a different page. In this scenario, you post back to the original page. The server-side code can process the *PostBack* and then execute the *Redirect*, as shown in the following example, where the NavigateTest4.aspx page contains a *Button* control that performs a redirect to the NavigateTest5.aspx page when the *Button* is clicked:

```vb
'VB
Protected Sub Button1_Click(ByVal sender As Object, _
        ByVal e As System.EventArgs) Handles Button1.Click
    Response.BufferOutput = True
    'process data
    Response.Redirect("NavigationTest5.aspx")
End Sub
```

```csharp
//C#
protected void Button1_Click(object sender, EventArgs e)
{
    Response.BufferOutput = true;
    //process data
    Response.Redirect("NavigationTest5.aspx");
}
```

Notice that the *BufferOutput* must be set to *true* in order to perform the redirect to ensure that no data is sent to the browser prior to executing the *Redirect* method. If data is sent to the browser prior to executing the *Redirect* method, an *HttpException* is thrown, indicating that you cannot redirect after the Hypertext Transfer Protocol (HTTP) headers are sent.

The redirect is accomplished by sending an HTTP response code of 302 to the browser along with the URL of the page to redirect to. The address that is displayed in the browser is updated to reflect the new URL location. Note that this comes at the cost of performing an extra round trip to the server.

The *PreviousPage* property does not get populated when using the *Redirect* method. To access data from the original page, you need to resort to traditional methods of passing data, such as placing the data into cookies, session state variables, or passing the data in the *QueryString*.

Issuing Server-Side Transfer

In your server-side code, you can switch control to a different Web page by using the *Transfer* method on the *HttpUtility* object. An instance of the *HttpUtility* class is stored on the *Page* object, in the *Server* property. Like the previous redirect example, you post back to the original page. The server-side code can process the *PostBack* and then execute the *Transfer* method, as shown in the following example, where the NavigateTest5.aspx page contains a *Button* control that performs a transfer to the NavigateTest6.aspx page when the *Button* is clicked.

```vb
'VB
Protected Sub Button1_Click(ByVal sender As Object, _
    ByVal e As System.EventArgs) Handles Button1.Click
  Server.Transfer("NavigationTest6.aspx", False)
End Sub
```

```csharp
//C#
protected void Button1_Click(object sender, EventArgs e)
{
    Server.Transfer("NavigationTest6.aspx", false);
}
```

The *Transfer* method accepts a Boolean parameter called *preserveForm* that you set to indicate your desire to keep the form and QueryString data. It is generally better to set this to *false*. You can also access the *PreviousPage* property to pass data between pages, just as you do when cross-page posting.

Using the Site Map Web Server Control

ASP.NET 2.0 provides a means to specify a site structure and a number of controls that perform navigation and display the site map on your Web page.

NOTE   New in ASP.NET 2.0

The Site Map is new in ASP.NET 2.0.

The following controls can be used to display site map data:

- **Menu**   Shows the site structure and allows the user to select a location to navigate to.
- **TreeView**   Shows the site structure in a collapsible tree format and allows the user to select a location to navigate to.
- **SiteMapPath**   Shows the current location and the path of pages to go through to get there as a breadcrumb-like trail. For example, if you are on the Microsoft Web site getting help on Visual Studio .NET, the site map path might display something like this:

```
Home > Visual Studio > Support
```

These controls typically provide client-side markup to navigate the Web site hierarchy. The *TreeView* and *Menu* controls use the *SiteMapDataSource* control as a source for the site map data that is displayed. By default, the *SiteMapDataSource* gets its data from the Web.sitemap file, which is a specially formatted XML file that is located in the root of the Web site. The *SiteMapPath* control gets its data directly from the Web.sitemap file.

You can add the Web.sitemap file to your Web application by right-clicking your Web site, selecting Add New Item | Site Map, and accepting the default name of Web.sitemap. The Web.sitemap looks like the following:

```
<?xml version="1.0" encoding="utf-8" ?>
<siteMap xmlns="http://schemas.microsoft.com/AspNet/SiteMap-File-1.0" >
    <siteMapNode url="" title=""  description="">
        <siteMapNode url="" title=""  description="" />
        <siteMapNode url="" title=""  description="" />
    </siteMapNode>
</siteMap>
```

Using the *SiteMap* Class

The *SiteMap* class provides programmatic access to the site navigation hierarchy. Its two primary properties are *RootNode* and *CurrentNode,* and both return *SiteMapNode* instances. The *SiteMapNode* object represents a node in the site map and has properties called *Title, Url,* and *Description.* To access nodes in the hierarchy, you can use the *SiteMapNode* instance's *ParentNode, ChildNodes, NextSibling,* and *PreviousSibling* properties. For example, the following code snippet can be used to navigate to the Web page that is listed as the parent Web page in the Web.sitemap file.

```
'VB
Protected Sub Button1_Click(ByVal sender As Object, _
        ByVal e As System.EventArgs) Handles Button1.Click
    Response.Redirect(SiteMap.CurrentNode.ParentNode.Url)
End Sub
```

```
//C#
protected void Button1_Click(object sender, EventArgs e)
{
    Response.Redirect(SiteMap.CurrentNode.ParentNode.Url);
}
```

> **Quick Check**
> - Which method of navigation requires the most communication between the browser and the Web server?
>
> **Quick Check Answer**
> - Client-side browser redirect requires the most communication because this is a server-side method that tells the browser to request a new page, thus causing multiple round trips to the server.

Lab: Working With Site Navigation

In this lab, you create a Web application using frames. The top frame contains a title for your Web application and a *SiteMapPath* control. The left frame contains a *TreeView* control for navigation. Clicking any node on the *TreeView* or *SiteMapPath* controls cause the main frame to load the desired page.

▶ **Exercise 1: Create the Web Application Project and Its Frames**

In this exercise, you create the Web application project. You also configure Default.aspx to be a frames page and add the top and left frames.

1. Open Visual Studio 2005 and create a new Web Application project called WorkingWithSiteNavigation using your preferred programming language.

   The new project will create a Web page called Default.aspx, which will be configured to be the frames page for the Web application.

2. Configure the Default.aspx page to have a top frame, a left frame, and a main frame. Remove the code-behind page as well. Your Default.aspx should look like the following:

```
<!DOCTYPE HTML PUBLIC "-//W3C//DTD HTML 4.01 Frameset//EN"
    "http://www.w3.org/TR/html4/frameset.dtd">
<html xmlns="http://www.w3.org/1999/xhtml">
<head id="Head1" runat="server">
    <title>Frame Page</title>
</head>
<frameset rows="70, *" >
  <frame src="TitlePage.aspx">
  <frameset cols="20%, 80%">
      <frame src="MenuPage.aspx" >
      <frame src="MainPage.aspx" name="MainFrame">
  </frameset>
  <noframes>
      This is a frames page.
```

```
    </noframes>
  </frameset>
</html>
```

3. Add a new Web page called TitlePage.aspx for the top frame.

4. On the TitlePage.aspx page, add a textual title called Working With Site Navigation. Set the font size for the title to xx-large and center the title text.

5. Add a new Web page called MenuPage.aspx for the left frame.

6. On the MenuPage.aspx page, add a *TreeView* control.

7. Select the *TreeView* control and click the symbol in the upper-right corner of the control to reveal the TreeView Tasks window. Click the drop-down list for the Choose Data Source option and click New Data Source. Click Site Map as the data source and click OK.

8. In the Source View window, locate the *<head>* element and add the following directive to specify that the hyperlinks use the MainFrame as their target window:

```
<base target="MainFrame"/>
```

9. Add a Site Map to the Web application by right-clicking the Web application in the Solution Explorer and clicking Add New Item. Click Site Map, keep the default file name of Web.sitemap, and click Add.

10. Change the Web.sitemap file to look like the following:

```
<?xml version="1.0" encoding="utf-8" ?>
<siteMap xmlns="http://schemas.microsoft.com/AspNet/SiteMap-File-1.0" >
    <siteMapNode url="~/MainPage.aspx" title="Main Page"
        description="This is the main page.">
      <siteMapNode url="~/Support.aspx" title="Support Page"
          description="The support page." >
        <siteMapNode url="~/Faqs.aspx" title="FAQs Page"
            description="The frequently asked questions page." />
      </siteMapNode>
      <siteMapNode url="~/Products.aspx" title="Products Page"
          description="The products page." />
    </siteMapNode>
</siteMap>
```

11. Add the following Web pages to the Web application: MainPage.aspx, Support.aspx, Faqs.aspx, and Products.aspx. On each of these pages, add a *SiteMapPath* control.

12. Build the Web application project.

▶ **Exercise 2: Test the Site Navigation**

In this exercise, you test the site navigation on the Web application.

1. Continue with the project from the previous exercise, or open the completed Lesson 2, Exercise 1 project from the CD.

2. Right-click the Default.aspx page, and select Start As Start Page.

3. Test the Web application by pressing F5 to display the Default.aspx frame page. You should see the frames page, as shown in Figure 6-5.

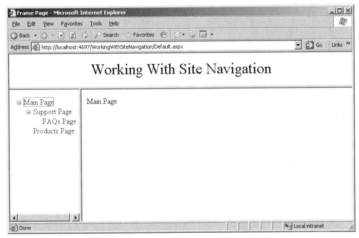

Figure 6-5   The frames page with the *TreeView* and *SiteMapPath* controls.

4. Try clicking the links on the *TreeView* control.

5. Try clicking the links on the *SiteMapPath* controls.

Lesson Summary

- You can provide client-side code or markup to request a new Web page.

- You can configure a control to perform cross-page posting for navigation to a new Web page.

- You can issue a client-side redirect from your server-side code to navigate to a new Web page.

- You can issue a server-side transfer to navigate to a new Web page.

- The *SiteMap* class can be used with the Web.sitemap file to programmatically navigate to a new Web page.

Lesson Review

You can use the following questions to test your knowledge of the information in Lesson 2, "Performing Site Navigation." The questions are also available on the companion CD if you prefer to review them in electronic form.

NOTE   Answers

Answers to these questions and explanations of why each answer is right or wrong are located in the "Answers" section at the end of the book.

---

1. Which of the following server-side methods can be used on the *HttpServerUtility* to navigate to a different Web page without requiring a round trip to the client?

   A. *Redirect*

   B. *NextPage*

   C. *Transfer*

2. Which control requires the Web.sitemap file to display site map information?

   A. *SiteMenuView*

   B. *SiteMapView*

   C. *SiteMenu*

   D. *SiteMapPath*

3. You want to provide an Up button for your Web pages to programmatically navigate up the site map. Which class can you use to access the site map to accomplish this?

   A. *NavigateSite*

   B. *SiteMap*

   C. *Map*

   D. *Navigator*

Chapter Review

To further practice and reinforce the skills you learned in this chapter, you can perform the following tasks:

- Review the chapter summary.
- Review the list of key terms introduced in this chapter.
- Complete the case scenarios. These scenarios set up real-world situations involving the topics of this chapter and ask you to create solutions.
- Complete the suggested practices.
- Take a practice test.

Chapter Summary

- You can use the validation framework to ensure data integrity at the client and at the server.
- You can provide site navigation via client-side code or markup, server-side code, or cross-page posting.

Key Terms

Do you know what this key term means? You can check your answers by looking up the term in the glossary at the end of the book.

- cross-page posting

Case Scenarios

In the following case scenarios you will apply what you've learned about input validation and site navigation. If you have difficulty completing this work, review the material in this chapter before beginning the next chapter. You can find answers to these questions in the "Answers" section at the end of this book.

Case Scenario 1: Determining the Proper User Name Validators to Implement

You are creating a new Web page that collects various data from users. On the registration page, the user name must be a valid e-mail address.

- Which validator controls will you implement on the user name text box?

Case Scenario 2: Determining the Proper Password Validators to Implement

You are creating a new Web page that collects various data from users. On the registration page, the user must supply a password and confirmation password. The password must contain at least one uppercase letter, one lowercase letter, and one number. The password must also be between 6 and 14 characters.

- Which validator controls will you implement on the password text box?

Case Scenario 3: Implementing a Site Map

You are creating a Web site for a customer and want to create a menu that contains a tree view of the locations that the user can navigate to. You also want to display a breadcrumb path to show the user the path to the page.

- Which controls will you use?

Suggested Practices

To successfully master the Program a Web Application, Implement Site Navigation and Input Validation exam objective and the Add and Configure Web Server Controls exam objective, complete the following tasks.

Create a Web Site and Program Redirection

For this task, you should complete Practice 1.

- **Practice 1**   Create a new Web page that collects data from users. Add a submit button and configure the button to perform a cross-page *PostBack*. Add code to the destination Web page that retrieves the data from the source Web page to prove that you can access this data.

Create a Data Collection Page with Validation

For this task, you should complete Practices 1 and 2. Complete Practice 3 to obtain extra experience with the *CustomValidator* control.

- **Practice 1** Create a new Web page that collects data from users. Practice adding the validators to restrict data entry to the known set of good data.
- **Practice 2** Disable all client-side validation and test server-side validation.
- **Practice 3** Add at least one *CustomValidator* and supply client-side and server-side validation code.

Implement the HyperLink Web Server Control

For this task, you should complete Practices 1 and 2.

- **Practice 1** Create a new Web page that and add several HyperLink Web server controls to the page.
- **Practice 2** Configure some HyperLink controls to navigate to different Web pages on the same Web site, and configure other HyperLink controls to navigate to a Web page on a different Web site.

Take a Practice Test

The practice tests on this book's companion CD offer many options. For example, you can test yourself on just the content covered in this chapter, or you can test yourself on all the 70-528 certification exam content. You can set up the test so that it closely simulates the experience of taking a certification exam, or you can set it up in study mode so that you can look at the correct answers and explanations after you answer each question.

MORE INFO **Practice tests**

For details about all the practice test options available, see "How to Use the Practice Tests" in this book's Introduction.

Chapter 7

ASP.NET State Management

Web pages rarely stand alone. Applications almost always need to track users who visit multiple pages within a Web site, whether to provide personalization, store information about a user, or track usage for reporting purposes.

At a high level, ASP.NET provides two different types of state management: client-side and server-side. Client-side state management stores information on the client's computer by embedding the information into a Web page, a Uniform Resource Locator (URL), or a cookie. Server-side state management tracks the user with a cookie or a URL but stores the information about a user in the server's memory or a database.

Exam objectives in this chapter:

- Manage state and application data.

  - Manage state of an application by using client-based state management options.

  - Manage state of an application by using server-based state management options.

  - Maintain state of an application by using database technology.

- Create event handlers for pages and controls.

  - Respond to application and session events.

Lessons in this chapter:

Before You Begin

To complete the lessons in this chapter, you should be familiar with Microsoft Visual Basic or C# and be comfortable with the following:

- Have Microsoft Windows XP and Microsoft Visual Studio 2005 installed on your computer with SQL Server 2005 Express Edition.
- Be familiar with the Visual Studio 2005 Integrated Development Environment (IDE).
- Have a basic understanding of Hypertext Markup Language (HTML) and client-side scripting.

> **Real World**
>
> *Tony Northrup*
>
> Back in the old days (you know, before the .NET Framework), tracking a user's visit across a Web site was a real pain because I had to write all the code to associate data with cookies. Of course, that only worked if the browser supported cookies—if I wanted to provide an alternate technique for tracking users, I had to write that code, too.
>
> State management in ASP.NET now provides those capabilities for developers, saving us the hassle of writing the same type of code over and over again. That's exactly what development frameworks should do—minimize redundant development so developers can focus on the more interesting coding. As you're working through this lesson, think about how long it would take you to duplicate all the state management functionality provided with the .NET Framework.

Lesson 1: Using Client-Side State Management

The most scalable way to perform state management is to store the data on the client. ASP.NET provides several techniques for storing state management information on the client:

- **View state**   ASP.NET uses *view state* to track values in controls. You can add custom values to view state, too.

- **Control state**   If you create a custom control that requires view state to work properly, you should use *control state* to ensure other developers don't break your control by disabling view state.

- **Hidden fields**   Like view state, *hidden fields* store data in an HTML form without displaying it in the user's browser. That data is available only when the form is processed.

- **Cookies**   *Cookies* store a value in the user's browser that the browser sends with every page request to the same server. Cookies are the best way to store state data that must be available for multiple Web pages on a Web site.

- **Query strings**   *Query strings* store values in the URL that are visible to the user. Use query strings when you want a user to be able to e-mail or instant message state data with a URL.

In this lesson, you will first learn when to choose client-side over server-side state management. Then you will learn how to implement view state, control state, hidden fields, cookies, and query strings.

After this lesson, you will be able to:

- Choose between client-side and server-side state management.
- Use view state to store custom values.
- Use control state to store values for custom controls even if view state is disabled.
- Use hidden fields to store values in a Web form.
- Use cookies to track state management data as a user browses multiple pages in a Web site.
- Use query strings to pass values to a page using a hyperlink.

Estimated lesson time: 30 minutes

Choosing Client-Side or Server-Side State Management

State management information, such as user name, personalization options, or shopping cart contents, can be stored at either the client or the server. If the state management information is stored on the client, the client submits the information to the server with each request. If the state management information is stored on the server, the server stores the information, but tracks the client using a client-side state management technique. Figure 7-1 illustrates both client-side and server-side state management.

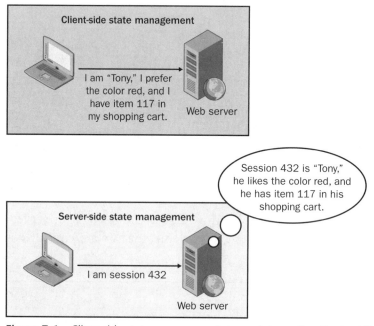

Figure 7-1 Client-side state management stores data on the client, while server-side state management requires the server to store the data.

Storing information on the client has the following advantages:

- **Better scalability** With server-side state management, each client that connects to the Web server consumes memory on the Web server. If a Web site has hundreds or thousands of simultaneous users, the memory consumed by storing state management information can become a limiting factor. Pushing this burden to the clients removes that potential bottleneck.

- **Supports multiple Web servers**   With client-side state management, you can distribute incoming requests across multiple Web servers with no changes to your application because the client provides all the information the Web server needs to process the request. With server-side state management, if a client switches servers in the middle of the session, the new server does not necessarily have access to the client's state information. You can use multiple servers with server-side state management, but you need either intelligent load-balancing (to always forward requests from a client to the same server) or centralized state management (where state is stored in a central database that all Web servers access).

Storing information on the server has the following advantages:

- **Better security**   Client-side state management information can be captured (either in transit or while it is stored on the client) or maliciously modified. Therefore, you should never use client-side state management to store confidential information, such as a password, authorization level, or authentication status.

- **Reduced bandwidth**   If you store large amounts of state management information, sending that information back and forth to the client can increase bandwidth utilization and page load times, potentially increasing your costs and reducing scalability. The increased bandwidth usage affects mobile clients most of all, because they often have very slow connections. Instead, you should store large amounts of state management data (say, more than 1 KB) on the server.

View State

As you might have already noticed, if a user clicks a button to submit an ASP.NET page, the page retains all its values and settings. For example, if you modify the text on a label and the user clicks a button, the modified text is still displayed when the page reappears. This happens because ASP.NET has a client-side state management technique built in: *ViewState*.

The *ViewState* property provides a dictionary object for retaining values between multiple requests for the same page. When an ASP.NET page is processed, the current state of the page and controls is hashed into a string and saved in the page as a hidden field. If the data is too long for a single field (as specified in the *MaxPageStateField-Length* property), then ASP.NET performs view state chunking to split it across multiple hidden fields. The following code sample demonstrates how view state adds data as a hidden form within a Web page's HTML:

```
<input type="hidden" name="__VIEWSTATE" id="__VIEWSTATE" value="/
wEPDwUKMTIxNDIyOTMOMg9kFgICAw9kFgICAQ8PFgIeBFR1eHQFEzQvNS8yMDA2IDE6Mzc6MTEgUE1kZGROWHn/
rt75XF/pMGnqjqH1H66cdw==" />
```

NOTE .NET 2.0

View state chunking is new in ASP.NET, version 2.0.

The sections that follow describe how to encrypt view state data, disable view state data, and add custom values to the view state.

Encrypting View State Data

You can enable view state encryption to make it more difficult for attackers and malicious users to directly read view state information. This adds processing overhead to your Web server; however, it is necessary if you plan to store confidential information in the view state. To configure view state encryption for an application, set the *<pages viewStateEncryptionMode>* attribute to Always in your Web.config file, as the following example shows:

```
<configuration>
  <system.web>
    <pages viewStateEncryptionMode="Always"/>
  </system.web>
</configuration>
```

Alternatively, you can enable view state encryption for a specific page by setting the value in the page directive, as the following sample demonstrates:

```
<%@ Page Language="C#" AutoEventWireup="true" CodeFile="Default.aspx.cs" Inherits="_Default"
ViewStateEncryptionMode="Always"%>
```

Because *ViewState* supports encryption, it is the most secure method of client-side state management. Encrypted *ViewState* is secure enough for most security requirements; however, it is always more secure to store data on the server.

Disabling ViewState Data

View state is enabled by default for every control, including Label controls, which you might never change. Unfortunately, view state adds overhead to ASP.NET forms. If you do not need to use view state, you should disable it by setting the *EnableViewState* property for each Web control to False. This reduces server processing time and decreases page size.

Reading and Writing Custom ViewState Data

You can also add and retrieve custom values with *ViewState*. If you have a value that you'd like to keep track of while the user is visiting a single ASP.NET Web page, adding a custom value to *ViewState* is the most efficient and secure way to do that. However, *ViewState* is lost if the user visits a different Web page, so it is useful only for temporarily storing values.

The following code demonstrates how to determine whether the time of the last visit was recorded in *ViewState*, how to display the value in a *Label* control named Label1, and then to set the value using the current time. To use this code, create a form with a *Label* control named Label1 and a *Button* control:

```vb
'VB
' Check if ViewState object exists, and display it if it does
If (Me.ViewState("lastVisit") IsNot Nothing) Then
    Label1.Text = CType(Me.ViewState("lastVisit"), String)
Else
    Label1.Text = "lastVisit ViewState not defined!"
End If

' Define the ViewState object for the next page view
Me.ViewState.Add("lastVisit", DateTime.Now.ToString())
```

```csharp
//C#
// Check if ViewState object exists, and display it if it does
if (ViewState["lastVisit"] != null)
    Label1.Text = (string)ViewState["lastVisit"];
else
    Label1.Text = "lastVisit ViewState not defined.";

// Define the ViewState object for the next page view
ViewState.Add("lastVisit", DateTime.Now.ToString());
```

While cookies must be strings, you can store a wide variety of serializable objects in *ViewState*. The following example stores a *DateTime* object in *ViewState* without converting it to a string and also uses a different technique for adding a *ViewState* value:

```vb
'VB
' Check if ViewState object exists, and display it if it does
If (Me.ViewState("lastVisit") IsNot Nothing) Then
    Dim lastVisit As DateTime = CType(Me.ViewState("lastVisit"), DateTime)
    Label1.Text = lastVisit.ToString()
```

```
Else
    Label1.Text = "lastVisit ViewState not defined!"
End If

' Define the ViewState object for the next page view
Me.ViewState("lastVisit") = DateTime.Now
```

```
//C#
// Check if ViewState object exists, and display it if it does
if (ViewState["lastVisit"] != null)
    Label1.Text = ((DateTime)ViewState["lastVisit"]).ToString();
else
    Label1.Text = "lastVisit ViewState not defined.";

// Define the ViewState object for the next page view
ViewState["lastVisit"] = DateTime.Now;
```

Quick Check

1. How do ASP.NET Web forms remember the settings for controls between user requests?

2. Is view state lost if a user refreshes a Web page? What if the user e-mails a URL to a friend?

Quick Check Answers

1. View state, which is enabled by default, remembers values for control properties on a form.

2. View state is maintained within a page's HTML, so it is lost if a page is refreshed or if the URL is copied.

Control State

If you create a custom control that requires *ViewState*, a developer who uses the control might break its functionality by disabling *ViewState* for the control or the entire page. To solve this, you can use the *ControlState* property to store state information for your control. *ControlState* allows you to persist property information that is specific to a control and cannot be turned off like the *ViewState* property. To use control state in a custom control, your control must override the *OnInit* method and call the *Register-RequiresControlState* method during initialization and then override the *SaveControl-State* and *LoadControlState* methods.

NOTE .NET 2.0

ControlState is new in ASP.NET version 2.0

ControlState takes away the developer's choice of turning off *ViewState* for a control. Typically, it's better to let developers choose how to use the controls. However, if a control simply cannot function without *ViewState*, you should implement *ControlState*.

Hidden Fields

ViewState stores information in the Web page using hidden fields. Hidden fields are sent back to the server when the user submits a form; however, the information is never displayed by the Web browser (unless the user chooses to view the page source). ASP.NET allows you to create your own custom hidden fields and store values that are submitted with other form data.

A *HiddenField* control stores a single variable in its *Value* property and must be explicitly added to the page. You can use hidden fields only to store information for a single page, so it is not useful for storing session data. If you use hidden fields, you must submit your pages to the server using Hypertext Transfer Protocol (HTTP) *POST* (which happens if the user presses a button) rather than requesting the page using *HTTP GET* (which happens if the user clicks a link). Unlike view state data, hidden fields have no built-in compression, encryption, hashing, or chunking, so users can view or modify data stored in hidden fields.

Cookies

Web applications can store small pieces of data in the client's Web browser by using cookies. A *cookie* is a small amount of data that is stored either in a text file on the client file system (if the cookie is persistent) or in memory in the client browser session (if the cookie is temporary). The most common use of cookies is to identify a single user as he or she visits multiple Web pages. You can also use cookies to store state information, user preferences, or an encrypted token indicating that the user has been successfully authenticated.

Figure 7-2 illustrates how Web clients and servers use cookies. First (Step 1), the Web client requests a page from the server. Because the client has not visited the server before, it does not have a cookie to submit. When the Web server responds to the request (Step 2), the Web server includes a cookie. The Web client submits that cookie with each subsequent request for any page on the same server (Steps 3, 4, and any future page views).

Figure 7-2   Web servers use cookies to track Web clients.

NOTE   Inside ASP.NET

As described in Lesson 2 of this chapter, ASP.NET uses cookies to track user sessions.

Cookies are the most flexible and reliable way of storing data on the client. However, users can delete the cookies on their computers at any time. Even if you store cookies with long expiration times, a user might decide to delete all cookies, wiping out any settings you might have stored in them. Therefore, if you rely on persistent cookies to store information about a user between visits, you should also allow users to log in to your Web application so you can restore persistent cookies in the event the users remove their cookies.

Reading and Writing Cookies

A Web application creates a cookie by sending it to the client as a header in an HTTP response. The Web browser then submits the same cookie to the server with every new request.

To create a cookie, add a value to the *Response.Cookies HttpCookieCollection*. To view a cookie sent back by the Web browser, read values in *Request.Cookies*. The following sample code (which belongs in the *Page_Load* event handler) demonstrates both defining and reading cookie values by setting a cookie named "lastVisit" to the current time. If the user already has the cookie set, the code displays the time the user last visited the page in the *Label1* control.

```vb
'VB
' Check if cookie exists, and display it if it does
If Not (Request.Cookies("lastVisit") Is Nothing) Then
    ' Encode the cookie in case the cookie contains client-side script
    Label1.Text = Server.HtmlEncode(Request.Cookies("lastVisit").Value)
Else
    Label1.Text = "No value defined"
End If
```

```
' Define the cookie for the next visit
Response.Cookies("lastVisit").Value = DateTime.Now.ToString
Response.Cookies("lastVisit").Expires = DateTime.Now.AddDays(1)

//C#
// Check if cookie exists, and display it if it does
if (Request.Cookies["lastVisit"] != null)
    // Encode the cookie in case the cookie contains client-side script
    Label1.Text = Server.HtmlEncode(Request.Cookies["lastVisit"].Value);
else
    Label1.Text = "No value defined";

// Define the cookie for the next visit
Response.Cookies["lastVisit"].Value = DateTime.Now.ToString();
Response.Cookies["lastVisit"].Expires = DateTime.Now.AddDays(1);
```

NOTE The *HttpCookie* class

This example shows the simplest and most common way of creating cookies. You can also create instances of the *HttpCookie* class and add them to the *HttpCookieCollection*.

The first time the user visits the page in the previous example, the code displays "No value defined" because the cookie has not yet been set. However, if you refresh the page, it displays the time of the first visit. Note that the code sample defines the *Expires* property for the cookie. You must define the *Expires* property and set it for the time period you would like the client to store the cookie if you want the cookie to persist between browser sessions. If you do not define the *Expires* property, the browser stores it in memory and the cookie is lost if the user closes his or her browser.

To delete a cookie, overwrite the cookie and set an expiration date in the past. You can't directly delete cookies because they are stored on the client's computer.

NOTE **Viewing and troubleshooting cookies**

As described in Chapter 1, "Introducing the ASP.NET 2.0 Web Site," you can use Trace.axd to view cookies for every page request.

Controlling Cookie Scope

Some Web sites store private information in cookies. For that reason, you don't want a browser to send your cookie to other Web sites. By default, browsers won't send a cookie to a Web site with a different hostname (although, in the past, vulnerabilities in browsers have allowed attackers to trick a browser into submitting another Web site's cookie).

You can control a cookie's scope to either limit the scope to a specific folder on the Web server or expand the scope to any server in a domain. To limit the scope of a cookie to a folder, set the *Path* property, as the following example demonstrates:

```vb
'VB
Response.Cookies("lastVisit").Value = DateTime.Now.ToString
Response.Cookies("lastVisit").Expires = DateTime.Now.AddDays(1)
Response.Cookies("lastVisit").Path = "/Application1"
```

```csharp
//C#
Response.Cookies["lastVisit"].Value = DateTime.Now.ToString();
Response.Cookies["lastVisit"].Expires = DateTime.Now.AddDays(1);
Response.Cookies["lastVisit"].Path = "/Application1";
```

With the scope limited to "/Application1", the browser submits the cookie to any page in the /Application1 folder, but not to pages in other folders, even if they are on the same server.

To expand the scope to an entire domain, set the *Domain* property, as the following example demonstrates:

```vb
'VB
Response.Cookies("lastVisit").Value = DateTime.Now.ToString
Response.Cookies("lastVisit").Expires = DateTime.Now.AddDays(1)
Response.Cookies("lastVisit").Domain = "contoso.com"
```

```csharp
//C#
Response.Cookies["lastVisit"].Value = DateTime.Now.ToString();
Response.Cookies["lastVisit"].Expires = DateTime.Now.AddDays(1);
Response.Cookies["lastVisit"].Domain = "contoso.com";
```

Setting the *Domain* property to "Contoso.com" causes the browser to submit the cookie to any server in the contoso.com domain, which might include www.contoso.com, intranet.contoso.com, or private.contoso.com. Similarly, you can use the *Domain* property to specify a full hostname, limiting the cookie to that specific server.

Storing Multiple Values in a Cookie

Though it depends on the browser, you typically can't store more than 20 cookies per site, and each cookie can be a maximum of 4 KB in length. To work around the 20-cookie limit, you can store multiple values in a cookie, as the following code demonstrates:

```vb
'VB
Response.Cookies("info")("visit") = DateTime.Now.ToString()
Response.Cookies("info")("firstName") = "Tony"
Response.Cookies("info")("border") = "blue"
Response.Cookies("info").Expires = DateTime.Now.AddDays(1)
```

```
//C#
Response.Cookies["info"]["visit"].Value = DateTime.Now.ToString();
Response.Cookies["info"]["firstName"].Value = "Tony";
Response.Cookies["info"]["border"].Value = "blue";
Response.Cookies["info"].Expires = DateTime.Now.AddDays(1);
```

Running the code in this example sends a cookie with the following value to the Web browser:

```
(visit=4/5/2006 2:35:18 PM)  (firstName=Tony)  (border=blue)
```

Cookie properties, such as *Expires*, *Domain*, and *Path*, apply for all values within a cookie. You can access individual values within the cookie using *Request.Cookies* in exactly the same way you define the values.

Query Strings

Query strings are commonly used to store variables that identify specific pages, such as search terms or page numbers. A query string is information that is appended to the end of a page URL. A typical query string might look like the following real-world example:

```
http://support.microsoft.com/Default.aspx?kbid=315233
```

In this example, the URL identifies the Default.aspx page. The query string (which starts with a question mark [?]) contains a single parameter named "kbid," and a value for that parameter, "315233." Query strings can also have multiple parameters, such as the following real-world URL, which specifies a language and query when searching the Microsoft.com Web site:

```
http://search.microsoft.com/results.aspx?mkt=en-US&setlang=en-US&q=hello+world
```

The values in this query string can be retrieved from within the ASP.NET page using the objects shown in Table 7-1.

Table 7-1 Sample Query String Values

Value Name	ASP.NET Object	Value
mkt	Request.QueryString["mkt"]	en-US
setlang	Request.QueryString["setlang"]	en-US
q	Request.QueryString["q"]	hello world

Query strings provide a simple but limited way to maintain state information between multiple pages. For example, they are an easy way to pass information from one page to another, such as passing a product number from a page that describes a product to a page that adds the item to a user's shopping cart. However, some browsers and client devices impose a 2083-character limit on the length of the URL. Another limitation is that you must submit the page using an *HTTP GET* command in order for query string values to be available during page processing. Therefore, you shouldn't add query strings to button targets in forms.

IMPORTANT   Always validate user input

You should expect users to modify data in query strings. For that reason, you must always validate data stored in query strings.

Query string data is included in bookmarks and when users e-mail URLs. In fact, it's the only way to enable a user to include state data when copying and pasting a URL to another user. For that reason, you should use query strings for any information that uniquely identifies a Web page, even if you are also using another state-management technique.

IMPORTANT   Practical query string character limits

Browsers have 2083-character limits on URLs, but you'll start to have problems with much shorter-length URLs if users e-mail them using plain-text e-mail or send them to other users via instant message. To allow a URL to be e-mailed, limit the length to 70 characters (including the http:// or https://). To allow a URL to be sent via instant message, limit the length to 400 characters.

Real World

Tony Northrup

While only the most sophisticated users are comfortable modifying cookies or hidden fields, many casual users know how to change query strings. For example, the first interactive Web application I ever wrote allowed a user to rate pictures on a scale from 1 to 10, and the user's rating was submitted as a query string value. For example, if the user rated a picture 7, the query string might read "page.aspx?pic=342&rating=7." One day I noticed a picture with a rating above 100–a clever user had manually changed the query string to include a very large value, and my application had added the rating to the database without validation. To fix the problem, I added code to reject any request with a rating more than 10 or less than 1.

A common mistake I see is that developers use query strings to allow users to navigate search results but do not validate the query strings properly. Often, query strings for search results have query strings for the search terms, the number of results per page, and the current page numbers. If you don't validate the query string, the user can set the number of results per page to a huge number, such as 10,000. Processing thousands of search results can take several seconds of your server's processing time and cause your server to transmit a very large HTML page. This makes it very easy for an attacker to perform a denial-of-service attack on your Web application by requesting the search page repeatedly.

Don't ever trust values from a query string; they must always be validated.

To write query string values, modify the URL for any hyperlink the user might click. For example, if you have a *HyperLink* control with *NavigateUrl* defined as "page.aspx," you can add the string "?user=tony" to the *HyperLink.NavigateUrl* property so that the full URL is "page.aspx?user=tony." Separate multiple query string values with ampersands (&). For example, the URL "page.aspx?user=tony&prefs=1&page=1252" passes three query string values to Page.aspx: user (with a value of "tony"), prefs (with a value of 1), and page (with a value of 1252).

One of the biggest drawbacks to using query strings is that there are no tools built into the .NET Framework to simplify the creation of query strings. You must manually add query string values to every hyperlink that the user might click.

To read a query string value, access the *Request.QueryStrings* collection just like you would access a cookie. To continue the previous example, the page.aspx page could process the "user" query string by accessing Request.QueryStrings("user") in Visual Basic or Request.QueryStrings["user"] in C#. For example, the following code displays values for the user, prefs, and page query strings in the *Label1* control:

```VB
'VB
Label1.Text = "User: " + Server.HtmlEncode(Request.QueryString("user")) + _
    ", Prefs: " + Server.HtmlEncode(Request.QueryString("prefs")) + _
    ", Page: " + Server.HtmlEncode(Request.QueryString("page"))
```

```C#
//C#
Label1.Text = "User: " + Server.HtmlEncode(Request.QueryString["user"]) +
    ", Prefs: " + Server.HtmlEncode(Request.QueryString["prefs"]) +
    ", Page: " + Server.HtmlEncode(Request.QueryString["page"]);
```

Security Alert   You should always encode cookie or query string values using *Server.HtmlEncode* before displaying the value in an HTML Web page to any user. *Server.HtmlEncode* replaces HTML code with special characters that a Web browser cannot process. For example, *Server.HtmlEncode* replaces a "<" sign with "&lt." If you display the value in a browser, the user sees the "<" sign, but the browser does not process any HTML code or client-side scripts.

To provide extra protection, the runtime throws a *System.Web.HttpRequestValidationException* if it detects HTML or client-side scripting in a query string. Therefore, you cannot pass HTML code in a query string. This can be disabled by an administrator, however, so you should not rely on it for protection.

Lab: Store State Management Data on the Client

In this lab, you use different client-side state management techniques to track the number of pages a user opens.

▶ **Exercise 1: Store Data in View State**

In this exercise, you add custom values to the *ViewState* object and then test the behavior when browsing to different pages.

1. Create a new ASP.NET Web site named ClientState in either C# or Visual Basic using Visual Studio 2005.

2. In the blank project, on the Default.aspx page, add a label named Label1, a button named Button1, and a hyperlink named HyperLink1. Set the *HyperLink1.Navigate-Url* property to "Default2.aspx."

3. Create a second Web form named Default2.aspx, add a label named Label1, a button named Button1, and a hyperlink named HyperLink1. Set the *HyperLink1.NavigateUrl* property to "Default.aspx."

4. In the *Page_Load* method for both Default.aspx and Default2.aspx, add code to store the current number of clicks in the *ViewState* object and display the clicks in the *Label* control. The following code demonstrates how to do this:

```VB
'VB
Protected Sub Page_Load(ByVal sender As Object, ByVal e As System.EventArgs) Handles
Me.Load
    If (ViewState("clicks") IsNot Nothing) Then
        ViewState("clicks") = CInt(ViewState("clicks")) + 1
    Else
        ViewState("clicks") = 1
    End If
    Label1.Text = "ViewState clicks: " + CInt(ViewState("clicks")).ToString
End Sub
```

```csharp
//C#
if (ViewState["clicks"] != null)
    ViewState["clicks"] = (int)ViewState["clicks"] + 1;
else
    ViewState["clicks"] = 1;
Label1.Text = " ViewState clicks: " + ((int)ViewState["clicks"]).ToString();
```

5. Build your Web site and visit the Default.aspx page. Click the button several times and verify that the clicks counter increments.

6. Click the hyperlink to load the Default2.aspx page. Notice that the counter returns to 1—the value stored in ViewState is lost because you opened a different page.

7. Click the hyperlink to return to Default.aspx. Notice that the counter is again reset. Switching between pages loses all ViewState information.

▶ **Exercise 2: Store Data in a Hidden Field**

In this exercise, you add a *HiddenField* control and use it to store state management data.

1. Continue editing the project you created in the previous exercise. Alternatively, you can open the completed Lesson 1, Exercise 1 project from the CD.

2. On the Default.aspx page, add a *HiddenField* control named HiddenField1.

3. In the *Page_Load* method for Default.aspx, add code to store the current number of clicks in the *HiddenField1* object and display the clicks in the *Label* control. The following code demonstrates how to do this:

```vb
'VB
Protected Sub Page_Load(ByVal sender As Object, ByVal e As System.EventArgs) Handles
Me.Load
    ' Store value in HiddenField
    Dim clicks As Integer
    Integer.TryParse(HiddenField1.Value, clicks)
    clicks += 1
    HiddenField1.Value = clicks.ToString

    Label1.Text = "HiddenField clicks: " + HiddenField1.Value
End Sub
```

```csharp
//C#
int clicks;
int.TryParse(HiddenField1.Value, out clicks);
clicks++;
HiddenField1.Value = clicks.ToString();

    Label1.Text = "HiddenField clicks: " + HiddenField1.Value
```

4. Notice that *HiddenField.Value* is a *String*, which requires converting data to and from the *String* type. This makes it less convenient than other methods of storing data.

5. Build your Web site and visit the Default.aspx page. Click the button several times and verify that the clicks counter increments. If you browse to other pages, the *HiddenField* value is lost.

▶ **Exercise 3: Store Data in a Cookie**

In this exercise, you use a cookie to track user clicks.

1. Continue editing the project you created in the previous exercise. Alternatively, you can open the completed Lesson 1, Exercise 2 project from the CD.

2. In the *Page_Load* method for both Default.aspx and Default2.aspx, add code to retrieve the current number of clicks from a cookie named "clicks," increment the value, and store the new value in the same cookie. Display the clicks in the *Label* control. The following code demonstrates how to do this:

```vb
'VB
Protected Sub Page_Load(ByVal sender As Object, ByVal e As System.EventArgs) Handles Me.Load
    ' Retrieve value from a cookie
    Dim cookieClicks As Integer
    If Not (Request.Cookies("clicks") Is Nothing) Then
        cookieClicks = Integer.Parse(Request.Cookies("clicks").Value) + 1
    Else
        cookieClicks = 1
    End If

    ' Define the cookie for the next visit
    Response.Cookies("clicks").Value = cookieClicks.ToString

    Label1.Text = "Cookie clicks: " + cookieClicks.ToString
End Sub
```

```csharp
//C#
// Retrieve value from a cookie
int cookieClicks;
if (Request.Cookies["clicks"] != null)
    cookieClicks = int.Parse(Request.Cookies["clicks"].Value) + 1;
else
    cookieClicks = 1;

// Define the cookie for the next visit
Response.Cookies["clicks"].Value = cookieClicks.ToString();

Label1.Text = "Cookie clicks: " + cookieClicks.ToString();
```

3. Build your Web site and visit the Default.aspx page. Click the button several times and verify that the clicks counter increments.

4. Click the hyperlink to load Default2.aspx. Notice that the counter is not reset. With cookies, you can browse to any page on the same Web site and access the same value.

▶ **Exercise 4: Store Data in a Query String**

In this exercise, you use a query string to track user clicks.

1. Continue editing the project you created in the previous exercise. Alternatively, you can open the completed Lesson 1, Exercise 3 project from the CD.

2. In the *Page_Load* method for both Default.aspx and Default2.aspx, add code to retrieve the current number of clicks from a query string parameter named "clicks," increment the value, and store the new value in the Hyperlink1.Navigate-Url. Display the clicks in the *Label* control. The following code demonstrates how to do this:

```VB
'VB
Protected Sub Page_Load(ByVal sender As Object, ByVal e As System.EventArgs) Handles
Me.Load
    ' Retrieve value from the query string
    Dim queryClicks As Integer
    If Not (Request.QueryString("clicks") Is Nothing) Then
        queryClicks = Integer.Parse(Request.QueryString("clicks")) + 1
    Else
        queryClicks = 1
    End If

    ' Define the query string in the hyperlink
    HyperLink1.NavigateUrl += "?clicks=" + queryClicks.ToString
    Label1.Text = "Query clicks: " + queryClicks.ToString
End Sub
```

```C#
//C#
// Retrieve value from the query string
int queryClicks;
if (Request.QueryString["clicks"] != null)
    queryClicks = int.Parse(Request.QueryString["clicks"]) + 1;
else
    queryClicks = 1;

// Define the query string in the hyperlink
HyperLink1.NavigateUrl += "?clicks=" + queryClicks.ToString();
Label1.Text = "Query clicks: " + queryClicks.ToString();
```

IMPORTANT   **Why does this example not use *Server.HtmlEncode*?**

Earlier, this lesson warned you to always use *Server.HtmlEncode* to encode cookies or query strings before displaying them in an HTML page. These exercises don't seem to practice what they preach, however. Instead, the exercises use strong typing to ensure there is no malicious code contained in the values before they are displayed. By converting the values from strings to integers and back to strings, there is no possibility that HTML code or client-side scripts can be displayed. If the user inserts malicious code in a cookie or query string, the runtime throws an exception when it attempts to parse the value, preventing the malicious code from being displayed. However, you must always use *Server.HtmlEncode* before directly displaying the string value of a cookie or query string.

---

3. Build your Web site, visit the Default.aspx page, and click the hyperlink to load Default2.aspx. Notice that the counter is incremented.

4. Click the hyperlink several times to switch between pages. Notice that the URL includes the number of clicks; this is visible to the user.

If the user bookmarks the link and returns to the page later, or even returns to the same URL on a different computer, the current clicks counter is retained. With query strings, you can e-mail or bookmark Web pages and have the state information stored in the URL. However, you must include the query string in any link the user might click on the page, or the information is lost.

Lesson Summary

■   Use client-side state management when scalability is the top priority. Use server-side state management when data must be protected.

■   ASP.NET uses view state by default to store information about controls in a Web form. You can add custom values to view state by accessing the *ViewState* collection.

■   Use control state when a custom control cannot function with view state disabled. To use control state in a custom control, your control must override the *OnInit* method and call the *RegisterRequiresControlState* method during initialization and then override the *SaveControlState* and *LoadControlState* methods.

■   Use hidden fields to store data in forms when view state is disabled. To use a hidden field, add the *HiddenField* control to a Web form.

■   Cookies store data on the client that the Web browser submits with every Web page request. Use cookies to track users across multiple Web pages. To create a cookie, add a value to the *Response.Cookies* collection. To read a cookie, access the *Request.Cookies* collection.

■ Query strings store small pieces of information in a hyperlink's URL. Use query strings when you want state management data to be bookmarked, such as when displaying multiple pages of search results. You must manually add query strings to a hyperlink. To read query strings, access the *Request.QueryStrings* collection.

Lesson Review

You can use the following questions to test your knowledge of the information in Lesson 1, "Using Client-Side State Management." The questions are also available on the companion CD if you prefer to review them in electronic form.

NOTE Answers

Answers to these questions and explanations of why each answer choice is right or wrong are located in the "Answers" section at the end of the book.

---

1. You need to store a user's user name and password as he or she navigates to different pages on your site so that you can pass those credentials to back-end servers. Which type of state management should you use? (Choose the best answer.)

   A. Client-side state management

   B. Server-side state management

2. You need to track non-confidential user preferences when a user visits your site to minimize additional load on your servers. You distribute requests among multiple Web servers, each running a copy of your application. Which type of state management should you use? (Choose the best answer.)

   A. Client-side state management

   B. Server-side state management

3. You are creating an ASP.NET Web form that allows a user to browse information in a database. While the user accesses the page, you need to track search and sorting values. You do not need to store the information between visits to the Web page. Which type of client-side state management would meet your requirements and be the simplest to implement? (Choose the best answer.)

   A. View state

   B. Control state

   C. Hidden fields

   D. Cookies

   E. Query strings

4.   You are creating an ASP.NET Web site with dozens of pages. You want to allow the user to set user preferences and have each page process the preference information. You want the preferences to be remembered between visits, even if the user closes the Web browser. Which type of client-side state management meets your requirements and is the simplest to implement? (Choose the best answer.)

   A. View state

   B. Control state

   C. Hidden fields

   D. Cookies

   E. Query strings

5.   You are creating an ASP.NET Web form that searches the product inventory and displays items that match the user's criteria. You want users to be able to bookmark or e-mail search results. Which type of client-side state management meets your requirements and is the simplest to implement? (Choose the best answer.)

   A. View state

   B. Control state

   C. Hidden fields

   D. Cookies

   E. Query strings

Lesson 2: Using Server-Side State Management

ASP.NET provides two ways to share information between Web pages without sending the data to the client: application state and session state. *Application state* information is available to all pages, regardless of which user requests a page. *Session state* information is available to all pages opened by a user during a single visit. Both application state and session state information are lost when the application restarts. To persist user data between application restarts, you can store it using profile properties.

After this lesson, you will be able to:

- Use application state to store information that should be accessible to all Web pages.
- Use session state to store information that should be accessible to all Web pages opened by a user during a single visit to your Web site.
- Describe the purpose of profile properties.

Estimated lesson time: 30 minutes

Application State

ASP.NET allows you to save values using application state, a global storage mechanism that is accessible from all pages in the Web application. Therefore, you can use application state to store information that must be maintained between server round trips and between requests for pages.

Application state is stored in the *Application* key/value dictionary (an instance of the *HttpApplicationState* class). You can add application-specific information to this structure to store it between page requests. Once you add your application-specific information to application state, the server manages it, and it is never exposed to the client. Application state is a great place to store information that is not user-specific. By storing it in the application state, all pages can access data from a single location in memory, rather than keeping separate copies of the data.

IMPORTANT Choosing application or session state

You should not store user-specific information in application state. Instead, you should use session state, as described later in this lesson. Any user might theoretically be able to access the *Application* object, so storing user information in the *Application* object could expose you to security risks.

Data stored in the *Application* object is not permanent and is lost any time the application is restarted. IIS regularly restarts ASP.NET applications to improve reliability, and applications are restarted if the computer is restarted. To persist information, read and write the values using application events, as described in the next section.

Responding to Application Events

ASP.NET provides three events that enable you to initialize *Application* variables (free resources when the application shuts down) and respond to *Application* errors:

- *Application_Start*   Raised when the application starts. This is the perfect place to initialize *Application* variables.

- *Application_End*   Raised when an application shuts down. Use this to free application resources and perform logging.

- *Application_Error*   Raised when an unhandled error occurs. Use this to perform error logging.

To implement these events, add the Global.asax file to your project by following these steps:

1. In Microsoft Visual Studio 2005, click Website, and then click Add New Item.

2. Click Global Application Class, and then click Add.

   Visual Studio adds a default Global.asax file that has methods for *Application_Start*, *Application_End*, and *Application_Error*, as well as *Session_Start* and *Session_End* (described later in this lesson). The following code demonstrates how to implement these services in the Global.asax file to keep track of users in the Application["UsersOnline"] object:

```
'VB
Sub Application_Start(ByVal sender As Object, ByVal e As EventArgs)
    Application("UsersOnline") = 0
End Sub

Sub Session_Start(ByVal sender As Object, ByVal e As EventArgs)
    Application.Lock()
    Application("UsersOnline") = CInt(Application("UsersOnline")) + 1
    Application.UnLock()
End Sub

Sub Session_End(ByVal sender As Object, ByVal e As EventArgs)
    Application.Lock()
    Application("UsersOnline") = CInt(Application("UsersOnline")) - 1
    Application.UnLock()
End Sub
```

```csharp
//C#
void Application_Start(object sender, EventArgs e)
{
    // Code that runs on application startup
    Application["UsersOnline"] = 0;
}

void Session_Start(object sender, EventArgs e)
{
    // Code that runs when a new session is started
    Application.Lock();
    Application["UsersOnline"] = (int)Application["UsersOnline"] + 1;
    Application.UnLock();
}

void Session_End(object sender, EventArgs e)
{
    // Code that runs when a session ends.
    // Note: The Session_End event is raised only when the sessionstate mode
    // is set to InProc in the Web.config file. If session mode is set to StateServer
    // or SQLServer, the event is not raised.
    Application.Lock();
    Application["UsersOnline"] = (int)Application["UsersOnline"] - 1;
    Application.UnLock();
}
```

Reading and Writing Application State Data

You can read and write application state data using the *Application* object (an instance of the *HttpApplicationState* class) just like you would read and write data to the *ViewState* object—as a collection. However, because multiple Web pages might be running simultaneously, you must lock the *Application* object when making calculations and performing updates, exactly as you need to lock a shared resource in a multi-threaded application. For example, the following code locks the *Application* update and increments a variable:

```vb
'VB
Application.Lock()
Application("PageRequestCount") = CInt(Application("PageRequestCount")) + 1
Application.UnLock()
```

```csharp
//C#
Application.Lock();
Application["PageRequestCount"] = ((int)Application["PageRequestCount"])+1;
Application.UnLock();
```

If you don't lock the *Application* object, it is possible for another page to change the variable between the time that the process reads the current value and the time it writes the new value, causing a calculation to be lost. You do not need to lock the *Application* object when initializing variables in *Application_Start*.

To read *Application* values, simply cast the value to the correct type. The following example demonstrates how to read an Integer that has been stored in *Application*:

```
'VB
CInt(Application("PageRequestCount"))
```

```
//C#
(int)Application["PageRequestCount"]
```

Session State

ASP.NET allows you to save values using session state, a storage mechanism that is accessible from all pages requested by a single Web browser session. Therefore, you can use session state to store user-specific information that must be maintained between server round trips and between requests for pages.

Session state is similar to application state, except that it is scoped to the current browser session. If different users are using your application, each user session has a different session state. In addition, if a user leaves your application and then returns later after the session timeout period, session state information is lost and a new session is created for the user.

Session state is stored in the *Session* key/value dictionary (an instance of the *HttpSessionState* class). You can add session-specific information to this structure to store it between page requests. Once you add your session-specific information to session state, the server manages it, and it is never exposed to the client.

You can use session state to accomplish the following tasks:

- Uniquely identify browser or client-device requests and map them to individual session instances on the server. This allows you to track which pages a user saw on your site during a specific visit.

- Store session-specific data on the server for use across multiple browser or client-device requests during the same session. This is perfect for storing shopping cart information.

- Raise appropriate session management events. In addition, you can write application code leveraging these events.

Once you add your application-specific information to session state, the server manages this object. Depending on which options you specify, session information can be stored in cookies, on out-of-process servers, or on computers running Microsoft SQL Server. Because session state can be centrally stored, it is perfect for storing data when using multiple front-end Web servers.

Reading and Writing Session State Data

The following code sample demonstrates how to store the time the user last loaded a page in a session variable and then later retrieve that value by casting it to the appropriate type. While this performs a similar function to the *ViewState* example in Lesson 1, the *Session* object is available to any page, the count is incremented whether the user submits a form or just clicks a link, and the count is stored on the server rather than the client:

```vb
'VB
' Check if Session object exists, and display it if it does
If (Session("lastVisit") IsNot Nothing) Then
    Label1.Text = Session("lastVisit").ToString()
Else
    Label1.Text = "Session does not have last visit information."
End If

' Define the Session object for the next page view
Session("lastVisit") = DateTime.Now
```

```csharp
//C#
// Check if Session object exists, and display it if it does
if (Session["lastVisit"] != null)
    Label1.Text = ((DateTime)Session["lastVisit"]).ToString();
else
    Label1.Text = "Session does not have last visit information.";

// Define the Session object for the next page view
Session["lastVisit"] = DateTime.Now;
```

To track a user's session, ASP.NET uses the ASP.NET_SessionId cookie with a random 24-byte value. Values stored in *Session* must be serializable.

Disabling Session State

If you don't use session state, you can improve performance by disabling session state for the entire application by setting the *sessionState mode* property to Off in the Web.config file, as the following example shows:

```xml
<configuration>
  <system.web>
    <sessionState mode="off"/>
  </system.web>
</configuration>
```

If you want to disable session state for only a particular page of an application, set the *EnableSessionState* page directive to False. You can also set the *EnableSessionState* page directive to ReadOnly to provide read-only access to session variables. The following code sample shows how to disable session state for a single page:

```
<%@ Page Language="C#" AutoEventWireup="true"  CodeFile="Default.aspx.cs"
Inherits="_Default" EnableSessionState = "False"%>
```

Configuring Cookieless Session State

By default, session state uses cookies to track user sessions. This is the best choice for the vast majority of applications. Almost all Web browsers support cookies, and those that don't are typically clients you don't want to track session data for, such as search engines or other robots.

However, you can enable a cookieless session state to have ASP.NET track sessions using a query string in the URL. The session ID is embedded in the URL after the slash that follows the application name and before any remaining file or virtual directory identifier. For example, the following URL has been modified by ASP.NET to include the unique session ID lit3py55t21z5v55vlm25s55:

```
http://www.example.com/s(lit3py55t21z5v55vlm25s55)/orderform.aspx
```

The following example shows a Web.config file that configures an ASP.NET application to use cookieless session identifiers.

```
<configuration>
  <system.web>
    <sessionState cookieless="true"
      regenerateExpiredSessionId="true" />
  </system.web>
</configuration>
```

Responding to Session Events

ASP.NET provides two events that help you manage user sessions:

- **Session_Start**   Raised when a new session begins. This is the perfect place to initialize session variables.

- **Session_End**   Raised when a session is abandoned or expires. Use this to free per-session resources.

To implement these events, add the Global.asax file to your project and write code in the appropriate event handler, as discussed in the section "Responding to Application Events," earlier in this lesson.

Choosing a Session State Mode

ASP.NET session state supports several different storage options for session data:

- **InProc**   Stores session state in memory on the Web server. This is the default, and it offers much better performance than using the ASP.NET state service or storing state information in a database server. InProc is fine for simple applications, but robust applications that use multiple Web servers or must persist session data between application restarts should use StateServer or SQLServer.

- **StateServer**   Stores session state in a service called the ASP.NET State Service. This ensures that session state is preserved if the Web application is restarted and also makes session state available to multiple Web servers in a Web farm. ASP.NET State Service is included with any computer set up to run ASP.NET Web applications; however, the service is set up to start manually by default. Therefore, when configuring the ASP.NET State Service, you must set the startup type to Automatic.

- **SQLServer**   Stores session state in a SQL Server database. This ensures that session state is preserved if the Web application is restarted and also makes session state available to multiple Web servers in a Web farm. On the same hardware, the ASP.NET State Service outperforms SQLServer. However, a SQL Server database offers more robust data integrity and reporting capabilities.

- **Custom**   Enables you to specify a custom storage provider. You also need to implement the custom storage provider.

- **Off**   Disables session state. You should disable session state if you are not using it to improve performance.

Configuring Session State Modes

You can specify which mode you want ASP.NET session state to use by assigning *SessionStateMode* enumeration values to the mode attribute of the *sessionState* element in your application's Web.config file. Modes other than *InProc* and *Off* require additional parameters, such as connection-string values. You can examine the currently selected session state by accessing the value of the *System.Web.SessionState.HttpSessionState.Mode* property.

For example, the following settings in a Web.config file cause the session state to be stored in a SQL server database identified by the specified connection string:

```
<configuration>
  <system.web>
    <sessionState mode="SQLServer"
      cookieless="true "
      regenerateExpiredSessionId="true "
      timeout="30"
      sqlConnectionString="Data Source=MySqlServer;Integrated Security=SSPI;"
      stateNetworkTimeout="30"/>
  </system.web>
</configuration>
```

While you can configure session state for your application, that is typically the responsibility of systems administrators. For example, a systems administrator might initially configure your Web application on a single server using the InProc mode. Later, if the server gets too busy or requires redundancy, the systems administrator adds a second Web server, configures the ASP.NET state service on a server, and modifies the Web.config file to use the StateServer mode. Fortunately, the session state mode is transparent to your application, so you won't need to change your code. Besides configuring the Web.config file, you don't need to change how your application deals with session states to support different modes.

Quick Check

1. Which typically consumes more memory: application state or session state?
2. Which might not work if a user has disabled cookies in his or her Web browser: application state or session state?

Quick Check Answers

1. Session state tends to use much more memory than application state, because copies of all variables are stored for each user.
2. Session state, by default, won't work if a Web browser that supports cookies has cookies disabled. Application state isn't user-specific, though, and doesn't need to be tracked in cookies. Therefore, application state works regardless.

Profile Properties

ASP.NET provides a feature called profile properties, which allows you to store user-specific data. This feature is similar to session state, except that the profile data is not lost when a user's session expires. The profile-properties feature uses an ASP.NET profile, which is stored in a persistent format and associated with an individual user. The ASP.NET profile allows you to easily manage user information without requiring you to design your own database. In addition, the profile makes the user information available using strongly typed classes that you can access from anywhere in your application. You can store objects of any type in the profile.

NOTE   .NET 2.0

Profile properties are new in ASP.NET version 2.0.

To use profile properties, you must configure a profile provider. ASP.NET includes a *SqlProfileProvider* class that allows you to store profile data in a SQL database, but you can also create your own profile provider class that stores profile data in a custom format and to a custom storage mechanism, such as an XML file, or even to a Web service.

Because data that is placed in profile properties is not stored in application memory, it is preserved through Internet Information Services (IIS) restarts and worker-process restarts without losing data. Additionally, profile properties can be persisted across multiple processes, such as in Web farms or Web gardens.

MORE INFO   Profile properties

For more information about profile properties, refer to Chapter 9, "Customizing and Personalizing a Web Application."

Lab: Store State Management Data on the Server

In this lab, you use different server-side state management techniques to track the number of pages a user has opened.

▶ **Exercise 1: Store Data in the Application Object**

In this exercise, you add custom values to the *Application* object and then test the behavior when browsing to different pages.

1. Create a new ASP.NET Web site named ServerState in either C# or Visual Basic using Visual Studio 2005.

2. In the blank project, on the Default.aspx page, add labels named Label1 and Label2, and a hyperlink named HyperLink1. Set the *HyperLink1.NavigateUrl* property to "Default2.aspx."

3. Create a second Web form named Default2.aspx, add labels named Label1 and Label2, and a hyperlink named HyperLink1. Set the *HyperLink1.NavigateUrl* property to "Default.aspx."

4. Add the Global.asax file to your project.

5. In the Global.asax file, in the *Application_Start* method, initialize an Integer named "clicks" in the Application object, as the following example shows:

```VB
'VB
Sub Application_Start(ByVal sender As Object, ByVal e As EventArgs)
    ' Code that runs on application startup
    Application("clicks") = 0
End Sub
```

```C#
//C#
void Application_Start(object sender, EventArgs e)
{
    // Code that runs on application startup
    Application["clicks"] = 0;
}
```

6. In the *Page_Load* method for both Default.aspx and Default2.aspx, add code to increment the number of clicks in the *Application* object. Don't forget to lock the application object before updating the value. Then display the value in Label1. The following code demonstrates how to do this:

```VB
'VB
Application.Lock()
Application("clicks") = CInt(Application("clicks")) + 1
Application.UnLock()

Label1.Text = "Application clicks: " + Application("clicks").ToString
```

```C#
//C#
Application.Lock();
Application["clicks"] = ((int)Application["clicks"]) + 1;
Application.UnLock();

Label1.Text = "Application clicks: " + Application["clicks"].ToString();
```

7. Build your Web site and visit the Default.aspx page. Click the hyperlink several times to switch between pages and verify that the clicks counter increments.

8. From a different computer, open the same page. Notice that the click count includes the clicks you made from the first computer because the *Application* object is shared among all user sessions.

9. Restart your Web server and visit the same page again. Notice that the click count is reset; the *Application* object is not persisted between application restarts.

▶ **Exercise 2: Store Data in the Session Object**

In this exercise, you add custom values to the *Session* object and then test the behavior when browsing to different pages.

1. Continue editing the project you created in the previous exercise. Alternatively, you can open the completed Lesson 2, Exercise 1 project from the CD.

2. In the Global.asax file, in the *Session_Start* method, initialize an Integer named "clicks" in the Session object, as the following example shows:

```
'VB
Sub Session_Start(ByVal sender As Object, ByVal e As EventArgs)
    ' Code that runs when a new session is started
    Session("clicks") = 0
End Sub
```

```
//C#
void Session_Start(object sender, EventArgs e)
{
    // Code that runs when a new session is started
    Session["clicks"] = 0;
}
```

3. In the *Page_Load* method for both Default.aspx and Default2.aspx, add code to increment the number of clicks in the *Session* object. Don't forget to lock the application object before updating the value. Then display the value in Label2. The following code demonstrates how to do this:

```
'VB
Protected Sub Page_Load(ByVal sender As Object, ByVal e As System.EventArgs) Handles
Me.Load
    Session("clicks") = CInt(Session("clicks")) + 1
    Label2.Text = "Session clicks: " + Session("clicks").ToString
End Sub
```

```
//C#
Session["clicks"] = ((int)Session["clicks"]) + 1;
Label2.Text = "Session clicks: " + Session["clicks"].ToString();
```

Notice that *HiddenField.Value* is a *String*, which requires converting data to and from the *String* type. This makes it less convenient than other methods of storing data.

4. Build your Web site and visit the Default.aspx page. Click the hyperlink several times to switch between pages and verify that both the *Application* and *Session* clicks counters increment.

5. From a different computer, open the same page. Notice that the *Application* click count includes the clicks you made from the first computer because the *Application* object is shared among all user sessions. However, the *Session* clicks counter includes only clicks made from that computer.

6. Restart your Web server and visit the same page again. Notice that both click counts are reset; the *Application* and *Session* objects are not persisted between application restarts.

Lesson Summary

■ You can use the *Application* collection to store information that is accessible from all Web pages but is not user-specific. To initialize *Application* variables, respond to the *Application_Start* event in your Global.asax file.

■ You can use the *Session* collection to store user-specific information that is accessible from all Web pages. To initialize Session variables, respond to the *Session_Start* event in your Global.asax file. You can store session information in the server's memory using the InProc session state mode, store it in an ASP.NET State Service server using the StateServer mode, store it in a database using the SQLServer mode, implement your own custom session state storage using Custom, or turn session state off completely.

Lesson Review

You can use the following questions to test your knowledge of the information in Lesson 2, "Using Server-Side State Management." The questions are also available on the companion CD if you prefer to review them in electronic form.

NOTE Answers

Answers to these questions and explanations of why each answer is right or wrong are located in the "Answers" section at the end of the book.

---

1. In which file should you write code to respond to the *Application_Start* event? (Choose the best answer.)

    A. Any ASP.NET server page with an .aspx extension

    B. Web.config

    C. Global.asax

    D. Any ASP.NET server page with an .aspx.vb or .aspx.cs extension

2. You need to store state data that is accessible to any user who connects to your Web application. Which object should you use? (Choose the best answer.)

    A. *Session*

    B. *Application*

    C. *Response.Cookies*

    D. *Response.ViewState*

3. You need to store user logon credentials that are provided by the user each time the user connects to your Web application. Which object should you use? (Choose the best answer.)

    A. *Session*

    B. *Application*

    C. *Response.Cookies*

    D. *Response.ViewState*

4. You need to write data to a database before a user's session times out. Which event should you respond to? (Choose the best answer.)

    A. *Application_Start*

    B. *Application_End*

    C. *Session_Start*

    D. *Session_End*

Chapter Review

To further practice and reinforce the skills you learned in this chapter, you can perform the following tasks:

- Review the chapter summary.
- Review the list of key terms introduced in this chapter.
- Complete the case scenarios. These scenarios set up real-world problem situations involving the topics of this chapter and ask you to create solutions.
- Complete the suggested practices.
- Take a practice test.

Chapter Summary

- State management enables you to access data between multiple Web requests. Client-side state management offers the best performance, while server-side state management offers improved security and the ability to store large amounts of data. ASP.NET includes five ways to store client-side state management data: control state, cookies, hidden fields, query strings, and view state.

- ASP.NET includes three server-side state management techniques. Application state is the best choice when you need to store information about multiple users between Web requests. Choose session state to store information about a single user's visit to your Web site. Use profile properties when you must persist information about a user between multiple visits.

Key Terms

Do you know what these key terms mean? You can check your answers by looking up the terms in the glossary at the end of the book.

- application state
- control state
- cookie
- hidden field
- query string
- session state
- view state

Case Scenarios

In the following case scenarios, you apply what you've learned about how to implement and apply ASP.NET state management. You can find answers to these questions in the "Answers" section at the end of this book.

Case Scenario 1: Remembering User Credentials

You are an application developer for Contoso, Ltd., a business-to-business retailer. You are writing an e-commerce Web application that retrieves inventory and customer data from a back-end database server. Recently, your Marketing Department has received requests from customers to provide enhanced account-management capabilities. Your manager asks you to interview key people and then come to his office to answer his questions about your design choices.

Interviews

Following is a list of company personnel you interviewed and their statements:

- **Marketing Manager** "We recently had a session with our most important customers to identify potential areas of improvement. One of the comments that we heard frequently was that they want a way to log in to our Web site and view past order information. I know I hate having to log in to Web sites every time I visit the Web page, so if we could remember their login information, I think the customers would be happier."

- **Development Manager** "This seems like a fair request; however, we need to keep security in mind. Don't do anything that would allow an attacker to steal a user's session and view his or her orders."

Questions

Answer the following questions for your manager.

1. What state management mechanism would you use to remember a user's login credentials?

2. How can you reduce the risk of a user's credentials being stolen?

3. How should you store information about previous orders?

Case Scenario 2: Analyzing Information for Individual Users and for All Users

You are an application developer working for Fabrikam, Inc., a consumer Web-based magazine. Recently, your Marketing Department personnel requested the ability to see a snapshot of what a user is currently doing on the Web site in real time. Additionally, they would like to display advertisements to that user based on the content viewed in the current session, and they would like the ability to analyze multiple different articles that a user might have read during that visit.

You discuss the needs with the Marketing Manager, who says:

"We have great tools for analyzing Web site logs, but we often want to know what's happening on the site in real time so that we can make instant decisions. For example, if we post a new article, we'd like to see how many users are currently viewing that page. Also, I think we can better cater our advertisements to customer needs by analyzing a user's path through our Web site. Is there any way to track what a user does in a session?"

Questions

Answer the following questions for your manager.

1. How can you analyze data for all users?

2. How can you analyze what an individual user has done?

Suggested Practices

To successfully master the Manage State and Application Data exam objective and the Respond to Application and Session Events exam subobjective, complete the following tasks.

Manage State by Using Client-Based State Management Options

For this task, you should complete Practice 1 to get a better understanding of how to implement control state. Complete Practices 2 and 3 to explore how real-world Web sites use cookies.

- **Practice 1**   Create a custom control and implement control state management.
- **Practice 2**   View your Temporary Internet Files folder (typically located in C:\Documents and Settings*username*\Local Settings). Examine cookies that

Web sites have stored on your computer and open the files in a text editor to view the information they contain.

- **Practice 3**   Disable cookies in your Web browser. Then visit several of your favorite Web sites to determine if the Web site behavior changes at all.

Manage State by Using Server-Based State Management Options

For this task, you should complete all of Practice 1 to get experience using the *Application* objects. Complete Practices 2 and 3 to gain experience working with user sessions.

- **Practice 1**   Using a Web application that you previously developed, add real-time application activity analysis functionality described in Case Scenario 2 so that you can open a Web page and view which pages users are currently viewing.

- **Practice 2**   Using a Web application that you previously developed, enable Web site personalization using the *Session* object. Allow a user to set a preference, such as background color, and apply that preference to any page the user might view.

- **Practice 3**   Disable cookies in your Web browser and visit the Web application you created in Practice 2. Attempt to set a preference and study how the application responds. Think about how an application might determine whether a browser supports sessions and what to do if the browser does not support sessions.

Maintain State by Using Database Technology

For this task, you should complete Practices 1 and 2.

- **Practice 1**   Configure a Web application to use a SQL state server.
- **Practice 2**   Configure a Web application to use the ASP.NET state service.

Respond to Application and Session Events

For this task, you should complete Practices 1 and 2.

- **Practice 1**   Using a Web application that you previously developed, add code to initialize variables to the *Application_Start* event. Add code to release resources in the *Application_End* event.

■ **Practice 2** Using a Web application that you previously developed, add code to initialize variables to the *Session_Start* event. Add code to release resources in the *Session_End* event.

Take a Practice Test

The practice tests on this book's companion CD offer many options. For example, you can test yourself on just the content covered in this chapter, or you can test yourself on all the 70-528 certification exam content. You can set up the test so that it closely simulates the experience of taking a certification exam, or you can set it up in study mode so that you can look at the correct answers and explanations after you answer each question.

MORE INFO Practice tests

For details about all the practice test options available, see the "How to Use the Practice Tests" section in this book's Introduction.

Chapter 8

Programming the Web Application

One of the unique aspects of programming a Web application is understanding the interactions between the Web browser and the Web server. ASP.NET provides you direct access to a great deal of information related to the client-server communications. To write efficient and reliable Web applications, you must understand how the different components of a Web application interact and how to examine and configure each component.

Exam objectives in this chapter:

- Program a Web application.

    - Detect browser types in Web Forms.

    - Ascertain the cause of an unhandled exception at the page level.

    - Programmatically access the header of a Web page.

    - Access encapsulated page and application context.

    - Use a page's *Async* attribute to create a page that has built-in asynchronous capabilities.

- Add and configure Web server controls.

    - Programmatically edit settings in a Web site's configuration file.

    - Write an ASP.NET handler to generate images dynamically for display on a Web page.

Lessons in this chapter:

Before You Begin

To complete the lessons in this chapter, you should be familiar with Microsoft Visual Basic or C# and be comfortable with the following tasks:

- Have Microsoft Windows XP and Microsoft Visual Studio 2005 installed with Microsoft SQL Server 2005 Express Edition.

- Be familiar with the Visual Studio 2005 Integrated Development Environment (IDE).

- Have a basic understanding of Hypertext Markup Language (HTML) and client-side scripting.

Lesson 1: Using Web Site Programmability

While you can do most programming tasks within an ASP.NET Web page, you often need to interact with ASP.NET directly and understand how ASP.NET interacts with Internet Information Services (IIS). This can allow you to accomplish the following types of tasks:

- Catch otherwise unhandled exceptions
- Examine or update application configuration settings
- Run tasks asynchronously
- Dynamically generate different file types

This lesson describes each of these ASP.NET programming tasks.

After this lesson, you will be able to:
- Catch unhandled exceptions at the page or application level.
- Read and modify settings in different configuration files.
- Enable asynchronous Web pages.
- Create custom ASP.NET handlers to respond to requests for nonstandard file types.

Estimated lesson time: 30 minutes

Page and Application Exception Handling

Exception handling is most effective when you catch exceptions for small blocks of code. For example, you should surround code that establishes a database connection with a *Try/Catch* block, so that you can present very specific error information to the user.

However, unhandled exceptions can still occur if there is an error in code that does not have a *Try/Catch* block. You can catch these errors at either the page or the application level.

To catch errors at the page level, create a *Page_Error* event handler in each page to handle the *Error* event. The event handler must accept an *Object* parameter and an *EventArgs* parameter. Typically, you do not need to examine either of these parameters within the event handler. Instead, you access the *Server.GetLastError()* method to retrieve the last error, and then call *Server.ClearError()* to remove the error from the queue. The following code sample demonstrates this by writing the error message using *Trace.Write*:

```vb
'VB
Private Sub Page_Error(ByVal sender As Object, _
    ByVal e As System.EventArgs) Handles MyBase.Error
    Trace.Write("ERROR: " & Server.GetLastError().Message)
    Server.ClearError()
End Sub
```

```csharp
//C#
private void Page_Error(object sender, EventArgs e)
{
    Trace.Write("ERROR: " + Server.GetLastError().Message);
    Server.ClearError();
}
```

Note that you can't display error messages in controls. Controls are not accessible from within *Page_Error*.

Exam Tip   Know that you retrieve the last error by calling *Server.GetLastError()* and then clear the last error by calling *Server.ClearError()*.

You can also catch unhandled exceptions at the application level, in case you'd rather not add *Page_Error* event handlers to each page. To do this, handle the *Application_Error* method in your application's Global.asax file. Typically, you should call *Server.Transfer* to redirect the user to a different Web page that handles the error, as the following code sample demonstrates:

```vb
'VB
Sub Application_Error(ByVal sender As Object, ByVal e As EventArgs)
    ' Code that runs when an unhandled error occurs
    Server.Transfer("HandleError.aspx")
End Sub
```

```csharp
//C#
void Application_Error(object sender, EventArgs e)
{
    // Code that runs when an unhandled error occurs
    Server.Transfer("HandleError.aspx");
}
```

Visual Studio 2005 automatically generates the *Application_Error* event handler for you when you add an item to your project using the Global Application Class template. In the page that handles the error, you should call *Server.GetLastError()* to retrieve the error, and then clear the error by calling *Server.ClearError()*, just as you would do for a *Page_Error* event handler.

Security Alert An attacker can potentially use any details about the inner workings of your application to which he or she gains access to identify a vulnerability. For this reason, attackers commonly use port scanning and system profiling to gain information about a target computer. Often, one of the most detailed sources of information for attackers is the error message.

Everyone has been frustrated by ambiguous error messages at some point. For example, consider this error message found in the author's application event log: Faulting application, version, faulting module, version 0.0.0.0, fault address 0x00000000. This message doesn't provide any information that would be useful for troubleshooting the problem. To avoid this frustration, and to facilitate troubleshooting, good developers provide very detailed error messages. Although this is a very user-friendly practice, it can also weaken the security of your application. You should not provide detailed error messages to end users, but you should allow administrators and developers to view error messages.

You can do this by using *Trace.Write* (if you, as the developer, will be reviewing the messages) or by using ASP.NET Web events, as described in Chapter 1, "Introducing the ASP.NET 2.0 Web Site."

Programming the Web.Config File Settings

You (or a systems administrator) can make many standard configuration changes using the ASP.NET Web Site Administration tool. For other changes, you need to edit the Web.config XML file. That works well when you need to manually make changes, but there are other times when you might want to programmatically edit configuration settings, such as in the following scenarios:

- During initial configuration of the Web.config file during setup, based on user input
- As part of a custom application administration tool to simplify management for systems administrators
- To automatically adjust the Web site configuration based on other network conditions

Fortunately, ASP.NET provides the ASP.NET Configuration API for this purpose. It is the same API that the ASP.NET MMC snap-in and the ASP.NET Web Site Administration tool use to make configuration changes.

You use a *System.Configuration.Configuration* object to read the Web.config file and write any changes you might make. To create a *Configuration* object for the current application, call *WebConfigurationManager*.

Once you have a *Configuration* object, you can read sections by calling the *GetSection* and *GetSectionGroup* methods. The current user or process must have Read permissions to all configuration files in the hierarchy. If you make any changes, call the *Save* method to persist those changes to the Web.config file (which requires permission to modify the file), or call the *SaveAs* method to save those changes to a new configuration file (which requires permission to create a new file). You might use *SaveAs* if you want to create new configuration settings that apply only to a subfolder.

For example, the following code sample (which requires the *System.Web.Configuration* namespace) displays the current authentication mode as defined in the <system.web><authentication> section, and then displays it in the *Label1* control:

```
'VB
Dim section As AuthenticationSection = _
    WebConfigurationManager.GetSection("system.web/authentication")
Label1.Text = section.Mode.ToString()
```

```
//C#
AuthenticationSection section =
    (AuthenticationSection) WebConfigurationManager.GetSection("system.web/authentication");
Label1.Text = section.Mode.ToString();
```

Each standard element in the Web.config file has its own class, and you must use that class to access the configuration information. In C#, this requires an explicit conversion after calling the *System.Web.Configuration.WebConfigurationManager.GetSection* method, as the previous code sample demonstrates. Table 8-1 lists these classes.

Table 8-1   Classes Used to Access Configuration Sections

Class	Configuration Section
AuthenticationSection	<system.web><authentication>
AnonymousIdentificationSection	<system.web><anonymousIdentification>
AuthorizationSection	<system.web><authorization>

Table 8-1 Classes Used to Access Configuration Sections

Class	Configuration Section
CacheSection	<system.web><cache>
CompilationSection	<system.web><compilation>
CustomErrorsSection	<system.web><customErrors>
DeploymentSection	<system.web><deployment>
GlobalizationSection	<system.web><globalization>
HealthMonitoringSection	<system.web><healthMonitoring>
HostingEnvironmentSection	<system.web><hostingEnvironment>
HttpCookiesSection	<system.web><httpCookies>
HttpHandlersSection	<system.web><httpHandlers>
HttpRuntimeSection	<system.web><httpRuntime>
IdentitySection	<system.web><identity>
MachineKeySection	<system.web><machineKey>
MembershipSection	<system.web><membership>
OutputCacheSection	<system.web><outputCache>
PagesSection	<system.web><pages>
ProcessModeSection	<system.web><processMode>
ProfileSection	<system.web><profile>
RolesManagerSection	<system.web><rolesManager>
SecurityPolicySection	<system.web><securityPolicy>
SessionPageStateSection	<system.web><sessionPageState>
SessionStateSection	<system.web><sessionState>
SiteMapSection	<system.web><siteMap>

Table 8-1   Classes Used to Access Configuration Sections

Class	Configuration Section
SqlCacheDependencySection	<system.web><sqlCacheDependency>
TraceSection	<system.web><trace>
TrustSection	<system.web><trust>
WebControlsSection	<system.web><webControls>
WebPartsSection	<system.web><webParts>
XhtmlConformanceSection	<system.web><xhtmlConformance>

Once you have created an instance of one of these classes, you can use the class's methods and properties to read or write configuration settings information.

Besides accessing the <system.web> section, you can access custom application settings using the *WebConfigurationManager.AppSettings* collection. The following code sample demonstrates how to display the MyAppSetting custom application setting (which you could add using the ASP.NET Web Site Configuration tool) in a *Label* control:

```
'VB
Label1.Text = WebConfigurationManager.AppSettings("MyAppSetting")
```

```
//C#
Label1.Text = WebConfigurationManager.AppSettings["MyAppSetting"];
```

Similarly, you can programmatically access connection strings using the *WebConfigurationManager.ConnectionStrings* collection:

```
'VB
Label1.Text = WebConfigurationManager.ConnectionStrings("Northwind").ConnectionString
```

```
//C#
Label1.Text = WebConfigurationManager.ConnectionStrings["Northwind"].ConnectionString;
```

Accessing the static *WebConfigurationManager* methods is the most efficient way to read configuration settings because it takes into account the entire hierarchy of system and application configuration settings and indicates your effective settings. If you want to make changes, however, you must choose a specific configuration location. To do this, create an instance of a *Configuration* object. To create an instance of the root

Web.config file that applies to all applications, call the static *WebConfigurationManager.OpenWebConfiguration* method and pass a null parameter to create a *Configuration* object. Then, use the *Configuration* object to create objects for individual sections. Edit values in those sections and save the changes by calling *Configuration.Save()*.

Quick Check

1. What type does *WebConfigurationManager.GetSection* return, and how should you handle it?

2. How can you programmatically update a connection string stored in the Web.config file?

Quick Check Answers

1. *WebConfigurationManager.GetSection* returns an *Object* type. You must cast it to a type specific to the configuration section.

2. Create a *Configuration* object. Then, update the connection string using the *ConnectionStrings* collection. Finally, call *Configuration.Save*.

The following code sample demonstrates how to enable tracing in the root Web.config file, assuming the application has the necessary security permissions (which it won't by default):

NOTE Providing administrative credentials

The *OpenWebConfiguration* method has overloads that allow you to specify a different server and to provide credentials.

```vb
'VB
Dim rootConfig As Configuration = WebConfigurationManager.OpenWebConfiguration(Nothing)
Dim section As TraceSection = (TraceSection)rootConfig.GetSection("system.web/trace")
section.Enabled = True
rootConfig.Save()
```

```csharp
//C#
Configuration rootConfig = WebConfigurationManager.OpenWebConfiguration(null);
TraceSection section = (TraceSection)rootConfig.GetSection("system.web/trace");
section.Enabled = true;
rootConfig.Save();
```

You can open other configuration files by passing the application path (but not the full file name). For example, if you want to edit the Web.config file for the MyApp application on the current Web server to enable tracing, you can use the following code sample (notice that only the parameter for the first line has changed):

```
'VB
Dim rootConfig As Configuration = WebConfigurationManager.OpenWebConfiguration("/MyApp")
Dim section As TraceSection = rootConfig.GetSection("system.web/trace")
section.Enabled = True
rootConfig.Save()
```

```
//C#
Configuration rootConfig = WebConfigurationManager.OpenWebConfiguration("/MyApp");
TraceSection section = (TraceSection)rootConfig.GetSection("system.web/trace");
section.Enabled = true;
rootConfig.Save();
```

This code adds the following line to the /MyApp/Web.config file (assuming the line does not yet exist):

```
<trace enabled="true" />
```

NOTE   Finding the application path

To retrieve the application path at run time, use the *Request.ApplicationPath* property. This property is described in more detail in Lesson 2 of this chapter.

Because there is a hierarchy of configuration files, there are different ways to handle saving settings. The *ConfigurationSaveMode* enumeration allows you to specify the save technique using one of these values:

- ■ *Full*   Causes all properties to be written to the configuration file. This is useful mostly for creating information configuration files or moving configuration values from one machine to another.

- ■ *Minimal*   Causes only properties that differ from inherited values to be written to the configuration file.

- ■ *Modified*   Causes only modified properties to be written to the configuration file, even when the value is the same as the inherited value.

To create a new configuration file, call the *Configuration.SaveAs* method and provide a location. The following code sample demonstrates how to call *Configuration.SaveAs* using the *ConfigurationSaveMode* enumeration.

```
'VB
Dim config As Configuration = WebConfigurationManager.OpenWebConfiguration("/MyApp")
config.SaveAs("c:\MyApp.web.config", ConfigurationSaveMode.Full, True)
```

```
//C#
Configuration config = WebConfigurationManager.OpenWebConfiguration("/MyApp");
config.SaveAs(@"c:\MyApp.web.config", ConfigurationSaveMode.Full, true);
```

Asynchronous Web Page Programming

Asynchronous programming allows a process to have multiple threads, enabling the process to do more than one action simultaneously. While asynchronous programming can be complicated, it can dramatically improve performance in situations where the process would otherwise need to wait for a relatively slow action, such as accessing a network resource, to occur.

If you have done asynchronous programming in Windows Forms applications, you can also use those techniques in ASP.NET Web forms. However, ASP.NET provides a different technique as well. Additionally, because ASP.NET Web pages may have dozens of users simultaneously, the considerations and benefits of asynchronous programming are different.

Improving Performance with Asynchronous Web Page Programming

In a Windows Forms application, you often use asynchronous programming to allow the application to respond to user input while a long-running process executes. In Web pages, the user can't interact with the page until page rendering is complete, so responding to user input isn't a valid reason for using asynchronous programming.

Instead, you should use asynchronous programming to improve the efficiency of long-running Web pages, even if each page only needs to perform one task at a time. In this case, the Web application becomes much more efficient during busy times when multiple pages are requested simultaneously because the thread pool is used more efficiently.

For example, if you are creating a Web page that must query a network resource (such as a Web service), IIS and ASP.NET can only render a limited number of pages simultaneously. Therefore, the thread pool can become completely consumed, creating a performance bottleneck. Once the thread pool is consumed, your server waits for pages to finish rendering before beginning to process other pages. Even though the server might have available processor cycles, requests are queued. By enabling asynchronous Web page programming, the server can begin rendering more pages simultaneously, improving efficiency and reducing page rendering time.

NOTE   Improving performance with thread pooling

Thread pooling can be tricky. When implementing asynchronous Web pages, use a performance testing tool such as the Web Capacity Analysis Tool or the Web Application Stress Tool to verify that performance improves under heavy load. Often, the overhead introduced by asynchronous programming can offset the benefits. Whether performance improves depends on many aspects of the application and Web server configuration. For more information about stress testing tools, read Microsoft Knowledge Base article 231282 at *http://support.microsoft.com/kb/231282.*

Enabling an Asynchronous Web Page

To enable asynchronous Web page programming, follow these steps:

1. Add the *Async="true"* attribute to the *@ Page* directive, as the following example shows:

    ```
    'VB
    <%@ Page Language="VB" Async="true" AutoEventWireup="false" %>
    ```

    ```
    //C#
    <%@ Page Language="C#" Async="true" AutoEventWireup="true" %>
    ```

2. Create events to start and end your asynchronous code that implements *System.Web.IHttpAsyncHandler.BeingProcessRequest* and *System.Web.IHttpAsyncHandler.EndProcessRequest*. These events must match the following signatures:

    ```
    'VB
    Function BeginGetAsyncData(ByVal src As Object, ByVal args As EventArgs, ByVal cb As
    AsyncCallback, ByVal state As Object) As IAsyncResult
    End Function

    Sub EndGetAsyncData(ByVal ar As IAsyncResult)
    End Sub
    ```

    ```
    //C#
    IAsyncResult BeginGetAsyncData(Object src, EventArgs args, AsyncCallback cb, Object
    state)
      { }

    void EndGetAsyncData(IAsyncResult ar)
      { }
    ```

3. Call the *AddOnPreRenderCompleteAsync* method to declare your event handlers, as demonstrated by the following code:

```
'VB
Dim bh As New BeginEventHandler(AddressOf Me.BeginGetAsyncData)
Dim eh As New EndEventHandler(AddressOf Me.EndGetAsyncData)
Me.AddOnPreRenderCompleteAsync(bh, eh)

//C#
BeginEventHandler bh = new BeginEventHandler(this.BeginGetAsyncData);
EndEventHandler eh = new EndEventHandler(this.EndGetAsyncData);
AddOnPreRenderCompleteAsync(bh, eh);
```

Dynamically Generate Images Using an ASP.NET Handler

Each image in an HTML page requires a separate browser request and a separate response from your Web server. By default, IIS does not pass requests for images to ASP.NET. Instead, IIS simply reads the image file from the file system and sends it directly to the Web browser.

In some cases, you might want to handle requests for images in ASP.NET instead. For example, you might need to dynamically generate a chart displaying performance information over a period of time, or you might want to dynamically create thumbnails in a photo album application. In these circumstances, you have two options:

- Dynamically generate the images in advance and save the images as files on the file system. IIS could then send the images to the user like any other picture file. To ensure the picture is available when requested by the Web browser, the image generation could be done during the request for the ASP.NET page with the embedded images.

- Configure ASP.NET to receive requests for images and generate the images dynamically for each request.

  To configure ASP.NET to receive requests for images, follow these high-level steps:

  1. Write code to dynamically generate the images.

  2. Configure IIS to pass requests for the required image types to ASP.NET.

  3. Configure ASP.NET to process requests for files with the required file extensions.

The sections that follow discuss these steps in more detail.

Dynamically Generating Images

To create a custom *Hypertext Transfer Protocol (HTTP) handler*, you create a class that implements the *IHttpHandler* interface to create a synchronous handler or the *IHttp-AsyncHandler* to create an asynchronous handler. Both handler interfaces require you to implement the *IsReusable* property and the *ProcessRequest* method. The *IsReusable* property specifies whether the *IHttpHandlerFactory* object (the object that actually calls the appropriate handler) can place your handlers in a pool and reuse them to increase performance or whether it must create new instances every time the handler is needed. The *ProcessRequest* method is responsible for actually processing the individual HTTP requests.

The following code demonstrates how to do this:

```vb
'VB
Public Class ImageHandler
    Implements IHttpHandler

    Public ReadOnly Property IsReusable() As Boolean _
            Implements System.Web.IHttpHandler.IsReusable
        Get
            Return False
        End Get
    End Property

    Public Sub ProcessRequest(ByVal context As System.Web.HttpContext) Implements _
            System.Web.IHttpHandler.ProcessRequest
        ' Set the MIME type
        context.Response.ContentType = "image/jpeg"
        ' TODO: Generate the image file using the Graphics namespace
        ' and then use context.Response to transmit the image
    End Sub
End Class
```

```csharp
//C#
public class ImageHandler : IHttpHandler
{
public ImageHandler()
{ }

    public bool IsReusable
    {
        get { return false; }
    }

    public void ProcessRequest(HttpContext context)
    {
        // Set the MIME type
        context.Response.ContentType = "image/jpeg";
```

```
        // TODO: Generate the image file using the Graphics namespace
        // and then use context.Response to transmit the image
    }
}
```

Configuring IIS to Forward Requests to ASP.NET

For performance reasons, IIS only passes requests for specific file types to ASP.NET. For example, IIS passes requests for .aspx, .axd, and .axd to the Aspnet_Isapi.dll file that performs the ASP.NET processing. For all other file types, including .htm, .jpg, and .gif, ASP.NET simply passes the file from the file system directly to the client browser.

Therefore, to handle image requests using ASP.NET, you must configure an IIS application mapping from the image file extension you need to the Aspnet_Isapi.dll file. To configure this, follow these steps:

1. Open the IIS Manager.

2. View the Web site or virtual folder properties.

3. Click the Directory tab, and then click Configuration.

4. On the Mappings tab of the Application Configuration dialog box, click Add.

5. In the Add/Edit Application Extension Mapping dialog box, add an association for the image file extension to the aspnet_isapi.dll file, as shown in Figure 8-1. You can copy the executable path from the .aspx file. Deselect the Check That File Exists check box. Then click OK.

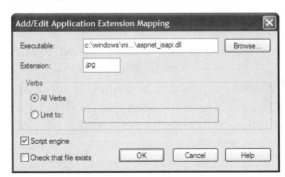

Figure 8-1   Configure an application mapping to process image requests in ASP.NET.

6. Repeat step 5 to add more application extension mappings, if necessary.

7. Click OK twice more to close all open dialog boxes.

Once you configure the application extension mapping, all requests for that file type are forwarded to ASP.NET. To enable normal image processing in most areas of your Web site, create a separate virtual directory just for dynamically generated images.

Configuring ASP.NET to Process Image Requests

After you configure IIS to forward image requests to ASP.NET, you must configure a handler for the file extension in your Web.config file. For each file extension or file name you want to register, create an *<add>* element in the <configuration><system.web><httpHandlers> section of your Web.config file, as the following example demonstrates:

```
<configuration>
    <system.web>
        <httpHandlers>
            <add verb="*" path="*.jpg" type="ImageHandler"/>
            <add verb="*" path="*.gif" type="ImageHandler"/>
        </httpHandlers>
    </system.web>
</configuration>
```

In this example, ASP.NET handles requests for files ending in .jpg or .gif by forwarding them to the *ImageHandler* class. For this to work properly, the *ImageHandler* assembly must be available in the application's Bin folder or the source code must be in the App_Code folder.

Real World

Tony Northrup

Dynamically generating images can be slow. If you plan to dynamically generate images, do performance testing on your Web site to ensure you can keep up with incoming requests. If the same image will be requested repeatedly, store the image file in the Cache object, as described in Chapter 13. In some circumstances, it might be more efficient to generate images using a service or a scheduled console application. On my personal photo album Web application, I pregenerate the most frequently accessed images, and only dynamically generate pictures when users need an unusual resolution.

Lab: Creating a Custom Handler

In this lab, you create a custom image handler to dynamically generate images that are part of ASP.NET Web pages.

▶ **Exercise 1: Create a Custom Image Handler**

In this exercise, you create an ASP.NET Web application that dynamically generates images.

1. Create a new ASP.NET Web application by connecting to a Web server, such as IIS, running on your local computer. Add the application to a new /pictures/ virtual directory. Do not create a file system–based Web site.

2. In Visual Studio, select the Website menu, and then choose Add New Item. In the Add New Item dialog box, click Class, and name the new class **ImageHandler**. Then, click Add. When prompted, choose to place the class in the App_Code folder.

3. Edit the automatically generated class declaration so that it implements the *IHttpHandler* interface, as the following shows:

```
'VB
Public Class HelloWorldHandler
    Implements IHttpHandler

//C#
public class ImageHandler : IHttpHandler
```

4. Use Visual Studio to automatically generate the required *IHttpHandler* members *IsReusable* and *ProcessRequest*.

5. Implement the *IsReusable* property by returning *False*. If you want to enable pooling, you return *True* instead.

```
'VB
Public ReadOnly Property IsReusable() As Boolean _
        Implements System.Web.IHttpHandler.IsReusable
    Get
        Return False
    End Get
End Property

//C#
public bool IsReusable
{
    get { return false; }
}
```

6. Implement the *ProcessRequest* method to return an image file using the *HttpContext.Response* object (passed to the method as a parameter). You can dynamically generate the image using the *System.Drawing* namespace. For simplicity, the following example demonstrates how to transmit an existing file located elsewhere on the file system (you may need to edit the path to a picture that exists on your Web server):

```vb
'VB
Public Sub ProcessRequest(ByVal context As System.Web.HttpContext) Implements _
        System.Web.IHttpHandler.ProcessRequest
    context.Response.ContentType = "image/jpeg"
    context.Response.TransmitFile("C:\Documents and Settings\" & _
        "All Users\Documents\My Pictures\Sample Pictures\blue hills.jpg")
End Sub
```

```csharp
//C#
public void ProcessRequest(HttpContext context)
{
    context.Response.ContentType = "image/jpeg";
    context.Response.TransmitFile(@"C:\Documents and Settings\" +
        @"All Users\Documents\My Pictures\Sample Pictures\blue hills.jpg");
}
```

NOTE Defining the MIME type

Note that this code sample sets the *context.Response.ContentType* property to *"image/jpeg."* You should use this property to define the correct MIME type so that the browser knows how to handle the file you send it. Otherwise, the browser might try to display it as text.

---

7. Add a Web.config file to your application if you do not already have a Web.config file. In Solution Explorer, select your solution. Then, select the Website menu, and choose Add New Item. In the Add New Item dialog box, click Web Configuration File, and then click Add.

8. In your Web.config file, add a handler that maps the .jpg file extension to your *ImageHandler* class. The following code demonstrates this:

```xml
<configuration>
    <system.web>
        <httpHandlers>
            <add verb="*" path="*.jpg" type="ImageHandler"/>
        </httpHandlers>
    </system.web>
</configuration>
```

9. Open Default.aspx in the designer, and drag an *Image* control to the page. Change the *ImageUrl* property to **Test.jpg**. This file does not exist, so nothing is displayed in the designer.

10. On the Web server that is hosting your application, open IIS Manager. Right-click the Pictures virtual directory, and then select Properties.

11. In the Pictures Properties dialog box, on the Directory tab, click the Configuration button. On the Mappings tab, click .Aspx, and then click Edit. Copy the executable path to the clipboard by selecting the text, right-clicking it, and then clicking Copy. Then, click Cancel.

12. In the Pictures Properties dialog box, click Add. Paste the executable path in the Executable text box by right-clicking it and then clicking Paste. In the Extension text box, type **.jpg**. Clear the Check That File Exists check box, and then click OK. Click OK twice more to close all open dialog boxes.

13. Return to Visual Studio and select the Default.aspx page. Press Ctrl+F5 to open the page in a browser. The page displays the dynamically generated image. View the page source to verify that the image file name does not exist on the file system.

Lesson Summary

- You can catch unhandled exceptions at the page level by responding to *Page_Error*, or at the application level by responding to *Application_Error*. In either event handler, you read the last error by calling *Server.GetLastError*. Then, you must remove it from the queue by calling *Server.ClearError*.

- You can use a *System.Configuration.Configuration* to examine and update configuration settings. To create a *Configuration* object, call *WebConfigurationManager.GetSection* and cast the returned object to the section-specific type. If you make an update to the configuration settings, write the changes by calling *Configuration.Save* or *Configuration.SaveAs*.

- Asynchronous Web pages can improve performance in scenarios where the thread pool might be limiting performance. To enable asynchronous pages, first add the *Async="true"* attribute to the @ *Page* directive. Then, create events to start and end your asynchronous code that implement *System.Web.IHttpAsyncHandler.BeingProcessRequest* and *System.Web.IHttpAsyncHandler.EndProcessRequest*. Finally, call the *AddOnPreRenderCompleteAsync* method to declare your event handlers.

■ By default, ASP.NET handles a limited number of file types, including .aspx, .ascx, and .axd. You can configure ASP.NET to handle any file type, which is useful if you need to dynamically generate normally static files, such as images. To configure ASP.NET to receive requests for images, first write code to dynamically generate the images. Then, configure IIS to pass requests for the required image types to ASP.NET. Finally, configure ASP.NET to process requests for files with the required file extensions.

Lesson Review

You can use the following questions to test your knowledge of the information in Lesson 1, "Using Web Site Programmability." The questions are also available on the companion CD if you prefer to review them in electronic form.

NOTE   Answers

Answers to these questions and explanations of why each answer choice is right or wrong are located in the "Answers" section at the end of the book.

---

1. You catch an unhandled exception in a *Page_Error* handler. How can you access the last error?

   A. *Server.GetLastError()*

   B. *Server.ClearError()*

   C. *Request.GetLastError()*

   D. *Application.GetLastError()*

2. Which of the following can you use to catch unhandled exceptions in an application? (Choose all that apply.)

   A. *Response_Error*

   B. *Page_Error*

   C. *Application_Error*

   D. *Server_Error*

3. Which of the following code samples correctly retrieves the current cookie configuration settings?

A. **VB**
```
Dim section As String = WebConfigurationManager.GetSection _
    ("system.web/httpCookies")
```

//C#
```
string section = WebConfigurationManager.GetSection("system.web/httpCookies");
```

B. **VB**
```
Dim section As HttpCookiesSection = _
    WebConfigurationManager.GetSection("httpCookies")
```

//C#
```
HttpCookiesSection section =
    (HttpCookiesSection) WebConfigurationManager.GetSection("httpCookies");
```

C. **VB**
```
Dim section As String = WebConfigurationManager.GetSection("httpCookies")
```

//C#
```
string section = WebConfigurationManager.GetSection("httpCookies");
```

D. **VB**
```
Dim section As HttpCookiesSection = _
    WebConfigurationManager.GetSection("system.web/httpCookies")
```

//C#
```
HttpCookiesSection section = (HttpCookiesSection)
    WebConfigurationManager.GetSection("system.web/httpCookies");
```

4. You need to have ASP.NET dynamically generate Word documents when a Web browser requests a file ending in a .Doc extension. How can you do this?

A. Implement the *IPartitionResolver* interface.

B. Implement the *IHttpModule* interface.

C. Implement the *IHttpHandler* interface.

D. Implement the *IHttpHandlerFactory* interface.

Lesson 2: Using Request Information

ASP.NET exposes a great deal of useful information in page, request, and application context. For example, you can identify the following types of information:

- The user's Internet Protocol (IP) address and browser type
- Any errors that occurred while generating the Web page response
- HTTP information sent by the client

Additionally, you can define or update the following types of information:

- Page title and style sheet
- HTTP headers
- The contents of the response

This lesson discusses the *Page, Browser, Response, Request, Server,* and *Context* objects.

After this lesson, you will be able to:

- Use the *Browser* object to identify client capabilities.
- Use Page and Application context to examine and update information, such as the details of the client request and the communications being sent back to the client.
- Access Web page headers to dynamically define the page title or the style sheet.

Estimated lesson time: 30 minutes

Determining the Browser Type

Though HTML standards exist, not all Web browsers display Web pages in exactly the same way. Additionally, different browsers have different capabilities. Sometimes, this is because two different competing browsers interpret standards differently. Other times, the browser may have restrictions imposed for security reasons or to better suit a mobile device.

To make sure your Web pages are displayed properly, it's important to test Web pages in every type of browser that your users might have. If you primarily rely on ASP.NET controls, you might never run into a problem. ASP.NET controls automatically adapt to different browser types and capabilities and provide the richest user interface possible for a given browser.

> ### Real World
>
> *Tony Northrup*
>
> Many people are very emotionally attached to a specific browser. If your Web application doesn't work properly in a user's browser, you can expect an angry e-mail. When testing different browsers, don't forget to also check different versions of Internet Explorer, including 64-bit versions. Different versions behave differently in some circumstances.

However, if you do run into a problem, it's important to correct it. Whenever possible, adjust your Web page so that a single version of the page renders correctly for all browser types. That might not always be possible. For example, if you want to add an ActiveX control to your Web page, you need to create a separate version of the Web page for clients that do not support ActiveX. This new version can be as simple as a Web page that indicates that ActiveX is required. Alternatively, you might make adjustments to display a functional, but slightly degraded, version of the Web page that the browser can support.

To display different versions of Web pages for different browsers, write code that examines the *Request.Browser HttpBrowserCapabilities* object. *Request.Browser* has many members that you can use to examine individual browser capabilities. Table 8-2 lists the most important *Request.Browser* methods; Table 8-3 lists the most important *Request.Browser* properties.

Table 8-2   *Request.Browser* **Methods**

Method	Description
GetClrVersions	Returns all versions of the .NET Framework common language runtime that are installed on the client.
IsBrowser	Gets a value indicating whether the client browser is the same as the specified browser.

Table 8-3 *Request.Browser* Properties

Property	Description
ActiveXControls	Gets a value indicating whether the browser supports ActiveX controls.
AOL	Gets a value indicating whether the client is an America Online (AOL) browser.
BackgroundSounds	Gets a value indicating whether the browser supports playing background sounds using the *<bgsounds>* HTML element.
Browser	Gets the browser string (if any) that was sent by the browser in the User-Agent request header. Note that some non-Microsoft browsers incorrectly identify themselves as Internet Explorer in order to improve productivity. Therefore, this string is not always accurate.
ClrVersion	Gets the version of the .NET Framework that is installed on the client.
Cookies	Gets a value indicating whether the browser supports cookies.
Crawler	Gets a value indicating whether the browser is a search engine Web crawler.
Frames	Gets a value indicating whether the browser supports HTML frames.
IsColor	Gets a value indicating whether the browser has a color display. *False* indicates that the browser has a grayscale display, which typically indicates a mobile device.
IsMobileDevice	Gets a value indicating whether the browser is a recognized mobile device.
JavaApplets	Gets a value indicating whether the browser supports Java.

Table 8-3 *Request.Browser* Properties

Property	Description
JavaScript	Gets a value indicating whether the browser supports JavaScript.
JScriptVersion	Gets the Jscript version that the browser supports.
MobileDeviceManufacturer	Returns the name of the manufacturer of a mobile device, if known.
MobileDeviceModel	Gets the model name of a mobile device, if known.
MSDomVersion	Gets the version of Microsoft HTML (MSHTML) Document Object Model (DOM) that the browser supports.
Tables	Gets a value indicating whether the browser supports HTML *<table>* elements.
VBScript	Gets a value indicating whether the browser supports Visual Basic Scripting edition (VBScript).
Version	Gets the full version number (integer and decimal) of the browser as a string.
W3CDomVersion	Gets the version of the World Wide Web Consortium (W3C) Extensible Markup Language (XML) Document Object Model (DOM) that the browser supports.
Win16	Gets a value indicating whether the client is a Win16-based computer.
Win32	Gets a value indicating whether the client is a Win32-based computer.

Quick Check

1. Which of the following browser capabilities can you *not* check using *Request.Browser*?

   ❏ Frames support

   ❏ Support for embedded images

   ❏ Tables support

   ❏ Cookies support

   ❏ JavaScript support

2. How can you determine if the client is a robot indexing your site for a search engine?

Quick Check Answers

1. Of the capabilities listed, the only one not provided by *Request.Browser* is support for embedded images.

2. Check *Request.Browser.Crawler*.

The properties exposed by the *Request.Browser* object indicate inherent capabilities of the browser but do not necessarily reflect current browser settings. For example, the *Cookies* property indicates whether a browser inherently supports cookies, but it does not indicate whether the browser that made the request has cookies enabled. People often disable cookies for security reasons, but the *Request.Browser* object still indicates that the browser supports cookies. For this reason, ASP.NET session state can be configured to test the client browser for cookie support.

MORE INFO   ASP.NET session support for cookies

For more information about ASP.NET sessions, refer to Chapter 7, "ASP.NET State Management."

Page and Application Context Overview

ASP.NET provides many objects that allow you to examine almost any detail of the current request and response that are available to the Web server. Table 8-4 lists useful objects that you can use to examine information relating to page and application context. While each of these objects is a member of other objects, they are also available in Visual Studio without providing a complete namespace.

Table 8-4 *Context* Objects

Object	Description
Response	Provides access to the HTTP response sent from the server to the client after receiving an incoming Web request. You can use this class to inject text into the page, to write cookies, and more. You can edit most aspects of the *Response*.
Request	Provides access to information that is part of the current page request as sent from the Web browser, including the request headers, cookies, client certificate, and query string. You can use this class to read what the browser sent to the Web server. These properties cannot be updated.
Server	Exposes utility methods that you can use to transfer control between pages, get information about the most recent error, encode and decode HTML text, and more. Most of the useful *Server* methods are static.
Context	Provides access to the entire current context (including the *Request* object). Most of the methods and properties provided by *Context* are also provided by other more frequently used objects, such as *Request* and *Server*.
Session	Provides information to the current user session. Also provides access to a session-wide cache you can use to store information, along with the means to control how the session is managed. For detailed information about the *Session* object, read Chapter 7.
Application	Provides access to application-wide methods and events for all sessions. Also provides access to an application-wide cache you can use to store information. For detailed information about the *Application* object, read Chapter 7.
Trace	Provides a way to display both system and custom trace diagnostic messages in the HTTP page output. For more information about the *Trace* object, read Chapter 1, "Introducing the ASP.NET 2.0 Web Site."

Response

The *Page.Response* property is an *HttpResponse* object that allows you to add data to the HTTP response being sent back to the client who requested a Web page. The *Response* object includes several useful methods:

- **BinaryWrite**   Writes binary characters to the HTTP response. To write a text string instead, call *Write*.

- **AppendHeader**   Adds an HTTP header to the response stream. You only need to use this if you need to provide a special directive to the Web browser that IIS does not add.

- **Clear**   Removes everything from the HTTP response stream.

- **ClearContent**   Removes the content from the response stream, not including the HTTP headers.

- **ClearHeaders**   Removes the headers from the response stream, not including the content.

- **End**   Completes the response and returns the page to the user.

- **Flush**   Sends the current output to the client without ending the request. This is useful if you want to return a partial page to the user; for example, if you had to perform a time-consuming database query or submit information to a credit card processing service, you could display, "Processing your transaction" using *Response.Write*, call *Response.Flush* to send it immediately to the user, process the transaction, and then display the transaction information when it is ready.

- **Redirect**   Instructs the Web browser to open a different page by returning an HTTP/302 code with the new Uniform Resource Locator (URL). This is an alternative to the *Server.Transfer* method, which causes ASP.NET to process a different page without the Web browser submitting a new request.

- **TransmitFile**   Writes a file to the HTTP response without buffering it.

- **Write**   Writes a file to the HTTP response with buffering.

- **WriteFile**   Instructs the Web browser to open a different page by returning an HTTP/302 code with the new URL. This is an alternative to the *Server.Transfer* method, which causes ASP.NET to process a different page without the Web browser submitting a new request.

- **WriteSubstitution**   Replaces strings in the response. This is useful if you are returning cached output, but you want to dynamically update that cached output. To initiate the replacement, call the *WriteSubstitution* method, passing it the callback method. On the first request to the page, the *WriteSubstitution* calls the *HttpResponseSubstitutionCallback* delegate to produce the output. Then, it adds a substitution buffer to the response, which retains the delegate to call on future requests. Finally, it degrades client-side cacheability from public to server-only, ensuring future requests to the page reinvoke the delegate by not caching on the client. As an alternative to using *WriteSubstituion*, you can use the *Substitution* control. For more information about caching, read Chapter 13.

The *Response* object also includes several useful properties:

- **Cookies** Enables you to add cookies that are sent back to the Web browser. If the Web browser supports cookies, it returns the exact same cookie to you using the *Request* object. For more information about cookies, read Chapter 7.

- **Buffer** If *True*, the response is buffered before sending it back to the user. If *False*, the response is sent back to the user in chunks. Typically, you should buffer the response, unless you are sending back a very large response, or the response will take a long time to generate.

- **Cache** Gets the caching policy of the Web page, such as the expiration time and privacy policy.

- **Expires** The number of minutes after which the browser should stop caching the page. Set this to the time period for which the page will be valid. If the page is constantly updated, set it to a very short period of time. If the page is static and rarely changes, you can increase this time to reduce the number of unnecessary page requests and improve the performance of your server.

- **ExpiresAbsolute** Similar to the *Expires* property, *ExpiresAbsolute* sets an absolute date and time after which the page cache is no longer valid.

- **Status** and **StatusCode** Gets or sets the HTTP status code that indicates whether the response was successful. For example, the status code 200 indicates a successful response, 404 indicates a file not found, and 500 indicates a server error.

Request

The *Page.Request* property is an *HttpRequest* object that allows you to add data to the HTTP response being sent back to the client who requested a Web page. The *Request* object includes several useful methods:

- *MapPath*   Maps the virtual path to a physical path, allowing you to determine where on the file system a virtual path is. For example, this allows you to convert /about.htm to C:\Inetpub\Wwwroot\About.htm.

- *SaveAs*   Saves the request to a file.

- *ValidateInput*   Throws an exception if the user input contains potentially dangerous input, such as HTML input, or input that might be part of a database attack. ASP.NET does this automatically by default, so you only need to manually call this method if you have disabled ASP.NET security features.

The *Request* object also includes several useful properties:

- *ApplicationPath*   Gets the ASP.NET application's virtual application root path on the server.

- *AppRelativeCurrentExecutionFilePath*   Gets the virtual path of the application root and makes it relative by using the tilde (~) notation for the application root (as in ~/page.aspx).

- *Browser*   Allows you to examine details of the browser's capabilities.

- *ClientCertificate*   Gets the client's security certificate, if the client provided one.

- *Cookies*   Enables you to read cookies sent from the Web browser that you have previously provided in a *Response* object. For more information about cookies, read Chapter 7.

- *FilePath*   Gets the virtual path of the current request.

- *Files*   If the client has uploaded files, this gets the collection of files uploaded by the client.

- *Headers*   Gets the collection of HTTP headers.

- *HttpMethod*   Gets the HTTP data transfer method (such as *GET, POST*, or *HEAD*) used by the client.

- *IsAuthenticated*   A Boolean value that is *True* if the client is authenticated.

- *IsLocal*   A Boolean value that is *True* if the client is from the local computer.

- *IsSecureConnection*   A Boolean value that is *True* if the connection uses secure HTTP (HTTPS).

- *LogonUserIdentity*   Gets the *WindowsIdentity* object that represents the current user.

- *Params*   A combined collection that includes the *QueryString*, *Form*, *ServerVariables*, and *Cookies* items. For more information about query strings and cookies, read Chapter 7.
- *Path*   The virtual path of the current request.
- *PhysicalApplicationPath*   The physical path of the application root directory.
- *PhysicalPath*   The physical path of the current request.
- *QueryString*   A collection of query string variables. For more information about query strings, read Chapter 7.
- *RawUrl* and *Url*   The URL of the current request.
- *TotalBytes*   The length of the request.
- *UrlReferrer*   Gets information about the URL of the client's previous request that linked to the current URL. You can use this to determine which page within your site or which external Web site brought the user to the current page.
- *UserAgent*   Gets the user agent string, which describes the browser the user has. Some non-Microsoft browsers indicate that they are Internet Explorer for compatibility.
- *UserHostAddress*   The client's IP address.
- *UserHostName*   The Domain Name System (DNS) name of the remote client.
- *UserLanguages*   A sorted string array of languages the client browser has been configured to prefer. ASP.NET can automatically display the correct language for a user. For more information, read Chapter 10, "Globalization and Accessibility."

Server

The *Page.Server* property is an *HttpServerUtil* object that provides static methods useful for processing URLs, paths, and HTML. The most useful methods are:

- *ClearError*   Clears the last error.
- *GetLastError*   Returns the previous exception, as described in Lesson 1 of this chapter.
- *HtmlDecode*   Removes HTML markup from a string. You should call *HtmlDecode* on user input before displaying it again to remove potentially malicious code.
- *HtmlEncode*   Converts a string to be displayed in a browser. For example, if the string contains a "<" character, *Server.HtmlEncode* convert it to the "&lt" phrase, which the browser displays as a less-than sign rather than treating it as HTML markup.

- *MapPath*   Returns the physical file path that corresponds to the specified virtual path on the Web server.

- *Transfer*   Stops processing the current page and starts processing the specified page. The URL is not changed in the user's browser.

- *UrlDecode*   Decodes a string encoded for HTTP transmission and sent to the server in a URL.

- *UrlEncode*   Encodes a string for reliable HTTP transmission from the Web server to a client through the URL.

- *UrlPathEncode*   URL-encodes the path portion of a URL string and returns the encoded string.

- *UrlTokenDecode*   Decodes a URL string token to its equivalent byte array using base 64 digits.

- *UrlTokenEncode*   Encodes a byte array into its equivalent string representation using base 64 digits suitable for transmission on the URL.

Context

The *Page.Context* property is an *HttpContext* object that provides access to a variety of objects related to the HTTP request and response. Many of these objects are redundant, providing access to *Page* members including *Cache*, *Request*, *Response*, *Server*, and *Session*. However, the *Context* object includes several unique methods:

- *AddError*   Adds an exception to the page, which can later be retrieved by calling *Server.GetLastError()* or cleared by calling *Server.ClearError()* or *Context.Clear-Error()*.

- *ClearError*   Clears the last error, exactly the same way as *Server.ClearError()*.

- *RewritePath*   Assigns an internal rewrite path and allows for the URL that is requested to differ from the internal path to the resource. *RewritePath* is used in cookieless session state to remove the session state value from the path URI.

The *Context* object also includes several unique properties:

- *AllErrors*   A collection of unhandled exceptions that have occurred on the page.

- *IsCustomErrorEnabled*   A Boolean value that is *true* if custom errors are enabled.

- *IsDebuggingEnabled*   A Boolean value that is *true* if debugging is enabled.

- *Timestamp*   The timestamp of the HTTP request.

Accessing Web Page Headers

HTML page header contains information that describes the page, including:

- Style sheet in use
- Page title (which typically appears in the browser title bar and is used when adding an Internet Explorer Favorite)
- Metadata that is used by search engines

With ASP.NET 2.0, you can edit page headers programmatically using the *Page.Header* control. You might use this to set the title of the page dynamically. For example, a Web page that displays a list of search results might contain the search query in the title so that each query can create a unique shortcut when added to Internet Explorer Favorites.

NOTE .NET 2.0

The *Page.Header* object is new with ASP.NET 2.0.

Table 8-5 lists the most important *Page.Header* members.

Table 8-5 *Page.Header* Properties

Property	Description
StyleSheet	The *StyleSheet* object that enables you to call the *CreateStyleRule* and *RegisterStyle* methods.
Title	The title of the page. This is used in the window title bar, in the Favorite name, and by search engines.

To set a page title programmatically, access *Page.Header.Title*, as the following code sample demonstrates:

```
'VB
Page.Header.Title = "Current time: " & DateTime.Now
```

```
//C#
Page.Header.Title = "Current time: " + DateTime.Now;
```

To set style information for the page (using the <head><style> HTML tag), access *Page.Header.StyleSheet*. The following code sample demonstrates how to use the *Page.Header.StyleSheet.CreateStyleRule* method to programmatically set the background color for a page to light gray and the default text color to blue:

```
'VB
' Create a Style object for the body of the page.
Dim bodyStyle As New Style()

bodyStyle.ForeColor = System.Drawing.Color.Blue
bodyStyle.BackColor = System.Drawing.Color.LightGray

' Add the style rule named bodyStyle to the header
' of the current page. The rule is for the body HTML element.
Page.Header.StyleSheet.CreateStyleRule(bodyStyle, Nothing, "body")

//C#
// Create a Style object for the body of the page.
Style bodyStyle = new Style();

bodyStyle.ForeColor = System.Drawing.Color.Blue;
bodyStyle.BackColor = System.Drawing.Color.LightGray;

// Add the style rule named bodyStyle to the header
// of the current page. The rule is for the body HTML element.
Page.Header.StyleSheet.CreateStyleRule(bodyStyle, null, "body");
```

The previous two code samples generate an HTML page with the following header:

```
<head><title>
Current time: 6/30/2006 4:00:05 PM
</title><style type="text/css">
body { color:Blue;background-color:LightGrey; }
</style></head>
```

Note that you only need to access *Page.Header.StyleSheet* if you need to set the style dynamically. Typically, you will set the style for a specific page by using the Visual Studio designer to edit the document's *Style* property with the Style Builder.

Lab: Examine Page and Application Context

In this lab, you update an application to display information about the request, response, and page context.

▶ Exercise 1: Display Page and Application Context

In this exercise, you update a Web page to display information about the current session.

1. Copy the Lesson 2, Exercise 1 Web site from the CD to your local computer in your preferred programming language, or if you're already installed this book's code to your hard disk, choose your prefered programming language. Open the Web site using Visual Studio, and edit the Default.aspx page. This page has a table with a series of Labels that you will use to display information.

2. In the *Page_Load* event handler, write code to display the HTTP status code and description using the *Response* object, as the following code sample demonstrates:

```
'VB
HttpStatusCode.Text = Response.StatusCode & ": " & Response.StatusDescription

//C#
HttpStatusCode.Text = Response.StatusCode + ": " + Response.StatusDescription;
```

3. Next, write code to display the timestamp using the *Context* object, as the following code sample demonstrates:

```
'VB
Timestamp.Text = Context.Timestamp.ToString

//C#
Timestamp.Text = Context.Timestamp.ToString();
```

4. Write code to display the URL referrer if it exists. If this is the user's first request, the *Request.UrlReferrer* object will be null, so you must check to determine if it is null before displaying it. This code sample demonstrates this:

```
'VB
If Not (Request.UrlReferrer Is Nothing) Then
    UrlReferrer.Text = Request.UrlReferrer.ToString
Else
    UrlReferrer.Text = "No referrer"
End If

//C#
if (Request.UrlReferrer != null)
    UrlReferrer.Text = Request.UrlReferrer.ToString();
else
    UrlReferrer.Text = "No referrer";
```

5. Write code to display the user languages. The *Request.UserLanguages* object is a collection of strings, so you must iterate through the strings to display them. The following code sample demonstrates this:

```
'VB
UserLanguages.Text = String.Empty
For Each s As String In Request.UserLanguages
    UserLanguages.Text &= s & "<br>"
Next
```

```
//C#
UserLanguages.Text = String.Empty;
foreach (string s in Request.UserLanguages)
    UserLanguages.Text += s + "<br>";
```

6. Write code to fill in the remaining labels using the *Request* object. You can use *Server.MapPath* to translate the virtual path to the physical path and use *Server.Url-Decode* to display HTTP headers in more readable text. This code sample demonstrates this:

```
'VB
HttpStatusCode.Text = Response.StatusCode & ": " & Response.StatusDescription

Timestamp.Text = Context.Timestamp.ToString

ApplicationPath.Text = Request.ApplicationPath
VirtualPath.Text = Request.FilePath
PhysicalPath.Text = Server.MapPath(Request.FilePath)
HttpHeaders.Text = Server.UrlDecode(Request.Headers.ToString).Replace("&",
"<br>")
HttpMethod.Text = Request.HttpMethod
IsAuthenticated.Text = Request.IsAuthenticated.ToString
IsLocal.Text = Request.IsLocal.ToString
IsSecureConnection.Text = Request.IsSecureConnection.ToString
LogonUserIdentity.Text = Request.LogonUserIdentity.ToString
TotalRequestBytes.Text = Request.TotalBytes.ToString
UserAgent.Text = Request.UserAgent
IpAddress.Text = Request.UserHostAddress

//C#
ApplicationPath.Text = Request.ApplicationPath;
VirtualPath.Text = Request.FilePath;
PhysicalPath.Text = Server.MapPath(Request.FilePath);
HttpHeaders.Text = Server.UrlDecode(Request.Headers.ToString()).Replace("&",
"<br>");
HttpMethod.Text = Request.HttpMethod;
IsAuthenticated.Text = Request.IsAuthenticated.ToString();
IsLocal.Text = Request.IsLocal.ToString();
IsSecureConnection.Text = Request.IsSecureConnection.ToString();
LogonUserIdentity.Text = Request.LogonUserIdentity.ToString();
TotalRequestBytes.Text = Request.TotalBytes.ToString();
UserAgent.Text = Request.UserAgent;
IpAddress.Text = Request.UserHostAddress;
```

7. Run the application and examine the values displayed. Next, run the application from a different computer with a different Web browser and notice how the values change. Think about how this information can be useful in real-world applications.

Lesson Summary

- You can use the *Browser* object to determine the client Web browser type and whether it supports cookies, ActiveX, JavaScript, and other capabilities that may affect its ability to render your Web pages correctly.

- You can use the *Request* object to examine details of the client Web browser's request to the Web server, including the request headers, cookies, the client certificate, query string, and more. You can use the *Response* object to send data directly to the client without using standard ASP.NET server controls. You can use the *Server* object's static methods to perform processing of HTML and URL data. The *Context* object provides several unique methods for adding errors and enabling debugging.

- Use the *Page.Header.StyleSheet* object to dynamically set the page's style sheet (including information such as the background color), and use the *Page.Header.Title* object to dynamically set the page title.

Lesson Review

You can use the following questions to test your knowledge of the information in Lesson 2, "Using Request Information." The questions are also available on the companion CD if you prefer to review them in electronic form.

NOTE Answers

Answers to these questions and explanations of why each answer choice is right or wrong are located in the "Answers" section at the end of the book.

---

1. Which of the following can you determine from the *Request.Browser* object? (Choose all that apply.)

   A. Whether the client has the .NET Framework CLR installed

   B. Whether the user is logged on as an administrator

   C. The user's e-mail address

   D. Whether the browser supports ActiveX

   E. Whether the browser supports JavaScript

2. You have created an ASP.NET search page and want to set the page title to "Search results: *<Query>*". How can you dynamically set the page title?

    A. *Page.Title*

    B. *Page.Header.Title*

    C. *Response.Header.Title*

    D. *Response.Title*

3. Which of the following *Response* methods causes ASP.NET to send the current response to the browser while allowing you to add to the response later?

    A. *Flush*

    B. *Clear*

    C. *End*

    D. *ClearContent*

Chapter Review

To further practice and reinforce the skills you learned in this chapter, you can perform the following tasks:

- Review the chapter summary.
- Review the list of key terms introduced in this chapter.
- Complete the case scenarios. These scenarios set up real-world situations involving the topics of this chapter and ask you to create solutions.
- Complete the suggested practices.
- Take a practice test.

Chapter Summary

- You can catch unhandled exceptions at the page level by responding to *Page_Error*, or at the application level by responding to *Application_Error*.
- If you need to view or change configuration settings, use *System.Configuration.Configuration* to examine and update configuration settings.
- Use asynchronous Web pages to improve performance in scenarios where the thread pool might be limiting performance.
- If you need to generate custom file types using ASP.NET, add an ASP.NET handler by inheriting from *IHttpHandler*, configuring the handler in your application's Web.config file, and configuring IIS to forward the requests for the appropriate file extension to ASP.NET.
- Use the *Browser* object to determine the client Web browser type and whether it supports cookies, ActiveX, JavaScript, and other capabilities.
- Use the *Request* object to examine details of the client Web browser's request to the Web server, including the request headers, cookies, the client certificate, query string, and more.
- Use the *Response* object to send data directly to the client, without using standard ASP.NET server controls.
- Use the *Server* object's static methods to perform processing of HTML and URL data.

- The *Context* object provides several unique methods for adding errors and enabling debugging.
- Use the *Page.Header* object to dynamically set the page's style sheet and title.

Key Terms

Do you know what these key terms mean? You can check your answers by looking up the terms in the glossary at the end of the book.

- asynchronous
- HTTP handler

Case Scenarios

In the following case scenarios, you will apply what you've learned about how to implement and apply serialization, as well as how to upgrade applications that make use of serialization. You can find answers to these questions in the "Answers" section at the end of this book.

Case Scenario 1: Dynamically Generating Charts

You are an application developer for Fabrikam, Inc., a financial services company. You have been asked to write an ASP.NET 2.0 application that enables users with Web browsers to view financial data graphically. For example, users should be able to visit the Web site to view a Web page displaying line charts comparing several different stock prices, or to view a comparison of home sales and mortgage rates.

Questions

Answer the following questions for your manager.

1. I'd like to display the charts as .gif images. How can you generate the charts?
2. The charts need to be dynamically generated. How can you display a dynamically generated .gif file in an ASP.NET Web page? What steps would you need to take to configure that?

Case Scenario 2: Dynamically Adjusting Pages Based on Browser Capabilities

You are an application developer for Fabrikam, Inc., a financial services company. The application you created in the previous scenario has been very successful. However, the IT group has received several user requests for improvements to your application. Users have requested:

- An ActiveX chart that enables users to adjust the scale dynamically.
- Scaled-down images for mobile clients.
- More contrast for charts created for grayscale clients.

Questions

Answer the following questions for your manager.

1. What specific property can you examine to determine whether the client supports ActiveX?

2. What property can you examine to determine whether the browser is running on a mobile client?

3. What property can you examine to determine whether the browser supports color or uses monochrome only?

Suggested Practices

To successfully master the Program a Web Application, Write an ASP.NET Handler to Generate Images Dynamically for Display on a Web Page, and Add and Configure Web Server Controls exam objectives, complete the following tasks.

Program a Web Application

For this task, you should complete all six practices.

- **Practice 1** Download and install a non-Microsoft Web browser. Then, use the browser to open the last several Web applications you have created. Note how different ASP.NET controls behave when viewed with different browsers. In particular, notice how Web Parts behave differently. Web Parts are described in Chapter 9, "Customizing and Personalizing a Web Application."

- **Practice 2** If you have a production ASP.NET Web site available, add code that creates a log of browser types and capabilities for each new user. Examine the variety of browsers and capabilities in your user base and think about how you might adjust your Web application to provide a better experience for all types of browsers.

■ **Practice 3**   Download one or two non-Microsoft browsers. Use those browsers to visit different Web sites and compare them side by side with Internet Explorer. Note how some Web sites display pages differently.

■ **Practice 4**   Using the last production ASP.NET Web site you created, add application-level error-handling to catch unhandled exceptions. Log exceptions to a file or database and let the application run for several days. Make note of whether any unhandled exceptions are occurring without your knowledge.

■ **Practice 5**   Create a synchronous ASP.NET Web page that displays the output from a Web service located on a different server. Test the performance of the Web page when 10 requests are issued simultaneously. Then rewrite the Web page to be asynchronous. Retest the Web page and note whether performance changes.

■ **Practice 6**   Deploy the ASP.NET Web page from the previous practice to both a Microsoft Windows 2000 Server computer running IIS 5.0 and a Microsoft Windows Server 2003 computer running IIS 6.0. Test the performance of both the synchronous and asynchronous versions of the page on the different operating systems and note how the different platforms perform.

Add and Configure Web Server Controls

For this task, you should complete both Practices 1 and 2.

■ **Practice 1**   Create a Web page that enables you to browse and edit the Web application's settings.

■ **Practice 2**   Create a Web setup project that prompts the user for input and configures the application's configuration file based on that user input.

Write an ASP.NET Handler to Generate Images Dynamically for Display on a Web Page

For this task, you should complete the practice to gain experience using HTTP handlers.

- **Practice 1**   Create an application that enables you to browse pictures on the Web server's local file system and view the pictures at different resolutions. Within the ASP.NET page's HTML, reference the images using query parameters that specify the file names and resolutions. Generate the pictures dynamically. Use the Trace.axd file to identify how long the Web server takes to resize images. Use the *Cache* object to improve the performance of files as they are retrieved.

Take a Practice Test

The practice tests on this book's companion CD offer many options. For example, you can test yourself on just the content covered in this chapter, or you can test yourself on all the 70-528 certification exam content. You can set up the test so that it closely simulates the experience of taking a certification exam, or you can set it up in study mode so that you can look at the correct answers and explanations after you answer each question.

MORE INFO   Practice tests

For details about all the practice test options available, see "How to Use the Practice Tests" in this book's Introduction.

Chapter 9
Customizing and Personalizing a Web Application

Modern Web applications are flexible, customizable, and personalized for individual users. You've probably seen personalized consumer Web sites, such as portal and news sites, where users can choose what types of content they want to see and even control the layout of Web pages. However, business applications are also moving in the direction of giving users the ability to customize how they view data and to see more of the information they care about most.

This chapter discusses four ways to provide customizable, personalized Web applications: master pages, themes, user profiles, and Web Parts.

Exam objectives in this chapter:
- Implement a consistent page design by using master pages.
  - ❏ Create a master page.
  - ❏ Add a ContentPlaceHolder control to a master page.
  - ❏ Specify default content for a ContentPlaceHolder.
  - ❏ Reference external resources in a master page.
  - ❏ Define the content of a particular page in a content page.
  - ❏ Create a content page.
  - ❏ Add content to a content page.
  - ❏ Reference a master page member from a content page.
  - ❏ Handle events when using master pages.
  - ❏ Create a nested master page.
  - ❏ Change master pages dynamically.
- Customize a Web page by using themes and user profiles.
  - ❏ Apply a theme declaratively.
  - ❏ Apply a theme programmatically.

❑ Apply a user-selected theme programmatically.

❑ Define custom themes.

❑ Define the appearance of a control by using skins.

❑ Enable users to personalize an application by using Web Parts.

❑ Track and store user-specific information by using user profiles.

❑ Personalize a Web page by dynamically adding or removing child controls in a Placeholder control at run time.

■ Implement Web Parts in a Web application.

❑ Track and coordinate all Web Parts controls on a page by adding a Web-PartManager control.

❑ Connect Web Parts to each other by using connection objects.

❑ Divide a page that uses Web Parts into zones by using WebPartZones.

❑ Present a list of available Web Parts controls to users by using CatalogPart controls.

❑ Enable users to edit and personalize Web Parts controls on a page by using EditorPart controls.

Lessons in this chapter:

Before You Begin

To complete the lessons in this chapter, you should be familiar with Microsoft Visual Basic or C# and be comfortable with the following tasks:

■ Have Microsoft Windows XP and Microsoft Visual Studio 2005 installed with SQL Server 2005 Express Edition and Internet Information Services (IIS).

■ Be familiar with the Visual Studio 2005 Integrated Development Environment (IDE).

■ Have a basic understanding of Hypertext Markup Language (HTML) and client-side scripting.

Real World

Tony Northrup

In the early '90s, having any Web site at all was an accomplishment, and all it took to impress people was an animated GIF. Near the mid-1990s, developers started adding simple scripting to create static Web sites that incorporated a few dynamic Web components, such as e-mail forms.

Over time, the Web development community has continued to raise the bar. Today, almost all Web pages incorporate some dynamic content. Almost all e-commerce and other business Web sites enable users to identify themselves to get permissions to view personalized versions of the Web site and to maintain their own accounts.

Creating a large personalized Web site like this would have been next-to-impossible with the Perl scripts most of us used in the early to mid-1990s. Today, with the .NET Framework, you can build dynamic, personalized Web sites with very little code. The Web sites are not only easier to create, but are more secure, reliable, and manageable. That means that, unlike some of the Perl scripts I wrote in the '90s, I probably won't have script kiddies hacking my site just for the fun of it.

Lesson 1: Using Master Pages

Many developers tend to focus primarily on functionality, not aesthetics. As a result, complex Web applications with dozens of pages can be both ugly and inconsistent. After all, if you discover a better way to provide site navigation while developing the thirteenth Web page in an application, you might not take the time to go back and adjust the first twelve pages.

ASP.NET master pages solve this problem by allowing you to create a consistent layout for all pages in your application. A single master page defines the look, feel, and standard behavior that you want for all pages (or a group of pages) in your application. You can then create individual content pages that contain just the information you want to fit into the template provided by the master page. When users request the content pages, ASP.NET merges the content with the master page.

This lesson describes how to create and use master pages and content pages.

Real World

Tony Northrup

All Web sites require consistency. Before master pages were available, I used to create custom controls for every component that would be repeated throughout a Web site, including the logo, the navigation bar, and the page footer. This way, if I needed to change an aspect of one of the common components, I could make the change in one place and have it reflected throughout the site.

That worked great unless I wanted to add or remove a component, or change the layout of the components. Then I'd have to go into every single Web page and make the change. After that, I'd have to test every Web page to make sure I hadn't made any mistakes.

Now master pages allow me to make centralized changes to the entire site by editing one file. It speeds up the development of content pages, too, because I don't have to worry about copying and pasting the structure for the shared controls.

After this lesson, you will be able to:

- Explain the purpose of master and content pages.
- Describe the process of creating master and content pages.
- Use different techniques for attaching content to a master page.
- Reference controls and properties on a master page from a content page.
- Explain how event handling works in master pages.
- Create nested master pages.
- Programmatically switch between master pages to provide user-selected templates.

Estimated lesson time: 45 minutes

Overview of Master and Content Pages

Master pages consist of two separate parts:

- **Master page** An ASP.NET file with a .master file extension. A *master page* contains a layout that includes text, HTML, and server controls. Instead of an "@ Page" directive, it contains an "@ Master" directive. The master page contains all top-level HTML elements for a page, including *<html>*, *<head>*, and *<form>*. A master page typically includes the page structure (usually an HTML table), company name and logo, and site navigation. To enable pages to insert content, a master page contains one or more *ContentPlaceHolder* controls. A master page inherits from the *MasterPage* class.

- **Content page** A *content page* defines the *ContentPlaceHolder* controls in a master page, essentially filling in the blanks. A content page is a standard .aspx file and is bound to the master page using the *MasterPageFile* attribute in the "@ Page" directive.

Figure 9-1 illustrates how master pages and content pages work together.

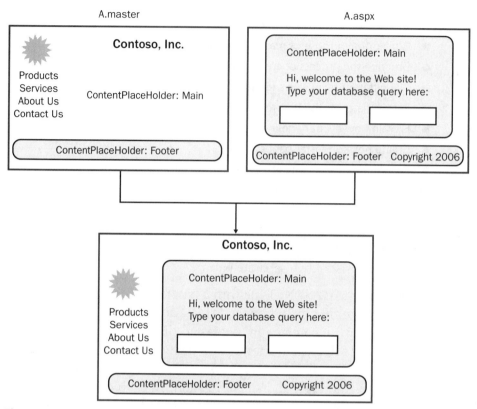

Figure 9-1 Master pages define a structure, and content pages fill in the blanks.

The following demonstrates a master page with two *ContentPlaceHolder* controls:

```
'VB
<% @ Master Language="VB" %>
<html>
<head runat="server">
  <title>Master page title</title>
</head>
<body>
  <form id="form1" runat="server">
    <table>
      <tr>
        <td><asp:contentplaceholder id="Main" runat="server" /></td>
        <td><asp:contentplaceholder id="Footer" runat="server" /></td>
      </tr>
    </table>
  </form>
</body>
</html>
```

```
//C#
<%@ Master Language="C#" %>
<html>
<head runat="server">
  <title>Master page title</title>
</head>
<body>
  <form id="form1" runat="server">
    <table>
      <tr>
        <td><asp:contentplaceholder id="Main" runat="server" /></td>
        <td><asp:contentplaceholder id="Footer" runat="server" /></td>
      </tr>
    </table>
  </form>
</body>
</html>
```

The following demonstrates a content page. Note that all text and controls must be within a *Content* control, or the page generates an error. Otherwise, the page behaves exactly like a standard ASP.NET page. Note the "@ Page" directive and *MasterPageFile* attribute.

```
'VB
<% @ Page Language="VB" MasterPageFile="~/Master.master" Title="Content Page 1" %>
<asp:Content ID="Content1" ContentPlaceHolderID="Main" Runat="Server">
    Main content.
</asp:Content>

<asp:Content ID="Content2" ContentPlaceHolderID="Footer" Runat="Server" >
    Footer content.
</asp:content>
```

```
//C#
<% @ Page Language="C#" MasterPageFile="~/Master.master" Title="Content Page 1" %>
<asp:Content ID="Content1" ContentPlaceHolderID="Main" Runat="Server">
    Main content.
</asp:Content>

<asp:Content ID="Content2" ContentPlaceHolderID="Footer" Runat="Server" >
    Footer content.
</asp:content>
```

Master pages provide functionality that developers have traditionally created by:

- Copying and pasting existing code, text, and control elements repeatedly.
- Using framesets.
- Using include files for common elements.
- Using ASP.NET user controls.

Advantages of master pages include the following:

- They allow you to centralize the common functionality of your pages so that you can make updates in just one place.

- They make it easy to create one set of controls and code and apply the results to a set of pages. For example, you can use controls on the master page to create a menu that applies to all pages.

- They give you fine-grained control over the layout of the final pages by allowing you to control how the placeholder controls are rendered.

- They provide object models that allow you to customize the master pages from individual content pages.

At run time, master pages are handled in the following sequence:

1. A user requests a page by typing the URL of the content page.

2. When the page is fetched, the "@ Page" directive is read. If the directive references a master page, the master page is read as well. If this is the first time the pages have been requested, both pages are compiled.

3. The master page with the updated content is merged into the control tree of the content page.

4. The content of individual *Content* controls is merged into the corresponding *ContentPlaceHolder* control in the master page.

5. The resulting merged page is rendered to the browser as a single page.

In general, the master page structure has no effect on how you construct your pages or program them. However, in some cases, if you set a page-wide property on the master page, it can affect the behavior of the content page, because the master page is the closest parent for the controls on the page. For example, if you set the *Enable-ViewState* property on the content page to *true* but set the same property to *false* in the master page, view state is effectively disabled because the setting on the master page takes priority.

The Process of Creating Master and Content Pages

At a high level, you will follow this process to create master and content pages with Visual Studio 2005:

1. Add a master page to your Web site with a .master extension.

2. To the master page, add layout tables, graphics, copyright information, and other content that should appear on multiple pages. Then add one or more *ContentPlaceHolder* controls where pages can add unique content.

3. Add a Web form to the Web site with an .aspx extension. Select the Select Master Page check box when creating the page and select your master page.

4. To the content page, add text, graphics, and controls to each *Content* control to map to the *ContentPlaceHolder* controls in the master page.

At the hands-on level, creating content is just as straightforward. In fact, you can create master and content pages without writing a single line of code. Exercise 1 of this lesson's lab walks you through the process step by step.

Quick Check

1. Which control must you have on a master page?
2. Which control must you have on a content page?

Quick Check Answers

1. You must have the *ContentPlaceHolder* control on a master page.
2. You must have the *Content* control, which is inserted into a *ContentPlaceHolder* control, on a content page.

Techniques for Attaching Content Pages to a Master Page

You can attach content pages to a master page at three levels:

- **At the page level** You can use a page directive in each content page to bind it to a master page, as in the following code example:

```
'VB
<%@ Page Language="VB" MasterPageFile="MySite.Master" %>
```

```
//C#
<%@ Page Language="C#" MasterPageFile="MySite.Master" %>
```

- **At the application level** By making a setting in the *<pages>* element of the application's configuration file (Web.config), you can specify that all ASP.NET pages (.aspx files) in the application automatically bind to a master page. If you use this strategy, all ASP.NET pages in the application that have *Content* controls are merged with the specified master page. (If an ASP.NET page does not contain

Content controls, the master page is not applied.) The element might look like the following:

```
<pages masterPageFile="MySite.Master" />
```

- **At the folder level** This strategy is like binding at the application level, except that you make the setting in a Web.config file in one folder only. The master-page bindings then apply to the ASP.NET pages in that folder.

Referencing Master Page Properties and Controls from Content Pages

Ideally, content pages depend upon the master page to define any application-specific settings. For example, if your master page has your company name in the upper-left corner, content pages read the company name from a master page property rather than having the company name hard-coded into every content page.

To reference master page properties from a content page, follow this process:

1. Create the property in the master page.
2. Add the "@ MasterType" declaration to the .aspx content page.
3. Reference the property from the content page using *Master.Property_Name*.

The sections that follow describe this process in more detail.

Creating a Property in the Master Page

Content pages can reference any public property declared in the master page class. For example, in the following code sample from a master page code-behind file, content pages can access both the address and the company name:

```vb
'VB
Public Address As String = "123 Anywhere"
Public Property CompanyName() As String
    Get
        Return CType(ViewState("CompanyName"), String)
    End Get
    Set(ByVal value As String)
        ViewState("CompanyName") = value
    End Set
End Property
```

```csharp
//C#
public String Address = "123 Anywhere";
public String CompanyName
{
```

```
    get { return (String)ViewState["companyName"]; }
    set { ViewState["companyName"] = value; }
}
```

NOTE **Avoid hard-coding information**

This example uses hard-coded variables to illustrate how to declare properties. Typically, properties such as company name and address should be defined in the application configuration.

Adding an "@ MasterType" Declaration in a Content Page

Before you can reference master properties in a content page, you must add the "@ MasterType" declaration to the .aspx content page below the "@ Page" declaration, as the following demonstrates:

```
'VB
<%@ Page Language="VB" MasterPageFile="~/Master1.Master" CodeFile="Home.aspx.vb"
Inherits="Home" Title="Contoso Home Page" %>
<%@ MasterType virtualpath="~/Master1.master" %>
```

```
//C#
<%@ Page Language="C#" MasterPageFile="~/Master1.Master" CodeFile="Home.aspx.cs"
Inherits="Home" Title="Contoso Home Page" %>
<%@ MasterType virtualpath="~/Master1.master" %>
```

You are now ready to reference master properties. However, the Visual Studio 2005 development environment might not recognize the property names until you save the Web page.

If you are creating multiple master pages that might be referenced by the same set of content pages, you should derive all master pages from a single base class. Then specify the base class name in the "@ MasterType" declaration. This enables the content page to reference the same properties regardless of which master page is being used.

Referencing Master Properties

Once you add the "@ MasterType" declaration, you can reference properties in the master page using the *Master* class. For example, the following code defines a Label control named *CompanyName* using the *CompanyName* public property defined in the master page:

```
'VB
CompanyName.Text = Master.CompanyName
```

```
//C#
CompanyName.Text = Master.CompanyName;
```

If you later change the master page associated with a content page, make sure you implement the same public properties to ensure the content pages continue to function correctly.

Referencing Controls in the Master Page

Besides properties, you can also reference and update controls in the master page from a content page by calling the *Master.FindControl* method and supplying the control name. *Master.FindControl* returns a *Control* object, which you need to cast to the correct type to create a new object. You can then read or update the object as if it were local.

The following code (which belongs in the *Page_Load* method of the content page) demonstrates this by updating a *Label* control in the master page named *Brand*:

```VB
'VB
Dim _Brand As Label = CType(Master.FindControl("Brand"), Label)
_Brand.Text = "Fabrikam"
```

```C#
//C#
Label _Brand = (Label)Master.FindControl("Brand");
_Brand.Text = "Fabrikam";
```

Use this technique any time a content page needs to customize information in a master page.

Handling Events When Working with Master Pages

Responding to events is only slightly more complicated when using master pages than when using standard ASP.NET pages, because events can occur in either the master page or a content page. Typically, however, responding to these events is intuitive.

Respond to control events, such as *Button_Click*, in the page containing the control. If the control is in the master page, add the code to respond to the control event in the master page. If the control is in the content page, add the code to respond to the control event in the control page.

When responding to page events, the sequence of events in the master and content page can be significant. The following is the sequence in which events occur when a master page is merged with a content page:

1. Master page controls *Init* event.
2. Content controls *Init* event.

3. Master page *Init* event.

4. Content page *Init* event.

5. Content page *Load* event.

6. Master page *Load* event.

7. Content controls *Load* event.

8. Content page *PreRender* event.

9. Master page *PreRender* event.

10. Master page controls *PreRender* event.

11. Content controls *PreRender* event.

Creating a Nested Master Page

Master pages can be nested, with one master page referencing another as its master. Nested master pages allow you to create componentized master pages. For example, a large site might contain an overall master page that defines the look of the site. Different site content partners can then define their own child master pages that reference the site master and that, in turn, define the look for that partner's content.

A child master page has the file name extension .master, as with any master page. However, the child master page also has a master attribute in the "@ Master" declaration. The following example demonstrates a child master page whose parent master page is named "Parent.master":

```
'VB
<%@ Master Language="VB" master="Parent.master"%>
<asp:Content id="Content1" ContentPlaceholderID="MainContent" runat="server">
   <asp:panel runat="server" id="panelMain" backcolor="lightyellow">
   <h2>Child master</h2>
     <asp:panel runat="server" id="panel1" backcolor="lightblue">
       <p>This is childmaster content.</p>
       <asp:ContentPlaceHolder ID="Content1" runat="server" />
     </asp:panel>
     <asp:panel runat="server" id="panel2" backcolor="pink">
       <p>This is childmaster content.</p>
       <asp:ContentPlaceHolder ID="Content2" runat="server" />
     </asp:panel>
   </asp:panel>
</asp:Content>
```

```
//C#
<%@ Master Language="C#" master="Parent.master"%>
<asp:Content id="Content1" ContentPlaceholderID="MainContent" runat="server">
```

```
    <asp:panel runat="server" id="panelMain" backcolor="lightyellow">
    <h2>Child master</h2>
      <asp:panel runat="server" id="panel1" backcolor="lightblue">
        <p>This is child master content.</p>
        <asp:ContentPlaceHolder ID="Content1" runat="server" />
      </asp:panel>
      <asp:panel runat="server" id="panel2" backcolor="pink">
        <p>This is child master content.</p>
        <asp:ContentPlaceHolder ID="Content2" runat="server" />
      </asp:panel>
    </asp:panel>
</asp:Content>
```

The child master page typically contains content controls that are mapped to content placeholders on the parent master page. In this respect, the child master page is laid out like any content page. However, the child master page also has content placeholders of its own to display content supplied by its own child pages.

Dynamically Changing Master Pages

You define the master page in a content page's "@ Page" declaration, but that doesn't mean you can't switch to a different master page programmatically. Changing master pages allows you to provide different templates for different users. For example, you might give users a choice of different colors and styles. You could also use different master pages to format data for different browsers or different mobile devices.

MORE INFO Mobile devices

For more information about creating Web pages for mobile devices, read Chapter 12, "Creating ASP.NET Mobile Web Applications."

To dynamically change master pages, follow these high-level steps:

1. Create two or more master pages with the same *ContentPlaceHolder* controls and public properties. Typically, you create one master page, copy it to create the second master page, and make any modifications necessary. Note that, from this point forward, you must make any changes to the *ContentPlaceHolder* controls or public properties to all master pages to ensure compatibility.

2. Optionally, provide a way for users to switch between master pages. If the master page should be the user's choice (for example, if color and layout are the primary differences), add links to your master pages to enable users to switch between pages. You need to define the current master page within the content page, however, so store the setting in the *Session* variable or in another object that is

accessible to both the master and content pages. For example, this code can be called from a link or button on the master page to set a *Session* variable to the name of a different master page. After you define the master page within the content page, reload the page:

```vb
'VB
Session("masterpage") = "Master2.master"
Response.Redirect(Request.Url.ToString)
```

```csharp
//C#
Session["masterpage"] = "Master2.master";
Response.Redirect(Request.Url.ToString());
```

3. Define the master page in the content page's *Page_PreInit* method. *Page_PreInit* is the last opportunity you have to override the default master page setting, because later handlers (such as *Page_Init*) reference the master page. For example, this code defines the master page based on the *Session* object:

```vb
'VB
Sub Page_PreInit(ByVal sender As Object, ByVal e As EventArgs)
    If Not (Session("masterpage") Is Nothing) Then
        MasterPageFile = CType(Session("masterpage"), String)
    End If
End Sub
```

```csharp
//C#
void Page_PreInit(Object sender, EventArgs e)
{
    if (Session["masterpage"] != null)
        MasterPageFile = (String)Session["masterpage"];
}
```

Exercise 2 in this lesson's lab walks you through this process step by step.

Lab: Using Master and Child Pages

In this lab, you create multiple master and child pages.

▶ **Exercise 1: Create master pages and a child page**

In this exercise, you create a new ASP.NET Web site with two master pages and a child page.

1. Create a new ASP.NET Web site named MasterContent in either C# or Visual Basic using Visual Studio 2005.

2. Add a new Master Page to your Web site named Professional.master.

3. In the design view for Professional.master, add a Label named CompanyName with a large font and the phrase **Contoso, Inc.** Then add a Label named Welcome with the phrase **Welcome, visitor!** Figure 9-2 demonstrates this.

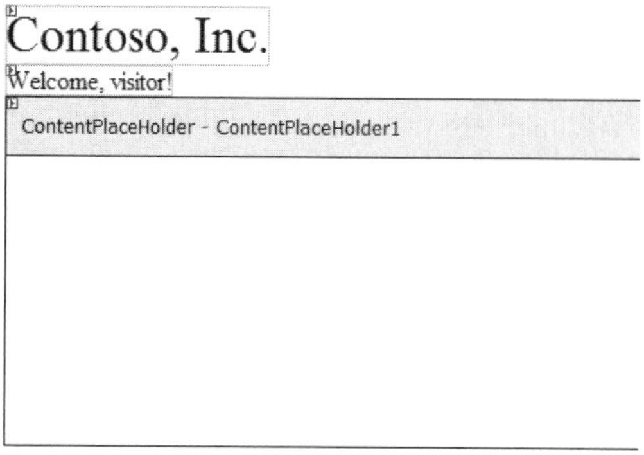

Figure 9-2   Create a sample master page.

4. Repeat the previous step to create an identical page named Colorful.master. Add *Label* controls with the same names. Then set the page background color and the font colors to your favorite colors.

5. Add a new Web Form to your Web site named Home.aspx. In the Add New Item dialog box, select the Select Master Page check box. In the Select A Master Page dialog box, select Professional.master.

6. To Home.aspx, add a TextBox named UserName, a DropDownList named Template, and a Button named Submit. Add two items to the DropDownList: Professional and Colorful. Optionally, add labels to improve the appearance of the form. Figure 9-3 demonstrates this.

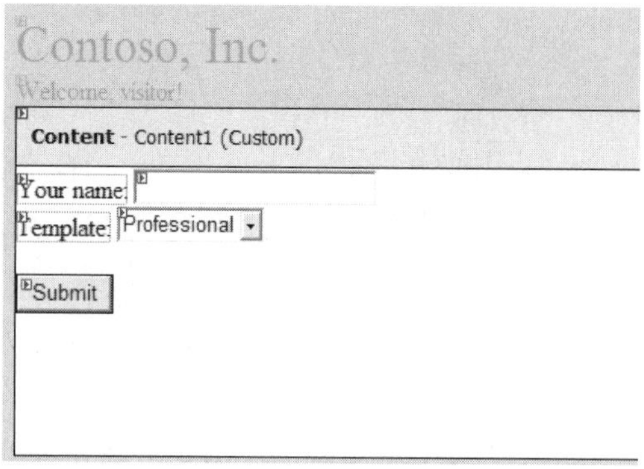

Figure 9-3   Create a sample content page.

7. Build your project and open the resulting Home.aspx page in a browser. Verify that it displays correctly, as shown in Figure 9-4. None of the controls do anything yet, however.

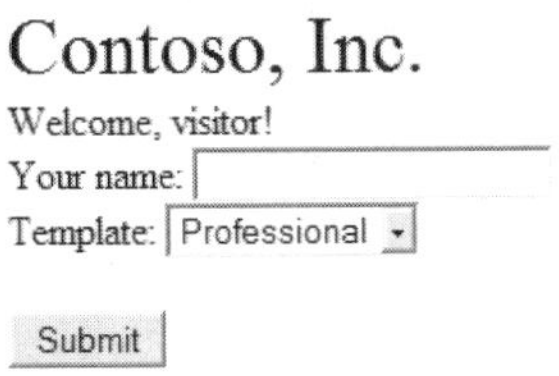

Contoso, Inc.

Welcome, visitor!

Your name: [   ]

Template: [Professional ▾]

[Submit]

Figure 9-4   Verifying that the content page displays within the default master page.

As this exercise demonstrated, master and content pages can be created in just a few minutes without writing any code.

▶ **Exercise 2: Modify Master Page Properties and Switch Master Pages**

In this exercise, you add functionality to a child page to change controls on a master page and to switch between two different master pages.

1. Continue working with the project you created in Exercise 1.

2. Double-click the Submit button to open the button's event handler.

3. In the *Submit_Click* method, add code that determines whether the user provided a value in the UserName text box. If the user did, use the name he or she typed to define a *Session* variable named *UserName*, and change the welcome message in the master page to read **Welcome, user_name!** The following code demonstrates this:

```vb
'VB
If Not (UserName.Text Is Nothing) Then
    Session("UserName") = UserName.Text
    Dim _Welcome As Label = CType(Master.FindControl("Welcome"), Label)
    _Welcome.Text = "Welcome, " + UserName.Text + "!"
End If
```

```csharp
//C#
if (UserName.Text != null)
{
    Session["UserName"] = UserName.Text;
    Label _Welcome = (Label)Master.FindControl("Welcome");
    _Welcome.Text = "Welcome, " + Session["UserName"] + "!";
}
```

4. Build your project and open the Home.aspx page. In the *UserName* text box, type your name, and then click the Submit button. Verify that the page successfully changes the *UserName* label in the master page. While this works now, it only

works within the Home.aspx content page. If a user loads a different page, the welcome message reverts to "Welcome, visitor!"

5. If you are using Visual Basic, edit the Home.aspx "@ Page" declaration to set the *AutoEventWireup* attribute to *true*. This is set to *true* by default in C#. Then create a *Page_Load* method in the code-behind file. This demonstrates the proper "@ Page" declaration:

```
<%@ Page Language="VB" MasterPageFile="~/Professional.master" AutoEventWireup="true"
CodeFile="Home.aspx.vb" Inherits="Home" title="Untitled Page" %>
```

6. Within the *Page_Load* method, check to see if there is a *Session* variable named *UserName*. If there is, change the welcome message in the master page to read **Welcome, *user_name*!** The following code demonstrates this:

```
'VB
Protected Sub Page_PreInit()
    If Not (Session("UserName") Is Nothing) Then
        Dim _Welcome As Label = CType(Master.FindControl("Welcome"), Label)
        _Welcome.Text = "Welcome, " + Session("UserName") + "!"
    End If
End Sub
```

```
//C#
protected void Page_PreInit()
{
    if (Session["UserName"] != null)
    {
        Label _Welcome = (Label)Master.FindControl("Welcome");
        _Welcome.Text = "Welcome, " + Session["UserName"] + "!";
    }
}
```

7. Build your application, and then open the Home.aspx page. In the UserName text box, type your name, and then click the Submit button. The page should change to show the name you typed. Browse to a different page, and then return to Home.aspx to verify that the user name is being retrieved from the *Session* object, and not *ViewState*.

8. In the Home.aspx design view, double-click the Template drop-down list. In the event handler, define the Template variable of the *Session* object using the selected value. The following code demonstrates this:

```
'VB
Session("Template") = Template.SelectedValue
```

```
//C#
Session["Template"] = Template.SelectedValue;
```

9. Create a *Page_PreInit* method. In the *Page_PreInit* method, check to see if there is a *Session* variable named *Template*. If there is, use it to change the *MasterPageFile* object to the selected template's filename. The following code demonstrates this:

```
'VB
If Not (Session("Template") Is Nothing) Then
    MasterPageFile = CType(Session("Template"), String) + ".master"
End If
```

```
//C#
if (Session["Template"] != null)
    MasterPageFile = (String)Session["Template"] + ".master";
```

10. Build your application, and then open the Home.aspx page. Switch to the Colorful template, and then click Submit. Then reload the page. Notice that the page does not change templates until after you reload it. This happens because the *Template_SelectedIndexChanged* method runs after the *Page_PreInit* method. Therefore, the *Page_PreInit* method cannot detect the *Session("Template")* (in Visual Basic) or the *Session["Template"]* (in C#) variable until the second time you load the page.

As you can see, using the master page model doesn't prevent you from accessing controls contained in the master page from the content page.

Lesson Summary

- Master pages provide templates that you can use to create consistent Web pages throughout an application.

- To use master pages, first create a master page and add layout tables and other common elements. Then add *ContentPlaceHolder* controls to the master page. To create the content pages, add standard Web forms, select the master page check box when creating the page, select the master page, and then add content to the page.

- You can attach content at the page level, the application level, or the folder level.

- To reference public properties in a master page, add the "@ MasterType" declaration to the content page and reference the property using *Master.Property_Name*. To reference controls in a master page, call *Master.FindControl* from the content page.

- Handle control events in the master or content page that contains the control.

- Nested master pages fit into the *ContentPlaceHolder* controls on a master page but can contain other content pages. To create a nested master page, add a master attribute to the "@ Master" page declaration and specify the parent master page.

- To programmatically change the master page for a content page, set the page's *MasterPageFile* property and reload the page.

Lesson Review

You can use the following questions to test your knowledge of the information in Lesson 1, "Using Master Pages." The questions are also available on the companion CD if you prefer to review them in electronic form.

NOTE   Answers

Answers to these questions and explanations of why each answer choice is right or wrong are located in the "Answers" section at the end of the book.

---

1. What is the relationship between master and content pages? (Choose the best answer.)

   A. One master page for multiple content pages

   B. One content page for multiple master pages

   C. Multiple content pages for multiple master pages

   D. One content page for one master page

2. Which of the following statements about referencing master page members is true? (Choose all that apply.)

   A. Content pages can reference private properties in the master page.

   B. Content pages can reference public properties in the master page.

   C. Content pages can reference public methods in the master page.

   D. Content pages can reference controls in the master page.

3. You are converting an existing Web application to use master pages. To maintain compatibility, you need to read properties from the master page. Which of the following changes are you required to make to .aspx pages to enable them to work with a master page? (Choose all that apply.)

   A. Add an "@ MasterType" declaration.

   B. Add an "@ Master" declaration.

   C. Add a *MasterPageFile* attribute to the "@ Page" declaration.

   D. Add a *ContentPlaceHolder* control.

4. You need to dynamically change the master page of a content page. In which page event should you implement the dynamic changing? (Choose the best answer.)

   A. *Page_Load*

   B. *Page_Render*

   C. *Page_PreRender*

   D. *Page_PreInit*

Lesson 2: Using Themes and User Profiles

An ASP.NET *theme* is a collection of properties that define the appearance of pages and controls in your Web site. A theme can include skin files, which define property settings for ASP.NET Web server controls, and cascading style sheet files (.css files) and graphics. By applying a theme, you can give the pages in your Web site a consistent appearance.

This lesson describes how to create themes and store information in user profiles.

Real World

Tony Northrup

At the time of this writing, my personal Web site is a mess. I made it years ago, when ASP.NET was brand new and themes weren't yet available.

Here's the thing: I hate the Times New Roman default font. I much prefer sans-serif fonts. So, I manually set the font for every control. But, because I was doing it manually, I overlooked some controls. Later, when I added new controls, I forgot to set the font correctly every time. So, my fonts are inconsistent.

That's one reason why themes are great—they save you time and they let you define your own defaults.

After this lesson, you will be able to:

- Use themes to specify attributes for controls on a single page or an entire Web site.
- Use user profiles to track information about a user between visits.
- Dynamically add controls to a specific location on a Web page.

Estimated lesson time: 45 minutes

Using Themes

Typically, all the Web pages in a Web site have a set of properties in common, including background color, font size and style, and foreground color. You can manually set the properties for every control on every page, but that isn't a good use of your time, and you'll probably overlook some settings.

Themes save you time and improve the consistency of a site by applying a common set of properties across all pages in a Web site or on a Web server to define the look of pages and controls. Basically, themes change the default appearance of controls. Themes can be made up of a set of elements:

- **Skins** Files with .skin extensions that contain property settings for buttons, labels, text boxes, and other controls. Skin files resemble control markups, but contain only the properties you want to define as part of the theme.
- **Cascading style sheets (CSS)** Files with .css extensions that ASP.NET automatically applies to all pages.
- **Images and other resources** You can add images (such as a corporate logo) or other resources to themes as necessary.

However, many themes simply have skin files to set default attributes for controls. The sections that follow describe different ways you can use themes and show you how to implement them.

Applying Control Attributes for Themes with ASP.NET

When you use themes, attributes for controls could be defined in a standard or style sheet theme defined in the "@ Page" directive, in a standard or style sheet theme defined in the Web.config file, or in the control properties themselves. Within ASP.NET, attributes and elements take precedence in the following order:

1. *Theme* attribute in the "@ Page" directive.
2. *<pages Theme="themeName">* element in the Web.config file.
3. Local control attributes.
4. *StyleSheetTheme* attribute in the "@ Page" directive.
5. *<pages StyleSheetTheme="themeName">* element in the Web.config file.

In other words, if you specify a *Theme* attribute in the "@ Page" directive, settings in the theme override any settings you've specified for controls on the page. However, by simply changing the *Theme* attribute to *StyleSheetTheme*, the control-specific settings take precedent over the theme settings.

For example, this directive applies a theme that would override control properties. In other words, if *SampleTheme* specifies that *Label* controls use a red font, but you specify a blue font for a *Label* control, the Labels appear with red font:

```
<%@ Page Theme="SampleTheme" %>
```

This directive applies a style sheet theme. Any changes you make to local control properties override settings in the style sheet theme. Therefore, continuing the previous example, a blue *Label* control appears blue even if *SampleTheme* specifies that *Label* controls are red:

```
<%@ Page StyleSheetTheme="SampleTheme" %>
```

However, *Label* controls that do not have a color specified appear as red. In this regard, if you choose to use a style sheet theme, your theme's properties are overridden by anything declared locally within the page. Similarly, if you use a standard theme (sometimes referred to as a "customization theme" in Microsoft Developer Network [MSDN] documentation), your theme's properties override anything within the local page and anything within any style sheet theme in use.

You can also disable themes for a specific page by setting the *EnableTheming* attribute of the "@ Page" directive to *false*:

```
<%@ Page EnableTheming="false" %>
```

Similarly, to disable themes for a specific control, set the control's *EnableTheming* property to *false*.

Creating a Theme

It takes only a few minutes to create a theme. If you plan to use the theme only within a single Web application, create an application theme within your application folder. If you need to access the theme from multiple Web applications, you can create a global theme instead. Once you have created your theme folders, add skin files and cascading style sheets. The sections that follow describe how to do this.

Creating an Application Theme   If you only need to access a theme from within a single Web application, you should create the theme within your Web application folders. To create an application theme, follow these steps:

1. Create an App_Themes folder in your Web application. In Visual Studio, right-click your Web site in the Solution Explorer, select Add ASP.NET Folder, and then select Theme.

2. Within your App_Themes folder, create a subfolder with your theme name. For example, you could name the theme "RedTheme" or "BlueTheme." You use this name for both the folder name and when referencing the theme in page declarations and configuration files. You can have multiple themes for a Web application, as Figure 9-5 illustrates.

Figure 9-5   Create multiple themes by adding subfolders to the App_Themes folder.

3. Within your theme subfolder, add skin files, style sheets, and images that make up your theme.

4. In each page that you want to apply the skin to, add the *Theme* or *StyleSheetTheme* attribute to the "@ Page" directive. To apply the theme to an entire Web application, add the *<pages Theme="themeName">* element or the *<pages StyleSheetTheme="themeName">* element to the Web.config file.

Creating a Global Theme   A global theme is available to all the Web sites on your Web server. To create a global theme, follow these steps:

Create a Themes folder using the path *iisdefaultroot*\aspnet_client\system_web*version*\Themes. For example, if the default Web root folder is in C:\Inetpub\wwwroot\ folder on the Web server and the version of the .NET Framework is 2.0.50727, the new Themes folder is C:\Inetpub\wwwroot\aspnet_client\system_web\2_0_50727\Themes.

NOTE   **Using global themes with file-based Web site development**

If you are creating a file-based Web site in your development environment, create the themes folders in the %windows%\Microsoft.NET\Framework*<version>*\ASP.NETClientFiles\Themes folder.

---

1. Within your Themes folder, create a subfolder with your theme name.

2. Within your theme subfolder, add skin files, style sheets, and images that make up your theme. You can't do this directly with the Visual Web Developer; however, you can create a theme for a Web application and then move it to the global folder.

3. In each page that you want to apply the skin to, add the *Theme* or *StyleSheetTheme* attribute to the "@ Page" directive. To apply the theme to an entire Web application, add the *<pages Theme="themeName">* element or the *<pages StyleSheetTheme="themeName">* to the Web.config file. The Visual Web Developer does not recognize the global theme name; however, ASP.NET processes it properly when you retrieve the page from IIS.

> **Quick Check**
>
> 1. In which folder should you place themes for an application?
> 2. In which folder should you place global themes?
>
> **Quick Check Answers**
>
> 1. Place themes for an application in the App_Themes folder.
> 2. Place global themes in the *iisdefaultroot*\aspnet_client\system_web*version* \Themes folder.

Creating a Skin File   Skin files are the most common theme components; they serve to define default settings for control appearance attributes. To create a skin file, create a .skin file in your theme folder with control and attribute definitions. A .skin file can contain several skins for multiple control types, or you can create a separate .skin file for each control.

There are two types of control skins:

- **Default skins**   A default skin automatically applies to all controls of the same type when a theme is applied to a page. A control skin is a default skin if it does not have a *SkinID* attribute. For example, if you create a default skin for a *Calendar* control, the control skin applies to all *Calendar* controls on pages that use the theme. Default skins are matched exactly by control type, so that a *Button* control skin applies to all *Button* controls, but not to *LinkButton* controls or to controls that derive from the *Button* object.

- **Named skins**   A named skin is a control skin with a *SkinID* property set. Named skins do not automatically apply to controls by type. Instead, you explicitly apply a named skin to a control by setting the control's *SkinID* property. Creating named skins allows you to set different skins for different instances of the same control in an application.

The following is a control skin for a *Button* control that defines the foreground and background colors:

```
<asp:Button runat="server"
    BackColor="lightblue"
    ForeColor="black" />
```

Similarly, you can define other attributes, including font attributes:

```
<asp:Button runat="server"
    BackColor="Red"
    ForeColor="White"
    Font-Name="Arial"
    Font-Size="9px" />
```

Control skins are exactly like ASP.NET source code for the controls; however, skins never define the control IDs. The easiest way to create a skin file is to follow these steps:

1. Add controls to an .aspx file.
2. Specify the appearance of the controls using the Visual Studio designer.
3. Create a new skin file. To do this with Visual Studio 2005, right-click the name of your theme in Solution Explorer, select Add New Item, and then select the Skin File template.
4. Copy the source for the controls to the skin file.
5. Remove the ID properties from the control definitions in the skin file. Be sure to leave the *runat="server"* attribute.

Adding a Cascading Style Sheet to Your Theme   A cascading style sheet (CSS) contains style rules that are applied to elements in a Web page. CSS styles define how elements are displayed and where they are positioned on the page. Instead of assigning attributes to each element on your page individually, you can create a general rule that applies attributes whenever a Web browser encounters an instance of an element or an element that is assigned to a certain style class.

To add a CSS to your Web site, right-click the name of your theme in Solution Explorer, select Add New Item, and then select the Style Sheet template. When the theme is applied to a page, ASP.NET adds a reference to the style sheet to the head element of the page.

MORE INFO   **Cascading Style Sheets**

CSS is not part of ASP.NET; CSS works for any type of Web site. It isn't specifically covered in the exam objectives and won't be covered in detail in this book. However, CSS is still extremely useful, and all Web developers should be familiar with CSS. For more information about CSS, see "Cascading Style Sheets Overview" at *http://msdn2.microsoft.com/en-US/library/240ww6sz(VS.80).aspx*.

Applying a Theme Programmatically

If you just want to provide a consistent appearance for your Web site, you should specify a theme in page declarations or configuration files. This provides a single interface for all users who visit your Web site.

You can also give users a choice of themes. While this isn't usually necessary for business Web sites, it's a great way to allow users to customize consumer-oriented portal, forum, and shopping sites.

To apply a theme programmatically, set the page's *Theme* property in the *Page_PreInit* method. The following code demonstrates how to set the theme based on a query string value; however, this works equally well using cookies or session state:

```vb
'VB
Protected Sub Page_PreInit(ByVal sender As Object, ByVal e As System.EventArgs) _
        Handles Me.PreInit
    Select Case Request.QueryString("theme")
        Case "Blue"
            Page.Theme = "BlueTheme"
        Case "Pink"
            Page.Pink = "PinkTheme"
    End Select
End Sub
```

```csharp
//C#
Protected void Page_PreInit(object sender, EventArgs e)
{
    switch (Request.QueryString["theme"])
    {
        case "Blue":
            Page.Theme = "BlueTheme";
            break;
        case "Pink":
            Page.Theme = "PinkTheme";
            break;
    }
}
```

Similarly, you can apply a theme to specific controls by setting the control's *SkinID* property in the *Page_PreInit* method. The following code shows how to set the skin for a control named *Calendar1*:

```vb
'VB
Sub Page_PreInit(ByVal sender As Object, ByVal e As System.EventArgs) _
        Handles Me.PreInit
    Calendar1.SkinID = "BlueTheme"
End Sub
```

```
//C#
void Page_PreInit(object sender, EventArgs e)
{
    Calendar1.SkinID = "BlueTheme";
}
```

To programmatically apply a style sheet theme (which works just like a theme but doesn't override control attributes), override the *StyleSheetTheme* property, and in the *Get* accessor, return the name of the style sheet theme. The following code example shows how to set a theme named BlueTheme as the style sheet theme for a page:

```
'VB
Public Overrides Property StyleSheetTheme() As String
    Get
        Return "BlueTheme"
    End Get
    Set(ByVal value As String)
    End Set
End Property
```

```
//C#
public override String StyleSheetTheme
{
  get { return "BlueTheme"; }
}
```

Using User Profiles

You can provide users with a custom experience in your Web site by defining and using profile properties, which you can use to track user information (address, city), preferences (color scheme, list of stocks to follow), or any custom information required by your application (shopping cart). Once you define profile properties, ASP.NET automatically associates individual instances of the profile properties with each user, and you can use code to set or get the values. ASP.NET persists property values in a data store (which you can configure), and the next time a user visits your site, ASP.NET automatically retrieves the profile property value for that user.

The sections that follow describe different ways you can utilize *user profiles* and shows you how to implement profiles.

Configuring the SQL Server Database

Though you can create your own ASP.NET profile provider, by default, ASP.NET stores profile information in a SQL Server database using the *SqlProfileProvider* class. If you are using a SQL Server 2005 Express Edition database that is installed using the default configuration on the same computer as the Web server (as it might be on your development computer), you don't need to do anything to configure the database.

However, if you are using a different database, such as the standard SQL Server 2005, you must create a database to be used by the *SqlProfileProvider*. You can create the database by running the Aspnet_regsql.exe command, which is found in the following path:

```
%windows%\Microsoft .NET\Framework\<version>
```

When you run the tool, you specify the -Ap option. The following command shows the syntax that you use to create the database required to store ASP.NET profiles using the *SqlProfileProvider*:

```
aspnet_regsql.exe -Ap
```

Comparing Authenticated and Anonymous Profiles

You can use profiles with either authenticated or non-authenticated users. If your Web application requires user authentication, you can immediately begin using profiles, because profiles are automatically enabled for authenticated users.

MORE INFO   Authentication

For more information about user authentication, read Chapter 11, "Implementing Authentication and Authorization."

To use profiles on a site that does not authenticate users, you must explicitly enable profiles. After you enable anonymous profiles, ASP.NET creates a unique identification for each user the first time he or she visits your site, and tracks the user with a cookie. The cookie is set to expire about 70 days after the user last visited your site. User profiles can also function without cookies by storing unique identifiers in the URL of the page request; however, the profile is lost when the user closes his or her browser.

Enabling Anonymous User Profiles

To use profiles for unauthenticated users, you first enable profiles in your Web.config file. To do this, add an *<anonymousIdentification>* element to your `<system.web>` section and set the *enabled* attributes to *true*, as is demonstrated here:

```
<configuration>
  <system.web>
    <anonymousIdentification enabled="true" />
  </system.web>
</configuration>
```

The *<anonymousIdentification>* element has several other attributes that you can define to control how cookies are used. However, the defaults are typically sufficient. Additionally, when you define properties, you must set the *allowAnonymous* attribute for each property to *true*.

Migrating Anonymous User Profiles to Authenticated User Profiles

If you enable anonymous user profiles and later require authentication, ASP.NET creates a new profile for the user. To avoid losing the user's profile information, respond to the *MigrateAnonymous* event which ASP.NET raises when the user logs in. The following code demonstrates how to migrate information when a user is authenticated:

```
'VB
Public Sub Profile_OnMigrateAnonymous(sender As Object, args As ProfileMigrateEventArgs)
    Dim anonymousProfile As ProfileCommon = Profile.GetProfile(args.AnonymousID)

    Profile.ZipCode = anonymousProfile.ZipCode
    Profile.CityAndState = anonymousProfile.CityAndState
    Profile.StockSymbols = anonymousProfile.StockSymbols

    ' Delete the anonymous profile. If the anonymous ID is not
    ' needed in the rest of the site, remove the anonymous cookie.
    ProfileManager.DeleteProfile(args.AnonymousID)
    AnonymousIdentificationModule.ClearAnonymousIdentifier()
End Sub
```

```
//C#
public void Profile_OnMigrateAnonymous(object sender, ProfileMigrateEventArgs args)
{
    ProfileCommon anonymousProfile = Profile.GetProfile(args.AnonymousID);

    Profile.ZipCode = anonymousProfile.ZipCode;
    Profile.CityAndState = anonymousProfile.CityAndState;
    Profile.StockSymbols = anonymousProfile.StockSymbols;

    // Delete the anonymous profile. If the anonymous ID is not
    // needed in the rest of the site, remove the anonymous cookie.

    ProfileManager.DeleteProfile(args.AnonymousID);
    AnonymousIdentificationModule.ClearAnonymousIdentifier();
}
```

Configuring Profile Properties

Before you can use profiles, you must first define the properties that you want to track for each user in the Web.config file. For example, if you want to track the user's first and last name in string values, and the date he or she first visited the site in a *DateTime* object, the `<profile>` section of the configuration file could look like this:

```
<configuration>
  <system.web>
     <profile>
       <properties>
         <add name="FirstName" />
         <add name="LastName" />
         <add name="FirstVisit" type="System.DateTime" />
       </properties>
     </profile>
  </system.web>
</configuration>
```

Notice that you don't have to explicitly declare the type for string values, but you do need to set the *type* attribute for any other class. By default, each property is enabled only for authenticated users. To enable properties to be used by anonymous users, set the *allowAnonymous* attribute to *true* for each property:

```
<anonymousIdentification enabled="true" />
<profile>
  <properties>
    <add name="FirstName" allowAnonymous="true" />
    <add name="LastName" allowAnonymous="true" />
    <add name="FirstVisit" type="System.DateTime" allowAnonymous="true" />
  </properties>
</profile>
```

You can also define groups of properties, as the following configuration segment demonstrates:

```
<profile enabled="true">
  <properties>
    <group name="Address">
      <add name="Street" />
      <add name="City" />
      <add name="PostalCode" />
    </group>
  </properties>
</profile>
```

In this example, you could access the street using *Profile.Address.Street*.

MORE INFO   **Adding user-defined types to profile properties**

You can also add custom classes to profiles. For more information, read "Defining ASP.NET Profile Properties" at *http://msdn2.microsoft.com/en-us/library/d8b58y5d(VS.80).aspx*.

Defining and Retrieving User Properties

Once you've configured which properties you want to track for users, you can programmatically define and retrieve these values using the *Profile* object, as the following example shows:

```VB
'VB
Profile.FirstName = firstNameTextBox.Text
Profile.LastName = lastNameTextBox.Text
greetingTextBox = "Welcome, " + Profile.FirstName + " " + Profile.LastName
```

```C#
//C#
Profile.FirstName = firstNameTextBox.Text;
Profile.LastName = lastNameTextBox.Text;
greetingTextBox = "Welcome, " + Profile.FirstName + " " + Profile.LastName;
```

Using profiles in this way is extremely easy compared to the alternatives, because you do not need to explicitly determine who the user is nor perform any database look-ups. Simply getting the property value out of a profile causes ASP.NET to perform the necessary actions to identify the current user and look up the value in the persistent profile store.

Dynamically Adding Controls

Another way to customize Web pages for users is to dynamically add controls. While you can add controls programmatically, the task is greatly simplified if you add a *PlaceHolder* control at design time. To use a *PlaceHolder* control to enable you to dynamically add other controls, follow these steps:

1. Add a *PlaceHolder* control to your Web page.

2. In your code (typically the *Page_Load* event handler), create an instance of the control you want to add to the page.

3. Call the *PlaceHolder.Controls.Add* method to add your control to the *PlaceHolder*'s location.

You can even add multiple controls using a single *PlaceHolder*, which is useful for building more complex dynamic pages. The following code demonstrates this by adding a Button, a Label containing an HTML line break, and then a second Button:

```VB
'VB
Protected Sub Page_Load(ByVal sender As System.Object, _
      ByVal e As System.EventArgs) Handles MyBase.Load
   Dim Button1 As Button = New Button()
   Button1.Text = "Button 1"
   PlaceHolder1.Controls.Add(Button1)
```

```
    Dim Literal1 As New Literal()
    Literal1.Text = "<br>"
    PlaceHolder1.Controls.Add(Literal1)

    Dim Button2 As New Button()
    Button2.Text = "Button 2"
    PlaceHolder1.Controls.Add(Button2)
End Sub

//C#
void Page_Load(object sender, EventArgs e)
{
    Button Button1 = new Button();
    Button1.Text = "Button 1";
    PlaceHolder1.Controls.Add(Button1);

    Literal Literal1 = new Literal();
    Literal1.Text = "<br>";
    PlaceHolder1.Controls.Add(Literal1);

    Button Button2 = new Button();
    Button2.Text = "Button 2";
    PlaceHolder1.Controls.Add(Button2);
}
```

Lab: Applying Themes and User Profiles

In this lab, you work with local and global themes, and then track information about users in profiles.

▶ Exercise 1: Apply local and global themes

In this exercise, you create two local themes to color buttons and labels: blue and green. You will test the themes, move them to the global location, and verify that they still work.

1. Create a new ASP.NET Web site named MyThemes in either C# or Visual Basic using Visual Studio 2005. Use Hypertext Transfer Protocol (HTTP) to store the files on a Web server (such as IIS installed on your local computer), rather than storing the Web site on your file system.

2. Add the App_Themes folder to your Web site and add two subfolders: BlueTheme and GreenTheme.

3. In both BlueTheme and GreenTheme, create skin files named Button.skin and Label.skin. Solution explorer should resemble Figure 9-6.

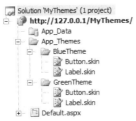

Figure 9-6   Create skin files for *Label* and *Button* controls in two custom themes.

4. Open Default.aspx in design view and add a *Label* and a *Button* control.

5. Edit the properties of the two controls so that they have dark blue text on a light blue background.

6. Switch to the source view of Default.aspx and copy the source code for your *Label* control to the clipboard.

7. Open the App_Themes\BlueTheme\Label.skin file. Paste the source code for your *Label* control into the file. Then remove the ID and Text attributes, as shown here:

    ```
    <asp:Label runat="server" BackColor="#C0FFFF" ForeColor="#0000C0"></asp:Label>
    ```

8. Switch to the source view of Default.aspx and copy the source code for your *Button* control to the clipboard.

9. Open the App_Themes\BlueTheme\Button.skin file. Paste the source code for your *Button* control into the file. Then remove the *ID* and *Text* attributes, as shown here:

    ```
    <asp:Button runat="server" BackColor="#C0FFFF" ForeColor="#0000C0" />
    ```

10. Repeat steps 5 through 9, but define green colors for the *Label* and *Button* controls and use the source code to create the Label.skin and Button.skin files in the GreenTheme.

11. Add a new Web Form to your application and name it Home.aspx. Add default *Label* and *Button* controls to the form. Then press Ctrl+F5 to save your files and view Home.aspx in your browser. Note that the *Label* and *Button* controls both appear with black text on a white background.

12. In the design view for Home.aspx, view the document properties and set the *StyleSheetTheme* attribute to BlueTheme. Then change the foreground color of the *Button* control to Red. Press Ctrl+F5 to save your files and view Home.aspx in your browser. Note that the style sheet theme affects both the foreground and background colors of the *Label* control, but it does not change the red text of the

Button control. Because you defined the foreground color of the *Button* control, the setting overrode the *StyleSheetTheme*.

13. In the design view for Home.aspx, view the document properties, remove the *StyleSheetTheme* attribute, and set the *Theme* attribute to BlueTheme. Press Ctrl+F5 to save your files and view Home.aspx in your browser. Note that the theme affects both the foreground and background colors of both controls, because the *Theme* attribute overrides control settings.

14. Using Windows Explorer, create a folder at the following location on your Web server: \wwwroot\aspnet_client\system_web\<*version*>\Themes. Move both the BlueTheme and GreenTheme folders from your application directory to this new global theme folder.

15. Now return to Visual Studio and press Ctrl+F5 to view Home.aspx in your browser. Note that the two controls are still affected by BlueTheme. Because the themes are now located in a global theme folder, any Web application can apply the theme.

16. View the source for Home.aspx, and look at the "@ Page" declaration. Manually change the *Theme* attribute to GreenTheme. You could also change this attribute using the designer. Now press Ctrl+F5 to view Home.aspx in your browser and verify that the controls are colored green.

As this exercise demonstrates, it takes only a few minutes to customize the appearance of all controls in a Web application.

▶ **Exercise 2: Create anonymous user profiles**

In this exercise, you enable user profiles for anonymous users and track information for Web site visitors.

1. Create a new ASP.NET Web site named TrackUsers in either C# or Visual Basic using Visual Studio 2005. For simplicity, store the Web site using the file system instead of HTTP or File Transfer Protocol (FTP).

2. If necessary, add a Web.config file to your project. Then configure it to enable anonymous user profiles. For example, you can use this Web.config file:

```
<configuration>
  <system.web>
    <anonymousIdentification enabled="true" />
  </system.web>
</configuration>
```

3. Edit the Web.config file to enable the following profile attributes:

    a. Name, as a String

    b. FirstVisit, as a DateTime object

Then save the Web.config file so that the properties are immediately available in Visual Studio. The following Web.config example demonstrates this:

```
<configuration>
  <system.web>
    <anonymousIdentification enabled="true" />
    <profile>
      <properties>
        <add name="Name" allowAnonymous="true" />
        <add name="FirstVisit" type="System.DateTime" allowAnonymous="true" />
      </properties>
    </profile>
  </system.web>
</configuration>
```

4. Add the following controls to the Default.aspx Web form:

   a. *TextBox* with an ID of nameTextBox.

   b. *Label* with an ID of greetingLabel. Remove the default text.

   c. *Button* with an ID of Button1.

5. Now create a method named *Greet_User* in the Default.aspx code-behind file to define the user's first visit if it hasn't already been defined, and then display the user's name and first visit time using the *greetingLabel* control. The following code demonstrates one way to do this:

```
'VB
Protected Sub Greet_User()
'Check if the user's name is defined, and greet him or her if it is
    If Profile.Name.Length > 0 Then
        greetingLabel.Text = "Welcome, " + Profile.Name + "! "
    Else
        greetingLabel.Text = "Welcome, unidentified user! "
    End If

'Define the first visit time if necessary
    If Profile.FirstVisit.Year < 1900 Then
        Profile.FirstVisit = DateTime.Now
    End If

'Display the first visit time
    greetingLabel.Text += "Your first visit was " + Profile.FirstVisit
End Sub

//C#
protected void Greet_User()
{
    // Check if the user's name is defined, and greet him or her if it is
    if (Profile.Name.Length > 0)
        greetingLabel.Text = "Welcome, " + Profile.Name + "! ";
    else
        greetingLabel.Text = "Welcome, unidentified user! ";
```

```
    // Define the first visit time if necessary
    if (Profile.FirstVisit.Year < 1900)
        Profile.FirstVisit = DateTime.Now;

    // Display the first visit time
    greetingLabel.Text += "Your first visit was " + Profile.FirstVisit;
}
```

6. If you are using Visual Basic, edit the Default.aspx "@ Page" declaration to set the *AutoEventWireup* attribute to *true*. This is set to *true* by default in C#. This demonstrates the proper "@ Page" declaration:

```
<%@ Page Language="VB" AutoEventWireup="true" CodeFile="Default.aspx.vb"
Inherits="_Default" %>
```

7. In the *Page_Load* method (which you need to create if you are using Visual Basic), call your *Greet_User* method.

```
'VB
Protected Sub Page_Load()
    Greet_User()
End Sub
```

```
//C#
protected void Page_Load(object sender, EventArgs e)
{
    Greet_User();
}
```

8. Using the design view for the Default.aspx file, double-click the button to create a *Click* event handler. In the event handler, use the contents of the *nameTextBox* control to define *Profile.Name*. Then call *Greet_User*. The following code demonstrates this:

```
'VB
Protected Sub Button1_Click(ByVal sender As Object, ByVal e As System.EventArgs) Handles
Button1.Click
    Profile.Name = nameTextBox.Text
    Greet_User()
End Sub
```

```
//C#
protected void Button1_Click(object sender, EventArgs e)
{
    Profile.Name = nameTextBox.Text;
    Greet_User();
}
```

9. Press Ctrl+F5 to build your Web page. Verify that the Web page greets you as an unidentified user and displays the current time as your first visit.

10. In the text box, type your name. Then click the button. The Web page displays your name and first visit time.

11. Verify that the profile persists between user visits. Close all instances of your Web browser, and then re-open the Web page. It greets you with your name and the time of your first visit.

12. In Window Explorer, open the App_Data application subdirectory. Note that it contains two files: Aspnetdb.mdf (the main SQL Server user profile database) and Aspnetdb_log.ldf (the database log file).

As you can see, user profiles are easy to implement, but extremely powerful.

Lesson Summary

- To create a theme, add an App_Themes subfolder to your application. Then add skin files, CSS pages, graphics, and other resources. Finally, apply the theme at the page or application level.

- To use user profiles, first configure a SQL Server database. If your Web site authenticates users, there's nothing more for you to do—you can begin accessing the *Profile* object immediately. If you need to provide profiles for anonymous users, enable anonymous identification in your Web.config file.

- To dynamically place controls in a specific location, add *PlaceHolder* controls to a Web page. Then call *PlaceHolder.Controls.Add* to add your control. This is an excellent way to customize pages based on user preferences.

Lesson Review

You can use the following questions to test your knowledge of the information in Lesson 2, "Using Themes and User Profiles." The questions are also available on the companion CD if you prefer to review them in electronic form.

NOTE Answers

Answers to these questions and explanations of why each answer choice is right or wrong are located in the "Answers" section at the end of the book.

---

1. Which of the following themes can override an attribute that you specified for a control? (Choose all that apply.)

   A. A theme specified using @ *Page Theme="MyTheme"*

   B. A theme specified using @ *Page StyleSheetTheme="MyTheme"*

   C. *<pages Theme="themeName">* element in the Web.config file

   D. *<pages StyleSheetTheme="themeName">* element in the Web.config file

2. Which of the following is a valid skin file? (Choose the best answer.)

   A. `<asp:Label ID="Label1" BackColor="#FFE0C0" ForeColor="Red" Text="Label"></asp:Label>`

   B. `<asp:Label ID="Label1" runat="server" BackColor="#FFE0C0" ForeColor="Red" Text="Label"></asp:Label>`

   C. `<asp:Label runat="server" BackColor="#FFE0C0" ForeColor="Red"></asp:Label>`

   D. `<asp:Label BackColor="#FFE0C0" ForeColor="Red"></asp:Label>`

3. You need to allow users to choose their own themes. In which page event should you specify the user-selected theme? (Choose the best answer.)

   A. *Page_Load*

   B. *Page_Render*

   C. *Page_PreRender*

   D. *Page_PreInit*

4. Which of the following Web.config files correctly enables the Web application to track the age of anonymous users in a variable of type Int32? (Choose the best answer.)

   A.
   ```
   <anonymousIdentification enabled="true" />
   <profile>
     <properties>
       <add name="Age" type="System.Int32" allowAnonymous="true" />
     </properties>
   </profile>
   ```

   B.
   ```
   <anonymousIdentification enabled="true" />
   <profile>
     <properties>
       <add name="Age" allowAnonymous="true" />
     </properties>
   </profile>
   ```

   C.
   ```
   <anonymousIdentification enabled="true" />
   <profile>
     <properties>
       <add name="Age" type="System.Int32" />
     </properties>
   </profile>
   ```

   D.
   ```
   <profile>
     <properties>
       <add name="Age" type="System.Int32" />
     </properties>
   </profile>
   ```

Lesson 3: Using Web Parts

Modern Web pages are collections of components. For example, examine your favorite news site—it probably has a navigation bar to the left, a title bar at the top, at least one column of news, and a footer. Additionally, many news and portal sites provide customized, optional components, such as weather reports and stock quotes.

ASP.NET *Web Parts* give you the ability to provide your users with control over the components that appear on a Web page. With Web Parts, users can minimize or completely close groups of controls. So, if they want to see the weather on your page, they can—or they can close it to save room for more valuable content. You can also provide a catalog of Web Parts to enable users to add groups of controls wherever they want on a page.

This lesson describes how to create and use Web Parts.

After this lesson, you will be able to:

■ Describe what Web Parts are and how they can be used.

■ Add Web Parts to a page.

■ Create a Web page that allows users to edit and rearrange Web Parts.

■ Connect Web Parts to each other to allow sharing of data.

■ Enable personalization for Web Parts to enable customized settings to be persisted.

Estimated lesson time: 90 minutes

What Are Web Parts?

Web Parts are components that users can display, hide, or move. As shown in Figure 9-7, Web Parts provide menus to the clients that enable them to control the components.

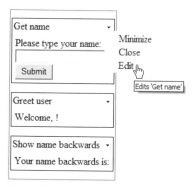

Figure 9-7 Web Parts generate client-side menus to enable customization.

You can also add a catalog to your Web pages to allow users to add Web Parts, as shown in Figure 9-8.

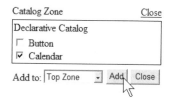

Figure 9-8 You can use a *CatalogZone* control to enable users to add Web Parts on demand, without writing any code.

Web Parts are commonly used for:

- A list of recent news articles relating to your organization.
- A calendar showing upcoming events.
- A list of links to related Web sites.
- A search box.
- Picture thumbnails from a photo gallery.
- Site navigation controls.
- A blog.
- News articles pulled from a Really Simple Syndication (RSS) feed.
- Local weather retrieved from a Web service.
- Stock market quotes and graphs.

Any control can act as a Web Part, including standard controls and custom controls. Using Web Parts doesn't necessarily require writing any code, because you can do so entirely with the Visual Studio designer.

Adding Web Parts to a Page

To add Web Parts to a page, follow these steps:

1. Add a *WebPartManager* control to the top of the page (it must appear before any Web Parts). This control is not visible to the user, but it is required to use Web Parts.

2. Create a layout table. Technically, a layout table isn't necessary, but in practice, it's the best way to arrange Web Parts.

3. Add *WebPartZone* containers to each cell in the layout table that you want to contain Web Parts. Add a descriptive *Title* attribute for each *WebPartZone* control.

4. Add controls to the *WebPartZone* containers to define default positions for your Web Parts. Add a descriptive *Title* attribute for each Web Part that you add.

As demonstrated by Exercise 1 in this lesson's lab, that's all you need to do to take advantage of Web Parts. However, you can do much more, including giving users the ability to customize Web Parts.

NOTE Hands-on learning

Web Parts configuration is one of those topics that are best learned by hands-on usage. In several places, this lesson suggests that you explore one of the three exercises in the lab at the end of the lesson. Instead of waiting to read the entire lesson, it is a good idea to skip forward and do the referenced exercise before continuing.

Enabling Users to Arrange and Edit Web Parts

Web Parts can have several different modes to allow users to control how Web Parts are displayed on the page. The modes are:

- **Browse (*BrowseDisplayMode*)** The standard way users browse Web pages. This is the default mode.

- **Design (*DesignDisplayMode*)** Enables users to drag and drop Web Parts into different locations. This mode is always available.

- **Edit (*EditDisplayMode*)** Like Design mode, Edit mode enables users to drag and drop Web Parts. Additionally, users can select Edit from the Web Parts menu to edit the title, size, direction, window appearance, and zone of Web Parts by using *AppearanceEditorPart* and *LayoutEditorPart* controls. To use this mode, you must add an *EditorZone* control to your Web page, and then add either or both *AppearanceEditorPart* and *LayoutEditorPart*.

- **Catalog (*CatalogDisplayMode*)**   Enables users to add additional Web Parts that you specify by using a *CatalogZone* control. This mode is available only after you add a *CatalogZone* to your Web page.

- **Connect (*ConnectDisplayMode*)**   Enables users to manually establish connections between controls by interacting with a *ConnectionZone* control. For example, Web Parts can be linked to show summary and detail information of the same report. This mode is only available after you add a *ConnectionZone* control to the page. For more information about Web Parts connections, see the section titled "Connecting Web Parts," later in this lesson.

When a user chooses to change modes, your application must programmatically set the *WebPartManager.DisplayMode* property.

To enable a user to enter different display modes and edit Web Parts, follow these steps:

1. Add a control to enable a user to switch between different Web Parts modes. Use *WebPartManager.SupportedDisplayModes* to retrieve the list of modes that are supported and provide a list of options to the user. When the user selects a mode, set *WebPartManager.DisplayMode* to the selected mode. You can retrieve the page's *WebPartManager* instance by calling the static *WebPartManager.Get-CurrentWebPartManager(Page)* method.

2. Add an *EditorZone* container to the page to hold editing tools. This control is hidden until the user selects the Edit mode.

3. Add an *AppearanceEditorPart* control to the *EditorZone* container to give a user the ability to adjust the border, size, direction, and title of Web Parts.

4. Add a *LayoutEditorPart* control to the *EditorZone* container to give a user the ability to adjust the minimized state of Web Parts and to move Web Parts to other *WebPartZone* containers.

5. Add a *CatalogZone* container to the page. Then add a *DeclarativeCatalogPart* control to the *CatalogZone* container to enable a user to add controls to the page. These controls are hidden until the user selects the Catalog mode.

6. Add a *ConnectionsZone* control to the page to enable a user to establish connections between controls. This control is hidden until the user selects the Connect mode.

For detailed instructions, walk through Exercise 2 of this lesson's lab.

Connecting Web Parts

One of the most powerful features of the Web Parts tool is the ability to build connections between Web Parts. To understand the possibilities, imagine building an internal application to manage employee payroll. You could have:

- A main Web Part so you can browse employee data.

- A Web Part that displays a chart of the selected employee's overtime pay.

- A Web Part that shows a pie chart illustrating how payroll, benefits, stock options, and pension fit into the employee's overall compensation.

- A Web Part that compares the employee's pay to other employees in the same position.

- A Web Part that compares the employee's pay to other employees in the same location.

With Web Parts connections, the user can select an employee file and have all the other Web Parts automatically update using that employee's information. Naturally, the user analyzing the data would have the ability to add, remove, and rearrange Web Parts.

Connections are also useful for consumer-oriented Web sites. For example, if you are building a portal site, you might have Web Parts that display localized information based on the user's postal code, including the weather, local news, and the phase of the moon. Rather than requiring the user to specify his or her postal code for each individual Web Part, all Web Parts can connect to a specialized Web Part that stores the users' postal codes.

Connections can be either static or dynamic. If a connection is static, you (as the developer) establish the connection during the development process, and it cannot be changed by the user. Static connections are permanent and cannot be deleted by users. Dynamic connections can be established by users and are enabled by adding a *ConnectionsZone* control to the Web page.

Creating a Static Connection

To create a static connection, follow these steps:

1. Create a provider Web Part. A Provider Web Part can derive from the *WebPart* class, or it can simply be a Web control. You must create a public method with the *ConnectionProvider* attribute that returns the value that the consumer receives. The following code demonstrates a provider method:

```vb
'VB
<ConnectionProvider("User name provider", "NameProvider")> _
Public Function GetName() As String
    ' Name contains the user's name, read from a TextBox control
    Return Name
End Function
```

```csharp
//C#
[ConnectionProvider("User name provider", "NameProvider")]
public string GetName()
{
    // Name contains the user's name, read from a TextBox control
    return Name;
}
```

2. Create a consumer Web Part. A Consumer Web Part can derive from the *WebPart* class or it can simply be a Web control. You must create a public method with the *ConnectionConsumer* attribute that accepts the same type that the provider's *ConnectionProvide* method returns. The following code demonstrates a consumer method:

```vb
'VB
<ConnectionConsumer("User name consumer", "NameConsumer")> _
Public Sub GetName(ByVal Name As String)
    greetingLabel.Text = "Welcome, " + Name + "!"
End Sub
```

```csharp
//C#
[ConnectionConsumer("User name consumer", "NameConsumer")]
public void GetName(string Name)
{
    // greetingLabel is an existing Label control
    greetingLabel.Text = "Welcome, " + Name + "!";
}
```

3. Create a Web page with a *WebPartManager* control. Add at least one *WebPartZone* container.

4. Add your provider and consumer Web Parts to *WebPartZone* containers.

5. Within the *WebPartManager* control source, add a *<StaticConnections>* element that includes a *WebPartConnection* control to declare the connection between the provider and consumer. The *WebPartConnection* control must have an *ID* attribute, an attribute to identify the provider control (*ProviderID*), an attribute to identify the provider method (*ProviderConnectionPointID*), an attribute to identify the consumer control (*ConsumerID*), and an attribute to identify the consumer method (*ConsumerConnectionPointID*). You should have one *WebPartConnection* control for each pair of connected controls. The following markup demonstrates this:

```
<asp:WebPartManager ID="WebPartManager1" runat="server">
    <StaticConnections>
        <asp:WebPartConnection
            ID="conn1"
            ProviderID="getName"
            ProviderConnectionPointID="NameProvider"
            ConsumerID="showName"
            ConsumerConnectionPointID="NameConsumer"
        />
    </StaticConnections>
</asp:WebPartManager>
```

This can seem confusing at first; however, Exercise 3 in this lesson's lab walks you through the process of creating controls that connect to each other and of configuring them in a Web page.

Exam Tip   For the exam, know exactly how to establish a static connection, which attributes you must assign to each method, and what you must add to the .aspx page source.

Enabling Dynamic Connections

To enable dynamic connections that a user can create or break, follow these steps:

1. Create a page with a provider and consumer connection as described in the previous section.

2. Optionally, establish a static connection between the provider and consumer, as described in the previous section. This acts as a default connection that a user can break if desired.

3. Add a *ConnectionsZone* control to the Web page.

4. Add a control to enable a user to enter the Connect mode, as described in "Using Different Display Modes," earlier in this lesson.

Establishing Dynamic Connections Between Web Parts

When a user views your page, he or she can enter Connect mode and use the *ConnectionsZone* control to edit connections. To edit a connection as a user, follow these steps:

1.   Switch the display mode to Connect.

2.   On the Web Parts menu for either the provider or the consumer, select Connect, as shown in Figure 9-9.

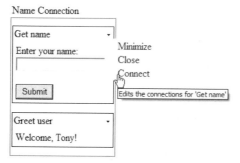

Figure 9-9   Select Connect from the Web Parts menu to edit the connection.

3.   The *ConnectionsZone* object appears, as shown in Figure 9-10.

Figure 9-10   Use the *Connections Zone* control to dynamically establish a connection.

4. If there is an existing connection, click the Disconnect button to break the current connection. Otherwise, click Create A Connection To A Consumer, select the consumer, and click Connect, as shown in Figure 9-11.

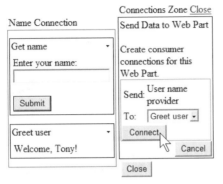

Figure 9-11   Click Connect to establish a dynamic connection between Web Parts.

5. When you are done editing connections, click Close.

The Web Parts are connected, just as if you had connected them statically.

Quick Check

1. Why would you want to use Web Parts?
2. Which component is required for all pages that use Web Parts?
3. What component do you need to enable a user to add new Web Parts to a page?

Quick Check Answers

1. Web Parts enable users to customize the components on a page and the layout of a page.
2. The *WebPartManager* control is required for all pages that use Web Parts.
3. The *CatalogZone* control enables a user to add new Web Parts to a page.

Personalizing Web Parts

Web Parts support personalization, where changes to the layout are stored for each user so that the user sees the same layout the next time he or she visits the page. Web Parts personalization is similar to, but separate from, user profiles. They both rely on client-side cookies and store data in a SQL Server database by default, however. Typically, users are authenticated using Windows or Forms authentication.

MORE INFO   User authentication

For more information about user authentication, refer to Chapter 11, "Implementing Authentication and Authorization."

Enabling Personalization for Custom Controls

By default, personalization remembers the location and other personalized Web Parts settings, as described in "Enabling Users to Arrange and Edit Web Parts," earlier in this chapter. You can also store custom data in the personalization database to enable controls to remember information about users. To each public property that you want to remember for individual users, simply add the *Personalizable* attribute, as the following simplified code demonstrates:

```vb
'VB
<Personalizable()> _
Property Zip() As String
    Get
        Return _zip
    End Get

    Set(ByVal value As String)
        _zip = value
    End Set
End Property
```

```csharp
//C#
[Personalizable]
public string Zip
{
    get
    {
        Return _zip;
    }

    set
    {
      _zip = value;
    }
}
```

Enabling Shared Personalization

Web Parts personalization is enabled by default, and authenticated users of a Web Parts page are able to personalize pages for themselves without any special configuration. However, individual or user-scoped personalization changes are visible only to the user who made them. If you want to provide webmasters (or any user) the power to make personalization changes that affect how everyone sees Web Parts, you can enable shared personalization in your application's Web.config file.

Within the <system.web> section of the configuration file, add an <authorization> section, and within that, add an *<allow>* element to specify which user or users have access to shared personalization scope, as the following example shows:

```
<authorization>
  <allow verbs="enterSharedScope" users="SomeUserAccount"
    roles="admin"  />
</authorization>
```

The specified user or users now have the ability to edit a page in shared personalization scope so that the changes they make are visible to all users.

Disabling Personalization for a Page

You can also disable personalization for a page, which is useful if you want to take advantage of personalization on some pages but not on others. To disable personalization on a page, view the properties for the page's *WebPartManager* control and set the *WebPartManager.Personalization.Enabled* attribute to *false*. The easiest way to do this is by using the designer, but the source code appears similar to the following:

```
<asp:WebPartManager ID="WebPartManager1" runat="server">
    <Personalization Enabled="False" />
</asp:WebPartManager>
```

Lab: Using Web Parts

In this lab, you create a Web page that uses Web Parts. You then expand the page capabilities to enable users to customize the page, and then add controls that communicate with each other.

▶ **Exercise 1: Create a Web Page with Web Parts**

In this exercise, you create a Web page that uses Web Parts and enables the user to arrange and modify the Web Parts.

1. Create a new ASP.NET Web site named MyWebParts in either C# or Visual Basic using Visual Studio 2005.

2. From the Toolbox, under WebParts, drag a *WebPartManager* control to the top of the page. This control isn't visible to users, but it must appear before any Web Part controls, or else the runtime throws an exception.

3. In the Default.aspx page, add a four-cell table using the "Header, footer, and side" template below the *WebPartManager* control.

4. From the Toolbox, under WebParts, drag *WebPartZone* controls to the top, left, and bottom cells. Set the IDs for these to *TopWebPartZone*, *LeftWebPartZone*, and *BottomWebPartZone*. Then set the *HeaderText* property for the zones to "Top zone," "Left zone," and "Bottom zone."

5. Now add two new Web User controls to your Web site named *CalendarWebPart* and *ButtonWebPart*. To each custom control, add several standard controls. These custom controls serve as examples only—in the real world, they do something clever like displaying the weather or querying a database. If you have created your own controls, feel free to use those instead.

6. Open Default.aspx in the design view. Drag *ButtonControl* to the Top Zone *WebPartZone* container and drag *CalendarControl* to the Left Zone *WebPartZone* container.

7. Press Ctrl+F5 to save your Web site and open Default.aspx in a browser. Notice that your two controls appear on the page. Click the menu button in the upper-right corner and experiment with minimizing and closing the Web Parts. Also notice that both Web Parts are currently labeled Untitled.

8. Return to Visual Studio and open Default.aspx in design view. To give the Web Parts meaningful display names, you need to edit the *Title* property. Click the instance of *CalendarControl*, view the properties, and notice that the title is not displayed. To edit the *Title* property, you must manually add it to the source code, as shown here:

```
<asp:WebPartZone ID="LeftWebPartZone" runat="server" HeaderText="Left zone">
    <ZoneTemplate>
        <uc2:CalendarControl title="Calendar" ID="CalendarControl1" runat="server" />
    </ZoneTemplate>
</asp:WebPartZone>
```

9. Create a title for both the *CalendarControl* and *ButtonControl* instances. Save the page and view it in a Web browser again to verify that the title appears.

▶ **Exercise 2: Enable Users to Customize Web Parts**

In this exercise, you extend an existing Web Parts application to enable user customization.

1. Open Visual Studio and continue working with the project you created in the previous exercise.

2. In the Default.aspx page, in design view, drag a *DropDownList* control to the right pane of the layout table. Set the *ID* property to *ModeList* and set the *AutoPostBack* property to *true*.

3. If you are using Visual Basic, edit the Default.aspx "@ Page" declaration to set the *AutoEventWireup* attribute to *true*. This is set to *true* by default in C#. This demonstrates the proper "@ Page" declaration:

```
<%@ Page Language="VB" AutoEventWireup="true" CodeFile="Default.aspx.vb"
Inherits="_Default" %>
```

4. Create two methods: *Page_Init* and *GenerateModeList*. In the *Page_Init* method (which is automatically called when the page is created, thanks to the *Auto-EventWireup* capability), add an event handler so that ASP.NET calls the *GenerateModeList* method during the *InitComplete* event. The following code demonstrates this:

```
'VB
Sub Page_Init(ByVal sender As Object, ByVal e As EventArgs)
    AddHandler Page.InitComplete, AddressOf InitComplete
End Sub

//C#
void Page_Init(object sender, EventArgs e)
{
    Page.InitComplete += new EventHandler(InitComplete);
}
```

5. Now, in the *GenerateModeList* method (which is called during the *InitComplete* event, based on the event handler you just added), write code to populate the *ModeList* control using the *SupportedDisplayModes* property of the *WebPartManager* control. Be sure to select the correct item in the list based on the current mode. The following sample code demonstrates this:

```
'VB
Protected Sub GenerateModeList(ByVal sender As Object, ByVal e As EventArgs)
    Dim _manager As WebPartManager = WebPartManager.GetCurrentWebPartManager(Page)
    Dim browseModeName As String = WebPartManager.BrowseDisplayMode.Name
    ModeList.Items.Clear()

    ' Fill the drop-down list with the names of supported display modes.
```

```
    For Each mode As WebPartDisplayMode In _manager.SupportedDisplayModes
        Dim modeName As String = mode.Name

        ' Make sure a mode is enabled before adding it.
        If mode.IsEnabled(_manager) Then
            Dim item As ListItem = New ListItem(modeName, modeName)
            ModeList.Items.Add(item)
        End If
    Next

    ' Select the current mode
    Dim items As ListItemCollection = ModeList.Items
    Dim selectedIndex As Integer =
items.IndexOf(items.FindByText(_manager.DisplayMode.Name))
    ModeList.SelectedIndex = selectedIndex
End Sub

//C#
protected void GenerateModeList(object sender, EventArgs e)
{
    WebPartManager _manager = WebPartManager.GetCurrentWebPartManager(Page);

    String browseModeName = WebPartManager.BrowseDisplayMode.Name;

    ModeList.Items.Clear();
    // Fill the drop-down list with the names of supported display modes.
    foreach (WebPartDisplayMode mode in _manager.SupportedDisplayModes)
    {
        String modeName = mode.Name;
        // Make sure a mode is enabled before adding it.
        if (mode.IsEnabled(_manager))
        {
            ListItem item = new ListItem(modeName, modeName);
            ModeList.Items.Add(item);
        }
    }

    // Select the current mode
    ListItemCollection items = ModeList.Items;
    int selectedIndex = items.IndexOf(items.FindByText(_manager.DisplayMode.Name));
    ModeList.SelectedIndex = selectedIndex;
}
```

6. In the Default.aspx design view, double-click the *ModeList* control to create an event handler for the *ModeList_SelectedIndxChanged* event. Then write code to set the current mode to the mode selected from the list, as the following code demonstrates:

```
'VB
Protected Sub ModeList_SelectedIndexChanged(ByVal sender As Object, ByVal e As
EventArgs)
    Dim _manager As WebPartManager = WebPartManager.GetCurrentWebPartManager(Page)
```

```
    Dim mode As WebPartDisplayMode =
_manager.SupportedDisplayModes(ModeList.SelectedValue)
    If Not (mode Is Nothing) Then
        _manager.DisplayMode = mode
    End If
End Sub
```

```csharp
//C#
protected void ModeList_SelectedIndexChanged(object sender, EventArgs e)
{
    WebPartManager _manager = WebPartManager.GetCurrentWebPartManager(Page);
    WebPartDisplayMode mode = _manager.SupportedDisplayModes[ModeList.SelectedValue];
    if (mode != null)
        _manager.DisplayMode = mode;
}
```

7. Press Ctrl+F5 to save your Web site and open Default.aspx in Internet Explorer (other browsers will probably not work correctly). Notice that your two controls appear on the page. Click the drop-down list and select Design. Then drag and drop your controls from one zone to another. Click the drop-down list again and return to Browse mode.

8. Return to Visual Studio and open Default.aspx in design view. From the Toolbox, under WebParts, drag an *EditorZone* control to the right cell below the *ModeList* control. Then drag *AppearanceEditorPart* and *LayoutEditorPart* controls to the *EditorZone* control.

9. Press Ctrl+F5 to save your Web site and open Default.aspx in your Web browser. Click the drop-down list and select Edit. Then click the menu button in the upper-right corner of the calendar control and click Edit. Notice that the *EditorZone*, *AppearanceEditorPart*, and *LayoutEditorPart* controls appear. Experiment with the controls to change their appearance and layout. Notice that adding this capability doesn't require writing any other code; you simply need to add the controls to the page. The *WebPartManager* control detects the presence of the *EditorZone* and automatically enables the Edit mode.

10. Return to Visual Studio and open Default.aspx in design view. From the Toolbox, under WebParts, drag a *CatalogZone* control to the right cell below the *EditorZone* control. Now, drag a *DeclarativeCatalogPart* control into the *CatalogZone* control.

11. Right-click the *DeclarativeCatalogPart* control, select Edit Template, and then select WebPartsTemplate. This enables you to add controls to the catalog. Then, from Solution Explorer, drag your *ButtonControl* and *CalendarControl* controls to the *CatalogZone* control. This adds the controls to the catalog. However, if you

view the catalog now, both controls are labeled Untitled. To assign titles, switch to source view and add *Title* attributes to both controls, as shown here:

```
<asp:DeclarativeCatalogPart ID="DeclarativeCatalogPart1" runat="server">
    <WebPartsTemplate>
        <uc1:ButtonControl ID="ButtonControl2" runat="server" title="Button" />
        <uc2:CalendarControl ID="CalendarControl2" runat="server" title="Calendar" />
    </WebPartsTemplate>
</asp:DeclarativeCatalogPart>
```

12. Press Ctrl+F5 to save your Web site and open Default.aspx in your Web browser. Click the drop-down list and select Catalog. The Catalog Zone you created appears and shows the available controls. Select the *Button* control, select Bottom Zone from the drop-down list, and then click Add. Continue experimenting with the control; switch back to Browse mode when you are done.

▶ **Exercise 3: Create Connected Web Parts**

In this exercise, you extend an existing Web Parts application to enable user customization.

1. Open Visual Studio and continue working with the project you created in the previous exercise.

2. Create three new Web User controls:
   - **GetName**   Add a *Label* control showing "Please type your name." Add a *TextBox* control named *NameTextBox*. Then add a *Button* labeled "Submit."
   - **GreetUser**   Add a *Label* control named *GreetLabel* displaying "Hello, unidentified user."
   - **ShowNameBackwards**   Add a *Label* control named *BackwardsLabel* showing "Please type your name to see it spelled backward."

3. In the *GetName* control, write code to store the text the user types in the text box when the user clicks the button. Then create a public method named *GetUserName* and set the *ConnectionProvider* attribute. In the *GetName* method, return the name the user typed. This control provides the user's name to the other two controls, so the user only has to type it once.

```
'VB
Partial Class GetName
    Inherits System.Web.UI.UserControl
    Private _name As String = String.Empty

    Public Overridable Property Name() As String
        Get
            Return _name
```

```
        End Get
        Set(ByVal value As String)
            _name = value
        End Set
    End Property

    <ConnectionProvider("User name provider", "NameProvider")> _
    Public Function GetUserName() As String
        Return Name
    End Function

    Protected Sub Button1_Click(ByVal sender As Object, ByVal e As System.EventArgs)
Handles Button1.Click
        If Not (NameTextBox.Text = String.Empty) Then
            _name = Page.Server.HtmlEncode(NameTextBox.Text)
        End If

    End Sub
End Class

//C#
public partial class GetName : System.Web.UI.UserControl
{
    string _name = String.Empty;

    public virtual string Name
    {
        get { return _name; }
        set { _name = value; }
    }

    [ConnectionProvider("User name provider", "NameProvider")]
    public string GetUserName()
    {
        return Name;
    }

    protected void Button1_Click(object sender, EventArgs e)
    {
        if (NameTextBox.Text != String.Empty)
            _name = Page.Server.HtmlEncode(NameTextBox.Text);
    }
}
```

4. In the *GreetUser* control, create a public method named *GetName* and set the *ConnectionConsumer* attribute. This control reads the user's name from the *Get-Name* control and displays it to the user as part of a greeting. Create the *GetName* method so that it accepts a string and uses it to create a greeting using the *Greet-Label* control, as the following code demonstrates:

```
'VB
Partial Class GreetUser
```

```
    Inherits System.Web.UI.UserControl

    <ConnectionConsumer("User name consumer", "NameConsumer")> _
    Public Sub GetName(ByVal Name As String)
        GreetLabel.Text = "Welcome, " + Name + "!"
    End Sub
End Class
```

```
//C#
public partial class GreetUser : System.Web.UI.UserControl
{
    // This method is identified by the ConnectionConsumer
    // attribute, and is the mechanism for connecting with
    // the provider.
    [ConnectionConsumer("User name consumer", "NameConsumer")]
    public void GetName(string Name)
    {
        GreetLabel.Text = "Welcome, " + Name + "!";
    }
}
```

5. In the *ShowNameBackwards* control, create a public *GetName* method as you did
    for *GreetUser*, with the same *ConnectionConsumer* attribute. Then write code to
    reverse the order of the user's name and display it in the *BackwardsLabel* control,
    as the following code demonstrates:

```
'VB
Partial Class ShowNameBackwards
    Inherits System.Web.UI.UserControl

    <ConnectionConsumer("User name consumer", "NameConsumer")> _
    Public Sub GetName(ByVal Name As String)
        Dim ForwardsName As Char() = Name.ToCharArray
        Dim BackwardsName As Char() = Name.ToCharArray
        Dim Length As Integer = Name.Length - 1
        Dim x As Integer = 0
        While x <= Length
            BackwardsName(x) = ForwardsName(Length - x)
            x = x + 1
        End While
        BackwardsLabel.Text = "Your name backward is: " + New String(BackwardsName)
    End Sub
End Class
```

```
//C#
public partial class ShowNameBackwards : System.Web.UI.UserControl
{
    // This method is identified by the ConnectionConsumer
    // attribute, and is the mechanism for connecting with
    // the provider.
    [ConnectionConsumer("User name consumer", "NameConsumer")]
    public void GetName(string Name)
    {
```

```
// Reverse the order of the user's name
char[] ForwardsName = Name.ToCharArray();
char[] BackwardsName = Name.ToCharArray();
int Length = Name.Length - 1;

for (int x = 0; x <= Length; x++)
    BackwardsName[x] = ForwardsName[Length - x];

// Display the name to the user
BackwardsLabel.Text = "Your name backward is: " + new string(BackwardsName);
    }
}
```

6. Open Default.aspx in design view and add the *GetName*, *GreetUser*, and *Show-NameBackwards* controls to the Bottom Zone. Specify titles for each control, as you did in Exercise 1.

7. Open Default.aspx in the source view. Within the *WebPartManager* control, add a <*StaticConnections*> element. Within the <*StaticConnections*> element, add two *WebPartConnection* controls that declare the connections between the GetName provider and the GreetUser and ShowNameBackwards consumers. The *WebPartConnection* control must have an *ID* attribute, an attribute to identify the provider control (*ProviderID*), an attribute to identify the provider method (*ProviderConnectionPointID*), an attribute to identify the consumer control (*ConsumerID*), and an attribute to identify the consumer method (*ConsumerConnectionPointID*). The following markup demonstrates this:

```
<asp:WebPartManager ID="WebPartManager1" runat="server">
    <StaticConnections>
        <asp:WebPartConnection
            ID="WebPartConnection1"
            ProviderID="GetName1"
            ProviderConnectionPointID="NameProvider"
            ConsumerID="GreetUser1"
            ConsumerConnectionPointID="NameConsumer"
        />
        <asp:WebPartConnection
            ID="WebPartConnection2"
            ProviderID="GetName1"
            ProviderConnectionPointID="NameProvider"
            ConsumerID="ShowNameBackwards1"
            ConsumerConnectionPointID="NameConsumer"
        />
    </StaticConnections>
</asp:WebPartManager>
```

8. Press Ctrl+F5 to save your Web site and open Default.aspx in your Web browser. In the *GetName* control, type your name and then click the button. Your name appears in the other two controls.

Lesson Summary

- Web Parts are controls that users can close, minimize, edit, and move.

- To add Web Parts to a page, add a *WebPartManager* control to the top of the page, add *WebPartZone* containers to the page, and then add controls to the *WebPartZone* containers.

- To enable users to edit or rearrange Web Parts, add a control to enable users to select different modes. Then add an *EditorZone* container to your page and add an *AppearanceEditorPart* or a *LayoutEditorPart* to the *EditorZone* container. To enable users to add more Web Parts, add a *CatalogZone* container and a *DeclarativeCatalogPart* to the container. To enable users to control how Web Parts are connected, add a *ConnectionsZone* control.

- To connect Web Parts to enable them to share data, first create provider and consumer Web Parts. Then add them to your Web page. Finally, configure the connections between the Web Parts by adding a *<StaticConnections>* element to the *WebPartManager* control.

- To use Web Parts personalization, enable authentication in your application and provide a data store to contain the personalization information. You can provide personalization in custom classes by adding the *Personalizable* attribute to public properties.

Lesson Review

You can use the following questions to test your knowledge of the information in Lesson 3. The questions are also available on the companion CD if you prefer to review them in electronic form.

NOTE Answers

Answers to these questions and explanations of why each answer choice is right or wrong are located in the "Answers" section at the end of the book.

---

1. Which of the following can be a Web Part? (Choose all that apply.)

    A. A custom control based on the Web User Control template

    B. A standard *Label* control

    C. A type derived from *WebPart*

    D. A master page

2. Which of the following are required to enable users to change the title of a Web Part? (Choose all that apply.)

   A. *LayoutEditorPart*

   B. *EditorZone*

   C. *CatalogZone*

   D. *AppearanceEditorPart*

3. You have developed a Web page with many different Web Part components. Some Web Parts are enabled by default, and you want to give a user the ability to display others. Which classes should you use? (Choose all that apply.)

   A. *LayoutEditorPart*

   B. *DeclarativeCatalogPart*

   C. *CatalogZone*

   D. *AppearanceEditorPart*

4. You have created a Web Part control that prompts the user for personalization information, including his or her name, region, and preferences. You want other controls to be able to read information from this control to customize the information they display. How should you modify your Web Part to enable other Web Parts to connect to it? (Choose the best answer.)

   A. Create a method that shares the user's information and add the *ConnectionConsumer* attribute to that method.

   B. Create a method that shares the user's information and add the *ConnectionProvider* attribute to that method.

   C. Create a public property that shares the user's information and add the *ConnectionConsumer* attribute to that method.

   D. Create a public property that shares the user's information and add the *ConnectionProvider* attribute to that method.

Chapter Review

To further practice and reinforce the skills you learned in this chapter, you can perform the following tasks:

- Review the chapter summary.
- Review the list of key terms introduced in this chapter.
- Complete the case scenarios. These scenarios set up real-world situations involving the topics of this chapter and ask you to create solutions.
- Complete the suggested practices.
- Take a practice test.

Chapter Summary

- Master pages enable you to have a consistent page structure and layout across all Web pages in your application with minimal effort. Any change to a master page can affect all pages the user visits. You can create multiple master pages and allow users to select templates according to their preferences.
- Themes, and specifically skins, can apply a set of attributes to all controls in a Web application. You should use themes to provide consistent, centrally managed appearances. To enable users to customize pages, you can dynamically change themes. User profiles track information about users and are particularly useful for storing user preferences.
- Web Parts are components that contain Web controls and can be easily moved around a page. Users can have as much or as little control over Web Parts as you choose to grant them.

Key Terms

Do you know what these key terms mean? You can check your answers by looking up the terms in the glossary at the end of the book.

- content page
- master page
- theme
- user profile
- Web Part

Case Scenarios

In the following case scenarios, you apply what you've learned about how to implement and apply customization and personalization. You can find answers to these questions in the "Answers" section at the end of this book.

Case Scenario 1: Meet Customization Requirements for an Internal Insurance Application

You are an application developer for Humongous Insurance. Six months ago, you released version 1.0 of a new .NET Web application that internal staff uses to perform several critical tasks, including:

- Looking up customer information when a subscriber calls.
- Managing the list of in-network physicians.
- Identifying subscribers who are behind on payments.
- Analyzing claims to identify areas of high cost.

Since the release of your application, you've been focused on fixing bugs. However, the application is now very stable, and you are beginning discussions with users to determine future features. At this stage, your manager would like you to meet with some users, analyze their requests, and determine how feasible these features might be when using the .NET Framework.

Interviews

Following is a list of company personnel who were interviewed and their statements:

- **Accounts Receivable Manager**   "We have about two dozen employees in accounts receivable who are primarily responsible for chasing down subscribers who are behind on their payments. Your current application works great; however, it doesn't meet everyone's needs equally. To clarify, we have different groups for people responsible for corporate accounts, public sector accounts, small business accounts, and individual subscribers. Depending on the group, these employees want to see different information on the page. If possible, I'd like to enable users to customize pages and have those preferences remembered for each time they visit the page."

- **Underwriter**   "I'm responsible for analyzing claims and determining how we need to adjust prices to cover the cost of claims. I primarily use your application's reporting features. I love them—all I ask is that you make them more flexible. Right now, if I select a type of claim, I can see a chart of how the costs for that type of claim have changed over time. I'd like to be able to view that chart, but also view whether the claim is regional in nature, and whether specific types of organizations have more of that type of claim than others. Right now, I have to open different windows to see these different reports. I'd like them all to appear on a single page when I click a claim type."

Questions

Answer the following questions for your manager.

1. How can you provide the personalization capabilities requested by the Accounts Receivable Manager?

2. How can you enable different components to communicate with each other, as described by the underwriter?

Case Scenario 2: Provide Consistent Formatting for an External Web Application

You are an application developer working for Humongous Insurance. You are responsible for updating an external Web application based on user requests. Currently, the Web application's primary features are:

- Enabling subscribers to search and identify providers.

- Providing a reference for subscribers who need to know what is and isn't covered.

- Enabling subscribers to contact customer service representatives with questions.

- Providing portals to subscribers to enable them to read updates about Humongous Insurance and general health care topics.

You have a backlog of e-mails from users. While you have quite a few positive e-mails, today you are reading through the negative e-mails to identify ways to update the application to better serve users.

E-mails

Following is a list of e-mails received from users:

- **ltrj@contoso.com** "Awful. There are so many different fonts that it looks like a ransom note. Why does every page look different? Get an editor."

- **eto1974@fabrikam.com**   "I don't care about your stupid press releases. Take them off the page."
- **rtwo22@cpandl.com**   "Nice website, but the colors are awful."

Questions

Answer the following questions for your manager.

1. How can you address the concerns about the inconsistency of fonts?
2. How can you ensure a developer does not set the incorrect font on a control?
3. How can you allow users to remove the list of press releases from a Web page?
4. How can you enable users to change the colors the Web site?

Suggested Practices

Complete the following tasks to successfully master the Customizing and Personalizing a Web Application exam domain, which includes the objectives Implement a Consistent Page Design by Using Master Pages, Customize a Web Page by Using Themes and User Profiles, and Implement Web Parts in a Web Application.

Implement a Consistent Page Design by Using Master Pages

For this task, you should complete Practices 1 and 2 to gain experience using master pages. Practice 3 shows you how to use master pages to change the layout of pages for different device types, and you should complete it if you are interested in client-specific rendering.

- **Practice 1**   Using a copy of the last Web application you created, implement a master page model and convert your existing .aspx pages to content pages.
- **Practice 2**   Using a copy of the last Web application you created, create multiple master pages and give users the option of switching between master pages based on their preferences for layout and color.
- **Practice 3**   Create a Web application that detects the client device and switches templates based on the client type. For traditional Web browsers, display a navigation bar on the left side of the screen. For mobile clients, display all content in a single row.

Customize a Web Page by Using Themes and User Profiles

For this task, you should complete at least Practices 1 and 2. If you want in-depth knowledge of how themes affect controls, complete Practice 3 as well.

- **Practice 1**   Using a copy of the last Web application you created, add a theme to configure all controls with consistent colors.
- **Practice 2**   Add authenticated user profiles to the last Web application you created. For example, you might use the user profile to track recent database queries and enable the user to select from a list of recent requests.
- **Practice 3**   Create a custom control and experiment with setting the attributes using themes.

Implement Web Parts in a Web Application

For this task, you should complete all three practices to gain experience using Web Parts.

- **Practice 1**   Using the Web Parts page you created in the Lesson 3 exercises, open the Web page using a non-Microsoft browser. Notice how ASP.NET renders the Web Part controls differently.
- **Practice 2**   Using the Web Parts page you created in Lesson 3, Exercise 3, expand the connected control capabilities so that the user's name is stored persistently.
- **Practice 3**   Using the Web Parts page you created in Lesson 3, Exercise 3, remove the static connections from Default.aspx. Then add a *ConnectionsZone* control to the page. View the page and use the *ConnectionsZone* control to manually establish the connections between the *GetName*, *GreetUser*, and *ShowNameBackwards* controls.

Take a Practice Test

The practice tests on this book's companion CD offer many options. For example, you can test yourself on just the content covered in this chapter, or you can test yourself on all the 70-528 certification exam content. You can set up the test so that it closely simulates the experience of taking a certification exam, or you can set it up in study mode so that you can look at the correct answers and explanations after you answer each question.

MORE INFO **Practice tests**

For details about all the practice test options available, see the section titled "How to Use the Practice Tests" in this book's Introduction.

Chapter 10
Globalization and Accessibility

Globalization allows your application to be used by people in different parts of the world who speak different languages, while accessibility enables users with different display and input devices to interact with a Web site. Globalization and accessibility are both important for the same reason: They make your applications useful for a wider audience. This chapter covers both of these important topics.

Exam objectives in this chapter:
■ Implement globalization and accessibility.

Lessons in this chapter:

Before You Begin

To complete the lessons in this chapter, you should be familiar with Microsoft Visual Basic or C# and be comfortable with the following tasks:

■ Have Microsoft Windows XP and Microsoft Visual Studio 2005 installed with Microsoft SQL Server 2005 Express Edition.

■ Be familiar with the Visual Studio 2005 Integrated Development Environment (IDE).

■ Have a basic understanding of Hypertext Markup Language (HTML) and client-side scripting.

Real World

Tony Northrup

The great thing about Web applications is that you can reach millions of users anywhere in the world. This is a challenge for developers, though, because we tend to make development choices based on our own preferences, with input from the people around us. For example, when choosing colors, I tend to stick to black text on a white background. (I'm a simple guy.) When thinking about how to make pages usable by non-technical people, I think of my father-in-law, who hasn't yet figured out how to turn off Caps Lock.

That isn't a good sampling of the user base for a Web application, however. Web applications often have international users and must support multiple languages and cultures. Supporting new languages and cultures involves more than substituting words from other languages and often requires different alphabets and layouts. You also need to keep in mind that many users have screen readers, alternative pointing devices, and other accessibility tools. Therefore, such users won't interact with a Web page as most people would.

Lesson 1: Configuring Globalization and Localization

Whether you're creating an intranet application for a multinational company or a public Web application for a global audience, you need to consider the best ways to address users in different cultures with different languages. ASP.NET provides the infrastructure to create Web applications that automatically adjust formatting and languages according to user preferences.

This lesson describes how to create Web applications that are suitable for varied cultures.

After this lesson, you will be able to:

- Use local and global resources to provide multiple languages of your Web application.
- Create a Web page structure that is flexible enough to support different languages.
- Programmatically set the language and culture of a Web page.

Estimated lesson time: 40 minutes

Using Resource Files

If you need to display an ASP.NET page in one of several different languages, you could prompt the user for his or her preferred language, and then write if-then statements to update the text of all controls. However, that would be complex, time-consuming, and would require that the person translating the Web site know how to write code.

ASP.NET uses resource files to make supporting multiple languages simpler. Visual Studio 2005 can automatically generate Extensible Markup Language (XML) resource files that contain text for your controls in different languages. You don't need to be a developer to update these resource files, so you can use non-technical translation staff to provide different versions of the site's user interface. When the user visits your site, the Web browser can provide the user's language preference. ASP.NET then automatically displays text using that language's resources, if they are available.

There are two types of resources: local and global. The sections that follow describe each of these types of resources.

Local Resources

Local resources are specific to a single Web page and should be used for providing versions of a Web page in different languages. Local resources must be stored in an App_LocalResources subfolder of the folder containing the Web page. Because you might have local resources for every page in your Web application, you might have App_LocalResources subfolders in every folder.

Resource files are named using the format *<PageName>*[*.language*].resx. Therefore, the following are all valid resource files for different language versions of the Default.aspx page:

- **Default.aspx.resx**   The base resource file to use if no other resource file better matches the user's language and culture.

NOTE   The term *culture*

In development, the term *culture* refers to regional language and formatting differences. For example, English spoken in the United States is slightly different than the English spoken in England or Australia. Each country might also have different standards for currency and formatting. For example, in the United States, numbers are written as 12,345.67. In parts of Europe, the comma and period are used differently, and the same number is written as 12.345,67. By specifying a culture, the .NET Framework automatically adjusts formatting as needed. You need to manually create culture-specific resources, however.

- **Default.aspx.de.resx**   A resource file for German. (The abbreviation for German is "de.")

- **Default.aspx.es.resx**   A resource file for Spanish. (The abbreviation for Spanish is "es.")

- **Default.aspx.es-mx.resx**   A resource file for Spanish (Mexico), specifically. (The abbreviation for the Spanish language in the country of Mexico is "es-MX.") If you have both this file and the Default.apsx.es.resx file, ASP.NET uses this resource file for users in Mexico, while all other Spanish-speaking cultures receive the Default.aspx.es.resx file.

Generating a Default Resource File   To automatically generate a resource file using Visual Studio 2005, follow these steps:

1. In the Visual Studio designer, click the designer surface or a control.

2. On the Tools menu, select Generate Local Resource.

    This causes Visual Studio to perform the following tasks:

    ❏ Create the App_LocalResources folder, if necessary.

❑ Generate an XML-based local resource file for the Web page in the App_LocalResources folder with *Text* and *ToolTip* values for all existing controls on the page, as well as the page title. The following example demonstrates this:

```
<data name="Button1Resource1.Text" xml:space="preserve">
  <value>My Default Button Text</value>
</data>
<data name="Label1Resource1.Text" xml:space="preserve">
  <value>My Default Label Text</value>
</data>
<data name="PageResource1.Title" xml:space="preserve">
  <value>My Globalized Web page</value>
</data>
```

❑ Change the declarations for all server controls to include the *meta:resourcekey* attribute, as the following example demonstrates:

```
<asp:Label ID="Label1" runat="server" meta:resourcekey="Label1Resource1"
Text="Label" />
<asp:Button ID="Button1" runat="server" meta:resourcekey="Button1Resource1"
Text="Button" />
```

If you add additional controls to the Web page after generating the resource file, Visual Studio does not automatically add resources for those controls. However, you can later select Generate Local Resource on the Tools menu to update the resource file with any new controls you have added. Typically, generating resource files is one of the last steps of the development process. Once you have multiple resource files, you need to add each new control to every resource file, and then translate the values for each culture. This is error-prone and can be very time-consuming.

Creating Resource Files for Other Cultures   Once you create a default resource file, you can copy and paste it to create resource files for other cultures. Then you need to update the resource values for the new culture. To copy the default resource file, follow these steps:

1. In Solution Explorer, right-click your default resource file, and then select Copy.

2. Right-click the App_LocalResources folder, and then select Paste.

3. Right-click the new resource file, and then select Rename. Type a new name, for the resource file, that includes the language and culture code before the file extension. For example, you might name the file **Default.aspx.fr.resx** to create a French-language version of the Default.aspx page. (The abbreviation for French is "fr.")

4. Double-click the new resource file to open it in Visual Studio. Visual Studio displays a table containing values and comments for each resource. Update the values for the new culture, and then save the resource file.

Repeat these steps to create resource files for every culture that you want to support. While Visual Studio provides a convenient interface for developers, translators can use any standard XML editor to update the resource files.

Testing Resource Files for Other Cultures   ASP.NET automatically determines the user's preferred culture based on information provided by the Web browser. To test other cultures, you need to update the preferred language in your Web browser by following these steps:

1. In Microsoft Internet Explorer, on the Tools menu, choose Internet Options.

2. Click Languages.

3. In the Language Preference dialog box, click Add.

4. In the Add Language dialog box, under Languages, click the language you want to test, and then click OK. This is shown in Figure 10-1.

Figure 10-1   Add a new preferred language to Internet Explorer to test your Web site.

5. In the Language Preference dialog box, under Language, click the language you want to test. Then click Move Up to move it to the top of the list, and then click OK.

Now you can visit the Web page and view the selected culture's resource file. When you are done testing, remember to reset your browser to your preferred language/culture.

Global Resources

Global resources can be read from any page or code that is in the Web site. You should only use global resources when you need to access a single resource from multiple Web pages. Global resources must be stored in the App_GlobalResources folder at the root of the application.

Using local resource files to automatically define values for controls is called *implicit localization*. With *explicit localization*, you define control properties by manually associating them with resources in global resource files. ASP.NET then automatically provides the correct cultural translation to end users.

To use explicit localization, first create a default global resource file. Then create resources files for individual cultures. Finally, associate control properties with resources.

Quick Check

1. In which folder should you store global resource files?
2. In which folder should you store local resource files?

Quick Check Answers

1. App_GlobalResources
2. App_LocalResources

The sections that follow describe how to create a global resource file, how to associate control properties with global resources, and how to programmatically access resources.

Create a Global Resource File   To create a global resource file, follow these steps:

1. In Solution Explorer, right-click the root of your Web site, click Add ASP.NET Folder, and then click App_GlobalResources.
2. Right-click the App_GlobalResources folder, and then click Add New Item.
3. Under Visual Studio installed templates, click Resource File.
4. In the Name box, type any file name with an .resx extension, such as Localized-Text.resx, and then click Add.
5. Double-click the new resource file to open it in Visual Studio. Visual Studio displays a table. Add values for the culture, and then save the resource file.

6. Copy and paste the resource default file to create resource files for different cultures. For each culture, add the culture identifier immediately before the .resx extension. For example, you might name a French global resource file Localized-Text.fr.resx. Then edit each global resource file to provide the translations.

Associating Control Properties with Global Resources Once you have defined global resources, you can associate control properties (such as *Label.Text*) with the global resource so that ASP.NET automatically displays the correct text for the user's culture. The ability to manually associate a control with a global resource is the key advantage to using global resources over local resources; you can assign multiple controls to a single resource. Therefore, if you have a *Label* that displays a greeting message on every page, you only need to define the message once for each culture, rather than defining it separately for each Web page.

To associate a control property with a global resource, follow these steps:

1. View a control's properties. In the (*Expressions*) property, click the ellipsis (...) button.

2. The Expressions dialog box appears. In the Bindable Properties list, click Text (or any other property that you want to bind to a resource). In the Expression Type list, select Resources.

3. Under Expression Properties, set *ClassKey* to your global resource file name (without the extension) and *ResourceKey* to the name of the resource within the resource file.

4. Click OK, as shown in Figure 10-2.

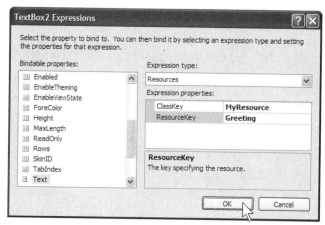

Figure 10-2 Use expressions to bind controls to global resources.

Visual Studio displays the default resource in the Designer and displays the culture-specific resources when users visit the Web page. Within the source, Visual Studio updates the control's *Text* property to <%$ Resource:*ClassKey, ResourceKey* %>. For example, if you ware binding a Label's *Text* property to a message named Greeting in the Resource.resx global resource, the source resembles:

```
<asp:Label ID="Label1" runat="server" Text="<%$ Resources:Resource, Greeting %>" />
```

Exam Tip Know the <%$ Resources:*Resource, Name* %> format for the exam.

Accessing Resource Values Programmatically You can also access resource values programmatically using the *Resources.Resource* object. After saving global resources, Visual Studio creates strongly typed members of the *Resources.Resource* object for every global resource value you add. For example, if you add a value named *Greeting*, you can assign the value to a *Label* control using the following code:

```
'VB
Label1.Text = Resources.Resource.Greeting
```

```
//C#
Label1.Text = Resources.Resource.Greeting;
```

NOTE The *Localize* control

To localize static text, use the *Localize* control. It functions similarly to the *Literal* control.

If the resources are not available at design time, or if you do not use Visual Studio to define the resources, you can use the *GetLocalResourceObject* and *GetGlobalResourceObject* methods to access global resources, and then cast them to the correct type. For example, the following code sample uses these methods to define two controls:

```
'VB
Button1.Text = GetLocalResourceObject("Button1.Text").ToString()
Image1.ImageUrl = CType(GetGlobalResourceObject("WebResourcesGlobal", "LogoUrl"), String)
```

```
//C#
Button1.Text = GetLocalResourceObject("Button1.Text").ToString();
Image1.ImageUrl = (String)GetGlobalResourceObject("WebResourcesGlobal", "LogoUrl");
```

To use the *GetLocalResourceObject* method, simply provide the name of the resource. To use *GetGlobalResourceObject*, provide both the file name (without the extension) and the resource name.

HTML Layout Best Practices

Globalization can be as simple as replacing text with text from another language and reformatting numbers and symbols. However, some languages, such as Arabic languages, require different layouts because text flows from right to left. To allow Web pages to be used by the widest variety of cultures, follow these guidelines:

- **Avoid using absolute positioning and sizes for controls** Rather than specifying control locations in pixels, allow the Web browser to position them automatically. You can do this by simply not specifying a size or location. The easiest way to determine if any controls have absolute positions is to view the source for a Web page. For example, the following illustrates a control that uses absolute positioning, which should be avoided:

```
<div id = idLabel style = "position: absolute; left: 0.98em; top: 1.21em; width: 4.8em;
height: 1.21em;">
```

- **Use the entire width and height of forms** Although many Web sites specify a number of pixels for the width of a form or table column, this can cause formatting problems for languages that use more letters or a different text layout. Instead of specifying a specific width, use 100 percent of the width of the Web browser, as the following sample demonstrates:

```
<table width=100%>
```

- **Size elements relative to the overall size of the form** When you do need to provide a specific size for a control, use relative proportions to allow the entire form to be easily resized. You can use this using style sheet expressions, as the following sample demonstrates:

```
<div style='
  height: expression(document.body.clientHeight / 2);
  width: expression(document.body.clientWidth / 2); '>
```

- **Use a separate table cell for each control** Doing this allows text to wrap independently and ensures correct alignment for cultures in which text layout flows from right to left.

- **Avoid enabling the *NoWrap* property in tables** Setting *HtmlTableCell.NoWrap* to *true* disables word wrapping. While it might work well in your native language, other languages can take more space and might not display correctly.

- **Avoid specifying the *Align* property in tables**   Setting a left or right alignment in a cell can override layout in cultures that use right-to-left text. Therefore, avoid them.

In summary, the less explicitly you configure layout, the better your page can be localized, because you leave layout decisions to the client browser.

Setting the Culture

Often, Web browsers are configured with the user's language preferences. However, many Web browsers are misconfigured. For example, an American tourist in Mexico might use a Web browser at an Internet café that has been configured for Spanish, even though the American would prefer to read English. For this reason, you should use the browser's setting as the default and allow users to override that default setting.

In an ASP.NET Web page, you use two different *Page* properties to set culture:

- **Culture**   Determines the results of culture-dependent functions, such as the date, number, and currency formatting. You can only define the *Culture* object with *specific cultures* that define both language and regional formatting requirements, such as "es-MX" or "fr-FR." You cannot define the *Culture* object with *neutral cultures* that define only a language, such as "es" or "fr."

- **UICulture**   Determines which global or local resources are loaded for the page. You can define *UICulture* with either neutral or specific cultures.

Define the *Culture* and *UICulture* properties by overriding the page's *InitializeCulture* method. From this method, define the *Culture* and *UICulture* properties, and then call the page's base *InitializeCulture* method. The following code sample demonstrates this, assuming that DropDownList1 contains a list of cultures:

```vb
'VB
Protected Overloads Overrides Sub InitializeCulture()
    If Not (Request.Form("DropDownList1") Is Nothing) Then
        ' Define the language
        UICulture = Request.Form("DropDownList1")

        ' Define the formatting (requires a specific culture)
        Culture = Request.Form("DropDownList1")
    End If
    MyBase.InitializeCulture()
End Sub
```

```csharp
//C#
protected override void InitializeCulture()
{
```

```
    if (Request.Form["DropDownList1"] != null)
    {
        // Define the language
        UICulture = Request.Form["DropDownList1"];

        // Define the formatting (requires a specific culture)
        Culture = Request.Form("DropDownList1");
    }
    base.InitializeCulture();
}
```

Normally, you should provide users with a list of cultures and languages for which you have configured resources. For example, if you have configured resources for English, Spanish, and French, you should only allow users to choose from one of those three options. However, you can also retrieve an array of all available cultures by calling the *System.Globalization.CultureInfo.GetCultures* method. Pass this method a *CultureTypes* enumeration that specifies which subset of available cultures you want to list. The most useful *CultureTypes* values are:

- **AllCultures**   All cultures included with the .NET Framework, including both neutral and specific cultures. If you use *AllCultures* in your code, be sure to verify that a selected culture is a specific culture before assigning it to the *Culture* object.

- **NeutralCultures**   Neutral cultures that provide only a language and not regional formatting definitions.

- **SpecificCultures**   Specific cultures that provide both language and regional formatting definitions.

You can also declaratively set the culture for a Web site or Web page. To define the culture for an entire Web site, add a <globalization> section to the Web.config file, and then set the *uiculture* and *culture* attributes, as the following sample demonstrates:

```
<globalization uiculture="es" culture="es-MX" />
```

To declare a culture for a Web page, define the *UICulture* and *Culture* attributes of the @ Page declaration, as shown here:

```
<%@ Page UICulture="es" Culture="es-MX" %>
```

By default, Visual Studio defines the *UICulture* and *Culture* page attributes as *auto*.

Lab: Creating a Web Page That Supports Multiple Cultures

In this lab, you create a multicultural Web page.

▶ **Exercise: Create a Web page for Both English and Spanish**

In this exercise, you create a Web page that displays language-specific text based on the user's browser preference, while allowing users to overwrite the default setting.

1. Create a blank ASP.NET Web site in Visual Studio 2005.

2. Open the Default.aspx form and add a *Label* control and a *DropDownList* control. Set the *DropDownList.AutoPostBack* property to *True*. You use the *Label* control to display a culture-specific greeting to the user, and you use the *DropDownList* control to allow the user to choose a specific language.

3. Click the Designer surface. Click the Tools menu, and then click Generate Local Resource.

4. In Solution Explorer, double-click Default.aspx.resx. For the *Label1Resource1.Text* value, type **Hello**. For the *PageResource1.Title* value, type **English**. Then save the Default.aspx.resx file.

5. In Solution Explorer, right-click Default.aspx.resx, and then click Copy. Right-click App_LocalResources and click Paste. Next, rename the new resource file to **Default.aspx.es.resx**.

6. Double-click Default.aspx.es.resx. For the *Label1Resource1.Text* value, type **Hola**. For the *PageResource1.Title* value, type **Español**. Then save the Default.aspx.es.resx file.

7. Press Ctrl+F5 to open your page in a Web browser. Notice that the *Label* displays Hello even though you never directly set the *Label1.Text* property. Also notice that the page title (shown in the Internet Explorer title bar) shows English.

8. In Internet Explorer, follow these steps:

   a. On the Tools menu, select Internet Options.

   b. In the Internet Options dialog box, click Languages.

   c. In the Language Preference dialog box, click Add.

   d. In the Add Language dialog box, under Languages, click Spanish (Mexico) [es-mx]. Then, click OK.

e. In the Language list, click Spanish, and then click Move Up to make it your preferred language.

f. Click OK twice to return to Internet Explorer.

9. Reload the Web page and verify that the page displays the Spanish resources you provided.

10. Return to Visual Studio and edit the source code for the Default.aspx page. Add the *System.Globalization* namespace to the page to allow you to use the *Culture-Info* object.

11. In the *Page_Load* event handler (which you can create in Visual Basic by double-clicking the Default.aspx Designer surface), write code to populate the *DropDownList1* control with a list of cultures, as the following code sample demonstrates:

```vb
'VB
For Each ci As CultureInfo In CultureInfo.GetCultures(CultureTypes.NeutralCultures)
    DropDownList1.Items.Add(New ListItem(ci.NativeName, ci.Name))
Next
```

```csharp
//C#
foreach (CultureInfo ci in CultureInfo.GetCultures(CultureTypes.NeutralCultures))
{
    DropDownList1.Items.Add(new ListItem(ci.NativeName, ci.Name));
}
```

NOTE   **Neutral vs. specific cultures**

This code sample provides *CultureTypes.NeutralCultures* to get a list of cultures that provide both language and culture info (for example "en-us" instead of just "en"). You can use *CultureTypes.SpecificCultures* instead if you want the user to pick both language and country. You can use neutral cultures to define the *UICulture* object, but you can only use specific cultures to define the *Culture* object.

---

12. Now override the *InitializeCulture* method to base the page's culture on the item selected from the *DropDownList1* control. Because we are defining only language, use the *UICulture* object, rather than the *Culture* object. Call the base *InitializeCulture* event after you have defined *UICulture*. The following code sample demonstrates this:

```vb
'VB
Protected Overloads Overrides Sub InitializeCulture()
    If Not (Request.Form("DropDownList1") Is Nothing) Then
        UICulture = Request.Form("DropDownList1")
    End If
    MyBase.InitializeCulture()
```

```
End Sub

//C#
protected override void InitializeCulture()
{
    if (Request.Form["DropDownList1"] != null)
    {
        UICulture = Request.Form["DropDownList1"];
    }
    base.InitializeCulture();
}
```

13. Press Ctrl+F5 to open your page in a Web browser. From the drop-down list, select English. The page reloads and displays the English greeting. Select Spanish again and notice that the page changes back to Spanish. The drop-down list and your implementation of *InitializeCulture* allow ASP.NET to automatically select the browser's preferred language, while giving users the option of overriding the default choice.

14. Repeat step 8 to reconfigure Internet Explorer to your normal language settings.

Lesson Summary

- Local resource files allow you to provide translations for controls on a Web page. Local resources provide translations for a single Web page and should be placed in the App_LocalResources folder within the page's folder. Local resource files are named using the format *<PageName>*[.*language*].resx. Global resources provide translations for phrases that can be assigned to any control in the Web application and should be placed in the App_GlobalResources folder at the root of the application.

- To make your page as easy to globalize as possible, follow these best practices:
    - Avoid using absolute positioning and sizes for controls.
    - Use the entire width and height of forms.
    - Size elements relative to the overall size of the form.
    - Use a separate table cell for each control.
    - Avoid enabling the *NoWrap* property in tables.
    - Avoid specifying the *Align* property in tables.

- To programmatically set the language, set the *UICulture* object to the neutral or specific culture abbreviation. To programmatically set the regional formatting preferences, set the *Culture* object to the specific culture abbreviation.

Lesson Review

You can use the following questions to test your knowledge of the information in Lesson 1, "Configuring Globalization." The questions are also available on the companion CD if you prefer to review them in electronic form.

NOTE Answers

Answers to these questions and explanations of why each answer choice is right or wrong are located in the "Answers" section at the end of the book.

---

1. You need to create a Web page that is available in both the default language of English and in German. Which of the following resource files should you create? (Choose all that apply.)

   A. App_LocalResources/Page.aspx.resx.de

   B. App_LocalResources/Page.aspx.resx

   C. App_LocalResources/Page.aspx.de.resx

   D. App_LocalResources/Page.aspx.en.resx

2. What must you do to enable users to choose their own language preferences? (Choose all that apply.)

   A. Define the *Page.Culture* property.

   B. Define the *Page.UICulture* property.

   C. Override the *Page.InitializeCulture* method.

   D. Override the *Page.ReadStringResource* method.

3. How can you define a control property using a global resource at design time?

   A. In Visual Studio, define the *DataValueField* property.

   B. In Visual Studio, define the *DataSourceID* property.

   C. In Visual Studio, edit the *Text* property.

   D. In Visual Studio, edit the *(Expressions)* property.

4. You add a global resource with the name Login by using Visual Studio. How can you access that global resource programmatically?

   A. *Resources.Resource.Login*

   B. *Resources.Resource("Login")*

   C. *Resources("Login")*

   D. *Resources.Login*

Lesson 2: Configuring Accessibility

Whether you are creating a public Web site for millions to use, or a small intranet Web application, you must strive to make it usable by the widest possible audience. By making your site accessible, you make it usable by those who prefer non-traditional input and display devices. For example, many a user does not use a conventional mouse, and other users use screen readers to read the text on Web sites, rather than displaying it on a monitor.

This lesson provides best practices for making your Web application accessible.

After this lesson, you will be able to:

- Describe public accessibility standards.
- Explain how ASP.NET controls provide accessibility by default.
- Create Web pages that support visual accessibility tools.
- Create Web pages that support accessibility tools for user input.
- Test the accessibility of individual Web pages or entire Web applications.

Estimated lesson time: 30 minutes

Public Accessibility Guidelines

Many people are working to make technology accessible to the widest audience possible. One of the most prominent groups is the World Wide Web Consortium (W3C), a Web standards organization. Through the Web Accessibility Initiative, the W3C has created the Web Content Accessibility Guidelines (WCAG).

MORE INFO   WCAG

The WCAG is very thorough; this book only attempts to cover the key points as they relate to ASP.NET development. For more information about WCAG, visit *http://www.w3.org/WAI/*.

The United States government has also created accessibility standards in Section 508 of the Rehabilitation Act. Depending on the organization for which you are developing a Web application, you may be required to conform your application to these standards. The Section 508 guidelines are conceptually similar to the WCAG guidelines.

MORE INFO Section 508 Guidelines

For more information about Section 508 guidelines, visit *http://www.section508.gov/*.

How ASP.NET Controls Support Accessibility

ASP.NET controls are designed to be accessible by default. For example, login controls such as *Login*, *ChangePassword*, *PasswordRecovery*, and *CreateUserWizard* use text boxes with associated labels to help a user who uses a screen reader or who does not use a mouse. These controls also use input controls with tab index settings to make data entry without a mouse easier.

Another way some ASP.NET controls support accessibility is by allowing users to skip link text. *Screen readers* typically read the text of links from the top to the bottom of a page, enabling users to choose a specific link. ASP.NET controls that include navigation links provide the *SkipLinkText* property, which is enabled by default and allows users to skip past the link text. The *CreateUserWizard*, *Menu*, *SiteMapPath*, *TreeView*, and *Wizard* controls each support skipping links. These links are not visible to users viewing the page with a traditional Web browser. For example, the following HTML source code (which has been slightly simplified) is generated by default when you add a *Menu* control to a Web page:

```
<a href="#Menu1_SkipLink">
    <img alt="Skip Navigation Links" src="/WebResource.axd?d=_9Q2Lm" width="0" height="0" />
</a>
… menu links …
<a id="Menu1_SkipLink"></a>
```

As the HTML demonstrates, a zero-pixel image file with the alt text "Skip Navigation Links" links to a location on the page immediately after the menu. While traditional browsers do not display the zero-pixel image, screen readers read the alt text and allow users to skip past the menu. The simplest way to follow this best practice is to use one of the ASP.NET controls that provides the *SkipLinkText* property. However, if you implement custom controls with navigation links, you can provide similar functionality.

Though ASP.NET controls are designed to be as accessible as possible, you, as the developer, must take advantage of some features by providing text descriptions of some controls. The next sections provide more detailed information.

Improving Visual Accessibility

Many users have tools to supplement or replace a traditional monitor. These tools include screen readers, magnifiers, and high-contrast display settings. To make your application as accessible as possible using these tools, follow these guidelines:

- **Describe every image by providing alt text using the *AlternateText* property** This is useful for users who have images disabled in browsers or otherwise cannot see the pictures. Screen readers, which use speech synthesis to verbally read text on a Web page, can read alt text descriptions. You can also set the *Image.Description-Url* property to specify an HTML page that further describes an image, but you should only configure it if you want to provide a longer description than is possible with *AlternateText*. If an image is not important (such as an image that forms a border), set the *GenerateEmptyAlternateText* property to *True* to cause screen readers to ignore it.

- **Use solid colors for background and use contrasting colors for text** All users appreciate easy-to-read text, especially users who may not be able to perceive low-contrast text. Therefore, you should avoid text that is a similar shade to the background color.

- **Create a flexible page layout that scales correctly when text size is increased** Internet Explorer and other browsers support the ability to increase text size, which makes text easier to read. This is useful both to users who have specialized accessibility settings and users with high-resolution displays.

- **Set the *Table.Caption* property to a description of the table** Screen readers can read the *Table.Caption* property to describe the purpose of the data contained in a table to users. This allows the user to quickly determine whether he or she wants to hear the contents of the table or skip past it.

- **Provide a way to identify column headers** You can create table headers by using the *TableHeaderRow* class and setting the *TableSection* property to the *Table-Header* enumeration of the *TableRowSection* class. This causes the table to render a *thead* element. When you create cells with the *TableCell* control, you can set each *AssociatedHeaderCellID* property for the cell to the ID of a table header cell. This causes the cell to render a header attribute that associates the cell with the corresponding column heading, simplifying table navigation for users with screen readers. The *Calendar*, *DetailsView*, *FormView*, and *GridView* ASP.NET server controls render HTML tables with these features.

■ **Avoid defining specific font sizes**   Use heading tags (such as <H1> or <H3>) instead of font sizes to support the user's formatting options. Heading tags are available from the Visual Studio Formatting toolbar.

■ **Avoid requiring client scripts**   Assistive technologies often cannot render client scripts, so you should use client script only for nonessential effects, such as mouse rollovers. For example, validator controls use client scripts to determine whether input meets specified requirements, and then to dynamically display error messages. However, screen readers and other assistive technologies might not render this correctly. Therefore, you should set the *EnableClientScript* property to *False* to improve accessibility. WCAG standards do not allow controls that require client scripts, so if you must comply with these standards, you should also avoid using the *LinkButton*, *ImageButton*, and *Calendar* controls.

NOTE   WCAG standards and client scripts

In practice, your users may not have problems with the client scripts included with ASP.NET server controls. These client scripts have been developed to comply with WCAG accessibility guidelines. However, total WCAG compliance does require you to avoid insisting on client script support.

If you cannot meet accessibility goals, consider providing alternative text-only Web pages. You can use global resources to allow both accessible and nonaccessible versions of a Web page to share the same text content.

Quick Check

1. What can you do to make a Web page more useful to users who use special displays or screen readers to make text more readable?

2. What can you do to make a Web page more useful to a user who does not use a mouse?

Quick Check Answers

1. First, avoid specifying font sizes or using colors that might be difficult to read. Second, provide descriptions for images, tables, and forms that screen readers can use.

2. Provide access keys for all controls that require user input and underline the access keys in associated labels. Define a logical tab order that allows the user to progress through the form using the Tab key. Additionally, specify default buttons for forms and *Panel* controls.

Improving the Accessibility of Forms Requiring User Input

Many users prefer not to use mice or have difficulties using pointing devices. For these users, it's critical that you make your Web application usable by keyboard alone. While providing keyboard shortcuts is common in Windows Forms applications, it's fairly uncommon in Web applications.

To make your application as accessible as possible using a keyboard, follow these guidelines:

- **Set the** *DefaultFocus* **property for a form to place the cursor in a logical location where data entry normally begins** *DefaultFocus* defines where the cursor starts when a user opens a Web page. Typically, you set the default focus to the topmost editable field on a page.

- **Define the tab order in a logical way so that a user can complete forms without using a mouse** Ideally, a user should be able to complete one text box, and then press the Tab key to jump to the next text box.

- **Specify default buttons for forms and** *Panel* **controls by setting the** *DefaultButton* **property** Default buttons can be accessed simply by pressing Enter. Not only does this make user input simpler for a user who doesn't use a mouse, but it can speed data entry.

- **Provide useful link text** Screen readers enable users to choose links by speaking hyperlinked text. Therefore, all hyperlinked text should describe the link. Avoid adding hyperlinks to text such as "Click here," because users with a screen reader will not be able to distinguish it from other links. Instead, provide the name of the link destination with the hyperlink, such as "Directions to Contoso headquarters."

- **Define access keys for button controls by setting the** *AccessKey* **property** You can use access keys for Web controls just like you would for a Windows Forms application. When you set the *AccessKey* property for a control, the user can hold down the Alt key and press the specified letter to immediately move the cursor to that control. The standard method of indicating a shortcut key is to underline a letter in the control. The next guideline describes how to provide shortcut keys for *TextBox* controls.

- **Use** *Label* **controls to define access keys for text boxes** *TextBox* controls do not have descriptions that can be easily read by screen readers. Therefore, you should associate a descriptive *Label* control with a *TextBox* control and use the *Label* control to define the *TextBox* control's shortcut key. To associate the *Label* with another control, define both the *AccessKey* and *AssociatedControlID* properties. Also, underline the access key in the *Label's* text using the underline HTML element (<*u*> and </*u*>). The following source demonstrates a *Label* control and an associated *TextBox* control:

```
<asp:Label
    AccessKey="N"
    AssociatedControlID="TextBox1"
    ID="Label1"
    runat="server"
    Text="<u>N</u>ame:">
</asp:Label>
 
<asp:TextBox ID="TextBox1" runat="server" />
```

■ **Whenever possible, use the *Panel* control to create subdivisions in a form and define the *Panel.GroupingText* property with a description of the controls in that panel** ASP.NET uses the *GroupingText* property to create <*fieldset*> and <*legend*> HTML elements, which can make forms easier for users to navigate. For example, you might define separate *Panel* controls to collect a user's shipping, billing, and credit card information in a checkout page. The following HTML demonstrates how ASP.NET renders the *Panel.GroupingText* property as a <*legend*> element:

```
<form name="form1" method="post" action="Default.aspx" id="form1">
<div id="Panel1" style="height:50px;width:125px;">
  <fieldset>
  <legend>
Shipping Information
  </legend>
        <input name="TextBox2" type="text" id="TextBox2" />
  </fieldset>
</div>
<div id="Panel2" style="height:50px;width:125px;">
  <fieldset>
  <legend>
Billing Information
  </legend>
        <input name="TextBox1" type="text" id="TextBox1" />
  </fieldset>
</div>
```

■ **Specify meaningful error messages in the *Text* and *ErrorMessage* properties of validator controls**   While the default asterisk (*) is sufficient to identify input controls that need to be completed for some users, it is not useful to users with screen readers. Instead, provide descriptive error messages, such as, "You must provide your e-mail address."

Real World

Tony Northrup

Making a Web site accessible takes only a few extra minutes and usually doesn't have a negative impact on users with traditional Web browsers. Contrary to popular belief, you don't need to use huge font sizes or black-and-white text. People with accessibility requirements typically already have their computers configured to meet their requirements.

The first key to accessibility is to avoid forcing small font sizes and difficult-to-read colors on users in such a way that it overrides their font size and color settings. Often, that's as easy as not specifying special formatting or colors, and just letting the Web browser make display choices based on user settings.

The second key to accessibility is providing multiple techniques for viewing and selecting objects. Provide hidden text descriptions for tables, forms, and images. Provide keyboard shortcuts for buttons and text boxes. A user who doesn't use a mouse will appreciate it, and others won't notice.

Testing Accessibility

Visual Studio can test Web pages or entire Web applications for compliance to WCAG and Section 508 standards. The sections that follow describe how to use Visual Studio to automatically test your work.

▶ **Checking the Accessibility of a Single Page**

To use Visual Studio to test the accessibility of a Web page, follow these steps:

1. In Visual Web Developer, open the page.

2. On the View menu, choose Error List.

3. On the Tools menu, choose Check Accessibility. The Accessibility Validation dialog box appears.

4. Select the check boxes for the type and level of accessibility checking that you want to perform, and then click Validate.

The results of the check are displayed in the Error List window.

▶ **Automatically Checking the Accessibility of a Web Application**

To use Visual Studio to automatically test the accessibility of a Web application when you build it, follow these steps:

1. In Solution Explorer, right-click the name of your Web site, and then choose Property Pages.

2. Click Accessibility.

3. Select the check boxes for the type and level of accessibility checking that you want to perform, and then click Apply.

4. Click Build.

5. Select one or both of the following check boxes, depending on whether you want to check individual pages and/or the entire Web site when building the Web site:

    ❑ Include Accessibility Validation When Building Page

    ❑ Include Accessibility Validation When Building Web

6. Click OK.

Now, when you build your Web application, Visual Studio automatically generates a list of errors. Accessibility errors won't prevent a successful build, and you have to manually view the Error List to examine any issues.

Lab: Improving the Accessibility of a Web Page

In this lab, you improve the accessibility of an ASP.NET Web application.

▶ **Exercise 1: Make an Accessible Checkout Page**

In this exercise, you update an existing e-commerce checkout page to make it more accessible by following accessibility best practices.

1. Copy the Chapter 10, Exercise 2, Lesson 1 partial project from the companion CD to a folder on your local computer. Then open the project in Visual Studio.

2. Open the Default.aspx page in Visual Studio, and then press Ctrl+F5 to view the page in a browser. Make note of the nonaccessible aspects of the page, including:

    ❑ Lack of panels to divide the form

    ❑ Noncontrasting colors

    ❑ Lack of alt text for images

    ❑ No tab order specified

    ❑ Labels not associated with text boxes

    ❑ No default focus

    ❑ No default button configured

3. First, add two *Panel* controls to the form, and then move the shipping address and billing address tables into their respective panels. Then, set the *GroupingText* property for the new *Panel* controls to *Shipping Address* and *Billing Address*. Panel controls help with accessibility by enabling users to easily navigate to different parts of a form, and the *GroupingText* property replaces the Shipping Address and Billing Address images, which screen readers cannot read.

4. Using the image editor of your choice, replace the Contoso-Logo.gif file with a logo that has colors with more contrast. The existing foreground and background colors are too similar and are not easily readable. You can also change the page background color to match the logo.

NOTE **Complying with logo requirements**

Many organizations have very strict logo requirements that specify the colors that must be used when displaying the logo. However, most organizations also have a high-contrast version of their logo. For more information, contact the public relations group within your organization.

---

5. Provide alt text for the logo by setting the *Image1.AlternateText* property to *Contoso, Inc. logo*.

6. Specify a tab order for the text boxes by setting the *TextBox.TabIndex* property for each text box. Make the top text box *1* and number the rest sequentially as you work down the page. Also, set the *TabIndex* properties for the two buttons at the bottom of the page.

7. Replace the text which is currently labeling the text boxes with *Label* controls. For each *Label* control, define a unique *AccessKey* property and underline that letter in the label. Also, define the *AssociatedControlID* property to associate each label with the correct *TextBox* control.

8. Finally, configure a default button and default focus. Switch to Source view and click the Form ASP.NET element. Then view the Properties window and set the *DefaultButton* property to *Button1* and set the *DefaultFocus* property to *TextBox1*.

9. Press Ctrl+F5 to open the Web page in your browser. Use the shortcut keys to navigate between fields. View the alt text for the logo by hovering your cursor over the logo.

10. Return to Visual Studio. Click the Tools menu, and then click Check Accessibility. Examine the errors and address any errors that seem valid.

Lesson Summary

- Two of the most prominent accessibility standards are the W3C's WCAG standards and the U.S. government's Section 508 standards.

- ASP.NET controls support accessibility whenever possible. For example, controls that provide multiple navigation links give users with screen readers the opportunity to skip the links.

- To make Web pages as visually accessible as possible, follow these guidelines:
  - Provide good alternative (ALT) text for all graphics.
  - Write useful link text.
  - Use tables and their alternatives correctly.
  - Avoid requiring client scripts

- To make Web pages accessible for users with different input tools, design good keyboard navigation by providing keyboard shortcuts, default buttons, and logical tab orders.

- Visual Studio can test your Web page or an entire Web application for WCAG or Section 508 compliance.

Lesson Review

You can use the following questions to test your knowledge of the information in Lesson 2, "Configuring Accessibility." The questions are also available on the companion CD if you prefer to review them in electronic form.

NOTE   Answers

Answers to these questions and explanations of why each answer choice is right or wrong are located in the "Answers" section at the end of the book.

---

1. Which *Image* properties can you define to enable screen readers to describe a picture on a Web page? (Choose all that apply.)

    A. *AccessKey*

    B. *AlternateText*

    C. *DescriptionUrl*

    D. *ToolTip*

2. Which of the following are accessibility features provided by ASP.NET? (Choose all that apply.)

    A. Controls provide properties that enable you to provide hidden descriptions that are available to screen readers.

    B. Controls are displayed in high contrast by default.

    C. Controls that include a list of links at the top provide hidden links to skip over the links.

    D. Controls display text in large font sizes by default.

3. For which of the following guidelines does ASP.NET provide automated testing? (Choose all that apply.)

    A. WCAG Priority 1

    B. WCAG Priority 2

    C. ADA

    D. Access Board Section 508

Chapter Review

To further practice and reinforce the skills you learned in this chapter, you can perform the following tasks:

- Review the chapter summary.
- Review the list of key terms introduced in this chapter.
- Complete the case scenarios. These scenarios set up real-world situations involving the topics of this chapter and ask you to create solutions.
- Complete the suggested practices.
- Take a practice test.

Chapter Summary

- Globalization enables users who speak other languages and have different formatting standards to use your Web application. ASP.NET provides local and global resources to simplify the process of providing translations for controls. Local resources enable you to translate single pages, while global resources provide translations that can be shared between multiple pages. Besides providing translations, you should also follow HTML layout best practices to improve the likelihood that your Web application is rendered correctly in other languages. While Web browsers automatically provide the user's language and regional preferences to the Web server, you should also allow a user to override that preference by choosing options from a list that specifies the *UICulture* and *Culture* objects.

- Accessibility enables users with different input and display devices to interact with your Web application. ASP.NET controls are designed with accessibility in mind. However, you, as a developer, must still define specific properties to improve the accessibility of Web pages. For example, you should always define the *Image.AlternateText* property, because screen readers verbally speak the image's description, helping users without conventional monitors to navigate the site.

Key Terms

Do you know what these key terms mean? You can check your answers by looking up the terms in the glossary at the end of the book.

- culture
- explicit localization
- global resources
- implicit localization
- local resources
- neutral culture
- screen reader
- specific culture

Case Scenarios

In the following case scenarios, you will apply what you've learned about how to implement and apply serialization, as well as how to upgrade applications that make use of serialization. You can find answers to these questions in the "Answers" section at the end of this book.

Case Scenario 1: Upgrade an Application for Multiple Languages

You are an application developer for Contoso, Inc. Contoso manufactures shelving and display units that are used by retail outlets. Traditionally, Contoso's sales staff has been focused entirely within the United States. Typically, a sales staff develops a relationship with a retail chain, and then provides access to the Contoso Web application for new orders and support. You are responsible for developing that Web application.

Contoso has decided to expand globally. At first, the company plans to expand into Canada, and, later, into Mexico. The sales staff is struggling, however, because Contoso's identity is too focused around the English-speaking United States. Sales staff in Canada complain that parts of Canada prefer to speak French, and the Web site is English-only. Similarly, Mexican sales staff have requested a Spanish Web site with regional settings aligned with those commonly used in Mexico.

Answer the following questions for your manager.

1. How can we provide a French version of our Web site?

2. How can translators provide updated text for the Web site?

3. How can users choose between the French and English versions of our Web site?

4. How can we distinguish between Mexican regional requirements and those of other Spanish-speaking countries, such as Spain?

Case Scenario 2: Making a Web Application Accessible

You are an application developer working for Humongous Insurance. Recently, management has begun an initiative to make all facilities and other resources usable with alternative input and display devices, using the United States government's Section 508 of the Rehabilitation Act as a guideline. Your intranet Web application is included within the scope of this initiative.

Questions

Answer the following questions for your manager.

1. How can we determine if any aspects of your Web application are not compliant with Section 508?

2. What does it mean for an application to be accessible?

3. Does the Web application have to be awkward to use with a traditional keyboard, mouse, and monitor if we make it accessible?

4. What types of things do you need to do to make your Web application Section 508 compliant?

Suggested Practices

To successfully master the Implement Globalization and Accessibility exam objective, complete the following tasks.

Implement Globalization and Accessibility

For this task, you should complete at least Practices 1, 2, and 3 for a better understanding of how to provide Web applications for multiple languages and cultures. If you want an understanding of the real-world complexity of providing Web application translations, complete Practice 4 as well. Then complete Practices 5, 6, and 7 to gain an understanding of how to best develop accessible Web applications.

- **Practice 1**   Update the Web application you created in Lesson 1 to also display French and German languages.

- **Practice 2**   Update the Web application you created in Lesson 1 to display a list of specific cultures, and add resources for multiple specific cultures.

- **Practice 3**   Configure Internet Explorer to use a different preferred language. Then, visit your favorite Web sites to see which sites provide alternate languages. Make note of which elements of the page have changed.

- **Practice 4**   Create an application to enable non-developer translators to create local and global resource files. Then, use the tool to provide an alternate language version of the last Web application you created.

- **Practice 5**   Experiment with the Windows XP accessibility tools. To use these accessibility tools, click the Start menu, click All Programs, click Accessories, and then click Accessibility.

- **Practice 6**   Visit this screen reader simulation to experience how screen readers can be used to interact with Web pages: *http://www.webaim.org/simulations/screenreader.php*.

- **Practice 7**   Using the last production Web application you created, use the Check Accessibility tool to identify any accessibility problems. Then, address as many of the accessibility problems as possible.

Take a Practice Test

The practice tests on this book's companion CD offer many options. For example, you can test yourself on just the content covered in this chapter, or you can test yourself on all the 70-528 certification exam content. You can set up the test so that it closely simulates the experience of taking a certification exam, or you can set it up in study mode so that you can look at the correct answers and explanations after you answer each question.

MORE INFO   **Practice tests**

For details about all the practice test options available, see "How to Use the Practice Tests" in this book's Introduction.

Chapter 11

Implementing Authentication and Authorization

When the Web was young, most Web sites were public spaces that did not require users to identify themselves. Today, most Web sites allow users to authenticate so that the users can gain access to private information, site customization, and members-only features.

With the Microsoft .NET Framework version 2.0, adding user-management capabilities to a Web application is easier than ever. As with earlier versions of the .NET Framework, ASP.NET integrates with Windows security, allowing users to authenticate automatically with their Windows or Active Directory user names and passwords. New to the .NET Framework is a set of Login controls and the *Roles* and *Membership* classes. Together, these tools enable you to build simple user management into a Web application without writing a line of code, or, you can provide complex, customized user management by building on the framework.

Exam objectives in this chapter:

- Establish a user's identity by using forms authentication.
  - ❑ Configure forms authentication for a Web application by using a configuration file.
  - ❑ Enable cookieless forms authentication by setting the *cookieless* attribute.
  - ❑ Use membership APIs and the *Membership* class to manage users.
  - ❑ Enable anonymous identification.
- Use authorization to establish the rights of an authenticated user.
  - ❑ Manage roles in the Web Site Administration Tool.
  - ❑ Ascertain whether a specific user is in a role.
  - ❑ Determine the roles for a specific user by using the *Roles* object or the *User* object.
  - ❑ Store role information in a cookie.

❑ Restrict access to files by using file authorization.

❑ Restrict access to portions of an application by using URL authorization.

■ Implement Microsoft Windows authentication and impersonation.

❑ Establish a user's identity by using Windows authentication.

❑ Use impersonation to control access to resources.

■ Use login controls to control access to a Web application.

❑ Use the *Login* Web server control.

❑ Use the *LoginView* Web server control to view a user's login status.

❑ Use the *PasswordRecovery* Web server control to allow a user to recover a password.

❑ Use the *LoginStatus* Web server control to display either a login or logout link.

❑ Use the *LoginName* Web server control to display a user's login name on a Web page.

❑ Use the *CreateUserWizard* Web server control as a UI for creating new Web application user accounts.

❑ Use the *ChangePassword* Web server control to allow a user to change his or her password.

❑ Specify the membership provider used for logging on.

❑ Configure a mail server so that login controls can be used to send e-mail messages to users.

Lessons in this chapter:

Before You Begin

To complete the lessons in this chapter, you should be familiar with Visual Basic (VB) or C# and be comfortable with the following tasks:

- Have Microsoft Windows XP and Microsoft Visual Studio 2005 installed with Microsoft SQL Server 2005 Express Edition.

- Be familiar with the Visual Studio 2005 Integrated Development Environment (IDE).

- Have a basic understanding of Hypertext Markup Language (HTML) and client-side scripting.

Real World

Tony Northrup

People are going to try to hack into your application. It happens to everyone. Even if your data isn't all that important, script kiddies (people who use automated tools to attempt to exploit security vulnerabilities) will explore your Web server and Web site.

For that reason, you must create all Web applications with security in mind. If you assume your site will be attacked, your odds of avoiding a compromise are much greater.

Lesson 1: Using ASP.NET Membership

The .NET Framework version 2.0 includes ASP.NET membership, which makes it easy to add user-management capabilities to your Web site. ASP.NET membership includes several different features:

- Wizard-based configuration of user-management capabilities.

- Browser-based user management and access control configuration.

- A set of ASP.NET controls that provides users with the ability to log in, log out, create new accounts, and recover lost passwords.

- The *Membership* and *Roles* classes, which you can use to access user-management capabilities within your code.

This lesson describes these features and shows you how to use them in your own Web applications.

MORE INFO   **Protecting Web servers**

This chapter strives to provide the information that you need to maximize the security of your Web applications. The topic of improving security for Web servers is massive, and most of the burden of protection falls on the shoulders of system administrators. For more information about protecting servers, read "Securing Your Web Server" in Microsoft Developer Network (MSDN) on the Microsoft Web site at *http://msdn.microsoft.com/library/en-us/secmod/html/secmod89.asp*. For more information about protecting ASP.NET applications, read "Building Secure ASP.NET Applications: Authentication, Authorization, and Secure Communication" at *http://msdn.microsoft.com/library/en-us/dnnetsec/html/SecNetch08.asp*.

> **After this lesson, you will be able to:**
> - List the login controls and describe each control's purpose.
> - Describe how the *Membership* class can be used.
> - Describe how the *Roles* class can be used.
> - Configure an ASP.NET Web application to support user management.
>
> **Estimated lesson time: 45 minutes**

Login Controls

ASP.NET version 2.0 provides controls, classes, and management tools for authenticating users with Web forms and then storing user information in a database, enabling you to track and authenticate users without relying on Active Directory or the Windows local user database. Before the .NET Framework version 2.0 was released, custom user *authentication* required creating many complex components from scratch, including:

- A login page.
- A user database.
- User-management tools.
- Password-management tools.

Creating these components was once very time-consuming. Additionally, it was risky to create these components from scratch, because a bug could compromise your application's security.

The .NET Framework includes controls and classes to simplify the process of adding login capabilities to your Web application. The login controls include:

- *Login*   A user interface that prompts for user names and passwords and enables users to select whether they want to be automatically authenticated the next time they visit. You can use the *Login* control with ASP.NET membership without writing any code, or you can write your own authentication code by adding a handler for the *Authenticate* event.
- *LoginView*   Enables you to display different information to users who are logged in. For example, you could use this link to go to site features that are available only to authenticated users.
- *LoginStatus*   Displays a login link for users who haven't been authenticated and a logout link for users who are currently logged in.
- *LoginName*   Displays the current user's user name, if logged in.
- *PasswordRecovery*   Enables password retrieval for a user by sending an e-mail message to the user or by having the user answer a security question.
- *CreateUserWizard*   Gathers information from a new user and creates a new account.
- *ChangePassword*   Enables a user who is logged in to change his or her password.

Additionally, you can use a *ValidationSummary* control to display detailed error information provided by some of these controls.

The functionality built into these controls enables you to create a Web site that enables users to create their own accounts, change and reset their passwords, and log on and log off without writing any code. Additionally, administrators can use the ASP.NET Web Site Administration Tool to manage user accounts and security settings from a Web browser without understanding how the underlying Web.config files work.

Quick Check

1. Which control would you use to provide a login link?
2. Which login controls are useful only to authenticated users?

Quick Check Answers

1. The *LoginStatus* control.
2. The *LoginName*, *ChangePassword*, and *LoginView* controls.

The *Membership* Class

There are several classes and interfaces for user management; however, the most important class is the *System.Web.Security.Membership* class.

NOTE .NET 2.0

The *Membership* class is new in the .NET Framework version 2.0.

Membership provides capabilities to add, remove, and find users. These capabilities are provided by the following static methods:

- **CreateUser** Adds a user to the database. Use this method if you create a custom page to enable users or administrators to add new accounts.

- **DeleteUser** Removes a user from the data store. Use this method if you create custom user management tools.

- **FindUsersByEmail** Gets a collection of membership users for whom the e-mail addresses contain the specified e-mail addresses to match.

- **FindUsersByName** Gets a collection of membership users for whom the user names contain the specified user names to match.

- **GeneratePassword** Creates a random password of the specified length. Use this if you are implementing custom controls to generate or reset passwords.

- **GetAllUsers** Returns a collection of all users in the database.

- **GetNumberOfUsersOnline** Returns the number of users currently logged on.

- **GetUser**   Returns a *MembershipUser* object representing the current logged-on user. Call this method any time you need to access the current user's account.

- **GetUserNameByEmail**   Gets a user name for which the e-mail address for the user matches the specified e-mail address.

- **UpdateUser**   Updates the database with the information for the specified user. Use this method if you create a page to enable users or administrators to modify existing accounts.

- **ValidateUser**   Verifies that the supplied user name and password are valid. Use this method to check a user's credentials if you create your own custom login controls.

The *Roles* Class

Role management consists of a set of classes and interfaces that establish roles for the current user and manage role information. In ASP.NET user management, roles function as user groups, enabling you to assign access controls to all users who are part of a specific role. The most useful of these classes is *System.Web.Security.Roles*, which provides capabilities to add users to or remove users from roles, create new roles, and determine which roles a user is a member of.

NOTE .NET 2.0

The *Roles* class is new in the .NET Framework 2.0.

Roles provides many static methods, including the following:

- **AddUserToRole, AddUsersToRoles, AddUsersToRole,** and **AddUsersToRoles**   Adds a user to a role

- **CreateRole**   Creates a new role

- **DeleteRole**   Deletes an existing role

- **FindUsersInRole**   Returns a collection of users in a role

- **GetAllRoles**   Returns a collection of all roles that currently exist

- **GetRolesForUser**   Returns a collection of roles for the current user

- **IsUserInRole**   Returns true if the user is a member of a specified role

- **RemoveUserFromRole, RemoveUsersFromRole, RemoveUserFromRoles,** and **RemoveUsersFromRoles**   Removes a user from a role

For example, if you want to add the current user to a role named Users, you could use the following code (assuming an instance of *CreateUserWizard* is named *CreateUserWizard1*):

```
'VB
Roles.AddUserToRole(CreateUserWizard1.UserName, "Users")
```

```
//C#
Roles.AddUserToRole(CreateUserWizard1.UserName, "Users");
```

You cannot use the *Roles* class to manage Windows user groups when using Windows authentication. Windows authentication is discussed in more detail in Lesson 2 of this chapter.

Ideally, you structure your Web application so that you can control access by configuring *authorization* for subfolders using the ASP.NET Web Site Administration Tool (described later in this lesson). This capability, combined with the built-in login controls, can enable you to create your Web application without using either the *Membership* class or the *Roles* class. However, you should be familiar with these classes and their functions so that you can provide customized user-management capabilities when required.

Configuring Web Applications to Use ASP.NET Membership

To create a Web site that uses ASP.NET membership, follow these high-level steps:

1. Create a Web site structure. If a portion of your Web site requires authentication or membership in a specific role, place the pages that should be protected in a separate subfolder. If authentication is optional (for example, a user forum where unauthenticated users can browse but not add messages), a separate subfolder is not required.

2. Configure ASP.NET Membership.

3. Create roles that function as user groups.

4. Optionally, create users and add them to the appropriate roles.

5. Create access rules to control which folders users and roles have access to.

6. Configure Simple Mail Transport Protocol (SMTP) e-mail settings to enable e-mail notification and password resetting. You can do this from the Application tab of the ASP.NET Web Site Administration Tool.

7. Create login pages using Visual Studio.

The sections that follow describe these steps in more detail.

Configuring ASP.NET Membership

To configure ASP.NET membership by using the Web Site Administration Tool, follow these steps:

1. Create an ASP.NET Web application using Visual Studio. If you plan to have separate subfolders for different groups (for example, a folder that only authenticated users are allowed to access, or a folder for application administration tool pages), create those folders first.

2. On the Website menu, select ASP.NET Configuration.

3. Select the Security tab and click the Use The Security Setup Wizard To Configure Security Step By Step link.

4. In Step 1, click Next.

5. In Step 2, select From The Internet to use ASP.NET membership (as shown in Figure 11-1) or select From A Local Area Network to use Windows authentication. Click Next.

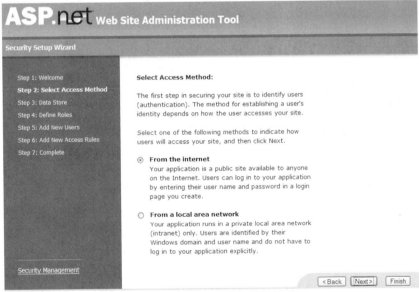

Figure 11-1 Choose From The Internet to create a custom user database or From A Local Area Network to use Windows authentication.

6. In Step 3, the wizard displays a message stating that user information will be stored using Advanced Provider Settings. By default, membership information is

stored in a Microsoft SQL 2005 Server Express Edition database file in the App_Data folder of your Web site. Click Next.

7. In Step 4, the wizard displays an option to create roles. Roles are essentially group memberships, and you'll need them for most membership scenarios. To enable roles, select the Enable Roles For This Web Site check box. Then click Next.

8. If you choose to enable roles, the wizard displays a page where you can create roles. For example, you might create roles for Users and Administrators, as shown in Figure 11-2. When you have created any roles you need, click Next.

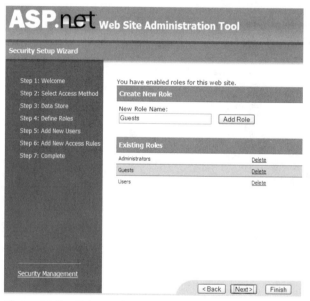

Figure 11-2   Create roles to group users into categories.

9. In Step 5, you can create user accounts by entering the requested information and then clicking Create User. You can also add user accounts later. When you have created any user accounts you need, click Next.

10. In Step 6, add access rules to control which users and roles can access which folders. Figure 11-3 illustrates rules restricting access to folders. When you have added your access rules, click Next.

Add New Access Rule

Select a directory for this rule:	**Rule applies to:**	**Permission:**
⊟ ☐ memberships	○ Role ⌄ Guests ⌄	○ Allow
☐ App_Data	○ User ⬚	⦿ Deny
☐ MemberPages	○ All Users	
	⦿ Anonymous Users	[Add This Rule]
	Search for users	

Rules that appear dimmed are inherited from the parent and cannot be changed at this level.

Permission	Users And Roles	Delete
Allow	Administrators	Delete
Deny	Users	Delete
Deny	Guests	Delete
Deny	[anonymous]	Delete
Allow	[all]	Delete

Figure 11-3   Add access rules to restrict access to folders.

11. In Step 7, click Finish. You return to the Security tab of the Web Site Administration Tool, where you can manage users, roles, and access rules.

Creating a Login Page

To create a login page, follow these steps:

1. Create a login page named Login.aspx. If you use another file name, you will need to configure the new file name in your Web.config file. For more information about configuring forms authentication, read Lesson 2 in this chapter.

2. On your login page, add a *Login* control. The *Login* control prompts the user for his or her credentials, as shown in Figure 11-4. The *Login* control includes features such as validation to ensure the user types a password.

Log In
User Name: jberry
Password: *********
☑ Remember me next time.
[Log In]

Figure 11-4   The *Login* control prompts the user for credentials.

MORE INFO   Changing the appearance of controls

You can use templates to change the appearance of login controls. For more information, refer to Chapter 9, "Customizing and Personalizing a Web Application."

---

3. Add a *ValidationSummary* control to your login page and set the *ValidationSummary.ValidationGroup* property to the ID of your *Login* control. This describes detailed error messages in the event the user forgets to type his or her password, or if another validation event occurs. For example, if a user forgets to type the password, the *Login* control displays a red asterisk by the Password field. If you add a *ValidationSummary* control, it displays the message "Password is required." Invalid credential errors display in the *Login* control itself, but not in the *ValidationSummary* control.

4. Optionally, add a *PasswordRecovery* control to the login page. If a user forgets his or her password, this control enables the user to type his or her user name and receive a new, random password via e-mail, as shown in Figure 11-5. Optionally, users can be required to answer a security question.

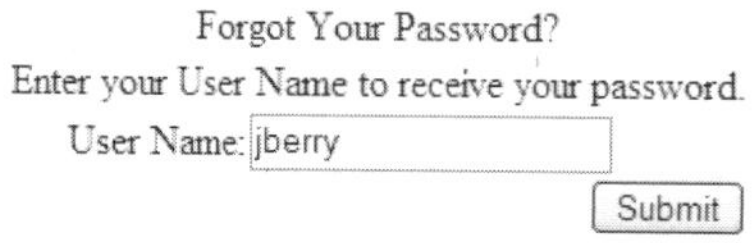

> Forgot Your Password?
> Enter your User Name to receive your password.
> User Name: jberry
>   Submit

Figure 11-5   The *PasswordRecovery* control can send e-mail to users who request their passwords.

5. Add a *LoginStatus* control to all pages of your site. The *LoginStatus* control gives users a link to access your login page if they have not yet authenticated. If you are using master pages, add the *LoginStatus* control to your master page.

6. That's all you have to do if you are using ASP.NET membership and you plan to handle user management by using the Web Site Administration Tool, because the *Login* control automatically handles authentication. If the user provides valid credentials, the user is logged in, and membership controls such as *LoginStatus* automatically reflect that.

7. If the user does not provide valid credentials, the *Login* control prompts to retype the password. You should create a handler for the *Login.LoginError* event and perform security auditing by adding an event to the Security event log. Similarly, you should respond to the *PasswordRecovery.UserLookupError* and *PasswordRecovery.AnswerLookupError* events. Otherwise, users can guess passwords and user names without administrators discovering it.

Creating a User Account-Creation Page

If you are creating a public Web application, you should create an account-creation page to enable users to add their own user accounts. To create a user account-creation page, follow these steps:

1. Create a user account-creation page. For example, you might name it NewUser.aspx.

2. On your user account-creation page, add a *CreateUserWizard* control. The *CreateUserWizard* control prompts the user for user name, password, e-mail, security question, and security answer, as shown in Figure 11-6. The *CreateUserWizard* control includes features such as validation to ensure the user types a password.

Sign Up for Your New Account

User Name:	mberg
Password:	*********
Confirm Password:	*********
E-mail:	mberg@contoso.com
Security Question:	What is my cat's name?
Security Answer:	Sam

The Password and Confirmation Password must match.

Create User

Figure 11-6 The *CreateUserWizard* control enables users to create accounts for themselves.

3. Create a handler for *ContinueButtonClick* event. At a minimum, you should redirect the user to a page linking to members-only content, as the following code demonstrates:

```vb
'VB
Protected Sub CreateUserWizard1_ContinueButtonClick(ByVal sender As Object, ByVal e As
EventArgs)
    Response.Redirect("Members/Default.aspx")
End Sub
```

```csharp
//C#
protected void CreateUserWizard1_ContinueButtonClick(object sender, EventArgs e)
{
    Response.Redirect("Members/Default.aspx");
}
```

By default, new user accounts do not belong to any roles. To add a new user to a role (such as a default Users role), add a handler for the *CreateUserWizard.CreatedUser* event, and then call the *Roles.AddUserToRole* method as described earlier in this lesson.

Creating a Password Change Page

To create a page to allow users to change their own passwords, follow these steps.

1. Create an account-management page. For example, you might name it ManageUser.aspx.

2. Add a *ChangePassword* control to the page.

3. Add a *ValidationSummary* control to your login page and set the *ValidationSummary.ValidationGroup* property to the ID of your *ChangePassword* control. This describes detailed error messages in the event the user forgets to type his or her password, or another validation event occurs. For example, if a user forgets to complete the Confirm New Password field, the *ChangePassword* control displays a red asterisk by the Confirm New Password field. If you add a *ValidationSummary* control, the *ValidationSummary* control displays the message "Confirm New Password is required." Invalid credential errors are displayed in the *Login* control itself, and not the *ValidationSummary* control, however.

4. Create a handler for *ContinueButtonClick* event. At a minimum, you should redirect the user to a page linking to members-only content.

Lab: Configuring Authentication in ASP.NET Applications

In these exercises, you create an ASP.NET Web application and then configure it to restrict access using role manager.

▶ **Exercise 1: Create a Web site that uses ASP.NET Memberships**

In this exercise, you create a new ASP.NET Web site and add support for ASP.NET Memberships.

1. Create an ASP.NET Web application using Visual Studio.

2. Create two subfolders named Members and Admin. To each subfolder, add a blank ASP.NET Web form named Default.aspx. Later, you'll access these pages to verify that ASP.NET requires proper authentication.

3. On the Website menu, select ASP.NET Configuration.

4. Select the Security tab and click the Use The Security Setup Wizard To Configure Security Step By Step link.

5. On Step 1, click Next.

6. On Step 2, select the From The Internet option button. Then click Next.

7. On Step 3, click Next.

8. On Step 4, select the Enable Roles For This Web Site check box. Then click Next.

9. On the Create New Role page, create two roles: Users and Administrators. Then click Next.

10. On Step 5, create two users: StandardUser and Admin. Provide your e-mail address for each and make note of the passwords you assign. Then click Next.

11. On Step 6, select the Admin directory. Create a rule that grants the Administrators role Allow access. Then create a rule that grants All Users Deny access. Note that the new Deny rule appears before the default Allow-All rule, which means users who are not members of the Administrators role have their access denied.

12. While still on Step 6, select the Members directory. Create a rule that grants the Users role Allow access. Then create a rule that grants All Users Deny access. Click Next.

13. On Step 7, click Finish.

14. You return to the Security tab of the Web Site Administration Tool. Click Create Or Manage Roles.

15. For the Administrator role, click Manage. Click All, and then select User Is In Role for Admin. Click Back.

16. For the Users role, click Manage. Click All, and then select User Is In Role for StandardUser and Admin. Click Back.

17. Click the Application tab. Click Configure SMTP E-mail Settings. Configure your SMTP server, type a From e-mail address, and then click Save. Click OK.

18. Return to Visual Studio and open the root Web.config file. Notice that the *roleManager* element is enabled and the *authentication* element is set to *Forms*.

19. Open Members/Web.config and Admin/Web.config. Notice that the Web Site Administration Tool created these files and used them to specify the permissions for each folder. You can also do this using a single Web.config file by specifying the *<location>* element, as described in the next lesson.

Now the Web site is ready to use ASP.NET memberships, and you have created users, roles, and access rules. Continue working with this Web site for the next exercise.

▶ **Exercise 2: Create Web forms that use *Login* controls**

In this exercise, you create Web forms using *Login* controls to take advantage of ASP.NET membership.

1. Continue working with the Web site you created in the previous exercise, which is configured to support ASP.NET membership and has users and roles added to the database. Alternatively, you can open the completed Lesson 1, Exercise 1 project from the CD.

2. Create a new ASP.NET Web form named Login.aspx. Add the following controls:

   A. A *Login* control

   B. A *PasswordRecovery* control

3. Open the root Default.aspx page. Add the following controls:

    A. A *HyperLink* control with the *Text* property set to **Members only** and the *NavigateUrl* set to **Members/Default.aspx**.

    B. A *HyperLink* control with the *Text* property set to **Administrators only** and the *NavigateUrl* set to **Admin/Default.aspx**.

    C. A *LoginStatus* control.

4. Press Ctrl+F5 to open Default.aspx in a Web browser.

5. On the Default.aspx page, click the Members Only link to attempt to access a protected page. Notice that ASP.NET detects that you are not authenticated and redirects you to the default Login.aspx page. Also notice that the URL includes a parameter named *ReturnUrl* that contains the page you were attempting to access.

6. On the Login.aspx page, in the User Name box, type **StandardUser**. Type your password in the Password box, and then click Log In. ASP.NET takes you to the Members/Default.aspx page, which is blank. However, because it does not return an error, you know you are successfully authenticated.

7. Click the Back button in your browser twice to return to the root Default.aspx page, and then click the Administrators Only link. Even though you are already authenticated, ASP.NET redirects you to the Login.aspx page because the StandardUser account does not have access to the Admin folder.

8. On the Login.aspx page, in the User Name box, type **Hacker**. Then click Log In. Notice that ASP.NET rejects your authentication attempt.

9. Under Forgot Your Password, type **Admin**, and then click Submit. Provide an answer to your security question, and then click Submit to request a new password. Check your e-mail for a message from the Web server containing your new password.

10. After you have your new password, use the new credentials to authenticate. ASP.NET takes you to the Admin/Default.aspx page, which is blank. However, because it does not return an error, you know you are successfully authenticated.

Lesson Summary

■   ASP.NET provides several login controls to enable you to easily build pages that support creating user accounts, logging in, logging out, and resetting passwords. These controls include *Login*, *LoginView*, *LoginStatus*, *LoginName*, *PasswordRecovery*, *CreateUserWizard*, and *ChangePassword*.

■ Use the *Membership* class when you need to perform user management tasks from within your code, such as creating, deleting, or modifying user accounts. This class enables you to create custom forms that provide similar functionality to that provided by the standard ASP.NET login controls.

■ Use the *Roles* class when you need to perform role-management tasks from within your code, such as adding users to roles, removing users from roles, creating new roles, or examining which roles a user is a member of.

■ The easiest way to configure a Web application to use ASP.NET user membership is to configure ASP.NET Membership using the Security Setup Wizard. Then create a login page using the *Login* control and, optionally, a *PasswordRecovery* control. Next, create a user account creation page using the *CreateUserWizard* control. Finally, create a page to enable users to change their passwords using the *ChangePassword* control.

Lesson Review

You can use the following questions to test your knowledge of the information in Lesson 1, "Using ASP.NET Membership." The questions are also available on the companion CD if you prefer to review them in electronic form.

NOTE Answers

Answers to these questions and explanations of why each answer choice is right or wrong are located in the "Answers" section at the end of the book.

---

1. Which of the following controls provides a link for unauthenticated users to log on? (Choose the best answer.)

    A. *Login*

    B. *LoginView*

    C. *LoginStatus*

    D. *LoginName*

2. You use the ASP.NET Web Site Administration Tool to configure ASP.NET membership with forms authentication. What should you name your login form so that you do not have to modify the Web.config file? (Choose the best answer.)

    A. Login.aspx

    B. LoginPage.aspx

      C. Default.aspx

      D. Auth.aspx

3. You are creating a Web form that enables users to log on to your Web site. Which of the following ASP.NET controls should you add to the page? (Choose two.)

      A. *Login*

      B. *CreateUserWizard*

      C. *LoginName*

      D. *PasswordRecovery*

4. You have created an ASP.NET Web form that enables users to create accounts with a *CreateUserWizard* control. After a new user creates an account, you want to redirect the user to a page listing the rules for your Web site. Which of the following events should you respond to? (Choose the best answer.)

      A. *CreateUserWizard.Unload*

      B. *CreateUserWizard.ContinueButtonClick*

      C. *CreateUserWizard.CreatedUser*

      D. *CreateUserWizard.Init*

Lesson 2: Using Windows, Forms, Passport, and Anonymous Authentication

Though ASP.NET membership is a perfect fit for many Web applications, ASP.NET actually supports four types of authentication:

- Windows authentication
- Forms authentication (which ASP.NET membership uses)
- Passport authentication
- Anonymous access

This lesson describes how to configure both Internet Information Services (IIS) and your applications for each of the standard Web authentication types.

After this lesson, you will be able to:

- Configure an ASP.NET Web application to require Windows authentication.
- Create an ASP.NET Web application that uses custom forms for user authentication.
- Configure an ASP.NET Web application to require Passport authentication.
- Configure Web applications for anonymous access.
- Configure impersonation so that ASP.NET uses non-default user credentials.
- Restrict access to Web applications, files, and folders by manually editing Web.config files.

Estimated lesson time: 45 minutes

Configuring Web Applications to Require Windows Authentication

If your application is targeted for use inside an organization, and users accessing the application have existing user accounts within the local user database of the Web server or Active Directory, you should authenticate users with Windows authentication. You can configure Windows authentication in two ways: within IIS and within your ASP.NET application. To provide defense in depth, use both techniques to require authentication.

When a Web application requires Windows authentication, the application rejects any request that does not include a valid user name and password in the request header. The user's browser then prompts the user for a user name and password. Because the browser prompts the user for credentials, you do not have to create a page to request the user's user name and password. Some browsers, such as Microsoft Internet Explorer, automatically provide the user's current user name and password when the server is located on the intranet. This seamlessly authenticates the user, relieving the need to retype the password for intranet site visits.

Additionally, because users are authenticated against the server's local user database or Active Directory domain, using Windows authentication saves you from creating a database to store user credentials. Leveraging the Windows authentication mechanism is, therefore, the simplest way to authenticate users. To configure IIS to require all users to authenticate on computers running Microsoft Windows Server 2003, follow these steps:

1. In the Administrative Tools program group, open the IIS Manager.

2. In the IIS Manager console, click to expand your server name, to expand Web Sites, and then to expand the Web site.

3. Right-click the site or folder name you are configuring authentication for and select Properties.

4. Click the Directory Security tab. In the Authentication And Access Control group, click the Edit button.

5. Clear the Enable Anonymous Access check box, which is selected by default.

6. Select the Integrated Windows Authentication check box, as shown in Figure 11-7. Optionally, select Digest Windows Authentication For Windows Domain Servers to enable authentication across proxy servers.

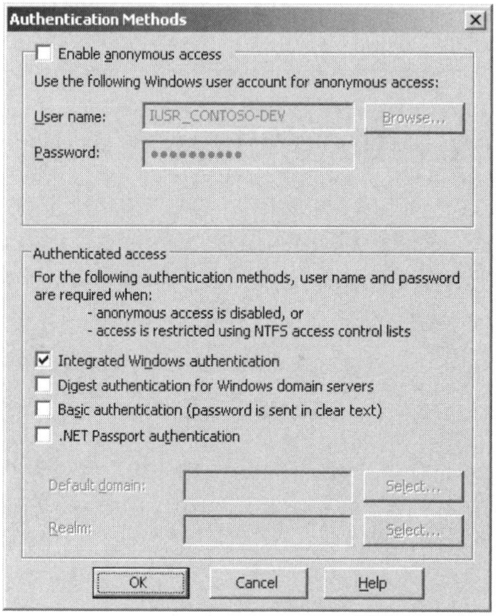

Figure 11-7   For best results, configure Windows authentication in both IIS and your application.

7. Click OK twice to return to the IIS Manager console.

At this point, all Web requests to the virtual directory will require Windows authentication, even if ASP.NET is configured for anonymous access only. Even though configuring IIS is sufficient to require users to present Windows credentials, it is good practice to edit the application's Web.config file to also require Windows authentication.

Real World

Tony Northrup

I've spent time as both a developer and a systems administrator. Each role has different responsibilities. Typically, systems administrators should be responsible for configuring Windows security for a Web application. This doesn't require them to write any code, because they can configure it using the IIS Manager and the ASP.NET Web Site Administration Tool.

So, if you're creating an application that should use Windows authentication, it's okay to leave it up to the systems administrator to configure. Not all systems administrators know how to properly configure it, however, so you should be familiar with the process and be able to demonstrate how it's done when you hand off application support. You do need to configure forms authentication and passport authentication, however, because those require application-specific configuration settings, such as specifying the login page. Typically, you would provide all the configuration information as part of your Web.config file.

To configure an ASP.NET application for Windows Authentication, edit the `<authentication>` section of the Web.config file. This section, like most sections related to ASP.NET application configuration, must be defined within the `<system.web>` section. The `<system.web>` section, in turn, must exist within the `<configuration>` section. This example shows the `<authentication>` section of the Web.config file configured to use Windows authentication:

```
<configuration>
    <system.web>
        <authentication mode="Windows" />
        <authorization>
            <deny users="?" />
        </authorization>
    </system.web>
</configuration>
```

The `<authorization>` section simply requires all users to be successfully authenticated. Specifying `<deny users="?" />` within `<authorization>` requires users to be authenticated, whereas specifying `<allow users="*" />` within `<authorization>` bypasses authentication entirely. The "?" symbol represents unauthenticated users, while the "*" symbol represents all users, both authenticated and unauthenticated.

You can also configure Windows authentication in your application's Web.config file by following these steps, which are more user-friendly:

1.   Create an ASP.NET Web application using Visual Studio.

2.   On the Website menu, select ASP.NET Configuration.

3.   Select the Security tab, and then click Select Authentication Type.

4.   Under How Will Your Users Access The Site, click From A Local Network. Then click Done, as shown in Figure 11-8.

Figure 11-8   Select From A Local Network to enable Windows authentication.

Creating Custom ASP.NET Forms to Authenticate Web Users

Windows authentication presents the end user with a browser-generated dialog box. Although giving the browser the responsibility of gathering the user's user name and password enables automatic authentication on intranet sites, it gives you, as a developer, very little flexibility. Web applications developed for external sites commonly use form-based authentication instead. Form-based authentication presents the user with an HTML-based Web page that prompts the user for credentials.

Once authenticated via forms authentication, ASP.NET generates a cookie to serve as an authentication token. The browser presents this cookie with all future requests to the

Web site, allowing the ASP.NET application to validate requests. This cookie can, optionally, be encrypted by a private key located on the Web server, enabling the Web server to detect an attacker who attempts to present a cookie that the Web server did not generate.

ASP.NET membership allows you to quickly add forms authentication to your Web application. Because Microsoft thoroughly tests the controls and classes involved in authentication and storing the user information, these controls are probably more secure than controls that any developer might make. Therefore, you should use ASP.NET membership whenever possible.

However, if you need complete control over how users are authenticated and managed, you can also create custom forms authentication controls and pages. In the sections that follow, you will learn how to configure an ASP.NET configuration file to require forms authentication, how to add user credentials to a Web.config file, and how to create an ASP.NET Web form to authenticate users.

Configuring a Web.Config File for Forms Authentication

To configure forms authentication, you have to create an authentication page that uses an HTML form to prompt the user for credentials. Therefore, forms authentication can be used on only those ASP.NET Web applications developed with this authentication method in mind. Although you can choose to rely on administrators to configure Windows or on anonymous authentication, you *must* distribute a Web.config file for your application to use forms authentication.

Administrators deploying your application should not need to modify the Web.config file, but they can control some aspects of how Forms authentication behaves, such as configuring the timeout period after which a user will need to log on again. A simple Web.config file requiring Forms authentication is shown here:

```
<configuration>
    <system.web>
        <authentication mode="Forms">
            <forms loginURL="LoginForm.aspx" />
        </authentication>
        <authorization>
            <deny users="?" />
        </authentication>
    </system.web>
</configuration>
```

In the preceding example, all users who have not yet signed in are redirected to the LoginForm.aspx page when they attempt to access any ASP.NET file. Typically, the form prompts the user for a user name and password and handles authentication within the application itself.

Regardless of the way the application handles the user's input, the user's credentials are sent to the server as a *Hypertext Transfer Protocol (HTTP)* request—without any automatic encryption. HTTP is the protocol Web browsers and Web servers use to communicate. The best way to ensure privacy of user credentials submitted by using forms authentication is to configure an Secure Sockets Layer (SSL) certificate within IIS and require *Hypertext Transfer Protocol Secure (HTTPS)* for the login form. HTTPS is an encrypted form of the HTTP protocol, which is used by virtually every e-commerce Web site on the Internet to protect private information about end users and to protect end users from submitting private information to a rogue server impersonating another server.

The user name and password can be checked against a database, a list contained in the Web.config file, an Extensible Markup Language (XML) file, or any other mechanism you create. Forms authentication is tremendously flexible; however, you are entirely responsible for protecting your authentication mechanism from attackers. Because proof of authentication is stored in a cookie provided by the Web server (by default), and that cookie generally contains only the user's user name, an attacker can potentially create a fake cookie to trick the Web server into considering the user as authenticated. ASP.NET includes the ability to encrypt and validate authentication cookies, but naturally, this protection includes some overhead for the Web server.

The type of encryption and validation used is controlled by the protection attribute of the `<authentication>` section. If the protection attribute is not set, it defaults to All. If the protection attribute is set to Encryption, the cookie is encrypted with 3DES. This encryption protects the privacy of the data contained in the cookie but performs no validation. If the protection attribute is set to Validation, as the following example demonstrates, the server verifies the data in the cookie upon each transaction to reduce the likelihood of it being modified between the time it is sent from the browser and the time it is received by the server. If the protection attribute is set to None, neither encryption nor validation is performed. This setting reduces the overhead on the server, but it is suitable only in situations where privacy is not a concern, such as Web site personalization. Note its usage here:

```
<authentication mode="Forms" protection="Validation" >
    <forms loginURL="LoginForm.aspx" />
</authentication>
```

By default, ASP.NET stores the authentication token in a cookie for most devices. However, if the browser does not support cookies, ASP.NET will store the authentication information as part of the URL. You can control this behavior by setting the *cookieless* attribute of the `<forms>` element to one of the following settings:

- **UseCookies** Always attempts to send a cookie to the client, even if the client indicates it cannot support cookies.

- **UseUri** Always stores the authentication token as part of the URL rather than a cookie. Technically, the token is stored in the Uniform Resource Identifier (URI), which is the last portion of the URL.

- **AutoDetect** If a browser indicates that it supports cookies, the AutoDetect setting causes ASP.NET to test whether the browser actually does support cookies. If it does not, or if the browser indicates that it does not support cookies, ASP.NET uses cookieless authentication instead.

- **UseDeviceProfile** The default setting, UseDeviceProfile, uses a cookie to prove authentication if the browser profile indicates that it supports cookies. You might find that some users have changed the default setting to not allow cookies. In this case, forms authentication does not work properly unless you change this setting to AutoDetect.

For example, the following section of a Web.config file enables cookieless forms authentication for all clients. This works well, but it causes the authentication token to be included in bookmarks and whenever the user sends a URL to another user:

```
<authentication mode="Forms" >
    <forms
     Cookieless="UseUri"
     loginURL="LoginForm.aspx" />
</authentication>
```

Another important attribute of the `<forms>` section is timeout, which defines, in minutes, the amount of idle time allowed between requests before the user is forced to log on again. If the `<forms>` section is `<forms loginUrl="YourLogin.aspx" timeout="10">`, the user is forced to log on again if he or she does not send any requests to the ASP.NET application within 10 minutes. This number should be decreased to reduce the risk of the browser being misused while the user is away from the computer. The `<forms>` section has other attributes, but LoginUrl, protection, and timeout are the most important.

Quick Check

1. By default, under what circumstances does forms authentication provide cookies to the browser?

2. If you have users who have disabled cookies in their browsers, what can you do to enable them to use forms authentication?

Quick Check Answers

1. By default, cookies are provided to browser types that support cookies, whether or not the browser has cookies enabled.

2. Use the AutoDetect setting.

Configuring User Accounts in the Web.Config File

To avoid creating a database to store user credentials, you can store the user credentials directly in the Web.config file. The passwords can be stored in one of three formats: clear text, encrypted with the MD5 one-way *hash algorithm*, or encrypted with the SHA1 one-way hash algorithm. Using one of the two hash algorithms to mask the user credentials reduces the likelihood that a malicious user with read access to the Web.config file will gather another user's login information. Define the hashing method used within the `<forms>` section, in the `<credentials>` section. An example is shown here:

```
<authentication mode="Forms">
    <forms loginUrl="login.aspx" protection="Encryption" timeout="30" >
        <credentials passwordFormat="SHA1" >
            <user name="Eric" password="07B7F3EE06F278DB966BE960E7CBBD103DF30CA6"/>
            <user name="Sam" password="5753A498F025464D72E088A9D5D6E872592D5F91"/>
        </credentials>
    </forms>
</authentication>
```

To enable administrators to use hashed password information in the Web.config file, your ASP.NET application must include a page or tool to generate these passwords. The passwords are stored in hexadecimal format and hashed with the specified hashing protocol. You can use the *System.Security.Cryptography* namespace to generate such a hash. The following console application demonstrates this by accepting a password as a command-line parameter and displaying the hash of the password. The resulting hash can be pasted directly into the Web.config file.

```vb
'VB
Imports System.Security.Cryptography
Imports System.Text

Module Module1
    Sub Main(ByVal args As String())
        Dim myHash As SHA1CryptoServiceProvider = New SHA1CryptoServiceProvider
        Dim password As Byte() = Encoding.ASCII.GetBytes(args(0))
        myHash.ComputeHash(password)
        For Each thisByte As Byte In myHash.Hash
            Console.Write(thisByte.ToString("X2"))
        Next
        Console.WriteLine()
    End Sub
End Module
```

```csharp
//C#
using System;
using System.Security.Cryptography;
using System.Text;

namespace HashExample
{
    class Program
    {
        static void Main(string[] args)
        {
            SHA1CryptoServiceProvider myHash=new SHA1CryptoServiceProvider();

            byte[] password  = Encoding.ASCII.GetBytes(args[0]);
            myHash.ComputeHash(password);

            foreach (byte thisByte in myHash.Hash)
                Console.Write(thisByte.ToString("X2"));
            Console.WriteLine();
        }
    }
}
```

Alternatively, you can call the *FormsAuthentication.HashPasswordForStoringInConfigFile* method to generate a password hash. This method is described in the next section.

IMPORTANT Storing credentials in a .config file

You should store credentials in a .config file only during testing. Protecting passwords with a hash is little deterrent to an attacker who can read the contents of the .config file, because hashed password databases exist that can quickly identify common passwords.

The FormsAuthentication Class

The *FormsAuthentication* class is the basis for all forms authentication in ASP.NET. The class includes the following read-only properties, which you can use to programmatically examine the current configuration:

- **FormsCookieName** Returns the configured cookie name used for the current application.
- **FormsCookiePath** Returns the configured cookie path used for the current application.
- **RequireSSL** Gets a value indicating whether the cookie must be transmitted using SSL (that is, over HTTPS only).

IMPORTANT Improving security if the Web server has an SSL certificate

Enable *RequireSSL* for best security. This will ensure that forms authentication is encrypted.

- **SlidingExpiration** Gets a value indicating whether sliding expiration is enabled. Enabling sliding expiration resets the user's authentication timeout with every Web request.

IMPORTANT Improving security (at the cost of convenience)

Disable *SlidingExpiration* for the highest level of security. This prevents a session from remaining open indefinitely.

Additionally, you can call the following methods:

- **Authenticate** Attempts to validate the credentials against those contained in the configured credential store, given the supplied credentials.
- **Decrypt** Returns an instance of a *FormsAuthenticationTicket* class, given a valid encrypted authentication ticket obtained from an HTTP cookie.
- **Encrypt** Produces a string containing an encrypted authentication ticket suitable for use in an HTTP cookie, given a *FormsAuthenticationTicket* object.
- **GetAuthCookie** Creates an authentication cookie for a given user name.
- **GetRedirectUrl** Returns the redirect URL for the original request that caused the redirect to the login page.
- **HashPasswordForStoringInConfigFile** Given a password and a string identifying the hash type, this routine produces a hash password suitable for storing in a configuration file. If your application stores user credentials in the Web.config

file and hashes the password, build this method into a management tool to enable administrators to add users and reset passwords.

■ **RedirectFromLoginPage**   Redirects an authenticated user back to the originally requested URL. Call this method after verifying a user's credentials with the *Authenticate* method. You must pass this method a string and a Boolean value. The string uniquely identifies the user, and the method uses it to generate a cookie based on that information. The Boolean value, if true, allows the browser to use the same cookie across multiple browser sessions. Generally, this unique piece of information should be the user's user name.

■ **RenewTicketIfOld**   Conditionally updates the sliding expiration on a *FormsAuthenticationTicket* object.

■ **SetAuthCookie**   Creates an authentication ticket and attaches it to the cookie's collection of the outgoing response. It does not perform a redirect.

■ **SignOut**   Removes the authentication ticket, essentially logging the user off.

Creating a Custom Forms Authentication Page

When using forms authentication, you must include two sections at a minimum:

■ A forms authentication page

■ A method for users to log off and close their current sessions

To create a forms authentication page, create an ASP.NET Web form to prompt the user for credentials and call members of the *System.Web.Security.FormsAuthentication* class to authenticate the user and redirect him or her to a protected page. The following code sample demonstrates an overly simple authentication mechanism that just verifies that the contents of *usernameTextBox* and *passwordTextBox* are the same, and then calls the *RedirectFromLoginPage* method to redirect the user to the page originally requested. Notice that the Boolean value passed to *RedirectFromLoginPage* is *true*, indicating that the browser saves the cookie after the browser is closed, enabling the user to remain authenticated if the user closes and reopens his or her browser before the authentication cookie expires.

```
'VB
If usernameTextBox.Text = passwordTextBox.Text Then
    FormsAuthentication.RedirectFromLoginPage(usernameTextBox.Text, True)
End If
```

```
//C#
if (usernameTextBox.Text == passwordTextBox.Text)
    FormsAuthentication.RedirectFromLoginPage(usernameTextBox.Text, true);
```

Although the authentication mechanism demonstrated in the previous code sample (verifying that the user name and password are equal) can never provide adequate protection for a Web application, it demonstrates the flexibility of forms authentication. You can check the user's credentials using any mechanism required by your application. Most often, the user name and a hash of the user's password is looked up in a database.

If user credentials are stored in the Web.config file, or you have configured them using ASP.NET membership, call the *FormsAuthentication.Authenticate* method to check the credentials. Simply pass to the method the user's user name and password. The method returns true if the user's credentials match a value in the Web.config file. Otherwise, it returns false. The following code sample demonstrates the use of this method to redirect an authenticated user. Notice that the Boolean value passed to *RedirectFromLoginPage* is false, indicating that the browser does not save the cookie after the browser is closed, requiring the user to reauthenticate if he or she closes and reopens the browser, thus improving security:

```VB
'VB
If FormsAuthentication.Authenticate(username.Text, password.Text) Then
    ' User is authenticated. Redirect user to the page requested.
    FormsAuthentication.RedirectFromLoginPage(usernameTextBox.Text, False)
End If
```

```C#
//C#
if (FormsAuthentication.Authenticate(username.Text,
password.Text))
{
    // User is authenticated. Redirect user to the page requested.
    FormsAuthentication.RedirectFromLoginPage(usernameTextBox.Text, false);
}
```

In addition to creating a page to authenticate users, provide a method for users to log off of the application. Generally, this is a simple "Log out" hyperlink that calls the *FormsAuthentication.SignOut* static method to remove the user's authentication cookie.

Configuring Web Applications to Require Passport Authentication

You can also authenticate users using a service from Microsoft called Passport. Passport is a centralized directory of user information that Web sites can use, in exchange for a fee, to authenticate users. Users can choose to allow the Web site access to personal information stored on Passport, such as the users' addresses, ages, and interests. Storing information about users worldwide within the Passport service relieves end users from maintaining separate user names and passwords on different sites. Further, it saves the user time by eliminating the need to provide personal information to multiple Web sites.

Exam Tip   Passport authentication probably won't be covered on the 70-528 exam.

MORE INFO   **Passport software development kit**

For more detailed information about the requirements of building a Web application that uses Passport, you can download and review the free Passport software development kit from MSDN on the Microsoft Web site at *http://support.microsoft.com/?kbid=816418*.

Configuring Web Applications for Only Anonymous Access

You can explicitly disable authentication for your application if you know that it will be used only by anonymous users. However, in most cases where your application does not require authentication, you should simply not provide an authentication configuration setting in the Web.config file and allow the system administrator to configure authentication with IIS.

This example shows a simple Web.config file that allows only anonymous access to an ASP.NET application:

```
<configuration>
    <system.web>
        <authentication mode="None" />
    </system.web>
</configuration>
```

Configuring Impersonation by Using .config Files

By default, ASP.NET applications make all requests for system resources from the ASP-NET account (IIS 5.0) or the Network Service account (IIS 6.0). This setting is configurable and is defined in the `<processModel>` item of the `<system.web>` section of the Machine.config file. The default setting for this section is:

```
<processModel autoConfig="true" />
```

Setting *autoConfig* to *true* causes ASP.NET to automatically handle *impersonation*. However, you can change *autoConfig* to *false* and set the *userName* and *password* attribute to define the account ASP.NET impersonates when requesting system resources on behalf of a Web user.

Automatic configuration is sufficient for most ASP.NET implementations. However, in many cases, administrators need to configure ASP.NET to impersonate the client's authenticated user account, IIS's anonymous user account, or a specific user account. This configuration is done by setting the *impersonate* attribute of the `<identity>` element of the Machine.config (for server-wide settings) or Web.config (for application- or directory-specific settings) files. To enable impersonation of the client's authenticated Windows account, or IIS's IUSR_*MachineName* account for anonymous access, add the following line to the `<system.web>` section of the Web.config file:

```
<identity impersonate="true" />
```

When IIS is configured for anonymous access, ASP.NET makes requests for system resources using the IUSR_*MachineName* account. When a user authenticates directly to IIS using a Windows logon, ASP.NET impersonates that user account. To enable ASP.NET to impersonate a specific user account, regardless of how IIS authentication is handled, add the following line to the `<system.web>` section of the Web.config file and replace the *DOMAIN*, *UserName*, and *Password* attributes with the account logon credentials:

```
<identity impersonate="true" userName="DOMAIN\UserName" password="Password"/>
```

Restricting Access to ASP.NET Web Applications, Files, and Folders

Authentication determines a user's identity, whereas authorization defines what the user might access. Before the .NET Framework, administrators controlled Web user authorization entirely with NTFS permissions. Although NTFS permissions are still a key part of configuring security for ASP.NET applications, these permissions are now complemented by ASP.NET's authorization capabilities. Authorization is now controlled with Web.config files, just like authentication. This enables authorization to work with any type of authentication—even if the authorization doesn't use the local user database or Active Directory directory service that NTFS permissions are based on. The use of Web.config files also makes copying file permissions between multiple Web servers as easy as copying files.

In the sections that follow, you will learn how to restrict access according to user and group names, to restrict access to specific files and folders using either a .config file or file permissions, and to use impersonation in an ASP.NET application.

Restricting Access to Users and Groups

The default Machine.config file contains the following authorization information:

```
<authorization>
    <allow users="*"/>
</authorization>
```

Unless you modify this section of the Machine.config file, or override the Machine.config file by adding this section to your application's Web.config file, all users permitted by your authentication configuration are allowed to interact with all parts of your ASP.NET Web application. The `<allow users="*">` subsection of the authorization section tells ASP.NET that all users who pass the authentication requirements are allowed access to all ASP.NET content.

To configure an ASP.NET application to provide access only to the users Eric and Sam, override the Machine.config security settings by editing the Web.config file in the root of the ASP.NET application and add the following lines within the `<system.web>` section:

```
<authorization>
    <allow users="Eric, Sam"/>
    <deny users="*"/>
</authorization>
```

The `<allow>` and `<deny>` subsections contain users and roles attributes. The users attribute should be set to a list of user names separated by commas, an asterisk (*) to indicate all authenticated or unauthenticated users, or a question mark (?) to indicate anonymous users. If Windows authentication is used, the user names should match names in the local user database or Active Directory directory service and need to include a domain name (that is, *DOMAIN\user* for domain accounts or *COMPUTER-NAME\user* for local user accounts).

The roles element contains a comma-separated list of roles. When Windows authentication is used, roles correspond to Windows user groups. In this case, the names must exactly match group names in the local user database or Active Directory. Provide the domain name for groups in the Active Directory, but do not specify the computer name for local groups. For example, to specify the IT group in the CONTOSO domain, use **CONTOSO\IT**. To specify the local users group, use **Users**.

If you are using Windows authentication, you must disable the *roleManager* element in your Web.config file to use role security to authorize Windows user groups. The *roleManager* element is disabled by default, so removing it from your Web.config file is sufficient to disable it. You can authorize Windows users with *roleManager* enabled, but it must be disabled to authorize Windows groups.

Controlling Authorization for Folders and Files by Using .config Files

The previous techniques are useful for controlling user access to an entire ASP.NET application. To restrict access to specific files or folders, add a `<location>` section to the `<configuration>` section of the Web.config file. The `<location>` section contains its own `<system.web>` subsection, so do not place it within an existing `<system.web>` section.

To configure access restrictions for a specific file or folder, add the `<location>` section to your Web.config with a single section: path. The path section must be set to the relative path of a file or folder; absolute paths are not allowed. Within the `<location>` section, include a `<system.web>` subsection and any configuration information that is unique to the specified file or folder. For example, to require forms authentication for the file ListUsers.aspx and restrict access to the user named admin, add the following text to the `<configuration>` section of the Web.config file:

```
<location path="ListUsers.aspx">
    <system.web>
        <authentication mode="forms">
            <forms loginUrl="AdminLogin.aspx" protection="All"/>
        </authentication>
        <authorization>
            <allow users="admin"/>
            <deny users="*"/>
        </authorization>
    </system.web>
</location>
```

When using multiple `<location>` sections, file and subfolders automatically inherit all settings from their parents. Therefore, you do not need to repeat settings that are identical to the parents' configurations. When configuring authorization, inheritance has the potential to lead to security vulnerabilities. Consider the following Web.config file:

```
<configuration>
  <system.web>
    <authentication mode="Windows" />
    <authorization>
      <deny users="?" />
    </authorization>
  </system.web>

  <location path="Protected">
    <system.web>
      <authorization>
```

```
        <allow roles="CONTOSO\IT" />
      </authorization>
    </system.web>
  </location>
</configuration>
```

In this example, there are actually *three* layers of inheritance. The first is the Machine.config file, which specifies the default `<allow users="*"/>`. The second layer is the first `<system.web>` section in the example, which applies to the entire application. This setting, `<deny users="?"/>`, denies access to all unauthenticated users. By itself, this second layer denies access to any user. However, combined with the Machine.config file, this layer allows access to all authenticated users and denies access to everyone else.

The third layer is the `<location>` section, which grants access to the CONTOSO\IT group. However, this section also inherits the `<deny users="?"/>` and `<allow users="*"/>` settings. Therefore, the effective settings for the Protected subfolder are the same as for the parent folder: all authenticated users have access. To restrict access to *only* users in the CONTOSO\IT group, you must explicitly deny access to users who are not specifically granted access, as the following code demonstrates:

```
<location path="Protected">
  <system.web>
    <authorization>
      <allow roles="CONTOSO\IT" />
      <deny users="*" />
    </authorization>
  </system.web>
</location>
```

NOTE Using file permissions

You can also control access to files and folders by setting NTFS file permissions. However, file permissions are typically managed by systems administrators. Additionally, because file permissions cannot be distributed as easily as a Web.config file and they can only be used with Windows security, they should not be relied upon as the primary method of file authorization for developers.

Lab: Controlling Authorization in ASP.NET Applications

In this lab, you modify an ASP.NET Web application to use Windows authentication.

▶ **Exercise: Create a Web site that uses ASP.NET memberships**

In this exercise, you update a previously created ASP.NET Web site to disable role manager and use Windows authentication instead.

1. Continue working with the Web site you created in Lesson 1, Exercise 2, which has been configured to support ASP.NET membership and has users and roles added to the database. Alternatively, you can open the completed Lesson 1, Exercise 2 project from the CD.

2. On the Website menu, select ASP.NET Configuration.

3. Click the Security tab, and then click Select Authentication Type.

4. Click From A Local Network, and then click Done.

5. In Visual Studio, examine the Web.config file. Notice that the *authentication* element has been removed, which means forms authentication is no longer enabled. Now remove the `<roleManager>` element so that the *roles* element refers to Windows groups, instead of the roles you added using role manager.

6. In Visual Studio, add a *LoginName* control to the Default.aspx page. This enables you to see the user account you are using to access the Web site.

7. With the Default.aspx page still open, press Ctrl+F5 to open the page in a browser. Notice that the *LoginName* control shows that you are automatically logged in using your Windows user account.

8. Click the Members Only link. If your current account is a member of the local Users group, you are allowed to access the page. Otherwise, ASP.NET denies you access.

9. Click the Administrators Only link. If your current account is a member of the local Administrators group, you are allowed to access the page. Otherwise, ASP.NET denies you access.

10. On the Website menu of Visual Studio, select ASP.NET Configuration. Click the Security tab. Notice that you can no longer use the Web Site Administration Tool to manage roles. When role manager is disabled, ASP.NET uses Windows groups as roles. Therefore, you must manage the groups using tools built into Windows, such as the Computer Management console.

11. On the Security tab of the Web Site Administration Tool, click Manage Access rules. Then click the Admin subfolder. Notice that it displays the existing rules. Click Add New Access Rule and notice that you can add a rule for specific users, all users, or anonymous users. You cannot, however, add rules to grant access to roles, because role manager has been disabled. To add access rules for Windows Groups using roles, you must manually edit the `<authorization>` section of the Web.config files.

This exercise worked because the role names you created in Lesson 1 are exactly the same as the default group names in the local Windows user database. Typically, you would not use the ASP.NET Web Site Administration Tool to create access rules. Instead, you would manually edit the Web.config files, as described in this lesson.

Lesson Summary

- You can configure an application to require Windows credentials from a user by either configuring IIS, configuring the Web.config file, or both.

- To create custom ASP.NET forms for user authentication, first configure your Web.config file to specify the authentication form. Then create an ASP.NET Web form to prompt the user for credentials and write code to verify the credentials and authenticate the user. You should also provide a way for users to log off.

- ASP.NET Web applications support Passport, which uses a centralized authentication service provided by Microsoft for a fee.

- If an application does not require authentication, you can explicitly configure it for anonymous access.

- By default, ASP.NET accesses resources using ASP.NET credentials. If you need to access resources from the user's account or from a specific user account, you can use impersonation, either from within your code or by configuring the Web.config file.

- To control which users can access folders and files in a Web application, you can use either NTFS file permissions or Web.config files.

Lesson Review

You can use the following questions to test your knowledge of the information in Lesson 2, "Using Windows, Forms, Passport, and Anonymous Authentication." The questions are also available on the companion CD if you prefer to review them in electronic form.

NOTE Answers

Answers to these questions and explanations of why each answer choice is right or wrong are located in the "Answers" section at the end of the book.

---

1. Which of the following Web.config segments correctly requires that all users be authenticated using a Windows user account? (Choose the best answer.)

A.
```
<authentication mode="Windows" />
<authorization>
    <deny users="*" />
</authorization>
```

B.
```
<authentication mode="Windows" />
<authorization>
    <allow users="*" />
</authorization>
```

C.
```
<authentication mode="Windows" />
<authorization>
    <deny users="?" />
</authorization>
```

D.
```
<authentication mode="Windows" />
<authorization>
    <allow users="*" />
</authorization>
```

2. By default, how does ASP.NET track which users have successfully authenticated using forms authentication? (Choose the best answer.)

   A. Provides an authentication token in the form of a cookie.

   B. Provides an authentication token in the URI.

   C. Provides an authentication token in the form of a cookie if the client's browser proves that it can store and return a cookie. Otherwise, stores the authentication token in the URI.

   D. Provides an authentication token in the form of a cookie if the client's browser type supports cookies. Otherwise, stores the authentication token in the URI.

3. Given the following Web.config file, what permissions do users have to the Marketing folder? (Choose the best answer.)

```
<configuration>
  <system.web>
    <authentication mode="Windows" />
    <authorization>
      <deny users="?" />
    </authorization>
  </system.web>

  <location path="Marketing">
    <system.web>
      <authorization>
        <allow roles="FABRIKAM\Marketing" />
        <deny users="*" />
      </authorization>
```

```
    </system.web>
  </location>
</configuration>
```

   A. Authenticated users and members of the FABRIKAM\Marketing group have access. All other users are denied access.

   B. Members of the FABRIKAM\Marketing group have access. All other users are denied access.

   C. All users, authenticated and unauthenticated, have access

   D. All users are denied access.

4. You are configuring NTFS file permissions for a Web application with the following Web.config file:

```
<configuration>
  <system.web>
    <authentication mode="Windows" />
    <authorization>
      <deny users="?" />
    </authorization>
  </system.web>

  <location path="Marketing">
    <system.web>
      <authorization>
        <allow roles="FABRIKAM\Marketing" />
        <deny users="*" />
      </authorization>
    </system.web>
  </location>
</configuration>
```

For the Marketing folder, you remove all file permissions, and then grant read access to the FABRIKAM\John and FABRIKAM\Sam user accounts. John is a member of the FABRIKAM\Domain Users and FABRIKAM\Marketing groups. Sam is only a member of the FABRIKAM\Domain Users group. Which of the following users can access Web forms located in the Marketing folder? (Choose the best answer.)

   A. Unauthenticated users

   B. Authenticated users

   C. Members of the FABRIKAM\Domain Users group

   D. FABRIKAM\John

   E. FABRIKAM\Sam

Chapter Review

To further practice and reinforce the skills you learned in this chapter, you can perform the following tasks:

- Review the chapter summary.
- Review the list of key terms introduced in this chapter.
- Complete the case scenarios. These scenarios set up real-world situations involving the topics of this chapter and ask you to create a solution.
- Complete the suggested practices.
- Take a practice test.

Chapter Summary

- Many Web sites identify individual users in order to personalize the Web sites, to enable users to view account information such as past orders, or to provide unique identities to individual users for communicating on a forum. ASP.NET provides membership capabilities to enable you to identify users with a username and password without writing any code. Once you've added membership capabilities to your site, you can use a wide variety of controls to your ASP.NET Web pages to enable users to create accounts, reset their passwords, log on, and log off.

- Authentication verifies a user's identity, and can grant the user access to protected areas of your Web site. ASP.NET provides several different authentication mechanisms to meet different requirements:

  - Windows authentication enables you to identify users without creating a custom page. Credentials are stored in the Web server's local user database or an Active Directory domain. Once identified, you can use the user's credentials to gain access to resources that are protected by Windows authorization.

  - Forms authentication enables you to identify users with a custom database, such as an ASP.NET membership database. Alternatively, you can implement your own custom database. Once authenticated, you can reference the roles the user is in to restrict access to portions of your Web site.

❑ Passport authentication relies on a centralized service provided by Microsoft. Passport authentication identifies a user with using his or her e-mail address and a password, and a single Passport account can be used with many different Web sites. Passport authentication is primarily used for public Web sites with thousands of users.

❑ Anonymous authentication does not require the user to provide credentials.

Key Terms

Do you know what these key terms mean? You can check your answers by looking up the terms in the glossary at the end of the book.

■ authentication

■ authorization

■ hash algorithm

■ impersonation

■ *Roles*

Case Scenarios

In the following case scenarios, you apply what you've learned about how to authenticate users and control access using authorization. You can find answers to these questions in the "Answers" section at the end of this book.

Case Scenario 1: Configuring Web Application Authorization

You are a developer for Southridge Video, a business that creates instructional videos. The business is deploying a new ASP.NET intranet application, and the administrators need some help configuring the security. The Web application has several subfolders, and each subfolder is managed by a different organization within Southridge. You meet with each of the managers and review the technical requirements to determine how you should configure security for that organization's subfolder.

Interviews

Following is a list of company personnel interviewed and their statements:

- **Wendy Richardson, IT Manager**   "My Web experts have created an ASP.NET intranet application in the /Southridge/ virtual folder of our Web server's default Web site. The application should be accessible only to users who have valid accounts in the SOUTHRIDGE Active Directory domain. Several of the internal groups have their own subfolders in the application, including IT. Check with each of the managers to determine how he or she wants security configured. For the IT subfolder, I just want members of the IT group in the Southridge domain to be able to access it."

- **Arif Rizaldy, Systems Administrators**   "Hey, I hear you're configuring a new Web application. Can you do me a favor and put all the configuration in a single Web.config file? I had to troubleshoot a security problem the other day and spent hours trying to figure out what it was because I forgot that there might be a Web.config file in any of the folders. One Web.config file is just easier for me to manage."

- **Anders Riis, Production Manager**   "For now, I'd like our Production subfolder to be accessible to members of the Production group. Oh, also, give Thomas access to it. Thomas is the Manager of Sales. I don't know what his user account name is."

- **Catherine Boeger, Customer Service Manager**   "Anyone who is an employee should be able to open the CustServ folder."

- **Thomas Jensen, Sales Manager**   "For now, only I should have access to the Sales folder. I'll probably change this later, but there's confidential information in there now. My user account is TJensen. Sometimes I have to enter it as Southridge-backslash-TJensen."

Technical Requirements

Create a single Web.config file for the application that configures permissions for each of the subfolders according to the requirements outlined in the following table. Require Windows authentication for every file in the application.

Table 11-1   Application Authorization Requirements for Southridge Video

Folder	Authorized Users
/Southridge/	All authenticated users

Table 11-1 Application Authorization Requirements for Southridge Video

Folder	Authorized Users
/Southridge/IT/	All members of the SOUTHRIDGE\IT group
/Southridge/Production/	All members of the SOUTHRIDGE\Production group and the SOUTHRIDGE\TJensen user account
/Southridge/CustServ/	All authenticated users
/Southridge/Sales/	Only the SOUTHRIDGE\TJensen user account

Questions

Configure security for Southridge Video, and then answer the following questions.

1. What does the Web.config file that you created look like?

2. Besides creating a Web.config file, how can you further protect the folders?

Case Scenario 2: Configuring Web Application Authentication

You are a developer for Northwind Traders. Your manager has asked you to create a simple ASP.NET Web page to display the contents of a text file. The text files are generated by a legacy system to report on various aspects of your company's financial status, so they are protected using NTFS file permissions. The IT Manager, Nino Olivotto, describes the problem:

"The financial people want to be able to view these text reports from our intranet, so it would be nice if you could create an ASP.NET Web form to allow that. Here's the catch, though. I don't want to change the permissions on the file so that just anyone can read it. The Web server doesn't have the file permissions to access to the files by default, and I don't want it to. Instead, I'd like to have the user provide Windows credentials, and have your application use those credentials to show the file. Oh—and name the project ShowReport. You can place it in the C:\Inetpub\Wwwroot\Show-Report\ folder."

You review the company's technical requirements before creating the ASP.NET Web application.

Technical Requirements

Create an ASP.NET Web application in the C:\Inetpub\Wwwroot\ShowReport\ folder using either C# or Visual Basic .NET. Create several text files in the ShowReport folder, remove all default NTFS permissions, and then add permissions so that only specific users can access the files. Use impersonation to take advantage of the user's Windows credentials to display the contents of the files.

Questions

Create the ASP.NET Web application and then answer the following questions to explain to the IT Manager how you created the application and why you did what you did.

1. What authentication method did you use? Why?

2. How did you implement impersonation? Why?

3. What XML code did you add to the Web.config file?

4. What code did you write to display the text files?

Suggested Practices

To successfully master the Implementing Authentication and Authorization exam domain, which includes the objectives Establish a User's Identity by Using Forms Authentication, Use Authorization to Establish the Rights of an Authenticated User, Implement Microsoft Windows Authentication and Impersonation, and Use Login Controls to Control Access to a Web Application, complete the following tasks.

Establish a User's Identity by Using Forms Authentication

For this task, you should complete at least Practices 1 and 3 to get a solid understanding of how forms authentication behaves. If you want a better understanding of how to implement custom user databases, complete Practice 2 as well.

- **Practice 1**   Create an ASP.NET Web application and implement custom forms authentication. For simplicity, store user names and passwords in a collection. Use the Web.config files to restrict access to specific files and folders and verify that the authorization features work properly.

- **Practice 2**   Extend the Web application you created in the previous practice to store user credentials in a database. Store the passwords using hashes so that they are less vulnerable to attack.

- **Practice 3** Use a browser that supports cookies to visit an ASP.NET Web site that uses forms authentication. Then disable cookies in the browser and attempt to visit the site. Change the *Cookieless* attribute of the `<forms>` element to *AutoDetect* and test the Web site again.

Use Authorization to Establish the Rights of an Authenticated User

For this task, you should complete all three practices to gain experience using authorization to protect portions of a Web application.

- **Practice 1** Create a custom Web form that provides common user-management features, such as displaying a list of users, allowing you to delete users, and adding users to roles.

- **Practice 2** Using the Web application you created in Lessons 1 and 2, delete the Web.config files in the Admin and Members folders. Then use `<location>` elements in the root Web.config file to configure identical access rules in a single file.

- **Practice 3** Create an ASP.NET Web application that uses Windows authentication. Then create several different groups and user accounts on the Web server. Experiment with NTFS file permissions and Web.config access rules to determine how ASP.NET behaves when one or both denies access to a user.

Implement Microsoft Windows Authentication and Impersonation

For this task, you should complete both practices to gain an understanding of how ASP.NET uses Windows authentication and impersonation.

- **Practice 1** Create an ASP.NET Web application that uses Windows authentication. Then, create several different groups and user accounts on the Web server. Write code that examines the user's account and displays the user name and whether the user is a member of built-in groups such as Users and Administrators.

- **Practice 2** Enable object access auditing on your development computer (or a development Web server) as described in Microsoft Knowledge Base article 310399 at *http://support.microsoft.com/?kbid=310399*. Create a folder on your computer and add a text file to it. Then enable success and failure auditing on the folder. Using the Web application you created in the previous example, write code to read the text file and display it on a Web page. Note whether the code succeeds or fails. Then view the Security event log to examine the auditing events and identify which user account ASP.NET used to access the file. Next, enable impersonation in your Web application and repeat the process to determine whether the user account changed.

Use Login Controls to Control Access to a Web Application

For this task, you should complete at least Practices 1 and 2. If you want experience with sending e-mail messages to new users, complete Practice 3 as well.

- **Practice 1**   Using the ASP.NET Web application you created in the Lesson 1 and 2 labs, create a template to modify the colors and fonts used by the controls.
- **Practice 2**   Using the ASP.NET Web application you created in the Lesson 1 and 2 labs, modify the text displayed by each of the controls to display messages in a different language.
- **Practice 3**   Respond to the *CreateUserWizard.CreatedUser* event to automatically send an e-mail to the new user welcoming him or her to your Web site.

Take a Practice Test

The practice tests on this book's companion CD offer many options. For example, you can test yourself on just the content covered in this chapter, or you can test yourself on all the 70-528 certification exam content. You can set up the test so that it closely simulates the experience of taking a certification exam, or you can set it up in study mode so that you can look at the correct answers and explanations after you answer each question.

MORE INFO   **Practice tests**

For details about all the practice test options available, see the section titled "How to Use the Practice Tests" in this book's Introduction.

Chapter 12

Creating ASP.NET Mobile Web Applications

Have you noticed that more and more people have handheld computers, cellular phones with Internet browsers, or messaging devices of some sort? Mobile computing is becoming increasingly popular. You can even purchase vehicles such as cars, trucks, and boats with mobile devices that are built into the dash.

Businesses are exploring the methods of keeping their employees mobile while increasing profitability. Businesses also see that they can increase sales from mobile customers. Customers may want to use mobile devices to buy tickets to sporting events, theaters, and so on. Mobile applications can also deliver traffic information and supply messaging capabilities. This chapter introduces mobile Web applications and discusses the challenges in creating mobile Web applications that can be accessed effectively from a vast array of device types.

Exam objectives in this chapter:
- Create a mobile Web application project.
- Use device-specific rendering to display controls on a variety of devices.
- Use adaptive rendering to modify the appearance of Web server controls.
- Use the mobile Web controls to display content on a device.

Lessons in this chapter:

Before You Begin

To complete the lessons in this chapter, you should be familiar with Microsoft Visual Basic or C# and be comfortable with the following tasks:

- Have Microsoft Windows XP and Microsoft Visual Studio 2005 installed with Microsoft SQL Server 2005 Express Edition.

- Be familiar with the Visual Studio 2005 Integrated Development Environment (IDE).

- Have a basic understanding of Hypertext Markup Language (HTML) and client-side scripting.

- Know how to create a new Web site.

- Be able to add Web server controls to a Web page.

Real World

Glenn Johnson

Internet availability is becoming more widespread in coffee shops and restaurants. Some cities have even launched citywide Internet initiatives. Internet access is great if you have a device that can access the Internet.

Imagine being in a restaurant, discussing the idea of going to see a movie, and being able to go online to see what's showing and then purchasing your tickets. It's doable today if you use your laptop computer, but if you try using your cell phone or PDA, you typically run into problems trying to display a Web page on a small device. Companies that create Web pages that display properly on small devices increase revenues from mobile users.

Lesson 1: Building Mobile Applications

In this lesson, you learn how to create a mobile application that can be rendered on a variety of devices.

After this lesson, you will be able to:

■ Create a mobile Web application.

  ❑ Use device-specific rendering to display controls on a variety of devices.

  ❑ Use adaptive rendering to modify the appearance of Web server controls.

  ❑ Use the mobile Web controls to display content on a device.

Estimated lesson time: 60 minutes

Introducing the Mobile Web Application

You can create a mobile Web application by starting a new ASP.NET Web application using your desired programming language, deleting the Default.aspx Web page, and adding Mobile Web Forms.

The mobile Web application project is very similar to a standard ASP.NET Web application. Many of the features of ASP.NET, such as tracing and debugging, are still available in a mobile Web application. The primary difference in mobile Web applications is that the Web form has a different behavior. The form's design view does not provide a strict graphical representation of the page, because the page renders differently on each mobile device. Given the variability of this reproduction, you should think of the form as being a representation of an item in a sequence of tasks.

Creating a Mobile Web Application

A mobile Web application is an ASP.NET Web site that contains mobile Web forms. Follow these steps to create a simple mobile Web application:

1. Create an ASP.NET Web site using your preferred programming language.
2. Remove the Default.aspx page that is added by the Web site template.
3. Add one or more mobile Web forms to the project.
4. On each mobile Web form, add the desired mobile controls.
5. Add code to the code-behind pages that executes in response to events that are raised by the mobile controls.

Viewing and Testing Mobile Web Applications

Internet Explorer can be used to view a mobile Web form. A user can change the default browser by selecting File | Browse With and choosing the desired browser. In addition to the browser settings that are listed, device emulators may be added.

Many of the mobile device manufacturers provide emulators that can be used to test mobile Web applications. Emulators display the mobile Web application as it would appear on the hardware device. If an emulator is set to be the default browser, it is displayed when pressing F5 to debug the mobile application.

OpenWave

One of the common cell phone emulator providers is OpenWave; you can download the latest phone emulators from *http://developer.openwave.com*. Figure 12-1 shows the generic phone emulator. In addition, OpenWave also provides skins for many popular phones.

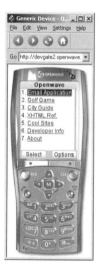

Figure 12-1   The OpenWave generic phone emulator.

When the generic phone is displayed, the Simulator Console window is also displayed, as shown in Figure 12-2. The Simulator Console window displays the raw Hypertext Transfer Protocol (HTTP) and header information, which can be helpful when attempting to diagnose problems.

Figure 12-2   The OpenWave Simulator Console window.

Device Emulator

The device emulator installs with Microsoft Visual Studio 2005 and is intended to be used primarily when testing applications developed for use with the Compact Framework, but it can also be used to test mobile Web applications. A .bat file can be created to handle the arguments that are required, such as the emulator type, the skin, and Ethernet usage, as follows:

DeviceEmulator.bat File

```
C:

cd "C:\Program Files\Microsoft Device Emulator\1.0"

rem The following is on the same line
DeviceEmulator "C:\Program Files\Microsoft Visual Studio
8\SmartDevices\Emulators\Images\PocketPC\2003\1033\PPC_2003_SE_WWE_ARMv4.bin" /skin
"C:\Program Files\Microsoft Visual Studio
8\SmartDevices\Skins\PocketPC_2003\PocketPC_2003\1033\PocketPC_2003_Skin.xml" /p
```

In this case, the emulator is on the C: drive, so the .bat file switches to the C: drive, then changes to the proper directory, launches the emulator with the Pocket PC 2003 image and the Pocket PC 2003 skin, and enables Ethernet connectivity with the /p switch.

The .bat file may be added as a browser type in Visual Studio 2005. After the emulator starts, the site may be browsed to by using the actual Internet Protocol (IP) address of the development computer. For example, instead of browsing to *http://localhost/MobileWebTest/Default.aspx*, the URL might be *http://192.168.1.2/MobileWebTest/Default.aspx*. If the development computer does not have an IP address, the Microsoft Loopback Adapter may be installed, and a fixed IP address and subnet mask may be assigned, which can then be used by the emulator to access the Web sites on the development machine.

The Pocket PC connection settings may also need to be set to use Work settings by selecting Start | Settings | Connections | Connections | Advanced | Select Networks, and then changing both settings to My Work Network, as shown in Figure 12-3.

Figure 12-3   The Pocket PC emulator with My Work Network selected.

Understanding Mobile Web Forms

Like the standard Web form, the mobile Web form is an .aspx file that is accessible by a URL and can optionally have a code-behind page. The mobile Web forms that you add to your Web site inherit from the *System.Web.UI.MobileControls.MobilePage* class initially contain single *mobile:Form* controls. Unlike the standard Web form that can only contain one form control, the mobile Web form can contain many *mobile:Form* controls. By default, the first *mobile:Form* control on the page is visible. You can switch from one *mobile:Form* to another by setting the *ActiveForm* property of the mobile Web form.

You can add many mobile controls to the *mobile:Form* control, but the number of mobile controls should be kept to a small number of organized controls. As mobile controls are added and deleted, the *mobile:Form* control automatically resizes. The *mobile:Form* control cannot be resized manually, as the *mobile:Form* control does not have resize handles. Mobile controls may not be positioned to absolute locations and therefore have one control to each line.

Within the mobile Web form, all controls in all *mobile:Form* controls are programmatically accessible from within the .aspx file and the code-behind file. This means that there can only be one control, called *txtName* on the mobile Web form, regardless of how many *mobile:Form* controls are on the page.

Although many *mobile:Form* controls can be added to a mobile Web form, it is important to remember that every time a page is instantiated, all of the controls on the mobile Web form are instantiated. This may hurt performance and resource usage, so you should refrain from creating a single mobile Form that contains every *mobile:Form* control for your entire Web application. If you have too many *mobile:Form* controls on a mobile Web form, you can move seldom-used *mobile:Form* controls to a different page. In general, it's best to place all forms on a single page except when transferring the user to a different phase of that application, when a different URL is required, or when performance is suffering.

Maintaining Session State

In a typical ASP.NET Web site, session state is maintained by issuing a session cookie to the browser. When the browser communicates to the Web server, the session cookie is passed to the Web server, and the Web server retrieves the session ID value from the session cookie to look up the session state data for your session.

Many mobile devices, such as cell phones, don't accept cookies, which cause problems with maintaining session state. The solution is to enable cookieless sessions. This can be accomplished by adding the following element to the Web.config file inside the *system.web* element:

```
<sessionState cookieless="true" />
```

With cookieless sessions, the session ID value is placed into the URL for the Web site instead of a cookie. You should plan on implementing cookieless sessions on all mobile applications to assure that your mobile Web site is compatible with the majority of mobile devices.

Understanding User Input Options

Mobile Web developers understand that mobile users input data differently from traditional computer users. Cell phones are typically more difficult to input data into. Many cell phones display only a few lines of text and some cell phones are able to display only one text box for user input at a time. This means that a *mobile:Form* with many controls can be broken apart, so it's important to focus on grouping controls that should be kept together. Mobile controls are organized by placing them into containers. Each container contains a logical group of controls, which helps the runtime render each mobile device page.

Pagination   You separate the *mobile:Form* content into smaller chunks by using pagination. Enabling pagination causes the runtime to format the output to the target device. Pagination is disabled by default but can be enabled by setting the *Paginate* property of each *mobile:Form* control to *true*.

For inputting data, pagination is typically not required, because many devices already contain mechanisms for allowing input of one item at a time. Pagination is best suited for *mobile:Form* controls that display lots of read-only data to keep a device from running out of memory.

In addition to enabling and disabling the pagination, custom pagination is also supported by the *List*, *ObjectList*, and *TextView* controls. These controls support internal pagination, which means that these controls provide pagination of their own items. These controls provide the ability to set the items per page and can raise the *LoadItems* events to load data.

Panels   Panels are containers that can be used to provide further grouping of controls for the purpose of enabling, disabling, hiding, and showing controls as a single group. Panels cannot be navigated to in the same way that forms can. You can use panels as a placeholder for dynamically created controls. The runtime attempts to display all controls that are with the panel on the same screen.

Styles   Styles can be used to change the visual appearance of a control. You can group styles and assign them to controls to provide a consistent appearance across your application. Implement styles by using the *StyleSheet* control or by using the *<Style>* tag. Only one *StyleSheet* control can be assigned to a mobile Web form. If the *StyleSheet* control is dropped onto a *mobile:Form* control, the *StyleSheet* displays an error message.

Styles are treated as hints. If the device supports the assigned style, the runtime attempts to assign the style to the controls as required. If the device does not support the assigned style, the runtime ignores the style.

A control inherits styles that are assigned to the container that the control is in. You can override a style by assigning a style directly to the control. When assigning styles, you can assign the styles directly to a property of the control, or assign the *StyleReference* property to a control.

Understanding Adaptive Rendering

Adaptive rendering is the act of rendering a control differently based on the browser that requested the Web page. In the following example, a mobile *Calendar* control is placed on a mobile Web form, and a cell phone requests the mobile Web form. The *Calendar* control renders as shown in Figure 12-4.

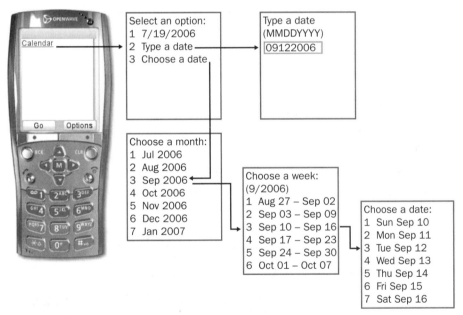

Figure 12-4   The mobile *Calendar* control rendered on a cell phone.

Notice that there is not enough space on the cell phone to render the current month, so the control is rendered as a hyperlink that simply states Calendar. If the user clicks this link, a menu is presented to give the user some options for entering the date. The user can simply select the current date, type in a date, or go through more menu screens to select a date.

If the same Web page is selected using Internet Explorer, the *Calendar* control renders as shown in Figure 12-5.

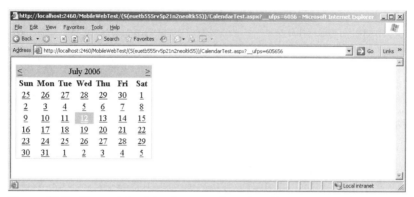

Figure 12-5   The mobile *Calendar* control rendered in Internet Explorer.

With Internet Explorer, the mobile *Calendar* control is rendered to display the current month, providing the same look as the regular *Calendar* control.

How does adaptive rendering work? When a browser requests a Web page, it sends an HTTP header called the *User-Agent*, which is a string that is used to identify the browser. The runtime uses the *User-Agent* string to look up the browser's capabilities. The capability settings for each browser can be viewed and set in the *browserCaps* element in the config files.

NOTE   New in ASP.NET 2.0

The browser capabilities structure has changed in ASP.NET 2.0.

In ASP.NET 2.0, *browserCaps* relies on XML files that contain a hierarchal structure of browser definitions. The default location of the XML files is as follows:

```
C:\WINDOWS\Microsoft.NET\Framework\v2.0.50727\CONFIG\Browsers\
```

Each of the XML files has a .browser extension; these files are used to build a class called *HttpBrowserCapabilities*, which is a factory class that creates an instance of *HttpBrowserCapabilities* and populates its properties based on the browser type. You can modify the existing .browser files and create new .browser files. The *HttpBrowserCapabilities* class is in an assembly called *ASP.BrowserCapsFactory.dll* that is installed in the global assembly cache. To regenerate the *ASP.BrowserCapsFactory.dll* assembly and its *HttpBrowserCapabilities* class based on changes to the .browser files, run the aspnet_regbrowsers command-line tool in the .NET Command Prompt window using the −*i* switch (install).

Implementing Device-Specific Rendering

Device-specific rendering is the ability to specify rendering for a control based on a device type. One way to use device-specific rendering is to query the various *Request.Browser* properties and perform actions based on the browser type. For example, a mobile *Label* control has been added to a mobile Web form. The following code has been added to the code-behind to display a different message based on whether the browser is a mobile device:

```vb
'VB
Partial Class LabelTest
    Inherits System.Web.UI.MobileControls.MobilePage

    Protected Sub Form1_Load(ByVal sender As Object, _
        ByVal e As System.EventArgs) Handles Form1.Load

        if (Request.Browser.IsMobileDevice) then
            Label1.Text = "A mobile device"
        else
            Label1.Text = "Not a mobile device"
        end if

    End Sub
End Class
```

```csharp
//C#
using System;

public partial class LabelTest :
    System.Web.UI.MobileControls.MobilePage
{
    protected void Page_Load(object sender, EventArgs e)
    {
        if (Request.Browser.IsMobileDevice)
        {
            Label1.Text = "A mobile device";
        }
        else
        {
            Label1.Text = "Not a mobile device";
        }
    }
}
```

Another way to perform device-specific rendering is to use the *DeviceSpecific* control. A single *DeviceSpecific* control can be nested inside any mobile control or in the *mobile:Form* to provide custom behavior based on a filter. The *DeviceSpecific* control can be explicitly dragged and dropped into the Source View of a mobile control, or you can implicitly create the *DeviceSpecific* control by setting the *PropertyOverrides* property of a control in the Properties window when in DesignView.

The *DeviceSpecific* control works with the *AppliedDeviceFilters* property that is available on each control. The *AppliedDeviceFilters* property gives the mobile control the ability to filter output based on the device that is being used. Figure 12-6 shows the Applied Device Filters dialog box that is available on most controls by clicking the ellipsis button (which features three dots) for the *AppliedDeviceFilters* property.

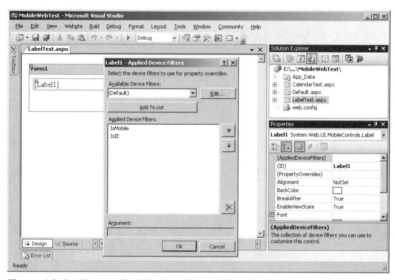

Figure 12-6   The Applied Device Filters dialog box allows overrides to be configured for specific devices.

Although the AppliedDeviceFilters window is accessible from any control, the creation of a filter adds an entry into the Web.config file for your site, and the filter is available to use on any mobile control on your site. The creation of the filters that are shown in Figure 12-6 resulted in the following entries in the Web.config file's *system.web* element:

```
<deviceFilters>
    <filter name="IsIE" compare="Browser" argument="IE" />
    <filter name="IsMobile" compare="IsMobileDevice" argument="true" />
</deviceFilters>
```

When a mobile control is being rendered, this list is viewed by the runtime to see if the device matches one of the *deviceFilters*. If a match is found, the *PropertyOverrides* is applied based on the settings that have been configured for the matching filter. Figure

12-7 shows the *PropertyOverrides* window for the IsIE filter and the IsMobile filter, as assigned to a *Label* control.

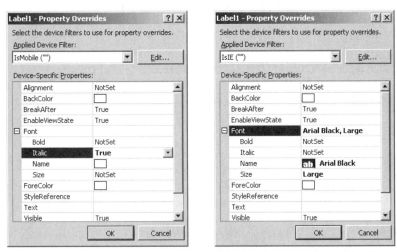

Figure 12-7   The PropertyOverrides window for the IsIE and IsMobile filters.

When the mobile Web form is displayed on a mobile device, the font is italicized. On Internet Explorer, the font is Arial Black with the font's size set to Large. Figure 12-8 shows the rendered output using a cell phone and using Internet Explorer.

Figure 12-8   The rendered output using a cell phone and using Internet Explorer.

When the *PropertyOverrides* property was set, the *DeviceSpecific* control was nested inside the *Label* control and *Choice* elements were added for the configuration of the filters, which can be viewed in the Source View window as follows:

```
<mobile:Form ID="Form1" Runat="server">
    <mobile:Label ID="Label1" Runat="server">
        <DeviceSpecific>
            <Choice Filter="IsMobile" Font-Italic="True" />
            <Choice Filter="IsIE" Font-Name="Arial Black" Font-Size="Large" />
        </DeviceSpecific>
    </mobile:Label>
</mobile:Form>
```

Using Mobile Controls

All mobile controls provide *Init*, *Load*, *Prerender*, and *Unload* events, in addition to custom events for specific controls.

You must adhere to the following guidelines when working with mobile controls:

- Always place mobile controls inside a *mobile:Form* control.

- Follow the cardinality and containment rules for each control. You can find these rules in the help function for each control. Be careful not to add a control when its cardinality rules dictate that the number of controls have reached the maximum.

- Do not add standard Web server controls or HTML server controls anywhere on a mobile page other than in an HTML template.

All controls have a *BreakAfter* property that is set to *true* by default. This means that all controls default to having one control per line; that is, they have a linear layout behavior. The linear behavior is typically desirable, since many devices are capable of displaying only a single control on a line.

Many of the mobile controls are similar to their standard Web server control counterparts. This helps developers leverage existing ASP.NET knowledge when building mobile applications. All of the validation controls have been implemented in ASP.NET 2.0 as well. The data-binding techniques are similar too. It's primarily the method of displaying data that is different in mobile applications.

The following sections describe many of the mobile controls that are included in ASP.NET 2.0.

Label Control

The *Label* control may be used to display a string to the user that cannot be edited by the user. When working with long strings, it is preferable to use the *TextView* control, because the *Label* control may not render as nicely.

The *Label* control has properties for various styles as well as *Alignment* and *Wrapping* properties.

TextBox Control

The *TextBox* control provides the user the ability to input a string. The *TextBox* control contains several style settings to allow customization of the *TextBox* view.

The *TextBox* contains a *Size* property to limit the width of the *TextBox* to the number of characters that *Size* is set to. The *TextBox* also contains a *MaxLength* property that limits the number of characters that can be entered into the *TextBox*.

The *TextBox* can be configured to only accept numeric input by setting the *Numeric* property to *true*.

The *TextBox* can also be used to set passwords by setting the *Password* property to *true*.

TextView Control

The *TextView* control provides the ability to display many lines of text. This control allows the use of some HTML formatting tags to control the output, such as *a* (hyperlink), *b* (bold), *br* (break), *i* (italic), and *p* (paragraph).

Command Control

The *Command* control represents a programmable button. On some devices, the *Command* button renders as a button, while on other devices, such as cell phones, it renders as a soft key that may be pressed. The *Text* property of the button is displayed on the control or in the soft key layout.

The *Command* control raises its *OnClick* event when the button is clicked and has an *ItemCommand* that propagates to the container when the button is clicked.

Image Control

The *Image* control displays an image based on the capabilities of the device. The image also supports the ability to have device filters assigned, which means that each type of device can have a different image. The *AlternateText* property should always be set on the *Image* control, because some devices may not support images, and some devices may not support the type of image that is being provided. For example, if a .gif file is being provided and the device only works with .wbmp files, the *AlternateText* is displayed.

List Control

The *List* control displays a static list of items. List items may be added to the *Items* property of the control or by binding data to the control. This list is paginated as required.

The *List* control supports data binding using the *DataSource, DataMember, DataText-Field* and *DataValueField* properties. While this list is primarily used to display static data with links, the *SelectionList* control (which we describe next) is intended to provide a selection list with options that are more similar to the menu type.

SelectionList Control

The *SelectionList* is very similar to the *List* control, except the *SelectionList* does not post back to the server. This means that a command button must be provided on the form.

The *SelectionList* also allows multiple selections, whereas the *List* control only allows a single selection. The *SelectionList* does not offer pagination, though the *List* control does.

By default, this control renders on most devices as a drop-down list box, which means that only one selection is available. The *SelectType* property of the *SelectionList* control can be used to change *CheckBox* or *MultiSelectListBox* to allow multiple selections.

This control also supports data binding using the *DataSource, DataMember, DataText-Field,* and *DataValueField* properties.

ObjectList Control

One might refer to the *ObjectList* control as being the *Mobile DataGrid*. This control is used to display tabular data. The *ObjectList* control is bound to data using the *Data-Source* and *DataMember* properties and contains a property called *LabelField,* which displays when the control is initially rendered. The *LabelField* is typically set to the primary key field, and when rendered, produces a list of primary key values as hyperlinks that can be clicked to see the rest of the data. Figure 12-9 shows the rendered output of the *ObjectList* on a cell phone when bound to the Northwind database using a SqlDataSource to retrieve CustomerID, CompanyName, ContactName, and ContactTitle from the Customers table.

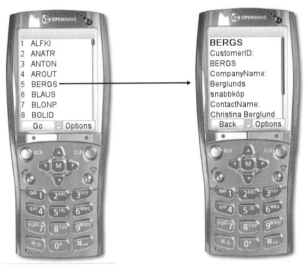

Figure 12-9   The *ObjectList* control when bound to the Customers table.

In Figure 12-9, notice that a list of CustomerID values are initially displayed, but selecting BERGS brings up a new screen that shows the details for BERGS . On the cell phone, the ContactTitle is not visible, but is displayed by pressing the down arrow.

Calendar Control

The *Calendar* control allows the user to specify a date. The presentation of the date selection may be very different, depending on the type of device, as shown earlier in the adaptive rendering topic (see Figure 12-4). The *Calendar* control renders as a series of forms, in which the user can drill down to a specific date. The user also has the ability to manually enter a date.

AdRotator Control

The *AdRotator* control can be used to place an advertisement on a device. This control is similar to ASP.NET's *AdRotator* control, except that the rendering adapts to the device.

The *AdRotator* can be assigned a series of images. The *AdRotator* control does not require a specific image type. The image can be assigned, based on the device type, by assigning device filters.

The *AdRotator* control requires an .xml file to configure the advertisements. This file can be the same file that is used by the standard *AdRotator* Web server control, in which the root element of the .xml file is called *Advertisements,* and the *Advertisements* element may contain many *Ad* elements. Each *Ad* element contains elements for each advertisement property, as follows:

Advertisements.xml

```xml
<?xml version="1.0" encoding="utf-8" ?>
<Advertisements xmlns="http://schemas.microsoft.com/AspNet/AdRotator-Advertisement-File-
1.2">
<Ad xmlns="">
<ImageUrl>~/images/AdventureWorks.gif</ImageUrl>
<MobileImageUrl>~/images/AdventureWorksMobile.gif</MobileImageUrl>
<NavigateUrl>http://www.adventure-works.com</NavigateUrl>
<AlternateText>Ad for Adventure Works Web site</AlternateText>
<Impressions>100</Impressions>
<Keyword>AdventureWorks</Keyword>
</Ad>
<Ad xmlns="">
<ImageUrl>~/images/Contoso.gif</ImageUrl>
<MobileImageUrl>~/images/ContosoMobile.gif</MobileImageUrl>
<NavigateUrl>http://www.contoso.com/</NavigateUrl>
<AlternateText>Ad for Contoso Ltd. Web site</AlternateText>
<Impressions>200</Impressions>
<Keyword>Contoso</Keyword>
</Ad>
<Ad xmlns="">
<ImageUrl>~/images/NorthwindTraders.gif</ImageUrl>
<MobileImageUrl>~/images/NorthwindTradersMobile.gif</MobileImageUrl>
<NavigateUrl>http://www.northwindtraders.com</NavigateUrl>
<AlternateText>Ad for Northwind Traders Web site</AlternateText>
<Impressions>300</Impressions>
<Keyword>Northwind</Keyword>
</Ad>
</Advertisements>
```

Figure 12-10 shows the *AdRotator* control on the cell phone and in Internet Explorer. Notice that the Advertisements.xml file has a user-defined element called *MobileImageUrl* and that smaller images were created for mobile devices. The IsMobile device filter is added to the *AdRotator* and the *PropertyOverrides* for the IsMobile device filter sets the *ImageKey* to *MobileImageUrl*.

Figure 12-10 The *AdRotator* control rendering on the cell phone and on Internet Explorer.

PhoneCall Control

The *PhoneCall* control provides a simple method of dialing a phone number on devices that support placing calls. The *PhoneCall* control has a *PhoneNumber* property that can be set to the phone number that is to be dialed. The phone number is displayed on the device as a hyperlink, but if the *Text* property is set, the *Text* is displayed as a hyperlink instead. The *SoftKeyLabel* property can be set to a custom string, such as *Call* for the function key, if the device supports function keys.

The *PhoneCall* control displays the contents of the *AlternateText* property if the device does not support phone calls. The *AlternateText* property defaults to {0} {1}, where {0} is the *Text* property and {1} is the *PhoneNumber* property.

Validation Controls

Validation controls are a very important part of standard ASP.NET 2.0 Web pages, and they are included as mobile controls as well. The following is a list of mobile validation controls:

RequiredFieldValidator   An entry is required in this field.

RangeValidator   The entry must be within the specified range.

CompareValidator   The entry is compared to another value.

CustomValidator   A custom validation function validates the entry.

RegularExpressionValidator   The entry must match the specified pattern.

ValidationSummary   This displays a summary of all input errors.

These controls are essentially the same as the controls that are available in ASP.NET 2.0, except that the mobile validator controls do not provide client-side validation. You can combine these controls as necessary. For example, a *TextBox* may have both the *RequiredFieldValidator* and the *RegularExpressionValidator*.

Data Binding

Data binding in ASP.NET 2.0 is essentially the same as data binding in ASP.NET. Most controls support the *DataSource* and *DataMember* properties, while some controls support the *DataTextField* and the *DataValue* fields as well. It is important to use the *IsPostBack* property and load data into the cache. Rather than binding all controls, only the controls for the current form should be bound.

Applying Best Practices to Mobile Applications

In many respects, writing applications for mobile use can become a challenging endeavor. The following list identifies some guidelines and best practices that you should consider.

- **Provide a Separate Desktop Presentation**   Although many devices are adaptive, desktop users want and expect a much richer presentation. It's usually best to provide two presentations: one for the desktop and one for the mobile devices.

- **Page Content**   Keep page content as simple as possible.

- **Data Access**   Instead of sending a complete result set to the user, only send the data record that the user is interested in. Only bind the required controls.

- **Adaptive Controls**   Test adaptive controls with several devices, including devices that display a few lines.

- **Default Values**   Present the user with default values whenever possible.

- **Evaluate *ViewState***   In many applications, better performance may be obtained by turning off *ViewState,* because this reduces the amount of data that is being transferred to a slow mobile device. Turning off *ViewState* may require the server to rebuild the data each time the user posts back to the server.

- **Use Caching**   Whenever possible, cache data access results to keep from retrieving data each time the user accesses the server.

- **Combine Many Forms on a Page**   It is much easier to share data between forms on a page than it is to share data between pages. However, there is a point where performance suffers. Look for places where it is easy to pass a few items to a new page.

- **Use Cookieless Sessions**   Many mobile devices do not support cookies, so it is important to use cookieless sessions.

- **Use Session Server**   Use Microsoft SQL Server to store state in a Web farm environment.

- **Using Hyperlinks to a Form**   A hyperlink can be created to a form by using the *#form3* syntax. If the page has a user control called *myControl*, which has forms, a hyperlink can be created using the *#myControl:form2* syntax.

- **Minimize Image Usage**   This use of images should be kept to a minimum due to the low bandwidth and screen resolution that is available on most mobile devices. Some mobile devices may not support images, while others may not support the image type that is being supplied, such as when a .gif file is used on a mobile device that only supports .wbmp files. Be sure to assign a value to the *AlternateText* property of all graphics.

Quick Check

1. What is a primary difference between the standard validator controls and the mobile validator controls?

2. What can you do to ensure that session state is maintained when mobile devices that don't accept cookies are accessing your mobile Web site?

Quick Check Answers

1. The mobile validation controls don't provide client-side validation.

2. You should enable cookieless sessions in the Web.config file.

Lab: Working with Mobile Web Applications

In this lab, you create a mobile Web site application. This application demonstrates the use of mobile controls to access and display data on a cell phone or browser. This application presents the user with the option of searching the products by name, product ID, or by drilling down through the categories to get to the products.

▶ **Exercise 1: Create the Web Site and add Controls**

In this exercise, you create the mobile Web site and add the controls.

1. Open Visual Studio 2005 and create a new Web site called **WorkingWithMobileWebApplications** using your preferred programming language. The new Web site will be created and a standard Web page called Default.aspx is displayed.

2. Delete the Default.aspx Web page.

3. Add a mobile Web form to the Web site, called Default.aspx, which replaces the Default.aspx page that you deleted in the previous step.

4. Switch to Design View, select the mobile form, and set its ID to **frmMainMenu** and its Title to **Select a Search Method**.

5. Add another mobile *Form* control to the page. Set this form's ID to **frmSearchName** and its Title to **Enter Name**.

6. Add another mobile *Form* control to the page. Set this form's ID to **frmSearchId** and its Title to **Enter ID**.

7. Add another mobile *Form* control to the page. Set this form's ID to **frmSearchCategory** and its Title to **Select a Category**.

8. Add another mobile *Form* control to the page. Set this form's ID to **frmResult** and its Title to **Search Result**.

9. Add a mobile *List* control to the frmMainMenu and set the ID to **lstMainMenu**. Add the following to the *Items* collection of lstMainMenu: *By Name* (value=1), *By ID* (value=2), and *By Category* (value=3).

10. Add a mobile *Label* control to frmSearchName and set its ID to **lblSearchName** and its Text to **Enter Name**.

11. Add a mobile *TextBox* control to frmSearchName and set its ID to **txtSearchName**.

12. Add a mobile *Command* control to frmSearchName and set its ID to **cmdSearchName** and its Text to **Search**.

13. Add a mobile *Label* control to frmSearchId and set its ID to **lblSearchId** and its Text to **Enter ID**.

14. Add a mobile *TextBox* control to frmSearchId and set its ID to **txtSearchId**.

15. Add a mobile *Command* control to frmSearchId and set its ID to **cmdSearchId** and its Text to **Search**.

16. Add a *List* control to frmSearchCategory and set its ID to **lstCategories**.

17. Add an *ObjectList* to frmResult and set its ID to **lstResult**.

Figure 12-11 shows the complete mobile *Form* controls.

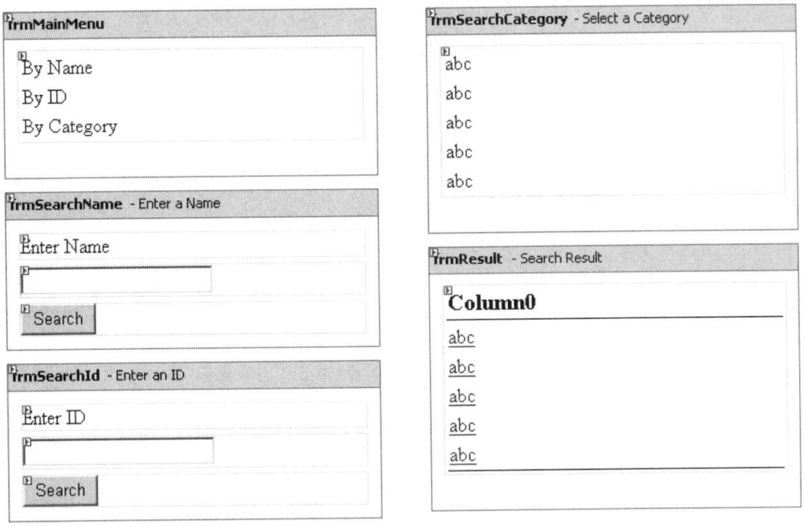

Figure 12-11 The completed mobile *Form* controls.

▶ **Exercise 2: Add the Code**

In this exercise, you add code to the code-behind page.

1. Continue with the project you started in Exercise 1.

2. Add the *Northwind* database to the App_Data folder.

3. Go to the code-behind page and add code to declare and initialize a *DataSet* with the Category and Product data, as shown in the following code sample:

```
'VB
Imports System.Data
Imports System.Data.SqlClient

Partial Class _Default
    Inherits System.Web.UI.MobileControls.MobilePage

    Private ds As New DataSet()

    Private Sub Page_Load( ByVal sender As System.Object, _
            ByVal e As System.EventArgs) _
            Handles MyBase.Load
        If Not Page.IsPostBack Then
            GetData()
        End If
```

```
        End Sub

    Public Sub GetData()
        Dim cn As New SqlConnection( _
          "Data Source=.\SQLEXPRESS;AttachDbFilename=" + _
          "|DataDirectory|NORTHWND.MDF;Integrated Security=True; " + _
          "User Instance=True")
        Dim Sql As String = "select * from categories"
        Dim da As New SqlDataAdapter(Sql, cn)
        da.Fill(ds, "Categories")
        Sql = "Select * from products"
        da.SelectCommand.CommandText = Sql
        da.Fill(ds, "Products")
    End Sub

End Class

//C#
using System;
using System.Data;
using System.Data.SqlClient;
using System.Web.UI.MobileControls;

public partial class _Default : System.Web.UI.MobileControls.MobilePage
{
    private DataSet ds = new DataSet();

    protected void Page_Load(object sender, EventArgs e)
    {
        if(!Page.IsPostBack)
        {
            GetData();
        }
    }

    public void GetData()
    {
        SqlConnection cn = new SqlConnection(
          @"Data Source=.\SQLEXPRESS;AttachDbFilename=" +
          "|DataDirectory|NORTHWND.MDF;Integrated Security=True;" +
          "User Instance=True");
        string Sql = "select * from categories";
        SqlDataAdapter da = new SqlDataAdapter(Sql, cn);
        da.Fill(ds, "Categories");
        Sql = "Select * from products";
        da.SelectCommand.CommandText = Sql;
        da.Fill(ds, "Products");
    }
}
```

4. Double-click the *lstMainMenu* control to insert the *ItemCommand* event handler method into the code-behind page. Add the following code to the code-behind page to create a new *DataSet* object and set the active form based on the selected item in the main menu:

```vb
'VB
Protected Sub lstMainMenu_ItemCommand(ByVal sender As Object, _
     ByVal e As System.Web.UI.MobileControls.ListCommandEventArgs) _
     Handles lstMainMenu.ItemCommand
  If e.ListItem.Value = 1 Then
     Me.ActiveForm = frmSearchName
  End If
  If e.ListItem.Value = 2 Then
     Me.ActiveForm = frmSearchId
  End If
  If e.ListItem.Value = 3 Then
     GetData()
     Me.ActiveForm = frmSearchCategory
     lstCategories.DataSource = ds.Tables("Categories").DefaultView
     lstCategories.DataTextField = "CategoryName"
     lstCategories.DataValueField = "CategoryID"
     lstCategories.DataBind()
  End If
End Sub

//C#
protected void lstMainMenu_ItemCommand(
    object sender, ListCommandEventArgs e)
{
    if (e.ListItem.Value == "1")
    {
        this.ActiveForm = frmSearchName;
    }
    if (e.ListItem.Value == "2")
    {
        this.ActiveForm = frmSearchId;
    }
    if (e.ListItem.Value == "3")
    {
        GetData();
        this.ActiveForm = frmSearchCategory;
        lstCategories.DataSource = ds.Tables["Categories"].DefaultView;
        lstCategories.DataTextField = "CategoryName";
        lstCategories.DataValueField = "CategoryID";
        lstCategories.DataBind();
    }
}
```

5. Add code to display the result of any search. The code uses a new method called the *ShowResults* method. This method simply sets the properties of the results *ObjectList* and binds as follows:

```vb
'VB
Public Sub ShowResults()
lstResult.DataSource = ds.Tables("Products").DefaultView
lstResult.LabelField = "ProductName"
lstResult.DataBind()
Me.ActiveForm = frmResult
End Sub
```

```csharp
//C#
public void ShowResults()
{
    lstResult.DataSource = ds.Tables["Products"].DefaultView;
    lstResult.LabelField = "ProductName";
    lstResult.DataBind();
    this.ActiveForm = frmResult;
}
```

6. Double-click the *cmdSearchName* control to add the event handler method. Add code to perform the search by name function that gets the data into the *DataSet*, set the *RowFilter* property of the product's default view, and bind the data. The code is as follows:

```vb
'VB
Protected Sub cmdSearchName_Click(ByVal sender As Object, _
        ByVal e As System.EventArgs) Handles cmdSearchName.Click
    GetData()
    ds.Tables("Products").DefaultView.RowFilter = _
     String.Format("ProductName like '{0}%'", txtSearchName.Text)
    ShowResults()
End Sub
```

```csharp
//C#
protected void cmdSearchName_Click(object sender, EventArgs e)
{
    GetData();
    ds.Tables["Products"].DefaultView.RowFilter =
     String.Format("ProductName like '{0}%'", txtSearchName.Text);
    ShowResults();
}
```

7. Double-click the *cmdSearchId* control and enter the code to change the *RowFilter* property, as shown in the following code:

```vb
'VB
Protected Sub cmdSearchId_Click(ByVal sender As Object, _
        ByVal e As System.EventArgs) Handles cmdSearchId.Click
```

```
      GetData()
      ds.Tables("Products").DefaultView.RowFilter = _
          String.Format("ProductID = {0}", txtSearchId.Text)
      ShowResults()
   End Sub


//C#
protected void cmdSearchId_Click(object sender, EventArgs e)
{
    GetData();
    ds.Tables["Products"].DefaultView.RowFilter =
        String.Format("ProductID = {0}", txtSearchId.Text);
    ShowResults();
}
```

8. Double-click the *lstCategories* control and add code for the search by category, which is similar to the previous code. The *DataSet* is populated, the *RowFilter* is set to the value of the category that was selected, and the data is bound as shown in the following code:

```
'VB
Protected Sub lstCategories_ItemCommand(ByVal sender As Object, _
        ByVal e As System.Web.UI.MobileControls.ListCommandEventArgs) _
        Handles lstCategories.ItemCommand
    GetData()
    ds.Tables("Products").DefaultView.RowFilter = _
     String.Format("CategoryID = {0}", e.ListItem.Value)
    ShowResults()
End Sub


//C#
protected void lstCategories_ItemCommand(object sender,
    ListCommandEventArgs e)
{
    GetData();
    ds.Tables["Products"].DefaultView.RowFilter =
     String.Format("CategoryID = {0}", e.ListItem.Value);
    ShowResults();
}
```

▶ **Exercise 3: Test the Mobile Web Application**

In this exercise, you run the Web page and test the mobile Web application.

1. Continue with the project from previous exercise.

2. Run the mobile Web form. Figure 12-12 shows the Main Menu rendered with the cell phone and Internet Explorer.

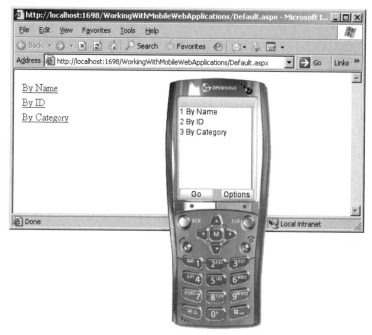

Figure 12-12   The Main Menu of the mobile Web application.

3.   Select By Name. Enter the letter **A** and press the Search button. Notice that the cell phone requires you to enter the letter and then select Option | Go. This performs the search and displays the result.

4.   Go back to the Main Menu and test the By ID and the By Category options.

Lesson Summary

- A mobile Web application has the ability to render to a wide variety of mobile devices.

- You can test your mobile application using Internet Explorer, various devices, or device emulators.

- To create a mobile Web application, create a standard ASP.NET Web site using your preferred programming language, and then replace the Default.aspx page with a mobile Web form.

- You can add many *mobile:Form* controls to a mobile Web form.

- You can enable state to a wide variety of mobile devices by using cookieless sessions.

- The mobile Web controls provide adaptive rendering for various device types.
- You have the ability to provide device-specific rendering, which allows you to override the default rendering.

Lesson Review

You can use the following questions to test your knowledge of the information in Lesson 1, "Building Mobile Applications." The questions are also available on the companion CD if you prefer to review them in electronic form.

NOTE Answers

Answers to these questions and explanations of why each answer choice is right or wrong are located in the "Answers" section at the end of the book.

---

1. You attempt to create a mobile Web site, but don't see a mobile Web site project template, so you create a standard Web site. What do you do to convert this site to a mobile Web site?

   A. Add mobile controls to the Default.aspx page that was created for the standard ASP.NET Web site.

   B. Add mobile Web forms to your Web site and add mobile controls to the mobile Web forms.

   C. In the Default.aspx page that was created for the standard ASP.NET Web site, change the form element to a *mobile:Form* element and add your mobile controls to this page.

   D. Obtain the latest service pack for Visual Studio 2005, which contains the mobile Web site template.

2. You have a mobile *Label* control on your mobile Web form, and you want the text to be different based on whether the browser is Internet Explorer or a mobile device. How can you perform this task? (Choose two.)

   A. In your code, add a test for Request.Browser.IsMobileDevice, and then set the *Text* property accordingly.

   B. In your code, call the *IsDevice* method on the mobile Web form and pass the *Device.Mobile* enumeration value, and then set the *Text* property accordingly.

    C. Read the *UserAgent* property on the *Request* object, and if the *UserAgent* is equal to *mobile*, set the *Text* property accordingly.

    D. Set the default *Text* value, and then define a mobile device in the *Applied-DeviceFilters*, and use this to set the *Text* property using the *PropertyOverrides* property of the mobile *Label* control.

3. You created a mobile Web site that appears to be working properly for your users. Joe just purchased a new state-of-the-art mobile device; when he attempted to view a *Calendar* control on your Web site, the control attempted to render a month view, but Joe's mobile device screen wasn't big enough to display the calendar. You decide to create a new .browser file that represents Joe's mobile device, and the settings will cause the calendar to render appropriately. How can you the get runtime to recognize the new .browser file settings?

    A. Add the name of the .browser file to the machine.config file in the *Browsers* element.

    B. Add the .browser file name to the Web.config file for your Web site in the *Browsers* element.

    C. Run the aspnet_regbrowsers command-line tool in the .NET Command Prompt window using the −i switch.

    D. Run the aspnet_regiis command-line tool in the .NET Command Prompt window using the −*registerbrowsers* switch.

Chapter Review

To further practice and reinforce the skills you learned in this chapter, you can perform the following tasks:

- Review the chapter summary.
- Review the list of key terms introduced in this chapter.
- Complete the case scenarios. These scenarios set up real-world situations involving the topics of this chapter and ask you to create solutions.
- Complete the suggested practices.
- Take a practice test.

Chapter Summary

- A mobile Web application has the ability to render to a wide variety of mobile devices.
- The mobile Web controls provide adaptive rendering for various device types.
- You have the ability to provide device specific rendering, which allows you to override the default rendering.

Key Terms

Do you know what these key terms mean? You can check your answers by looking up the terms in the glossary at the end of the book.

- adaptive rendering
- device-specific rendering

Case Scenarios

In the following case scenarios, you apply what you've learned in this chapter. You can find answers to these questions in the "Answers" section at the end of this book.

Case Scenario 1: Determining the Mobile Control to Use

You are creating a mobile Web application that will be used by real estate agents to enter search criteria into their mobile devices, such as price range, quantity of rooms, lot size, and city. After entering the criteria, the data is sent to the Web server and the Web server responds with a list of houses that meet the search criteria.

   1.   What control would you use to display the results?

Case Scenario 2: Determining How Many Web Pages to Create

You are creating a mobile Web application that will be accessible using desktop computers, notebook computers, PDAs, smartphones with Windows Mobile 5, and cell phones with mobile browsers. Your boss is concerned that, for every Web page, you may need to provide a device specific Web page.

   1.   How can you implement the Web site with a minimum amount of Web pages?
   2.   How should you implement the Web site?

Suggested Practices

The exam objectives in this chapter are:

- Create a mobile Web application project.
- Use device-specific rendering to display controls on a variety of devices.
- Use adaptive rendering to modify the appearance of Web server controls.
- Use the mobile Web controls to display content on a device.

To successfully master these exam objectives, complete the following tasks.

Create a Mobile Web Application Project

For this task, you should complete Practice 1.

Practice 1

- Create a new mobile Web application using the programming language of your choice.

Exploring Adaptive Rendering

For this task, you should complete Practices 1 and 2.

Practice 1

- Create a new mobile Web application using the programming language of your choice.
- Add a calendar mobile to a mobile form.
- Run the mobile Web application to view the calendar using Internet Explorer.

Practice 2

- Download and install OpenWave's latest phone emulator from *http://developer .openwave.com*.
- Run the mobile Web application to view the calendar using the phone emulator.

Implement Device-Specific Rendering

For this task, you should complete Practices 1 and 2.

Practice 1

- Create a new mobile Web application using the programming language of your choice.
- Add a calendar mobile to a mobile form.
- Add device specific rendering based on a specific device to change the style of the calendar.
- Run the mobile Web application to view the calendar using Internet Explorer.

Practice 2

- Download and install OpenWave's latest phone emulator from *http://developer .openwave.com*.
- Try debugging your application using the phone emulator.

Create a Data-Collection Page with Validation

For this task, you should complete Practices 1 and 2.

Practice 1

- Create a new mobile Web application that collects data from users to perform queries and displays the query results to the users.

Practice 2

- Practice adding mobile validator controls to restrict data entry to the known set of good data.

Take a Practice Test

The practice tests on this book's companion CD offer many options. For example, you can test yourself on just the content covered in this chapter, or you can test yourself on all the 70-528 certification exam content. You can set up the test so that it closely simulates the experience of taking a certification exam, or you can set it up in study mode so that you can look at the correct answers and explanations after you answer each question.

MORE INFO   Practice tests

For details about all the practice test options available, see "How to Use the Practice Tests" in this book's Introduction.

Chapter 13

Monitoring, Deploying, and Caching Applications

After you've developed and tested your application, it's time to deploy it. In most real-world environments, deployment involves moving an application from a staging environment to one or more Web servers. Microsoft Visual Studio and the .NET Framework provide several different ways to deploy your Web application to meet the requirements of a wide variety of environments.

Once you've deployed your application, you need to keep it running. Server applications must integrate into an environment's monitoring infrastructure, so ASP.NET provides several different *event providers* to send notifications to the Event Log, to a database, or to an e-mail address. You can create custom events and event providers, too.

For busier Web applications, performance is critical. Upgrading hardware isn't always feasible, but you can significantly reduce the processing requirements of your application by using caching. ASP.NET provides two types of caching to improve the efficiency of your application.

Exam objectives in this chapter:
- Use a Web setup project to deploy a Web application to a target server.
  - Create a Web setup project.
  - Configure deployment properties for a Web setup project.
  - Install a Web application on a target server.
- Copy a Web application to a target server by using the Copy Web tool.
- Precompile a Web application by using the Publish Web utility.
- Optimize and troubleshoot a Web application.
  - Customize event-level analysis with the ASP.NET health-monitoring API.
  - Use performance counters to track the execution of an application.
  - Optimize performance by using the ASP.NET *Cache* object.

Lessons in this chapter:

Before You Begin

To complete the lessons in this chapter, you should be familiar with Microsoft Visual Basic or C# and be comfortable with the following tasks:

- Have Microsoft Windows XP and Microsoft Visual Studio 2005 installed with Microsoft SQL Server 2005 Express Edition.

- Be familiar with the Visual Studio 2005 Integrated Development Environment (IDE).

- Have a basic understanding of Hypertext Markup Language (HTML) and client-side scripting.

Real World

Tony Northrup

As a developer, you probably want to focus on writing code rather than on deploying and managing it. The best thing you can do to allow yourself to focus on creating new applications is to make your applications as deployable and manageable as possible. Speak with the IT members who will be installing and maintaining your application, and ask them what you can do as a developer to simplify those processes. Trust me; if you take a few hours to address operational requirements now, you'll save yourself many meetings after your application is released.

Lesson 1: Deploying Web Applications

As you've been working through the exercises on this book, you have probably been running applications on your local computer. You never had to deploy your sample applications, because you could run them in place.

Only the simplest of production environments use a single server, however. Most enterprise Web applications have deployment, staging, and production servers. Highly available and high-scalability applications often run on multiple Web servers simultaneously. Additionally, many developers release Web applications commercially, so that other people can deploy them on their own servers. In each of these scenarios, you must create a plan to deploy your application and any updates that you release in the future.

This lesson describes the different techniques available to deploy Web applications.

After this lesson, you will be able to:

- Create a Web Setup Project and use the resulting files to deploy your application.
- Update and deploy Web applications in environments with multiple developers and servers using the Copy Web tool.
- Precompile Web applications using the Publish Web Site tool.

Estimated lesson time: 40 minutes

Using Web Setup Projects

Depending on the scenario, .NET Framework Web applications can be extremely easy to deploy. Because they are typically entirely file-based, you can deploy a Web application to a Web server by simply copying the files. Do you need to make an application update? In most cases, you can simply overwrite the old file. If you're maintaining a Web application on a single server, there's no need to run a setup process, edit the registry, or add items to the Start menu.

This simplicity provides a great deal of flexibility. If your Web application is to be deployed to an array of Web servers (in which multiple Web servers host the same Web site for scalability and availability), you can use any file-synchronization tool to copy the files between servers. Administrators don't need to log on to servers, change registry entries, or restart servers to deploy applications, so making updates and deploying new applications is easy.

There are times, however, when you may need more control over how your application is deployed. You may need to configure the Web server, deploy files to other locations, add registry entries, or download and install prerequisites. You might also need to create a Windows Installer (.msi) file so that IT can deploy the application using tools such as Active Directory software distribution or Microsoft Systems Management Server (SMS). Finally, if you are creating a Web application that users might download from the Internet and install on their own computers, a Windows Installer file enables the setup to be performed automatically, even if the user does not know how to configure a Web server.

The sections that follow describe how to create a Web Setup Project, how to configure deployment properties, how to configure deployment conditions, and how to deploy Web applications.

Creating a Web Setup Project

A Web Setup Project is very similar to a standard Setup Project that you might make for a Windows Forms application; however, it provides specialized capabilities required by Web applications. To add a Web Setup Project to a Web site, follow these steps:

1. Open your Web site in Visual Studio.

2. In Visual Studio, select the File menu, choose Add, and then choose New Project.

3. Under Project Types, expand Other Project Types, and then select Setup And Deployment. Under Templates, choose Web Setup Project. In the Name field, type a name for your project, as shown in Figure 13-1. Then click OK.

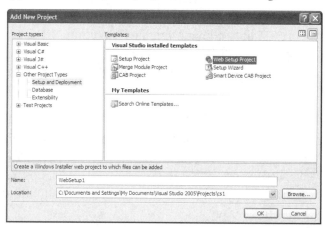

Figure 13-1   Add a new project to your Web site to create a Web Setup Project.

4. Visual Studio adds the project to your Web site and displays the File System editor. Right-click Web Application Folder, click Add, and then click Project Output.

5. In the Add Project Output Group dialog box, with Content Files selected, click OK.

Now that you have created a Web Setup Project with your project's output, you can add additional folders, files, and assemblies that are not part of your project output to the Web Setup Project. This might be necessary if, for example, you had a separate folder containing images that you have not added to your Web site project.

Web Setup Projects are not automatically built when you build your Web application. Instead, you must select the Web Setup Project in Solution Explorer and choose Build. The build output in Visual Studio shows you where the .msi file is generated. By default, it is always placed in the same folder that contains your solution file, which is a subfolder of your Visual Studio 2005\Projects\ folder.

Configuring Deployment Properties

Many Web applications do not require custom configuration. More complex Web applications might have complex dependencies (such as particular operating system versions or service packs), require custom registry entries, or need administrator configuration. You can use Web Setup Projects to deploy Web applications to meet any of these requirements. The sections that follow discuss how to do this in more detail.

Configuring Launch Conditions   You can specify launch conditions to restrict the computers your Web application can be installed on. For example, you can check for specific versions of Windows or verify that specific service packs are present.

To add launch conditions, follow these steps:

1. Select your setup project in Solution Explorer.

2. Select the View menu, choose Editor, and then choose Launch Conditions.

3. The Launch Conditions Editor appears, as shown in Figure 13-2.

Figure 13-2   Use the Launch Conditions Editor to configure requirements for your target computer.

The Launch Conditions Editor has two related nodes:

■ **Search Target Machine** Defines criteria to search for prior to installation. By default, this node contains Search For IIS. You can add file, registry, and Windows Installer search conditions. Typically, you pair a search condition that determines whether a change is necessary with a launch condition that performs the change.

■ **Launch Conditions** Based on a search condition or other criteria (such as the operating system version), the launch condition defines conditions that must be met prior to installation. Launch conditions can provide a useful message to the user if a requirement is missing. It can then automatically retrieve a Web page. By default, Web Setup Projects include conditions for the .NET Framework and Internet Information Services (IIS).

Typically, you must add an item to each of these two nodes to require a single component. For example, if you want to verify that a specific Dynamic-Link Library (DLL) is present, you must create a search condition under Search Target Machine and store the result of the search in a property. Then you must create a launch condition that specifies the search condition's property, displays an error message to the user if the required file is missing, and optionally installs the required component from the Internet.

To add a file launch condition, follow these steps:

1. In the Launch Conditions Editor, right-click Requirements On Target Machine, and then select Add File Launch Condition.

   The Launch Conditions Editor adds a search condition to the Search Target Machine node and a launch condition to the Launch Conditions node. The new search condition's *Property* value has a default name of FILEEXISTS1, which links it to the *Condition* property of the launch condition.

2. Rename both the new search condition and the new launch condition so that the names indicate the file you are searching for.

3. Select the new search condition and view the Properties window. Configure the properties as described in Table 13-1.

   Table 13-1   **File Search Condition Properties**

Property	Description
FileName	The name of the file to look for. Just specify the filename with extension, and not the folder.

Table 13-1   File Search Condition Properties

Property	Description
Folder	The folder to search for the file in. You can search subfolders by specifying the Depth field.
Depth	The number of nested folders within the specified folder to search.
MinDate, MaxDate	The minimum and maximum last modified date of the file.
MinSize, MaxSize	The minimum and maximum size of the file.
MinVersion, MaxVersion	The minimum and maximum version of the file.
Property	The name of the property that stores the results of this search. You specify this property name in the corresponding launch condition.

4. Select the new launch condition and view the Properties window. Configure the properties as described in Table 13-2.

Table 13-2   Launch Condition Properties

Property	Description
Condition	The condition that must evaluate to *true* for installation to continue. By default, this is the name of a property assigned to a search condition, and if the search does find the required file or other object, the launch condition is fulfilled. You can specify more complex conditions to check for operating system version, service pack levels, and other criteria. For more information, read "Configuring Deployment Conditions" later in this lesson.
InstallUrl	Optional. If the *Condition* is not met, the setup project retrieves this Uniform Resource Locator (URL) to install the required component.
Message	The message that is displayed to the user if the launch condition is not met.

To add a search condition, follow these steps:

1. Right-click Search Target Machine, and then select Add File Search, Add Registry Search, or Add Windows Installer Search.

2. Type a name for your search condition, and then press Enter.

3. With the new search condition selected, view the Properties window to configure your search condition. The exact properties vary depending on the type of condition, but each allows you to specify that specific files, registry entries, or Windows Installer globally unique identifiers (GUIDs) are available.

   To add a launch condition that must be met prior to installing your Web application, follow these steps:

4. Right-click Launch Conditions, and then select Add Launch Condition.

5. Type a name for your launch condition, and then press Enter.

6. With the new launch condition selected, view the Properties window to configure your launch condition. Set the *Condition* property to match the *Property* value of a search condition or specify a different condition, as described in "Configuring Deployment Conditions" later in this lesson. To download software to resolve the missing launch condition, provide a URL in the *InstallUrl* property. In the *Message* property, type a message to be displayed to the administrator who is installing your Web application.

Adding Custom Setup Wizard Pages   Administrators responsible for deploying and managing your Web applications can customize settings by editing your Web.config file. To enable simpler configuration at setup time, you can add custom setup wizard pages. With these pages, you can prompt users to custom-configure information, and then provide that information as parameters for custom actions. Combined, custom setup wizard pages and custom actions enable you to perform the following types of tasks at setup time:

- **Display a license agreement**   A Web Setup Project provides a dialog template for requiring the user to accept a license agreement.

- **Modify settings in the Web.config file**   You can use user input to modify configuration settings without requiring administrators to know how to configure an Extensible Markup Language (XML) file.

- **Perform custom configuration**   Prompt the user for information that might be stored in the registry or in another unusual location.

- **Activate or register your application**   Prompt the user for a product key or registration information. Prompts can be either required or optional.

To add a custom setup wizard page, follow these steps:

1. In Solution Explorer, choose your setup project.

2. Select the View menu, choose Editor, and then choose User Interface.

3. The User Interface Editor appears, as shown in Figure 13-3. The User Interface Editor displays the different setup phases for both standard and administrative installs.

Figure 13-3   Use the User Interface Editor to add pages to the setup wizard.

4. Right-click the setup phase you want to add a page to, and then click Add Dialog. Normally, you add dialog boxes to the Start phase under the Install node. You can add only a splash page, a license agreement page, or a Read Me page to the Administrative Install.

5. In the Add Dialog window, click the dialog box template you want to add. The different templates allow for collecting different types of information and can only be customized by hiding some controls and displaying different labels. After clicking a template, click OK.

6. Select your new dialog and view the Properties window. You configure all aspects of the dialog box using the dialog box Properties window; Visual Studio does not provide a designer. To control the information for which the dialog box prompts the user, edit the labels and property names for the dialog box. For the text box and radio button series of dialog boxes, you can configure the label for each field (for example, *Edit1Label* or *Button1Label*), the name the value is to be stored in (for example, *Edit1Property* or *ButtonProperty*), and the

default value (for example, *Edit1Value* or *DefaultValue*). The License Agreement template allows you to specify a license agreement file, and the Splash template allows you to display a bitmap file.

7. To control the order of your custom dialog box, right-click it and then click Move Up or Move Down.

When you run the Web setup project, your custom dialog boxes appear as setup wizard pages. If you configured pages to collect custom information from users, you can reference that data in custom actions, as described in the next section.

Adding Custom Actions   Web Setup Projects provide a great deal of flexibility and can meet most setup requirements. If you have more demanding requirements, such as submitting registration information to a Web service or validating a product key, you can add a custom action. Custom actions can run in any of the four phases of setup:

- **Install**   This phase performs the bulk of the work done during setup by adding files and creating configuration settings required by your application to run.

- **Commit**   After the Install phase is complete and all changes required to run your application have been made, the Commit phase finalizes these changes. After the Commit phase, setup cannot be rolled back and the application should be uninstalled with Add Or Remove Programs.

- **Rollback**   The Rollback phase runs only if setup fails or is cancelled. In such a case, the Rollback phase occurs instead of the Commit phase and removes any new files or settings.

- **Uninstall**   This phase removes files and settings from the computer when the application is removed with Add Or Remove Programs. Often, uninstall routines leave settings and databases in place so that they can be restored if the application is later reinstalled.

To add a custom action, follow these steps:

1. Select your setup project in Solution Explorer.
2. Select the View menu, choose Editor, and then choose Custom Actions.
3. The Custom Actions Editor appears. The Custom Actions Editor displays the four setup phases. Right-click the phase you want to add a custom action to, and then select Add Custom Action.

4. In the Select Item In Project dialog box, select the executable or script. To add an assembly that is part of your current project, select the /bin/ folder, click Add Output, select the project, and then select Primary Output.

If you add more than one custom action to a single phase, you can rearrange the custom actions by right-clicking them and then clicking Move Up or Move Down.

Adding Registry Entries   Storing information in the registry used to be the preferred way of storing application settings. However, the best practice for configuring .NET Framework applications is to store settings in configuration files. There may still be times when you need to add registry entries during setup, however. For example, you might need to configure an aspect of the operating system or another application.

To configure a Web Setup Project to add a registry entry during setup, follow these steps:

1. In Solution Explorer, select your setup project.
2. Select the View menu, choose Editor, and then choose Registry.
3. The Registry Settings Editor appears. You cannot browse the computer's full registry structure. Therefore, to add a registry setting in a nested key, you need to add each nested key. For example, to add a setting to HKEY_LOCAL _MACHINE\SOFTWARE\Microsoft\ASP.NET\, you need to add the SOFT-WARE, Microsoft, and ASP.NET keys to the HKEY_LOCAL_MACHINE hive in the Registry Settings Editor.
4. Right-click the key you want to add a setting to, select Add, and then select String Value, Environment String Value, Binary Value, or DWORD Value. Type the name of the value, and then press Enter.
5. To define the value, select the registry value, view the Properties window, and set the *Value* property. To make the installation of the value conditional, define the *Condition* property.

By default, registry keys are not removed when an application is uninstalled. To automatically remove a registry key, select the key and view the Properties window. Then set the *DeleteAtUninstall* property to *True*.

Configuring Deployment Conditions

You can configure deployment conditions to require specific operating system versions, specific service pack levels, and other criteria. Table 13-3 lists commonly used conditions.

Table 13-3   Windows Installer Conditions

Condition	Description
VersionNT	Version number for Microsoft Windows NT-based operating systems, including Microsoft Windows 2000, Windows XP, and Microsoft Windows Server 2003.
Version9X	Version number for early Windows consumer operating systems, including Microsoft Windows 95, Microsoft Windows 98, and Microsoft Windows Me.
ServicePackLevel	Version number of the operating system service pack.
WindowsBuild	Build number of the operating system.
SystemLanguageID	Default language identifier for the system.
AdminUser	Tool that determines whether the user has administrative privileges.
PhysicalMemory	Size of the installed RAM in megabytes.
IISVERSION	Version of IIS, if installed.

MORE INFO   Windows Installer properties

For a detailed list of properties, see the Property Reference in the MSDN Library at *http://msdn.microsoft.com/library/en-us/msi/setup/property_reference.asp*.

To evaluate environment variables, preface the variable name with a "%" symbol, as this example illustrates:

```
%HOMEDRIVE = "C:" (verify that the home drive is C:\)
```

To simply check a property for a specific value, you can use the "=" operator, as the following example shows:

```
IISVERSION = "#6" (check for IIS 6.0)
VersionNT = 500 (check for Windows 2000)
```

You can also check for ranges:

```
IISVERSION >= "#4" (check for IIS 4.0 or later)
Version9X <= 490 (check for Windows Me or earlier)
```

You can also check for multiple conditions using Boolean operators: Not, And (True if both values are True), Or (True if either value is True), Xor (True if exactly one value is True), Eqv (True if both values are the same), and Imp (True if the left term is False or the right term is True). The following example demonstrates these Boolean operators:

```
WindowsBuild=2600 AND ServicePackLevel=1 (check for Windows XP with Service Pack 1)
```

Deploying Web Applications Using a Web Setup Project

When you build a Web Setup Project, two files are generated:

- **Setup.exe** An executable file that installs the files and settings you added to your Web Setup Project. When it is being run, the setup wizard guides the user through the installation process and prompts him or her for any required configuration settings, such as the Web site and folder, as shown in Figure 13-4. Users can add command-line parameters to automate the installation.

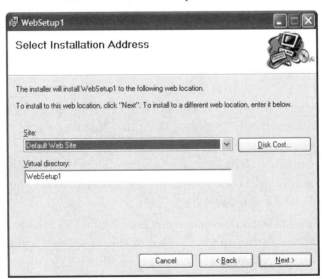

Figure 13-4 Web Setup Projects enable a Web application to be installed using a setup wizard.

- **WebSetupProjectName.msi** The Windows Installer file containing any files you added to your Web Setup Project. A user can install this file by double-clicking it and launching the setup wizard, exactly as if he or she were running the

Setup.exe file. Alternatively, network administrators can distribute it using Active Directory software distribution or Microsoft Systems Management Server.

Though users are more familiar with using Setup.exe to install an application, the Windows Installer file is smaller, far more versatile, and is familiar to most systems administrators. The only disadvantage to deploying the application with the .msi file is that the target Web server must have Windows Installer. Most Web servers already have this component, however.

What Is Windows Installer?

Windows Installer, also known as *Microsoft Installer* or *MSI*, is a technology and file format for installing applications on Windows computers. Most new applications, including almost all new Microsoft applications, include Windows Installer files. The inclusion of a Windows Installer package (.msi) file with an application greatly simplifies deployment in enterprise environments by enabling administrators to automatically install the application in a variety of ways.

NOTE   **Windows Installer behavior**

Windows Installer packages (.msi) are not executable files, even though they behave exactly like Setup.exe files. When you launch an .msi file, the operating system opens the file with Windows Installer (Msiexec.exe).

Windows Installer packages provide the following to enable flexible application deployment:

- **Transforms**   A transform is a collection of changes that administrators deploying your application can apply to a base Windows Installer package. They can do this without your assistance and without accessing your Web Setup Project files directly. Transforms for Windows Installer package files are similar to answer files that you might have used to automate the installation of an operating system such as Microsoft Windows XP.

- **Properties can be defined on the command line**   Properties are variables that Windows Installer uses during an installation. A subset of these, called public properties, can be set on the command line. This enables you to allow administrators to pass nonstandard parameters to your setup procedure, and enables automated installations even when you have custom requirements.

- **Standardized command-line options**   Command-line options are used to specify variables, switches, and file and path names and control the actions of the installation at run time.

Table 13-4 displays the most important Windows Installer command-line options and details Windows Installer capabilities such as reinstalling, repairing, and removing applications. For example, for every application installed by Windows Installer, the command-line option to perform an installation without displaying a user interface (UI) is /qn. The command-line option to create verbose log files is /lv*.

Table 13-4   Windows Installer Command-Line Options

Option	Parameters	Definition
/i	{package| ProductCode}	Installs or configures a product. For example, to install a product from A:\Example.msi, use the following command: `msiexec /i A:\Example.msi`
/a	package	Performs an administrative installation.
/f	[p][o][e][d][c] [a][u][m][s][v] {package| ProductCode}	Repairs a product. This option ignores any property values entered on the command line. p: Reinstall only if file is missing. o: Reinstall if file is missing or if an older version is installed. e: Reinstall if file is missing or an equal or older version is installed. d: Reinstall if file is missing or a different version is installed. c: Reinstall if file is missing or the stored checksum does not match the calculated value. a: Force all files to be reinstalled. u: Rewrite all required user-specific registry entries. m: Rewrite all required computer-specific registry entries. s: Overwrite all existing shortcuts. v: Run from source and recache the local package. For example, you can repair the installation package using the following command: `msiexec /fpecms Example.msi`

Table 13-4 Windows Installer Command-Line Options

Option	Parameters	Definition
/x	{package| ProductCode}	Uninstalls a product. For example, you can remove or uninstall a package using the following command: `msiexec /x Example.msi`
/L	`[i][w][e][a][r] [u][c][m][p][v] [+][!]logfile`	Specifies the path to the log file. The following flags indicate which information to log: i: Status messages w: Nonfatal warnings e: All error messages a: Startup of actions r: Action-specific records u: User requests c: Initial user interface parameters m: Out-of-memory p: Terminal properties v: Verbose output +: Append to existing file !: Flush each line to the log *: Wildcard; log all information except for the v option. To include the v option, specify `/L*v`. For example, to install a package and create a log file that contains the information related to the status, out-of-memory, and error messages, use the following command: `msiexec /i Example.msi /Lime logfile.txt`

Table 13-4 Windows Installer Command-Line Options

Option	Parameters	Definition
/p	PatchPackage	Applies a patch. To apply a patch to an installed administrative image, you must combine options as follows: /p: PatchPackage /a: package For example, to apply a patch to an administrative installation package, use the following syntax: `msiexec /p <PatchPackage> /a Example.msi`
/q	{n|b|r|f}	Sets user interface level. qn: No user interface. qb: Basic user interface. qr: Reduced user interface with a modal dialog box displayed at the end of the installation. qf: Full user interface with a modal dialog box displayed at the end. qn+: No user interface except for a modal dialog box displayed at the end. qb+: Basic user interface with a modal dialog box displayed at the end. qb-: Basic user interface with no modal dialog boxes. For example, to display the basic user interface options during the package installation, use the following command: `msiexec /qb Example.msi`
/? or /h	none	Displays the Windows Installer version and copyright information. For example, to display the version and copyright information, use the following command: `msiexec /?`

Quick Check

1. What launch conditions do Web Setup Projects include by default?
2. What are the four phases of a Web Setup Project deployment?

Quick Check Answers

1. By default, Web Setup Projects check for IIS and the .NET Framework.
2. Install, Commit, Rollback, and Uninstall.

Deploying Web Applications Using the Copy Web Tool

Web Setup Projects are useful if you are providing a Web application to many users (for example, allowing people to download the application from the Web and install it). If you are responsible for updating a specific Web site for your organization, it's impractical to log on to the Web server and install a Windows Installer package each time you make an update.

For internal applications, you can edit the Web application directly on the Web server. However, changes you make are immediately implemented in your production Web application, and this includes any bugs that might be there. To enable yourself to test a Web application, you can edit a local copy of the Web application on your computer and publish changes to the production Web server using the Copy Web tool. You can also use the Copy Web tool to publish changes from a staging server to a production Web server, or between any two Web servers.

The Copy Web tool can copy individual files or an entire Web site to or from a source Web site and a remote Web site. You can also choose to synchronize files, which involves copying only changed files and detecting possible versioning conflicts in which the same file on both the source and remote site have been separately edited. The Copy Web tool cannot merge changes within a single file; only complete files can be copied.

To set up the Copy Web tool by configuring a remote Web site, follow these steps:

1. In Visual Studio 2005, open a Web application. The Web application can be on your local computer or a remote Web site.

2. In Solution Explorer, right-click your Web application, and then select Copy Web Site. Alternatively, you can select the Website menu, and then choose Copy Web Site.

3. The Copy Web page appears and displays two panes: Source Web Site and Remote Web Site. First, you must configure a remote Web site. At the top of the window, click Connect.

4. The Open Web Site dialog appears. Select one of the following four options, and then click Open.

   ❑ **File System** A destination Web site on a local hard drive or a shared folder. A network drive connected to a shared folder on the remote Web server is the fastest way to transfer a Web site to a server on your intranet. You must have previously configured the Web application on the server and shared the Web application folder. This technique transfers your source code across the network in clear text.

   ❑ **Local IIS** A destination Web application running within IIS on your local computer. You can use this interface to create a new Web application on your local server.

   ❑ **FTP Site** A destination remote Web site where the server is configured to run a File Transfer Protocol (FTP) server and allow uploads and downloads to the Web application folder. You must have previously configured the Web application on the server and shared the Web application folder. This technique transfers your user credentials and your source code across the network in clear text, and, therefore, is not recommended.

   ❑ **Remote Site** An interface where you can transfer files to and from a remote Web application using FrontPage extensions, provided you have configured the Web server to allow this type of update. You can use this interface to create a new Web application on your server. To prevent your source code from being sent across the network in clear text, configure the Web site with a Secure Sockets Layer (SSL) certificate and select the Connect Using Secure Sockets Layer check box in the Open Web Site dialog box.

Once you have configured a connection, Visual Studio remembers it in the future. Figure 13-5 shows the Copy Web tool.

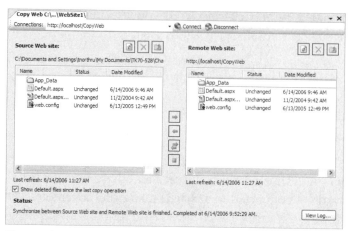

Figure 13-5   Use the Copy Web tool to synchronize two Web sites.

Once you are connected, you can copy or synchronize files between the source and the remote Web site in several different ways:

- **Copy individual files**   Select files in either the source or the remote Web site, and then click the directional Copy Selected Files buttons.

- **Copy the entire site**   Right-click the Source Web Site pane, and then click Copy Site To Remote. To copy the Remote Web Site to the source Web site, right-click the Remote Web Site pane, and then click Copy Site To Source.

- **Synchronize individual files**   Select files in either the source or remote Web site, and then click Synchronize Selected Files.

- **Synchronize the entire site**   Right-click the Source Web Site pane, and then click Synchronize Site.

When copying or synchronizing files, it's possible for there to be versioning conflicts if another developer modifies the remote copy of a file that you edited. Visual Studio doesn't have the capability to merge or analyze these changes. Therefore, the Copy Web tool simply notifies you of the conflict and lets you choose whether to overwrite the remote file with your local file, overwrite your local file, or not overwrite either file. Unless you know exactly what changed on a file, you should never overwrite it. Instead, you should analyze the file, determine what changed, and attempt to manually merge the changes. Otherwise, you might overwrite a coworker's development effort.

Precompiling Web Applications

The first time a page is requested from a new or updated Web application, ASP.NET compiles the application. Compiling doesn't typically take long (often less than a second or two), but the first few Web page requests are delayed while the application is compiled. To avoid this delay, you can precompile your Web application when you publish it to a server.

To precompile and publish a Web application, follow these steps:

1. In Visual Studio 2005, open a Web application. The Web application can be on your local computer or a remote Web site.

2. In Solution Explorer, right-click your Web application, and then select Publish Web Site. Alternatively, you can select the Build menu, and then choose Publish Web Site.

3. On the Publish Web Site dialog box, specify a location to publish to. If you click the ellipsis button ("..."), you can browse the File System, Local IIS, an FTP Site, or a Remote Site, exactly as you would using the Copy Web tool.

4. In the Publish Web Site dialog box, select your options:

   ❑ **Allow This Precompiled Site To Be Updatable**   Specifies that the content of .aspx pages are not compiled into an assembly; instead, the markup is left as is, allowing you to change HTML and client-side functionality after precompiling the Web site. Selecting this check box is equivalent to adding the -u option to the aspnet_compiler.exe command.

   ❑ **Use Fixed Naming And Single Page Assemblies**   Specifies that batch builds are turned off during precompilation in order to generate assemblies with fixed names. Themes and skin files continue to be compiled to a single assembly. This option is not available for in-place compilation.

   ❑ **Enable Strong Naming On Precompiled Assemblies**   Specifies that the generated assemblies are strongly named by using a key file or key container to encode the assemblies and to ensure that they have not been tampered with. After you select this check box, you can do the following:

   Specify the location of a key file to use to sign the assemblies. If you use a key file, you can select Delay signing, which signs the assembly in two stages: first with the public key file, and then with a private key file that is specified later during a call to the aspnet_compiler.exe command.

Specify the location of a key container from the system's cryptographic service provider (CSP) to use to name the assemblies.

Specify whether to mark the assembly with the *AllowPartiallyTrustedCallers* property, which allows strongly named assemblies to be called by partially trusted code. Without this declaration, only fully trusted code can use such assemblies.

5. Finally, click OK to compile and publish the Web site.

Publishing a Web site is an easy way to move a Web site from a development server to a staging or production server.

Lab: Deploying Web Applications

In these exercises, you deploy applications using two techniques: a Web Setup Project and the Copy Web tool.

▶ **Exercise 1: Create a Web Setup Project**

In this exercise, you create a new ASP.NET Web site and a Web Setup Project.

1. In Visual Studio 2005, create a new Web site.

2. In Visual Studio, select the File menu, select Add, and then select New Project.

3. Under Project Types, expand Other Project Types, and then select Setup And Deployment. Under Templates, click Web Setup Project. In the Name field, type **MyWebSetup**. Then click OK.

4. Visual Studio adds the project to your Web site and displays the File System editor. Right-click Web Application Folder, select Add, and then select Project Output.

5. In the Add Project Output Group dialog box, with Content Files selected, click OK.

   If you were to build and install your project at this point, it would copy the Default.aspx page and code-behind file to the location specified by the user during setup.

6. In the File System Editor, expand the Web Application Folder. Right-click Bin, select Add, and then select File. Navigate to your Windows folder and select the System.ini file. Click Open.

7. In the File System Editor, right-click the Web Application Folder, select Add, and then select Web Folder. Name the folder **Images**.

8. Right-click the Images folder, select Add, and then select File. In your Windows folder, select Gone Fishing.bmp. Then click Open.

9. Now add a launch condition. Select the View menu, choose Editor, and then choose Launch Conditions.

10. Select the View menu, choose Editor, and then choose Launch Conditions.

11. In the Launch Conditions Editor, right-click Requirements On Target Machine, and then select Add File Launch Condition.

12. Rename the new search condition **Search for Browscap**.

13. Select the new search condition and view the Properties window. Set the *File-Name* property to **Nothing.ini** (this file doesn't exist, but you'll fix the error later). Set the *Folder* property to [**SystemFolder**], and set the *Depth* property to **4**. This searches the system folder and all subfolders four levels deep for a file named Browscap.ini, which should be present on any Web server. Note that the Property value is set to FILEEXISTS1.

14. Rename the new launch condition **Browscap Condition**.

15. Select the new launch condition and view the Properties window. Set the *Install-Url* property to **http://support.microsoft.com/kb/826905**, which contains information about the Browscap.ini file. In the real world, you would provide a link with instructions on how to fulfill the requirement. Set the *Message* property to **You must have a Browscap.ini file**. Notice that the *Condition* property is set to FILEEXISTS1, which corresponds to the search condition *Property* value.

16. In Solution Explorer, right-click your setup project and then select Build. In the Output window, make note of the folder containing the output files.

17. Open the output folder and examine the files that are present.

In the next exercise, you install the Web application.

▶ **Exercise 2: Deploy a Web Setup Project**

In this exercise, you install a Web application using a Windows Installer file. To complete this exercise, you must have completed Exercise 1.

1. Open the folder that contains the .msi file you created in Exercise 1 and double-click it.

2. Setup launches and detects the missing file dependency. Click OK. Then click Close.

3. Return to Visual Studio and change the *FileName* property for your search condition to **Browscap.ini**. Then rebuild your Web project.

4. Rerun the .msi file. This time, the computer should meet the setup requirements because the Browscap.ini file exists in a subfolder of the system folder. Click Next.

5. On the Select Installation Address page, notice that you have the opportunity to select the Web site and virtual directory. Choose a unique virtual directory and make note of it. Click Next.

6. On the Confirm Installation page, click Next.

7. On the Installation Complete page, click Close.

8. Open the Internet Information Services console. Find the virtual directory you installed the Web application to. Verify that Default.aspx and the code-behind file are present in the root directory. Then verify that the /bin/ folder exists and contains the System.ini file. Also, verify that the /Images/ folder exists and contains the Gone Fishing.bmp file.

As you can see, deploying a Web application can be as easy as installing a Windows Forms application. While this process takes you through a manual installation of a Windows Installer package, you and other administrators can also deploy the .msi file in a totally automated manner.

▶ **Exercise 3: Deploy a Web Application Using Copy Web**

In this exercise, you deploy a Web application to a Web server by using the Copy Web tool.

1. In Visual Studio 2005, create a new Web site or continue working with the Web site you created in the previous exercises.

2. In Solution Explorer, right-click your Web application, and then select Copy Web Site.

3. The Copy Web page appears and displays two panes: Source Web Site and Remote Web Site. First, you must configure a remote Web site. At the top of the window, click Connect.

4. The Open Web Site dialog appears. Click Local IIS.

5. In the upper-right corner, click Create New Web Application. Name the application **CopyWeb**. You only need to do this the first time you copy a Web site.

6. With the CopyWeb virtual directory selected, click Open.

7. Now the http://localhost/CopyWeb virtual directory is selected as the remote Web site. To copy files to the remote location, right-click the Source Web Site pane, and then select Synchronize Site. Copy Web transfers all files to the local Web server. Make note of the Date Modified value for the Default.aspx page.

8. Open Windows Explorer and navigate to the folder containing your CopyWeb application (C:\Inetpub\wwwroot\CopyWeb\ by default). Open the Default.aspx page in Notepad. Between the <div> and </div> markups, add "Hello, world!" to simulate changes being made on the Web server. Then close Notepad and save your changes.

9. In Visual studio, double-click Default.aspx in the Solution Explorer. In the Designer, type **This change was made to the local copy**. Then save the page.

10. In Solution Explorer, right-click your Web application, and then select Copy Web Site. Note that both the source and remote Web sites have updated Date Modified values for the Default.aspx pages, the Status for each page is set to Changed, and a question mark appears beside the files. In the real world, these signs enable you to discover a potential versioning conflict before synchronizing the Web site.

11. Right-click the Source Web Site pane, and then select Synchronize Site.

12. The Resolve Synchronization Conflicts dialog box appears. Notice that it detects the versioning conflict and prompts you to choose which file to keep. However, it does not give you the opportunity to examine the two files to identify which version to keep. Additionally, it does not attempt to merge any changes. Because of this, it is important to communicate with other developers to ensure two people do not work on the same files at the same time. Click Use Source.

13. Open a Web browser and visit *http://127.0.0.1/CopyWeb/Default.aspx*. Notice that the Web page displays the changes you made to the source Web site when you chose to overwrite the remote Web site's content.

Lesson Summary

- Web Setup Projects allow you to create executable Setup.exe files and Windows Installer packages that administrators can use to easily deploy your applications to a Web server.

- The Copy Web tool can synchronize a Web site between a remote server and your local computer. This is perfect if you want to do deployment and testing on your local computer, and then upload the Web site to a remote Web server. Copy

Web tool is useful in environments with multiple developers because it detects versioning conflicts.

■ Precompiling a Web application removes the delay that occurs when ASP.NET compiles an application after the first user request. To precompile a Web application, use the Publish Web Site tool.

Lesson Review

You can use the following questions to test your knowledge of the information in Lesson 1, "Deploying Web Applications." The questions are also available on the companion CD if you prefer to review them in electronic form.

NOTE   Answers

Answers to these questions and explanations of why each answer choice is right or wrong are located in the "Answers" section at the end of the book.

---

1. You need to add a registry entry to make your application function. In which phase of the Web Setup Project should you add the registry entry?

    A. Install

    B. Commit

    C. Rollback

    D. Uninstall

2. You need to make a change to an operating system-related registry entry to make your application function. You want to ensure you remove this change if setup is cancelled or the application is removed from the computer. In which phases should you undo your registry modification? (Choose all that apply.)

    A. Install

    B. Commit

    C. Rollback

    D. Uninstall

3. Which of the following deployment tools enable multiple developers to work on a site simultaneously while detecting potential versioning conflicts?

    A. Setup Project

    B. Web Setup Project

    C. Copy Web tool

    D. Publish Web Site tool

4. Which of the following deployment tools has the potential to improve responsiveness of the Web site to end users?

    A. Setup Project

    B. Web Setup Project

    C. Copy Web tool

    D. Publish Web Site tool

Lesson 2: Building Web Applications for Monitoring

After you deploy your application, you (or a systems administrator) needs to monitor, maintain, and, likely, troubleshoot it. You can make the operations phase of an application's life cycle much easier by building monitoring capabilities into your application. Using health-monitoring and performance counters, you can give those responsible for supporting your application insight into its inner workings.

After this lesson, you will be able to:

■ Customize how ASP.NET notifies you about important events and which events are considered important.

■ Create custom performance counters and monitor those performance counters.

Estimated lesson time: 30 minutes

Customizing Event Analysis

As a developer, it's easy to be focused on creating and deploying applications. After you deploy an application, however, systems administrators are typically responsible for managing the application. To make their lives easier, and to help them diagnose and fix problems without your assistance, you can add ASP.NET health-monitoring capabilities to your application. With ASP.NET health monitoring, developers and systems administrators can:

■ Monitor live ASP.NET applications, individually or across a Web farm, to ensure that they are working properly.

■ Diagnose ASP.NET applications that appear to be failing.

■ Log events that do not necessarily relate to errors in an ASP.NET application but can be useful to examine.

There are several different ways administrators might want to be notified about events, including:

■ An event added to an event log

■ An e-mail notification

■ An event stored in a database

Additionally, there are dozens of different events that might be noteworthy, such as:

- Starting or ending a Web application
- Successful and unsuccessful authentication attempts
- ASP.NET errors
- Custom application events

By default, ASP.NET only has two types of events enabled: *All Errors* (any ASP.NET error) and *Failure Audits* (unsuccessful authentication attempts). However, you can enable other types of events and control the event providers that each event uses.

The sections that follow describe ASP.NET event providers, Web events, and how to configure them.

ASP.NET Event Providers

Rather than requiring you to write code to perform any number of different event notification mechanisms, the .NET Framework includes several event providers, as described in Table 13-5. Both the events that are built into ASP.NET and custom events that your application generates can be sent through any of these providers.

Table 13-5   ASP.NET Event Providers

Event Provider	Description
EventLogWebEventProvider	Writes Web event data to the Windows event log. By default, this provider is configured to write all errors to the Windows event log. Security operation errors are logged under the event name *Failure Audits* and all other errors are logged under the event name *All Errors*.
	To read event log data, you can view data using the Windows Event Viewer or read event log data programmatically.
SqlWebEventProvider	Logs Web event data to a Microsoft SQL Server database. By default, this provider logs data to the SQL Server Express database in the Web application's App_Data folder. It does not subscribe to any events by default.

Table 13-5 ASP.NET Event Providers

Event Provider	Description
WmiWebEventProvider	Passes Web events to Windows Management Instrumentation (WMI), converting them to WMI events. By default, this provider does not subscribe to any events.
SimpleMailWebEvent-Provider and *TemplatedMail-WebEventProvider*	Sends an e-mail message when Web events are raised. By default, these providers are not configured and do not subscribe to any events.
TraceWebEventProvider	Passes event data to the ASP.NET page tracing system. By default, this provider is not configured and does not subscribe to any events. Tracing provides you with the ability to start and stop event tracing sessions, to instrument applications to provide trace events, and to consume trace events. You can use the events to debug an application and perform capacity and performance analysis.

Additionally, you can create your own custom event providers by inheriting from the *WebEventProvider* or *BufferedWebEventProvider* classes. Custom event providers can log events to a custom log file, send event data to third-party monitoring systems, and meet other specific requirements that might be provided by your IT department.

MORE INFO How to create custom event providers

For more information about creating custom event providers, read Extending ASP.NET Health Monitoring at *http://msdn2.microsoft.com/en-us/ms228095.aspx*.

ASP.NET Web Events

ASP.NET includes many different types of events that can be sent through any of the event providers. These events are listed in Table 13-6.

Table 13-6   ASP.NET Web Events

Event Class	Description
WebApplicationLifetimeEvent	Represents a significant event in the lifetime of an ASP.NET application. Application lifetime events include events such as application startup and shutdown events. If an application is terminated, you can determine why by viewing the related event-message field.
WebAuditEvent	Serves as the base class for all ASP.NET health-monitoring audit events.
WebAuthenticationFailure-AuditEvent	Provides information about ASP.NET authentication failures.
WebAuthenticationSuccess-AuditEvent	Provides information about successful authentication events.
WebBaseErrorEvent	Serves as the base class for all the health-monitoring error events.
WebBaseEvent	Serves as the base class for the ASP.NET health-monitoring events.
WebErrorEvent	Provides information about errors caused by problems with configuration or application code. An example is the error issued by ASP.NET when an error is found in a page.
WebFailureAuditEvent	Provides information about security failures.
WebHeartbeatEvent	Serves as a timer for the ASP.NET health-monitoring system. These events are raised at an interval defined by the *heartbeatInterval* attribute of the <healthMonitoring> configuration section.
WebManagementEvent	Serves as the base class for events that carry application and process information.
WebRequestErrorEvent	Defines the event that carries information about Web-request errors.

Table 13-6   ASP.NET Web Events

Event Class	Description
WebRequestEvent	Serves as the base class for events providing Web-request information.
WebSuccessAuditEvent	Provides information about successful security events. An example of this is a successful URL authorization for a Web request.
WebViewStateFailure-AuditEvent	Provides Web application view state failure information.

Additionally, you can create your own custom Web events by deriving a class from one of the base event classes shown in Table 13-6, such as *WebManagementEvent* or *WebAuditEvent*.

Configuring Health-Monitoring Events

Health-monitoring events are configured in the <healthMonitoring> section of a Web.config file. The <healthMonitoring> section can have several sections:

- **<bufferModes>**   Sometimes events can occur rapidly and repeatedly. These events can slow down the server or your monitoring infrastructure, causing even more problems. By configuring the <bufferModes> section, you can configure how *SqlWebEventProvider* and *MailWebEventProvider* events are buffered so that they are stored up and transmitted in batches. You can add custom buffer modes and then associate them with a provider in the <providers> section.

- **<providers>**   This section configures event providers. By default, it contains the *EventLogProvider*, *LocalSqlServer*, and *WmiWebEventProvider* classes. You can add more standard event providers to this section (such as *SimpleMailWebEventProvider*) or add your custom event providers.

- **<profiles>**   Profiles define how many events can occur within a specific time limit. By default, this section contains the Default and Critical profiles. Use Default for most events; it prevents an event from occurring more than once every 10 minutes (as defined by the *minInterval* attribute). Use Critical when you need to see every single event that occurs. These profiles probably meet your requirements; however, you can add more profiles and specify them in custom rules if necessary.

- **<rules>** This section associates event types with event providers. By default, the *All Errors* and *Failure Audits* events are associated with the *EventLogProvider*, which causes the events to be added to the local Event Log. You can edit this section to configure custom health monitoring.

- **<eventMappings>** This section associates event names (such as *All Errors* and *Failure Audits*) with the classes that implement them (*System.Web.Management.WebBaseEvent* and *System.Web.Management.WebFailureAuditEvent*, respectively). You only need to edit this section if you create your own custom event.

By default, Visual Studio does not add this section to your Web.config file when you create a Web project. However, ASP.NET does have default settings. The following configuration sample shows only a portion of the default settings to demonstrate how to configure each of these sections:

```
<healthMonitoring heartbeatInterval="0" enabled="true">
  <bufferModes>
    <add name="Critical Notification"
      maxBufferSize="100"
      maxFlushSize="20"
      urgentFlushThreshold="1"
      regularFlushInterval="Infinite"
      urgentFlushInterval="00:01:00"
      maxBufferThreads="1" />
    <add name="Notification"
      maxBufferSize="300"
      maxFlushSize="20"
      urgentFlushThreshold="1"
      regularFlushInterval="Infinite"
      urgentFlushInterval="00:01:00"
      maxBufferThreads="1" />
  </bufferModes>

  <providers>
    <add
    name="EventLogProvider"
    type="System.Web.Management.EventLogWebEventProvider,
      System.Web,Version=2.0.0.0,Culture=neutral,
      PublicKeyToken=b03f5f7f11d50a3a" />
    <add
      ConnectionStringName="LocalSqlServer"
      maxEventDetailsLength="1073741823"
      buffer="false"
      bufferMode="Notification"
      name="SqlWebEventProvider"
      type="System.Web.Management.SqlWebEventProvider,
        System.Web,Version=2.0.0.0,Culture=neutral,
        PublicKeyToken=b03f5f7f11d50a3a" />
  </providers>
```

```xml
<profiles>
  <add
    name="Default"
    minInstances="1"
    maxLimit="Infinite"
    minInterval="00:01:00"
    custom="" />
  <add
    name="Critical"
    minInstances="1"
    maxLimit="Infinite"
    minInterval="00:00:00"
    custom="" />
</profiles>

<rules>
  <add
    name="All Errors Default"
    eventName="All Errors" provider="EventLogProvider"
    profile="Default"
    minInstances="1"
    maxLimit="Infinite"
    minInterval="00:01:00"
    custom="" />
  <add
    name="Failure Audits Default"
    eventName="Failure Audits"
    provider="EventLogProvider"
    profile="Default"
    minInstances="1"
    maxLimit="Infinite"
    minInterval="00:01:00"
    custom="" />
</rules>

<eventMappings>
  <add
    name="All Events"
    type="System.Web.Management.WebBaseEvent,
    System.Web,Version=2.0.0.0,Culture=neutral,
      PublicKeyToken=b03f5f7f11d50a3a"
    startEventCode="0"
    endEventCode="2147483647" />
  <add
    name="All Errors"
    type="System.Web.Management.WebBaseErrorEvent,
    System.Web,Version=2.0.0.0,Culture=neutral,
      PublicKeyToken=b03f5f7f11d50a3a"
    startEventCode="0"
    endEventCode="2147483647" />
  <add
    name="All Audits"
    type="System.Web.Management.WebAuditEvent,
```

```
      System.Web,Version=2.0.0.0,Culture=neutral,
      PublicKeyToken=b03f5f7f11d50a3a"
    startEventCode="0" endEventCode="2147483647" />
  <add
    name="Failure Audits"
    type="System.Web.Management.WebFailureAuditEvent, System.Web,Version=2.0.0.0,
      Culture=neutral, PublicKeyToken=b03f5f7f11d50a3a"
    startEventCode="0"
    endEventCode="2147483647" />
  </eventMappings>
</healthMonitoring>
```

Real World

Tony Northrup

I've been on both the development and management side of Web application. Your first instinct might be to monitor every possible event, but take it from me: You need to be careful about configuring too many monitoring alerts.

Sending alerts, and even adding events to the Event Log, takes processor time and can slow a server down. There's a certain sense of irony when you're awakened by a pager in the middle of the night to troubleshoot a failed server, only to discover that it is bogged down by a monitoring process that is constantly sending alerts about a noncritical problem.

Additionally, if you generate too many events, administrators have a hard time identifying the important ones. I've often seen systems administrators overlook a significant event because it was buried among thousands of events that could have been ignored.

Providing Custom Performance Counters

For years, administrators have used performance counters to monitor the performance of computers, networks, and applications, as shown in Figure 13-6. Developers also use performance counters to help identify bottlenecks in their applications' performances.

With the .NET Framework 2.0, it's easy to add custom performance counters and to update the performance data from within your code. Now you (or an administrator) can monitor any aspect of your application's performance. This can enable administrators to more easily identify bottlenecks and problems, which simplifies trouble-shooting, improves bug reports, and makes it easier to tune performance.

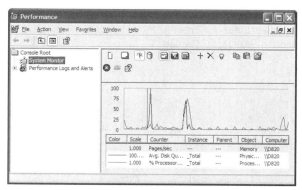

Figure 13-6   You can use the Performance console to monitor performance counters.

The sections that follow describe how to monitor standard and custom performance counters and how to add and update custom performance counters.

Monitoring Performance Counters

Once you create performance counter objects, you must provide data for these counters to be useful. First, you must add a *PerformanceCounter* object to your application. When developing a Windows Forms application, you can add a *Performance-Counter* object to a form using the Designer. However, when developing an ASP.NET Web form, you must add the *PerformanceCounter* object programmatically.

The following code sample reads the ASP.NET Requests Queued performance counter and displays the value in the *queuedLabel* control:

```vb
'VB
Dim pc As PerformanceCounter = New PerformanceCounter("ASP.NET", "Requests Queued")
queuedLabel.Text = pc.RawValue.ToString
```

```csharp
//C#
PerformanceCounter pc = new PerformanceCounter("ASP.NET", "Requests Queued");
queuedLabel.Text = pc.RawValue.ToString();
```

You can use Server Explorer in Visual Studio or the Performance console in the Administrative Tools start menu to browse the available performance counters on a computer.

Adding Performance Counters using the Designer

You can add performance counters and categories using Server Explorer. To add counters, follow these steps:

1. Open Server Explorer and expand the node for the server you want to view.

2. Right-click the Performance Counters node and select Create New Category. If you have already created a category, right-click it, and then select Edit Category.

3. The Performance Counter Builder dialog box appears. Enter a name and description for the category you want to create.

4. Click New. Type a name for the counter you want to create within the category. Then choose a type from the Type drop-down list and type a description for the counter.

5. Click OK.

This is convenient if you are configuring a single server; however, these changes are not automatically replicated on servers to which you might later deploy your application. If you need to create performance counters during the setup process or within your application, you should create them programmatically, as described in the next section.

Adding Custom Performance Counter Categories

You can't add performance counters to built-in categories. Instead, you should create a new category specifically for your application and place all your custom counters in that category.

To add a custom performance counter category and a single counter, call the static *PerformanceCounterCategory.Create* method. The *PeformanceCounterCategory* class is in the *System.Diagnostics* namespace. Provide the category name, a description of the category, a name for the counter, and a description of the counter. The following code sample demonstrates this:

```vb
'VB
PerformanceCounterCategory.Create("CategoryName", "CounterHelp", _
    PerformanceCounterCategoryType.MultiInstance, "CounterName", "CounterHelp")
```

```csharp
//C#
PerformanceCounterCategory.Create("CategoryName", "CounterHelp",
    PerformanceCounterCategoryType.MultiInstance, "CounterName", "CounterHelp");
```

If you want to add multiple counters to a single category, create an instance of *CounterCreationDataCollection* and add multiple *CounterCreationData* objects to the collection. The following code sample demonstrates this:

```vb
'VB
Dim counters As CounterCreationDataCollection = New CounterCreationDataCollection
counters.Add(New CounterCreationData("Sales", _
    "Number of total sales", PerformanceCounterType.NumberOfItems32))
counters.Add(New CounterCreationData("Active Users", _
    "Number of active users", PerformanceCounterType.NumberOfItems32))
counters.Add(New CounterCreationData("Sales value", _
    "Total value of all sales", PerformanceCounterType.NumberOfItems32))
PerformanceCounterCategory.Create("MyApp Counters", _
    "Counters describing the performance of MyApp", _
    PerformanceCounterCategoryType.SingleInstance, counters)
```

```csharp
//C#
CounterCreationDataCollection counters = new CounterCreationDataCollection();
counters.Add(new CounterCreationData("Sales",
    "Number of total sales", PerformanceCounterType.NumberOfItems32));
counters.Add(new CounterCreationData("Active Users",
    "Number of active users", PerformanceCounterType.NumberOfItems32));
counters.Add(new CounterCreationData ("Sales value",
    "Total value of all sales", PerformanceCounterType.NumberOfItems32));
PerformanceCounterCategory.Create("MyApp Counters",
    "Counters describing the performance of MyApp",
    PerformanceCounterCategoryType.SingleInstance, counters);
```

To check whether a category already exists, use the *PerformanceCounterCategory.Exists* method.

Quick Check

1. Which class would you use to create a custom performance counter?
2. Which class would you use to read performance counter data?

Quick Check Answers

1. *PerformanceCounterCategory*, specifically, the *PerformanceCounterCategory.Create* method, using the overload that accepts a *CoutnerCreationDataCollection* object.
2. The *PerformanceCounter* object.

Providing Performance Counter Data

After you create a custom performance counter, you can update the data as needed. You don't need to constantly update it—just do so when the value changes. Performance counter data is sampled only every 400 milliseconds, so if you update the value more frequently than that, it won't significantly improve the accuracy.

To update a performance counter, create a *PerformanceCounter* object just as you would for reading a performance counter value. However, you must set the *ReadOnly* property to *False*. You can do this using the overloaded *PerformanceCounter* constructor that takes a Boolean parameter, as shown below, or you can set the *ReadOnly* property after creating the object.

```vb
'VB
Private pc As PerformanceCounter = New PerformanceCounter("MyApp Counters", "Sales", False)
```

```csharp
//C#
PerformanceCounter pc = new PerformanceCounter("MyApp Counters", "Sales", false);
```

After creating the *PeformanceCounter* object, you can set the value directly by defining the *RawValue* property. Alternatively, you can call the *Decrement*, *Increment*, and *IncrementBy* methods to adjust the value relative to the current value. The following code sample demonstrates how to use each of these methods:

```vb
'VB
Dim pc As PerformanceCounter = New PerformanceCounter("MyApp Counters", "Sales", False)
pc.RawValue = 7
pc.Decrement
pc.Increment
pc.IncrementBy(3)
```

```csharp
//C#
PerformanceCounter pc = new PerformanceCounter("MyApp Counters", "Sales", false);
pc.RawValue = 7;
pc.Decrement();
pc.Increment();
pc.IncrementBy(3);
```

Lab: Monitoring Web Applications

In this lab, you create ASP.NET Web applications that modify the default health-monitoring notifications and update a custom performance counter.

▶ **Exercise 1: Send E-Mail for Health-Monitoring Notifications**

In this exercise, you create a new ASP.NET Web site and configure it to send e-mail messages for all health-monitoring events.

1. Create an ASP.NET Web application using Visual Studio.

2. On the Website menu, select ASP.NET Configuration.

3. Click the Application tab. Then click Configure SMTP E-mail Settings, Configure your Simple Mail Transfer Protocol (SMTP) server, type a From e-mail address, and then click Save. Click OK.

4. In Visual Studio, open your Web.config file. Add a <healthMonitoring> section to the Web.config file within the <system.web> section, as shown:

```
<configuration xmlns="http://schemas.microsoft.com/.NetConfiguration/v2.0">
    <system.web>
        <healthMonitoring enabled="true" heartbeatInterval="0">
        </healthMonitoring>
    </system.web>
</configuration>
```

5. Within the <healthMonitoring> section, add a <providers> section. This is necessary because there is no e-mail provider configured by default. Specify the *to* and *from* attributes with your own e-mail address. This demonstrates how to configure it:

```
<providers>
  <add
    name="My E-mail Provider"
    type="System.Web.Management.SimpleMailWebEventProvider"
    to="destination@contoso.com"
    from="source@contoso.com"
    buffer="false"
    subjectPrefix="WebEvent has fired"
  />
</providers>
```

6. Within the <healthMonitoring> section, add a <rules> section with a single rule that associates the *All Events* event type with your newly configured provider. Set the *eventName* attribute of the new rule to *All Events* (which matches an item in the default section of the <eventMappings> section of the root Web.config file). Set the *provider* attribute to match the *name* attribute of your provider. This demonstrates how to configure it:

```
<rules>
  <add
    name="Testing Mail Event Providers"
    eventName="All Events"
    provider="My E-mail Provider"
```

```
      profile="Default"
      minInstances="1"
      maxLimit="Infinite"
      minInterval="00:01:00"
      custom=""
   />
</rules>
```

7. In Visual Studio, open the Default.aspx page. Then press Ctrl+F5 to open the page in a Web browser. This generates an event that is sent through the mail event provider that you added.

8. Wait a few moments, and then check your e-mail. Depending on your e-mail server, this may take several minutes. You'll receive one or more e-mail notifications indicating that ASP.NET is compiling and starting your application.

▶ **Exercise 2: Create Custom Performance Counters**

In this exercise, you create a new ASP.NET Web site, create a new performance counter, update the new performance counter, and view the updated value.

1. Create an ASP.NET Web application using Visual Studio.

2. On the Default.aspx page, add a *Button* control named Button1. Then double-click *Button* to create a *Click* event handler.

3. Add the *System.Diagnostics* namespace to the page.

4. In the *Click* event handler, add code to check whether the performance counter category named MyApp Counters exists. Create one if it does not yet exist. Within that category, add three counters: Sales, Active Users, and Sales Value.

```VB
'VB
' Check whether the custom counter already exists
If Not PerformanceCounterCategory.Exists("MyApp Counters") Then
    ' Create the new counter category with three counters
    Dim counters As CounterCreationDataCollection = New CounterCreationDataCollection
    counters.Add(New CounterCreationData("Sales", "Number of total sales", _
        PerformanceCounterType.NumberOfItems32))
    counters.Add(New CounterCreationData("Active Users", "Number of active users", _
        PerformanceCounterType.NumberOfItems32))
    counters.Add(New CounterCreationData("Sales Value", "Total value of all sales", _
        PerformanceCounterType.NumberOfItems32))
    PerformanceCounterCategory.Create("MyApp Counters", _
    "Counters describing the performance of MyApp",
    PerformanceCounterCategoryType.SingleInstance, counters)
End If
```

```
//C#
if (!PerformanceCounterCategory.Exists("MyApp Counters"))
{
    // Create the new counter category with three counters
    CounterCreationDataCollection counters = new CounterCreationDataCollection();
    counters.Add(new CounterCreationData("Sales",
        "Number of total sales", PerformanceCounterType.NumberOfItems32));
    counters.Add(new CounterCreationData("Active Users",
        "Number of active users", PerformanceCounterType.NumberOfItems32));
    counters.Add(new CounterCreationData("Sales Value",
        "Total value of all sales", PerformanceCounterType.NumberOfItems32));
    PerformanceCounterCategory.Create("MyApp Counters",
        "Counters describing the performance of MyApp",
        PerformanceCounterCategoryType.SingleInstance, counters);
}
```

5. Also add code to increment the Sales counter in your new custom performance counter category within the *Click* event handler.

```
'VB
' Create a performance counter object to read and write performance data
Dim pc As PerformanceCounter = New PerformanceCounter("MyApp Counters", "Sales", False)

' Increase the value of the performance counter
pc.Increment()
```

```
//C#
// Create a performance counter object to read and write performance data
PerformanceCounter pc = new PerformanceCounter("MyApp Counters", "Sales", false);

// Increase the value of the performance counter
pc.Increment();
```

6. Finally, within the *Click* event handler, update the *Button1.Text* value to display the current value of the Sales counter.

```
'VB
' Display the current value in the Button control
Button1.Text = pc.RawValue.ToString
```

```
//C#
// Display the current value in the Button control
Button1.Text = pc.RawValue.ToString();
```

7. Press Ctrl+F5 to run your application. Click the button several times; notice that the value increments each time.

8. Open Server Explorer and expand the node for your computer. Expand the Performance Counters node. Right-click MyApp Counters, and then click Delete.

Lesson Summary

- ASP.NET applications raise a variety of different events and can alert administrators to these events using a variety of different notification mechanisms. You can customize the default configuration to cause different events to notify you, or change the way event notifications are created. For example, you can easily configure ASP.NET to send you an e-mail when an event occurs. You can also create custom event types and notification mechanisms.

- Administrators can monitor performance counters to view statistics about an application's health and performance. ASP.NET includes many standard performance counters, and you can add custom performance counters that contain data specific to your application.

Lesson Review

You can use the following questions to test your knowledge of the information in Lesson 2, "Building Web Applications for Monitoring." The questions are also available on the companion CD if you prefer to review them in electronic form.

NOTE Answers

Answers to these questions and explanations of why each answer choice is right or wrong are located in the "Answers" section at the end of the book.

---

1. Which of the following event providers is enabled by default?

    A. *EventLogWebEventProvider*

    B. *SqlWebEventProvider*

    C. *WmiWebEventProvider*

    D. *SimpleMailWebEventProvider*

2. You need to monitor unsuccessful attempts to gain access to a portion of your Web site that requires authentication. Which of the following Web event types should you monitor?

    A. *WebAuthenticationSuccessAuditEvent*

    B. *WebAuthenticationFailureAuditEvent*

    C. *WebHeartbeatEvent*

    D. *WebRequestEvent*

3. You want to programmatically add a performance counter category with multiple counters. Which class should you use to specify the counters?

    A. *PerformanceCounterCategory*

    B. *CounterSample*

    C. *CounterCreationDataCollection*

    D. *CounterCreationData*

4. Which tool can you use to create performance counters?

    A. The Performance console

    B. Server Explorer

    C. Solution Explorer

    D. File System Editor

Lesson 3: Using Caching to Improve Performance

Caching stores frequently accessed data in memory where it can be retrieved faster than it could be from a file or database. For example, if you frequently query the Inventory database table in an e-commerce application, you might be able to improve performance by caching the table in memory so that future queries can be done from the memory cache.

You can cache data manually by copying a database or a file into a variable and then accessing that variable from memory. However, as you begin to use the object, you discover that there's a lot of complexity in caching. For example, what happens if you need to perform an update? If you update a database and don't update the cache, then the cache is inaccurate (also known as *stale*).

Fortunately, the .NET Framework 2.0 provides the *Cache* object, which enables you to easily take advantage of the improved performance caching can offer without requiring you to write code to deal with the complexities of caching.

ASP.NET provides two different types of caching:

- **Application caching**   A collection that can store any object in memory and automatically remove the object based on memory limitations, time limits, or other dependencies.
- **Page output caching**   ASP.NET can store a copy of rendered pages to reduce the time required to render the page in future requests.

This lesson describes both application caching and page output caching.

After this lesson, you will be able to:

- Use application caching to improve the performance of database queries and other time-consuming data retrieval.
- Use page output caching to improve the performance of page rendering.

Estimated lesson time: 40 minutes

Application Caching

To use the application cache, add and retrieve objects from the *Cache* collection. A single *Cache* object exists for each application, so items in the *Cache* can be shared between user sessions and requests.

Before using a cached value stored in the *Cache* collection, you must verify that it is not null. If a value is null, that value either hasn't been cached or it has expired. Therefore, you must retrieve the object from the original source rather than from *Cache*.

The following code sample demonstrates how to cache and retrieve a string in the *Cache* collection:

```vb
'VB
Cache("Greeting") = "Hello, world!"
If Not (Cache("Greeting") Is Nothing) Then
    value = CType(Cache("Greeting"), String)
Else
    value = "Hello, world!"
End If
```

```csharp
//C#
Cache["Greeting"] = "Hello, world!";
if (Cache["Greeting"] != null)
    value = (string)Cache["Greeting"];
else
    value = "Hello, world!";
```

Of course, you wouldn't normally cache a static string; you'd normally cache a file or an object that's based on a relatively slow database or network query. You can cache any type object, but you must cast it to the correct type when accessing it.

The previous example demonstrates that you can use the *Cache* object just like a standard collection, as long as you verify that the object being accessed isn't null. You can access much more sophisticated functionality, however, by using the *Add* and *Insert* methods. Each of these methods enables you to automatically remove an item from the cache after a specific period of time, or when a file, database object, or another cache object expires.

To use the *Cache.Insert* method, provide the following parameters (parameters vary depending on the overload used):

- **A key**   The *String* that you'll use to access the cached object in the *Cache* collection.
- **An *Object* to be cached**   The *Object* that you want to retrieve later.

- **A dependency (optional)**   A *CacheDependency* object that identifies a file or cache key, and that, when the file or cache key is changed, triggers this object to be removed from the cache. If you cache a file, you should configure a dependency for the file so that it is removed from cache after being modified, ensuring that your cache never becomes stale. This can be null.

- **An absolute expiration date (optional)**   The time (in a *DateTime* object) at which the object should be removed from the cache, regardless of whether it has been recently accessed. Set this to *System.Web.Caching.Cache.NoAbsoluteExpiration* if you don't want to use it.

- **A time span (optional)**   The time span (in a *TimeSpan* object) after which the object should be removed from the cache if it has not been accessed. Set this to *System.Web.Caching.Cache.NoSlidingExpiration* if you don't want to use it.

- **A priority (optional)**   A *CacheItemPriority* enumeration value that you can use to determine which objects are removed first when memory starts to run low. Lower-priority objects are removed sooner. Set this to *System.Web.Caching.CacheItem-Priority.Default* if you don't want to use it.

- **A callback method (optional)**   An event handler that is called when the object is removed from the cache. This can be null if you don't want to specify a callback method.

For example, the following code sample demonstrates how to make a *cache dependency* based on a file. If the file changes, the object is removed from cache.

```vb
'VB
Cache.Insert("FileCache", "CacheContents", New System.Web.Caching.CacheDependency( _
    Server.MapPath("SourceFile.xml")))
```

```csharp
//C#
Cache.Insert("FileCache", "CacheContents", new System.Web.Caching.CacheDependency(
    Server.MapPath("SourceFile.xml")));
```

You can also create multiple dependencies for a single object. The following example demonstrates how to use an *AggregateCacheDependency* object to add an item to the cache that is dependent on both an item named *CacheItem1* and a file named Source-File.xml.

```vb
'VB
Dim dep1 As CacheDependency = New CacheDependency(Server.MapPath("SourceFile.xml"))
Dim keyDependencies2 As String() = {"CacheItem1"}
Dim dep2 As CacheDependency = New System.Web.Caching.CacheDependency(Nothing, _
    keyDependencies2)
Dim aggDep As AggregateCacheDependency = New System.Web.Caching.AggregateCacheDependency()
```

```
aggDep.Add(dep1)
aggDep.Add(dep2)
Cache.Insert("FileCache", "CacheContents", aggDep)
```

```
//C#
System.Web.Caching.CacheDependency dep1 =
    new System.Web.Caching.CacheDependency(Server.MapPath("SourceFile.xml"));
string[] keyDependencies2 = { "CacheItem1" };
System.Web.Caching.CacheDependency dep2 =
    new System.Web.Caching.CacheDependency(null, keyDependencies2);
System.Web.Caching.AggregateCacheDependency aggDep =
    new System.Web.Caching.AggregateCacheDependency();
aggDep.Add(dep1);
aggDep.Add(dep2);
Cache.Insert("FileCache", "CacheContents", aggDep);
```

If you want a cached object to be used for a specific amount of time because it will become outdated, pass the *Cache.Insert* method for a time in the future at which the object should expire. The *DateTime.Now* object has a variety of methods for adding a specific number of minutes to the current time, as the following example demonstrates:

```
'VB
Cache.Insert("FileCache", "CacheContents", Nothing, DateTime.Now.AddMinutes(10.0), _
    TimeSpan.Zero)
```

```
//C#
Cache.Insert("FileCache", "CacheContents", null, DateTime.Now.AddMinutes(10d),
    TimeSpan.Zero);
```

If you want your most frequently used cached objects to stay in your cache longer, specify a time span. The time span is the time after the last read request that the cached object will be retained. This example shows you how to keep an object in cache for five minutes after the last request:

```
'VB
Cache.Insert("CacheItem7", "Cached Item 7", _
    Nothing, System.Web.Caching.Cache.NoAbsoluteExpiration, New TimeSpan(0, 10, 0))
```

```
//C#
Cache.Insert("CacheItem7", "Cached Item 7",
    null, System.Web.Caching.Cache.NoAbsoluteExpiration, new TimeSpan(0, 10, 0));
```

The *Cache.Add* method works exactly the same as the *Cache.Insert* method, except that it returns the defined value. That makes the *Cache.Add* method easier to use when you want to add an item to a cache and also defines another variable with a single line of code.

Quick Check

1. How can you cause a cached object to be automatically invalidated after a specific amount of time?

2. Where is *Cache* data stored—in memory, on the hard disk, in a database, or on a state server?

3. What types of data can you store in the *Cache* collection?

4. What must you do before you retrieve an object from the *Cache* collection?

Quick Check Answers

1. Call the *Cache.Add* or *Cache.Insert* methods and provide a dependency.

2. The *Cache* object is stored in memory.

3. You can store any type of data in the *Cache* collection. However, when you retrieve it, you must cast it to the correct type.

4. You must verify that the object is not null. If it is null, you must retrieve it from the original source rather than from *Cache*.

Page Output Caching

After a Web browser retrieves a page, the browser often keeps a copy of the page on the local computer. The next time the user requests the page, the browser simply verifies that the cached version is still valid, and then displays the cached page to the user. This improves the responsiveness of the site by decreasing the time required to load the page. It also reduces the load on the server because the server is not required to render a page.

Client-side caching requires that each individual user retrieve a dynamically generated version of your page. If one user visits your Web site 100 times, your Web server only has to generate the page once. If 100 users visit your Web site once, your Web server needs to generate the page 100 times.

To improve performance and reduce rendering time, ASP.NET 2.0 now supports page output caching. With page output caching, ASP.NET can keep a copy of a rendered ASP.NET Web page in memory. The next time a user requests it—even if it's a different user—ASP.NET can return the page almost instantly. If a page takes a long time to render (for example, if you make multiple queries), this can significantly improve performance.

Caching pages on the server has drawbacks, however. If your page shows dynamic information or is customized for individual users, you don't want the same version of the page sent to every user. Fortunately, ASP.NET gives you flexible configuration options to meet almost any requirements. You can even implement user controls to cache parts of a page while generating other portions dynamically.

Real World

Tony Northrup

If you have a simple ASP.NET Web site, page output caching might not be worth the trouble. However, if your application does significant processing or sends requests to a database, page output caching could reduce the load on your server by 10 times or more.

I run a personal Web site with an ASP.NET photo album application. Each page has several different dynamic elements and must make multiple database queries. To keep the application responsive on my old server, I wrote a significant amount of ASP.NET 1.1 code to optimize performance whenever possible by minimizing database queries. With declarative page output caching (which is new in the .NET Framework 2.0), I could have avoided writing that code and simply relied on page output caching to cache each page until an update was required. That would have decreased rendering time by at least 80 percent while still enabling the dynamic features of the site.

Declaratively Configuring Caching for a Single Page

To configure ASP.NET to cache a single page, add the @ *OutputCache* directive to the top of the page and configure the attributes shown in Table 13-7.

Table 13-7 *OutputCache* Attributes

Attribute	Description
Duration	The number of seconds to cache the page. This is the only required parameter.
Location	One of the *OutputCacheLocation* enumeration values, such as *Any*, *Client*, *Downstream*, *Server*, *None*, or *ServerAndClient*. The default is *Any*.

Table 13-7 *OutputCache* **Attributes**

Attribute	Description
CacheProfile	The name of the cache settings to associate with the page. The default is an empty string ("").
NoStore	A Boolean value that determines whether to prevent secondary storage of sensitive information.
Shared	A Boolean value that determines whether user control output can be shared with multiple pages. The default is *False*.
VaryByParam	A semicolon-separated list of strings used to vary the output cache. By default, these strings correspond to a query string value sent with *Get* method attributes, or a parameter sent using the *Post* method. When this attribute is set to multiple parameters, the output cache contains a different version of the requested document for each combination of specified parameters. Possible values include none, an asterisk (*), and any valid query string or *Post* parameter name. Either this attribute or the *VaryByControl* attribute is required when you use the @ *Output-Cache* directive on ASP.NET pages and user controls. A parser error occurs if you fail to include it. If you do not want to specify a parameter to vary cached content, set the value to *none*. If you want to vary the output cache by all parameter values, set the attribute to an asterisk (*).
VaryByControl	A semicolon-separated list of strings used to vary a user control's output cache. These strings represent the ID property values of ASP.NET server controls declared in the user control.
SqlDependency	A string value that identifies a set of database and table name pairs that a page or control's output cache depends on. Note that the *SqlCacheDependency* class monitors the table in a database that the output cache depends on, so that when items in a table are updated, those items are removed from the cache when using table-based polling. When using notifications (in Microsoft SQL Server 2005) with the value *CommandNotification*, ultimately a *SqlDependency* class is used to register for query notifications with the SQL Server 2005 server.

Table 13-7 *OutputCache* Attributes

Attribute	Description
VaryByCustom	Any text that represents custom output caching requirements. If this attribute is given a value of browser, the cache is varied by browser name and major version information. If a custom string is entered, you must override the *GetVaryByCustomString* method in your application's Global.asax file.
VaryByHeader	A semicolon-separated list of Hypertext Transfer Protocol (HTTP) headers used to vary the output cache. When this attribute is set to multiple headers, the output cache contains a different version of the requested document for each combination of specified headers.

The *Location, CacheProfile,* and *NoStore* attributes cannot be used in user controls (.ascx files). The *Shared* attribute cannot be used in ASP.NET pages (.aspx files).

The following example demonstrates how to cache a page for 15 minutes, regardless of the parameters passed to the page:

```
<%@ OutputCache Duration="15" VaryByParam="none" %>
```

If the page might display differently based on parameters, provide the names of those query parameters in the *VaryByParam* attribute. The following example caches a different copy of the page for different values provided in the location or count query parameters:

```
<%@ OutputCache Duration="15" VaryByParam="locationTextBox;countTextBox" %>
```

The *VaryByParam* query parameters typically match the names of input controls, such as a *TextBox* control.

To cache a portion of an ASP.NET Web page, move the portion of the page that you want to cache into an .ascx user control. Then add the @ *OutputCache* directive to the user control. That user control will be cached separately from the parent page.

Programmatically Configuring Caching for a Single Page

If you need to make run-time decisions about output caching, you can do so using the *Response.Cache* object. The available programmatic methods do not correspond directly to the attributes provided by the @ *OutputCache* directive, but they provide basic functionality:

- **Response.Cache.SetExpires**   Use this method to specify the number of seconds that the page is to be cached.

- **Response.Cache.SetCacheability**   Use this method to specify an *HttpCacheability* enumeration value, such as *HttpCacheability.Public* (which enables caching at both the client and the server) or *HttpCacheability.Server* (which enables caching at the server but disables caching at the client).

- **Response.Cache.SetValidUntilExpires**   Pass this method a *True* value to configure the cache to ignore cache-invalidation headers.

Using Substitution to Update Caches

Some pages may not be eligible for caching because they have simple elements that must be dynamically generated. As an alternative to creating separate user controls for the dynamic element and configuring different caching policy for those user controls, you can use substitution. ASP.NET provides two cache substitution techniques:

- **The *Response.WriteSubstitution* method**   You add static placeholders to your page in places where dynamic content is required, and then use the *Response.Write-Substitution* method to specify a method that replaces portions of a cached page with dynamically generated content. To specify the substitution method, call *WriteSubstitution* and pass a callback method with an *HttpResponseSubstitution-Callback* signature.

NOTE Substitution with cached user controls

You can't use substitution to update cached user controls where output caching is applied at the user control level.

- **The *Substitution* control**   *Substitution* controls are similar to *Label* controls, but *Substitution* controls are exempt from output caching. The only useful property is *Substitution.MethodName*, which you use to specify the method that generates the content that is inserted at the location of the *Substitution* control. The method specified by *MethodName* must accept an *HttpContext* parameter and return a *String*. The *String* value is inserted into the response at the *Substitution* control location when the cached page is returned to the user. The following code demonstrates how to specify a substitution method that displays the current time in a *Substitution* control named *Substitution1*:

```vb
'VB
Sub Page_Load(ByVal sender As Object, ByVal e As System.EventArgs)
    ' Specify the callback method.
    Substitution1.MethodName = "GetCurrentDateTime"
End Sub


' The Substitution control calls this method to retrieve the current date and time.
' This section of the page is exempt from output caching.
Shared Function GetCurrentDateTime(ByVal context As HttpContext) As String
    Return DateTime.Now.ToString()
End Function
```

```csharp
//C#
void Page_Load(object sender, System.EventArgs e)
{
    // Specify the callback method.
    Substitution1.MethodName = "GetCurrentDateTime";
}


// The Substitution control calls this method to retrieve
// the current date and time.
// This section of the page is exempt from output caching.
public static string GetCurrentDateTime (HttpContext context)
{
    return DateTime.Now.ToString();
}
```

The *AdRotator* control also performs post-cache substitution, by default, in order to constantly display new ads.

Programmatically Invalidating Cached Pages

Often, you want to cache pages, but specific events might require you to stop using the cached page. For example, a page that displays results from a database query should only be cached until the results of the database query change. Similarly, a page that processes a file should be cached until the file is changed. Fortunately, ASP.NET gives you several ways to invalidate cached pages.

The sections that follow describe how to make caching choices before returning a page and how to create a cache page output file dependency.

Determining Whether to Return a Cached Page Prior to Rendering   To directly control whether a cached version of a page is used or whether the page is dynamically regenerated, respond to the *ValidateCacheOutput* event and set a valid for the *HttpValidationStatus* attribute. Then, from the *Page.Load* event handler, call the *AddValidationCallback* method and pass an *HttpCacheValidateHandler* object with your method.

The following example demonstrates how to create a method to handle the *Validate-Page* event:

```vb
'VB
Public Shared Sub ValidatePage(ByVal context As HttpContext, _
        ByVal data As [Object], ByRef status As HttpValidationStatus)
    If Not (context.Request.QueryString("Status") Is Nothing) Then
        Dim pageStatus As String = context.Request.QueryString("Status")

        If pageStatus = "invalid" Then
            status = HttpValidationStatus.Invalid
        ElseIf pageStatus = "ignore" Then
            status = HttpValidationStatus.IgnoreThisRequest
        Else
            status = HttpValidationStatus.Valid
        End If
    Else
        status = HttpValidationStatus.Valid
    End If
End Sub
```

```csharp
//C#
public static void ValidateCacheOutput(HttpContext context, Object data,
        ref HttpValidationStatus status)
{
    if (context.Request.QueryString["Status"] != null)
    {
        string pageStatus = context.Request.QueryString["Status"];

        if (pageStatus == "invalid")
            status = HttpValidationStatus.Invalid;
        else if (pageStatus == "ignore")
            status = HttpValidationStatus.IgnoreThisRequest;
        else
            status = HttpValidationStatus.Valid;
    }
    else
        status = HttpValidationStatus.Valid;
}
```

Notice that this code sample uses logic to specify one of the *HttpValidationStatus* values to control how the page is cached:

- **HttpValidationStatus.Invalid** Causes the cache to be invalidated so that the page is dynamically generated. The newly generated page is stored in the cache, replacing the earlier cached version.

- **HttpValidationStatus.IgnoreThisRequest** Causes the current page request to be dynamically generated without invalidating the previously cached version of the page. The dynamically generated page output is not cached, and future requests might receive the previously cached output.

- **HttpValidationStatus.Valid**   Causes ASP.NET to return the cached page.

The following sample demonstrates how to configure that event handler so that it is called when ASP.NET determines whether to use the cached version of the page:

```vb
'VB
Protected Sub Page_Load(ByVal sender As Object, _
    ByVal e As System.EventArgs) Handles Me.Load

    Response.Cache.AddValidationCallback( _
        New HttpCacheValidateHandler(AddressOf ValidatePage), Nothing)
End Sub
```

```csharp
//C#
protected void Page_Load(object sender, EventArgs e)
{
    Response.Cache.AddValidationCallback(
        new HttpCacheValidateHandler(ValidateCacheOutput),
        null);
}
```

ASP.NET calls the method you specified when it determines whether to use the cached version of the page or a new, dynamically generated version of the page.

Creating a Cache Page Output Dependency   To create a cache page output dependency, call one of the following *Response* methods:

- **Response.AddCacheDependency**   Makes the validity of a cached response dependent on a *CacheDependency* object.

- **Response.AddCacheItemDependency** and **Response.AddCacheItemDependencies**   Makes the validity of a cached response dependent on one or more other items in the cache.

- **Response.AddFileDependency** and **Response.AddFileDependencies**   Makes the validity of a cached response dependent on one or more files.

Configuring Caching for an Entire Application

You can also configure output caching profiles that you can easily reference from pages in your application. This provides centralized configuration of output caching. To create a cache profile, add the <caching><outputCacheSettings><outputCacheProfiles> section to your Web.config file's <system.web> element, as the following sample demonstrates:

```
<caching>
    <outputCacheSettings>
        <outputCacheProfiles>
            <add name="OneMinuteProfile" enabled="true" duration="60"/>
        </outputCacheProfiles>
    </outputCacheSettings>
</caching>
```

Caching profiles support most of the same attributes as the *@ OutputCache* directive, including *Duration, VaryByParameter, VaryByHeader, VaryByCustom, VaryByControl, SqlDependency, NoStore,* and *Location.* Additionally, you must provide a *Name* attribute to identify the profile, and you can use the *Enabled* attribute to disable a profile if necessary.

Once you create a cache profile, reference it from within a page using the *CacheProfile* attribute of the *@ OutputCache* directive, as the following example demonstrates. You can override specific attributes on a per-page basis.

```
<%@ OutputCache CacheProfile="OneMinuteProfile" VaryByParam="none" %>
```

Lab: Using Page Output Caching to Improve Performance

In this lab, you configure page output caching for a simple ASP.NET Web application.

▶ **Exercise: Enable Page Output Caching**

In this exercise, you enable page output caching for an ASP.NET Web page.

1. Copy the Lesson3-Exercise1 sample project from this book's CD to your computer's hard drive in either Visual Basic or C#, or if you're already installed this book's code files to your hard drive, choose a programming language.

2. Use Visual Studio 2005 to open the project. Press Ctrl+F5 to run the project. Note that each time you choose a different item from the list, the name of the chosen page and the current time are displayed at the top of the list.

3. Stop debugging and edit the Default.aspx page in Source view. Add a page output cache directive to the top of the page so that the page is automatically cached for 10 seconds. Do not specify any dependencies. The following code sample demonstrates how to do this:

```
<%@ OutputCache Duration=10 VaryByParam="none" %>
```

4. Press Ctrl+F5 to open the page in a Web browser. Choose Page Two from the list and notice that the page updates correctly. Immediately choose Page Three from the list and notice that the page name does not change and that it continues to display the previous time. Make note of the time and repeatedly choose different pages from the list until 10 seconds have passed. After 10 seconds, notice that the page updates correctly and again shows the current time. This demonstrates that page output caching is working correctly; however, the caching prevents the form from functioning.

5. Stop debugging and edit the Default.aspx page in Source view. Modify the page output cache to specify the name of the *DropDownList* control, *PageChoiceDrop-DownList*. The following code sample demonstrates how to do this:

```
<%@ OutputCache Duration=10 VaryByParam="PageChoiceDropDownList" %>
```

6. Press Ctrl+F5 to open the page in a Web browser. Choose Page Two from the list and notice the time displayed. Immediately choose Page Three from the list and notice that the page updates correctly. Quickly choose Page Two from the list again. If you chose Page Two within 10 seconds of the first time you chose it, you will see the previous time. Because of the change you made to the *OutputCache* declaration, ASP.NET caches a separate version of the page for each value of the *PageChoiceDropDownList* control that you choose, and each expires 10 seconds after it is generated. Click the Submit button repeatedly until 10 seconds pass and the page is regenerated.

Lesson Summary

■ You can use the *Cache* object to store any other object, and then access the cached object from other Web pages. The *Cache* object is an excellent way to reduce the number of database queries and file accesses. Use the *Cache.Add* and *Cache.Insert* methods to add an object to the cache with a dependency to ensure the cached object does not become stale.

■ Page output caching stores a copy of a rendered page or user control and serves it up without modification in future requests. Page output caching practically eliminates rendering time, even if the ASP.NET program logic is extremely time-consuming. Configure dependencies to ensure page output caching does not serve outdated results.

Lesson Review

You can use the following questions to test your knowledge of the information in Lesson 3, "Using Caching to Improve Performance." The questions are also available on the companion CD if you prefer to review them in electronic form.

1. You are creating an ASP.NET Web page that displays a list of customers generated by a database query. The user can filter the list so that only customers within a specific state are displayed. You want to maximize the performance of your Web application by using page output caching. You want to ensure users can filter by state, but you are not concerned about displaying updates to the list of customers because the customer list doesn't change very frequently. Which declarative @ *OutputCache* attribute should you configure?

    A. *VaryByParam*

    B. *VaryByHeader*

    C. *SqlDependency*

    D. *VaryByCustom*

2. You need to programmatically configure page output caching. Which object would you use?

    A. *Request*

    B. *Response*

    C. *Application*

    D. *Server*

3. You want to cache an object but have it automatically expire in 10 minutes. How can you do this? (Choose all that apply.)

    A. Directly define the *Cache* item.

    B. Call *Cache.Get*.

    C. Call *Cache.Insert*.

    D. Call *Cache.Add*.

4. Which tool can you use to create performance counters? (Choose all that apply.)

   A. An HTTP header

   B. A file

   C. A time span

   D. A registry key

   E. Another object in the *Cache*

Chapter Review

To further practice and reinforce the skills you learned in this chapter, you can perform the following tasks:

- Review the chapter summary.
- Review the list of key terms introduced in this chapter.
- Complete the case scenarios. These scenarios set up real-world situations involving the topics of this chapter and ask you to create a solution.
- Complete the suggested practices.
- Take a practice test.

Chapter Summary

- You can deploy Web applications in a variety of different ways. The simplest way to deploy a Web application is to simply copy the files. Alternatively, you can use the Copy Web tool to synchronize the files between two Web sites, enabling you to keep separate development and staging servers. The Copy Web tool also works well in environments with multiple developers, because it can detect versioning conflicts. The Publish Web tool is capable of precompiling a Web site, which reduces the delay that occurs when a user requests the first page from a Web site. If you have more complex setup requirements, you can create a Web Setup Project and deploy the Setup.exe file or the Windows Installer file to Web servers.

- There are several ways you can monitor applications after deployment. First, you can configure Web events and event providers to add events to the event log, send events to a database, or e-mail yourself notifications of events. With custom event providers, you can integrate ASP.NET application events into any monitoring infrastructure. You can also use performance counters in your application by either monitoring standard performance counters or adding your own performance data.

- Caching is one of the most effective ways to improve performance. ASP.NET provides two different types of caching: application caching (implemented using the *Cache* object) and page output caching. Application caching requires writing code, but it gives you detailed control over how objects are cached. Page output caching keeps a copy of rendered HTML from an ASP.NET page or user control. Both types of caching are extremely useful for reducing the time required to submit redundant database queries and access files.

Key Terms

Do you know what these key terms mean? You can check your answers by looking up the terms in the glossary at the end of the book.

- application caching
- cache dependency
- caching
- event provider
- page output caching
- precompiling
- stale

Case Scenarios

In the following case scenarios you will apply what you've learned about optimizing and deploying Web applications. You can find answers to these questions in the "Answers" section at the end of this book.

Case Scenario 1: Deploying a Web Application

You are a developer for Southridge Video. You are the sole developer of the company's external Web site, which allows customers to rent videos online. The reliability of the application is critical, so the quality assurance team must test any changes you make on a staging server before you make changes to the production Web server.

You frequently work from your home. Unfortunately, Southridge's virtual private network (VPN) is unreliable, so you must do your development on your laptop computer. You can only access the staging and production Web servers from the internal network or the VPN, but that's not a problem because you don't need to make updates to those servers very frequently. Additionally, you don't have a broadband connection, so you need to avoid sending large updates across the connection when it is working.

Questions

Answer the following questions.

1. Which tool would you use to update the staging server?

2. Which tool should the quality assurance people use to update the production server?

Case Scenario 2: Improving the Performance of a Public Web Site

You are a developer for Southridge Video. Fortunately, the site has been getting busier and busier. Currently, both the Web server and the back-end database are hosted on a single computer. Unfortunately, you've discovered that the server that runs it isn't powerful enough to meet peak demand. During the busiest hours, you discover that processor utilization is very high.

You discuss the problems with other people at your organization. Following is a list of company personnel interviewed and their statements:

- **Arif Rizaldy, Database Administrator** "I did some analysis on the SQL Server database performance like you asked. The biggest problem is that when a user clicks on a movie genre on the Web site, such as Comedy or Drama, your application performs a very processor-intensive query to find the appropriate movies. I've optimized the indexes already, so there's nothing we can do besides upgrading the server or querying the database less often."

- **Wendy Richardson, IT Manager** "The company is doing well, but we don't have any budget to upgrade the server. So, find a way to make the application more efficient."

Questions

Answer the following questions for your manager.

1. Is there a way you can use the application *Cache* object to improve performance?

2. How can you make sure stale cache information isn't sent to users after the company adds new movies?

3. Each page on the Web site is personalized with the current users' preferences. Is there a way you can use page output caching to improve performance?

Suggested Practices

To successfully master the Tracing, Configuring, and Deploying Applications exam domain, complete the following tasks.

Use a Web Setup Project to Deploy a Web Application to a Target Server

For this task, you should complete at least Practices 1 and 2 to get a solid understanding of how to use Web Setup Projects. If you want a better understanding of how applications are distributed in enterprises and you have sufficient lab equipment, complete Practice 3 as well.

- **Practice 1**   Create a Web Setup Project that prompts the user to provide database connection information, and then stores the connection information as part of a connection string in the Web.config file.

- **Practice 2**   Using the last real-world application you created or one of the applications you created for an exercise in this book, create a Web Setup Project for it. Deploy it to different operating systems, including Windows 2000, Windows XP, and Windows Server 2003. Verify that the deployed application works on all platforms. If it does not work, modify your Web Setup Project to make it work properly. Make note of how the Web Setup Project handles computers that lack the .NET Framework 2.0.

- **Practice 3**   Create a Web Setup Project and generate a Windows Installer file. If you have sufficient lab equipment, use Active Directory software distribution to distribute the Web application automatically to multiple servers.

Copy a Web Application to a Target Server by Using the Copy Web Tool

For this task, you should complete both practices to gain experience using the Copy Web tool.

- **Practice 1**   Use the Copy Web tool to create a local copy of your last real-world Web application. With your computer disconnected from the network, make an update to the Web site. Then, use the Copy Web tool to update that single file on the remote Web server.

■ **Practice 2**   Using a local copy of a Web site, make an update to different files on both your local copy and the remote Web site. Then, use the Copy Web tool to synchronize the local and remote Web site.

Precompile a Web Application by Using the Publish Web Utility

For this task, you should complete the practice to gain an understanding of the performance gains that can be realized by precompiling an application.

■ **Practice**   Enable tracing in a Web application. Then, modify the Web.config file and save it to force the application to restart. Open a page several times, and then view the Trace.axd file to determine how long the first and subsequent requests took. Next, use the Publish Web Site tool to precompile the application. Open a page several times, and then view the Trace.axd file to determine how long the first and subsequent requests took with the precompiled application.

Optimize and Troubleshoot a Web Application

For this task, you should complete at least Practices 2, 3, and 4. If you want experience working with standard performance counter data, complete Practice 1 as well.

■ **Practice 1**   Create a Web page that draws performance counter data graphically, similar to the Performance console.

■ **Practice 2**   Using the last real-world ASP.NET Web application you created, add custom performance counters so that you can monitor the inner details of your application.

■ **Practice 3**   Using the last real-world ASP.NET Web application you created, view the Trace.axd file and make note of how long it takes each page to render. Focusing on the pages which take the longest, add page output caching to improve performance. If you can't cache entire pages, move sections of a page into user controls and cache the user controls. Allow regular users to open the cached pages and note whether performance improves significantly.

■ **Practice 4**   Using the last real-world ASP.NET Web application you created that accesses a database, use the *Cache* object to store a copy of database results. View the Trace.axd page before and after the change to determine if the caching improves performance.

Take a Practice Test

The practice tests on this book's companion CD offer many options. For example, you can test yourself on just the content covered in this chapter, or you can test yourself on all the 70-528 certification exam content. You can set up the test so that it closely simulates the experience of taking a certification exam, or you can set it up in study mode so that you can look at the correct answers and explanations after you answer each question.

MORE INFO Practice tests

For details about all the practice test options available, see the "How to Use the Practice Tests" section in this book's Introduction.

Answers

Chapter 1: Lesson Review Answers

Lesson 1

1. **Correct Answer: D**
   - A. **Incorrect:** This is not a valid property name.
   - B. **Incorrect:** This is not a valid property name.
   - C. **Incorrect:** This is not a valid property name.
   - D. **Correct:** This property is true if data is being sent to the Web server or false if the page is simply being requested.

Lesson 2

1. **Correct Answer: C**
   - A. **Incorrect:** This requires Front Page Server Extensions on the remote computer.
   - B. **Incorrect:** This is only applicable for Web sites that are created on the local developer computer.
   - C. **Correct:** You can create a Web site on a remote computer using FTP if Front Page Server Extensions are not installed on the remote computer.
   - D. **Incorrect:** This is for local Web servers only.

2. **Correct Answer: D**
   - A. **Incorrect:** This is for local Web servers only.
   - B. **Incorrect:** This is only applicable for Web sites that are created on the local developer computer.
   - C. **Incorrect:** This option is only usable when creating a Web site on a remote computer using FTP instead of Front Page Server Extensions.
   - D. **Correct:** This option works with Front Page Server Extensions on the remote computer.

3. **Correct Answer: B**
   - A. **Incorrect:** There is no such model.

      B. **Correct:** The code-behind model provides separation of client-side and server-side code.

      C. **Incorrect:** This model does not provide separation.

      D. **Incorrect:** There is no such model.

4. **Correct Answer: A**

      A. **Correct:** ASP.NET 2.0 supports sites containing Web pages that are written using different programming languages.

      B. **Incorrect:** The code-behind page does not need to be rewritten.

      C. **Incorrect:** The files do not need to be rewritten.

      D. **Incorrect:** Web references are only used with Web services.

Lesson 3

1. **Correct Answer: C**

      A. **Incorrect:** This file is used in a Web application only.

      B. **Incorrect:** This file never affects any Window applications.

      C. **Correct:** Making changes to the Machine.config file affects Windows and Web applications.

      D. **Incorrect:** This is an ASP file and has no effect on .NET applications.

2. **Correct Answer: B**

      A. **Incorrect:** This file is used for default Web settings.

      B. **Correct:** This file is used to change settings that affect only the current Web application.

      C. **Incorrect:** Setting changes to the Machine.config file can affect Windows and Web applications.

      D. **Incorrect:** This is an ASP file and has no effect on .NET applications.

3. **Correct Answer: D**

      A. **Incorrect:** There is no such tool.

      B. **Incorrect:** This program is used to create and edit word processing documents, not modify Web applications.

      C. **Incorrect:** This is used to make global setting changes to Visual Studio 2005.

D. **Correct:** This tool presents a user-friendly GUI that can be used to modify a Web site's settings.

Lesson 4

1. **Correct Answer: A**

    A. **Correct:** Use the ASP.NET trace facility to view life-cycle event timings.

    B. **Incorrect:** This is a waste of your time.

    C. **Incorrect:** There is no such attribute in the Web.config file.

    D. **Incorrect:** There is no such setting in the Web site properties.

2. **Correct Answer: D**

    A. **Incorrect:** You must make enabled="true" and localOnly="false."

    B. **Incorrect:** You must make pageOutput="false" and localOnly="false."

    C. **Incorrect:** You must make mostRecent="true."

    D. **Correct:** The settings are correct.

3. **Correct Answer: C**

    A. **Incorrect:** The Control Tree shows information about each control on the Web page, but not the posted data.

    B. **Incorrect:** The Headers Collection does not contain the posted data.

    C. **Correct:** The Form collection contains the posted data.

    D. **Incorrect:** The Server Variables don't contain the posted data.

Chapter 1: Case Scenario Answers

Case Scenario 1: Creating a New Web Site

1. The Web site type will be File-based. The following list describes how the File-based Web site type fulfills the requirements:

    ❑ File-based Web sites do not require IIS to be installed on the developer machines.

    ❑ Each developer can debug independently with the File-based Web site. If you attempt to use a centralized server with IIS installed, you will run into problems when multiple developers attempt to debug at the same time.

Case Scenario 2: Placing Files in the Proper Folders

1. You will place the ShoppingCart.dll file in the Bin folder, the database files in the App_Data folder, and the wrapper file in the App_Code folder.

   A primary benefit to adhering to the ASP.NET 2.0 folder structure is that a user who attempts to browse to any of these folders will receive an HTTP 403 Forbidden error.

Chapter 2: Lesson Review Answers

Lesson 1

1. **Correct Answer: C**

   A. **Incorrect:** This is not a valid option when right-clicking.

   B. **Incorrect:** This is not a valid operation to convert to HTML server control.

   C. **Correct:** Right-click and select Run As Server Control to convert the HTML element.

   D. **Incorrect:** This is not a valid option in the Properties window.

2. **Correct Answer: A**

   A. **Correct:** Simply set the AutoPostBack property of the control to true.

   B. **Incorrect:** There is no method called *ForcePostBack*.

   C. **Incorrect:** There is no property called PostBackAll.

   D. **Incorrect:** The client makes no attempt to communicate with the server until you set the AutoPostBack property to true.

3. **Correct Answer: C**

   A. **Incorrect:** There is no *ShowControl* method on the TextBox.

   B. **Incorrect:** There is no property called VisibleControl on the TextBox.

   C. **Correct:** The TextBox instance must be added to the *Controls* collection of form1 or the *Controls* collection of any server control that exists on the page.

   D. **Incorrect:** There is no *AddControl* method on the Web page.

Lesson 2

1. **Correct Answer: D**

   A. **Incorrect:** There is no such property.

   B. **Incorrect:** There is no such property.

   C. **Incorrect:** There is no such property.

   D. **Correct:** Set the GroupName.

2. **Correct Answer: B**

   A. **Incorrect:** There is no such type of button.

   B. **Correct:** Command Button controls can be used.

   C. **Incorrect:** There is no such type of button.

   D. **Incorrect:** There is no such type of button.

3. **Correct Answer: D**

   A. **Incorrect:** This is not the easiest way.

   B. **Incorrect:** There is no such selection.

   C. **Incorrect:** There is no such operation.

   D. **Correct:** Simply double-click the control to add the event handler for the default event.

Chapter 2: Case Scenario Answers

Case Scenario 1: Determining the Type of Controls to Use

1. The Web site uses Web server controls because this is a new Web application and the Web server controls provide a more consistent programming model.

   □ To collect the customer names and addresses, use *Label* controls as captions and use *TextBox* controls to capture the data.

   □ Use *CheckBox* control for the active indicator and for the vertical market categories because a true/false setting is required and the *CheckBox* control limits the user to checking (true) or clearing (false) the *CheckBox* control.

   □ Use *RadioButton* controls for mutually exclusive selection of the quantity of computers that the customer has.

Case Scenario 2: Selecting the Proper Events to Use

1. You should place the code to dynamically create the controls in the *Page_Init* event handler because that's where controls are typically created. After the *Page_Init* event handler has been executed, all controls should be instantiated.

2. You should place the code to set the control properties into the *Page_Load* event handler. When the Page_Load event handler fires, all controls should already be instantiated.

Chapter 3: Lesson Review Answers

Lesson 1

1. **Correct Answer: B**

   A. **Incorrect:** Use an HTML table instead.

   B. **Correct:** It's best to use the *Table*, *TableRow*, and *TableCell* controls when creating a custom control.

   C. **Incorrect:** Use an HTML table instead.

   D. **Incorrect:** Use a *GridView* control instead.

2. **Correct Answer: D**

   A. **Incorrect:** Although you could employ this method, it could be difficult to execute and certainly isn't the best way to accomplish this task.

   B. **Incorrect:** The product lines are not rectangular, so this would not be an option.

   C. **Incorrect:** The *MultiView* only shows one *View* at a time, so this would not be a good solution.

   D. **Correct:** The *ImageMap* provides the ability to define hot spot areas and the *PostBackValue* can be used to get the area that was clicked.

3. **Correct Answer: C**

   A. **Incorrect:** In the available answers, this is not the easiest control to implement.

   B. **Incorrect:** This control can't provide Wizard-like behavior.

   C. **Correct:** The Wizard control simplifies your solution.

   D. **Incorrect:** No such control exists.

Lesson 2

1. **Correct Answer: C**

   A. **Incorrect:** *HotSpot* objects cannot be hidden or shown.

   B. **Incorrect:** The *Calendar* control can't be used to provide random selection of the image to be displayed.

   C. **Correct:** The *AdRotator* provides random selection of images.

   D. **Incorrect:** The *ImageButton* is not appropriate for this function.

2. **Correct Answer: C**

   A. **Incorrect:** The *DetailsView* only shows one record at a time.

   B. **Incorrect:** The *Table* control does not provide edit capabilities.

   C. **Correct:** The *GridView* control is the best choice.

   D. **Incorrect:** The *ImageButton* is not appropriate for this function.

3. **Correct Answer: A**

   A. **Correct:** The *DropDownList* can display a list that uses a minimum amount of space.

   B. **Incorrect:** The *RadioButtonList* control does not provide a list in a minimum amount of space.

   C. **Incorrect:** The *FormView* control does not provide a list in a minimum amount of space.

   D. **Incorrect:** The *TextBox* control does not provide a list.

Chapter 3: Case Scenario Answers

Case Scenario 1: Determining How to Prompt for Data

- You could divide the prompts by category and create a separate Web page for each category. This solution splits your code and data over several pages and can add to the overall complexity of the Web site.

- You could implement a solution using the *MultiView* control and create a separate *View* for each category. The *MultiView* and *View* do not have a user interface, so you have complete flexibility with regard to the graphical interface of the Web page.

- You could implement the *Wizard* control and create a *WizardStep* control for each category. The *Wizard* contains the behavior for moving between steps and offers a more complete solution.

Case Scenario 2: Implementing a Calendar Solution

1. This solution can use the *Calendar* control in every situation where a date or dates are required to be entered by the user, and in every situation where a schedule is being displayed to a Web site user. The following list describes some of these situations where you can use the *Calendar* control:

   ❏ Prompt for class start date.

   ❏ Prompt for class end date.

   ❏ Display of training provider's class schedule.

   ❏ Display of contractor's schedule.

2. Although you could use the *Table* control in these situations, you would need to write lots of code to get the functionality that the *Calendar* control provides natively, so the *Calendar* control is the best solution.

Case Scenario 3: Implementing a Master/Detail Solution

1. This solution is probably best suited to use the *GridView* for the customers and the orders because the ability to display this data as a list is a requirement.

   The *GridView* does not natively support the abiltiy to add new data records, but you can modify the *GridView* to provide this functionality. You can also supply a *Button* control that simply adds an empty data record and then places the record in edit mode.

   Another solution is to provide a *DetailsView* or *FormView* control in addition to the *GridView* controls for the customers and orders. The *DetailsView* and *FormView* provide the ability to add new rows, and you can edit all of the fields.

Chapter 4: Lesson Review Answers

Lesson 1

1. **Correct Answer: D**

   A. **Incorrect:** The *DataColumn* won't help with the navigation.

B.   **Incorrect:** The *DataColumn* won't help with the navigation.

C.   **Incorrect:** The *DataColumn* won't help with the navigation.

D.   **Correct:** You can use the *DataRelation* to navigate from the child to the parent or from the parent to the child.

2.   **Correct Answer: A**

A.   **Correct:** Primary keys must exist or the changed data will be appended into the destination *DataSet* instead of being merged.

B.   **Incorrect:** The *DataSet* schemas do not need to match, and you can specify what to do about the differences.

C.   **Incorrect:** The destination *DataSet* does not need to be empty.

D.   **Incorrect:** The *DataSet* does not need to be merged back to the same *DataSet* that created it.

3.   **Correct Answer: C**

A.   **Incorrect:** The *DataTable* object does not have a *Sort* method.

B.   **Incorrect:** The *DataSet* object does not have a *Sort* method.

C.   **Correct:** The *DataView* can be used for each sort.

D.   **Incorrect:** The *DataTable* object does not have a *Sort* method.

Lesson 2

1.   **Correct Answers: B and D**

A.   **Incorrect:** No such method.

B.   **Correct:** The *Close* method cleans up resources.

C.   **Incorrect:** Is not proactive and can orphan connections.

D.   **Correct:** The *using* block calls the *Dispose* method.

2.   **Correct Answer: A**

A.   **Correct:** The *InfoMessage* event displays informational messages as well as the output of the SQL print statement.

B.   **Incorrect:** No such event.

C.   **Incorrect:** No such event.

D.   **Incorrect:** No such event.

3. **Correct Answer: D**

    A. **Incorrect:** No such key.

    B. **Incorrect:** No such key.

    C. **Incorrect:** No such key.

    D. **Correct:** You must set *Asynchronous=true*.

Lesson 3

1. **Correct Answer: B**

    A. **Incorrect:** Cannot be used to create a new XML document.

    B. **Correct:** Use the *XmlDocument* class to create a new document from scratch.

    C. **Incorrect:** No such class.

    D. **Incorrect:** No such class.

2. **Correct Answer: C**

    A. **Incorrect:** No such type.

    B. **Incorrect:** No such type.

    C. **Correct:** Use the *XmlConvert* class.

    D. **Incorrect:** No such type.

Chapter 4: Case Scenario Answers

Case Scenario 1: Determining Ways to Update the Database

- You can load the XML file into a *DataSet* and then use a *SqlDataAdapter* to retrieve all changes and send the changes to the database.

- You can read the XML file into an *XmlDocument* object and use the DOM to parse the data and write code to send the changes to the database.

- You can use the *XmlTextReader* to read the XML file node by node, capturing the data and sending it to the database.

Case Scenario 2: Storing a DataSet to a Binary File

- Store the DataSet as a binary file by using the BinaryFormatter object.

■ You must set the RemotingFormat property of the DataSet to SerializationFormat.Binary to force the DataSet to be serialized as binary.

Chapter 5: Lesson Review Answers

Lesson 1

1. **Correct Answer: D**

    A. **Incorrect:** Not a valid extension.

    B. **Incorrect:** Not a valid extension.

    C. **Incorrect:** Not a valid extension.

    D. **Correct:** The .ascx extension is the proper extension for a user control.

2. **Correct Answer: C**

    A. **Incorrect:** Although you could use this method, it would be difficult to do and certainly is not the best way to accomplish this task.

    B. **Incorrect:** Although you could use this method, it would be difficult to do and certainly is not the best way to accomplish this task.

    C. **Correct:** The templated user control exposes the data to the Web page designer, who can then specify the format of the data in a template.

    D. **Incorrect:** This user control does not natively expose the style property, and if you choose to expose the property, you can only set an overall format for the user control, not a format for each of the data elements that are being exposed.

3. **Correct Answer: D**

    A. **Incorrect:** No such directive.

    B. **Incorrect:** No such directive.

    C. **Incorrect:** No such directive.

    D. **Correct:** Use the @Register directive to set a reference to the User Control that you are employing.

Lesson 2

1. **Correct Answer: C**

    A. **Incorrect:** Not a valid attribute.

B. **Incorrect:** Not the correct attribute.

C. **Correct:** Use the *ToolboxBitmap* attribute to set the image.

D. **Incorrect:** Not a valid attribute.

2. **Correct Answer: D**

A. **Incorrect:** No such method.

B. **Incorrect:** No such method.

C. **Incorrect:** No such method.

D. **Correct:** The *Render* method must be overridden and you must provide code to display your control.

3. **Correct Answer: A**

A. **Correct:** The CreateChildControls method must be overridden with code to create the child controls and set their properties.

B. **Incorrect:** No such method.

C. **Incorrect:** No such method.

D. **Incorrect:** No such method.

Chapter 5: Case Scenario Answers

Case Scenario 1: Sharing Controls Between Applications

- You should consider developing a custom composite control, because the composite control can easily contain other controls, and the layout is always the same.

  If you create a user control, you won't be able to compile it to a .dll file to install it into the GAC.

  You should not consider creating a templated control because of the goal to keep the layout consistent.

Case Scenario 2: Providing Layout Flexibility

- You should consider creating a templated user control or a templated control. Either method can be used to present the data to the Web page designers. Because this is a single site solution, the easiest, and therefore the best, solution is to implement the templated user control.

Chapter 6: Lesson Review Answers

Lesson 1

1. **Correct Answer: C**

   A. **Incorrect:** Not a valid operation.

   B. **Incorrect:** Not a valid operation.

   C. **Correct:** The *CustomValidator* can be used to perform a database lookup.

   D. **Incorrect:** Not a valid operation.

2. **Correct Answer: A**

   A. **Correct:** You need to test the *IsValid* property of the Web page before executing code in your event handler methods.

   B. **Incorrect:** The *IsValid* property is not set yet; exiting the *Load* event handler method still allows the event handler methods to execute.

   C. **Incorrect:** Although this will appear to correct the problem, a would-be hacker could disable client-side validation and the server-side problem would still exist.

   D. **Incorrect:** This is the default setting and does not correct the problem.

3. **Correct Answer: B**

   A. **Incorrect:** The *Text* property should be an asterisk and the *ErrorMessage* should be the detailed error message.

   B. **Correct:** Setting the *Text* property to an asterisk places the asterisk next to the control and setting the *ErrorMessage* to the detailed error message causes the detailed errors to be placed into the *ValidationSummary* control at the top of the Web page.

   C. **Incorrect:** The *Text* property should be an asterisk and the *ErrorMessage* should be the detailed error message.

   D. **Incorrect:** The *Text* property should be an asterisk and the *ErrorMessage* should be the detailed error message.

Lesson 2

1. **Correct Answer: C**

   A. **Incorrect:** Not a valid method.

   B. **Incorrect:** Not a valid method.

   C. **Correct:** Use the *Transfer* method to switch to the different Web page.

   D. **Incorrect:** Not a valid method.

2. **Correct Answer: D**

   A. **Incorrect:** No such control.

   B. **Incorrect:** No such control.

   C. **Incorrect:** No such control.

   D. **Correct:** The *SiteMapPath* control is automatically bound to the Web.sitemap file.

3. **Correct Answer: B**

   A. **Incorrect:** Not a valid class.

   B. **Correct:** The *SiteMap* class provides programmatic access to the site map.

   C. **Incorrect:** Not a valid class.

   D. **Incorrect:** Not a valid class.

Chapter 6: Case Scenario Answers

Case Scenario 1: Determining the Proper User Name Validators to Implement

- The *RequiredFieldValidator* ensures that non-whitespace has been entered.

  The *RegularExpressionValidator* can be used, and the *ValidationExpression* can be set to *Internet e-mail address*.

Case Scenario 2: Determining the Proper Password Validators to Implement

- The *RequiredFieldValidator* ensures that non-whitespace has been entered.

  A *CustomValidator* with code to check for the character types and length as specified.

Case Scenario 3: Implementing a Site Map

- You can use the *TreeView* control with the *SiteMapDataSource*, and a *SiteMapPath* control to display the breadcrumb path.

Chapter 7: Lesson Review Answers

Lesson 1

1. **Correct Answer: B**

   A. **Incorrect:** Client-side state management requires the client to transmit the user name and password with each request. It also requires the client to store the information locally, where it might be compromised.

   B. **Correct:** Server-side state management provides better security for confidential information by reducing the number of times the information is transmitted across the network.

2. **Correct Answer: A**

   A. **Correct:** Client-side state management is an excellent choice for storing non-confidential information. It is much easier to implement than server-side state management when multiple Web servers are involved, and it minimizes load on the servers.

   B. **Incorrect:** You could use server-side state management; however, it would require a back-end database to synchronize information between multiple Web servers. This would increase the load on your servers.

3. **Correct Answer: A**

   A. **Correct:** View state is the simplest way to store this information. Because it is enabled by default, you might not need to write any code to support state management for your form.

   B. **Incorrect:** You can use control state; however, it requires extra coding and is only necessary if you are creating a control that might be used in a Web page that has view state disabled.

   C. **Incorrect:** You can store the information in hidden fields; however, that requires writing extra code. View state supports your requirements with little or no additional code.

D. **Incorrect:** Cookies require extra coding and are only required if you need to share information between multiple Web forms.

E. **Incorrect:** You can use query strings to store user preferences. However, you need to update every link on the page that the user might click. This is very time-consuming to implement.

4. **Correct Answer: D**

A. **Incorrect:** View state can only store information for a single Web form.

B. **Incorrect:** Control state can only store information for a single control.

C. **Incorrect:** Hidden fields can only store information for a single Web form.

D. **Correct:** Unless you specifically narrow the scope, the user's browser submits information stored in a cookie to every page on your Web site. Therefore, each Web form processes the user preference information. If you configure the cookie expiration to make it persistent, the browser submits the cookie the next time the user visits your Web site.

E. **Incorrect:** You can use query strings to store user preferences. However, you need to update every link on the page that the user might click. This is very time-consuming to implement.

5. **Correct Answer: E**

A. **Incorrect:** View state information is not stored in the URL, and therefore is lost if the URL is bookmarked.

B. **Incorrect:** Control state information is not stored in the URL, and therefore is lost if the URL is bookmarked.

C. **Incorrect:** Hidden fields are not stored in the URL, and therefore are lost if the URL is bookmarked.

D. **Incorrect:** Cookies are not stored in the URL, and therefore are lost if the URL is bookmarked.

E. **Correct:** Query strings are stored in the URL. While they are not the easiest type of client-side state management to implement, they are the only way to enable state management data to be easily bookmarked and e-mailed.

Lesson 2

1. **Correct Answer: C**

   A. **Incorrect:** You cannot respond to the *Application_Start* event from within a Web form.

   B. **Incorrect:** You cannot write code in the Web.config file.

   C. **Correct:** The proper place to respond to *Application* or *Session* events is the Global.asax file.

   D. **Incorrect:** You cannot respond to the *Application_Start* event from within a Web form.

2. **Correct Answer: B**

   A. **Incorrect:** *Session* data is only available to a single user session.

   B. **Correct:** *Application* data is available to all users.

   C. **Incorrect:** Cookies are only available to single users.

   D. **Incorrect:** View state data is only available to individual users.

3. **Correct Answer: A**

   A. **Correct:** *Session* data is only available to a single user session.

   B. **Incorrect:** *Application* data is available to all users.

   C. **Incorrect:** Cookies are only available to a single user.

   D. **Incorrect:** View state data is only available to individual users.

4. **Correct Answer: D**

   A. **Incorrect:** *Application_Start* is called when the application loads. You cannot access the Session object from the *Application_Start* event handler.

   B. **Incorrect:** *Application_End* is called when the application shuts down. You cannot access the Session object from the *Application_End* event handler.

   C. **Incorrect:** *Session_Start* is called when a user first connects.

   D. **Correct:** The *Session_End* event handler is called when a user's session times out, and it's the perfect opportunity to persist data about a user's session. However, to prevent data from being lost if the server is shut down in the middle of a user session, you should persist session data after every page request.

Chapter 7: Case Scenario Answers

Case Scenario 1: Remembering User Credentials

1. You should use cookies, because they are stored on the client and can persist between multiple visits.

2. First, you should not store the users' credentials in cookies. Instead, you should store tokens that prove they have authenticated. Second, you can require Secure Sockets Layer (SSL) for your Web application so that all communications are encrypted. Third, you can narrow the scope of the cookies so that the browser only submits them to the SSL-protected portion of your Web site.

3. You should not use state management techniques to store previous orders. Instead, you should retrieve that information directly from the database.

Case Scenario 2: Analyzing Information for Individual Users and for All Users

1. You can use the *Application* object to store and analyze data related to all users. For each page view, you could update a custom collection within the *Application* object to track which page a user is currently viewing.

2. You can use the *Session* object to analyze what a user has done. For each page view, you could add the page that the user visits to a custom collection in the *Session* object, and then analyze that collection to make advertisement decisions.

Chapter 8: Lesson Review Answers

Lesson 1

1. **Correct Answer: A**

   A. **Correct:** *Server.GetLastError* retrieves the most recent error message. After processing it, you call *Server.ClearError* to remove the error from the queue.

   B. **Incorrect:** You should call *Server.ClearError* to remove an error from the queue after processing it. However, you must first call *Server.GetLastError* to handle the error.

   C. **Incorrect:** The *GetLastError* method is a member of the *Server* object, not the *Request* object.

    D. **Incorrect:** The *GetLastError* method is a member of the *Application* object, not the *Request* object.

2. **Correct Answers: B and C**

    A. **Incorrect:** Errors occur at the Page or Application level, but not the Response level.

    B. **Correct:** You can catch errors at the Page level using the *Page.Error* event.

    C. **Correct:** You can catch errors at the Page level using the *Server.Error* event.

    D. **Incorrect:** Errors occur at the Page or Application level, but not the Server level.

3. **Correct Answer: D**

    A. **Incorrect:** The *WebConfigurationManager.GetSection* method returns an object that must be cast to a section-specific type. It does not return a string.

    B. **Incorrect:** To identify the <httpCookies> section, you must reference "system.web/httpCookies" because <httpCookies> exists within <system.web>.

    C. **Incorrect:** The *WebConfigurationManager.GetSection* method returns an object that must be cast to a section-specific type. It does not return a string. Additionally, to identify the <httpCookies> section, you must reference "system.web/httpCookies" because <httpCookies> exists within <system.web>.

    D. **Correct:** To retrieve a section from the master Web.config file, call *WebConfigurationManager.GetSection*. This method returns an object that must be cast to the correct type. In Visual Basic, the casting happens automatically. However, it must be done explicitly in C#.

4. **Correct Answer: C**

    A. **Incorrect:** *IPartitionResolver* defines methods that must be implemented for custom session-state partition resolution, and does not relate to handling custom file types.

    B. **Incorrect:** *IHttpModule* provides module initialization and disposal events, enabling you to respond to *BeginRequest* and *EndRequst* HTTP events before and after a Web page is generated. You would not use it to handle a custom file type.

C. **Correct:** Implement the *IHttpHandler* interface to generate custom file types. Additionally, you must configure IIS to forward requests for .doc files to ASP.NET.

D. **Incorrect:** *IHttpHandlerFactory* is used as part of *IHttpHandler*, but it has no functionality itself.

Lesson 2

1. **Correct Answers: A, D, and E**

   A. **Correct:** You can check the *Request.Browser.ClrVersion* property to determine if the .NET Framework CLR is installed.

   B. **Incorrect:** The *Browser* object does not indicate whether the user is logged on as an administrator. The client's Web browser does not provide this information to the Web server.

   C. **Incorrect:** The *Browser* object does not provide the user's e-mail address. The client's Web browser does not send this information to the Web server.

   D. **Correct:** You can check the *Request.Browser.ActiveXControls* property to determine if the browser supports ActiveX controls.

   E. **Correct:** You can check the *Request.Browser.JavaScript* property to determine if the browser supports JavaScript.

2. **Correct Answer: B**

   A. **Incorrect:** *Title* is a member of *Page.Header*, not *Page*.

   B. **Correct:** You can dynamically set the page title by accessing *Page.Header.Title*.

   C. **Incorrect:** *Header* is a member of *Page*, not *Response*.

   D. **Incorrect:** *Title* is a member of *Page.Header*, not *Response*.

3. **Correct Answer: A**

   A. **Correct:** *Flush* sends any output currently stored in the *Response* object to the browser. You can add to it later.

   B. **Incorrect:** *Clear* removes all output from the *Response* object without sending it to the user.

   C. **Incorrect:** *End* sends all output to the Web browser, but also terminates the transaction, preventing you from later adding to it.

    D. Incorrect: Like *Clear*, *ClearContent* removes output from the Response object without sending it to the user.

Chapter 8: Case Scenario Answers

Case Scenario 1: Dynamically Generating Charts

1. You could use the *Graphics* class to generate line charts. For more complex charts, you could use third-party charting libraries.

2. You could create an ASP.NET handler for the .gif file extension. To do this, create a new class that derives from *IHttpHandler* and uses the *Response* object to return the chart image. Then, add a handler to the Web.config file associating the .gif file extension to your new class. Finally, configure IIS to forward requests for .gif files to ASP.NET.

Case Scenario 2: Dynamically Adjusting Pages Based on Browser Capabilities

1. *Request.Browser.ActiveXControls*

2. *Request.Browser.IsMobileDevice*

3. *Request.Browser.IsColor*

Chapter 9: Lesson Review Answers

Lesson 1

1. **Correct Answer: C**

    A. Incorrect: You often develop multiple master pages for a content page to provide different layouts and colors.

    B. Incorrect: While you can have multiple master pages for each content page, you can also have multiple content pages for each master page.

    C. Correct: Master and content pages have a many-to-many relationship.

    D. Incorrect: While you can have one content page per master page, that defeats the purpose of master and content pages.

2. **Correct Answers: B, C, and D**

   A. **Incorrect:** Content pages cannot reference private properties or methods in the master page.

   B. **Correct:** Content pages can reference public properties in the master page.

   C. **Correct:** Content pages can reference public method in the master page.

   D. **Correct:** Content pages can use the *Master.FindControl* method to reference controls in the master page.

3. **Correct Answers: A and C**

   A. **Correct:** The "@ MasterType" declaration is required to access the properties in the master page.

   B. **Incorrect:** You only need to add the "@ Master" declarations to the master page, not the content pages.

   C. **Correct:** Content pages must have a *MasterPageFile* attribute in the "@ Page" declaration that points to the master page.

   D. **Incorrect:** The master page, not the content pages, has the *ContentPlaceHolder* control.

4. **Correct Answer: D**

   A. **Incorrect:** *Page_Load* occurs after the content page has bound to the master page. If you attempt to change the master page, the runtime throws an exception.

   B. **Incorrect:** *Page_Render* occurs after the content page has bound to the master page. If you attempt to change the master page, the runtime throws an exception.

   C. **Incorrect:** *Page_PreRender* occurs after the content page has bound to the master page. If you attempt to change the master page, the runtime throws an exception.

   D. **Correct:** *Page_PreInit* is the last opportunity to change the master page. After this event, the page binds with the master page, preventing you from changing it.

Lesson 2

1. **Correct Answers: A and C**

    A. **Correct:** Themes specified using the *Theme* attribute override control attributes.

    B. **Incorrect:** Themes specified using the *StyleSheetTheme* attribute do not override control attributes.

    C. **Correct:** Themes specified using the *Theme* attribute override control attributes.

    D. **Incorrect:** Themes specified using the *StyleSheetTheme* attribute do not override control attributes.

2. **Correct Answer: C**

    A. **Incorrect:** Skin files should not include the ID attribute, and skin files must include the *runat="server"* attribute.

    B. **Incorrect:** Skin files should not include the ID attribute.

    C. **Correct:** Skin files must include the *runat="server"* attribute but should not include the ID attribute.

    D. **Incorrect:** Skin files must include the *runat="server"* attribute.

3. **Correct Answer: D**

    A. **Incorrect:** *Page_Load* occurs too late in the rendering process to change the theme.

    B. **Incorrect:** *Page_Render* occurs too late in the rendering process to change the theme.

    C. **Incorrect:** *Page_PreRender* occurs too late in the rendering process to change the theme.

    D. **Correct:** *Page_PreInit* is the proper method to specify the theme.

4. **Correct Answer: A**

    A. **Correct:** User profiles are disabled by default for anonymous users. To enable anonymous user profiles, add the *<anonymousIdentification enabled="true" />* element to the <system.Web> section of the Web.config file. Then in the <profile><properties> section, add the variables you want to track and set *allowAnonymous="true"* for each variable.

B. **Incorrect:** You must specify the type of all variables except strings.

C. **Incorrect:** You must set *allowAnonymous="true"* for each variable that anonymous users will access.

D. **Incorrect:** You must add the <anonymousIdentification enabled="true" /> element to the <system.Web> section of the Web.config file. Additionally, you need to set *allowAnonymous="true"* for each variable that anonymous users will access.

Lesson 3

1. **Correct Answers: A, B, and C**

A. **Correct:** Custom controls can act as Web Parts.

B. **Correct:** Labels and any standard controls can act as Web Parts, though they are not very useful.

C. **Correct:** You can derive a class from the *WebPart* class, and then use the class as a Web Part.

D. **Incorrect:** A content page cannot act as a Web Part. Instead, you should move the page into a control.

2. **Correct Answers: B and D**

A. **Incorrect:** The *LayoutEditorPart* control enables users to change the chrome state and zone of a control. It does not provide the ability to change the Web Part's title.

B. **Correct:** You must add an *EditorZone* container to the Web page. Then, add an *AppearanceEditorPart* control to the *EditorZone*.

C. **Incorrect:** *CatalogZone* enables users to add new Web Parts to a page, but it does not enable them to change Web Part titles.

D. **Correct:** The *AppearanceEditorPart* control enables users to set the titles of Web Parts.

3. **Correct Answers: B and C**

A. **Incorrect:** The *LayoutEditorPart* control enables a user to change the chrome state and zone of a control. It does not provide the ability to add Web Parts.

B. **Correct:** The *DeclarativeCatalogPart* control enables a user to add Web Parts when the page is in Catalog mode.

C. **Correct:** The *CatalogZone* container is required to hold the *DeclarativeCatalogPart* control, which enables a user to add Web Parts.

D. **Incorrect:** The *AppearanceEditorPart* control enables the user to edit the appearance of existing Web Parts, but does not enable a user to add new Web Parts.

4. **Correct Answer: B**

A. **Incorrect:** The *ConnectionConsumer* attribute should be applied to the method that receives the provider Web Part's data.

B. **Correct:** You should apply the *ConnectionProvider* attribute to a public method to allow consumers to access the method.

C. **Incorrect:** You cannot use properties for connections between Web Parts.

D. **Incorrect:** You cannot use properties for connections between Web Parts.

Chapter 9: Case Scenario Answers

Case Scenario 1: Meet Customization Requirements for an Internal Insurance Application

1. You can use a combination of user profiles and customizable Web Parts to meet their requirements.

2. Connected Web Parts can provide what you need. You can have a provider Web Part that enables the underwriter to choose a claim type, and consumer Web Parts that retrieve the currently selected claim type and display related statistics.

Case Scenario 2: Provide Consistent Formatting for an External Web Application

1. You can use themes and add a .skin file that defines fonts for different controls.

2. If you apply a theme using the *<pages Theme="themeName">* element in the Web.config file, it overrides control attributes.

3. You can use customizable Web Parts to enable users to remove unwanted controls.

4. To enable users to change colors on a Web site, use programmatically applied themes and user profiles. Then, users can customize their profiles and ASP.NET remembers their preferences for future visits.

Chapter 10: Lesson Review Answers

Lesson 1

1. **Correct Answers: B and C**

   A. **Incorrect:** The language abbreviation must precede the .resx extension.

   B. **Correct:** The default language file should not have a language extension.

   C. **Correct:** To create a German language file, add the language extension (de) between the page file name and the .resx extension.

   D. **Incorrect:** You do not need to add a language abbreviation to the resource name for the default language.

2. **Correct Answers: B and C**

   A. **Incorrect:** The *Page.Culture* property defines cultural formatting, such as how numbers are formatted. It is not required for defining a language.

   B. **Correct:** The *Page.UICulture* property defines the language resource file that is used.

   C. **Correct:** ASP.NET pages initialize the culture in the *InitializeCulture* method. You should override this method, set the *UICulture* property, and then call the base *Page.InitializeCulture* method.

   D. **Incorrect:** The *Page.ReadStringResource* method is not related to defining language.

3. **Correct Answer: D**

   A. **Incorrect:** The *DataValueField* property is only used when a control is linked to a *DataSource*.

   B. **Incorrect:** The *DataSourceID* property is only used when a control is linked to a *DataSource*.

   C. **Incorrect:** While you could programmatically define the *Text* property using a global resource, at design time, you should use the *(Expressions)* property.

   D. **Correct:** Visual Studio provides an editor for the *(Expressions)* property that enables you to link any other property to a global resource.

4. **Correct Answer: A**

   A. **Correct:** Visual Studio automatically creates strongly named objects within *Resources.Resource* for every value you create..

B. **Incorrect:** While you can access global resources using strings, you need to call the *GetGlobalResourceObject* method.

C. **Incorrect:** While you can access global resources using strings, you need to call the *GetGlobalResourceObject* method.

D. **Incorrect:** Visual Studio does not create strongly typed objects under *Resources* directly. Instead, they are within *Resources.Resource*.

Lesson 2

1. **Correct Answers: B and C**

   A. **Incorrect:** ASP.NET uses the *Image.AccessKey* parameter to provide a keyboard shortcut for an image.

   B. **Correct:** ASP.NET uses the *Image.AlternateText* parameter to create the alt text for an image. Screen readers typically describe images using the alt text.

   C. **Correct:** *DescriptionUrl* links to an HTML page that provides a long description of an image. ASP.NET uses this link to create the *longdesc* HTML attribute.

   D. **Incorrect:** *ToolTip* is not related to accessibility. *ToolTip* defines data that Internet Explorer displays when you hover your pointer over an image.

2. **Correct Answers: A and C**

   A. **Correct:** Controls such as *Image* provide properties that you can use to provide a description for those who cannot see the image.

   B. **Incorrect:** ASP.NET controls are not displayed in high contrast by default. However, they are designed to support high-contrast mode by default.

   C. **Correct:** Controls such as *CreateUserWizard, Menu, SiteMapPath, TreeView,* and *Wizard* support skipping links.

   D. **Incorrect:** ASP.NET controls do not display text in large font sizes by default. However, they are designed to support browsers configured to display large font sizes.

3. **Correct Answers: A, B, and D**

   A. **Correct:** Visual Studio can automatically test Web applications for compliance with WCAG Priority 1 guidelines.

   B. **Correct:** Visual Studio can automatically test Web applications for compliance with WCAG Priority 2 guidelines.

C. **Incorrect:** ADA, the Americans with Disabilities Act, provides accessibility guidelines for facilities, transportation, and more. However, it does not provide Web application accessibility guidelines.

D. **Correct:** Visual Studio automatically tests Web applications for compliance with Section 508 guidelines.

Chapter 10: Case Scenario Answers

Case Scenario 1: Upgrade an Application for Multiple Languages

1. You can use local and global resources to provide translations for your Web site. Use local resources to provide page-specific translations, and use global resources to provide phrases that are used on multiple pages.

2. Translators need to update the local and global resource files. These are standard XML files, so any XML editor can do it. You can also create an application to facilitate the translations.

3. Web browsers often are configured for language preferences. ASP.NET can automatically detect this preference and use the preferred language if the resource is available. Additionally, you should allow a user to specify a language.

4. Specific cultures distinguish both languages and regional requirements, as opposed to neutral cultures, which only distinguish the language.

Case Scenario 2: Making a Web Application Accessible

1. Visual Studio includes tools to test individual Web pages. Additionally, you can configure Visual Studio to automatically test a Web application for Section 508 compliance during the build process.

2. Accessible applications can be used with alternative input and display devices.

3. No, accessible applications do not require users with traditional input and display devices to make any sacrifices. Most accessibility features take the form of hidden textual descriptions and access keys, which users who do not need them will probably not notice.

4. You need to provide textual descriptions for all visual elements, such as forms, tables, and images. Additionally, you should make the Web application usable without the use of a mouse.

Chapter 11: Lesson Review Answers

Lesson 1

1. **Correct Answer: C**

    A. **Incorrect:** The *Login* control prompts the user for a user name and password.

    B. **Incorrect:** The *LoginView* control enables you to display custom content for authenticated or unauthenticated users.

    C. **Correct:** The *LoginStatus* control displays "Login," with a link to log in if the user is unauthenticated, or "Logout" to authenticated users.

    D. **Incorrect:** The *LoginName* control displays the user's name when he or she is authenticated. The control is not visible when a user is not authenticated.

2. **Correct Answer: A**

    A. **Correct:** If no filename is specified in the Web.config file, ASP.NET redirects unauthenticated users to the Login.aspx page, regardless of whether the page exists.

    B. **Incorrect:** ASP.NET directs users who need to log in to the page named Login.aspx by default.

    C. **Incorrect:** ASP.NET directs users who need to log in to the page named Login.aspx by default.

    D. **Incorrect:** ASP.NET directs users who need to log in to the page named Login.aspx by default.

3. **Correct Answers: A and D**

    A. **Correct:** The *Login* control is required on a login page, because it prompts the user for the user name and password.

    B. **Incorrect:** The *CreateUserWizard* control enables a user to create an account for his or herself. However, it is a very large control, and a user should only need to access it once. Therefore, it should be placed on its own page.

    C. **Incorrect:** The *LoginName* control is not a good choice for a login page because it displays an authenticated user's name. Because the user is not yet logged on when accessing the login page, there would not be a user name to display, and the control would not be visible.

D. **Correct:** The *PasswordRecovery* control is a good choice for a login page because it can be used to recover a password in the event the user forgets his or her password.

4. **Correct Answer: B**

A. **Incorrect:** The *Unload* event is called when the control is unloaded and does not allow you to redirect the user after a successful account creation.

B. **Correct:** After a user creates an account, he or she is notified of the successful account creation and prompted to click the Continue button. The *ContinueButtonClick* event is called when the user clicks that button. You should always create an event handler, because otherwise, users are returned to the same page.

C. **Incorrect:** The *CreatedUser* event is called when a user account is successfully created. However, it is called before the user has been notified of the account creation. Therefore, you should respond to *ContinueButtonClick* instead.

D. **Incorrect:** The *Init* event is called when the page is initialized, which would occur before the user account had been created. Therefore, redirecting the user in response to this event prevents him or her from being able to create an account.

Lesson 2

1. **Correct Answer: C**

A. **Incorrect:** The "*" special character refers to all users, authenticated or unauthenticated. Therefore, this Web.config file blocks all users.

B. **Incorrect:** The "*" special character refers to all users, authenticated or unauthenticated. Therefore, this Web.config file grants access to all users without prompting them for credentials.

C. **Correct:** The "?" special character refers to all unauthenticated users. Therefore, this Web.config file correctly blocks unauthenticated access.

D. **Incorrect:** The "?" special character refers to all unauthenticated users. Therefore, this Web.config file grants access to unauthenticated users without prompting them for credentials.

2. **Correct Answer: D**

    A. **Incorrect:** By default, cookies are used for browsers that support them. For browsers that do not support them, the authentication token is stored in the URI. You can configure cookies to always be used by setting the *cookieless* attribute of the *<forms>* element to *UseCookies*.

    B. **Incorrect:** By default, the authentication token is only stored in the URI if the browser does not support cookies. You can configure cookies to never be used by setting the *cookieless* attribute of the *<forms>* element to *UseUri*.

    C. **Incorrect:** This behavior is useful, but it is not the default setting. To configure this behavior, set the *cookieless* attribute of the *<forms>* element to *AutoDetect*.

    D. **Correct:** This is the default behavior, and is equivalent to setting the *cookieless* attribute of the *<forms>* element to *UseDeviceProfile*.

3. **Correct Answer: B**

    A. **Incorrect:** Authenticated users who are not members of the FABRIKAM\Marketing group are denied access, because the <deny users="*" /> element overrides the <allow users="?" /> default element in the Machine.config file.

    B. **Correct:** Only members of the FABRIKAM\Marketing group are allowed access, because the settings in the *<location>* element override the settings in the parent folders.

    C. **Incorrect:** The <deny users="*"> element in the <location> element blocks users who are not members of the FABRIKAM\Marketing group.

    D. **Incorrect:** The <allow roles="FABRIKAM\Marketing" /> element takes precedence over the <deny users="*"> element, granting members of the FABRIKAM\Marketing group access.

4. **Correct Answer: D**

    A. **Incorrect:** Unauthenticated users do not have access because the Web.config file denies them access. Additionally, NTFS permissions also denies them access.

    B. **Incorrect:** Authenticated users do not have access because the Web.config file denies them access to the Marketing folder. Additionally, NTFS permissions denies them access, because the NTFS permissions grant access only to John and Sam.

C. **Incorrect:** Members of the Domain Users group do not have access because the Web.config file denies them access to the Marketing folder. Additionally, NTFS permissions also denies them access, because the NTFS permissions grant access only to John and Sam..

D. **Correct:** John has access because he is granted permissions through ASP.NET because of his membership in the FABRIKAM\Marketing group. Additionally, he is granted NTFS permission to access the folder.

E. **Incorrect:** Sam does not have access because the Web.config file denies him access to the Marketing folder. However, he can access the Web pages from a shared folder, because NTFS permissions grant him access. Only ASP.NET blocks access.

Chapter 11: Case Scenario Answers

Case Scenario 1: Configuring Web Application Authorization

1. Your Web.config file should resemble the following:

```xml
<?xml version="1.0" encoding="utf-8" ?>
<configuration>

  <system.web>
    <authentication mode="Windows" />
    <authorization>
        <deny users="?" />
    </authorization>
  </system.web>

  <location path="IT">
    <system.web>
<authorization>
<allow roles="SOUTHRIDGE\IT" />
<deny users="*" />
</authorization>
    </system.web>
  </location>

  <location path="Production">
    <system.web>
<authorization>
<allow roles="SOUTHRIDGE\Production" />
<allow users="SOUTHRIDGE\TJensen" />
<deny users="*" />
</authorization>
    </system.web>
```

```
</location>

<location path="Sales">
  <system.web>
<authorization>
<allow users="SOUTHRIDGE\TJensen" />
<deny users="*" />
</authorization>
  </system.web>
 </location>
</configuration>
```

You also could have explicitly created a <location> section for the CustServ folder. However, because its permissions are identical to those of the parent folder, creating the <location> section is unnecessary.

2. You can use NTFS file permissions to further restrict access to the folders. This would provide defense-in-depth protection.

Case Scenario 2: Configuring Web Application Authentication

1. You should use Windows authentication, because you need the user to provide Windows credentials that the application can use to access the file.

2. Although you could configure impersonation in the application's Web.config file, that would grant the application unnecessary privileges and would give all users the same rights to the files. Instead, you should leave impersonation disabled in the Web.config file and implement impersonation only for the section of code that requires the user's elevated privileges.

3. You should configure the <authentication> and <authorization> sections as follows:

```
<configuration>
    <system.web>
        <authentication mode="Windows" />
        <authorization>
            <deny users="?" />
        </authentication>
    </system.web>
</configuration>
```

4. The following code works if added to the *Page_Load* method, assuming you create a *TextBox* objects named *filenameTextBox* and *reportTextBox*:

```
'VB Imports System.Security.Principal
Imports System.IO
…
' Impersonate the user with the account used to authenticate.
Dim realUser As WindowsImpersonationContext
```

```
realUser = CType(User.Identity, WindowsIdentity).Impersonate

' Perform tasks that require user permissions.
' Read the requested file.

Dim reader As StreamReader = File.OpenText(filenameTextBox.Text)
reportTextBox.Text = reader.ReadToEnd
reader.Close()

' Undo the impersonation, reverting to the normal user context.
realUser.Undo()
 //C# using System.Security.Principal;
using System.IO;
...
// Impersonate the user with the account used to authenticate.
WindowsImpersonationContext realUser;
realUser = ((WindowsIdentity)User.Identity).Impersonate();

// Perform tasks that require user permissions.
// Read the requested file.
StreamReader reader = File.OpenText(filenameTextBox.Text);
reportTextBox.Text = reader.ReadToEnd();
reader.Close();

// Undo the impersonation, reverting to the normal user context.
realUser.Undo();
```

Chapter 12: Lesson Review Answers

Lesson 1

1. **Correct Answer: B**

   A. **Incorrect:** Mobile controls must be added into *mobile:Form* elements.

   B. **Correct:** The mobile Web form contains a *mobile:Form* element that mobile controls can be added to.

   C. **Incorrect:** The standard Default.aspx page inherits from the System.Web.UI.Page, but must inherit from the System.Web.UI.MobileControls.MobilePage.

   D. **Incorrect:** Not a valid operation.

2. **Correct Answers: A and D**

   A. **Correct:** You can add a test for Request.Browser.IsMobileDevice and set the *Text* property based on its value.

   B. **Incorrect:** The mobile Web form does not contain an *IsDevice* method.

    C. **Incorrect:** The *UserAgent* property on the *Request* object will not be set to *mobile* for mobile devices.

    D. **Correct:** You can set the default *Text* value, and then define a mobile device in *the AppliedDeviceFilters,* and use this to set the *Text* property using the *PropertyOverrides* property of the mobile *Label* control.

3. **Correct Answer: C**

    A. **Incorrect:** Not a valid operation.

    B. **Incorrect:** Not a valid operation.

    C. **Correct:** You must run the aspnet_regbrowsers command-line tool in the .NET Command Prompt window using the −i switch.

    D. **Incorrect:** No such switch exists for the aspnet_regiis tool.

Chapter 12: Case Scenario Answers

Case Scenario 1: Determining the Mobile Control to Use

1. Use the *ObjectList* control because this control is capable of displaying tabluar data to a mobile device.

Case Scenario 2: Determining How Many Web Pages to Create

1. To create a Web site with the minimum number of Web pages, you can produce a single set of Web pages that are compatible with all devices by using mobile controls exclusively.

2. You should consider creating two sets of Web pages. One set would be for the desktop and notebook computers that have more processing power and hardware that can produce richer Web pages with more animation. The other set of Web pages would be for all other devices and would use the mobile controls which can render device specific Web pages.

Chapter 13: Lesson Review Answers

Lesson 1

1. **Correct Answer: A**

    A. **Correct:** Any installation changes you make should occur in the Install phase.

    B. **Incorrect:** If you can break an aspect of setup into separate installation and commit phases, you should do that. However, registry entries are simple changes and you can do them entirely in the Install phase.

    C. **Incorrect:** The Rollback phase is used to remove changes made during the Install phase if setup is cancelled or otherwise fails.

    D. **Incorrect:** The Uninstall phase is called when a user removed an application from Add/Remove Programs.

2. **Correct Answers: C and D**

    A. **Incorrect:** You would perform the initial change in the Install phase and record the previous value so that it could be removed later. However, you do not undo your registry modification in this phase.

    B. **Incorrect:** The Commit phase finalizes setup changes and should not be used for undoing setup modifications.

    C. **Correct:** The Rollback phase is used to remove changes made during the Install phase if setup is cancelled or otherwise fails. Therefore, you should undo your registry modification here if the change has already taken place.

    D. **Correct:** The Uninstall phase is called when a user removes an application from Add/Remove Programs. Therefore, you should undo your registry modification here.

3. **Correct Answer: C**

    A. **Incorrect:** Setup Projects are used to deploy Windows Forms applications, not Web applications.

    B. **Incorrect:** Web Setup Projects package Web sites in executable setups and Windows Installer files. You can use a Web Setup Project to deploy a Web application to a Web server. However, it does not assist the development process by detecting versioning conflicts.

    C. **Correct:** The Copy Web tool detects when a version of a file has been modified on the Web server after it is synchronized with the local copy of a file. Therefore, it can detect versioning conflicts when multiple developers work on a single site.

    D. **Incorrect:** The Publish Web Site tool is used to precompile and deploy Web sites. However, it does not have the ability to detect versioning conflicts.

4. **Correct Answer: D**

    A. **Incorrect:** Setup Projects are used to deploy Windows Forms applications, not Web applications.

    B. **Incorrect:** Web Setup Projects package Web sites in executable setups and Windows Installer files. You can use a Web Setup Project to deploy a Web application to a Web server; however, it does not precompile the Web site.

    C. **Incorrect:** The Copy Web tool detects when a version of a file has been modified on the Web server after it was synchronized with the local copy of a file. It does not enable you to precompile the Web site, however.

    D. **Correct:** The Publish Web Site tool is used to precompile and deploy Web sites. Precompiling reduces the delay when the first user requests a Web page, improving initial responsiveness of a site.

Lesson 2

1. **Correct Answer: A**

    A. **Correct:** By default, ASP.NET adds events to the event log.

    B. **Incorrect:** ASP.NET does not add events to a database by default.

    C. **Incorrect:** ASP.NET does not use the *WmiWebEventProvider* by default.

    D. **Incorrect:** ASP.NET does not send e-mails for events by default.

2. **Correct Answer: B**

    A. **Incorrect:** Successful audits occur when a user is successfully authenticated. To monitor unsuccessful events, use failure auditing.

    B. **Correct:** Failure audits, such as those that use the *WebAuthenticationFailureAuditEvent* class, occur when a user attempts to authenticate but provides invalid credentials.

C. **Incorrect:** *WebHeartbeatEvent* serves as a timer for the ASP.NET health-monitoring system and does not provide security events.

D. **Incorrect:** *WebRequestEvent* serves as the base class for events providing Web-request information and does not provide security events.

3. **Correct Answer: C**

A. **Incorrect:** Use the *PerformanceCounterCategory* class to call the static *Create* method. However, you must pass a parameter of type *PerformanceCounter-Category* to specify the counters.

B. **Incorrect:** *CounterSample* is a structure.

C. **Correct:** The *CounterCreationDataCollection* class stores an array of performance counters and can be used by the *PerformanceCounterCategory.Create* method to create multiple counters.

D. **Incorrect:** You can use *CounterCreationData* to create a single performance counter. However, you must use *CounterCreationDataCollection* to create multiple performance counters.

4. **Correct Answer: B**

A. **Incorrect:** You can use the Performance console to view, but not to add, performance counters.

B. **Correct:** To add a performance counter manually, use Server Explorer.

C. **Incorrect:** You cannot use Solution Explorer to add a performance counter. Instead, you must use Server Explorer.

D. **Incorrect:** You cannot use File System Editor to add a performance counter. Instead, you must use Server Explorer.

Lesson 3

1. **Correct Answer: A**

A. **Correct:** In this example, your primary concern is that a different copy of the page is cached for each state that the user might select. The state would be provided as a parameter; therefore, configuring the *VaryByParam* attribute with the name of the control containing the state input provides optimal caching.

B. **Incorrect:** The *VaryByHeader* attribute is used to dynamically generate the page if an item in the page's header varies. In this case, the header is not unique for different states, and you cannot use the attribute to configure the correct type of caching.

C. **Incorrect:** The *SqlDependency* attribute might seem like the correct attribute because the Web page is based on a SQL query. However, in this scenario, you are not concerned about updating the page if the database is updated. You are only concerned with updating the page output if the user chooses to filter the customer list, which is provided by a parameter, not the database.

D. **Incorrect:** The *VaryByCustom* attribute enables you to implement custom control over how pages are cached. While you could implement a custom method to meet your requirements, this would be time-consuming and inefficient. The capability you need is provided by the *VaryByParam* attribute.

2. **Correct Answer: B**

A. **Incorrect:** The *Request* object contains methods and parameters that describe the user's request. To configure page output caching, you must use the *Response* object instead.

B. **Correct:** The *Response* object contains methods such as *Response.Cache.Set-Expires* and *Response.AddCacheDependency* that enable you to configure page output caching programmatically.

C. **Incorrect:** The *Application* collection allows you to share data between all pages and processes in your application. Page output caching is configured on a per-page basis using the *Response* object.

D. **Incorrect:** The Server object contains methods such as *UrlDecode* and *UrlEncode* that are useful for processing server file paths. To configure page output caching, you must use the *Response* object instead.

3. **Correct Answers: C and D**

A. **Incorrect:** You can directly define *Cache* items. However, this technique does not provide for automatic expiration. When you directly define a *Cache* item, it stays cached until you remove it manually.

B. **Incorrect:** The *Cache.Get* method allows you to retrieve cached items, not define them.

C. **Correct:** You can use the *Cache.Insert* method to add an object to the cache and specify one or more dependencies, including an expiration time span.

D. **Correct:** You can use the *Cache.Add* method to add an object to the cache and specify one or more dependencies, including an expiration time span. Unlike *Cache.Insert*, *Cache.Add* also returns the cached value, which might make it easier to use in your code.

4. **Correct Answers: B, C, and E**

A. **Incorrect:** You can configure page output caching to vary with an HTTP header. However, the *Cache* object cannot use HTTP headers as dependencies.

B. **Correct:** You can create file dependencies for cache objects.

C. **Correct:** You can make a *Cache* object expire after a specific time span or at a specific time.

D. **Incorrect:** You cannot configure a *Cache* object to expire when a registry key is changed.

E. **Correct:** You can configure a *Cache* object to expire when a different object expires.

Chapter 13: Case Scenario Answers

Case Scenario 1: Deploying a Web Application

1. You can use either the Copy Web tool or the Publish Web Site tool to update the staging server. However, the Copy Web tool is more bandwidth-efficient because it only copies changed files.

2. The Publish Web Site tool is the best way for the quality assurance people to update the production Web server. That tool enables the site to be precompiled, which can improve performance.

Case Scenario 2: Improving the Performance of a Public Web Site

1. Yes. You can use the *Cache* object to store a copy of database query results, and then quickly retrieve those results the next time they are required.

2. The database administrator mentioned that you are using SQL Server, so you could configure a dependency on the database table that contains the list of movies.

3. Yes. If you create user controls for cacheable components, such as the portion of the page that displays a list of movies, that user control can be cached while the rest of the page is dynamically generated.

Glossary

ACID properties   An acronym that describes the four essential properties of a transaction: atomicity, consistency, isolation, and durability.

adaptive rendering   The act of rendering a control differently, based on the browser that requests the Web page.

application caching   A technique for programmatically storing objects in the *Cache* object for later retrieval directly from memory.

application state   A global storage mechanism that is accessible from all pages in the Web application.

asynchronous   Running multiple processes simultaneously to improve performance by reducing bottlenecks.

authentication   The process of identifying users based on their credentials. Typically, the credentials are user names and passwords.

authorization   The process of determing whether an authenticated user is allowed to access a specific resource. Even though a user is authenticated, he or she might not be authorized to open a file or Web page.

cache dependency   A file, database, time span, or other object that determines when an object is removed from a cache.

caching   A technique for storing frequently accessed data in memory, where it can be retrieved faster than it could be from a file or database.

child node   A node that is contained within another node.

composite control   A control that can contain constituent controls; the constituent controls are added to the composite control via code to the class file that defines the control. The class file is compiled to a .dll that can be shared among applications and can optionally be installed in the global assembly cache (GAC).

connection pooling   The process of reusing existing active connections instead of creating new connections when a request is made to the database.

constraint   Preserves data integrity by limiting the data that is considered acceptable.

content page   A page that closely resembles a standard .aspx page but provides content for *ContentPlaceHolder* controls located in a master page.

control state   Data stored within a custom control that cannot be disabled as view state can be.

cookie   Data that a Web server stores on a Web client. Web clients transmit cookies back to the server with every page request, enabling the server to track a user as he or she visits different pages on a site.

cross-page posting   A control is configured to post back to a Web page that is different from the Web page that the control was defined on.

culture   In development, this term refers to regional language and formatting differences. For example, English spoken in the United States is slightly different than the English spoken in England or Australia. Each country might also have different standards for currency and formatting. For example, in the United States, a number might be written as 12,345.67. In parts of Europe, the comma and period are used differently, and the same number is written as 12.345,67.

custom Web control   A control that inherits from Web control, and to which you can either write all of the code to render the control, or inherit from an existing Web control and provide extra behavior as necessary.

DataColumn   An object that defines the data to be held in a *DataTable*.

DataRow   An object that contains the data that is held in a *DataTable*.

DataTable   An object that represents tabular data as an in-memory table of rows, columns, and constraints.

device-specific rendering   The ability to specify rendering for a control based on a device type.

DiffGram   An XML document that contains all of the data from your *DataSet* object, including the original *DataRow* object information.

Distributed Authoring and Versioning (DAV)   A set of extensions to HTTP/1.1 that simplify Web site development when developers are working in team scenarios.

Document Object Model (DOM)   Delineates the standards provided by W3C that define the structure and provide a standard programming interface that can be used in a wide variety of environments and applications for XML documents.

event provider   A class that handles a Web event by storing it or notifying an administrator of the event.

explicit localization   This manually associates controls with global resources. You should use explicit localization when you may want to display a single resource on multiple pages.

expression column   Is also known as a derived or calculated column. Is a *DataColumn* in which the content is based on a formula and does not represent atomic data elements that can be modified. Expression columns can be used when the required data is not in the correct format.

global resources   Strings or other objects that can be accessed from any page in an application. In the context of globalization, global resources provide centralized storage for phrases that have been translated into multiple languages.

hash algorithm   A cryptographic technique for obscuring data in such a way that the original data cannot be determined. Hash algorithms are frequently used to protect passwords.

hidden field   Data stored within a Web form that is not visible to the user as he or she views the page in the Web browser.

HTML server control   This looks like its matching HTML tag, but it also contains the *runat="server"* attribute and provides a server-side object that you can programmatically access.

HTTP handler   A class based on *IHttpHandler* that enables ASP.NET to generate responses for custom file types.

Hypertext Transfer Protocol (HTTP)   A text-based communication protocol that is used to request Web pages from the Web server and send responses back to the Web browser.

impersonation   The process of using the end user's credentials to identify a process to resources. For example, if a Web application needs to read a table in a database and only members of the Managers group have permission to read the table, the Web application needs to impersonate the authenticated user in order to access the table.

implicit localization   This describes ASP.NET's ability to automatically associate controls with local resources. Implicit localization is the best way to provide page-by-page translations.

IsPostBack   A property contained on an ASP.NET Web page that is used to determine if data is being sent back to the Web server or if the Web page is simply being requested.

leaf node   A node that contains no children.

local resources   Strings or other objects that relate to a single Web page. In the context of globalization, ASP.NET can automatically display local resources associated with controls in the user's preferred language.

master page   A template that contains one or more *ContentPlaceHolder* controls. Content pages fill in the *ContentPlaceHolder* controls to create a full page. Master pages enable multiple pages in a Web site to have a consistent structure and reduce the time required to create redundant page elements.

method Is also known as a *verb* or a *command*; indicates what action is to be performed by the Web server using the URL that follows the method.

Multipurpose Internet Mail Extensions (MIME) type Is an indicator of the type of resource that is being sent to the Web browser; has a two-part designator "type/subtype," where the first part is the resource type and the second part is the resource sub-type.

naming container This defines a unique namespace for control names. Within a naming container, every control must be uniquely identifiable.

neutral culture This describes a culture that specifies only a language. Unlike specific cultures, neutral cultures do not specify currence or number formatting. Neutral cultures have two-letter abbreviations, such as "es" for Spanish, "fr" for French, and "en" for English.

page output caching A feature of ASP.NET that stores copies of rendered ASP.NET pages so that they do not have to be dynamically generated for future requests.

parent node A node that contains other nodes.

PostBack Sends data back to the server. Although its name comes from the POST method, it is possible to perform a PostBack using the GET method as well.

precompiling A feature of the Publish Web tool that compiles an ASP.NET Web application before the first request, reducing the delay that occurs when a user requests the first Web page.

primary key Consists of one or more columns in which the data provides a unique identity for each data row.

provider classes Are classes that you can use to transfer data between a data store and the client application.

QueryString A collection of key=value statements, separated by ampersand (&) characters, that can be passed to the Web server by concatenating a question mark (?) to the end of the URL and then concatenating the QueryString.

request Handles the communication from the Web browser to the Web server. Is also represented in ASP.NET as the Request object.

response Handles communication from the Web server to the Web browser. Is also represented in ASP.NET as the Response object.

Roles A class that identifies group membership for ASP.NET applications.

root node A node that is not contained by any other node and is an ancestor of all other nodes.

screen reader   This is a specialized Web browser tool that either translates text on a Web page into spoken words or drives a braille display.

server control   A control that is programmable by writing server-side code to respond to events from the control.

session state   Data stored within the *Session* object that is accessible only from pages viewed by a user during a specific visit to your Web site.

specific culture   This defines a culture that specifies both language and culture-specific formatting requirements. Each specific culture has a two-letter language abbreviation and a two-letter culture abbreviation. For example, "en-US" represents the English language for United States residents, while "en-GB" represents the English language for Great Britain residents.

stale   A cached object that is not consistent with the data source. Typically, a cached object becomes stale when the source is updated but the cache is not invalidated.

template control   A control that allows the separation of the user interface (presentation) from the control data and code. Templated controls do not natively provide a user interface. Instead, the user interface is supplied by a page developer through inline templates, which allow a page developer to customize the user interface for the control.

theme   A set of skins, CSS pages, images, and other resources that define defaults for controls or override specific control settings to provide a consistent appearance for all pages in a Web application.

transaction   An atomic unit of work that must be completed in its entirety. The transaction succeeds if it is committed and it fails if it is aborted.

user control   A template control that provides extra behavior to allow constituent (individual) controls to be added to the user control in the GUI designer, which are then added to the user control's template file, the .ascx file. The .ascx file is similar to the Web page's .aspx file and can have a code-behind page. To achieve reusability, the .ascx and code-behind files must be included in each project that requires the user control.

user profile   User-specific information that ASP.NET can store persistently in a database. User profiles are perfect for tracking user preferences, demographic information, and personal data.

ViewState   The mechanism by which Web page object and child control object data can be maintained between page requests. Any object data that cannot be represented as Hypertext Markup Language (HTML) in the Web page is eligible to be placed into ViewState.

Web browser   Provides a platform-independent means of displaying Web pages that were written with HTML.

WebForm   A Web page that may contain HTML markup, client-side code, or server-side code, and may be composed of a single file when using the in-line programming model, or a pair of files when using the code-behind programming model.

Web Part   A component containing a Web control that users can hide, move, and customize.

Web server   Receives and handles requests from the browser via HTTP.

Web server control   A Server control that offers more functionality and a more consistent programming model than HTML server controls. Web server controls may also render as many HTML tags and may also include client-side JavaScript code.

Index

Symbols & Numbers

& (ampersand), for separating query strings, 511
' (apostrophe), need for escaping, 463
* (asterisk), for all users, 702
? (question mark), for unauthenticated users, 702
3DES encryption, 704

A

\<a> element
    from AdRotator control, 177
    from HyperLink control, 482
absolute path, for saving file with FileUpload control, 126
absolute positioning of controls, 66
    and layout for globalization, 658
AcceptChanges method, 241
AccessDataSource, 160
accessibility, 649, 665–674
    ASP.NET controls support for, 666
    exercise, 672–674
    forms requiring user input, 669–670
    public guidelines, 665
    testing, 671–672
        single page, 671
        Web applications, 672
    visual, 667–668
Accessibility Validation dialog box, 671
AccessKey property
    of HotSpot control, 112
    of Web controls, 669
    of Web server control, 70
ACID properties of transaction, 326
Active Directory, for authentication, 700
active mode, vs. passive mode, 22–23
ActiveForm property, of mobile Web form, 732
ActiveViewIndex property, of View control, 133
ActiveX controls, separate Web page version without, 559
ActiveXControls property, of Request.Browser object, 560
Add method, for Rows collection, 233
Add New Item dialog box, 596
Add Project Output Group dialog box, 765, 782
AddCacheDependency method, of Response object, 816
AddCacheItemDependencies method, of Response object, 816

AddCacheItemDependency method, of Response object, 816
Added DataRowState enumeration value, 236
Added DataViewRowState enumeration value, 250
Add/Edit Application Extension Mapping dialog box, 551
AddError method, of Context object, 568
AddFileDependencies method, of Response object, 816
AddFileDependency method, of Response object, 816
AddUser(s)ToRole(s) method (Roles class), 687
AddValidationCallback method, 814
Administrators role, rule granting Allow access, 695
AdminUser condition, for Windows Installer, 772
ADO recordset, OleDbDataAdapter object to access, 315–317
ADO.NET
    primary provider classes and interfaces, 281
    Transaction object, 326–328
AdRotator control, 177–180, 814
    hierarchy, 177
    mobile control, 743–745
AggregateCacheDependency object, 807
AJAX (Asynchronous JavaScript and XML), 5
Align property, and layout for globalization, 659
All Errors event, 789
All Users role, rule granting to Deny access, 695
AllCultures, as CultureTypes value, 660
AllErrors method, of Context object, 568
Allow access
    rule granting to Administrator role, 695
    rule granting to Users role, 695
\<allow> section, in Web.config file, 713
allowAnonymous attribute, for user profile property, 612
AllowDBNull property, for DataColumn objects, 232
AllowPaging property, of DetailsView control, 190
AllowPartiallyTrustedCallers property, 782
AlternateText element, for AdRotator control XML file, 178
AlternateText property
    of HotSpot control, 112
    of Image control, 106
    of images, 667
    of mobile Image control, 741
    of PhoneCall control, 745
AlternatingItemTemplate, 162
ampersand (&), for separating query strings, 11, 511
And Boolean operator, to check Windows Installer conditions, 773

Additional Resources for C# Developers

Published and Forthcoming Titles from Microsoft Press

Microsoft® Visual C#® 2005 Express Edition: Build a Program Now!
Patrice Pelland ● ISBN 0-7356-2229-9

In this lively, eye-opening, and hands-on book, all you need is a computer and the desire to learn how to program with Visual C# 2005 Express Edition. Featuring a full working edition of the software, this fun and highly visual guide walks you through a complete programming project—a desktop weather-reporting application—from start to finish. You'll get an unintimidating introduction to the Microsoft Visual Studio® development environment and learn how to put the lightweight, easy-to-use tools in Visual C# Express to work right away—creating, compiling, testing, and delivering your first, ready-to-use program. You'll get expert tips, coaching, and visual examples at each step of the way, along with pointers to additional learning resources.

Microsoft Visual C# 2005 *Step by Step*
John Sharp ● ISBN 0-7356-2129-2

Visual C#, a feature of Visual Studio 2005, is a modern programming language designed to deliver a productive environment for creating business frameworks and reusable object-oriented components. Now you can teach yourself essential techniques with Visual C#—and start building components and Microsoft Windows®–based applications—one step at a time. With *Step by Step*, you work at your own pace through hands-on, learn-by-doing exercises. Whether you're a beginning programmer or new to this particular language, you'll learn how, when, and why to use specific features of Visual C# 2005. Each chapter puts you to work, building your knowledge of core capabilities and guiding you as you create your first C#-based applications for Windows, data management, and the Web.

Programming Microsoft Visual C# 2005 Framework Reference
Francesco Balena ● ISBN 0-7356-2182-9

Complementing *Programming Microsoft Visual C# 2005 Core Reference*, this book covers a wide range of additional topics and information critical to Visual C# developers, including Windows Forms, working with Microsoft ADO.NET 2.0 and Microsoft ASP.NET 2.0, Web services, security, remoting, and much more. Packed with sample code and real-world examples, this book will help developers move from understanding to mastery.

Programming Microsoft Visual C# 2005 *Core Reference*
Donis Marshall ● ISBN 0-7356-2181-0

Get the in-depth reference and pragmatic, real-world insights you need to exploit the enhanced language features and core capabilities in Visual C# 2005. Programming expert Donis Marshall deftly builds your proficiency with classes, structs, and other fundamentals, and advances your expertise with more advanced topics such as debugging, threading, and memory management. Combining incisive reference with hands-on coding examples and best practices, this *Core Reference* focuses on mastering the C# skills you need to build innovative solutions for smart clients and the Web.

CLR via C#, Second Edition
Jeffrey Richter ● ISBN 0-7356-2163-2

In this new edition of Jeffrey Richter's popular book, you get focused, pragmatic guidance on how to exploit the common language runtime (CLR) functionality in Microsoft .NET Framework 2.0 for applications of all types—from Web Forms, Windows Forms, and Web services to solutions for Microsoft SQL Server™, Microsoft code names "Avalon" and "Indigo," consoles, Microsoft Windows NT® Service, and more. Targeted to advanced developers and software designers, this book takes you under the covers of .NET for an in-depth understanding of its structure, functions, and operational components, demonstrating the most practical ways to apply this knowledge to your own development efforts. You'll master fundamental design tenets for .NET and get hands-on insights for creating high-performance applications more easily and efficiently. The book features extensive code examples in Visual C# 2005.

Programming Microsoft Windows Forms
Charles Petzold ● ISBN 0-7356-2153-5

CLR via C++
Jeffrey Richter with Stanley B. Lippman
ISBN 0-7356-2248-5

Programming Microsoft Web Forms
Douglas J. Reilly ● ISBN 0-7356-2179-9

Debugging, Tuning, and Testing Microsoft .NET 2.0 Applications
John Robbins ● ISBN 0-7356-2202-7

For more information about Microsoft Press® books and other learning products,
visit: **www.microsoft.com/books** *and* **www.microsoft.com/learning**

Additional Resources for Visual Basic Developers

Published and Forthcoming Titles from Microsoft Press

Microsoft® Visual Basic® 2005 Express Edition: Build a Program Now!
Patrice Pelland • ISBN 0-7356-2213-2

Featuring a full working edition of the software, this fun and highly visual guide walks you through a complete programming project—a desktop weather-reporting application—from start to finish. You'll get an introduction to the Microsoft Visual Studio® development environment and learn how to put the lightweight, easy-to-use tools in Visual Basic Express to work right away—creating, compiling, testing, and delivering your first ready-to-use program. You'll get expert tips, coaching, and visual examples each step of the way, along with pointers to additional learning resources.

Microsoft Visual Basic 2005 *Step by Step*
Michael Halvorson • ISBN 0-7356-2131-4

With enhancements across its visual designers, code editor, language, and debugger that help accelerate the development and deployment of robust, elegant applications across the Web, a business group, or an enterprise, Visual Basic 2005 focuses on enabling developers to rapidly build applications. Now you can teach yourself the essentials of working with Visual Studio 2005 and the new features of the Visual Basic language—one step at a time. Each chapter puts you to work, showing you how, when, and why to use specific features of Visual Basic and guiding as you create actual components and working applications for Microsoft Windows®. You'll also explore data management and Web-based development topics.

Programming Microsoft Visual Basic 2005 *Core Reference*
Francesco Balena • ISBN 0-7356-2183-7

Get the expert insights, indispensable reference, and practical instruction needed to exploit the core language features and capabilities in Visual Basic 2005. Well-known Visual Basic programming author Francesco Balena expertly guides you through the fundamentals, including modules, keywords, and inheritance, and builds your mastery of more advanced topics such as delegates, assemblies, and My Namespace. Combining in-depth reference with extensive, hands-on code examples and best-practices advice, this *Core Reference* delivers the key resources that you need to develop professional-level programming skills for smart clients and the Web.

Programming Microsoft Visual Basic 2005 Framework Reference
Francesco Balena • ISBN 0-7356-2175-6

Complementing *Programming Microsoft Visual Basic 2005 Core Reference*, this book covers a wide range of additional topics and information critical to Visual Basic developers, including Windows Forms, working with Microsoft ADO.NET 2.0 and ASP.NET 2.0, Web services, security, remoting, and much more. Packed with sample code and real-world examples, this book will help developers move from understanding to mastery.

Programming Microsoft Windows Forms
Charles Petzold • ISBN 0-7356-2153-5

Programming Microsoft Web Forms
Douglas J. Reilly • ISBN 0-7356-2179-9

Debugging, Tuning, and Testing Microsoft .NET 2.0 Applications
John Robbins • ISBN 0-7356-2202-7

Microsoft ASP.NET 2.0 *Step by Step*
George Shepherd • ISBN 0-7356-2201-9

Microsoft ADO.NET 2.0 *Step by Step*
Rebecca Riordan • ISBN 0-7356-2164-0

Programming Microsoft ASP.NET 2.0 *Core Reference*
Dino Esposito • ISBN 0-7356-2176-4

For more information about Microsoft Press® books and other learning products,
visit: **www.microsoft.com/books** *and* **www.microsoft.com/learning**

Microsoft Press products are available worldwide wherever quality computer books are sold. For more information, contact your book or computer retailer, software reseller, or local Microsoft Sales Office, or visit our Web site at **www.microsoft.com/mspress**. To locate your nearest source for Microsoft Press products, or to order directly, call 1-800-MSPRESS in the United States. (In Canada, call **1-800-268-2222**.)

Additional Resources for Web Developers
Published and Forthcoming Titles from Microsoft Press

Microsoft® Visual Web Developer™ 2005 Express Edition: Build a Web Site Now!
Jim Buyens • ISBN 0-7356-2212-4

With this lively, eye-opening, and hands-on book, all you need is a computer and the desire to learn how to create Web pages now using Visual Web Developer Express Edition! Featuring a full working edition of the software, this fun and highly visual guide walks you through a complete Web page project from set-up to launch. You'll get an introduction to the Microsoft Visual Studio® environment and learn how to put the lightweight, easy-to-use tools in Visual Web Developer Express to work right away—building your first, dynamic Web pages with Microsoft ASP.NET 2.0. You'll get expert tips, coaching, and visual examples at each step of the way, along with pointers to additional learning resources.

Microsoft ASP.NET 2.0 Programming
Step by Step
George Shepherd • ISBN 0-7356-2201-9

With dramatic improvements in performance, productivity, and security features, Visual Studio 2005 and ASP.NET 2.0 deliver a simplified, high-performance, and powerful Web development experience. ASP.NET 2.0 features a new set of controls and infrastructure that simplify Web-based data access and include functionality that facilitates code reuse, visual consistency, and aesthetic appeal. Now you can teach yourself the essentials of working with ASP.NET 2.0 in the Visual Studio environment— one step at a time. With *Step by Step*, you work at your own pace through hands-on, learn-by-doing exercises. Whether you're a beginning programmer or new to this version of the technology, you'll understand the core capabilities and fundamental techniques for ASP.NET 2.0. Each chapter puts you to work, showing you how, when, and why to use specific features of the ASP.NET 2.0 rapid application development environment and guiding you as you create actual components and working applications for the Web, including advanced features such as personalization.

Programming Microsoft ASP.NET 2.0
Core Reference
Dino Esposito • ISBN 0-7356-2176-4

Delve into the core topics for ASP.NET 2.0 programming, mastering the essential skills and capabilities needed to build high-performance Web applications successfully. Well-known ASP.NET author Dino Esposito deftly builds your expertise with Web forms, Visual Studio, core controls, master pages, data access, data binding, state management, security services, and other must-know topics—combining definitive reference with practical, hands-on programming instruction. Packed with expert guidance and pragmatic examples, this *Core Reference* delivers the key resources that you need to develop professional-level Web programming skills.

Programming Microsoft ASP.NET 2.0
Applications: *Advanced Topics*
Dino Esposito • ISBN 0-7356-2177-2

Master advanced topics in ASP.NET 2.0 programming—gaining the essential insights and in-depth understanding that you need to build sophisticated, highly functional Web applications successfully. Topics include Web forms, Visual Studio 2005, core controls, master pages, data access, data binding, state management, and security considerations. Developers often discover that the more they use ASP.NET, the more they need to know. With expert guidance from ASP.NET authority Dino Esposito, you get the in-depth, comprehensive information that leads to full mastery of the technology.

Programming Microsoft Windows® Forms
Charles Petzold • ISBN 0-7356-2153-5

Programming Microsoft Web Forms
Douglas J. Reilly • ISBN 0-7356-2179-9

CLR via C++
Jeffrey Richter with Stanley B. Lippman
ISBN 0-7356-2248-5

Debugging, Tuning, and Testing Microsoft .NET 2.0 Applications
John Robbins • ISBN 0-7356-2202-7

CLR via C#, Second Edition
Jeffrey Richter • ISBN 0-7356-2163-2

For more information about Microsoft Press® books and other learning products, visit: **www.microsoft.com/books** *and* **www.microsoft.com/learning**

System Requirements

We recommend that you use a computer that is not your primary workstation to do the practice exercises in this book because you will make changes to the operating system and application configuration.

Hardware Requirements

The following hardware is required to complete the practice exercises:

- Computer with a 600 MHz or faster processor
- 192 MB of RAM or more
- 2 GB of available hard disk space
- DVD-ROM drive
- 1,024 x 768 or higher resolution display with 256 colors
- Keyboard and Microsoft mouse, or compatible pointing device

Software Requirements

The following software is required to complete the practice exercises:

- One of the following operating systems:
  - Microsoft Windows 2000 with Service Pack 4
  - Microsoft Windows XP with Service Pack 2
  - Microsoft Windows XP Professional x64 Edition (WOW)
  - Microsoft Windows Server 2003 with Service Pack 1
  - Microsoft Windows Server 2003, x64 Editions (WOW)
  - Microsoft Windows Server 2003 R2
  - Microsoft Windows Server 2003 R2, x64 Editions (WOW)
  - Microsoft Windows Vista
- Microsoft Visual Studio 2005 (A 90-day evaluation edition of Visual Studio 2005 Professional Edition is included on DVD with this book.)

What do you think of this book?
We want to hear from you!

Do you have a few minutes to participate in a brief online survey? Microsoft is interested in hearing your feedback about this publication so that we can continually improve our books and learning resources for you.

To participate in our survey, please visit:

www.microsoft.com/learning/booksurvey

And enter this book's ISBN, 0-7356-2334-1. As a thank-you to survey participants in the United States and Canada, each month we'll randomly select five respondents to win one of five $100 gift certificates from a leading online merchant.* At the conclusion of the survey, you can enter the drawing by providing your e-mail address, which will be used for prize notification *only*.

Thanks in advance for your input. Your opinion counts!

Sincerely,

Microsoft Learning

Learn More. Go Further.

To see special offers on Microsoft Learning products for developers, IT professionals, and home and office users, visit: *www.microsoft.com/learning/booksurvey*